MANAGING

CULTURAL

DIFFERENCES

SEVENTH EDITION

SEVENTH EDITION

MANAGING CULTURAL DIFFERENCES

GLOBAL LEADERSHIP STRATEGIES FOR THE 21ST CENTURY

ROBERT T. MORAN, PH.D.
PHILIP R. HARRIS, PH.D.
SARAH V. MORAN, M.A.

AMSTERDAM • BOSTON • HEIDELBERG • LONDON
NEW YORK • OXFORD • PARIS • SAN DIEGO
SAN FRANCISCO • SINGAPORE • SYDNEY • TOKYO

Butterworth-Heinemann is an imprint of Elsevier
30 Corporate Drive, Suite 400, Burlington, MA 01803, USA
Linacre House, Jordan Hill, Oxford OX2 8DP, UK

 Recognizing the importance of preserving what has been written, Elsevier
prints its books on acid-free paper whenever possible.

Library of Congress Cataloging-in-Publication Data
Application submitted

British Library Cataloguing-in-Publication Data
A catalogue record for this book is available from the British Library.

ISBN 13: 978-0-7506-8247-3
ISBN 10: 0-7506-8247-7

For information on all Butterworth–Heinemann publications
visit our Web site at www.books.elsevier.com

Printed in the United States of America
07 08 09 10 11 10 9 8 7 6 5 4 3 2 1

To my children Elizabeth, Sarah, Molly, Rebecca and Benedict. Learners and teachers, receivers and givers, all multilingual citizens in our global world.

Robert T. Moran

In honor of Dr. Dorothy Lipp Harris, my late wife and elegant professor who supported me in writing this text for a quarter century and taught with it in graduate school. And to her sister, Jeanne Lipp Conover, who first introduced me into the concept of culture *when I was a Fulbright professor in Japan, 1962 . . . Plus in appreciation to two cosmopolitans who inspire me to continue writing in my 80s – my present wife, Janet Belport Harris and my stepson, Jason Winter Belport.*

Philip R. Harris

To my parents, whose global humanitarian lives have influenced me profoundly, and to every person who has crossed my path whose diversity of backgrounds, ethnicities, cultures, and world views have opened my eyes and mind. You have all taught me that through respect and developing a deep understanding of what makes each of us unique, that humankind, in all our wonderful diversity, can find ways to harmoniously live and work together.

Sarah V. Moran

CONTENTS

FOREWORD

Eighty years ago when the business world was in its post-industrial adolescence—and when Textron was founded as the world's first conglomerate—you could make some basic assumptions about people you would encounter throughout your workday. Most companies were regionally focused then, from suppliers to customers to employees. And that meant limited exposure to other ideas and approaches to problem solving. It meant you knew all the rules of engagement.

Today it's another story entirely. Textron has corporate offices in far-off places like China and Poland. We have manufacturing facilities in areas as varied as Pueblo, Mexico and Huddersfield, United Kingdom. Our Leadership Program puts recent college graduates in six-month rotations around the world. Our employees cover the spectrum of cultures and backgrounds—age, color, creed, faith.

Engagement on this global scale means working with variables impossible to predict, account for, and control.

Diversity, as the authors of this book point out, is a testament to how humans have dealt with and adjusted to universal problems for millennia, such as climate, geography, ongoing quests for food and shelter. Sometimes evidence of this is clear just by looking at one another. For instance, Scandinavians developed, physically, to live in the bright sunlight of a frozen north, and you can see this in pale blue eyes perfect for filtering light reflected off snow.

Sometimes our ancestral adaptation is more difficult to spot, as in the rigid traditional structure of Hindu society in India. For centuries, people there pursued lines of work based not on capability, but on his or her place in a strict, complicated caste system.

The good news is that walls such as this have come down all around the world, and businesses are reaping the rewards of talents the world over without restrictions of time zone or language. Right now I imagine there's someone in Vancouver on the phone with an airline booking agent in Mumbai making a reservation to travel to Venezuela for a new supply chain opportunity. When she arrives, she'll stay in touch with the corporate office via Blackberry while conducting meetings in fluent Spanish with the aid of a dictionary on her laptop.

There is no precedent for this. There are no examples to follow. Businesses of all sizes are grappling with how to maximize the opportunities—and minimize the challenges—of cultural differences. We're realizing that diversity can be a potent and differentiating competitive edge. And we're beginning to ask all the right questions in search of the right answers.

This conversation has begun in earnest because the world is opening its mind. We aren't just thinking outside the box, we're picking it up to see what's underneath, then tearing it apart and building something new altogether! And it's all happening because we've realized that business can no longer be held back by traditional solutions. Imagine the problems you can tackle when you assemble a team with a Western approach to problem solving—one that's time-bound, linear, and focuses on an end result—and join it with an Eastern approach to problem solving—one that seeks harmony, honors process, and values team relationships more than concrete solutions. Six Sigma is one example of this kind of adaptation, and the results have been tremendous for Western-based companies like Textron.

The book you're holding is a valuable guidebook for this new landscape. The authors approach a far-reaching, complicated subject in a truly inspiring way. It's filled with communication tools, fundamental concepts, and a map for the road ahead.

Ours is a connected world, one that allows companies to tackle the traditional problems of business—staffing, sourcing, attracting new customers, and innovating new solutions—in a truly revolutionary way. Authors Moran, Harris, and Moran understand that the challenge isn't simply attracting and recruiting a diverse, talented workforce around the globe, but retaining it. And that anyone who views globalization as a quick solution and follows it in blind pursuit of cheap labor is going to follow it right over a cliff. Opening our minds to the power of diversity and the possibility of the global workplace opens us to the transformational change required to succeed and grow.

I have nothing but enthusiasm for the road ahead. It's one we must all walk together with conviction and attention as we harness the power of cultural difference.

Lewis B. Campbell
Chairman, President and CEO
Textron Inc.

PROLOGUE

We are pleased and honored to present to readers of all cultures, the 7th edition of *Managing Cultural Differences*. In our complex and troubled global world, we hope some of the ideas, if utilized, will make a positive difference in the personal and professional worlds of all who explore their meaning and value.

When first published in 1979, our book recognized the importance of **culture**, and its impact on human behavior and performance in a business context. Only in this 21st Century are we beginning to realize that we create the worlds in which we live, but on the basis of our unique cultural codes! Our message has never been more relevant. In today's world, the human family struggles with two contrary forces – globalization and diversity, versus increasing racism, ethnic hatreds, and immigrant bashing. May those who seriously read this volume learn how to encourage the former and curb the latter.

Culture is not just a tool for coping, but a means for creating awareness and learning. It underpins all human activities, and explains much of our behavior. Our favorite analogy is to compare this concept to a beautiful jewel – hold it to the light, turn it around, and reveal its multiple dimensions. With each new writing of this text, we plumb culture's depths for meaning, and discover more applications – from national, to organizational, to team and work culture.

Numerous trends underscore the importance of effective intercultural relations to improve the quality of our lives, particularly with reference to job performance and productivity. We are grateful to more than a million readers, as well as university and college professors whose adoptions of this text worldwide in many institutions of higher education, confirming the validity of our message. Further our thanks to the many HRD consultants and trainers who have shared our thoughts with managers and other personnel in global corporations.

The material covered has been extensively updated – more maps for geographic areas and more profiles of countries within a region. The number of pages has increased, from the opening chapter on the "Global Leaders and Culture," to the "Epilogue," both of which summarize the book's themes and projects ahead. The expanded 7th edition is still organized within two units, "Cultural Impacts on Global Management," consisting of ten chapters; and "Regional Cultural Specifics" with lengthened coverage in the final six chapters. The United Nations recognizes 226 nations in the world; obviously, we could not treat all their unique cultures in this text. Instead, we choose a representative sample to provide culture specifics in terms of six major regions – North America, Latin America, Asia, Europe, the Middle East, and Africa.

Just as organizations are being "re-invented and re-engineered," so too is this publication. Yet, in our content, especially in the many exhibits, we still seek a balance of theory and practice, as well as between research findings and models. Perhaps this may partially explain why *Managing Cultural Differences* has been so popular and lasted so long. Although this work has always been written for both practitioners and students, we recognize that many of our readers are instructors in various departments of universities and colleges, or in corporate human resource development (HRD).

We welcome your continued evaluation as to how *Managing Cultural Differences*, both as a book and as a series, can better serve your needs.

Robert T. Moran, Ph.D.
Scottsdale, Arizona, U.S.A.

Philip R. Harris, Ph.D.
LaJolla, California, U.S.A.

Sarah V. Moran, M.A.
Montreal, Quebec, Canada

ACKNOWLEDGMENTS

The seventh edition would not have been possible without the talent and commitment of many people whom we wish to acknowledge.

Karen Maloney, our editor at Elsevier/Butterworth Heinemann is always engaging and personal to speak with and gentle, yet clear in her requests and expectations of authors. Dennis McGonagle, also of Elsevier gets answers to all questions and responds quickly to requests. Jay Donahue is a project manager/leader at Elsevier and used his best skills in bringing our materials forward. We thank the Elsevier team.

We especially thank Lewis B. Campbell, Chairman, President and CEO of Textron Inc. for writing the Foreword. His words were few but they brilliantly integrated trends in our global world with concepts in our book. Thanks Lewis.

Over the years many individuals have allowed us to use portions of their research. We wish to thank Nancy Baldwin, Maria Brightbill, Wayne Conway, Joseph Douress, Terry Finnegan, Ralph Krueger, Richard Lewis, Carl Nelson and Corrine Pfund, Laurel Cool, Mary Mitchell, Mary Pietanza, Jeni Chavez, Cecile C. Ramirez de Arellano, Jie Zhang Yuanlim, Kim Sung-do, B.W. Lee, Yoon Park, Rebekhab Henry, Regina Sy-Facunda, Raj Kohli, William Everett, Ferando Garcia-Pretel, Eduardo Magailanes, Sato Masatoshi, Barbara Goodman, Karin Romano, Ardnt Luebbers, Larissa Koursova, ByungKi An, John Bechtold, Biswajiit Mukherjie, Eric-Jan Van der Byl, Kristen Kelly, Elizabeth Moran de Longeaux, Sebastien de Longeaux and Molly Hanley.

We thank Jamie Gelbtuch for checking the demographics. We are confident of their accuracy. Molly Moran Hyland prepared the index. A good index helps readers find interesting topics quickly.

In the seventh edition, graduates of Thunderbird, Chris Menn and Maryellen Toffle wrote the excellent sections on Brazil and Italy based on their years of living and working in these countries. These sections are among the best "culture specific" profiles in the book.

We also acknowledge and thank the many professors and other users of the text and Instructor's Guide who gave us feedback about our work. We have incorporated many of these suggestions in the seventh edition. We especially thank the professors who use the text and the Instructor's Guide and who allowed us to interview them about changes and improvements.

Many feature articles in two outstanding international magazines, namely, *The Economist* of London and the *National Geographic* of Washington, D.C. have been most helpful.

Finally, Judith E. Soccorsy, always in good cheer, skillfully assisted from beginning to end. Thank you.

Robert T. Moran, Philip R. Harris, Sarah V. Moran

Unit 1

Cultural Impacts on Global Management

"A global manager is set apart by more than a worn suitcase and a dog-eared passport."

Harvard Business Review, August 2003

"We don't look so much at what and where people have studied, but rather at their drive, initiative, cultural sensitivity. . . ."

Stephen Green, Group CEO, HSBC
Harvard Business Review, August 2003

GLOBAL LEADERS AND CULTURE

Vérité en-deça des Pyrénées, erreur au delà. (There are truths on this side of the Pyrenees that are falsehoods on the other.)[1]

In 1492 Christopher Columbus set sail for India, going west . . . he called the people he met "Indians" and came home and reported to his king and queen. "The world is round." I set off for India 512 years later . . . I went east . . . I came home and reported only to my wife and only in a whisper: "The world is flat."[2]

The real voyage of discovery consists not in seeking new landscapes but in having new eyes.—Marcel Proust, French novelist, 1871–1922

More people will graduate in the United States in 2006 with sports exercise degrees than electrical engineering degrees. So, if we want to be the massage capital of the world, we're well on our way.[3]

The world is

flat.

LEARNING OBJECTIVES

In the twenty-first century, leaders in business, government and the professions cope with the phenomenon of globalization. It prompts them to cross borders more frequently and to communicate with persons from other cultures either in person or electionally.

This chapter provides a rationale and an imperative for all individuals working "globally" to understand and respect their counterparts and to develop the skills required to work effectively in today's complex world. Ways to analyze and understand other cultures are presented, along with how to use the suggested strategies. Seeing global issues through "multiple lens" or "by hearing with new ears" is also important.

Why does the world appear flat to some, round to others, and what are the advantages or disadvantages of either? Thomas Friedman writes about his insights during an interview with Nandan Nilekani, CEO of Infosys Technologies Limited.

"Outsourcing is just one dimension of a much more fundamental thing happening today in the world," Nilekani explained. "What happened over the last (few) years is that there was a massive investment in technology, especially in the bubble era, when hundreds of millions of dollars were invested in putting broadband connectivity around the world, undersea cables, all those things." At the same time, he added, computers became cheaper and dispersed all over the world, and there was an explosion of software-e-mail, search engines like Google, and proprietary software that can chop up any piece of work and send one part to Boston, one part to Bangalore, and one part to Beijing, making it easy for anyone to do remote development. When all of these things suddenly came together around 2000, added Nilekani, they created a platform where intellectual work, intellectual capital, could be delivered from anywhere. It could be disaggregated, delivered, distributed, produced and put back together again—and this gave a whole new degree of freedom to the way we do work, especially work of an intellectual nature . . . And what you are seeing in Bangalore today is really the culmination of all these things coming together.[4]

The point is the playing field in the global marketplace is being leveled for some and thus "flat." That is an advantage for many and a disadvantage for others. In either view, cultural competing is a requirement. Culture does count.

Culture does count.

The authors of this book have worked for global organizations for many years. In the 1960s and early 1970s, we had to convince many business and government leaders that "culture counts." From the industrialized world, the perspective often voiced was "we tell them what to do and if they want to work with us, they do it." This is rarely the situation today.

We no longer have to convince anyone with any global experience that *culture counts*. And when organizations, nongovernmental organizations (NGOs), and political organizations ignore, dismiss, or minimize culture, the costs are often significant. This chapter will present proven frameworks, models, and paradigms relevant to working skillfully in today's global business and geopolitical world. We believe managing cultural differences skillfully for all individuals, organizations, nongovernmental organizations (NGOs), and governments from all countries is a human and business imperative. Understanding the environment is a fundamental requirement for maintaining a competitive advantage. To successfully adapt to changes in the environment is a requirement for survival. Culture impacts relationships and business operations. Schein states it profoundly:

At the root of

the issue, we are

likely to find

communication

failures and

cultural

misunderstandings.

Consider any complex, potentially volatile issue—Arab relations, the problems between Serbs, Croats, and Bosnians, corporate decision making, getting control of the U.S. deficit, or health-care costs, labor/management relations, and so on. At the root of the issue, we are likely to find communication failures and cultural misunderstandings that prevent the parties from framing the problem in a common way, and thus make it impossible to deal with the problem constructively.[5]

McNamara et al. cite a dialogue about the Vietnam War between Colonel Herbert Schandler and Colonel Quach Hai Luong that illustrates dramatically the importance of culture in perception.[6] The dialogue took place in Hanoi in 1998, when military historians from the United States and Vietnam came together to try to understand the lessons of the Vietnam War to be carried forward to the twenty-first century.

> Colonel Quach Hai Luong: I want to ask you: What do you think the American objectives were in Vietnam?
>
> Colonel Herbert Schandler: Our objectives in Vietnam, as stated by our various presidents, were the following. First, to establish an independent, noncommunist South Vietnam whose people had the ability to choose their own leaders and form of government. A second objective was to *convince* North Vietnam—not to defeat or crush or obliterate North Vietnam—but to *convince* North Vietnam not to impose its will on the South by means of military force. We had no burning desire even to harm North Vietnam in any way. We just wanted to demonstrate to you that you could not win militarily in the South.
>
> Colonel Quach Hai Luong: But Colonel Schandler, if I may say so, this was a critical difference between your understanding of the situation and our understanding of it. Let me put it this way: your fundamental assumption is that Vietnam was two distinct—two rightfully independent—countries. On that basis, your objectives and strategies follow. We did not make that distinction. We saw only one country. All our strategies were based on this basic premise: that Vietnam is one country, unfortunately and artificially divided in two. Our war was for the purpose of protecting our independence and maintaining our national unity.

Now imagine, how different the outcomes of the Vietnam War might have been if at the beginning of this conflict the military leaders and negotiators of their respective countries had used sophisticated problem-solving skills and dug deeper to understand the cultural meanings and implications of their actions and behind their public statements about the war. The same might be said of present conflicts in Afghanistan and Iraq.

Also supporting the notion that "culture" is important is Alan Greenspan, former chairman of the United States Federal Reserve. Greenspan stated that he originally believed that capitalism was "human nature."[7] After the collapse of the Soviet economy, however, he concluded that "it was not human nature at all, but culture." Culture is finding it's place of significance in the experience of global individuals.

Cultures have always been distinct, mostly separate and independent. Over the past 100 years, and especially during the last 25, cultures and nations have remained unique but have become increasingly more interconnected in complex and nonobvious ways. This book covers many topics, but the threads of culture, differences, and leadership run throughout.

> "In the early 1990s I happened to come across early 1960s economic data on Ghana and South Korea, and I was astonished to see how similar their economies were at that time. These two countries had roughly comparable levels of per capita gross national product (GNP); similar divisions of their economy among primary products, manufacturing, and services; and overwhelmingly primary product exports, with South Korea producing a few manufactured goods. They were also receiving comparable levels of economic aid. Thirty years later, South Korea had become an industrial giant with the fourteenth largest economy in the world. No such changes had occurred in Ghana, whose per capita GNP was now about one-fifteenth that of South Korea's. How could this extraordinary difference in development be explained? Undoubtedly, many factors played a role, but it seemed to me that culture had to be a large part of the explanation. South Koreans value thrift, investment, hard work, education, organization, and discipline. Ghanaians had different values.[8] In short, culture counts."

Diamond's[9] statement that, "We all know that history has proceeded very differently for peoples from different parts of the globe," is one we can all agree with. The specific data that humans all came from Africa is not disputed. Diamond questions why did different people develop in different ways. His answer, "History followed different courses for different peoples because of differences in peoples' environments, not because of biological differences among peoples themselves."[10]

Change is also a part of our daily lives and impacts all. If culture counts managing cultural differences or skillfully leading in a global world becomes of paramount importance. Most of the following events took place after the year 2000 and share aspects of culture, differences, conflict, consequences, and leadership.

- ■ SARS (Severe Acute Respiratory Syndrome) which sometimes can lead to the death of an infected person migrates from China through Hong Kong to Taipei, Singapore, Canada, and other countries.
- ■ EU has expanded to 25 countries with many more countries desiring inclusion.
- ■ Hong Kong is returned to the People's Republic of China.
- ■ Good Friday Peace Accords signed in Northern Ireland.
- ■ North Korea restarts its nuclear program.

- The World Trade Center and the Pentagon are attacked by terrorists.
- A coalition of nations undertakes a "War on Terror" in Afghanistan against the Taliban regime and the al-Qaeda terrorism network.
- AIDS continues to ravage many countries, including Africa, and is spreading to India, China, Russia, and many other countries.
- Saddam Hussein, the United States invades Iraq. Onsay and Uday Hussain, his sons, are killed by U.S. troops.
- The Darfur crisis begins in the Sudan with Arabs and black Muslims fighting.
- The H5N1 strain of bird flu emerges in Southeast Asia.
- Bombs are set off in railway stations in Madrid, killing 202 and injuring more than 1400.
- Terrorist seize a grammar school in Breslan, Russia.
- Afghanistan holds a democratic presidential election.
- The Indian Ocean tsunami kills more than 275,000.
- London terrorist bombings kill 52 and injure approximately 700.
- Hurricane Katrina, a Category 5 hurricane, causes catastrophic damage in Louisiana, Mississippi, and Alabama.
- The Prophet Muhammad cartoon controversy sparks riots.
- An earthquake in Pakistan kills more than 81,000 people and leaves approximately 3 million homeless.
- Hamas wins 76 of 132 seats in the Palestinian legislative elections.
- Nuclear technology continues to proliferate.

CULTURE AND ITS CHARACTERISTICS

Culture is a distinctly human means of adapting to circumstances and transmitting this coping skill and knowledge to subsequent generations. Culture gives people a sense of who they are, of belonging, of how they should behave, and of what they should be doing. Culture impacts behavior, morale, and productivity at work, and includes values and patterns that influence company attitudes and actions. Culture is dynamic. Cultures change . . . but slowly.

Culture is often considered the driving force behind human behavior everywhere.

Culture is often considered the driving force behind human behavior everywhere. The concept has become the context to explain politics, economics, progress and failures. In that regard Huntington[11] has written:

> It is my hypothesis that the fundamental source of human conflict in this new world will not be primarily ideological or primarily economic. The great divisions among humankind and the dominating source of conflict will be culture.
>
> Culture and cultural identities . . . are shaping the patterns of cohesion, disintegration, and conflict in the post-cold war world. Global politics is being reconfigured along cultural lines . . . peoples and countries with

similar culture are coming together. Peoples and countries with different cultures are coming apart.

Prior to entering a new market, forming a partnership or buying a company, organizations spend time and money on "due diligence." The accuracy and sophistication of the financial market, product, and other aspects of this business endeavor are essential in the decision making, and are often a key determinant of eventual success. What is forgotten or minimized in both the business and politics is "cultural due diligence." The following models or frameworks on cultural analysis might be important in any due diligence exercise that has a cultural component. Chomsky[12] demonstrates his ability to master an incredible wealth of factual knowledge, and his skills exemplify political due diligence. Lewis[13] demonstrates the importance of cultural due diligence for business.

The following ten categories are a means for understanding either a macroculture or a microculture and can be useful for studying any group of people, whether they live in the rural South of the United States, India, the bustling city of Hong Kong, Banglore, Arusha in Tanzania or Bagdad in Iraq.

Sense of Self and Space. The comfort one has with self can be expressed differently by culture. Self-identity and appreciation can be manifested by humble bearing in one culture and by macho behavior in another. Independence and creativity are countered in other cultures by group cooperation and conformity. Americans have a sense of space that requires more distance between individuals, while Latins and Vietnamese will stand closer together. Some cultures are very structured and formal, while others are more flexible and informal.

Communication and Language. The communication system, verbal and nonverbal, distinguishes one group from another. Apart from the multitude of "foreign" languages, some nations have fifteen or more major spoken languages (within one language group there are dialects, accents, slang, jargon, and other such variations). Furthermore, the meanings given to gestures, for example, often differ by culture. So, while body language may be universal, its manifestation differs by locality. Subcultures, such as the military, have terminology and signals that cut across national boundaries (such as a salute or the rank system).

Dress and Appearance. This includes the outward garments and adornments, or lack thereof, as well as body decorations that tend to be culturally distinctive. We are aware of the Japanese kimono, the African headdress, the Englishman's bowler and umbrella, the Polynesian sarong, and the Native American headband. Some tribes smear their faces for battle, while some women use cosmetics to manifest beauty. Many subcultures wear distinctive clothing: the formal look of business, the jeans worn by youth throughout the world, and uniforms that segregate everyone from students to police.

Food and Feeding Habits. The manner in which food is selected, prepared, presented, and eaten often differs by culture. One man's pet is another person's delicacy. Americans love beef, yet it is forbidden to Hindus, while the forbidden food in Muslim and Jewish culture is normally pork, eaten extensively by the Chinese and others. Many restaurants cater to diverse diets and offer "national" dishes to meet varying cultural tastes. Feeding habits also differ, ranging from hands and chop sticks to full sets of cutlery. Even when cultures use a utensil such as a fork, one can distinguish a European from an American by which hand holds the implement.

Time and Time Consciousness. Sense of time differs by culture: some are exact and others are relative. Generally, Germans are precise about the clock, while many Latins are more casual. In some cultures, promptness is determined by age or status. Thus, in some countries, subordinates are expected on time at staff meetings, but the boss is the last to arrive. Yet, there are people in some other cultures who do not bother with hours or minutes, but manage their days by sunrise and sunset.

Time, in the sense of seasons of the year, varies by culture. Some areas of the world think in terms of winter, spring, summer, and fall; but for others the more meaningful designations may be rainy or dry seasons. In the United States, for example, the East and Midwest may be very conscious of the four seasons, while those in the West or Southwest tend to ignore such designations—Californians are more concerned with rainy months and mudslides or dry months and forest fires.

Many industries operate on round-the-clock schedules. This is the concern of chronobiologists who specialize in research on the body's internal clock by analysis of body temperature, chemical composition of blood serum and urine, sleepiness, and peak periods of feeling good. Drastic changes in time, such as can be brought on by shift work, can undermine both performance and personal life, leading to serious accidents on the job.

Relationships. Cultures fix human and organizational relationships by age, gender, status, and degree of kindred, as well as by wealth, power, and wisdom. The family unit is the most common expression of this characteristic, and the arrangement may go from small to large—in a Hindu household, the joint family includes under one roof, mother, father, children, parents, uncles, aunts, and cousins. In fact, one's physical location in such houses may also be determined, with males on one side of the house, females on the other. There are some places where the accepted marriage relationship is monogamy, while in other cultures it may be polygamy or polyandry (one wife, several husbands).

In some cultures, the authoritarian figure in the family is the head male, and this fixed relationship is then extended from home to community, explaining why some societies prefer to have a dictator head up the national family. Relationships between and among people vary by category—in some cultures, the elderly are honored, whereas in others they are ignored; in some cultures, women must wear veils and appear deferential, while in others the female is considered the equal, if not the superior of the male.

The military subculture has a classic determination of relationships by rank or protocol, such as the relationship between officers and enlisted personnel. Even when off duty, on base the recreational facilities are segregated for officers, noncommissioned, and enlisted personnel. The formalization of relationships is evident in some religious subcultures with titles such as reverend, guru, pastor, rabbi, or bishop.

Values and Norms. The need systems of cultures vary, as do the priorities they attach to certain behavior in the group. Those operating on a survival level value the gathering of food, adequate covering, and shelter, while those with high security needs value material things, money, job titles, as well as law and order. Many countries are in the midst of a values revolution. In some Pacific Island cultures, the greater one's status becomes, the more one is expected to give away or share.

In any event, from its value system, a culture sets norms of behavior for that society. These acceptable standards for membership may range from work ethic or pleasure to absolute obedience or permissiveness for children; from rigid submission of the wife to her husband to a more equal relationship. Because conventions are learned, some cultures demand honesty with members of one's own group but accept a more relaxed standard with strangers. Some of these conventions are expressed in gift-giving; rituals for birth, death, and marriage; guidelines for privacy; a show of respect or deference; expression of good manners, and so on. The globalization process and telecommunications are leading to the development of some shared values that cross borders and express planetary concerns, such as protection of the environment.[7]

From its value system, a culture sets norms of behavior for that society.

Beliefs and Attitudes. Possibly the most difficult classification is ascertaining the major belief themes of a people and how this and other factors influence their attitudes toward themselves, others, and what happens in their world. People in all cultures seem to have a concern for the supernatural that is evident in their religions and religious practices. In the history of human development, there has been an evolution in our spiritual sense so that today many individuals use terms like cosmic consciousness to indicate their belief in the transcendental powers. Between these two extremes in the spiritual continuum, religious traditions in various cultures consciously or unconsciously influence our attitudes toward life, death, and the hereafter. Western culture seems to be largely influenced by the Judeo-Christian-Islamic traditions, while Eastern or Asian cultures have been dominated by Buddhism, Confucianism, Taoism, and Hinduism. Religion, to a degree, expresses the philosophy of a people about important facets of life—it is influenced by culture and vice versa.

Mental Process and Learning. Some cultures emphasize one aspect of brain development over another so that one may observe striking differences in the way people think and learn. Anthropologist Edward Hall maintains that the mind is internalized culture, and the mental process involves how people organize and process information. Life in a particular locale defines the rewards and punishment for learning or not learning certain information or in a certain way, and this is confirmed and reinforced by the culture. For example, Germans stress logic, while logic for a Hopi Indian is based on preserving the integrity of their social system and all the relationships connected with it. Some cultures favor abstract thinking and conceptualization, while others prefer rote memory and learning. What seems to be universal is that each culture has a reasoning process, but then each manifests the process in its own distinctive way.

Work Habits and Practices. Another dimension of a group's culture is its attitude toward work—the dominant types of work, the division of work, and the work habits or practices, such as promotions or incentives. Work has been defined as exertion or effort directed to produce or accomplish something. Some cultures espouse a work ethic in which all members are expected to engage in a desirable and worthwhile activity. In other societies this is broadly defined to include cultural pursuits in music and the arts or sports. For some cultures, the worthiness of the activity is narrowly measured in terms of income produced, or the worth of the individual is assessed in terms of job status. In Japan, the cultural loyalty to family is transferred to the organization that employs the person and the quality of one's performance—it is expressed in work group participation, communication, and consensus.

Another way of observing a culture is to note the manner and method of offering praise for accomplishments, which can include testimonial dinners, pay increases, commendations, and medals.

These ten general classifications are a basic model for assessing a particular culture. It does not include every aspect of culture, nor is it the only way to analyze culture. This approach enables one to examine a people systemically. The categories are a beginning means of cultural understanding as one travels and visits different cultures. Likewise, the model can be used to study the microcultures within a majority national culture. All aspects of culture are interrelated, and to change one part is to change the whole. There is a danger in trying to compartmentalize a complex concept like culture, while trying to retain a sense of its whole. Culture is a complex system of interrelated parts that must be understood holistically.

Culture is a complex system of interrelated parts that must be understood holistically.

SYSTEMS APPROACH TO CULTURE

There are many different anthropological approaches to cultural analysis, and many prefer to use a coordinated systems approach as an alternative to understanding other cultures. A system, in this sense, refers to an ordered assemblage or combination of correlated parts that form a unitary whole.[14]

Kinship System—the family relationships and the way a people reproduce, train, and socialize their children. The typical North American family is a nuclear and rather independent unit. In many countries, there may be an extended family that consists of several generations held together through the male line (patrilineal) or through the female line (matrilineal). Such families have a powerful influence on child rearing, and often on nation building. Family influences and loyalties can affect job performance or business negotiations.

Educational System—how young or new members of a society are provided with information, knowledge, skills, and values. Educational systems may be formal and informal within any culture. How people learn varies by culture.

Economic System—the manner in which the society produces and distributes its goods and services. The Japanese economic system is in some ways an extension of the family and is group-oriented. Until recently, the world was divided into capitalistic or socialistic economic blocks, and economies were labeled *First World* (advanced free enterprise systems); *Second World* (socialist or communistic societies based on centralized planning and control; and *Third World* (developing nations moving from the agricultural to industrial or post-industrial stages). These categories are now outdated. Today, economies are mixed—some supposed Third World economies have high technology sectors, as in India and China; and Second World, formerly in the European Eastern Bloc, are in transition to free market systems, such as in Poland or Lithuania. Another trend beyond national economies is toward regional economic cooperatives or association that cut across national and ideological boundaries, such as is happening with NAFTA and the European Union. Macroeconomics is the study of such systems.

Political System—the dominant means of governance for maintaining order and exercising power or authority. Some cultures are tribal where chiefs rule, others have a ruling royal family with an operating king, while some prefer democracy.

Religious System—the means for providing meaning and motivation beyond the material aspects of life, that is, the spiritual side of a culture or its approach to the supernatural. This transcending system may lift a people to great heights of accomplishment, as is witnessed in the pyramids of Egypt and the Renaissance of Europe. It is possible to project the history and future of India, for instance, in terms of the impact of

How people learn varies by culture.

SYSTEMS APPROACH

its belief in reincarnation, which is enshrined in its major religion. Diverse national cultures can be somewhat unified under a shared religious belief in Islam or Christianity, for example. In some countries, Islam is becoming the basis for governance, legal, and political systems. In others, religion dominates legal and political systems, such as Judaism in Israel or Roman Catholicism in the Republic of Ireland. The influence of religion is culturally weakening in some states, as with Roman Catholicism in France and Lutheranism in Sweden. Religion can also be a source of divisiveness and conflict in society, for example, Northern Ireland; the former Yugoslavia (especially Bosnia and Kosovo); and Africa (including Algeria and Rwanda). Unfortunately, history demonstrates that in the name of religion, zealots and extremists may engage in culturally repressive behavior, such as religious persecutions, ethnic cleansing, terrorism of nonbelievers, and even "holy" wars.

Association System—the network of social groupings that people form, whether in person or electronically. These may range from fraternal and secret societies to professional/trade associations. Some cultures are very group oriented and create formal and informal associations for every conceivable type of activity (e.g., the culture in the United States). In some countries, families organize into clans, finding it difficult to work together for the common national good, as in Afghanistan and Iraq. Other societies are individualistic and avoid such organizing, such as in France.

Health System—the way a culture prevents and cures disease or illness, or cares for victims of disasters or accidents. The concepts of health and wholeness, well-being, and medical problems differ by culture. Some countries have witch doctors, spiritual remedies, and herb medications. Others, like India, have fewer government-sponsored social services, while Britain has a system of socialized medicine. The United States is in the midst of a major transition in its health-care and delivery system, and there is increasing emphasis on universal coverage, prevention and wellness health models, and alternative holistic medical treatments. Medical practitioners can be culturally biased. For example, Western medicine tended to ignore folk medicine, especially in Asia and Africa. Fortunately, in this century modern health-care workers are more open and are even practicing cross-cultural medicine. If the method or cure relieves pain and suffering without causing harm, they are willing to try and even adopt it.

Recreational System—the ways in which a people socialize or use their leisure time. What may be considered play in one culture may be viewed as work in another and vice versa. In some cultures "sport" has considerable political implications, in others it is solely for enjoyment, while in still others it is big business. Some cultures cherish the creative and performing arts, providing financial support for artists and musicians. Certain types of entertainment, such as a form of folk dancing, seem to cut across cultures. Global communications are forcefully impacting the media and entertainment industries. Music, sports, films, and special cultural or athletic events can be quickly broadcast world-wide. As a result, the youth subculture has similar tastes that go beyond national differences. The mass media and Internet become forums for electronic commerce and exchange in terms of leisure and recreation.

★KEY CULTURAL TERMINOLOGY★

The specialists who make a formal study of culture use terms that may be helpful to those trying to comprehend the significance of this phenomena in business or international life.

Patterns and Themes

Some cultural anthropologists search for a single integrated pattern to describe a particular culture. Thus, the Pueblo Indians may be designated as "Apollonian"—people who stick to the "middle of the road" and avoid excess or conflict in their valuing of existence. To pinpoint a consistent pattern of thought and action in a culture is difficult, so other scholars prefer to seek a summative theme. This is a position, declared or implied, that simulates activity and controls behavior; it is usually tacitly approved or openly promoted in the society. One can note that in most Asian cultures there is a "fatalism" theme, while in the American business subculture the theme is profits or the "bottom line."

Explicit and Implicit

Some aspects of culture are overt, while others are covert. Anthropologists remind us that each different way of life makes assumptions about the ends or purposes of human existence, about what to expect from each other, and about what constitutes fulfillment or frustration. Some of this is explicit in folklore and may also be manifest in law, regulations, customs, or traditions. Other aspects are implicit in the culture, and one must infer such tacit premises by observing consistent trends in word and deed. The distinction between public and hidden culture points up how much of our daily activity is governed by patterns and themes, the origin or meaning of which we are only dimly aware, if not totally unaware. Such culturally governed behavior facilitates the routine of daily living so that one may perform in a society many actions without thinking about them. This cultural conditioning provides the freedom to devote conscious thinking to new and creative pursuits. It is startling to realize that some of our behavior is not

Some aspects of culture are overt, while others are covert.

entirely free or consciously willed by us. At times this can be a national problem, such as when a society finally realizes that implicit in its culture is a form of racism, which requires both legislation and education to rectify. Most cultures tend to discriminate against certain groups and believers, and this too may be covert. Thus, there is a global movement to rectify such bias toward women, gays, and ethnic or racial minorities, as well as any outsider or foreigner.

Micro- or Subcultures

Within a larger society, group, or nation sharing a common majority or macroculture, there may be subgroupings of people possessing characteristic traits that distinguish them from the others. These subcultures may be described in group classification by age, class, gender, race, or some other entity that differentiates this micro- from the macroculture. Youth, or more specifically teenagers, share certain cultural traits, as do other ethnic groups. There are many microcultures, such as white- or blue-collar workers, police or the military, college students or the drug culture. Within a particular religious culture, there may be many sects or subcultures. As with any profession or vocational field that also has unique cultures, there are differing specialties and focus that are subcultures of the main group. Academia has a general culture and many subdivisions by discipline of study or specialization. The application of this concept is endless.

Universals and Diversity

The paradox of culture is the commonalties that exist in the midst of its diffusion or even confusion. There are generalizations that may be made about all cultures that are referred to as *universals*: age-grading, body adornments, calendar, courtship, divisions of labor, education, ethics, food taboos, incest and inheritance rules, language, marriage, mourning, mythology, numerals, penal sanctions, property rights, supernatural beliefs, status differentiation, toolmaking and trade, visiting, weaning, etc. Thus, certain activities occur across cultures, but their manifestation may be unique in a particular society. And that brings us to the opposite concept of cultural *diversity*. Some form of sports or humor or music may be common to all peoples, but the way in which it is accomplished is distinctive in various cultural groupings.

Rational/Irrational/Nonrational Behavior

There are many definitions of culture. Consider it as historically created designs for living that may be rational, irrational, and nonrational. *Rational* behavior in a culture is based on what that group considers reasonable for achieving its goals. *Irrational* behavior deviates from the accepted norms of a society and may result from an individual's deep frustration in trying to satisfy needs; it would appear to be done without reason and possibly largely as an emotional response. *Nonrational* behavior is neither based on reason, nor against reasonable expectations—it is dictated by one's own culture or subculture. A great deal of behavior is of this type, and we are unaware of why we do it, why we believe what we do, or that we may be biased or prejudiced from the perspective of those outside our cultural group. How often and when to take a bath frequently is a cultural dictate, just as what food constitutes breakfast. What is rational in one culture may be irrational in another, and vice versa.

Tradition

This is a very important aspect of culture that may be expressed in unwritten customs, taboos, and sanctions. Tradition can program a people as to what are proper behavior and procedures relative to food, dress, and to certain types of people, what to value, avoid, or de-emphasize. As the song on the subject of "tradition" from the musical *Fiddler on the Roof* extols:

> Because of our traditions, we keep our sanity.... Tradition tells us how to sleep, how to work, how to wear clothes... How did it get started? I don't know—it's a tradition.... Because of our traditions, everyone knows who he is and what God expects of him![15]

Traditions provide a people with a "mind-set" and have a powerful influence on their moral system for evaluating what is right or wrong, good or bad, desirable or not. Traditions express a particular culture, giving its members a sense of belonging and uniqueness. But whether one is talking of a tribal or national culture, a military or religious subculture, traditions should be reexamined regularly for their relevance and validity. Mass global communications stimulate acquisition of new values and behavior patterns that may more rapidly undermine ancient, local, or religious traditions, especially among women and young people worldwide.

The following struck the authors' imagination when a manager for a high tech company brought it to our attention namely, tradition and superstition express themselves when numbering floors in a hotel. We added some observations of our own as well (see Exhibit 1.1).

Some of these cultural variables have been researched and a "cultural profile" developed by Schmitz[16] for many countries. There are ten concepts in the model.

1. <u>Environment</u>. Social environments can be categorized according to whether they view and relate to people, objects, and issues

Traditions provide a people with a "mind-set."

It is quite normal in the United States to see the 13th floor absent in the selection of floors on the elevator directory panel. This is due, of course, to our cultural bias regarding the number 13 being "unlucky." By omitting it in the numbering sequence of the hotel floors, one avoids the anxiety of a superstitious customer. After entering the Hai-Li Hotel elevator in China and punching in my floor selection, I quickly noticed that not only was number 13 absent, but 14 was as well. As one rose to the higher floors in the hotel, one passed from floor number 12 to floor number 15. I mentioned this to my friends, and they assured me that the Chinese culture had an aversion to an unlucky number as well, only it was number 14. So our culturally astute hotel had decided to delete both numbers, thus showing their sensitivity (and respect) to both cultures, while showing favor to neither. Similarly in some countries, the custom is to designate the entrance floor as the "ground" floor, while the next floor becomes labeled the "first" floor, as the numbering continues upward. This is confusing to foreigners from countries where the entrance area from the street is known as the "first floor"; the problem worsens when more floors are being built underground, and as you enter, the visitor may find him or herself on the second or even third floor. Even basements are being built downward in levels 1, 2, 3, etc., and may be given exotic names after fruit or flowers. All this shakes up the staid, but makes the world more interesting.

A present orientation is indicated by placing a focus on short-term and quick results.

from the orientation of **control** (change environment), **harmony** (build balance), or **constraint** (external forces set parameters).

2. Time. A **past** orientation is indicated by placing a high value on preestablished processes and procedures. A **present** orientation is indicated by placing a focus on short-term and quick results. A **future** orientation is indicated by placing a focus on long-term results.

3. Action. Social environments can be distinguished by their approach to actions and interactions. An emphasis on relationships, reflection, and analysis indicates a **being** orientation. A focus on task and action indicates a **doing** orientation.

4. Communication. An emphasis on implicit communication and reliance on nonverbal cues indicates **high-context** orientation. A **low-context** orientation is indicated by a strong value on explicit communication.

5. Space. Cultures can be categorized according to the distinctions they make between **public** and **private** spaces.

6. <u>Power</u>. Social environments can be categorized by the way they structure power relationships. A **hierarchy** orientation is indicated by a high degree of acceptability of differential power relationships and social stratification. An **equality** orientation is indicated by little tolerance for differential power relationships and the minimizing of social stratification.

7. <u>Individualism</u>. An emphasis on independence and a focus on the individual indicate an **individualistic** orientation. An emphasis on affiliation and subordination of individual interest to that of a group, company, or organization indicates a **collectivistic** orientation.

8. <u>Competitiveness</u>. An emphasis on personal achievements, individual assertiveness, and success indicate a **competitive** orientation. Valuing quality of life, interdependence, and relationships indicates a **cooperative** orientation.

9. <u>Structure</u>. Environments that value adherence to rules, regulations, and procedures are considered **order** oriented and prefer predictability and minimization of risk. Environments that value improvisation exhibit a **flexibility** orientation and tend to reward risk taking, tolerate ambiguity, and value innovation.

10. <u>Thinking</u>. Cultures can expect, reinforce, and reward either a **deductive** approach (an emphasis on theory, principles, concepts, and abstract logic) or an **inductive** approach (emphasis on data, experience, and experimentation). They may also either emphasize a **linear** approach (analysis and segmentation of issues) or a **systemic** approach (synthesis, holism, and the "big picture").

Of course, it is important to keep in mind these constructs are not rigid and material diversity illustrates this. Though of the concepts along a continuum, where extremes are unlikely and placement is relative, it is this which leads us to Hofstede's research.

Hofstede's Early Research

To create opportunities for collaboration, global leaders must learn not only the customs, courtesies, and business protocols of their counterparts from other countries, but they must also understand the national character, management philosophies, and mind-sets of the people. Dr. Geert Hofstede, a European research consultant, has helped identify important dimensions of national character. He firmly believes that "culture counts" and has identified four dimensions of national culture:

1. <u>Power distance</u>—indicates "the extent to which a society accepts that power in institutions and organizations is distributed unequally."

He firmly believes that "culture counts" and has identified four dimensions of national culture.

2. Uncertainty avoidance—indicates "the extent to which a society feels threatened by uncertain or ambiguous situations."

3. Individualism—refers to a "loosely knit social framework in a society in which people are supposed to take care of themselves and of their immediate families only." Collectivism, the opposite, occurs when there is a "tight social framework in which people distinguish between in-groups and out-groups; they expect their in-group (relatives, clan, organizations) to look after them, and in exchange for that owe absolute loyalty to it."

4. Masculinity—with its opposite pole, *femininity*, expresses "the extent to which the dominant values in society are assertiveness, money and material things, not caring for others, quality of life, and people."

A significant dimension related to leadership in Hofstede's original study of 40 countries is the power distance dimension. He assigned an index value to each country on the basis of mean ratings of employees on a number of key questions.

Exhibit 1.2 shows the positions of the 40 countries on the power distance and uncertainty avoidance scales, and Exhibit 1.3 shows the countries' positions on the power distance and individualism scales.

The United States ranked fifteenth on power distance, ninth on uncertainty avoidance (both of these are below the average), fortieth on individualism (the most individualist country in the sample), and twenty-eighth on masculinity (above average).

In Hofstede's study the United States ranked fifteenth out of 40 on the power distance dimension. If this had been higher, then the theories of leadership taught in the United States might have been expected to be more Machiavellian. We might also ask how U.S. leaders are selected. Most are selected on the basis of competence, and it is the position of the person that provides his or her authority in the United States, which is, theoretically at least, an egalitarian society. In France, which has a higher power distance index score, there is little concern with participative management but great concern with who has the power.

Even today, French industry and the managers who run it are a mixture of the old and the new. France is still, in some ways, a country of family empires with many paternalistic traditions. There is also a remnant of a feudalistic heritage that is deeply rooted within the French spirit, which could account for the very conservative and autocratic nature of their business methodology. Hofstede has shown that in countries with lower power distance scores than the United States, such as Sweden and Germany, there is considerable acceptance of leadership styles and management models that are even more participative than presently exist. Industrial democracy and codetermination is a style that does not find much sympathy in the United States.

EXHIBIT 1.2

POSITIONS OF 40 COUNTRIES ON THE POWER DISTANCE AND UNCERTAINTY AVOIDANCE SCALES

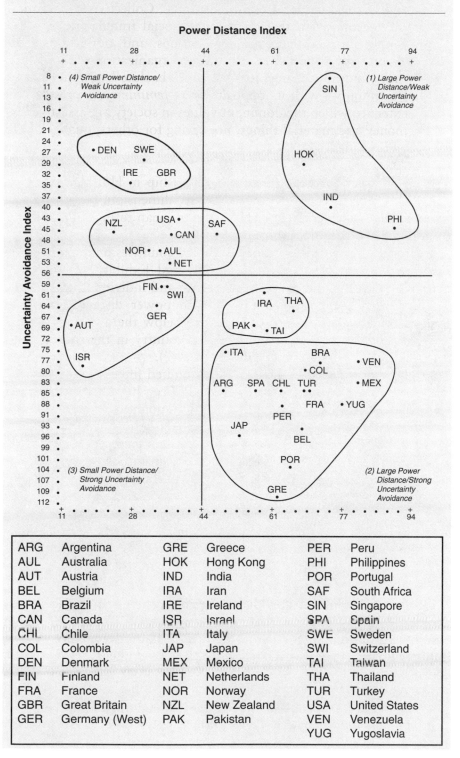

ARG	Argentina	GRE	Greece	PER	Peru
AUL	Australia	HOK	Hong Kong	PHI	Philippines
AUT	Austria	IND	India	POR	Portugal
BEL	Belgium	IRA	Iran	SAF	South Africa
BRA	Brazil	IRE	Ireland	SIN	Singapore
CAN	Canada	ISR	Israel	SPA	Spain
CHL	Chile	ITA	Italy	SWE	Sweden
COL	Colombia	JAP	Japan	SWI	Switzerland
DEN	Denmark	MEX	Mexico	TAI	Taiwan
FIN	Finland	NET	Netherlands	THA	Thailand
FRA	France	NOR	Norway	TUR	Turkey
GBR	Great Britain	NZL	New Zealand	USA	United States
GER	Germany (West)	PAK	Pakistan	VEN	Venezuela
				YUG	Yugoslavia

EXHIBIT 1.3

POSITIONS OF 40 COUNTRIES ON THE POWER DISTANCE AND INDIVIDUALISM SCALES

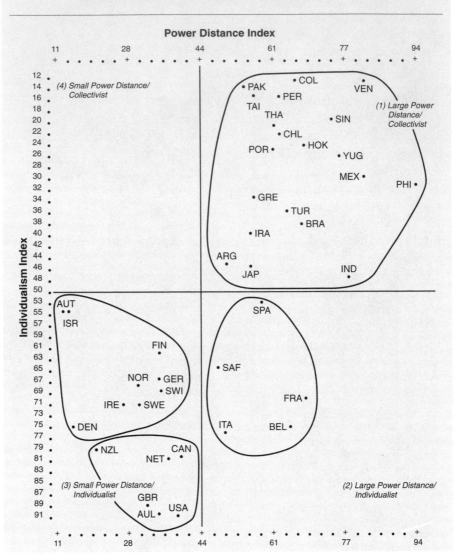

Hofstede has demonstrated that in Germany there is high uncertainty avoidance and, therefore, industrial democracy is brought about first by legislation. In Sweden, where uncertainty avoidance is low, industrial democracy was started with local experiments. Hofstede[17,18] continues:

The crucial fact about leadership in any culture is that it is a complement to subordinateship. The Power Distance Index scores . . . are in fact based on the values of people as *subordinates*, not on the values of superiors. Whatever a naive literature on leadership may try to make us believe, a leader cannot choose his style at will; what is feasible depends to a large extent on the cultural conditioning of his/her subordinates. I therefore show . . . a description of the type of subordinateship that, other things being equal, a leader can expect to meet in societies at three different levels of Power Distance, and to which his/her leadership has to respond. The middle level represents what most likely is found in the U.S. environment.

Where does this leave us as global managers? Perhaps we pick and choose, and adopt what is appropriate in the home culture. The matter is brought into focus as we examine a specific management system. The underlying assumptions regarding leadership in the United States are clearly seen in the practice of management by objectives. This assumes that a subordinate is independent enough to negotiate meaningfully with a superior (not too high of a power distance), that both the superior and the subordinate are willing to take risks (a low uncertainty avoidance), and that performance is important to both (high masculinity).

Hofstede continues to demonstrate the importance of cross-cultural research as management by objectives (MBO) is applied to Germany.

> Let us now take the case of Germany. This is also a below-average Power Distance country, so the dialogue element in MBO should present no problem. However, Germany scores considerably higher on Uncertainty Avoidance; consequently, the tendency towards accepting risk and ambiguity will not be present to the same extent. The idea of replacing the arbitrary authority of the boss by the impersonal authority of mutually agreed-upon objectives, however, fits the low Power Distance, high Uncertainty Avoidance cultural cluster very well. The objectives become the subordinates' "superego."

The consequences of Hofstede's conclusions are significant. Leadership, decision making, teamwork, organization, motivation, and in fact everything managers do is learned. Management functions are learned, and they are based on assumptions about one's place in the world. Managers from other business systems are not "underdeveloped" American managers.

Bond's Confucian Cultural Patterns

Another researcher, Michael H. Bond, believes that the taxonomies developed by Western scholars have a Western bias.[19] In his research, he found four dimensions of cultural patterns: integration, human-heartedness, interpersonal harmony, and group solidarity. The *integration dimension* refers in a broad sense to the continuum of social

Managers from other business systems are not "underdeveloped" American managers.

stability. If a person scores high on this dimension, he or she will display and value the behaviors of tolerance, noncompetitiveness, interpersonal harmony, and group solidarity. *Human-heartedness* refers to the values of gentleness and compassion. People who score high on this dimension value patience, courtesy, and kindness toward others. *Moral discipline* refers to the essence of restraint and moderation in one's regular daily activities. If one scores high on this dimension, the behaviors valued are following the middle way, regarding personal desires as negative. The *Confucian work dynamic* refers to an individual's attitude and orientation toward work and life. According to Bond, the behaviors that are exhibited along this continuum are consistent with the teachings of Confucius.

Kong Fu Zen, renamed Confucius by Jesuit missionaries, was a Chinese civil servant who lived during the Warring States Period about 2500 years ago. He sought to determine ways in which Chinese society could move away from fighting among themselves so that through discipline, human relationships, ethics, politics, and business average themselves harmoniously. He was well known for his wisdom and wit and was regularly surrounded by followers who recorded his teachings. Confucianism is a set of practical principles and ethical rules for daily life.

Confucius taught that people should be educated, skilled, hardworking, thrifty, modest, patient, and unrelenting in all things. Human nature is assumed to be inherently good, and it is the responsibility of the individual to train his or her character in these standards of behavior.

Exhibit 1.4 represents a framework for understanding cultural differences along several dimensions and will be valuable for any person working in the global world.

Many other researchers including Fons Trompenaars and Charles Hampden-Turner have studied culture and written persuasively on culture's impact on global business in the twenty-first century.

GLOBAL LEADERS AS INFLUENCERS

A challenge global leaders experience today is how to influence across cultures and functions the individuals with whom they work and their global partners. Aware of the cultural influences on the personalities, motivations, and values of their counterparts, skillful leaders are able to influence others, whether it is by giving orders and directions to individuals under their authority or by "influencing with authority." Leaders know what they want to accomplish but how to achieve it and who are the key people they need to influence to succeed is a routine unknown.

According to Cohen and Bradford[20] the following points are key in successfully influencing others.

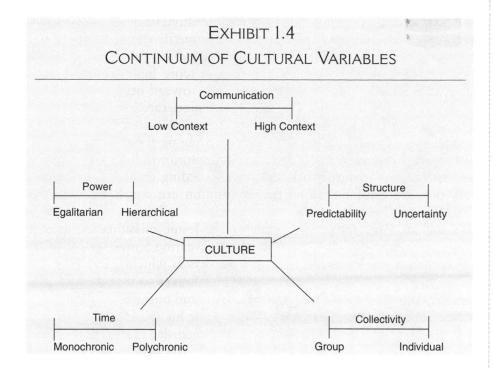

EXHIBIT 1.4
CONTINUUM OF CULTURAL VARIABLES

Communication
Low Context — High Context

Power
Egalitarian — Hierarchical

Structure
Predictability — Uncertainty

CULTURE

Time
Monochronic — Polychronic

Collectivity
Group — Individual

- Assume any individual, even an adversary, can be an ally.
- Be clear what you want.
- Understand the "cultures" of all those to be influenced.
- Identify your own and others currencies.
- Build the relationships and develop partners.
- Use formal and informal influencing skills.

SUCCESSFULLY INFLUENCE OTHERS Cohen & Bradford

Exhibit 1.5 shows a model of influence without authority.

All leaders have some power, which is the ability to influence others, inside or outside of an organization or enterprise whether it is a business, government agency or a nation, to do what you want them to do when you want them to do it. The total power of any individual is a combination of formal power or power associated with position plus informal power, which is personal and a function of one's skills, expertise and credibility.

Verma[21] states there are eight sources of power.

There are eight sources of power.

- Legitimate power—derives from position or status
- Persuasive—derives from personal skills and ability in winning others cooperation
- Contact/network—derives from who we know and our connections
- Information—derives from the information we have and knowledge of how organizations work
- Expertise—derives from knowledge
- Referent—derives from our reputation in an organization

SOURCES OF POWER Verma

■ Coercive—derives from our ability to punish
■ Reward—derives from our ability to reward

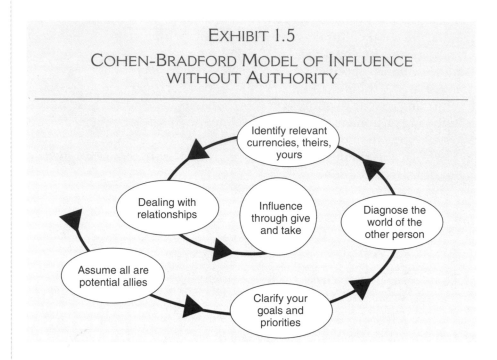

EXHIBIT 1.5
COHEN-BRADFORD MODEL OF INFLUENCE
WITHOUT AUTHORITY

CULTURAL UNDERSTANDING AND SENSITIVITY

"Ethnocentric" is defined as "Belief in the inherent superiority of one's own group and culture..."

The global leader, sensitive to cultural differences, appreciates a people's distinctiveness and effectively communicates with individuals from different cultures. A global leader does not impose his/her own cultural attitudes and approaches. Thus, by respecting the cultural differences of others, we will not be labeled as "ethnocentric," defined in *The Random House Dictionary* as:

> Belief in the inherent superiority of one's own group and culture; it may be accompanied by a feeling of contempt for those considered as foreign; it views and measures alien cultures and groups in terms of one's own culture.

Through cross-cultural experiences, we become more broad-minded and tolerant of cultural "uniqueness." When this is coupled with some formal study of the concept of culture, we not only gain new insights for improving our human relations, but we become aware of the impact of our native culture. Cultural understanding may minimize the impact of culture shock and maximize intercultural experiences, as well as increase professional development and organizational effectiveness.

Cultural sensitivity should teach us that culture and behavior are relative and that we should be more tentative, and less absolute, in human interaction.

The first step in managing cultural differences effectively is increasing one's general cultural awareness. We must understand the concept of culture and its characteristics before we can fully benefit from the study of cultural specifics and a foreign language.

Further, we should appreciate the impact of our specific cultural background on our own mind-set and behavior, as well as those of colleagues and customers with whom we interact in the workplace.[22] This takes on special significance within a more diverse business environment, often the result of increasing migration from less developed to more developed economies.

CROSS-CULTURAL LEARNING

To increase effectiveness across cultures, *training* must be the focus of the job, while *education* thought of with reference to the individual, and *development* reserved for organizational concerns. Whether one is concerned with intercultural training, education, or development, all employees should learn about the influence of culture and be effective cross-cultural communicators if they are to work with minorities within their own society or with foreigners encountered at home or abroad. For example, there has been a significant increase in foreign investments in the United States—millions of Americans now work within the borders of their own country for foreign employers. All along the U.S.-Mexican border, twin plants have emerged that provide for a flow of goods and services between the two countries.

A new reality of the global marketplace is the Information Highway and its impact on jobs and cross-cultural communications. Many skilled workers in advanced economies are watching their positions migrate overseas, where college educated nationals are doing high technology tasks for less pay. The Internet has changed how global business is and will be conducted for many decades.

Not considering computer language, most international exchanges take place with individuals using English as a second language. While a few corporate representatives will travel abroad, the main communication will occur by means of satellites on the Internet through modems connected to laptop or personal computers. Offshore operations done electronically in developing countries are stimulated by growing software applications that turn skilled tasks into routine work. Cross-cultural sensitivity is essential when participating in teleconferences or video conferences. Electronic media also require appropriate etiquette and protocols to create cultural synergy.

The first step in managing cultural differences effectively is increasing one's general cultural awareness.

To stay competitive globally more and more corporations are increasing their investments and activities in foreign countries. U.S. engineers can work on a project during the day, and then send it electronically to Asia or elsewhere for additional work while they sleep. Such trends represent an enormous challenge for cross-cultural competence. C-Bay Systems in Annapolis, Maryland, for instance, transmits U.S. physicians' dictations about patients to their subsidiary operations in India where they are transcribed into English, sent back to headquarters by computer, then the completed version is sent on to the medical office from which the communication originated.

Another example of "going global" is seen in personalized service firms such as law and accounting. These professions are increasingly engaging in cross-border activities, hiring local practitioners who comprehend their own unique culture, language, and legal or accounting systems. The need for international expertise and capital is one reason for this trend. Companies of professionals are forming alliances with their foreign counterparts such as the Alliance of European Lawyers. To be successful, the acquisition process then requires an integration of *national*, *organizational*, and *professional cultures*. Under these circumstances, culture becomes a critical factor ensuring business success, particularly with the twenty-first century trend toward economies of scale favoring large, multidisciplinary and multinational professional service organizations.[23]

In only 10% of 191 nations are the people ethnically or racially homogenous. Never before in history have so many inhabitants traveled beyond their homelands, either to travel or work abroad, or to flee as refugees. In host countries, the social fabric is being reconfigured and strained by massive waves of immigrants, whether legal or illegal.[24]

It is estimated that Chinese now constitute 3% of New York City's population, with a quarter million of them concentrated in Manhattan Island's Chinatown, which overflows into older ethnic neighborhoods. This is the largest Chinese expatriate group outside Southeast Asia.[25]

Many corporate and government leaders, business students and citizens still operate with dated mind-sets regarding the world, the people in various societies, the nature of work, the worker, and the management process itself. The Industrial Age has given way to the Information Age, and we can only speculate on its replacement in the next one hundred years. Possibly the Space Age? Capra and Steindl Rast[26] state:

> Now, in the old paradigm it was also recognized that things are interrelated. But conceptually you first had the things with their properties, and then there were mechanisms and forces that interconnected them. In the new paradigm we say the things themselves do not have intrinsic properties. All the properties flow from their relationships. This is what I mean by understanding the properties of the parts from the dynamics of the whole, because these relationships are dynamic relationships. So

In only 10% of 191 nations are the people ethnically or racially homogenous.

the only way to understand the part is to understand its relationship to the whole. This insight occurred in physics in the 1920s and this is also a key insight of ecology. Ecologists think exactly in this way. They say an organism is defined by its relationship to the rest.

Thus, today's leaders are challenged to create new models of management systems. For that to happen, managers and other professionals must become more innovative and recognize the contribution of each individual or unit to the effective workings of the whole.

As the late Peter Drucker consistently observed, the art and science of management is in its own revolution, and many of the assumptions on which management practice was based are now becoming obsolete.

Foreign competition and the need to trade more effectively overseas have forced most corporations to become more culturally sensitive and globally minded. Managing people from different cultures is receiving the attention of business students as well as those in education and human resource development. Global management is a component in most executive education training programs worldwide.

According to Rhinesmith:[27]

> Global managers must reframe the boundaries of their world . . . of space, time, scope, structure, geography and function; of functional, professional, and technical skills from a past age; of thinking and classification relative to rational to intuitive, national versus foreign, we versus they; of cultural assumptions, values and beliefs about your relations with others, and your understanding of yourself.

How do companies foster and create effective global managers? What is a global manager? Companies with worldwide operations are pondering these questions, plus many others. They find that the human resource component of the answer is, at times, more limiting than the capital investment in globalization. Bartlett and Ghoshal[28] state:

> Clearly, there is no single model for the global manager. Neither the old-line international specialist nor the more recent global generalist can cope with the complexities of cross-border strategies. Indeed, the dynamism of today's marketplace calls for managers with diverse skills. Responsibility for worldwide operations belongs to senior business, country, and functional executives who focus on the intense interchanges and subtle negotiations required. In contrast, those in middle management and front-line jobs need well-defined responsibilities, a clear understanding of their organization's transnational mission, and a sense of accountability.

Percy Barnevik, former President and CEO of Asea Brown Boveri (ABB), responded when asked if there is such a thing as a global manager:[29]

> Global managers are made, not born. This is not a natural process. We are herd animals. We like people who are like us. But there are many things you can do. Obviously, you rotate people around the world. There is no substitute for line experience in three or four countries to create a global perspective. You also encourage people to work in mixed nation-

Global managers must reframe the boundaries of their world . . .

Global managers are made, not born.

ality teams. You *force* them to create personal alliances across borders, which means that sometimes you interfere in hiring decisions.

You also have to acknowledge cultural differences without becoming paralyzed by them. We've done some surveys, as have lots of other companies, and we find interesting differences in perception. For example, a Swede may think a Swiss is not completely frank and open, that he doesn't know exactly where he stands. That is a cultural phenomenon. Swiss culture shuns disagreement. A Swiss might say, "Let's come back to that point later, let me review it with my colleagues." A Swede would prefer to confront the issue directly. How do we undo hundreds of years of upbringing and education? We don't, and we shouldn't try to. But we do need to broaden understanding.

Sheridan[30] found three clusters of leadership competencies and included intrapersonal competencies, interpersonal competencies and social competencies. The following Seven C's apply not only to U.S. leaders but any global leaders. Her summary is shown in Exhibit 1.6.

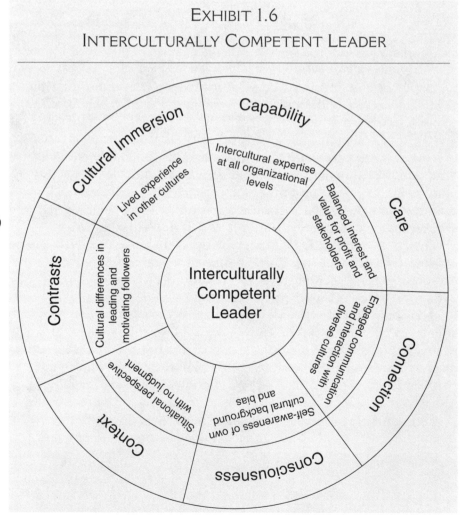

EXHIBIT 1.6
INTERCULTURALLY COMPETENT LEADER

KEY CONCEPTS FOR GLOBAL LEADERSHIP

The following ten concepts contain the underlying message of this book. An awareness of and an application of these concepts to one's organization has direct relevance to the effectiveness of global managers, international lawyers, economic and community development specialists, engineers and technicians, public health officials, and ultimately everyone working in today's multicultural environment. An understanding and utilization of these concepts is critical to successful global performance.

Global Leadership—being capable of operating effectively in a global environment while being respectful of cultural diversity. This is an individual who can manage accelerating change and differences. The global leader is open and flexible in approaching others, can cope with situations and people disparate from his or her background, and is willing to reexamine and alter personal attitudes and perceptions.

Cross-Cultural Communication—recognizing what is involved in one's image of self and one's role, personal needs, values, standards, expectations, all of which are culturally conditioned. Such a person understands the impact of cultural factors on communication and is willing to revise and expand such images as part of the process of growth. Furthermore, he or she is aware of verbal and nonverbal differences in communication with persons from another culture. Not only does such a person seek to learn another language, but he or she is cognizant that even when people speak the same language, cultural differences can alter communication symbols and meanings and result in misunderstandings.

Cultural Sensitivity—integrating the characteristics of culture in general, with experiences in specific organizational, minority, or foreign cultures. Such a person understands the cultural influences on behavior. This individual translates such cultural awareness into effective relationships with those who are different.

Acculturation—effectively adjusting and adapting to a specific culture, whether that be a subculture within one's own country or abroad. Such a person is alert to the impact of culture shock in successfully managing transitions. Therefore, when operating in an unfamiliar culture or dealing with employees from diverse cultural backgrounds, this person develops the necessary skills and avoids being ethnocentric.

Cultural Influences on Management—understanding that management philosophies are deeply rooted in culture and that management practices developed in one culture may not easily transfer to another. However, this insight can be used to appreciate the universal character of management and to identify with the subculture of modern managers. In the global marketplace, all management is multicultural.

Acculturation— effectively adjusting and adapting to a specific culture.

Effective Intercultural Performance—applying cultural theory and insight to specific cross-cultural situations that affect people's performance on the job. Such a person makes provisions for the foreign deployment process, overseas adjustment and culture shock, and the reentry of expatriates.

Changing International Business—coping with the interdependence of business activity throughout the world, as well as the subculture of the managerial group. There is an emerging universal acceptance of some business technology, computers, and management information systems, for example. Yet, the global manager appreciates the effect of cultural differences on standard business practice and principles, such as organizational loyalty.

Cultural Synergy—building upon the very differences in the world's people for mutual growth and accomplishment by cooperation. Cultural synergy through collaboration emphasizes similarities and common concerns and integrates differences to enrich human activities and systems. By combining the best in varied cultures and seeking the widest input, multiple effects and complex solutions can result. Synergy is separate parts functioning together to create a greater whole and to achieve a common goal. For such aggregate action to occur, cross-cultural skills are required.

Work Culture—applying the general characteristics of culture to the specifics of how people work at a point in time and place. In the macro sense, work can be analyzed in terms of human stages of develop-ment—the work cultures of hunter, farmer, factory worker, and knowledge worker. In the micro sense, work cultures can be studied in terms of specific industries, organizations, or professional groups.

Global Culture—understanding that while various characteristics of human culture have always been universal, a unique global culture with some common characteristics may be emerging. The influences of mass media and telecommunications, including the fax, e-mail, the Internet, and CNN/TV, are breaking down barriers between peoples and their diverse cultures. Global managers are alert to serving this commonality in human needs and markets with strategies that are transnational.

GLOBAL ORGANIZATIONS

The corporate culture of global organizations affects how an organization copes with competition and change, whether in terms of technology, economics, or people. Terpstra and David[31] recommend that people in global businesses be triply socialized—to their culture, their business culture, and their corporate culture. When we operate in the global marketplace it is imperative that we be informed about these three cultures of our customers, competitors, venture partners, suppliers, or government officials. Trompenaars[32] states:

> As markets globalise, the need for standarisation in organisational design, systems and procedures increases. Yet managers are also under pressure to adapt their organisation to the local characteristics of the market, the legislation, the fiscal regime, the socio-political system and the cultural system. This balance between consistency and adaptation is essential for corporate success.

As we transition from a postindustrial culture to an information culture, McCarthy[33] envisions knowledge as culture. She states that knowledge is a powerful force, creating and affecting culture's attitudes and forms. Knowledge—its creation, storage, and use—becomes basic economic activity contributing to social transformation. Knowledge workers in various professions and technologies cut across the traditional boundaries of both nationality and discipline.

By the end of the millennium, the number of global organizations was countless. However, in 1994 there were 37,000 transnational corporations with 207,000 affiliates that controlled one-third of all private sector assets, and had worldwide sales of U.S. $5.5 trillion.[34] With great vision in 1974, Barnett and Muller forecasted this postindustrial trend, and separately Wriston spoke of its influence. Barnett and Muller:[35]

> The global corporation is the first institution in human history dedicated to centralized planning on a world scale. Because its primary activity is to organize and to integrate economic activity around the world in such a way as to maximize global profit, it is an organic structure in which each part is expected to serve the whole. . . . The rise of such planetary enterprises is producing an organizational revolution as profound for modern man as the Industrial Revolution and the rise of the nation-state itself.

Thirty years ago, Walter B. Wriston, when chairman of Citibank observed:[36]

> The world corporation has become a new weight in an old balance and must play a constructive role in moving the world toward the freer exchange of both ideas and the means of production so that the people of the world may one day enjoy the fruits of a truly global society.

In discussing the evolution of the various corporations, the four types of corporations are cited—ethnocentric, polycentric, regiocentric, and geocentric.[37]

Ethnocentric corporations. These corporations are home-country oriented. Ethnocentric managers believe that home-country nationals are more intelligent, reliable, and trustworthy than foreign nationals. All key management positions are centered at the domestic headquarters. Home-country nationals are recruited and trained for all international positions. The ethnocentric approach is fostered by many internal and external influences. The CEO may be limited by the biases of the owners and stockholders. Labor unions may impose intense pressure in favor of domestic employment. Home government policy may force emphasis on the domestic market.

The ethnocentric philosophy is exhibited in many international companies. There is great difficulty for standard international companies communicating in different languages and in accepting cultural differences. International strategic alternatives are limited to entry modes such as exporting, licensing, and turnkey operations because "it works at home, so it must work overseas."

Polycentric corporations. These are host-country oriented corporations. Profit potential is seen in a foreign country, but the foreign market is too hard to understand. The polycentric firm establishes multinational operations on condition that host-country managers "do it their way." The polycentric message is: "Local people know what is best for them. Let's give them them the responsibility and leave them alone as long as they make us a profit."

The polycentric firm is a loosely connected group with quasi-independent subsidiaries as profit centers. Headquarters is staffed by home-country nationals, while local nationals occupy the key positions in their respective local subsidiaries. Host-country nationals have high or absolute sovereignty over the subsidiary's operations. There is no direction from headquarters and the only controls are financially oriented. No foreign national can seriously aspire to a senior position at headquarters.

The polycentric approach often results from great external pressures, such as laws in different countries requiring local management participation. Engineering standards may have to be determined locally. The host-country government may be a major customer and therefore influences the ways of doing business.

The polycentric philosophy is often exhibited in multinational corporations (MNCs). MNCs face a heterogeneous environment where product needs and preferences are diverse. In addition, governmental restrictions may be severe. Strategically, the MNC competes on a market-by-market basis because it believes that "local people know what is best for them."

Regiocentric corporations. These corporations capitalize on the synergistic benefits of sharing common functions across regions. A regiocentric corporation believes that only regional insiders can effectively coordinate functions within the region. For example, a regiocentric organization might select a Japanese subsidiary to manage its Asian

4 TYPES OF CORPORATIONS

Multinational corporations face a heterogeneous environment where product needs and preferences are diverse.

operations and a French subsidiary to manage its European operations. The regiocentric message is: "Regional insiders know what neighboring countries want."

The regiocentric firm is highly interdependent on a regional basis. Regional headquarters organize collaborative efforts among local subsidiaries. The regional headquarters is responsible for the regional plan, local research and development, product innovation, cash management, local executive selection and training, capital expenditure plans, brand policy, and public relations. The world headquarters takes care of world strategy, country analysis, basic research and development, foreign exchange, transfer pricing, intercompany loans, long-term financing, selection of top management, technology transfer, and establishing corporate culture.

Geocentric corporations. Being world oriented, a geocentric corporation's ultimate goal is to create an integrated system with a worldwide approach. The geocentric system is highly interdependent. Subsidiaries are no longer satellites and independent city-states. The entire organization is focused on both worldwide and local objectives. Every part of the organization makes a unique contribution using its unique competencies. The geocentric message is: "All for one and one for all. We will work together to solve problems anywhere in the world."

Geocentrism requires collaboration between headquarters and subsidiaries to establish universal standards with permissible local variations. Diverse regions are integrated through a global systems approach to decision making. Good ideas come from and flow to any country. Resources are allocated on a global basis. Geographical lines are erased and functional and product lines are globalized.

Within legal and political limits, the best people are sought to solve problems. Competence is what counts, not national origin. The reward system motivates managers to surrender national biases and work for worldwide objectives.

The geocentric firm overcomes political barriers by turning its subsidiaries into good citizens of the host nations. It is hoped that the subsidiary will become a leading exporter from the host to the international community. Furthermore, the geocentric organization will provide base countries with an increasing supply of hard currency, new skills, and knowledge of advanced technology.

Self-Perception and Others' Perception of You

Intentions are important but, like culture, perceptions count. And for the present and foreseeable future, what happens in our global world will be to a large extent influenced by Americans. The United States is involved in many global economic, political, and religious disputes and conflicts. But in this complex, rapidly changing yet

A geocentric corporation's ultimate goal is to create an integrated system with a worldwide approach.

interconnected global world, the influence of even the most powerful is highly limited.

The *Far Eastern Economic Review*[38] cited many Asian leaders on the subject of what they thought of the United States at this time. Here are some brief examples.

> In the Muslim world a feeling of impotence in the face of U.S. military might, coupled with a feeling of injustice (a second unjust war imposed on a Muslim country), will only result in more al-Qaeda recruits.
>
> The question that many are now asking is: "Has September 11 been used as an excuse for the U.S. to fulfill its imperial ambitions and was the whole war against terrorism hyped up to convince its public that this unjust war is justified?" *Imran Khan, party leader, member of Pakistan's national assembly, and former cricket captain*
>
> The United States has lost all moral credibility. Never again will countries in the developing world believe that the United States is a defender of the values it preaches abroad. *Farish A. Noor, Malaysian political scientist and human rights activist*
>
> But the war against Iraq makes me uncomfortable. I do not object to a war if necessary. But I do not like war which is the result of clumsy, unskilled political maneuvering. It may slow down the progress of positive thinking within Vietnamese society towards America. *Nguyen Tran Bat, chairman of the Investconsult Group, a Hanoi-based business and legal consultancy that has assisted such American clients as Citibank, Coca-Cola, and Ford Vietnam*

The current Gulf war has its first collateral damage not in the body counts in the desert battlefield but in the irreparable loss of the legitimacy and confidence that the UN has earned for itself during the past half century. From now on the United States is most likely to be dragged into every conflict around the world. There will be no UN to offer a mediating role to any conflict. *Surin Pitsuwan, former Thai foreign minister*

Now consider these comments which provide a contrast.[39]

> Americans almost alone in the world, have a serious . . . even simplistic belief that their country is a force for enduring good. They acknowledge it does not always get it right, that at times its antics fall far short of its highest ideals, but all but the most hardened cynics really believe in America as a force for freedom and prosperity and in the universality of these goals. This belief is born of the country's history, religion, and culture. . . . It is this self-faith as much as anything that defines and differentiates Americans from most of the rest of the world. There is not much doubt that outside the United States, American intentions, especially under the Bush administration, are regarded with a degree of suspicion and resentment . . . it is not hard to see why this self-belief evinces such cynicism around the world. The United States record—supporting tyrants, even in places such as Iraq—where it eventually topples them—is hardly unblemished. At times, America's commitment to liberty has looked a little selective.

At times, America's commitment to liberty has looked a little selective.

Denial

Most individuals, at some time in their lives, deny realities. In families, children deny that their parents are alcoholic, women deny that their husbands are abusive. Similarly, in business organizations and academic institutions, "realities" are suppressed, "feelings" are stuffed, and intellectualization exercises force new realities into old paradigms.

The following humorous parody illustrates the denial of a country's competitiveness problem and a misdiagnosis. This example is American, but it can easily apply to most countries.

The American Way

The Americans and the Japanese decided to engage in a competitive boat race. Both teams practiced hard and long to reach their peak performance. On the big day they both felt ready.

The Japanese won by a *mile*.

Afterward, the American team was discouraged by the loss. Morale sagged. Corporate management decided that the reason for the crushing defeat had to be found, so a consulting firm was hired to investigate the problem and recommend corrective action.

The consultant's findings: The Japanese team had eight people rowing and one person steering; the American team had one person rowing and eight people steering.

After a year of study and millions spent analyzing the problem, the consulting firm concluded that too many people were steering and not enough were rowing on the American team.

So, as race day neared again the following year, the American team's management structure was completely reorganized. The new structure: four steering managers, three area steering managers, one staff steering manager and a new performance review system for the person rowing the boat to provide work incentive.

The next year the Japanese won by *two* miles.

Humiliated, the American corporation laid off the rower for poor performance and gave the managers a bonus for discovering the problem.

In this oversimplification, in the first race the Americans were overconfident and denied they had a competitiveness problem. In preparation for the second race, there was a serious misdiagnosis. Hamel states it well.

To fully understand our competitive advantage/disadvantage, we have to go deeper, and look at our "genetic Coding"—i.e., our beliefs, our managerial frames. It is these beliefs that restrict our perceptions of reality and degrees of freedom. To be successful, a company needs "genetic variety." Our challenge must be to get outside our restrictive managerial frames.

If you want to enlarge your managerial frames, you must be curious about how the *rest of the world thinks*—and you must *have humility*. The real competitive problem is not that our institutional environment is hopelessly unhelpful, but that our managerial frames are hopelessly *inappropriate to the next round of global competition.*[40]

CONCLUSIONS

Two additional skills are of fundamental importance today for global people. The first skill is *listening* to understand. Many global leaders, particularly of nation-states, do not seem to possess this skill to a high degree. Listening is a symbol of respecting the dignity of others.

The second is the skill of locating and using many very sophisticated *cultural interpreters*. It is impossible for any individual, given the complexity of culture, to have a free understanding of other systems. However, cultural interpreters, individuals from each culture, can teach leaders. Having listened and been a student with cultural interpreters as teachers, the global leader is equipped to face the many opportunities and challenges that will be continually presented.

Having a sense of culture and its related skills is a unique human attribute. Culture is fundamentally a group problem-solving tools for coping in a particular environment. It enables people to create a distinctive world around themselves, to control their own destinies, and to grow. Sharing the legacy of diverse cultures advances our social, economic, technological, and human development. Culture can be analyzed in a macrocontext, such as in terms of national groups, or in a micro sense, such as within a system or organization. Increasingly, we examine culture in a global sense from the perspective of work, leadership, or markets.

Because management philosophies and practices are culturally conditioned, it stands to reason that there is much to be gained by including cultural studies in all management or professional development. This is particularly relevant during the global transformation under way. Culturally skilled leaders are essential for the effective management of emerging global corporations as well as for the furtherance of mutually beneficial world trade and exchange. In these undertakings, the promotion of cultural synergy by those who are truly global managers will help us to capitalize on the differences in people, while ensuring their collaborative action.

In summary, here are parallel reasons why all managers should advance their culture learning, or why global organizations should include it in their human resource development strategies:

Culture gives people a sense of identity.

- ■ Culture gives people a sense of identity, whether in nations or corporations, especially in terms of the human behavior and values to be encouraged. Through culture organizational loyalty and performance can be improved.
- ■ Cultural knowledge provides insight into people. The appropriate business protocol can be employed that is in tune with local character, codes, ideology, and standards.
- ■ Cultural awareness and skill can be helpful in influencing organizational culture. Furthermore, subsidiaries, divisions, departments, or

specializations have subcultures that can foster or undermine organizational goals and communications.

■ Cultural concepts and characteristics are useful for the analysis of work culture in the disappearing industrial and emerging meta-industrial work environments.

■ Cultural insights and tools are helpful in the study of comparative management techniques so that we become less culture bound in our approach to leadership and management practice.

■ Cultural competencies are essential for those in international business and trade.

■ Cultural astuteness enables one to comprehend the diversity of market needs and to improve strategies with minority and ethnic groups at home or foreign markets abroad.

■ Cultural understanding is relevant to all relocation experiences, whether domestic or international. This is valid for individual managers or technicians who are facing a geographic transfer, as well as for their families and subordinates involved in such a culture change.

■ Cultural understanding and skill development should be built into all foreign deployment systems. Acculturation to different environments can improve the overseas experience and productivity, and facilitate reentry into the home and organizational culture.

■ Cultural capabilities can enhance one's participation in international organizations and meetings. This is true whether one merely attends a conference abroad, is a delegate to a regional or foreign association, is a member in a world trade or professional enterprise, or is a meeting planner for transnational events.

■ Cultural proficiency can facilitate one's coping with the changes of any transitional experience.

Learning to manage cultural differences is a means for all persons to become more global in their outlook and behavior, as well as more effective personally and professionally. When cultural differences are understood and utilized as a *resource*, then all benefit.[41]

Learning to manage cultural differences is a means for all persons to become more global in their outlook.

MIND STRETCHING

1. Do you believe the world is really "flat," and what does this mean?
2. Is it possible to see events and issues through a multiple lens?
3. When confronted with cultural differences why do we often dig in and believe our way is right rather than listen?
4. What is your opinion regarding the Prophet Mohammed cartoon controversy?
5. In five years, with your "futurist hat" on, how would you describe our "global world."

REFERENCES

1. Pascal, B. *Pensées*, 60, 1670, p. 294.
2. Freidman, T. "It's a Flat World, After All," *The New York Times Magazine*, April 3, 2005.
3. www.theglobalist@theglobalist.com Globalist Interview > Global Business, A CEO's Responsibilities in the Age of Globalization, Jeffrey Immelt, March 17, 2006.
4. Freidman, T. *The World is Flat, A Brief History of the Twenty-First Century*, New York: Farrar, Strauss and Giroux, 2005, pp. 6–7.
5. Schein, E. H. "On Dialogue, Culture and Organizational Learning," *Organizational Dynamics*, Fall, 1993, Vol. 22, Is. 2, pp. 40–51.
6. McNamara, R. S., Blight, J. G., and Brigham, R. K. *Argument Without End*, New York: Public Affairs, 1999, p. 191.
7. Brooks, D. Ít's Culture That Counts," *International Herald Tribune*, February 21, 2006.
8. Harrison, L. and Huntington, S. P. (eds). *Culture Matters*, New York: Basic Books, 200, p. 111.
9. Diamond, J. *Guns, Germs, and Steel*, New York: Norton and Company, 1999, p. 13.
10. Ibid, p. 25.
11. Huntington, S. *The Clash of Civilizations and the Remaking of World Order*, New York: Simon & Schuster, 1996.
12. Chomsky N., Mitchell, P. R., and Schoeffel, J. (eds.). *Understanding Power*, New York: Vintage, 2002.
13. Lewis, R. D. *The Cultural Imperative*, Yarmouth, ME: Intercultural Press, 2003.
14. Miller, J. G. *Living Systems*, Niwot, CO: University Press of Colorado, 1994. See also *Systems Research and Behavioral Science*, Wiley Interscience, Buffins Lane, Chichester, West Sussex, UK PO19 1UD.
15. Stein, J. "Tradition," *Fiddler on the Roof*. Harnick, S., lyrics, Bock, J., music, 1964.
16. Schmitz, J. *Cultural Orientations Guide*, Princeton, NJ: Princeton Training Press, 2003, pp. 10–12.
17. Hofstede, G. *Cultures Consequences: International Differences in Work-Related Values*. Beverly Hills, CA: Sage Publications, 1984. See also Hofstede, G. *Cultures and Organizations: Software of the Mind*, London: McGraw-Hill, 1991.
18. Hofstede, G. *Cultures and Organizations: Software of the Mind*, London: McGraw-Hill, 1991.
19. Lustig, M. W., Koester, J. *Intercultural Competence: Interpersonal Communication Across Cultures*, Fifth Edition, New York: Allyn and Bacon, 2005.
20. Cohen, A. R. and Bradford, D. L. *Influence without Authority*, Hoboken, NJ: John Wiley & Sons, Inc., 2005.
21. Verma, V. K. *Managing the Project Team*, Newton Square, PA: PMI Publications, 1997.
22. Thiederman, S. *Bridging Cultural Barriers to Success: How to Manage the Multicultural Workforce*, Lexington, MA: Lexington Books. 1990. *Prof-*

iting in America's Multicultural Workplace, Lexington, MA: Lexington Books, 1991.

23. *The Economist*, August 29, 1998, p. 59.

24. Harris, P. R. *The Cultural Diversity Handbook*, Simons, G., Abramms, B., Hopkins, A., and Johnson D. (eds.). Princeton, NJ: Pacesetter Books, 1996.

25. *National Geographic*, August 1998, p. 62.

26. Capra, F. and Rast, D. Steindl. *Belonging to the Universe*, San Francisco, CA: Harper, 1991.

27. Rhinesmith, S. H. *A Manager's Guide to Globalization*, Second Edition, Chicago, IL: Irwin/ASTD, 1996, p. x.

28. Bartlett, C. A. and Ghoshal, S. "What Is a Global Manager?" *Harvard Business Review*, September/October 1992, p. 131.

29. Taylor, W. "The Logic of Global Business: An Interview with ABB's Percy Barnevik," *Harvard Business Review*, March/April, 1991, p. 95.

30. Sheridan, E. "The Intercultural Leadership Competencies for U.S. Leaders in the Era of Globalization," Ph.D. dissertation, 2005.

31. Terpstra, V. and David, K. *The Cultural Environment of International Business*, Cincinnati, OH: South-Western Publishing, 1985.

32. Trompenaars, F. *Riding the Waves of Culture*, London: Economist Books, 1997, p. 3.

33. McCarthy, E. D. *Knowledge as Culture: The New Sociology of Knowledge*, London: Routledge, 1996

34. *The Economist*, July 30, 1994, p. 57.

35. Barnett, R. J. and Muller, R. E. *Global Reach: The Power of the Multinational Corporation*, New York: Simon & Schuster, 1974.

36. Wriston, W. B., "The World Corporation—New Weight in an Old Balance," *Sloan Management Review*, Winter 1974.

37. Moran, R. T., Harris, P. R., and Stripp, W. G. *Developing the Global Organization: Strategies for Human Resource Professionals*. Houston, TX: Gulf Publishing Co., 1993.

38. "What Do You Think of America Now?" *Far Eastern Economic Review*, April 2, 2003, pp. 12–18.

39. Baker, G. "The land of the free enjoys the thrill of being a force for good," *Financial Times*, April 12/13, 2003.

40. Hamel, G. "Pushing the envelope of global strategy and competitiveness." A summary of remarks by Gary Hamel for the Executive Focus International 1993 Executive Forum, February 12, 1993.

41. Gesteland, R. R. *Cross-Cultural Business Behavior—Marketing, Negotiating, and Managing Across Cultures*, Copenhagen, DK: The Copenhagen Business School Press (Handelshojskolens Forlag), 1999.

GLOBAL LEADERS AND COMMUNICATIONS

LEARNING OBJECTIVES

Most leaders of organizations spend upwards of 70% of their time communicating. This chapter provides an overview of interpersonal AND intercultural communication. If we became "fluent" in low-/high-context communication, in making "isomorphic attributions" (or predicting accurately how leaves may interpret message) and in listening, our world might indeed be different. In this chapter we identify communication errors and describe approaches to using new communication media.

Our world's population exceeds six billion.

Our world's population exceeds six billion. This is hard to imagine for most. However, if the global population was only 1000 people, it would include:

584 Asians
124 Africans
150 Eastern and Western Europeans and former Soviets
84 Latin Americans
52 North Americans
6 Australians and New Zealanders

About 50% of the people speak the following languages:

165 Mandarin
86 English

83 Hindi/Urdu
64 Spanish
58 Russian
37 Arabic

The other half speaks Bengali, Portuguese, Indonesian, Japanese, German, French, and 200 other languages. Communication, indeed, would be challenging in this global village.[1]

Trade and exchange across cultural lines have played a crucial role in human history, being perhaps the most important external stimuli to change. . . . External stimuli, in turn, has been the most important single source of change and development in art, science, and technology. . . .

On the negative side, cross-cultural trade and communication pose special problems. People with a different way of life are strangers by definition; their ways seem unpredictable, and the unpredictable is probably dangerous as well. Communication itself is difficult. Even after an appropriate median comes into existence, like having a second language in common, understanding is hard to come by. Strangers . . . are still not to be trusted in the same full sense that neighbors and kinfolk can be trusted.[2]

Perhaps the importance of international business communication can best be highlighted by contrasting some economic developments in the global marketplace:

- The pace of economic change has accelerated. It took the United Kingdom 58 years to double its output per worker, the United States 47 years, Japan 34 years, South Korea 11 years, and China less than 10 years.[3]
- In the past, food preferences were considered very culturally oriented. Coca-Cola, McDonalds, and Pizza Hut have proven that tastes can be changed.[4]
- In some segments of the electronics industry, the shelf life of new products is 16 months. If products are not developed and introduced within this time frame they risk not being highly competitive.[4]
- Because of new communication technologies, people are increasingly communicating across cultures and borders.
- The era of globalization shapes everyone's domestic politics, commerce, environment, and international relations.[5]

With our globally interdependent economy, it is imperative that we understand our world trade partners. But those working internationally and participating in these intercultural experiences have found many challenges working or living in a foreign environment. Communication across cultural boundaries is difficult. Differences in customs, behavior, and values result in problems manageable only through effective cross-cultural communication and interaction.

Cross-cultural trade and communication pose special problems.

A cross-cultural
faux pas *results*
when we fail to
recognize that
persons of other
cultural
backgrounds
have goals,
customs,
thought patterns,
and values
different from
our own.

A recent study

People are often unaware when misunderstandings occur or "errors" are committed while working with persons from different cultures. A cross-cultural *faux pas* results when we fail to recognize that persons of other cultural backgrounds have goals, customs, thought patterns, and values different from our own. This is particularly true in a diverse workforce with increasing numbers of expatriate workers not familiar with the home culture, its language, and communication systems.

The personnel files of multinational corporations and government agencies are replete with documentation of intercultural communication misunderstandings. Some are not serious, while others result in organizational and personal tragedies and affect company presidents and ambassadors, as well as tourists. Interpersonal work or social relations with the host nationals usually go sour because of ineffective communication and a misreading of verbal and nonverbal communication signals, not because of personality factors.

Before a person is able to communicate effectively with people from different cultures, it is important to know something about them and where they live on planet Earth. Individuals from some nations, including many in the United States, have serious gaps in geographic literacy. A recent study by the National Geographic Society[6] found:

- One in ten young Americans could not find the United States on a blank world map.
- Only 13% could locate Iraq.
- Only 17% could locate Afghanistan.
- Only 30% could locate New Jersey.
- Only 71% could locate the Pacific Ocean.

But 30% were aware that the island on the 2002 *Survivor* show was in the South Pacific.

Once the basic geography of a people is known, the following is a list of questions that require a little more knowledge and sophistication. They are adapted from the booklet, "So You're Going Abroad: Are You Prepared?"[7] Can you answer the questions for any country in which you have done business?

1. There are many contemporary and historical people of whom a country is proud. Can you name: a politician, a musician, a writer, a religious leader, a sports figure?
2. Are you familiar with that country's basic history? Date of independence? Relationship to other countries?
3. What are some routine courtesies that people are expected to observe in that country?
4. How do they greet each other? Foreigners?
5. What do you know about their major religions?
6. Are there role differences between men and women?

7. What kinds of foods are traditional?
8. What kind of humor is appreciated?
9. What is the relationship between that country and your country?

CULTURAL DIFFERENCES AS COMMUNICATION RESOURCES

In the past, many assumed that cultural differences were barriers that impeded communication and interaction. Today, effective global leaders believe that cultural differences, if well managed, are resources, not handicaps. In one's homeland, both students and workers can be taught how to communicate more effectively with colleagues and customers, as well as how to create cultural synergy with those from different racial, ethnic, or national backgrounds. Training, briefing, and adequate preparation for an overseas assignment will make the experience positive and enlightening. However, an effective communicator working with American nationals in the United States is not necessarily an effective communicator working with Japanese or Saudi Arabians in the United States, Japan, or Saudi Arabia.

Comprehending Communication

Studies of what managers do each day indicate that 75% of their time is spent writing, talking, and listening, that is communicating. In fact, all business ultimately comes down to transactions or interactions between individuals. The success of the transaction depends almost entirely on how well managers understand each other.

To better understand the global leader's role as a communicator, it is vital that we comprehend what is involved in the complex process of communication. As shown in the next section, it is a dynamic exchange of energy, ideas, information—knowledge—between and among peoples. It is verbal and nonverbal and occurs at different levels—informal or formal, intellectual or emotional.

Most communication is manifest through symbols that differ in their meaning according to time, place, culture, or person. Human interaction is characterized by a continuous updating of the meaning of these symbols. In the past 25 years, we have expanded our capacities for symbolic communication beyond what was accomplished in the previous 2500 years. The human species is extending its communication capabilities beyond print to that of electronic technology; in the process our whole thought pattern is being transformed.

Despite the technological wonders of today's communications, international relations require us to deal with one another on a person-to-person basis. For this to be effective interaction, we have to overcome

Today, effective global leaders believe that cultural differences, if well managed, are resources, not handicaps. All business ultimately comes down to transactions or interactions between individuals. The success of the transaction depends almost entirely on how well managers understand each other.

language and stereotype barriers. This may require the mental elimination of terms like "foreigner" or "alien" and more appropriately viewing the individual as having a background that is different.

Axioms of Communication

Every person is a versatile communicator. Language sets us apart from other creatures and seemingly is characteristic of the more developed brain. But humans have a wide range of communication skills that go beyond words to include gestures, signs, shapes, colors, sounds, smells, pictures, and many other communication symbols. The diversity of human culture in this regard may be demonstrated by the "artist" who may communicate both thought and feeling in paintings, sculpture, music, and dance. Through such media, artists project themselves into people, things, and surroundings. They project their way of thinking, their temperament and personality, joys and sorrows into the world around them.

Every person operates within his or her own private world or perceptual field. This is what is referred to as life space, and it applies to individuals as well as to organizations and nations. Every individual communicates a unique perspective of the world and reality. Every culture reflects the group view of the world. From time to time, one must check whether one's view of the world, or that of an organization, synchronizes with the collective reality. This is particularly essential when "objective reality" is subject to the phenomenon of accelerating change. Cultural groups may have distorted views of world reality, as did China during the period of the Maoist Cultural Revolution.

Every person projects himself or herself into human communication. We communicate our image of self, including our system of needs, values, and standards; our expectations, ideals, and perceptions of peoples, things, and situations. We project this collective image through body, bearing, appearance, tone of voice, and choice of words.

Every person is a medium or instrument of communication, not just a sender and receiver of messages. If a person is comfortable with himself or herself and congruent, people usually respond positively. If one is uncomfortable and incongruent, people will respond negatively. The more aware the individual is of the forces that affect behavior at work within himself or herself, the more able that person is to control his or her own life space.

Every generation perceives life differently. For example, the previous concepts of behavioral communication can be applied to a generation of people. The people of each generation project a unique image of "their" world at a certain point in time. This image reflects a generation's system of needs, values, standards, and ideals. The children of the "Depression Age" experienced life differently from today's children

Every person operates within his or her own private world or perceptual field.

COMMUNICATION AXIOMS

and thus the problem of communication between the generations and even cultures becomes more understandable. The supervisor of a young worker, for example, may project his or her generation's view of the world (past oriented) and finds it difficult to facilitate communication by coming into the reality of the younger employee (future- and global-oriented).

Communication is at the heart of all organizational operations and international relations. It is the most important tool we have for getting things done. It is the basis for understanding, cooperation, and action. In fact, the very vitality and creativity of an organization or a nation depends on the content and character of its communications. Yet, communication is both hero and villain: it transfers information, meets people's needs, and gets things done, but far too often it also distorts messages, causes frustration, and renders people and organizations ineffective.

The Communication Process

Communication is a process of circular interaction involving a sender, receiver, and message. In human interaction, the sender or receiver may be a person or a group of people. The message conveys meaning through the medium or symbol used to send it (the how), as well as in its content (the what). Because humans are such intelligent, symbol-making creatures, the message may be relayed verbally or non-verbally, using words (oral or written), pictures, graphs, statistics, signs, or gestures. Humans are versatile communicators; we can communicate with nature, animals, and other humans. Humankind's capacity to communicate ranges from smoke signals and the sound of drums to television and the Internet. As a dynamic being, humans constantly invent new and improved ways of communicating. Regardless of the communication symbol, a sender and receiver are normally involved.

Both sender and receiver occupy a unique field of experience, different for each person. Essentially, it is a private world of perception through which all experience is filtered, organized, and translated; it is what psychologists call the individual's life space. This consists of the person's *psychological environment* as it exists for him or her. Each person experiences life in a unique way and psychologically structures his or her own distinctive perceptual field. Among the factors that compose one's field of experience are one's family and educational, cultural, religious, and social background. The individual's perceptual field affects the way he or she receives and dispenses all new information. It influences both the content and the media used in communicating.

An individual's self-image, needs, values, expectations, goals, standards, cultural norms, and perception effect the way input is received and interpreted. Essentially, persons *selectively perceive* all new data, determining that which is relevant to, and consistent with, their own

Communication is at the heart of all organizational operations and international relations. Communication is a circular process of interaction.

perceptual needs. Two people can thus receive the same message and derive from it two entirely different meanings. They actually perceive the same object or information differently. Communication, then, is a complex process of linking up or sharing perceptual fields between sender and receiver. The effective communicator builds a bridge to the world of the receiver. When the sender is from one cultural group and the receiver from another, the human interaction is intercultural communication.

Once the sender conveys the message, the receiver analyzes the message in terms of his or her particular field of experience and pattern of ideas—usually, decoding the message, interpreting it for meaning and encoding or sending back a response. Thus, communication is a circular process of interaction.

The communicator, whether as an individual from a cultural group or as a member of an organization, exhibits or transmits many kinds of behavior. First, the intended message is communicated on verbal and nonverbal levels. We also communicate unintended behavior, or subconscious behavior, on verbal and nonverbal levels. In other words, communication at any level involves a whole complex of projections. There is a "silent language" being used also in the process of human interaction, including tone of voice, inflection of words, gestures, and facial expressions. Some of these factors that affect the real meaning and content of messages are referred to as "body language"—the positioning of various parts of the sender's physique conveys meaning. The person is both a medium of communication and a message, and the way in which one communicates is vastly influenced by our cultural conditioning.

GLOBAL COMMUNICATION

Klopf[8] defines communication as "the process by which persons share information meanings and feelings through the exchange of verbal and nonverbal messages." The individual working and communicating in a multicultural environment must★"remember that the message that ultimately counts is the one that the other person gets or creates in their mind, not the one we send."[9]★

The following are practical guidelines for developing skills for more effective intercultural communication. These statements briefly outline several important characteristics of intercultural communication. Some are obvious, others are not, but all, if internalized and understood, will result in more effective communication.

■ *No matter how hard one tries, one cannot avoid communicating.* All behavior in human interaction has a message and communicates

No matter how hard one tries, one cannot avoid communicating.

CHARACTERISTICS OF INTERCULTURAL COMMUNICATION

something. Body language communicates as well as our activity or inactivity. All behavior is communication because all behavior contains a message, whether intended or not.

■ *Communication does not necessarily mean understanding.* Even when two individuals agree that they are communicating or talking to each other, it does not mean that they have understood each other. Understanding occurs when the two individuals have the same interpretation of the symbols being used in the communication process, whether the symbols are words or gestures.

■ *Communication is irreversible.* One cannot take back one's communication (although sometimes we wish one could). However, one's message can be explained, clarified, or restated. Once communicated, the message is part of the communicator's experience and it influences present and future meanings. For example, disagreeing with a Saudi Arabian in the presence of others is an "impoliteness" in the Arab world and may be difficult to remedy.

■ *Communication occurs in a context.* One cannot ignore the context of communication that occurs at a certain time, in some place, using certain media. Such factors have message value and give meaning to the communicators. For example, a business conversation with a French manager in France during an evening meal may be inappropriate.

■ *Communication is a dynamic process.* Communication is not static and passive, but rather it is a continuous and active process without beginning or end. A communicator is not simply a sender or a receiver of messages but can be both at the same time.

Each of us has been socialized in a unique environment. Important aspects of the environment are shared, and these constitute a particular culture. Culture poses communication problems because there are so many variables unknown to the communicators. As the cultural variables and differences increase, the number of communication misunderstandings also increase.

Every person is part of many different identity groups simultaneously, thus learning and becoming part of all their cultures. Each of us is culturally unique because each adopts or adapts differently the attitudes, values, and beliefs of the groups to which we belong. Thus, all communication becomes intercultural because of the various group identities of those communicating. Our challenge is to examine the differences that make us unique and discover ways to be more effective in overcoming the barriers these differences create.[10] That is why,

when we travel to another culture or interact with people from another culture in our culture, we cannot base our predictions of their behavior on our cultural rules and norms. This inevitably leads to misunderstanding. If we want to communicate effectively, we must use our

Communication does not necessarily mean understanding. Each of us has been socialized in a unique environment. Important aspects of the environment are shared, and these constitute a particular culture.

knowledge of the other culture to make predictions. If we have little or no knowledge of the other person's culture, we have no basis for making predictions.[11]

CULTURAL FACTORS IN COMMUNICATION

Intercultural communication is a process whereby individuals from different cultural backgrounds attempt to share meanings. Lustig and Koester[12] provide definitions of communications. For example, *intercultural* communication is "the presence of at least two individuals who are culturally different from each other on such important attributes as their value orientations, preferred communication codes, role expectations, and perceived rules of social relationship," exemplified by a Japanese and an English negotiator discussing a joint venture. *Intracultural* communication occurs between culturally similar individuals. The study of child-rearing practices in different cultures would be referred to as *cross-cultural* or communication that pertains to the "study of a particular idea or concept within many cultures." *Interracial* communication refers to the "differences in communication between members of racial and ethnic groups," such as African Americans and Asian Americans.

In the classical anthropological sense, culture refers to the cumulative deposit of knowledge, beliefs, values, religion, customs, and mores acquired by a group of people and passed on from generation to generation. Imagine yourself participating in the following cross-cultural situations that affect communication and understanding between two culturally different individuals.

Culture refers to the cumulative deposit of knowledge, beliefs, values, religion, customs, and mores acquired by a group of people and passed on from generation to generation.

Cross-Cultural Management

■ You are involved in a technical training program in China, and one of your responsibilities is to rate persons under your supervision. You have socialized on several occasions, spending time with one of the Chinese you are supervising. He is an extremely friendly and hard-working individual, but has difficulty exercising the leadership expected of him. On the rating form you indicated this, and his supervisor discussed it with him. Subsequently, he came to you and asked how you could have criticized his leadership skills. You indicated that you had an obligation to report deficiencies and areas of improvement. What cultural differences might cause misperceptions of performance appraisal and evaluation?

■ You are in Saudi Arabia attempting to finalize a contract with a group of Saudi businessmen. You are aware that these people are excellent negotiators; however, you find it difficult to maintain eye contact with your hosts during conversations. Furthermore, their increasing physical proximity to you is becoming more uncomfortable. You also have noticed that a strong handgrip while shaking hands is not returned. When invited to a banquet, because you are left-handed, you use your left hand while eating. Your negotiations are not successfully concluded. What may have been the reason for this? What cultural aspects are evidenced in this interaction, which if known could improve your communication with your Arab clients?

■ You are the manager of a group of Puerto Rican workers in a New York factory, but you only speak English. You resent the use of Spanish among your subordinates. Why do your subordinates feel more comfortable in their native language? How could your company facilitate their instruction in the English language? Or should it?

■ You are from a "developed country," and in your overseas travel to many countries for business you can feel deep resentment that seems to be directed at you, your government, and your country. How do you respond to situations like this?

In the past, many businesspeople were not overly concerned with the way culture influenced individual or organizational behavior. But now serious and costly errors have made those working in a multicultural environment aware that insensitivity and lack of cultural knowledge can do much to injure, permanently or temporarily, the relationship with their coworkers and colleagues. These questions may prove helpful and expedient.

1. What must I know about the social and business customs of country X?
2. What skills do I need to be effective as a negotiator in country Y?
3. What prejudices and stereotypes do I have about the people in country Z?
4. How will these influence my interaction?

COMMUNICATION KEYS—LOW/HIGH CONTEXT AND LISTENING

Anthropologist Edward Hall makes a vital distinction between high and low-context cultures, and how this matter of *context* impacts communications. A high-context culture uses high-context communications: information is either in the physical context or internalized in the person with little communicated in the explicit words or message. Japan, Saudi Arabia, Spain, and China are cultures engaged in high-context communications. On the other hand, a low-context culture

Context impacts

communications.

HIGH
CONTEXT
VS.
LOW
CONTEXT

employs low-context communications: most information is contained in explicit codes, such as words. Canada and the United States as well as many European countries engage in low-context communications.

When individuals communicate they attempt to find out how much the listener knows about whatever is being discussed. In a low-context communication the listener knows very little and must be told practically everything. In high-context cultures the listener is already "contexted" and doesn't need to have much background information. Communication between high- and low-context people is often fraught with impatience and irritation because low-context communicators may give more information than is necessary, while high-context communicators may not provide enough information or background.

Communication between high- and low-context people is often fraught with impatience and irritation

When communicating with individuals of our own culture, we can more readily assess the communication cues so that we know when our conversation, our ideas and words, are being understood and internalized. However, when communicating across cultures, communication misunderstandings can occur. They are usually not serious and can be rectified. Exhibit 2.1 illustrates a communication misunderstanding that had grave results. Excerpted is the transcript of the conversation between the captain, copilot, and controller on the Avianca flight that crashed on Long Island in 1991.

The communication misunderstanding involves the high and low context of communication styles. It can be seen from this dialogue between the pilot, copilot, and controller that there was a crucial error of misunderstanding between the copilot who was Colombian (native

EXHIBIT 2.1

Captain to Copilot:
"Tell them we are in emergency."

Copilot to Controller:
"We are running out of fuel . . ."

Controller:
"Climb and maintain 3000."

Copilot to Controller:
"Uh, we're running out of fuel."

Controller:
"I'm going to bring you about 15 miles northeast and then turn you back . . . Is that fine with you and your fuel?"

Copilot:
"I guess so."
The jet ran out of fuel and crashed.

language Spanish—high context), and the American controller, who was a low-context communicator. "Emergency" is low context. "We are running out of fuel" is more high context (literally, all airplanes, once they take off, are running out of fuel). The controller's last question, "Is that fine with you and your fuel?" is more high context.

The controller could have asked, "Are you declaring a fuel emergency?" If the controller had asked this question, perhaps the copilot would have responded "yes" because he or she had just heard the pilot say, "Tell them we are in emergency." Exhibit 2.2 provides another excellent example of a low/high context communication.

EXHIBIT 2.2
MIDDLE EAST LOW/HIGH CONTEXT COMMUNICATION

"How many days did it take?"

"I will tell you. We watered at al Ghaba in the Amairi. There were four of us, myself, Salim, Janazil of the Awamir, and Alaiwi of the Afar; it was in the middle of summer. We had been to Ibri to settle the feud between the Rashid and the Mahamid started by the killing of Fahad's son."

Musallim interrupted, "That must have been before the Riqaishi was Governor of Ibri. I had been there myself the year before. Sahail was with me and we went there from . . ."

But al Auf went on, "I was riding the three-year-old I had bought from bin Duailan."

"The one the Manahil raided from the Yam?" Bin Kabina asked.

"Yes. I exchanged it later for the yellow six-year-old I got from bin Ham. Janazil rode a Batina camel. Do you remember her? She was the daughter of the famous grey which belonged to the Harahaish of the Wahiba."

Mabkhaut said, "Yes, I saw her last year when he was in Salala, a tall animal; she was old when I saw her, past her prime but even then a real beauty."

Al Auf went on, "We spent the night with Rai of the Afar."

Bin Kabina chimed in, "I met him last year when he came to Habarut; he carried a rifle, 'a father of ten shots,' which he had taken from the Mahra he had killed in the Ghudun. Bin Mautlauq offered him the grey yearling, the daughter of Farha, and fifty *riyals* for this rifle, but he refused."

Al Auf continued, "Rai killed a goat for our dinner and told us . . .", but I interrupted: "Yes, but how many days did it take you to get to Bai?" He looked at me in surprise and said, "Am I not telling you?"[13]

Unless global

leaders are

aware of

the subtle

differences,

communication

misunderstandings

between low-

and high-context

communicators

can result.

Unless global leaders are aware of the subtle differences, communication misunderstandings between low- and high-context communicators can result. Japanese communicate by not stating things directly, while Americans usually do just the opposite—"spell it all out." The former looks for meaning and understanding in what is not said—in the nonverbal communication or body language, in the silences and pauses, in relationships and empathy. The latter emphasizes sending and receiving accurate messages directly, usually by articulating words. The following is a more sophisticated example of high-low context communication. It is taken from the wonderful book, *Arabian Sands*, by Wilfred Thesinger.[13] Read the situation carefully.

A third example in Exhibit 2.3 of low/high communication context involves a Chinese Human Resource director and a western HR director working for the same company.

EXHIBIT 2.3

A QUESTION FROM A WESTERNER TO A CHINESE HR DIRECTOR CONCERNING ATTENDANCE AT A TRAINING PROGRAM

Question: "Do you think Mr. Sim will be able to come to the course next week as I would like to make hotel reservations for him and the hotel is quite full?"

Answer: "It is possible he may have to attend a meeting in Shanghai."

Follow up question two days later and before the course begins:

Question sent by email: "I am following up my earlier conversation and am wondering if Mr. Sim will be attending the course."

Answer by email: "As I told you previously he will NOT attend."

Result: A significant misunderstanding between the Chinese HR director and the Westerner. The HR director ignored the Westerner at work for several days.

Exhibit 2.4 illustrates the cultural variations in management style between Mexicans and Americans.

For low context communicators to understand high context messages it is important to listen and observe the environment. Education seems to emphasize articulation over the acquisition of listening skills, which are essential to international negotiations. Lyman Steil pioneered scientific research on listening and discovered that it is the communication competency that is used most, but taught least in the United States. He summarized his findings in Exhibit 2.5. In high context cultures, listening skills are highly valued and learned from an early age.

EXHIBIT 2.4
MANAGEMENT STYLES

Aspect	Mexico	United States
Work/Leisure	Works to live Leisure considered essential for full life Money is for enjoying life	Lives to work Leisure seen as reward for hard work Money often end in itself
Direction/ Delegation	Traditional managers autocratic Younger managers starting to delegate responsibility. Subordinates used to being assigned tasks, not authority	Managers delegate responsibility and authority Executive seeks responsibility and accepts accountability
Theory vs. Practice	Basically theoretical mind Practical implementation often difficult	Basically pragmatic mind Action-oriented problem-solving approach
Control	Still not fully accepted Sensitive to being "checked upon"	Universally accepted and practiced
Staffing	Family and friends favored because of trustworthiness Promotions based on loyalty to superior	Relatives usually barred. Favoritism is not acceptable. Promotion based on performance
Loyalty	Mostly loyal to superior (person rather than organization) Beginnings of self-loyalty	Mainly self-loyalty Performance motivated by ambition
Competition	Avoids personal competition; favors harmony at work	Enjoys proving her/himself in competitive situations
Training and Development	Training highly theoretical. Few structured programs	Training concrete, specific. Structured programs general
Time	Relative concept. Deadlines flexible	Categorical imperative. Deadlines and commitments are firm
Planning	Mostly short-term because of uncertain environment	Mostly long-term in stable environment

Source: Abbot-Moran, *Uniting North American Business*, Butterworth-Heinemann, 2002, p. 71.

Now look at Exhibit 2.5 for the four categories used in this research. What is missing in this analysis? It would seem to be electronic transmission, which involves all four communication skills. The new mobile phones enable people to see, hear, and talk to the other party. The computer cuts across borders and cultures, transmitting messages, documents, visuals, and even sound. It is a means of multiple global communications for individuals and groups.

EXHIBIT 2.5
COMMUNICATION SKILLS

	Listening	Speaking	Reading	Writing
Learned	1st	2nd	3rd	4th
Used	Most	Next most	Next least	Least
(%−100)	(−45%)	(−30%)	(−16%)	(−9%)
Taught	Least	Next least	Next most	Most

We learn to listen and talk before we read and write. Should we have difficulties with reading, writing, and talking, we will receive special assistance while at school. Why is listening not accorded the same attention, the same importance as speaking, reading, and writing?

Listening is a

complex activity.

Listening is a complex activity. The average person speaks approximately 12,000 sentences every day at about 150 words per minute, while the listener's brain can absorb around 400 words per minute. What do we do with this spare capacity? Many of us do nothing. We become bored. A good listener is seldom bored. He or she uses this extra capacity to listen to the entire message and to more fully analyze the meanings behind the words.

Listening means different things to different people. It can mean different things to the same person in different situations. There are various types of listening behaviors:

VARIOUS
TYPES
OF
LISTENING

1. *Hearing* is a physiological process by which sound waves are received by the ear and transmitted to the brain. This is not really listening in and of itself, though the two are often equated. Hearing is merely one step in the process.
2. *Information gathering* is a form of listening. Its purpose is the absorption of stated facts. Information gathering does not pertain to the interpretation of the facts and is indifferent as to the source.
3. *Cynical listening* is based upon the assumption that all communication is designed to take advantage of the listener. It is also referred to as defensive listening.

4. *Offensive listening* is the attempt to trap or trip up an opponent with his own words. A lawyer, when questioning a witness, listens for contradictions, irrelevancies, and weakness.

5. *Polite listening* is listening just enough to meet the minimum social requirements. Many people are not listening—they are just waiting for their turn to speak and are perhaps rehearsing their lines. They are not really talking to each other, but at each other.

6. *Active listening* involves a listener with very definite responsibilities. In active listening, the listener strives for complete and accurate understanding, for empathy, and assistance in working out problems.

Active listening, is what our normal listening mode should be but rarely is.

Listening is, above all, a sharing of oneself. It is impossible for one to become an active listener without becoming involved with the speaker. Listening demonstrates the respect and concern that words alone cannot fully express. It has the unique power of diminishing the magnitude of problems. By speaking to someone who listens, a person has the sense of already accomplishing something.

Listening fulfills another vital function as well. The listener provides feedback to the speaker concerning the speaker's success in transmitting his or her message clearly. In doing this, the listener exerts great control over future messages that might or might not be sent. Feedback will influence the speaker's confidence, delivery, content of the words, and nonverbal facets of communication.

Simons, Vázquez, and Harris state that in working within our own culture we are very perceptive.[14] We know what ideas are being accepted or rejected and when others are following our conversation. However, when communicating across cultures there is the real possibility of reading people incorrectly, and they us. Problems arise when one does not pay close enough attention or actively listen to what an individual is trying to communicate. Instead, when at work, in focusing on getting the job done and meeting business deadlines and agendas, one can easily pretend to listen or listen halfheartedly. Today the workplace is a mix of individuals from different cultures, of different ages and genders, and with different work values. One must listen at three levels in cross-cultural exchanges.

1. *Pay attention* to the person and the message. One may subconsciously ignore a speaker whose thought process or thinking patterns are more convoluted or subtle than one's own. Also, the behavior of the speaker may be so emotional or subdued that one may selectively listen or not listen at all. To further complicate the listening process, an individual may speak with an

In active listening, the listener strives for complete and accurate understanding, for empathy, and assistance in working out problems.

accent, causing the listener to struggle to determine the words and put them in an understandable order.

2. *Emphasize and create rapport.* Empathy, especially with people who have visible differences in language and culture, can build trust and loyalty. The verbal and nonverbal cues of the speaker reveal his or her thinking patterns. Attempting to emulate cues, after reading them properly and matching their style, increases the comfort and effectiveness of communication, especially a cross-cultural one.

3. *Share meaning.* Share your understanding of the speaker's message. Paraphrasing is an "active listening" skill that enables the listener to check the accuracy of his or her understanding of the message.

ATTRIBUTION

Triandis[15] cites the following interesting cross-cultural situation. In many cultures domestic help does most of the tasks around a home, including the cleaning of shoes. In the United States, such employees usually do not clean shoes as part of their responsibilities. If Mr. Kato, a Japanese businessman, were a house guest of Mr. Smith, an American businessman, and asked the "cleaning person" to shine his shoes, there could be a problem. It is, or at least could be, an inappropriate request. However, the crucial question is, what *attributions* does the cleaning person make concerning Mr. Kato's request? There are probably two possibilities. One is that he or she could say Mr. Kato is ignorant of American customs, and in this case the person would not be too disturbed. The cleaning person could respond in a variety of ways, including telling the Japanese guest of the American custom, ignoring the request, and speaking to his or her employer. However, if the cleaning person attributes Mr. Kato's request to a personal characteristic (he is arrogant), then there will be a serious problem in their interpersonal relationship. If a person from one culture is offended by a person from another culture and believes the offense is caused by culture ignorance, this is usually forgiven. If one "attributes" the offense or "error" to arrogance, there will be serious problems.

Attribution theory is concerned with how people explain things that happen. We interpret behavior in terms of what is appropriate for a role. Mr. Kato expected that it would be acceptable to ask the cleaning person to shine his shoes. From the perspective of the cleaning person, this is not acceptable. When each one's expectations were not realized they attributed motives to the "offender" based on their cultural construct. It helps to answer such questions as:

LISTENING @ 3 LEVELS

Attribution theory is concerned with how people explain things that happen.

1. Why did Mr. Kato ask the cleaning person to shine his shoes?
2. Why did I pass or fail an examination?
3. Why can't Molly read?

There are many ways of perceiving the world. Given the almost limitless possibilities, we must subconsciously and habitually "screen" and organize the stimuli.

Attribution theory helps explain what happens and is applicable to cross-cultural management situations for the following reasons:

1. *All behavior is rational and logical from the perspective of the behaver.* At a seminar involving Japanese and American business people, an American asked a Japanese what was most difficult for him in the United States. The Japanese replied that "the most difficult part of my life here is to understand Americans. They are so irrational and illogical." The Americans listened with amusement and surprise.

2. *Persons from different cultures perceive and organize their environment in different ways, so that it becomes meaningful to them.* To be effective in working with people from different cultures requires that we make *isomorphic attributions* of the situation, i.e., we put ourselves "in the other person's shoes." Isomorphic attributions result in a positive evaluation of the other person because they help us to better understand his or her verbal and nonverbal behavior.

Triandis[16] provides another attribution in Exhibit 2.6. As background Greeks perceive supervisory roles as more authoritarian than Americans, who prefer participatory decision making. Read the verbal conversation first, then the attributions being made by the American and the Greek.

These examples illustrate that each statement in cross-cultural communication leads to an intimation that does not match the attribution of the other. These are extreme examples of nonisomorphic attributions, and accordingly work to the detriment of the relationship.

The intercultural skill of making isomorphic attributions is vital to appropriate protocol and effective technology transfer.[17] Exhibit 2.7 provides an example of a discussion between an American and a Japanese.

Levels of Culture and Human Interaction

Using the analogy that culture is like an iceberg (part of it is seen but most is not), the *technical* level of culture is the part of the iceberg that is visible. The technical aspects of a culture can be taught, and there is little emotion attached to this level. Few intercultural misunderstandings arise at this level because the reason for any misunderstanding is usually quite easy to determine. Managers operate at the technical

All behavior is rational and logical from the perspective of the behaver.

levels of culture when discussing the tolerance points of certain metals; however, when two managers are interacting over a period of time, it is difficult to remain exclusively at the technical level.

Continuing with the analogy of the cultural iceberg, the *formal* level of culture is partially above and partially below sea level. We learn

The formal level of culture is partially above and partially below sea level.

EXHIBIT 2.6
ATTRIBUTION IN GLOBAL MANAGEMENT

Verbal Conversation	Attribution
American: How long will it take you to finish this report?	*American*: I asked him to participate. *Greek*: His behavior makes no sense. He is the boss. Why doesn't he *tell* me?
Greek: I do not know. How long should it take?	*American*: He refuses to take responsibility. *Greek*: I asked him for an order.
American: You are in the best position to analyze time requirements.	*American*: I press him to take responsibility for his own actions. *Greek*: What nonsense! I better give him an answer.
Greek: 10 days.	*American*: He lacks the ability to estimate time; this time estimate is totally inadequate.
American: Take 15. Is it agreed you will do it in 15 days?	*American*: I offer a contract. *Greek*: These are my orders: 15 days.

In fact the report needed 30 days of regular work. So the Greek worked day and night, but at the end of the 15th day, he still needed one more day's work.

Verbal Conversation	Attribution
American: Where is the report?	*American*: I am making sure he fulfills his contract. *Greek*: He is asking for the report.
Greek: It will be ready tomorrow.	Both attribute that it is not ready.
American: But we had agreed it would be ready today.	*American*: I must teach him to fulfill a contract. *Greek*: The stupid, incompetent boss! Not only did he give me wrong orders, but he does not even appreciate that I did a 30-day job in 16 days.
The Greek hands in his resignation.	The American is surprised. *Greek*: I can't work for such a man.

aspects of our culture at the formal level usually by trial and error. We may be aware of the rules for a particular behavior, such as the rituals of marriage, but we do not know why. The emotion at the formal level of culture is high and violations result in negative feelings about the violator even though the violation is often unintentional. It is difficult to admit when the violated rule is local (i.e., an aspect of one culture

Emotion at the formal level of culture is high and violations result in negative feelings about the violator.

EXHIBIT 2.7
DISCUSSION BETWEEN A JAPANESE AND AMERICAN FIRM

A representative of a Japanese firm is discussing a business deal with a representative of an American firm. Americans value honesty and directness, while Japanese value harmony and group consensus. This was written during a seminar by a participant from an actual experience.

Verbal Conversation	Attribution
American: Well, what do you think of this deal between our companies?	A: I wonder if they are as committed to the contract as we are.
	J: He knows our company's position in these dealings. Why does he ask me?
Japanese: Our firm is honored to do business with such a prestigious American company.	J: I will remind him of our group's agreement.
	A: That's nice, but doesn't he have any thoughts of his own on the matter.
American: Thank you, but how do you personally feel about the contract?	A: He must not understand that I want his opinion on the deal. I will rephrase the question.
	J: We have agreed on the matter. Perhaps the Americans are still unsure.
Japanese: The company is pleased that we have been chosen to represent your firm in Japan, and we wish to do the best job we can.	J: Our board is in agreement.
	A: I know his firm's position. I just wonder what he thinks. Maybe I better try again and be more direct about it.
American: I'm sure your firm will represent us well, but do you feel that the terms of the contract are equitable?	A: Is this guy stupid or something? Or maybe he's trying to hide something.
Japanese: This is what our two companies have agreed upon. Therefore it must be the agreement.	J: Maybe he will feel better about the contract if I remind him that it was mutually agreed upon.
	A: He's really afraid to level with me.

and not another) and therefore does not apply to everyone. A business representative visiting France who uses a social occasion to discuss business with a French executive is violating a rule at the formal level of that culture.

The *informal* level of culture lies below "sea level," where actions and responses are automatic and almost unconscious. The rules of such behavior are usually not known, although we realize when something is wrong. Informal rules are learned through a process called modeling. One example of culture at the informal level is the male and female role behavior. In France, for instance, when is it appropriate for the American manager to begin calling her colleague "Denise," instead of "Mademoiselle Drancourt?" Emotion is usually intense at the informal level when a rule is broken, and the relationship between the persons involved is affected. Violations are interpreted personally; calling a person by his or her first name too soon could be interpreted as overly friendly and offensive.

VARIABLES IN THE COMMUNICATION PROCESS

Samovar and Porter[18] identify a number of variables in the communication process whose values are determined to some extent by culture. Each variable influences our perceptions, which in turn influence the meanings we attribute to behavior. Seeking to work effectively in a multicultural environment, one should recognize these and study the cultural specifics for the country or area to be visited.

Attitudes are psychological states that predispose us to behave in certain ways. An undesirable attitude for managers working in a multicultural environment is ethnocentrism or self-reference criterion. This is the tendency to judge others by using one's own personal or cultural standards. For example, instead of attempting to understand the Japanese within their own cultural context, an ethnocentric person tries to understand them as similar to or different from Americans. It is vital to refrain from constantly making comparisons between our way of life and that of others. Rather, one must understand other people in the context of their unique historical, political, economic, social, and cultural backgrounds. In that way it is possible to become more effective interactors.

Stereotypes are sets of attitudes that cause us to attribute qualities or characteristics to a person based on the group to which that individual belongs. Stereotypes are outsiders' beliefs about groups. Stereotypes are certain generalizations that allow us to organize and understand our environment. For humans to survive, we need to be able to form instant judgments about a situation, object, or person and to commit those judgments to memory. We draw on these stereotypes during similar situations so that we can quickly make judgments and act appropriately. Stereotypes aid us in predicting behavior by reducing our uncertainty. It was once said that "Stereotypes are in some ways a shorthand for us, but they have absolutely nothing to do with the person sitting across from you at the negotiating table."

Many studies of comparative management discuss "management" largely in terms of the system in the United States, which thus becomes the basis of comparison for management practices in other countries. Such studies facilitate the development of stereotypes because an underlying assumption is that the American management system is the norm and other systems are compared to the United States.

Social organization of cultures is another variable that influences one's perceptions. A *geographic society* is composed of members of a nation, tribe, or religious sect; a *role* society is composed of members of a profession or the elite of a group. Managers are members of the same role society, i.e., the business environment, but they are often members of different geographic societies. At one level communication between managers from two different cultures should be relatively smooth. On another level, significant differences in values, approach, pace, priorities, and other factors may cause difficulties.

Thought patterns or forms of reasoning may differ from culture to culture. The Aristotelian mode of reasoning prevalent in the West is not shared by people in the East. What is reasonable, logical, and self-evident to an American may be unreasonable, illogical, and not self-evident to a Japanese.

Roles in a society and expectations of a culture concerning behavior affect communication. Some roles have very prescriptive rules. For example, the *meishi* or name card of the Japanese businessperson identifies his or her position in a company and determines the degree of respect that is appropriately due the individual.

Language skill in a host country is acknowledged as important by global leaders, but many believe that a competent interpreter can be helpful and, at times, necessary.

Space is also a factor in the communication process. Americans believe that a comfortable space around them is approximately two feet. The United States is a noncontact society. Latin Americans and Middle Easterners, for example, are contact societies and are comfortable with close physical proximity to others. Touching is common between males and handshakes are frequent.

Time sense also impacts human interaction. North American cultures perceive time in lineal-spatial terms, in the sense that there is a past, a present, and a future. Being oriented toward the future, and in the process of preparing for it, one saves, wastes, makes up, or spends time. Zen treats time as a limitless pool in which certain things happen and then pass. A different time orientation can cause confusion when doing business in other cultures.

Thought patterns or forms of reasoning may differ from culture to culture.

Nonverbal signals or gestures are used in all cultures, and understanding the differences can help us become better cross-cultural communicators.

> Words representing perhaps 10% of the total (communication) emphasize the unidirectional aspects of communication—advocacy, law and adversial relationships—while behavior, the other 90%, stresses feedback on how people are feeling, ways of avoiding confrontation and the inherent logic that is the birthright of all people. Words are the medium of business, politicians, and our world leaders. All in the final analysis deal in power . . . The nonverbal, behavioral part of communication is the provenance of the common man and the core culture that guides life.
>
> Edward T. Hall[19]

Do your actions really speak louder than your words? A classic study by Dr. Albert Mehrabian found the *total impact* of a message on a receiver is based on 7% words used; 38% how the words are said—tone of voice, loudness, inflection, and other paralinguistic qualities; and 55% nonverbal—facial expressions, hand gestures, body position, etc.

Nonverbal signals or gestures are used in all cultures, and understanding the differences can help us become better cross-cultural communicators. An example of similar body language cues having different cultural reactions was reported by Furnham,[20] who states that "Research in the U.S. has shown that tips tend to be larger if the waiter touches the diner . . . and if the waiter gives a big and 'authentic' initial smile." However, in the UK that same body language exhibited by a waiter may result in no tip at all. Body language is frequently culturally distinct. International body language can fall under three categories, two of which can create problems.

1. A gesture can mean something different to others than it does to you. For example, the A-OK gesture, as used in the United States, means that things are fine, great, or that something has been understood perfectly. But Brazilians interpret it as an obscene gesture, and to the Japanese it means money.
2. A gesture can mean nothing to the person observing it. Scratching one's head or drawing in breath and saying "saa" are common Japanese responses to embarrassment. One can miss these cues as these gestures may have no particular meaning in one's native culture.
3. A gesture can mean basically the same in both cultures and the meaning is accurately communicated with few possible misunderstandings.

Hand and Arm Gestures

Most persons use their hands when speaking to punctuate the flow of conversation, refer to objects or persons, mimic and illustrate words or ideas. Often, gestures are used in place of words. Generally, Japanese speakers use fewer words and fewer gestures than American speakers; French use more of both and Italians much more.

In the United States, patting a small child on the head usually conveys affection. But in Malaysia and other Islamic countries, the head, considered the source of one's intellectual and spiritual powers, is sacred and should not be touched.

Australians signal "time to drink up" by folding three fingers of the hand against the palm, leaving the thumb and little finger sticking straight up and out. In China, the same gesture means six.

To get someone's attention or to summon a waiter or waitress is often a problem. This task requires different gestures in different countries. For example, in restaurants in North American countries, one would call a waiter or waitress quietly, "sir," "miss," "waiter," raise a finger to catch their attention, or tilt one's head to one side. Do not snap your fingers. On the Continent one would clink a glass or cup with a spoon or your ring. In the Middle East clapping one's hands is effective. In Japan extend your arm slightly upward, palm down, and flutter your fingers. In Spain and Latin America extend your hand, palm down, and rapidly open and close your fingers.

In a *Financial Times* advertisement, a major banking institution provided the following to illustrate the importance of local knowledge. One gesture in three countries has three different meanings.

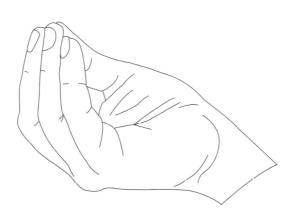

EGYPT

Be patient

GREECE

That's just perfect

ITALY

What exactly do you mean?

Often, gestures are used in place of words.

Eye Contact

In many Western cultures, a person who does not maintain good eye contact is regarded as slightly suspect. Those who avoid eye contact are unconsciously considered unfriendly, insecure, untrustworthy, inattentive, and impersonal. In contrast, Japanese children are taught in school to direct their gaze at the region of their teacher's Adam's apple or tie knot, and, as adults, Japanese lower their eyes when speaking to a superior, a gesture of respect.

In Latin American cultures and some African cultures, such as Nigeria, prolonged eye contact from an individual of lower status is considered disrespectful. In the United States, it is considered rude to stare—regardless of who is looking at whom. In contrast, the polite English person is taught to pay strict attention to a speaker, to listen carefully, and to blink his or her eyes to let the speaker know he or she has been understood as well as heard. Americans signal interest and comprehension by bobbing their heads or grunting.

A widening of the eyes can also be interpreted differently. For example, take the case of an American and a Chinese discussing the terms of a proposed contract. Regardless of the language in which the transaction is carried out, the U.S. negotiator may interpret a Chinese person's widened eyes as an expression of astonishment instead of its true meaning of politely suppressed Asian anger.

GUIDELINES FOR ENGLISH AND FOREIGN LANGUAGES

Much of the world's international business is conducted in English. When the mother languages in international business are different, generally the most commonly understood language is English. When Swedes negotiate with the Saudis in Saudi Arabia, the language most likely used is English. Following are twenty propositions for "internalizing" the use of English.[21]

1. Practice using the most common 3000 words in English, that is, those words typically learned in the first two years of language study. Be particularly careful to avoid uncommon or esoteric words; for example, use "witty" rather than "jocose," or "effective" rather than "efficacious."

2. Restrict your use of English words to their most common meaning. Many words have multiple meanings, and nonnative speakers are most likely to know the first or second most common meanings. For example, use "force" to mean "power"

or "impetus" rather than "basic point." Other examples include using "to address" to mean "to send" (rather than "to consider") or using "impact" to mean "the force of a collision" (rather than "effect").

3. Whenever possible, select an action-specific verb (e.g., "ride the bus") rather than a general action verb (e.g., "take the bus"). Verbs to avoid include "do," "make," "get," "have," "be," and "go." For example, the verb "get" can have at least five meanings (buy, borrow, steal, rent, retrieve) in "I'll get a car and meet you in an hour."

4. In general, select a word with few alternate meanings (e.g., "accurate"—one meaning) rather than a word with many alternate meanings (e.g., "right"—27 meanings).

5. In choosing among alternative words, select a word with similar alternate meanings rather than a word with dissimilar alternate meanings. For example, "reprove" means to rebuke or to censure—both similar enough that a nonnative speaker can guess the meaning accurately. In contrast, "correct" can mean either to make conform to a standard, to scold, or to cure, leaving room for ambiguity in interpretation by a nonnative speaker.

6. Become aware of words whose primary meaning is restricted in some cultures. For example, outside of the United States, "check" most commonly means a financial instrument and is frequently spelled "cheque."

7. Become aware of alternate spellings of commonly used words and the regions in which those spellings are used: for example, colour/color, organisation/organization, centre/center.

8. Resist creating new words by changing a word's part of speech from its most common usage; for example, avoid saying "a warehouse operation" or "attachable assets."

9. Avoid all but the few most common two-word verbs such as "to turn on/off (the lights)" or "to pick up" meaning "to grasp and lift."

10. Maximum punctuation should be used, e.g., commas that help clarify the meaning, but could technically be omitted, should be retained.

11. Redundancy and unnecessary quantification should be avoided as they are confusing to the nonnative speaker trying to determine the meaning of the sentence. For example, factories cannot operate at greater than capacity—"peak capacity" is redundant.

12. Conform to basic grammar rules more strictly than is common in everyday conversation. Make sure that sentences express a complete thought, that pronouns and antecedents are used

correctly, and that subordination is accurately expressed. For example, the sentence, "No security regulations shall be distributed to personnel that are out of date," needs to be rewritten as, "Do not distribute out-of-date security regulations to personnel."

13. Clarify the meaning of modal auxiliaries; for example, be sure that the reader will understand whether "should" means moral obligation, expectation, social obligation, or advice.

14. Avoid "word pictures," constructions that depend on invoking a particular mental image (e.g., "run that by me," "wade through these figures," "slice of the free world pie"). The use of absurd assumptions is a particular form of mental imagery likely to cause misunderstandings if taken literally; for example, "suppose you were me" or "suppose there were no sales."

15. Avoid terms borrowed from sports (e.g., "struck out," "field that question," "touchdown," "can't get to first base," "ballpark figure"), the military (e.g., "run it up the flag pole," "run a tight ship"), or literature (e.g., "catch-22").

16. When writing to someone you do not know well, use their last name and keep the tone formal while expressing personal interest or concern. Initial sentences can express appreciation (e.g., "We are extremely grateful to your branch . . .") or personal connection (e.g., "Mr. Ramos has suggested . . ."). Closing phrases can express personal best wishes (e.g., "With warmest regards, I remain sincerely yours . . .").

17. Whenever the cultural background of the reader is known, try to adapt the tone of the written material to the manner in which such information (i.e., apology, suggestion, refusal, thanks, request, directive) is usually conveyed in that culture. For example, apologies may need to be sweeping and unconditional (e.g., "My deepest apologies for any problems . . ."); refusals may need to be indirect (e.g., "Your proposal contains some interesting points that we need to study further . . .").

18. If possible, one should determine and reflect the cultural values of the reader on such dimensions as espousing controlling versus qualitative changes. When in doubt, a variety of value orientations should be included: "I want to thank you [individual] and your department [collective] . . ."

19. When the cultural background of the reader is known, try to capture the spoken flavor of the language in writing. For example, communications to Spanish speakers would be more descriptive, expressive, and lengthy than those to German-speakers.

20. Whenever possible, either adopt the cultural reasoning style of your reader or present information in more than one format. For

example, the following sentence contains both a general position statement and inductive reasoning: "Trust among business partners is essential; and our data show that our most successful joint ventures are those in which we invested initial time building a personal trusting relationship."

21. Oral presentations should be made plainly, clearly, and slowly, using visual aids whenever possible.
22. Paraphrase in intercultural conversations, encouraging your counterpart to do the same with your input.
23. Important international business communications by telephone should be confirmed by fax or written reports.
24. International meetings should be facilitated with a written summary, preferably in the language of the receiver or client.
25. Written brochures, proposals, and reports should be translated into the native language of the receiver or client.

Foreign Language Competency

To survive and communicate, the average European speaks several languages. The typical Japanese studies English as well as other languages. This is not true of most U.S. citizens who, even when they study a foreign language, often lack fluency.

Although English is becoming a global language, bear in mind that many speak it as a second language. Also, American English is different from, though rooted in, British English, which is further modified as it is used in the British Commonwealth nations. Thus, in countries where "English" is the official language, human resource leaders should consider training programs for those workers whose native language is not English. Group sessions or self-learning modules can be presented by organizations under the title, "Improving Communications at Work." This instruction should also include improving pronunciation skills of nonnative employees.

The use of interpreters can further reduce misunderstanding in business and international relations. But translations are given in a cultural context, and linguistic specialists themselves require cross-cultural training. Both international education and business can be facilitated by competent simultaneous interpretation. New equipment for simultaneous interpreting, graphic presentations, and reporting have done much to foster international communication. The global use of the computer creates a universal language of another type. And through the wizardry of electronic technology, forthcoming inventions will translate for us.

The following announcements in English illustrate the problems in intercultural communication.[22]

Poorly translated materials can cause problems for corporations. For example, when Coca-Cola introduced its product into the Asian

Although English is becoming a global language, bear in mind that many speak it as a second language.

market, the Chinese characters sounded correct, but actually read, "Bite the wax tadpole." Pepsi-Cola had a comparable communication disaster when it moved into the Thai market using the American slogan, "Come alive, you're in the Pepsi generation." Only later did Pepsi discover that the real Thai translation said, "Pepsi brings your ancestors back from the dead."

TECHNOLOGY AND INTERCULTURAL COMMUNICATION

The following underscores the challenges and prospects in current communication technologies, particularly relative to the intercultural factors. Cross-cultural skills and sensitivity are just as much in demand when people meet electronically as when they meet in person.

Communicating via Electronic Mail

Citizens of the global village increasingly use e-mail for business

Citizens of the global village increasingly use e-mail for business and personal reasons, with Internet subscriptions predicted to increase significantly every year. When e-mailing across cultures avoid ambiguous messages, be specific, and provide background or context for the communication so there can be no misinterpretation. Summarize information in different words to clarify, remembering that body language and voice intonation are not present to nuance the message.

Computers and Language

New communications technologies constantly expand our capacity for exchanges with one another regardless of distance. They enable us to transmit our *brains* and the information stored there rather than moving our *bodies* from place to place. The wonders of modern telecommunications are wide ranging—from telegraph, typewriter, telephone, television to radio, personal computers, electronic mail, and facsimile machines. Movies have moved from theaters to cassettes or diskettes that can be played on one's television or computer monitor; CD-ROM disks offer a wide range of learning and entertainment for a personal computer. A combination of communication satellites and computers, plus fiber optics on the ground, enhance our global interactions. Instead of using a keyboard, we can now talk to our computers in our own language. The emerging generation of communicating devices are called "thin client appliances"—fixed screen Web phones, smart mobile telephones—energy efficient and supposedly easy to use. Processing power for computing doubles every 18 months, while the speed and simplicity of message transmission increases as well. The cost of this communication also goes down, thanks to advances in cheap chips and high-bandwidth connections.

To plumb the depths of information on the global computer network, most messages and stored data are in English. Most people of the world do not speak English and are therefore handicapped in their use of the Internet. English, the language of science and business, is also the language of the computer world. To meet the demand for more multicultural media, a consortium of computer companies has developed Unicode, a universal digital code that allows computers to represent the letters and characters of virtually all of the world's languages. As a result of new multilingual software, people are adding databases and home pages or Web sites in their own languages, enabling greater numbers to communicate on the World Wide Web. Automatic translation capabilities now allow messages transmitted in one language to be received in another.[23] One such popular software is Easy Translator 4.0, by Transparent Language, Inc.

Video Conferencing

Video conferencing is forecast to grow 60% each year through the twenty-first century. In 1998, equipment sales were already a $5 billion industry. Frost & Sullivan Market Intelligence predict for the near future that North America will buy 50% of the video conferencing systems; Europe 26%; Pacific Rim countries 20%; while the rest of the world accounts for the remaining 4%.

Exxon Chemical employees use video conferencing more than 1600 times per year, saving more than $4 million in travel costs. For example, a 90-minute trans-Pacific video conference in Hong Kong will cost $500 compared to three executive's expenses for travel and lodging at approximately $12,000. Annually, the corporation has more than 3000 electronic meetings at 45 video centers worldwide. Team problem solving and short reviews are important benefits of this technology. Combined with interactive computers, a person in Europe can change numbers on a spreadsheet sketched on a board in the United States.[24]

Team problem solving and short reviews are important benefits of this technology.

AUDIO CONFERENCING

Now a team of researchers at PARC, a commercial research laboratory in Palo Alto, California, has developed a model for understanding and dealing with several simultaneous conversations. Like the many "chit-chats" one listens and participates in a typical, noisy cocktail party, groups of conversing people spontaneously form and break up as one overhears adjacent speakers, or gets bored with a discussion and moves away. Researcher Paul Aoki notes that the people sharing a *floor* sound noticeably louder to each other because they are in close proximity and facing one another. In contrast, the typical conference call is at the same volume, making it almost impossible for more than one person to speak at a time, thus inhibiting casual conversation.

Dr. Aoki's innovative system is called *Mad Hatter*, which mimics the context of normal conversation by changing the volume of sound, and permitting overlapping in speaking. Also by considering time lapses between individual input, the new system is able to switch *floors*, enabling several conversations to go on at once. Plans call for spotting common words featured in such conversations, and keeping track of differences in intonation. Not only business, but gossip too, may soon be easier in the global village.

Video-bridging is making it possible to connect multiple locations without degrading audio and video quality. This century will demonstrate the capability of 300 linkups in the same video conference. Inexpensive equipment will permit knowledge workers to turn their offices and homes into video studios, conducting video conferences from desktop computers with colleagues around the world. Other forms of teleconferencing may occur through use of telephones, computers, and shortwave radio. One problem has been the slowness of dialogue as each participant listens to only one speaker, to avoid confusion of several persons talking at once. Now a new technological improvement may overcome that difficulty.[25]

New information technologies are like two-edged swords—they can facilitate or complicate transcultural communications!

HANDLING TWO SWORDS AT THE SAME TIME—A GLOBAL SHIFT[26]

Is it possible to learn to shift one's style to fit different international situations? Is it possible to do what Miyamoto Musashi, a famous sev-

New information technologies are like two-edged swords—they can facilitate or complicate transcultural communications!

entccnth century Japanese samurai did? He developed the Nitoryu style of swordmanship, or the act of handling two swords at the same time.

To be skillful, effective, and successful in one's own culture by being assertive, quick, and to the point is one mode of behavior. To be equally successful in another culture by being unassertive, patient, and somewhat indirect is another mode entirely—like intentionally handling two swords at the same time. Yo Miyoshi says he modifies his behavior to suit his audience: "When I discuss something with the head office in the United States, I try to be Western. But when I deal with my people in the company here, I am Oriental or Japanese."

Miyoshi is able to shift his style or to handle two swords at the same time. He had to learn this behavior. In trying to teach "old dogs new tricks," we should focus on the teacher instead of the "dog." The following exercise is one way to focus on the teacher. The words listed below are some of the adjectives that could describe an international manager. Read the list and circle the ones that you believe apply to yourself.

Assertive, energetic, decisive, ambitious, confident, aggressive, quick, competitive, inpatient, impulsive, quick-tempered, intelligent, excitable, informal, versatile, persuasive, imaginative, original, witty, colorful, calm, easy-going, good-natured, tactful, unemotional, good listener, inhibited, shy, absented-minded, cautious, methodical, timid, lazy, procrastinator, enjoy responsibility, resourceful, individualist, broad interests, limited interests, good team worker, enjoy working alone, sociable, cooperative, quiet, easily distracted, serious, idealistic, ethnocentric, cynical, conscientious, flexible, mature, dependable, honest, sincere, reliable, adaptable, curious.

Using these qualities skillfully is handling one sword—the sword that makes you successful in your business culture. The next step in the exercise is to think of the next international trip you will be taking and consider the people you will be meeting. Now, go back to the same list of words and place a check beside those qualities that you believe these people will look for in you.

But we all carry basic personality characteristics—the sword that made us successful, our aggressiveness and competitiveness, for example. But in another culture the second sword we are expected to carry might be characterized by qualities such as gentleness, cooperativeness, followership, indirectness, and commitment to relationships.

Culture can be likened to an enormous, subtle, extraordinarily complex computer.

CONCLUSIONS

The most basic skill that global leaders must cultivate is cross-cultural communication. To facilitate our interactions with persons who do not share our values, assumptions, or learned ways of behaving requires new competencies and sensitivities so that the very cultural differences become resources. The complexities of the communication process have been reviewed here from the perspectives of cross-cultural behaviors and factors; listening, attribution and foreign language skill levels, and variables when interacting; body language and gestures.

This chapter has emphasized the possibilities and the pitfalls in intercultural communication, whether in personal or electronic encounters. New media have increased the prospects for positive or negative interchanges across cultures, both macro and micro. Culturally sensitive senders and receivers are still vital in the communication process. Global leaders should give a high priority to intercultural communication proficiency, as Hall and Hall observe:

Global leaders should give a high priority to intercultural communication proficiency

> Each cultural world operates according to its own internal dynamic, its own principles, and its own laws—written and unwritten. . . . Any culture is primarily a system for creating, sending, storing, and processing information. Communication underlies everything. . . . Culture can be likened to an enormous, subtle, extraordinarily complex computer. It programs the actions and responses of every person, and these programs can be mastered by anyone wishing to make the system work.[27]

And as the late Janice Hepworth observed:

> Each culture is a unique arrangement of "components" characterizing different lifestyles which distinguish one culture from another. "Components" is a broad term used here to refer to attitudes, values, beliefs, and institutions that each culture creates and defines to serve its own particular needs. The problems for intercultural communication arise out of unique definitions and arrangements made by each culture. . . . While this may seem obvious to you, the "rightness" of your way of doing things can stand in the way of intercultural communication.[28]

MIND STRETCHING

As you have read in this chapter, you of course understand yourself as formed in large part by your socialization in a particular culture. Therefore, we have a list of questions for you to consider. We ask that you take the time and look into the mirror to become better acquainted with your own style of communication and the societal and cultural influences that influence who you are, what you communicate about, how you communicate your thoughts. In this manner, you will best understand how to improve yourself as a cross-cultural communicator within the global business context.

1. How does your culture tell you how to communicate and behave and what are the messages that you feel are consistently reinforced?

2. How do you prefer to communicate? Direct? Indirect?
3. How does your religion influence your values? Your beliefs? Your behavior? Who you associate with?
4. In your personal life, do you have many friends who are different from you? How are they different? Are they different in personality, ethnicity, culture, or are most of your friends of your own cultural background? Why?
5. How much time do you spend to understand another person's perspective? Or do you prefer to try to persuade others to change and adopt your own perspective?

Everyone finds it easier to communicate and interact with people who have a similar personality, ethnicity, and culture. We also prefer to be around people who share our religion, our beliefs and our worldview. The challenge is to learn how to move beyond the inherent conflict that arises when two different people interact, and ultimately create an environment where all divergent parties can find the common ground. The first step is to understand your own culture and communication style, and what barriers you may have toward positive cross-cultural communication interaction.

Not only is the field of intercultural communication changing, but the relationship between culture and communication is—and probably always will be—complex and dynamic. We live in a rapidly changing world in which intercultural contract will continue to increase, creating heightened potential for both conflict and communication.[29]

> *Everyone finds it easier to communicate and interact with people who have a similar personality, ethnicity, and culture.*

REFERENCES

1. Meadows, D. H. "If the World Were a Village of 1000 People," *Futures by Design: The Practice of Ecological Planning*, Aberley, D. (ed.). Philadelphia, PA: New Society Publishers, 1994.
2. Curtin, P. D. *Cross-Cultural Trade in World History*. Cambridge University Press, United Kingdom, 1984, p. 1.
3. Schnitzer, M. C. *Comparative Economic Systems*. Cincinnati, OH: South-Western College Publishing, 1997.
4. Bartlett, C. A. and Ghoshal, S. *Managing Across Borders*. Boston, MA: Harvard Business School Press, 1989.
5. Friedman, T. L. *The Lexus and the Olive Tree*. New York: Anchor Books, 2000.
6. *Arizona Republic*, November 21, 2002.
7. Moran, R. T. "So You're Going Abroad: Are You Prepared?" Self-published, Tenth Printing, 2003.
8. Klopf, D. W. *Intercultural Encounters*. Englewood, CO: Morton Publishing Co., 1991.

9. Simons, G. F., Vázquez, C., and Harris, P. R. *Transcultural Leadership*. Houston, TX: Gulf Publishing Co., 1993.

10. Singer, M. R. *Perception & Identity in Intercultural Communication*. Yarmouth, ME: Intercultural Press, 1998.

11. Gudykunst, W. B. *Bridging Differences: Effective Intergroup Communications*. Thousand Oaks, CA, Sage Publications, 1994. See also Bennett, M. J. (ed.) *Basic Concepts of Intercultural Communication*. Yarmouth, ME: Intercultural Press, 1998.

12. Lustig, M. W. and Koester, J. *Intercultural Competence*. New York: Addison Wesley, 1998.

13. Thesinger, W. *Arabian Sands*. London: Penguin Books, 1991.

14. Simons, G. F., Vázquez, C., and Harris, P. R. *Transcultural Leadership*. Houston, TX: Gulf Publishing Co., 1993. See also Elashmawi, F. and Harris, P. R. *Multicultural Management 2000*. Houston, TX: Gulf Publishing Co., 1998.

15. Triandis, H. C. (ed.) *Variations in Black and White—Perceptions of the Social Environment*. Urbana, IL: University of Illinois Press, 1976.

16. Ibid.

17. Nelson, C. A. *Protocol for Profit—A Manager's Guide to Competing Worldwide*. London: International Thomson Business Press, 1998.

18. Samovar, L. A. and Porter, R. E. *Intercultural Communication: A Reader*. Belmont, CA: Wadsworth Publishing Co., 1988.

19. Hall, E. T. *Dance of Life*. Garden City, NY: Anchor Press/Doubleday, 1983.

20. Furnham, A. "Actions speak louder than words," *Financial Times*, April 4, 1999.

21. Riddle, D. I. and Lanham, Z. D. *The Journal of Language for International Business*, "Internationalizing Written Business English: 20 Propositions for Native English Speakers," 1985.

22. Landers, A. *Los Angeles Times*, "At Times Everything Gets Lost in the Translation," January 28, 1996.

23. Pollack, A. W. *New York Times*, August 7, 1995, C1/6.

24. Meyers, G. *Exxon Magazine*, summer 1998, pp. 10–11.

25. "Uncrossed Wires," in "Science and Technology," *The Economist*, June 21, 2003, p. 72.

26. Moran, R. T. "Handling Two Swords at the Same Time," Original and modified, 2003.

27. Hall, E. T. and Hall, M. R. *Hidden Differences—Doing Business with the Japanese*. Garden City, NY: Anchor/Doubleday, 1987.

28. Hepworth, J. *International Communication* (1990) and *Things to Know About Americans* (1991), Denver, CO: University Centers, Inc. See also Lustig, M. W. and Koester, J. *Intercultural Competence*. New York: HarperCollins, 1999.

29. Martin, J. N. and Nakayama, T. K. *Intercultural Communication in Contexts*. McGraw-Hill, Boston, 2004, p. xviii.

GLOBAL LEADERSHIP IN NEGOTIATIONS

Business and leisure travel to China is booming. In 2005, there were a record of 120,000,000 foreign visitors to China. In 1978, there were 230,000 foreign visitors to China.[1]

The significant increase in business travel is not only to China. Globalization has resulted in increased business travel to many countries in order to buy, sell, form mergers or acquisitions, build relationships, and many other activities. Most of these business relationships will be some form of negotiations.

Today's leaders seek business ventures in the global arena, crisscrossing the world to negotiate and bargain. Hundreds of billions of dollars have been spent in 2006.[2] Many claim the success rate of mergers and acquisitions to be less than 50% for successful integration, although little hard data is available. Shelton, Hall, and Darling state "these mergers typically failed to achieve the targeted results."

Appreciating the complexities of labor negotiations in the home culture or negotiating a contract in a foreign country has made these leaders understand the competency and skill needed to effectively work out these situations.

In the twenty-first century global leaders increasingly do their negotiating *electronically*, by telephone, fax, e-mail, and video conferencing. One of the most powerful communication tools for this purpose is the Internet. It offers quick and easy negotiation opportunities with manufacturers, suppliers, customers, and even government regulators. But it also requires more openness, transparency, and trust in business

Although globalization opens many opportunities, it also creates many complex challenges.

communications and negotiations. The Internet and computers are altering the entire situation of international negotiations.

LEARNING OBJECTIVES

To understand the importance of "culture" when negotiating with individuals in today's global world. Dealing with conflicts, having a high degree of emotional intelligence, and being able to "profile" accurately one's negotiating counterparts are significant ingredients in negotiating success.

The chapter is intended to be conceptual and immediately useful whether negotiating at home or abroad, and to persuade readers that global negotiating is a necessary learned skill.

CONFLICT RESOLUTION AND NEGOTIATIONS[3]

By definition all successful negotiation involves at least some resolution of conflicts.

By definition all successful negotiation involves at least some resolution of conflicts. Unsuccessful negotiation involves at least one conflict, large or small, that has not been resolved.

Like leadership and power, conflict is a fascinating subject for research and discussion in organizations. Traditionally, the social scientists who have studied conflict have been keenly aware of its destructive element which is observed in wars, strikes, family disruption, and disharmony. We will identify some themes reflecting the U.S. viewpoint with regard to conflict and suggest ways that other cultures resolve disputes. Rensis Likert stated many years ago, "The strategies and principles used by a society and all its institutions for dealing with disagreements reflect the basic values and philosophy in that society."[4]

What is conflict? Like the word culture there is no single agreed-upon definition. Thomas[5] states, "Conflict is the process that begins when one party perceives that the other has frustrated, or is about to frustrate, some concern of his." This frustration may result from actions that range from intellectual disagreement to physical violence. Another definition of "conflict" holds that it results when two or more persons or things attempt to occupy the same space at the same time. The management of conflict is a major issue at the personal and organizational level and all negotiations involve a resolution of conflicting interests and needs.

Most U.S. negotiators view conflict as a healthy, natural, and inevitable part of relationships and negotiations. This constructive approach to conflict views the positive attributes in any conflict situation. The belief that conflict is constructive requires that problems be addressed directly and that people can be motivated to search for solutions to these problems. Constructive disagreement may in fact be an integral part of American organizations. Stewart states, "When faced with a problem, Americans like to get to its source. This means facing the facts, meeting the problem head on, putting the cards on the table, and getting information straight from the horse's mouth. It is also desirable to face people directly, to confront them intentionally.[6]

However, conflict in organizations is perceived to have disadvantages when there are wide differences in viewpoints or perspectives and these are carried to the extreme. In this case, conflict is perceived as destructive, as the conflict creates a high level of stress for the individuals involved, which in turn affects their ability to perform. This undermines the cooperative dimension necessary in work groups and results in time and energy being devoted to resolutions which could have been spent on organizational objectives. Such a situation also thwarts the decision-making process. Conflict resolution should be viewed as a win–win situation.

With the change in emphasis from the elimination of conflict to the management of conflict, Thomas[7] identified two models of conflict between social units. The process model appears as:

$$\text{Frustration} \rightarrow \text{Conceptualization} \rightarrow \text{Behavior} \rightarrow \text{Outcome} \rightarrow \text{Frustration}$$
$$\uparrow \qquad \qquad \uparrow$$
$$\text{Other's Reactions}$$

The frustration of one party leads to a conceptualization of the situation, to some behavior, to the reaction of the other party, and then to agreement or the lack of agreement. In the latter case, the conflict episode is continued with further frustration, a new conceptualization, etc. The process model is concerned with the influence of an event (e.g., the conceptualization of the problems, etc.). The structural model attempts to understand conflict by studying how underlying conditions shape events. "The structural model is concerned with identifying the pressures and constraints which bear upon the parties' behavior, for example, social pressures, personal predispositions, established negotiation procedures and rules, incentives and so on."[8] The structural model attempts to predict the effect of these conditions on the behavior of the individuals involved in conflict. Thomas maintains that the two models complement each other.

Thomas and Kilman suggest a two-dimensional scheme, with one dimension being the cooperative-uncooperative striving to satisfy the other's concern, and the second being the degree to which one assertively pursues one's own concerns.[9] In Exhibit 3.1 the assertive style (4) is competitive and represents a desire to satisfy one's concern at the expense of the other. The cooperative style (2) attempts to satisfy

Conflict resolution should be viewed as a win–win situation.

the other but not one's own concern. A compromising style (3) is a preference for moderate but incomplete satisfaction of both parties. Labor-management disputes in the United States characterize this style. A collaborative style (5) attempts to fully satisfy the concerns of both parties and is most synergistic. The avoidance style (1) is an indifference to the concerns of either party. The cooperative style as opposed to uncooperative is an Eastern mode of resolving conflict, and the assertive mode is more Western.

The effective global manager must achieve a synergistic solution, diagnosing conflict accurately and determining a strategy for managing the conflict.

Conflict Management in the Arab World

In the Arab world, the role of the mediator is important in resolving conflict.

In the Arab world, the role of the mediator is important in resolving conflict. Thus, "the greater the prestige of the mediator, and the deeper the respect he commands, the better the chances that his efforts at mediating a dispute will be successful."[10] Some highly regarded families and groups carry on ascribed status as mediators. The mediator must be impartial and beyond pressures, including monetary ones, from either side in the dispute. The mediator will often promote compromise by appealing to the wishes of other respected parties; for example, "Do it for the sake of . . . your father/brother." The ethical force of such an argument ("for the sake of") has three underlying assumptions, all of which remain unspoken but nonetheless understood by the disputants.

EXHIBIT 3.1
A TWO-DIMENSIONAL SCHEMATIC SHOWING VARIOUS "STYLES" OF CONFLICT RESOLUTION

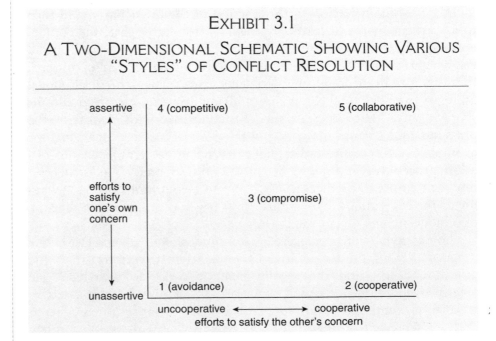

MANAGING CULTURAL DIFFERENCES

1. Each individual is obligated by ties of kinship to act in a manner that his kinsmen find gratifying.
2. The kinsmen, especially the older ones, are interested in the settlement of any conflict involving their kin group because every conflict represents a potential danger to the honor of the family.
3. By modifying one's position, the disputant can manifest generosity that, in turn, redounds the honor of kin and bedouin values.

Conflict Management in Japan

To understand typical behavioral responses to conflict situations in Japan requires a basic understanding of the history and cultural environment of Japan.[11] Accordingly, it is necessary to first ascertain the key psychological and cultural variables that affect Japanese conflict management phenomena, and then to determine how they interrelate with each other to create various deviations within a larger cultural norm. The Japanese conflict management system includes both institutionalized conflict management structures and behavioral conflict management techniques.

Styles of Handling Conflict in Japan

Five styles of handling conflict are used in Japan: avoiding, compromising, obliging, integrating, and dominating; and of these five styles the Japanese prefer the avoiding style. In repeated examples of Japanese managers response to the statement, "organizations would be better off if conflict could be eliminated," Japanese agree very strongly.

Avoiding

On a behavioral level, the Japanese commonly employ a number of techniques to avoid conflict. Many of these techniques are not uncommon in cultures around the world, but they provide particular insight into Japanese conflict management.

One of their most effective techniques is sometimes referred to as triadic management. To avoid confrontation between two people, the Japanese often create a triad with another outside individual to manage the situation. Conflict between the two parties may be communicated through the third party in an indirect manner. The third party may take a more active role as an arbiter in situations where there is an apparent stalemate. In such a situation, the third party who is respected by both of the other individuals may provide a breakthrough by presenting her- or himself as the person on whose behalf the other two parties are to resolve the conflict. She or he urges the conflicting parties to relent so that she or he can "save face" (*kao*), with an implicit threat

To understand typical behavioral responses to conflict situations in Japan requires a basic understanding of the history and cultural environment of Japan.

that she or he will take offense if her or his intervention is not heeded. To prevent humiliation to the arbiter, both parties may comply, even though they might prefer to remain in conflict with one another. Although this triadic management technique is by no means unique to Japan, it is utilized extensively, and provides one of the greatest vehicles for conflict management within the culture. Those skilled in global negotiations often use this method in Japan.

Compromising

A variant of triadic management, known as displacement, often can manifest itself in a variety of ways. Usually, the displacement will take place in the form of an offended individual attempting to convey his or her anger or resentment to a third party, who is in a far more favorable position to transfer the feelings of the injured party to the injuring party in a manner that is less conflicting.

Obliging

Another technique often utilized to avoid direct confrontation is commonly referred to as conflict acceptance. Instead of rejecting or correcting an undesirable state of affairs, the individual persuades her- or himself or is advised by someone else to accept the situation. This somewhat fatalistic or deterministic approach is rooted in the strong Buddhist influence on the culture throughout the history of Japan.

Integrating

Another less utilized technique employed to avoid direct confrontation may be referred to as self-aggression or self-confrontation. In this technique, one party expresses a grievance against another by exaggerated compliance.

Dominating

This style of conflict resolution is contrary to the very nature of the Japanese character and consequently is not used.

NEGOTIATING ACROSS CULTURES

Negotiation is a process in which two or more entities come together to discuss common and conflicting interests

Negotiation is a process in which two or more entities come together to discuss common and conflicting interests in order to reach an agreement of mutual benefit. In international business negotiations, the negotiation process differs from culture to culture in language, cultural conditioning, negotiating styles, approaches to problem solving, implicit assumptions, gestures and facial expressions, and the role of ceremony and formality.

For international negotiations to produce long-term synergy, and not just short-term solutions, individuals involved in the negotiation need to be aware of the multicultural facets in the process. The negotiator must understand the cultural space of his or her counterparts. It is our belief that negotiating is a skill, and it can be improved. Nelson[12] defines global negotiations as "a process by which one individual tries to persuade another to change his or her ideas of behavior. It is a process in which two partners with different needs and viewpoints try to reach agreement on matters of mutual interest. They want to do business or they would not be talking in the first place. Success in international business results from the ability to bring two people together, but all too often, the obstacle is our perception of people from other countries. Frequently, one party enters into a negotiation with expectations of the other party that are completely unrealistic!" The purpose of this section is to suggest some of the cultural variables and considerations.

Fisher[13] addresses five considerations for analyzing cross-cultural negotiations: (1) the players and the situation; (2) styles of decision making; (3) national character; (4) cross-cultural noise; and (5) interpreters and translators. Each consideration presents questions that should be answered before entering international negotiations.

The Players and the Situation

Fisher asserts that there is a cultural dimension in the way negotiators view the negotiation process. This raises several issues. Form, hospitality, and protocol are important to the success of international negotiations. Difficulties sometimes arise because there is a difference in what negotiators expect of a negotiation's social setting. The negotiator should discover what the foreign negotiator expects and then provide a tension-free environment that encourages cooperation and problem solving.

There also may be a national style in choosing negotiators and in selecting negotiating teams. Negotiators can anticipate a counterpart's behavior by researching biographical data and analyzing the negotiator's organizational or institutional role. In the case of negotiating teams, it is useful to discover how corporate culture affects internal dynamics.

Styles of Decision Making

Fisher contends that there are patterns in the way officials and executives structure their negotiation communication systems and reach institutional decisions. The organizational culture of a foreign corporation may provide formal rules and regulations guiding its decision-making process. A negotiator can find ways to influence a foreign

Negotiators can anticipate a counterpart's behavior by researching biographical data and analyzing the negotiator's organizational or institutional role.

corporation's decisions by analyzing its corporate culture and structuring arguments to fit within established guidelines.

Furthermore, there are general cultural patterns by which individual negotiators develop personal styles of decision-making behavior. By discovering how foreign counterparts look at facts and analyze data, successful negotiators can provide information that will increase the probability of a successful outcome.

National Character

Studies of national character call attention to both the patterns of personality that negotiators tend to exhibit and the collective concerns that give a nation a distinctive outlook in international relationships. Foreign negotiators concerned with international image may be preoccupied with discussions of their national heritage, identity, and language. Cultural attitudes, such as ethnocentrism or xenophobia, may influence the tone of the argument.

Fisher maintains that foreign negotiators display many different styles of logic and reasoning. They frequently find that discussions are impeded because the two sides seem to be pursuing different paths of logic. Negotiation breakdown may result from the way issues are conceptualized, the way evidence and new information are used, or the way one point seems to lead to the next.

During the discussions, the foreign counterpart may pay more attention to some arguments than to others. Greater weight may be given to legal precedence, expert opinion, technical data, amity, or reciprocal advantage. A good international negotiator will discover what is persuasive to the foreign counterpart and use that method of persuasion.

Negotiators may place different values on agreements and hold different assumptions about the way contracts should be honored.

Negotiators may place different values on agreements and hold different assumptions about the way contracts should be honored. The negotiator must find out what steps the counterpart intends to take in implementing the agreement. A signature on a piece of paper or a handshake may signify friendship rather than the closing of a contract.

Cross-Cultural Noise

Noise consists of background distractions that have nothing to do with the substance of the foreign negotiator's message. Factors such as gestures, personal proximity, and office surroundings may unintentionally interfere with communication. The danger of misinterpretation of messages necessitates analysis of various contextual factors.

Interpreters and Translators

Fisher points to limitations in translating certain ideas, concepts, meanings, and nuances. Subjective meaning may not come across through words alone. Gestures, tone of voice, cadence, and double entendres are all meant to transmit a message. Yet these are not included in a translation.

Sometimes a negotiator will try to communicate a concept or idea that does not exist in the counterpart's culture. For example, the American and English concept of "fair play" seems to have no exact equivalent in any other language. How then can an English national expect "fair play" from a foreign counterpart?

Interpreters and translators may have difficulty transmitting the logic of key arguments. This is especially true in discussions of abstract concepts such as planning and international strategy. The parties may think that they have come to an agreement when in fact they have entirely different intentions and understandings.

Fisher's five-part framework provided scholars and consultants with a launching pad for both theory-building and practical applications.

ASSUMPTIONS AND NEGOTIATING

When people communicate, they make certain assumptions about the other's process of perceiving, judging, thinking, and reasoning patterns. These assumptions are made without realization. Correct assumptions facilitate communication, but incorrect assumptions lead to misunderstandings, and miscommunication often results.

The most common assumption is projective cognitive similarity, that is, one assumes that the other perceives, judges, thinks, and reasons the same way he or she does. Persons from the same culture, but with a different education, age, background, and experience, often have difficulty communicating. American managers experience greater difficulties communicating with managers from other cultures than with managers from their own culture. However, in some regards American managers share more interests with other members of the world managerial subculture than with their own workers or union leaders. The effects of our cultural conditioning are so pervasive that people whose experience has been limited to the rules of one culture can have difficulty understanding communication based on another set of rules.

To create cultural synergistic solutions to management problems and international negotiating, U.S. managers must identify and understand what is American about America, what common cultural traits are shared by Americans, and what values and assumptions are their foundation. Mark Twain stated, "The only distinguishing characteristic of the American character that I've been able to discover is a fondness for ice water." There are many more.

Awareness of cultural influences is essential for transferring concepts, technology, or ideas. Depending on the cultures, there may be an

Sometimes a negotiator will try to communicate a concept or idea that does not exist in the counterpart's culture.

overlap of values in a specific area, and therefore the problems related to transferring ideas will be minimal. However, in some instances the gap will be significant and cause serious problems. According to Graham,[14] there are four problems in international business negotiations: (1) language, (2) nonverbal behavior, (3) values, and (4) thinking and decision making.

The problems increase in importance and complexity because of their subtle nature. For instance, it is easy to ascertain the language differences between the French and the Brazilians. The solution is either state-of-the-art translating headsets or interpreting/translating teams to accommodate each side. The problem is obvious and relatively easy to address.

Cultural differences concerning nonverbal behavior often are not as obvious; we are not as aware of these behaviors. In face-to-face negotiations, we give off and receive nonverbal behavioral cues. Some argue that these cues are the critical messages of a negotiation. The nonverbal signals from our counterparts can be so subtle that we may feel a sense of discomfort but may not know exactly why. For example, when a Japanese negotiator fails to make eye contact, it may produce a sense of unease in the foreigner but it may simply be shyness on the part of the Japanese. Often nonverbal intercultural friction affects business negotiations but goes undefined and more often uncorrected.

Laver and Trudgill in Scheu-Lottgen and Hernandez-Campoy also point out that during conversations one must act almost as a detective, considering the words and speech but also attempting to establish, from an array of clues, the state of mind and the profile and perspective of the other's identity.[15]

The difference in values is even more obscure and harder to understand. For example, Americans value objectivity, competitiveness, equity, and punctuality and often presume that other cultures hold the same values in high esteem. Regarding punctuality Graham states, "Everyone else in the world knows no negotiation tactic is more useful with Americans. Nobody places more value on time. Nobody has less patience when things slow down."[16]

Generally, during a complex negotiation Westerners divide the large tasks up into smaller ones. One can move through the smaller tasks, finishing one and moving on to the next, sensing accomplishment along the way. Issues are resolved at each step in the process, and the final agreement is the sum of the sequence. However, in Eastern thinking, all issues are discussed, often with no apparent order, and concessions, when made, occur at the conclusion of negotiations. The Western approach is sequential and the Eastern is holistic—the two are worlds apart. Therefore, American negotiators have difficulty measuring progress during negotiations with the Japanese, and the differences in the thinking and decision-making processes can result in blunders. For the Japanese, the long-term goal is a mutually beneficial ongoing busi-

In face-to-face negotiations, we give off and receive nonverbal behavioral cues. Some argue that these cues are the critical messages of a negotiation.

ness relationship. "The economic issues are the *context*, not the *content* of the talks." Conversely, to Americans, negotiations are a problem-solving activity, with the best solution for both parties as the goal.

EXAMPLE OF "CULTURAL BAGGAGE"

Graham and Herberger[17] suggest a combination of characteristics typical of American negotiators. They are part of the cultural baggage such nationals bring to the negotiating table and, according to Graham and Herberger, typify the American "John Wayne" style of negotiating.

"I can go it alone." Many U.S. executives seem to believe they can handle any negotiating situation by themselves, and they are outnumbered in most negotiating situations.

"Just call me John." Americans value informality and equality in human relations. They try to make people feel comfortable by playing down status distinctions.

"Pardon my French." Americans aren't very talented at speaking foreign languages.

"Check with the home office." American negotiators get upset when halfway through a negotiation the other side says, "I'll have to check with the home office." The implication is that the decision makers are not present.

"Get to the point." American negotiators prefer to come directly to the point, getting to the heart of the matter quickly.

"Lay your cards on the table." Americans expect honest information at the bargaining table.

"Don't just sit there, speak up." Americans don't deal well with silence during negotiations.

"Don't take no for an answer." Persistence is highly valued by Americans and is part of the deeply ingrained competitive spirit that manifests itself in every aspect of American life.

"One thing at a time." Americans usually attack a complex negotiation task sequentially; that is, they separate the issues and settle them one at a time.

"A deal is a deal." When Americans make an agreement and give their word, they expect to honor the agreement no matter what the circumstances.

"I am what I am." Few Americans take pride in changing their minds, even in difficult circumstances.

These comments on American negotiators may appear to be harsh. They are not intended to isolate Americans as lacking in global negotiating skills. In today's marketplace other nationalities can learn, as well as Americans how to negotiate more effectively and skillfully.

Americans value objectivity, competitiveness, equity, and punctuality and often presume that other cultures hold the same values in high esteem.

EXHIBIT 3.2
THE U.S. NEGOTIATOR'S GLOBAL REPORT CARD

Competency	Grade
Preparation	B–
Synergistic approach (win–win)	D
Cultural I.Q.	D
Adapting the negotiating process to the host country environment	D
Patience	D
Listening	D
Linguistic abilities	F
Using language that is simple and accessible	C
High aspirations	B+
Personal integrity	A–
Building solid relationships	D

In Exhibit 3.2 Acuff[18] is not complimentary in his report card on American negotiators' skills.

With hope, as we are broadened by the global experience, we are getting better at understanding the national character of our negotiating counterparts, confronting cultural stereotypes, and putting the negotiating process into a cultural context.

FRAMEWORK FOR INTERNATIONAL BUSINESS NEGOTIATIONS

A successful negotiation is a "win–win situation" in which both parties gain. Many factors affect a negotiation's outcome.

There are varied negotiation postures, bases from which to negotiate. One framework by Weiss and Stripp[19] maintains there are 12 variables in every international negotiation that impact the negotiation and can therefore significantly influence the outcome either positively or negatively.

■ *Basic Conception of Negotiation Process.* There are two opposing approaches to the concept of negotiation: strategic and synergistic. In the strategic model, resources are perceived as limited. The sides are competitive and as a result of bargaining, one side is perceived as getting a larger portion of the pie. In the synergistic model, resources are unlimited. Each party wants to cooperate so that all can have what they want. Counterparts look for alternative ways to obtain the desired results.

- *Negotiator Selection Criteria.* These criteria include negotiating experience, seniority, political affiliation, gender, ethnic ties, kinship, technical knowledge, and personal attributes (e.g., affability, loyalty, and trustworthiness). Each culture has preferences and biases regarding selection.
- *Significance of Type of Issue.* Defining the issues in negotiation is critical. Generally, substantive issues focus on control and use of resources (space, power, property). Relationship-based issues center on the ongoing nature of mutual or reciprocal interests. The negotiation should not hinder relationships and future negotiations.
- *Concern with Protocol.* Protocol is the accepted practices of social behavior and interaction. Rules of protocol can be formal or informal. Americans are generally less formal than Germans, for example.
- *Complexity of Language.* Complexity refers to the degree of reliance on nonverbal cues to convey and interpret intentions and information in dialogue. These cues include distance (space), eye contact, gestures, and silence. There is high- and low-context communication. Cultures that are high context in communication (China) are fast and efficient communicators and information is in the physical context or preprogrammed in the person. Low-context communication, in contrast, is information conveyed by the words without shared meaning implied. The United States is a low-context culture.
- *Nature of Persuasive Arguments.* One way or another, negotiation involves attempts to influence the other party. Counterparts can use an emotional or logical approach.
- *Role of Individuals' Aspirations.* The emphasis negotiators place on their individual goals and need for recognition may also vary. In some cases, the position of a negotiator may reflect personal goals to a greater extent than corporate goals. In contrast, a negotiator may want to prove he or she is a hard bargainer and compromise the goals of the corporation.
- *Bases of Trust.* Every negotiator at some point must face the critical issue of trust. One must eventually trust one's counterparts, otherwise resolution would be impossible. Trust can be based on the written laws of a particular country or it can be based on friendship and mutual respect and esteem.
- *Risk-Taking Propensity.* Negotiators can be perceived as either "cautious" (low risk takers), or "adventurous" (high risk takers). If a negotiator selects a solution that has lower rewards but higher probability of success he or she is not a risk taker. If the negotiator chooses higher rewards but a lower probability of success, then he or she is "adventurous" and a risk taker.
- *Value of Time.* Each culture has a different way of perceiving and acting on time. Monochronic cultures emphasize making agendas

One way or another, negotiation involves attempts to influence the other party. Counterparts can use an emotional or logical approach.

and being on time for appointments, generally seeing time as a quantity to be scheduled. Polychronic cultures stress the involvement of people rather than preset schedules. The future cannot be firm, so planning takes on little consequence.

- *Decision-Making System.* Broadly understood, decision-making systems can be "authoritative" or "consensual." In authoritative decision making, an individual makes the decision without consulting with his or her superiors. However, senior executives may overturn the decision. In consensus decision making, negotiators do not have the authority to make decisions unless they consult their superiors.
- *Form of Satisfactory Agreement.* Generally, there are two broad forms of agreement. One is the written contract that covers possible contingencies. The other is the broad oral agreement that binds the negotiating parties through the quality of their relationship.

Negotiation Insight for India, China, France and Nigeria

Is there a "national character" of a people?

Can statements be made about a group of people or a "culture" that is mostly accurate? Is there a "national character" of a people, that is, a system of beliefs, attitudes and values that are dominant in a country or nation as a result of common experiences.

In the definition of national character there are three assumptions: (1) all people belonging to a certain culture are alike in some respects; (2) they are somewhat different from other cultures in the same respects; (3) the characteristics ascribed to them are in some way related to the fact that they are citizens of a given country.

During negotiations, however, all anyone can observe is human behavior. We see what people do. What are the determinants of human behavior? We believe one has to consider three factors: culture (a national character); personality (no two people from the same culture are exactly alike); and context (where does the behavior take place? In New York? Sao Paulo? Tokyo? Jeddah?).

What follows is a summary of aspects of Indian, Chinese, French, and Nigerian "national character." Remember that "personality" and "context" are also determinants of behavior.

Framework Applied to Indian Negotiators
1. Basic Concept of the Negotiation Process
   - Building relationships and establishing rapport
   - Having conversations important
   - "Facilitation payments" often requested
   - Correct manners a requirement
2. Negotiator Selection Criteria
   - Technical experts always present

- Status differences among team members a factor
- Decisions made by senior management

3. Significance of Type of Issue
   - Price bargaining, reliability, credit, and local service important
   - Working rapport important
4. Concern with Protocol
   - Formality a norm
   - Friendly atmosphere
5. Complexity of Language
   - Concern with maintaining harmony
   - When Indians say "no problem" this is not to be taken literally
6. Nature of Persuasive Arguments
   - Maturity, wisdom, and self control are valued behaviors
7. Role of Individual Aspirations
   - No attempt to "stand out"
   - Decision making at higher levels
8. Bases of Trust
   - Trust must be earned
9. Risk-taking Propensity
   - Many are fatalists and are willing to take risks
10. Value of Time
    - Punctuality is important but patience is often required
11. Decision-making System
    - Highly centralized with only modest responsibility delegated to lower levels
12. Form of Satisfactory Agreement
    - Detailed agreements are the norm

Framework Applied to Chinese Negotiators
1. Basic Concept of the Negotiation Process
   - Intelligence gathering
   - Statements emphasizing "friendship"[20]
   - Hard bargaining
2. Negotiator Selection Criteria
   - Technical expertise
   - In times of turbulence/change political reliability
3. Significance of Type of Issue
   - Relationship based issues receive attention
   - Connections (guanxi) important
4. Concern with Protocol
   - High concern with proper etiquette
   - Use "home court" as advantage
5. Complexity of Language
   - Very high context with implicit and unstated desires and approaches

6. Nature of Persuasive Arguments
   ■ "No compromising" to establish economic value
7. Role of Individual Aspirations
   ■ Individual aspirations are resurfacing but "standing out" is unusual
8. Bases of Trust
   ■ Past record is important
9. Risk-taking Propensity
   ■ High avoidance of risk-taking resulting in meticulous and tough negotiating tactics and strategy
10. Value of Time
    ■ Long view of time and masters at the art of stalling
11. Decision-making System
    ■ Appearance of participative decision-making but reality is an authoritative system with higher levels always controlling
12. Form of Satisfactory Agreement
    ■ Carefully worded contracts but legal infrastructure lacking

Framework Applied to French Negotiators
1. Basic Concept of the Negotiation Process
   ■ A logical problem that can be solved with proper preparation and research
   ■ Conflict is constructive
2. Negotiator Selection Criteria
   ■ Technical expertise
   ■ The status and level of the person in the organization is important
3. Significance of Type of Issue
   ■ Technical and theoretical aspects of the discussion are of paramount importance
4. Concern with Protocol
   ■ Formality and politeness with proper attention to manners
5. Complexity of Language
   ■ A heated debate and accomplished rhetoric are valued
6. Nature of Persuasive Arguments
   ■ Combative and methodical debate
7. Role of Individual Aspirations
   ■ Individual accomplishments and one's personal power are important
8. Bases of Trust
   ■ Past performance and accomplishments
   ■ Trust is earned over time and usually not "given" at the beginning of a business relationship
9. Risk-taking Propensity
   ■ Risk is avoided

10. Value of Time
    - ◼ Long-term planning and often slow decision making
11. Decision-making System
    - ◼ Final decisions made at a high level in an organization
12. Form of Satisfactory Agreement
    - ◼ Detailed contractual agreements

Framework Applied to Nigerian Negotiators
1. Basic Concept of the Negotiation Process
    - ◼ Negotiation is a way of life
    - ◼ Early phases of negotiation are characterized by cooperation then leading to conflict resolution
    - ◼ "Dash" or expediting payments is common
2. Negotiator Selection Criteria
    - ◼ Age is equated with wisdom
3. Significance of Type of Issue
    - ◼ Establishing personal rapport and sincerity are key factors in success
4. Concern with Protocol
    - ◼ Formality and courtesy are necessary at all times
5. Complexity of Language
    - ◼ High emphasis on spoken word; meanings are subtle with a high degree of ambiguity
6. Nature of Persuasive Arguments
    - ◼ The love of using the language and arguments is apparent
7. Role of Individual Aspirations
    - ◼ Tribal and family loyalties dominant
8. Bases of Trust
    - ◼ Business relationships following from personal friendships and some remnants of a colonial hostility still evident
9. Risk-taking Propensity
    - ◼ Being risk-aversive is a tribal and religion-related characteristic
10. Value of Time
    - ◼ Time viewed as an abundant commodity with little being hurried
11. Decision-making System
    - ◼ Decision making centralized with very little delegation
12. Form of Satisfactory Agreement
    - ◼ Verbal agreements are more important than complex written legal documents

Interpreters and Translators During Negotiations

The importance of an interpreter in business negotiations cannot be overemphasized. It is the interpreter who can assist with the accurate communication of ideas between the two teams. A linguistic interpreter

The importance of an interpreter in business negotiations cannot be overemphasized.

can also be a cultural interpreter, letting the negotiators know of actual or potential cultural misunderstandings. It is advisable to remember the following points concerning the use of interpreters:

- Brief the interpreter in advance about the subject. Select an interpreter knowledgeable about the product or subject.
- Speak clearly and slowly.
- Avoid little-known words.
- Explain the major idea two or three different ways, as the point may be lost if discussed only once.
- Avoid talking more than a minute or two without giving the interpreter a chance to speak.
- While talking, allow the interpreter time to make notes about what is being said.
- Do not lose confidence if the interpreter uses a dictionary.
- Permit the interpreter to spend as much time as needed in clarifying points whose meanings are obscure.
- Do not interrupt the interpreter as he or she translates to avoid misunderstandings.
- Avoid long sentences, double negatives, or the use of negative wordings when a positive form could be used.
- Avoid superfluous words. Your point may be lost if wrapped up in generalities.
- Try to be expressive and use gestures to support your verbal messages.
- During meetings, write out the main points discussed. In this way both parties can double-check their understanding.
- After meetings, confirm in writing what has been agreed.
- Do not expect an interpreter to work for over two hours without a rest.
- Consider using two interpreters if negotiation is to last an entire day or into the evening so that when one tires the other can take over.
- Don't be concerned if a speaker talks for five minutes and the interpreter covers it in half a minute.
- Be understanding if the interpreter makes a mistake.
- Ask the interpreter for advice if there are problems.

Successful Negotiations Procedures

Negotiations bring together two parties, each with an expectation of the outcome. On examination the two parties evaluate their leverage, authority, and tactics. To close a negotiation that was the best possible deal for both sides means that, most likely, neither side feels cheated or duped and that a spirit of fairness pervaded the negotiation. When international negotiations take place, the cultural differences and implications can spin the negotiation in unanticipated directions. Weiss has

Negotiations bring together two parties, each with an expectation of the outcome.

established five steps for analyzing and developing a culturally responsive strategy for international negotiations.[21]

- *Study your own culture's negotiation script.* When we are in our home culture we behave almost automatically. Studying observations about our home culture by outsiders as well as our own self-examinations will enable a negotiator to construct an accurate national profile. What does your side bring to the party?
- *Learn the negotiation script of your counterpart.* A first-time negotiator should build a profile of his or her counterparts from the ground up. An experienced negotiator should review and research his or her counterparts, adding new information. Beware of cultural biases. What does this party bring to the negotiations?
- *Consider the relationship and circumstance.* Whether you are the buyer or the seller in a negotiation will affect the relationship, and an adjustment of strategy will have to occur. Any previous negotiating relationship with a counterpart, as well as their home culture and its familiarity with yours, will also affect the outcome. What is the context of the relationship?
- *Predict the counterpart's approach.* If your counterpart's approach is similar to yours, or you perhaps can influence the selection of the approach, these deliberations will preview the possible interactions during preparation for the negotiation. Generally, approaches will be complementary or conflicting.
- *Choose your strategy.* After completing the first four steps, the selection of the strategy must be feasible given the cross-cultural dimensions of the negotiations and the counterpart's approach, be appropriate to the relationship, and, with hope, be a win–win for both parties.

The following is a summary of a research project that analyzed actual negotiations.[22] The researchers' methods allowed them to differentiate between skilled negotiators and average negotiators by using behavior analysis techniques as they observed the negotiations and recorded the discussion. They identified "successful" negotiators as those who:

- Were rated as effective by both sides.
- Had a "track record" of significant success.
- Had a low incidence of "implementation" failures.

A total of 48 negotiators who met all of these three success criteria were studied. They included union representatives (17), management representatives (12), contract negotiators (10), and others (9).

The 48 successful negotiators were studied over a total of 102 separate negotiating sessions. In the following description, the successful negotiators are called the "skilled" group. In comparison, the negotiators who either failed to meet the criteria or about whom no criterion data were available were called the "average" group.

During the Planning Process

The research showed that the skilled negotiators gave more than three times as much attention to common-ground areas as did average negotiators.

Negotiation training emphasizes the importance of planning.

■ Planning Time—No significant difference was found between the total planning time of skilled and average negotiators prior to actual negotiation.
■ Exploration of Options—The skilled negotiator considers a wider range of outcomes or options for action than does the average negotiator.
■ Common Ground—The research showed that the skilled negotiators gave more than three times as much attention to common-ground areas as did average negotiators.
■ Long-Term or Short Term?—With the average negotiator, approximately one comment in 25 met the criteria of a long-term consideration, namely a comment that involved any factor extending beyond the immediate implementation of the issue under negotiation.
■ Setting Limits—The researchers asked negotiators about their objectives and recorded whether their replies referred to single-point objectives (e.g., "We aim to settle at 83") or to a defined range (e.g., "We hope to get 85 but we would settle for a minimum of 77"). Skilled negotiators were significantly more likely to set upper and lower limits—to plan in terms of range. Average negotiators, in contrast, were more likely to plan their objectives around a fixed point.
■ Sequence and Issue Planning—The term "planning" frequently refers to a process of sequencing—putting a number of events, points, or potential occurrences into a time sequence. Critical path analysis and other forms of network planning are examples.

Typical sequence plan used by average negotiators

A then B then C then D Issues are linked.

Typical issue plan used by skilled negotiators

A
D   B
C

Issues are independent and not linked by sequence.

The clear advantage of issue planning over sequence planning is flexibility.

Face-to-Face Behavior

Skilled negotiators show marked differences in their face-to-face behavior, compared with average negotiators. They use certain types of behavior significantly more frequently while they tend to avoid other types.

- Irritators—Certain words and phrases that are commonly used during negotiation have negligible value in persuading the other party, but do cause irritation. Probably the most frequent example of these is the term "generous offer" used by a negotiator to describe his or her proposal.
- Counterproposals—During negotiation, one party frequently puts forward a proposal and the other party immediately responds with a counterproposal. Researchers found that skilled negotiators made immediate counterproposals much less frequently than average negotiators.
- Argument Dilution—This way of thinking predisposes us to believe that there is some special merit in quantity. Having five reasons for doing something is considered more persuasive than having only one reason. One may feel that the more he or she can put on his or her scale, the more likely it is to tip the balance of an argument in his or her favor. The researchers found that the opposite was true. The skilled negotiator used fewer reasons to back up each of his or her arguments.
- Reviewing the Negotiation—The researchers asked negotiators how likely they were to spend time reviewing the negotiation afterward. Over two-thirds of the skilled negotiators claimed that they always set aside some time after a negotiation to review it and consider what they had learned. Just under half of average negotiators, in contrast, made the same claim.

This research clearly indicates some of the behaviors of skilled negotiators. Negotiators need to practice these behaviors, and others, to increase their skills.

Wederspahn suggests that human resource development programs within global corporations should include an International Negotiations Workshop with a cultural overview of the counterpart party in negotiations.[23] The model is based on the high low-context approach to culture discussed elsewhere in our book. **Position-based negotiation** is based on the win–lose paradigm—the more one party receives, the more the other has to give up in the pursuit of self interest and maximizing advantage. The main focus is on position—advancing, defending, and rationalizing it. Concessions made should be compensated by corresponding gains. Objective and impersonal data should be used to justify one's demands and trade-offs. Tactics include overstating

Skilled negotiators made immediate counterproposals much less frequently.

demands, multiple fall-back positions, pressure and dramatics displays, hidden agendas, bluffing and keeping one's opponents off-balance. In contrast, **interest-based negotiation** assumes that a mutually advantageous agreement is possible and desirable; expectations are for collaboration that is win–win and that brings benefits to both parties. This approach looks to long-term payoff in the relationship, so that there is mutual openness and information sharing to better understand each other's needs, constraints, and aspirations. Trust building includes visits to each other's facilities; establishing explicit and objective standards of fairness; designing systems to share gain/risk, giving and receiving help from one another, as well as socializing and creating a common strategy and culture. Surprises are avoided, pressure is not used, and agreements/contracts are flexible and adaptable to changing circumstances.

THE PRICE OF FAILED NEGOTIATIONS

War is a conflict in the extreme and often results when diplomacy and negotiations have failed. Recent research has suggested that serious conflict, such as war or occupation, can produce years of traumatic experiences, especially for many who have engaged in the extreme conflict. David Berceli, a trauma therapist and expert on Arab/American relations, has written on this in Exhibit 3.3.

EXHIBIT 3.3

WAR FORGES A NEW ERA IN CORPORATE ARAB/AMERICAN RELATIONSHIPS

In the United States, "roughly 3.6 days of work impairment per month associated with Post Traumatic Stress Disorder (PTSD)[a] translates into an annual productivity loss in excess of $3 billion."[b] These figures and subsequent loss in productivity increase dramatically in countries throughout the world that have been ravaged by war, political violence, or sectarian armed conflict. Due to recent events in the Middle East, international corporations operating there need to seriously consider the staggering toll that emotional pain and suffering will have on the functional and productive capacity of their employees.

"There is no avoiding the traumatic aftermath of war; it reaches into every segment of society."[c] Work impairment due to secondary comorbid disorders of PTSD such as anxiety, depression, irritability, disturbed sleep, and elevated mood disorders all damage the cognitive and interpersonal skills of employees. This has a staggering impact on the social structure and eventually the economy of any corporation or society. As a result of this reality, whether they want to or not, corporations operating in war-torn countries of the Middle East will be forced to implement programs and procedures to deal with the systemic consequences of the trauma their employees have experienced. . . .

Since the average duration of each trauma episode is reported to be more than seven years, "the typical person with PTSD has a duration of active symptoms for more than two decades. The process of healing therefore will have to be measured in terms of generations rather than years."[d] Beginning with the rebuilding of Iraq, corporate social responsibility and financial profitability should be seen as inseparable ideologies because of the severe and systemic trauma experienced by the Iraqi people. With some simple but strategic trauma behavior modifications, over time corporations will be able to break down antagonism and build alliances across opposing sides. They will be able to use the trauma of their employees as a common opportunity for gain. If they know what they are doing, they can use these opportunities to "reduce contentious behaviors and increase conciliation."[e]

[a]Post Traumatic Stress Disorder is the re-experiencing of disrupting emotions or behaviors following the initial trauma.
[b]This report is from the Department of Health Care Policy, R. Kessler, Harvard Medical School, Boston, MA. It can be found in the *Journal of Clinical Psychiatry*, 2000, 61 (suppl. 5): 4–12.
[c]Levine, P. "We Are All Neighbors," Foundation for Human Enrichment, 2002, p. 3.
[d]This report is from the Department of Health Care Policy, R. Kessler, Harvard Medical School, Boston, MA. It can be found in the *Journal of Clinical Psychiatry*, 2000, 61 (suppl. 5): 4–12.
[e]Baldwin, D. "Innovation, Controversy and Consensus in Traumatology," *The International Electronic Journal of Innovations in the Study of the Traumatization Process and Methods for Reducing or Eliminating Related Human Suffering*, Vol. 3:1, Article 3.

Emotional Intelligence and Negotiations

Everyone knows the meaning of IQ (Intelligence Quotient) and the importance of technical skills and intelligence to perform many job responsibilities. Some in an organization are referred to as "techies." Many also have personal experience with individuals who are very intelligent and have good technical skills but have failed in a leadership position.

Coleman[24] researched about 200 global companies and found that the traditional attributes associated with leadership—intelligence, vision, toughness, etc.—are insufficient. He states effective leaders must have a higher degree of emotional intelligence as well. According to Coleman there are five components of emotional intelligence.

There are five components of emotional intelligence.

1. Self-awareness or the ability to recognize and understand one's moods, emotions, as well as their effect on others. This is characterized by self-confidence and a realistic assessment.

2. Self-regulation or the ability to control or redirect disruptive impulses and moods and the propensity to suspend judgment. This is characterized by trustworthiness, integrity, and a comfort with ambiguity.
3. Motivation or the ability to work for reasons that go beyond money or status. This is characterized by a strong drive to achieve and optimism even in the face of failure.
4. Empathy or the ability to understand the emotional makeup of other people. This is characterized by expertise in building and retaining talent.
5. Social skills or proficiency in managing relationships and building networks. This is characterized by skills in leading change and expertise in building and leading teams.

CONCLUSIONS

Emotional intelligence contributes to a skillful negotiator's toolbox.

Roger Fisher,[25] the negotiating guru, in an interview about emotions and negotiations stated, "I don't have people criticizing me for talking about emotions . . . no one says it's a soft, fuzzy side." In short, keeping your feelings hidden, saying "Don't become emotional" during a heated argument may become obsolete.

This perspective is supported by Fromm[26] who wrote, "Emotions provide important information to us and to the other side. If we are able to express our emotions in a constructive way and at an appropriate time in the negotiation, rather than destroying or hurting the negotiation process it can greatly enhance it."

Emotional intelligence contributes to a skillful negotiator's toolbox. The instruments and questionnaire to measure one's emotional intelligence or emotional competence are easily available and recommended to all global negotiators.

MIND STRETCHING

1. As a negotiator list your strengths and your weaknesses. Write an action plan to become a more skillful negotiator.
2. Become an astute observer of human behavior. As you observe the behavior of others in different situations what are the determinants? culture? personality? context?
3. How can you increase your styles of resolving conflicts when negotiating across cultures?
4. Apply the concepts in the chapter to any global dispute. Why are there as many unresolved issues?
5. Do our global business and political leaders have a high degree of observable emotional intelligence?

REFERENCES

1. *The Arizona Republic*, Asia Times Online, April 24, 2006.
2. www.mergerstat.com
3. Moran, R. T. and Harris, P. R. *Managing Cultural Synergy.* Houston, TX: Gulf Publishing Company, 1982. Material updated in 2006.
4. Likert, R. and Likert, J. G. *New Ways of Managing Conflict.* New York: McGraw-Hill, 1976.
5. Thomas, K. W. *Conflict and Conflict Management.* Los Angeles: University of California, Working Paper, 74-3, 1974.
6. Stewart, E. C. *American Cultural Patterns: A Cross-Cultural Perspective.* LaGrange Park, IL: Intercultural Network, 1979.
7. Thomas, *Conflict and Conflict Management.*
8. Ibid.
9. Kilmann, R. H. and Thomas, K. W. *A Forced-Choice Measure of Conflict-Handling Behavior: The "Mode" Instrument.* Los Angeles Graduate School of Management, Working Paper, 1973, pp. 12–73.
10. Patai, R. *The Arab Mind.* New York: Charles Scribner & Sons, 1976.
11. Moran, R. T., Allen, J., Wichmann, R., Ando, T., and Sasano, M. "Japan," *Global Perspectives on Organizational Conflict.* Rahim, A. and Blum, A. (eds.). London: Praeger, 1994. Material updated in 2006.
12. Nelson, C. A. *Protocol for Profit—A Manager's Guide to Competing Worldwide.* London: International Thomson Business Press, 1998.
13. Fisher, G. *International Negotiation: A Cross-Cultural Perspective.* Chicago: Intercultural Press, 1980.
14. Graham, J. *"Vis-à-Vis:* International Business Negotiations," *International Business Negotiations*, Ghauri, P. and Usunier, J. C. (eds.), Oxford, UK: Pergamon, 1996.
15. Scheu-Lottgen, U. D. and Hernandez-Campoy, J. M. "An Analysis of Sociocultural Miscommunication: English, Spanish and German," *International Journal of Intercultural Relations*, Vol. 22, No. 4, November 1998.
16. Graham, J. *"Vis-à-Vis:* International Business Negotiations," *International Business Negotiations*, Ghauri, P. and Usunier, J. C. (eds.). Oxford, UK: Pergamon, 1996.
17. Graham, J. and Herberger, R. "Negotiating Abroad—Don't Shoot from the Hip," *Harvard Business Review*, July–August 1983.
18. Acuff, F. L. *How to Negotiate with Anyone, Anywhere Around the World.* New York: AMACOM, 1993.
19. Weiss, S. and Stripp, W. *Negotiation with Foreign Business Persons: An Introduction for Americans with Propositions on Six Cultures.* New York University/Faculty of Business Administration, February 1985.
20. In an excellent unpublished paper (2006), Neil R. Abramson, Simon Fraser University, British Columbia, reviewed the literature on Chinese-American negotiations. He found "the literature was evenly divided on whether the Chinese sincerely seek trusting based relationships as a condition for successful negotiations or whether this is a bargaining tactic."
21. Weiss, S. E. "Negotiating with 'Romans'—Part 2," *Sloan Management Review*, Massachusetts Institute of Technology, Spring 1994.

22. *Behavior of Successful Negotiators*. Huthwaite Research Group Report, 1976, 1982.
23. Wederspahn, Gary M. "The Fine Art of International Negotiation," *HR News/Society for Human Resource Management*, January 1993, pp. C6, 7.
24. Coleman, D. "Inside the Mind of the Leader," *Harvard Business Review*, January 2006.
25. www.news.harvard.edu/gazette/2005/10.13/03-reason.html
26. Fromm, D. "Dealing With Your Emotions in Negotiations," *The Negotiation Magazine*, November 2005.

GLOBAL LEADERS AND THE CHANGING KNOWLEDGE CULTURE

How do you turn transition into an advantage? By looking at every change, looking out every window. And asking: could this be an opportunity? Is this new thing a genuine change, or simply a fad? And the difference is very simple: a change is something people do, and a fad is something people talk about. . . .

—Peter F. Drucker[1]

LEARNING OBJECTIVES

To understand that in this emerging knowledge culture, open-mindedness to change and its management is essential. This chapter considers changes in our personal and organizational life spaces, as well as strategies for becoming transformational global leaders during this momentous shift to a knowledge work environment.

The twenty-first century is dominated by accelerating change, driven by continuing and rapid scientific and technological innovations. Those who would be global leaders need not only to plan and cope with change, but to increase their management skills for this transition to a knowledge economy and industries. Perhaps the greatest challenge is for people to be more flexible in their mind-sets, and willing to build continuing change into their lifestyles.

The twenty-first century is dominated by accelerating change.

The concepts of culture, communication, and change are all interconnected, each influencing the other whether within an individual or group, an institution or a system, a nation or a region, a planetary community or an interplanetary solar system. For example, changes in communication technologies are impacting both national and work cultures. Thus, this chapter focuses especially on the role of the global manager or professional seeking to exercise leadership in managing contemporary cultural changes.

A community or institution's culture facilitates or inhibits change. As we progress in this new millennium, the increasing pace of social and technological change requires leaders who do not merely plan and cope with change, but use it for positive and competitive advantage. By implication, this calls for an altering of mind-sets, norms, and roles, so as to improve the quality of life whether on or off the job. Like individuals, institutions whose cultures are adaptive usually outperform their counterparts. People can be trained and prepared for a culture of continuing and dynamic change, a constant of human evolution. But this means that the family, educational, work, political, and social environments in which they function must be transformed if they are to be relevant. Such is essential if the needs of members—be they employees, volunteers, customers, or suppliers—are to be serviced better and faster.[2]

People can be trained and prepared for a culture of continuing and dynamic change

CHANGES IN LIFE SPACES

When computer systems and area networking were first introduced into organizations, each produced a change in role relationships. When management information systems became available to office personnel by means of desk or laptop computers, the increased data available for decision making affected managerial relationships. For example, when Information Technology (IT) became dominant at work, a new field of Knowledge Management (KM) was devised. Curley et al. define its tools and processes as:[3]

> Knowledge management is the conscious management of a key corporate asset—knowledge—for the purpose of advancing organizational learning, strengthening the organization's ability to sustain and expand its core competencies and securing competitive advantage. . . . The management of this asset is about the management of information and relationships.

Each new innovation or technology brought into a company, agency, or association, alters the present equilibrium or status quo within that institution's culture. Similarly, when domestic firms start operating beyond homeland borders and enter the international marketplace, there occurs not only a transformation of corporate strategy, policies, and procedures, but structural changes in the way business is done. So too, when women, minorities, and foreigners in greater numbers became part of a more diverse workforce, relationships and attitudes changed among the majority of employees. As women were increasingly promoted to higher levels of management, the working relationships between women and men were influenced, along with business itself. All such actions provoke alterations in institutional culture. Thus, when managers, salespersons or technicians, as well as their families, are deployed overseas for a lengthy assignment, there is a profound transposition in their relationships to their world and the local "foreigners" in it. In fact, in all the above examples, people's personal, organizational, and national images changed in the process. Exhibit 4.1 offers further insights into modifications in the workplace.

Exhibit 4.1
Changing the Work Environment

Deindustrialization—the shrinkage of industrial jobs—is popularly perceived as a symptom of economic decline. On the contrary, it is a natural stage in economic development. As a country gets richer, it is inevitable that a smaller proportion of workers will be needed in the manufacturing sector. . . . It is much easier to automate manufacturing than services, replacing men by machines. . . . An increasing slice of value added in manufacturing consists of service activities, such as design, marketing, finance, and after-sales support. . . .

But in developed economies today, telecoms, software, banking and so on can create more wealth than making jeans or trainers. Writing a computer program creates more value than producing a computer disc. . . . Future prosperity will depend not on how economic activity is labeled, but on economies' ability to innovate and its capacity to adjust.

Just look at the makeup of the workforce in advanced countries. More people work in services—in America as many as 80%. Since 1996, the number of manufacturing jobs has shrunk close to one-fifth in America, Britain, and Japan. In the euro zone, the average loss has been 5%.

Another aspect of change is female participation in the labor force. In the United States, it is 62%; in the United Kingdom, 61%; but only 55% in Japan where women in the workforce lag behind. In the latter nation, less than 10% of managers are women, compared with 54% in America. Workers' demands for better working conditions are also on the rise throughout Asia.

Deindustrialization is a natural stage in economic development.

The nature of change is that it is inevitable and constant. It is part of the human condition. But during each stage of human development, the pace of change picks up. In the hunting/gathering period, change occurred over millions of years. Whereas in the centuries dominated by agricultural or farming activities, changes happened over thousands of years. During the industrial period, the work environment was modified by machines over a few hundred years. Now in the postindustrial or Information Age, changes occur in decades or less. This phenomenon is called the *acceleration or compression of change*. Today's managers and professionals function in a global marketplace that has altered more rapidly and extensively than any other period in human history. To survive and develop, leaders not only need new skills for coping with change, but must learn to create an environment that is open to dynamic change, both within their systems, as well as within their own lifestyles and those of their colleagues.

Dimensions of Change

Each of us creates the world around us based on culture codes. This chapter views planned change in the context of three interactive cultures: (1) *cyberculture*—the knowledge work culture within an urban, technological, superindustrial society; (2) *national culture*—the people and place in which one seeks to live and conduct business; (3) *organizational culture*—the work structure and environment in which we function and earn our living. Increasingly, these three interacting cultures often are not the ones in which we were born and socialized. Since human behavior can be modified, we are challenged by the impact of these cultural changes, especially if we aspire to a leadership role. People need not passively react, but have the means to temper or tamper with these influences. Specifically, modern management theory maintains that people have a responsibility to be *proactive agents of change*. That is, we can initiate actions to correct obsolescence and overcome culture lag in any system of which we are a part.

Not all change is desirable. Critical choices have to be made about the overall wisdom of an alteration or proposal. Because accelerating change is a reality of our century, we seek to plan and modify change so that it will not cause disastrous dislocation in the lives of people, their organizations, or societies. When citizens or employees become so frustrated with the status quo and the lack of change, they often revolt, rising against those who hold back progress and improvement. Many changes—for better or worse—are man-made. For example, owing to severe climate changes, the world's inhabitants have experienced a series of catastrophic natural disasters in recent years—from tsunamis and massive flooding to volcanic eruptions and tornadoes. The resulting destruction and trauma are changing peoples lives and economies profoundly. The unprecedented humanitarian aid and volunteering that have occurred globally have also brought the human family closer together. Science and technology is also attempting to delimit the harm associated with natural disasters by inventing better warning and control systems.

Perhaps the reader should start by assessing his or her attitudes toward personal and organizational change. It is a challenge to reeducate ourselves and to reevaluate our psychological constructs—the way we read meaning into the events and experiences of our lives.[4] Whether as persons, organizations, or even nations, we live in unique life spaces that impact our behavior.

Human Factors in Change

We have a set of highly organized constructs around which we organize our "private" worlds. Literally, we construct a mental system for putting order, as we perceive it, into these life spaces. This intellectual synthesis relates to our images of self, family, role, organization, nation, and universe. Such constructs then become psychological anchors or reference points for our mental functioning and well-being. Our unique construct systems exert a pushing/pulling effect on all other ideas and experiences we encounter. We assign meaning almost automatically to the multiple sensations and perceptions that bombard us daily.

Not only do individuals have such unique filters for their experiencing, but groups, organizations, and even nations develop these mental frameworks through which information coming from the environment is interpreted. Intense interactions of various segments within our varied grouping form sets that enable us to achieve collective goals. In this way, a group, organizational, or national "style," or type of behavior emerges. Through their communication, people share themselves, so that individual perceptions converge into a type of "consensus" of what makes sense to them in a particular environment and circumstance. *Culture then transmits these commonly shared sets of perceptions and relationships.*

But because human interaction is dynamic, pressures for change in such constructs build up in both individuals and institutions. For example, when a manager from Grand Rapids, Michigan, is transferred for three years to Riyadh, Saudi Arabia, or Bangalore, India, that person is challenged to change many of his or her constructs about life and people. The same may be said for the corporate culture when a company attempts to transplant operations from Paris, France, to the Middle East or Asia. These forces for change can be avoided, resisted, or incorporated into the person's perceptual field. If the latter happens,

Organizations, and even nations, develop these mental frameworks through which information coming from the environment is interpreted.

When leaders do
not prepare their
people for
necessary and
inevitable
change, the
consequences
can be
disastrous.

then change becomes a catalyst for restructuring our constructs, giving us an opportunity for growth. In other words, individuals and institutions can adapt and develop.

When leaders do not prepare their people for necessary and inevitable change, the consequences can be disastrous. For example, many national, educational, political, and religious systems suffer from "culture lag." That is, as the human mainstream has moved ahead to a new stage of development, this particular community is locked into a past mind-set. In the twenty-first century, many countries are burdened with obsolete and archaic religious, political, educational, and economic systems. In Asia, for instance, inadequate banking and lending practices hold back prosperity for their citizens. In the Middle East, ultratraditional religious views and practices diminish the role of women, deterring development of female potential and positive contributions. In Europe, centuries-old educational systems are badly in need of reform and updating. In Africa, the tribal ruling system has broken down, and the instability has led to a series of military coups and local despots, along with social chaos and ethnic killings. In North America, open door policies to foreigners and visitors are being undermined by fears of terrorism, forcing modernization of immigration and travel regulations, as well as security practices.

When a society or a system is imprisoned by its traditions, attitudes, and beliefs from the past, it may produce unsavory results. Terrorists or anarchists, for example, often come from countries where the needs of people, especially the young, are so frustrated that violence erupts. The sense of despair or righteousness may turn naïve youth into suicide bombers who destroy property and take human life. The subculture of global terrorism recruits young men and even women who are alienated and conditioned to an ideology of violence. At the same time, many perceive themselves as oppressed, and so they resort to rioting, fire bombings of property, and even the taking of innocent lives— witness the black power movement of the 1960s in the inner-city ghettos of America; the Irish Catholic minority and the IRA fighting of Northern Ireland; and the immigrant revolts that recently occurred in both Great Britain and France—which provides further insights into negative results when societies resist change and do not satisfy human needs.

Ordinarily, leaders skilled in planning change not only facilitate peoples' preparation and acceptance of change, but reduce stress and waste of human energy in making the new adjustments. Maximum two-way communication about the proposed role change can create readiness for its eventual implementation. Therefore, the negative impact of sudden change is lessened or defused. While proposing innovations, leaders can endeavor to reduce the uncomfortable threat to those involved. Harmful behavior or reactions, such as apathy or sabotage, protest or revolt, may then be minimized. As this was being written in November 2005, General Motors was again going through a massive restructuring process, including closing and merging of 12 plants, along major reductions in its labor force—30,000 layoffs. But how well did GM management and auto industry unions prepare their people to deal with such radical but necessary changes and the traumas connected with these latest attempts at survival and renewal for the giant automaker?

What's different about this knowledge culture? It is important for contemporary administrators, managers, and professionals to appreciate that throughout much of human history, most of the planet's inhabitants were raised in hierarchical societies, where personal choice and progress were limited and one's place in society was immutable. For generations, people survived by remaining within their prescribed roles, adapting to the thought pattern, belief, and action of their local cultural group. Except for some less developed countries, all this is changing—humankind is in the midst of a mind-boggling transformation that offers seemingly unlimited choices and opportunities. We change our environment and are changed by it. We create technology, and we are physically and psychologically altered by it. In the process, traditional customs, values, and attitudes may be disrupted or abandoned. Yet, as our culture and social institutions change, our capacity for such learning is seemingly inexhaustible. Global leaders are in the forefront of this phenomenon. But those on the cutting edge of innovation and advancement need to be mindful of the human dimensions involved in its implementation.

In today's *changing knowledge culture*, people are also challenged to alter the way they perceive or think about their work and how it is to be performed. The shifting context of the work environment has been described as the new work culture.[5] The driving forces behind these social and technological changes are:

■ Globalization of markets, consumerism, and workforces.
■ Transformation of traditional organizational hierarchy into a more participative, multinational, or global network.
■ Fragmentation of work and creation of a global job market.
■ Ascendancy of knowledge and information services as primary global products.

One outcome of such trends is the reshaping of views of our various roles in the family, community, or workplace

Role Changes

For five decades, researchers have studied the changing roles of men and women, discovering that gender differences are mostly in our minds and cultures, rather than in biological realities.

In today's changing knowledge culture, people are also challenged to alter the way they perceive or think about their work.

Limitations in *gender roles* are largely created and kept in place by social, not biological, forces. As such, they are more readily subject to change. Scholars have demonstrated the resulting harm for persons and organizations when individuals are typecast and culture-bound in their career aspirations. Further, social progress is deterred when such attitudes prevail, as we have seen historically in the caste system of India and the class system of England. Fortunately, within modern societies changes in this regard are rapid, as workers move beyond traditional role concepts while assertively seeking equal opportunity and empowerment.

Similar representations may be made of *organization roles*, and their place in society. Because human systems are collections of people, institutions may also suffer identity crises. Caught between a disappearing bureaucracy and an emerging "adhocracy," the institution may experience down turns in sales; poor morale and declining productivity; membership reductions; bankruptcy threats; obsolete product lines and services; and increasing frustration with unresponsive management. Organizations, then, are challenged to go through planned renewal to project new images of their positive roles among both personnel and the public. Simply hiring a public relations firm to redesign corporate image with the public is insufficient—organization members have to be involved in the process of institutional change!

So too with *national roles*. When a country's social fabric unravels or wavers, national identities may experience crises. Examples abound, such as when:

When a country's social fabric unravels or wavers, national identities may experience crises.

■ The United States' "loss of face" in Vietnam; the seizure of U.S. diplomats in Iran; the 9/11 double bombings of New York City's World Trade Center and the Pentagon; and the treatment of prisoners or insurgents in the "war on terrorism."
■ Great Britain lost its empire and colonies, nearly bankrupting the nation; or the country's inappropriate policies and responses to the influx of immigrants from British Commonwealth nations.
■ Japan's economic and technological progress threatens its traditional culture; and its youth reject "feudal" customs and practices.
■ U.S.S.R. and Communist totalitarian rule collapsed, leading to the formation of a Russian Federation with the loss of many states in the old Eastbloc.
■ East Germany's disappearance as a state, and its incorporation into The Federal Republic of Germany.
■ Yugoslavia breaks up into smaller Balkan states because hostilities and ethnic cleansing led to widespread human suffering, as well as economic and political chaos requiring UN and NATO interventions.
■ Iraq and North Korea being labeled as *rouge* states and subject to UN sanctions, boycotts, inspections.

■ Iran, when too-rapid modernization and secularization under the Shah caused a backlash of religious fundamentalism, leading to revolution and regime change.

People of various countries have sought to rediscover their collective selves in this postnation period. So geographers continuously redraw maps to reflect the changes in national borders. In some lands, the struggle for national identity is epitomized in a name change, as from Congo to Zaire or Rhodesia to Zimbabwe. Elsewhere, as in the former U.S.S.R., especially the Baltic Republics of Lithuania, Latvia, and Estonia, the countries became independent, with citizens seeking greater ethnic identity and autonomy. Whereas in the People's Republic of China, turmoil centers around information access, private enterprise, and democratization versus totalitarian control by the Communist Party. Often the identity struggles within or among nations produces violence based on ancient rivalries or on tribal, clan, or even religious affiliation. Such regressive behavior not only transgresses the UN Declaration on Human Rights, but acts to reverse changes toward a modern, multicultural society.

Even *global roles* are being altered by the phenomenon of "globalization." The late management philosopher, Peter Drucker, provided a disturbing but pertinent analysis of ongoing changes in world society.[6] He examined our altered perceptions of government's role, especially how politicians are falling behind the new realities. For example, he presaged the "decolonization" of the Soviet empire, anticipating the breakup of that huge country into European and Asian parts. National economies, he observed, are shaped increasingly by global events and the changing roles of owners, workers, managers, and the corporation itself. Drucker described a world of knowledge workers in companies reorganized to be leaner and more specialized, including within the expanding nonprofit and volunteer sectors. It is a work culture in which roles are less rigidly specified, while participative management reigns.

To meet the requirements of the Information Age, some reengineering advocates call for a business revolution—that is a change in *vocational roles*. In this postindustrial world, many forms of commerce, professions, and public service are experiencing their own identity problem. By clarifying our understanding of what we are as a business or professional enterprise, our journey into the future will be less hazardous. When our actions, adjustments, and reactions derive from a philosophy in tune with the world around us, we discover our identity as individuals and institutions. In this search for a more relevant career or business identity, we seek answers to these questions. What business are we in? What are we as an organization? What should we become? How do we develop a more diverse and effective workforce? Who are our customers? Where are our markets? Do we fear entering the global

Global roles are being altered by the phenomenon of "globalization."

marketplace because it requires coping with diverse cultures, customs, and even import/export regulations?

Environmental Forces Influencing Change

Global leaders with foresight gather information about the real environment, local and worldwide, that may cause changes in strategies, polices, and technologies. They analyze and anticipate trends that influence their futures. Some positive forces of change drive us to increase or decrease workforce, to be more aware or responsive to community needs. In other words, global leaders create *adaptive systems*! This implies overcoming resistive and negative forces seeking to restrain necessary shifts in production and manufacturing, as well as making necessary alterations in roles, rules, regulations, and even markets.

As a case in point, many corporations, nongovernmental organizations (NGOs), and other institutions go global to survive. Over a decade ago, Moran and Riesenberger described twelve environmental forces impacting organizations and influencing change that are still evident today.[7] Some *proactive environmental* forces are:

1. *Global sourcing*—organizations are seeking nondomestic sources of raw materials because of cost and quality.
2. *New and evolving markets* are providing unique growth opportunities.
3. *Economies of scale*—today's marketplace requires different approaches, resulting in competitive advantages in price and quality.
4. *Movement toward homogeneous demand*—globalization is resulting in similar products being required worldwide.
5. *Lowered transportation costs*—world transportation costs of many products have fallen significantly because of innovations.
6. *Government tariffs and taxes*—the protectionist tendencies of many governments are declining, as evidenced by the North American Free Trade Agreement (NAFTA) and the European Union (EU) policies and agreements.[8]
7. *Telecommunications*—falling prices as a result of privatization and new technologies are impacting globalization.
8. *Homogeneous technical standards*—the International Organization for Standardization (ISO) has been successful in developing global standards (known as ISO 9000).

Some *reactive forces* present in the global environment are:

1. *Competition for nondomestic organizations*—new competitive threats are regularly experienced by organizations.

2. *Risk for volatile exchange rates*—the constant fluctuation of exchange rates in many countries impacts profits.
3. *Customers are becoming more global consumers*—globalization is impacting customers in ways that "local content" in subsidiary-produced goods is increasing.
4. *Global technological change*—technological improvements coming from many areas of the world are requiring organizations to adjust their strategies to survive.

In a knowledge culture, smart global leaders do environmental scans. That is, they employ future research methods or consultants to help them to anticipate the future. They try to identify trends that will affect their businesses or organizations in the near- or long-term future. For example, they anticipate developing movements—such as the growth of environmental and ecological awareness and coalitions; the rise of activists organized to protect human or animal rights; and the development of space resources.

Smart global leaders do environmental scans.

Transforming Business Culture

Breakthroughs in paradigms, inventions, and technologies trigger rapid change in our professional lives and practices. Leading-edge thinkers maintain that the computer and the Internet are among the most transforming inventions in human history. Seemingly, they have the capacity to change everything—the way we work, the way we learn and play, and perhaps the way we sleep and cohabit. Andrew Grove, a founder and former chairman of Intel, predicted what has come to pass—that all corporations would become Internet companies. The global power of the Internet with its Web sites and chat rooms now dominates our lives, whether commerically or otherwise. Grove uses the term *Internet time* when referring to change, citing his own experience as a chip maker when the Pentium processor was in full-scale production.[9] As CNN reported the story worldwide, a minor design error resulted in "a rounding error in division once every nine billion times." After this global report, the new Pentium users immediately requested replacement chips. Intel's response was to quickly set up a "war room" to instantly answer a flood of inquiries on the subject. Gradually, they replaced chips with this minor defect by the hundreds of thousands. This crisis not only shows the planetary power of satellite communications, but the kind of global leadership necessary to *manage such change*!

Writing about global electronic connecting, Symonds[10] observed, "The Internet is turning business upside down and inside out. It is fundamentally changing the way companies operate, whether in high tech or metal bashing. This goes far beyond buying and selling over the

Internet, and deep into the processes and culture of an enterprise." Some of the sociotechnical changes Symonds underscores are:

- Connecting through the Internet with buyers and sellers as well as trading partners.
- Using the Internet to lower costs dramatically across integrated supply and demand chains.
- Developing e-business (electronic) at hyper-growth rates by inter-company trade over the Internet.
- Using Web sites to enrich the multimedia experience by integrating customer/suppliers, databases, monitoring sites visited, supporting online transactions, integrating personal/telephone call center operations, and supporting multiple payment operations.
- Establishing organizational *intranets* to improve departmental and personnel exchanges, manage travel and expenses, employee benefits, and share the latest information.

This whole process of instant, electronic communication is also transforming organizational cultures and business strategies. It fosters synergistic relations by the practice of connecting and collaborating. It encourages the formation of *information partnerships* between suppliers and customers, as well as between systems. It facilitates customized services, outsourcing for both personnel and manufacturing, and inventory control, as well as innovation with new products and services. The emerging e-speak technology connects us with electronic experts from mediators and brokers to physicians and consultants. Through networking the software permit industry, service organizations, and non-profit institutions become part of a worldwide, dynamic ecosystem.

Space technology produced the satellite industry, and in turn, a communication revolution that is connecting in new ways business, government, and academia, particularly researchers in both the private and public sectors all over the globe. In fact, researchers at the Salk Institute in La Jolla, California, have an automated computer program that currently recognizes 62 facial cues of any human being filmed on video. Such computer image analysis has myriad applications from health care to law enforcement. Universities are also daily creating new communication technologies and applications. For example, the University of California-San Diego has a Link Family Computer System to connect electronically various segments of its community for information exchanges. Components include StudentLink, FinancialLink, EmployeeLink, TravelLink, and DataLink, as well as EZPay for paperless financial transactions. This is a Web-based system providing easy access to information about a wide range of institutional operations and resources. It is another dimension of using modern media to streamline business practice, decrease costs, and increase productivity, while enhancing customer satisfaction and employee accountability and morale.

Online learning is another manifestation of this phenomenon. Electronic education is used for self-learning, organizational training, and career development, as well as university courses and degrees.[11] All of the above are additional indicators of why global leaders must learn to be high performers themselves in managing continuing technical change.

Utilizing Change Strategies

Global leaders should not only be sources of innovation, but also be skilled in using change strategies and methods. Agents of change may apply their efforts to alter personal, organizational, and national cultural goals. Operating globally in diverse cultures and circumstances necessitates appropriate adaptation of organizational objectives, management procedures, corporate processes, and technologies. Global leaders must learn to be as knowledgeable as possible wherever they are located, even if it means creative circumvention of local constraints. Innovators may respect the established system while working to bend or beat it to make it more responsive to satisfying human need.

Global leaders should be skilled in using change strategies and methods.

The *New York Times* once ran this interesting advertisement:

> WANTED—CHANGE AGENTS—Results-oriented individuals able to accurately and quickly resolve complex tangible and intangible problems. Energy and ambition necessary for success!

What then would be the responsibilities of such persons if employed? Obviously to bring about planned change in an organization or culture. That would imply examining the prospects for alterations in the status quo within these basic categories: *structure* (the system of authority, communication, roles, and work flow) . . . *technology* (problem-solving mechanisms, tools, and computers) . . . *tasks* (activities accomplished, such as manufacturing, research, service) . . . *processes* (techniques, simulations, methods, scenario-building procedures, such as management information systems) . . . *environment* (internal or external atmosphere) . . . *people* (personnel or human resources involved).

Having decided on which category or combinations will be the focus of one's energy for change, the leader might follow these additional steps: (a) identify specific changes that appear desirable to improve effectiveness; (b) create a readiness in the system for such change; (c) facilitate the internalization of the innovation; and (d) reinforce the new equilibrium established through the change. This process to be utilized is *force field analysis*—a systematic way to analyze the driving and resisting forces for change within individual or group life space as well as institutional or national space. The skilled change maker is also aware that any change introduced in one element of the previous chain affects the other factors. The parts of complex systems are interdependent, so the innovator attempts to forecast the ripple effect. Successful change agents take a multidimensional approach, considering legal, economic, and technological aspects of the change without ignoring its social, political, and personal implications. They also operate on certain assumptions:

- People are capable of planning and controlling their own destinies within their own life space.
- Behavioral change, knowledge, and technology should be incorporated into the planning process.
- Human beings are continually in the midst of cultural change or evolution.

The implication of the latter statement is that the people involved in the change process may be suspicious of simplistic solutions as a result of the information/media blitz to which they have been exposed. They may already be suffering from information overload, experiencing a sense of powerlessness and loss of individuality. Essentially, the effective change maker may employ three change models to bring about a shift in the status quo:

- *Power*—political or legal, physical or psychological influence or coercion to bring about change, which may be legitimate or illegitimate. It depends on the purpose of change, its ingredients, and the method of application. For example, legislative power may be used to promote equal employment opportunity or to prevent a disease epidemic, while authority of role or competence may be called upon to overcome resistance to change.
- *Rationale*—the appeal to reason and the common good. This approach must recognize that people are not always altruistic and that self-interest may block acceptance of the proposed change, no matter how noble or worthwhile for the majority.
- *Reeducative*—conditioning by training, education, and positive rewards becomes the means to not only create readiness for the change, but to provide the information and skills to implement it.

Each approach has its strengths and weaknesses, so a combination of the models may be most effective. Bellingham proposes examination of business drivers on strategy, structure, system, and personnel requirements in terms of new skills, styles, and the need for renewal.[12] To maximize commitment to change, ten competencies are developed among personnel.

1. Mobilize people behind a shared vision, strategy, and structure—especially by involvement.
2. Empower people by defining job directions/boundaries, as well as by providing autonomy and support.
3. Recognize individual and team contributions by clarifying requirements, expectations, motivators, and rewards.
4. Build capacity by developing people, especially by attending to health needs (physical, emotional, intellectual, and spiritual).
5. Create a learning organization by using a systems approach that seeks input, knowledge, and partnerships.
6. Realign the culture through review of stated values and operating principles, as well as by translating norms and expected behaviors.
7. Create a cultural revolution by diagnosis, training, and targets.
8. Promote understanding by describing events and identifying feeling.
9. Facilitate acceptance by moving ahead on commitment and putting the past behind.
10. Enable the change to happen, moving to the new, demonstrating the benefits, and providing transitional steps for implementation.

There are a variety of methods and techniques to facilitate planned change. An approach can be as simple as "imagineering" at a staff meeting about changes likely to become realities in a decade, based on present trend indicators. Or it may be using the more elaborate Delphi technique, in which a questionnaire is developed with about a dozen situations likely to occur in the future of a company or a culture. Members or experts may then be asked to rate on a percentage basis the probability of the event's happening. Results are then tabulated and median percentages for each item determined. A report of results is circulated among participants, and they are asked to again rate the alternative possibilities after studying peer responses.

Today, the words "reengineering" or "reinventing" the organization are used to describe planned system-wide change. One consultant maintains that reengineering is not about downsizing, reorganizing, or restructuring. It is about thinking outside of the box, rethinking your work and company. It is a fundamental and radical redesigning of all the processes of business to obtain improvements in critical measures of performance (cost, quality, capital, service, and speed). It is throwing away what is and replacing it. For instance, if IBM, Merck, Boeing, etc. did not already exist today, how would they be created and structured?

There are a variety of methods and techniques to facilitate planned change.

Organizational Culture Changes

Responding to change in today's organizations is difficult. At times, corporations that do not change or transform themselves effectively open the door to merger or acquisition by another company. In the worst scenario, such companies and associations go bankrupt. The annual *Fortune 500* list is filled with examples of firms that no longer exist because of inability to keep up with changing markets, technologies, or personnel needs.

According to Beatty and Ulrich,[13] four principles can serve as the framework if change and renewal are to be understood and implemented in mature organizations. Although stated over twenty years ago, their guidelines are still applicable to all human systems.

Organizations renew by focusing on the customer's perspective and demands. To sustain a competitive advantage, organizations must be devoted to customer or client needs in unique ways. When a mind-set is embedded in employees that affects their work habits, they can be encouraged to focus more on the perspectives of those they seek to serve, despite political boundaries and internal company policies. For such a change, Hewlett Packard asked their teams to pretend they were the buyers of a particular product. As customers they were to shop their four major competitors and evaluate why they chose one supplier over another, what the image of the supplier/competitor was, and the reasons for their choice. After going through this analysis from a purchaser's perspective, teams were better able to understand the perceived mind-sets of their competitors, which gave them insight into their own customers' needs.

Organizations renew by increasing their capacity for change. Like humankind, systems have internal clocks that determine how swiftly change will move from definition to action. Today, organizations want to reduce the cycle time for how and when decisions are made and activities completed so they can move more quickly from idea conception to production, thereby increasing their capacity for adaptation and flexibility. "Alignment, symbiosis and reflexiveness" can be helpful in this process. Alignment refers to the common goals of the company. When organizations have a sense of alignment they can move toward shared goals in a shorter time frame because less time is spent building commitment and more time can be spent on work. Symbiosis is the speed with which organizations can remove barriers inside and outside the company to effect change. The Ford Taurus is a good example. To reduce boundaries and speed up internal clocks, Ford chose a cross-functional team removing boundaries between departments to design and deliver the car. Consequently, the Taurus moved from conception to production in 50% less time than established internal clocks. Reflexiveness is the time to reflect and learn from past activities, ensuring a sense of continuity.

Organizations renew by adjusting both the hardware and software within their company. These researchers refer to the hardware as issues of strategy, structure, and systems. These domains of activity are malleable and measurable and can be heralded with high visibility,

The Taurus moved from conception to production in 50% less time than established internal clocks.

for example, timely announcement of new alterations in any or all of these three issues. Unless the hardware is connected to the appropriate software, however, computers are useless. The same is true of the less visible domains of the organization—the software, which includes employee behavior and mind-set. Change begins by altering hardware, but often not enough resources are spent making sure that employee behavior, mind-set, and work activities match the change.

Organizations need empowered employees to act as leaders at all levels. Employees are to be trusted and empowered to act on issues that affect their work performance. Leaders have the obligation of articulating a vision and of ensuring that the vision will be implemented. Leaders must be credible, effective communicators, articulating changes so that they are readily understood and accepted.

For organization renewal to succeed, leaders at all levels must be both inspirational and able to express the new vision/strategy mind-set, encouraging their followers to give the extra effort needed to make the vision a reality. Change agents are more apt to alter the status quo within organizations or institutions when they endeavor to:[14]

- include in the planning process everyone concerned about the change
- avoid discrepancies between words and actions relative to the change
- set realistic time frames for bringing about the change
- integrate the activities involved in the change with available budget and resources
- avoid overdependence on external or internal specialists
- avoid data gaps between the top, middle, and lower levels of the system
- avoid forcing innovations into old structures incapable of handling them
- avoid simplistic, cookbook solutions to the problems connected with change
- realize that effective human relations are a condition for change, not an end
- apply change intervention strategies appropriately
- identify personnel capable of diagnosing the need for change
- capitalize on the pressures both from within and without the system for the change
- search the system at all levels for the leadership to effect the change
- promote collaborative efforts between line and staff in planning and implementing changes
- take strategic risks to inaugurate necessary change, while maintaining a realistic, long-term perspective relative to the change

For organization renewal to succeed, leaders at all levels must be inspirational and credible, effective communications.

Introducing

change in

multicultural

organizations is

more difficult

than in domestic

organizations.

■ initiate systems to reward people who cooperate in carrying out the change and establishing more effective behaviors
■ collect data to support and evaluate the change
■ set measurable objectives and targets relative to the change that are both tangible and immediate.

Introducing change in multicultural organizations is more difficult than in domestic organizations. The change agent then needs to consider the cultural underpinnings resisting the change and make appropriate interventions. Technological, economic, market, and social forces, such as mass immigrations, drive changes in the workplace. Pritchett & Associates, a Dallas-based consultancy in organizational change, specializes in downsizing, turnarounds, and mergers during the "Age of Instability." In an employee handbook on the subject, Pritchett and Pound, write that myths about change influence mind-sets, and must be dispelled.[15] They advise workers that the reality is: *change is dynamic and here to stay; controlling emotions helps workers to control the fluid situation; progress often masquerades as trouble; company changes require that workers also change; problems are a natural side effect of implementing change.*

Management usually tries to be as straightforward as the situation permits, while making tough decisions about the alterations. Workers can be part of the problem or the solution. Both managers and workers must act as a team to make the change plan succeed. In the shift toward an emerging global economy and work culture, Pritchett advises that *new work habits* are essential. In another handbook, he provides these ground rules for worker success in our changing world:

■ Become a quick-change artist—be flexible and adaptable.
■ Commit fully to your job—it makes work satisfying and ensures success.
■ Speed up—accelerate with the organization.
■ Accept ambiguity and uncertainty—change is the only certainty.
■ Behave like you are in business for yourself—assume personal responsibility.
■ Stay in school—lifelong learning is essential.
■ Hold yourself accountable for outcomes—set goals and targets.
■ Add value—contribute more than you cost.
■ See yourself as a service center—customers are a source of job security.
■ Manage your own morale—be responsible for your attitude control.
■ Continuously strive for performance improvement.
■ Be a fixer, not a finger-pointer—assume ownership of problems.
■ Alter your expectations—rely on yourself to develop work skills for success in the information age!

In this emerging knowledge culture, global leaders are engaged in a continuing change process, primarily through strategic planning and management. Since the introduction of any change threatens both the existing culture and power structure, strategic response to change needs to be both decisive and planned. Therefore, foresighted leaders anticipate resistance to change, diagnose it, and then "manage" or incorporate it into the system. Professor Marios Katsioloudes wrote *Global Strategic Planning*, and he provided cultural perspectives on this important process when applied to both for profit and nonprofit organizations. The challenge faced by global leaders with strategic change is evident somewhat in Exhibit 4.2 concerning the world corporation, Siemens.

Our cultural conditioning affects our attitudes toward the phenomenon of change, as well as our concept of leadership. For our purposes here, the *Random House Dictionary* definition may provide a base for

EXHIBIT 4.2[16]

CULTURE CHANGE IN A CONGLOMERATE

Dedicated followers of corporate fashion no doubt see little reason to get excited about Siemens. Worse still to be a conglomerate that is not only European but based in Germany, the continent's sickest economy. Yet, for all that, could it be that Siemens's moment has now arrived? That is certainly the belief of Heinrich von Pierer, chief executive since 1992 and maker of everything from trains to power generators to mobile telephones. Initially he imagined he could change the group's notoriously bureaucratic culture within two or three years, at last he has finally done it in ten. The firm is certainly a giant. Even after recent layoffs of 30,000 people, Siemens still has a workforce of 430,000—75,000 in America where it is one of the largest foreign employers. Siemens's turnover last year was €84 billion ($79 billion) from its thirteen operating divisions. Its balance sheet is strong and it reported €2.6 billion of post-tax profits last year despite tough market conditions. Heinrich von Pierer has transformed the internal culture in a way that helped it avoid the worst follies of its rivals and build upon its present platform of expansion. Strong risk management is at the heart of this change. Although the firm gives plenty of latitude to its divisional and regional managers, it now monitors closely the signing of contracts and the execution of projects.

A leader *is one who guides, directs, conducts, while* leadership *is the position or function or ability to influence or lead others*

understanding—a *leader* is one who guides, directs, conducts, while *leadership* is the position or function or ability to influence or lead others. Just as there is some cultural difference between American and European understanding of both leaders and leadership, so there is even greater diversity about these terms between Western and Eastern cultures. R. D. Lewis reminds us that whereas with the former, leadership is supposedly based on "meritocratic" achievement, while the latter accept that leadership resides with strong persons at the top of a hierarchy. The Asian cultural view is influenced by Confucianism that seeks a stable society through hierarchy of five unequal relationships, extending from ruler and father to older brother, husband, and senior friend. Lewis underscores the cultural contrasts that affect the exercise of leadership in terms of values, communication styles, and organizational patterns. Exhibit 4.3 summarizes this seminal thinking.

This exhibit contains generalizations based on Lewis's research and experiences in more than a dozen countries as an interculturalist and linguist. Obviously, within both Western and Eastern cultures there will be many exceptions. Within Asia, there are national differences to be observed. Furthermore, the listings under Asian culture may be found somewhat applicable in the Near and Middle Eastern countries. However, these insights do underscore why there would be differences in leadership perception between the two cultural groupings. For example, in the more traditional Asian cultures, change might be more feared and resisted, while occurring more limitedly and slowly, unless revolutions determine otherwise. In the twenty-first century, China is rapidly changing as it moves somewhat toward a market economy. But these contrasts also provide clues for improving behavior and performance when living or working in the opposite cultural environment. By seeking to understand the other cultural position, a Westerner in Asia might focus on relationship and harmony building, as well as observing, when feasible, local precedents and customs. In this way, one learns to appreciate the other's life space and the limitations of one's own cultural conditioning.

For almost 60 years, behavioral science research in the West has focused on the function of leadership.[17] The consensus is that leadership style should be situational, that is, appropriate to the time, place, culture, and people involved. Thus, the leader should operate within a continuum as described in Exhibit 4.4. However, in an advanced, technological society, the middle-to-right-side range of the continuum is considered preferable, especially when dealing with knowledge workers. The words in the center of the model highlight the dominant style in each leadership posture from telling to complete delegation. The movable, diagonal line symbolizes the delicate balance between the leader's authority and the group's freedom. This balance shifts according to whether the authority is shared or centered in the

EXHIBIT 4.3

VALUES, COMMUNICATION STYLES, AND ORGANIZATIONAL PATTERNS

WESTERN CULTURAL VIEWS	ASIAN CULTURAL VIEWS
Values	
Democracy	Hierarchy
Equality	Inequality
Self-determination	Fatalism
Individualism	Collectivism
Human Rights	Acceptance of Status
Equality for Women	Male Dominance
Social Mobility	Established Social Class
Status through Achievement	Status through Birth or Wealth
Facts and Figures	Relationships
Social Justice	Power Structures
New Solutions	Good Precedents
Vigor	Wisdom
Linear Time	Cyclic Time
Results Orientation	Harmony Orientation
Communication Styles	
Direct	Indirect
Blunt	Diplomatic
Polite	Very Courteous
Talkative	Reserved
Extrovert	Introvert
Persuasive	Recommending
Medium-Strong Eye Contact	Weak Eye Contact
Linear-Active	Reactive
Unambiguous	Ambiguous
Decisive	Cautious
Problem Solving	Accepting of the Situation
Interrupts	Does Not Interrupt
Half Listens	Listens Carefully
Quick to Deal	Courtship Dance
Concentrates on Power	Concentrates on Agreed Agenda
Organizational Patterns	
Individual as a Unit	Company and Society as a Unit
Promotion by Achievement	Promotion by Age or Seniority
Horizontal or Matrix Structures	Vertical Structures
Profit Orientation	Market Share Priority
Contracts as Binding	Contracts as Renegotiable
Decisions by Competent Individuals	Decisions by Consensus
Specialization	Job Rotation
Professional Mobility	Fixed Loyalty

Source: Lewis, R. D. "Cultural Orientations Affecting Leadership Styles," The Cultural Imperative. Boston, MA: Nicholas Brealy/Intercultural Press, 2003.

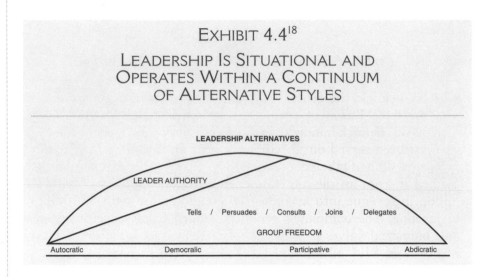

LEADERSHIP ALTERNATIVES

LEADER AUTHORITY

Tells / Persuades / Consults / Joins / Delegates

GROUP FREEDOM

Autocratic   Democralic   Participative   Abdicratic

The trend is now away from leadership centered in a single person to members of a group contributing toward the leadership function by sharing talent and resources.

ruling person or elite class of people. For example, the authoritarian type sets policy and *tells* the group members what he wants done. Whereas in a group that has much freedom and authority is wholly shared, the leader almost abdicates control in favor of total delegation. In the West, particularly within high tech organizations, this style is called team management, very much the norm in a knowledge culture.

The trend is now away from leadership centered in a single person to members of a group contributing toward the leadership function by sharing talent and resources. The research of social scientists confirms that participation and involvement of members in the decision-making process may result in more effective and productive performance. In terms of participative management, this principle is expressed as follows: those who will be substantially affected by decisions should be involved in making those decisions. But it takes a skillful and competent executive to implement such an ideal, and in many cultures such an approach is resisted.

Until recently, it was assumed that global leaders had a sense of ethics and social responsibility to their personnel, customers, and community. That expectation was undermined by greedy, unethical, and illegal executive behavior that ignored corporate honesty and responsibility. Both citizens and regulators have been shocked by corporate cultures guilty of massive accounting frauds and financial collusion, often with assistance from their giant auditing firms (such as with Enron, Global Crossing, WorldCom, and Adelphia). It is evident their organizational cultures were based on greed, deception, malfeasance, and intimidation. Exhibit 4.5 provides a mini case of such failure in real corporate leadership.

EXHIBIT 4.5
THE CASE OF THE GREEDY EXECUTIVES

Mark Belnick, the general counsel for Tyco International, hurried into the Boca Raton office of the company's chairman, L. Dennis Kozlowski. Belnick handed him a copy of a grand-jury subpoena that had just been served on the company naming Kozlowski personally.

Kozlowski had taken command of Tyco ten years earlier and transformed it from an obscure former government laboratory with $3 billion in revenue into an industrial conglomerate with $36 billion in revenue. The company's products ranged from security systems and industrial valves to medical equipment. Tyco's market capitalization was $1.5 billion when Kozlowski took charge; by 2001 it was $106 billion. Most of Kozlowski's compensation was in approximately $400 million of Tyco stock and options.

Later, a second indictment charged Kozlowski with personally defrauding Tyco of more than $300 million. Belnick was indicted for falsifying records. As details emerged, Kozlowski, more than any other executive who had prospered in the great bull market of the nineties, came to personify an epoch of corporate fraud, executive greed, and personal extravagance. It was a role almost no one would have predicted for him.

As Tyco's business fortunes rose, so did the expenditures of its CEO. In 1998, Kozlowski spent millions of dollars on a hundred-and-thirty foot J-Class sloop. The boat was extremely costly to maintain, even for someone with Kozlowski's income, but he saw it as a legitimate business expense, some of which could be charged to Tyco. Kozlowski had also embarked on a campaign of charitable activities, and here too, the line between Kozlowski's personal donations and Tyco corporate donations blurred. Tyco's lawyers ultimately determined that beginning in 1997, Kozlowski handed out $43 million in personal donations that actually came from Tyco. [Meanwhile, the chairman became busily involved in acquisitions—some corporate that promoted spectacular growth increasing Tyco's stock share value; some personal in the purchase of costly homes and art charged off to the company by questionable and sometimes illegal scheming. Ultimately the deviant behavior of the chairman and some associates resulted in a series of negative legal accusations.]

Tyco filed a report with the Securities and Exchange Commission that Dennis Kozlowski as chairman, Mark Swartz as chief financial officer, and Mark Belnick as general counsel, "engaged in a pattern of improper and illegal conduct by which they enriched themselves at the expense of the company." In an accompanying civil law suit, Tyco accused them of "egregious violations of trust reposed in him

Since the above story was written, the culprits therein have all been convicted and now are in prison, a fitting example to other unethical and greedy executives!

Source: Stewart, J. B. "Spend! Spend! Spend!" *The New Yorker*, February 17–24, 2003, pp. 132–147.

On the other hand, since the September 11, 2001, attacks on the United States, some public administrators have demonstrated remarkable civic leadership, such as former mayor of New York City, Rudolph Giuliani.

Synergistic Leadership

In a knowledge culture, leaders promote synergy or collaboration. Synergistic organizations also encourage self-actualization. But throughout this process, human systems must educate and train their members in new interpersonal and organizational skills so that adherents can communicate and cooperate across cultures and act together for mutual benefit. Such leadership also implies helping participants to conserve and develop human and natural resources for the common good. Finally, it means that leaders must acquire and practice a partnership form of power; namely, that of group initiative and cooperative action for mutual learning. Those with management responsibility are challenged to act as mentors or coaches for their members, so as to earn their commitment. Empowerment is the key.

Another change indicator in human resource development today is increasing emphasis on use of left- and right-brain learning activities. It appears that certain capacities are associated with either side of the cortex. Similarly, every person has qualities that are associated with both the female and male psyche. Holistic learning of males would include cultivation of those aspects commonly associated with the feminine character, and vice versa for the female. Furthermore, it has also been observed that one of the major problems with global leadership, whether political or corporate, is its male domination. Many decision makers tend to be chauvinistic and skewed toward the male perception of "reality" and the male approach to problem solving. If we are to have synergistic leadership, male/female thinking and powers must be integrated. Perhaps the world's persistent, unsolved problems—mass unemployment, hunger, violence, aggression, underutilization of human capital, among others—exist partly because our attempts to manage them have been so lopsided. That is, over one-half of the human race, women, are too frequently excluded from power and the decision-making process. Synergy is thwarted as long as outmoded cultural beliefs, attitudes, and traditions make false distinctions of a person's intrinsic worth based on gender. Such misconceptions have led to a human resource development movement worldwide toward diversity management and training.

Synergistic leaders in a knowledge economy promote planned change in the work culture that

- Emphasizes quality of life, rather than just quantity of goods/services.
- Promotes concepts of interdependence and cooperation rather than just competition.
- Encourages work and technology in harmony with nature, ever conscious of environmental/ecological considerations.
- Is conscious of corporate social responsibility goals rather than just technical efficiency and production.
- Creates an organizational culture that encourages self-achievement and fulfillment through participation, in contrast to dogmatism and dependency.
- Restates relevant traditional values, such as personal integrity, work ethic, respect for other's property, individual responsibility, and social cohesion.
- Encourages the capacity for intuition, creativity, flexibility, openness, group sensitivity, and goal-oriented planning for change.

The exercise of leadership in today's complex systems in transition is a challenge. It is an illusion that a single leader or decision maker can alone make the difference. Contemporary leadership failures, especially in the political or corporate arenas, stemming from incompetence or corruption disillusion the average citizen. In the twenty-first century, only the combined brainpower of multiple knowledge workers or teams is appropriate, so that many become involved with their unique resources and mobilized toward complex solutions. Contemporary changes in markets and workers call for a new type of management development.

Innovative leaders assist people and their social institutions to build upon, yet to transcend their cultural past. Anthropologist Edward Hall recalled that formerly one stayed relatively close to home so behaviors around us were fairly predictable. But today we constantly interact personally or through electronic media with strangers, often at great distances from our home, even at the other side of the globe. Such extensions have widened our range of human contact and caused our

The exercise of leadership in today's complex systems in transition is a challenge.

"world" to shrink, especially because of the twin impacts of mass communications and transportation. Today, global leaders require *transcultural insights and skills* for coping with such changed circumstances, shared readily with their colleagues. To be comfortable with changing cultural diversity and dissonance, we must literally move beyond the perceptions, imprints, and instructions of our own culture and personally change our mind-sets.

Cultures worldwide are in the midst of profound change, but nowhere is this more evident than in the workplaces of free-market economies. So while the pace of change varies around the world, its focus and challenges differ by region, community, and institution. But wherever the change occurs, it requires leaders who will create a culture of innovation and entrepreneurship. Then people will be open to continuous change, seeking creative solutions that contribute the next wave in human advancement.

LEADERSHIP IN CHANGING ORGANIZATIONAL CULTURE

If global managers are to be effective leaders, they need to understand (1) the influence of culture on organizations; and (2) how to use that culture to improve performance, productivity, and service. Effective leaders are continuously renewing, restructuring, and improving their corporate, agency, or association cultures. Such organizational culture manifests the values, attitudes, beliefs, myths, rituals, performance, artifacts, and numerous other institutional attitudes. Furthermore, this happens within larger changes in the new work environment which we call *the knowledge culture*.

Now consider what these individuals have in common.

- Hari just received his MBA from an American university and is employed in his own country of Pakistan for a Middle Eastern airline.
- Mary has just been appointed as a top manager in the Indonesian branch office of a Canadian company.
- Frank has been an American expatriate for six years and has just been reassigned to corporate headquarters in Paris, France.
- Mohammed, an Egyptian who was educated in Britain, is posted temporarily for additional training at a factory of his transnational employer in Taipei, Taiwan.
- Svetlia, an engineer, has been promoted to head up an international team in a Russian corporation partnering with a major American aerospace company.
- Lee is leaving his native Korea to supervise a construction crew of his fellow nationals in Saudi Arabia, where his company has a subcontract with a U.S. petroleum manufacturer.

- Alicia, a Hispanic high school graduate, has just been recruited to work in a government law enforcement agency that until now has been dominated by Anglo males.
- Vlad, a Lithuanian, has just been hired by the European Union to work in their Brussels headquarters.

All these individuals face problems of integration into unfamiliar national and/or organizational cultures. Perhaps, it would be better to think of it as a challenge of acculturation. Their approach to the different institutional contexts and coworkers can facilitate their success or failure in the new situation.

Leonand Nadler, a human resource pioneer, warned us decades ago that we all carry our "cultural baggage" into a system, thereby imposing limitations on our own or other's creativity. Everything the reader has learned previously in this text about culture in general can be applied to organizational culture. Institutional culture affects manager, employee, supplier, and customer behavior, as well as community relationships. Furthermore, such issues have regional, national, and international implications. The global corporate culture of Coca-Cola impacts and is influenced by the regional culture of Atlanta, Georgia, where its headquarters and principal activities are located. That same corporate culture interfaces with American regional cultures in its domestic marketing, as well as when it produces and sells its soft drinks abroad, whether in China or Mexico. We have already discussed environmental influences on a system's culture.

We all carry our "cultural baggage."

Further, the *organization's culture has a powerful impact on the members' morale and productivity*. It even affects the organization's image of itself, which in turn is communicated to its public. Those associated with the organization can either accept or reject its culture. If it is the former, then the member may conform or modify that culture. If it is the latter, then its personnel become frustrated or leave the organization.

Organizations are actually *microcultures* that operate within the larger context of a national *macroculture*. Thus, an organizational culture may be a Mexican government agency, an American multinational or foundation, a British university or trust, the Roman Catholic Church or an Islamic charity, a Russian or French airline, the Swedish Employers Federation, or the Association of Venezuelan Executives. Other transcultural organizations attempt to be synergistic in their structural makeup, such as UNESCO, the International Red Cross, the European Union, NATO, OPEC, or even ASEAN. Exhibit 4.6 illustrates many of the aspects of organizational culture, regardless of where an entity is located.

There are aspects of an organization's culture that are formal, explicit, and overt, just as there are dimensions that are informal, implicit, and covert. Fundamentally, the organization viewed as an

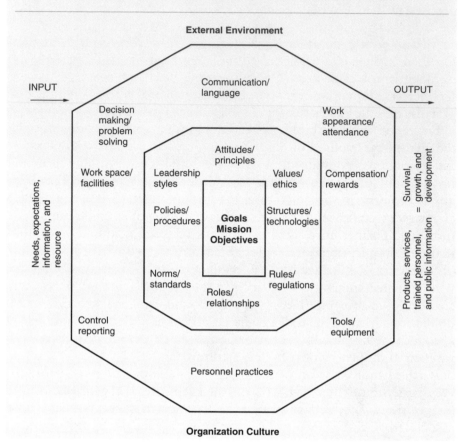

energy exchange system, inputs into a social system information and resources. Physical and psychic energy or *input* pour into the institution, along with capital, to be transformed into *output* as work, goods, or services. In attempting to achieve its goals and mission, the organization's culture is further influenced by leadership practices, norms and standards, rules and regulations, attitudes and principles, ethics and values, policies and practices, structures and technologies, products (artifacts) and services, roles and relationships. To facilitate these activities, cultural mandates or traditions are established concerning dress codes, work hours, work space, and facilities, tools and equipment, communication procedures and special language, rewards and recognitions, as well as various personnel provisions. The resulting cultural behavior and activities are manifested in the outputs, such as products, services, personnel, or public information.

A global corporation as large as General Motors, for example, has many subcultures in the form of divisions for manufacturing, marketing, and other functions, as well as numerous factories and plants. It may have many domestic and foreign subsidiaries that also have unique subcultures. The largest transnational corporations adapt themselves to the culture and circumstances in which they operate, while trying to retain that which gives them their distinctiveness and accomplishments. The GM culture is quite different from that of competitors within its own country, such as Ford Motor Company, but it is especially different from a comparable company abroad, such as Toyota of Japan. The formal aspects of such culture are like the tip of an iceberg—its overt activities are written objectives, technological processes, raw materials, and manpower skills. But then there are informal or covert elements that involve attitudes and feelings, values, and group norms that dominate the organization and affect both productivity and quality control. When General Motors, for example, opened a subsidiary plant in Juarez, Mexico, it developed a Mexican-American management team to create a plant culture appropriate to that community. It provided the Mexican and American managers and their spouses with language and culture training to enhance the success of the intercultural operation.

Today most successful corporate cultures are in the process of transition to postindustrial work environments dominated by change and innovation. To attune themselves to this larger knowledge culture, many global organizations are renewing themselves. Contemporary organizations cope with more than the cultural differences in companies or divisions that occur because of acquisitions, mergers, or foreign expansion. They also struggle to transform an industrial into a technological work culture centered on information processing and microelectronics. Increasingly, the century calls for high-performance, high-commitment work cultures that are creatively redesigning work and organizational structure. Such sociotechnical systems stimulate and direct human energy within an environment of continuous "learning" that rewards quality thinking and team performance. This necessitates a change in the managerial mind-set that gains competitive advantage by viewing people as human assets to be linked with technical resources in a collaborative work system.

Whether in a corporation, association, or government agency, culture is multifaceted and can be diagnosed in various ways, such as in terms of the subsystems that compose it. One model, proposed in our opening chapter, suggested ten major classifications or categories of culture for organizational analysis, and we will discuss it in the last section again.

Transnational Differences in Organizational Cultures

Because the *microculture* is a reflection of the *macroculture*, it stands to reason that geographical location of an organization will be affected

A global corporation as large as General Motors, for example, has many subcultures.

When a manager goes abroad, outside his or her native culture, the organizational culture that person represents should adapt to local circumstances.

by the culture of the surrounding community. There is continuous interaction between the majority and minority cultures, each influencing the other. Thus, when a manager goes abroad, outside his or her native culture, the organizational culture that person represents should adapt to local circumstances. Furthermore, the institutional cultures in the host country with whom the expatriate interfaces are quite unique manifestations of the indigenous culture. Should this person, who is a foreigner in a strange land, work for one of the local companies or government agencies as a consultant or even an employee, then that individual should expect that things will be done quite differently from "back home." People in the native organization will behave differently from colleagues in one's own country. These cultural factors are key to successful marketing and sales abroad.

The state of technological, economic, and social development of a nation will also affect the organizational culture. First World nations, for instance, may have more corporations using a more flexible, fluid, participative model of management, while developing countries might still use the industrial or traditional bureaucratic modes. Typical managerial activities such as planning and innovating, organizing and controlling, recruiting and selecting, evaluating and rewarding/ punishing, leading and relating, communicating, problem solving and decision making, negotiating and managing conflict, supervision and training are all conducted within the context of the dominant local culture. Thus, multinational organizations need adaptation to that people's perception of their world, their motivational orientation, their ways of associating, their value and activity emphasis. Their behavior stems their own unique socialization. In varying degrees, local companies, associations, or government agencies mirror the images and imprints of that culture's inhabitants.

Perhaps some examples of such cross-cultural differences in organizations and their workers will best illustrate this point. In the traditional Latin American organization that is rapidly disappearing, the supervisor-subordinate relationships are such that an employee would never directly approach a foreman or manager to discuss a problem—in the old authoritarian mode, one does not question the boss. In Japan of the past, the corporation's first duty was to its employees, and it was not considered demeaning for the worker to identify with the organization that employs him or her. In Japanese industry, the adversary labor-management relationship is considered unhealthy and an elitist attitude from the industrial revolution. For the most part, corporate, not government, enterprises provide for employee welfare. In fact, corporate elitism is frowned on, and group harmony is accented. Bear in mind that all such attitudes are changing rapidly in the twenty-first century.

Consider that a language is a means of communicating within a particular culture. There are approximately 3,000 different languages, and cach represents a different perceptual world. Many nations may share an official language, such as English, but have a variety of versions of it, such as British or American. In India, the official language is Hindi, but English is a "link" language among fifteen major languages and numerous dialects. Organizations in that country may be expected to speak the official language, but only 30% of the population does, so personnel in many companies will probably speak the local language and all that it implies. Thus, in the matter of organizational communications, a social institution may reflect the nation's language homogeneity or heterogeneity.

Social systems also utilize the local cultures approach to *time* and *time consciousness*. In some countries, company representatives may start a meeting within an hour of the agreed time, and the sequence of one's arrival at that staff conference may depend on one's status in the organization, or one's age. The length of the workday differs among cultures—in some, the starting and stopping times are exact, and may be spelled out in a union contract, whereas in others it may be more relaxed, even going by the sunrise and sunset, or the heat of the day, or the seasons.

The rhythm of life for a people is determined by their stage of human development; therefore, for populations in the preindustrial communities, time is shaped by the natural cycles of agriculture, whereas in industrialized nations, the artificial time of the clock and the assembly line regulate workers. In the superindustrial society of today, time becomes a scarce resource, while in underdeveloped nations, time is seemingly less relevant and more abundant. Sociologist Daniel Bell reminds American "clockwatchers" that the computer with its nanoseconds is considered a time-saver in organizational cultures of high technology. For some populations, the rhythm of life is linear, but for others it is cyclical.

In his insightful book, *The Cultural Imperative*, Richard Lewis offers a helpful analysis of contrasts in human behavior through three interactive categories or types: linear-active, multiactive, and reactive. This model is a way to predict and clarify behavior, avoid giving offense, and is a means for obtaining synergy through more unified actions. These three classifications not only cut across national and organizational cultures, but racial, religious, philosophical, and class divides. *Linear-active* people Lewis describes as task-oriented, highly organized planners who complete one action at a time in a linear agenda. They prefer authentic communications, information exchanges where the parties take turns talking and listening; depend on logic, facts and figures, even confrontation if necessary, but are open to compromise; and partly conceal feelings and emotions. Generally, the cultures of northern Europe and North America would seem to prefer this approach, though there are many exceptions within these populations, especially with mass immigrations.

For some populations, the rhythm of life is linear, but for others it is cyclical.

Multiactives are emotional, loquacious, and impulsive persons who attach much importance to human relations and compassion; they do not follow agendas well, tending to do several tasks at the same time; their conversations are roundabout, animated with interruptions and several speaking at the same time; uncomfortable with silence. It would appear that such is the dominant behavior among Latins and Africans.

Reactives are primarily respectful listeners who are intent on establishing the positions of others; they rarely initiate action or discussion, preferring to react to others' opinions before formulating their own. Many Asians and Finnish people would seem to fit into this last categorization.

The culture of a work system must be sensitive to and adapted to the mainstream culture in which it operates.

The culture of a work system must be sensitive to and adapted to the mainstream culture in which it operates. Organizational leaders everywhere can learn from each other, regardless of where in the world the entity functions. The transnational corporation crosses borders, moving beyond the culture of a single country, while operating comfortably in the multicultures of many nations. Yet such global corporations do develop a unique microculture of their own, with diversified subsidiaries—local or regional companies or divisional cultures. Ideally, the organizational model and environment are a synergy of the diverse macrocultures in which it functions, as well as varying managerial approaches to business, government, and people. Thus, far-flung business activities require a new organizational strategy that is more cosmopolitan, able to accommodate cross-cultural realities. Japanese business leaders, for example, are gradually changing their attitudes toward mergers and acquisitions. Although their culture and language disinclined them toward such actions, farsighted executives now realize their necessity as part of the global marketplace. The restructured Japanese organizations may produce both synergy and strength.

The multinational entity becomes a successful conglomerate by integrating and synthesizing the organizational cultures of its many parts. For example, through acquisitions, or strategic alliances, the global corporation consists of varied overseas subsidiaries or partnerships. The central or core base operation then impacts considerably the organizational culture of its affiliates, allowing those companies or partners abroad input to influence the headquarters' culture, policies, and decisions.

Adaptive Systems

The multinational enterprise adapts to the larger culture in which it functions, depending on its experiences with that external environment. Twenty-five years ago, Terpstra[19] identified five factors, which are still relevant, to be considered in international business.

Cultural Variability—the degree to which conditions within a macroculture are at a low, high, stable, or unstable rate. The more turbulent the macroculture, for instance, the more unpredictable are business operations. The internal structure and processes in that situation requiring rapid adjustment to change would demand open channels of communication, decentralized decision making, and predominance of local expertise.

Cultural Complexity—requires a response from corporate leaders that considers the covert and overt approaches of the national culture.

Cultural Hostility—the degree to which conditions locally are threatening to organizational goals, norms, values, etc. Depending on how the transnational corporation is perceived, the indigenous environment may range from munificent to malevolent in terms of acceptability, cooperation, political climate, material and human resources, capital, and goodwill. In response, the organizational culture may range from integration and collaboration to tightening up and finally being forced to leave.

Cultural Heterogeneity—the degree to which cultures are dissimilar or similar. It is easier for a transnational corporation to deal with a culture that is relatively homogeneous, or like the base culture (e.g., English-based multinationals would have an edge possibly in British Commonwealth nations). But when a culture is diverse and disparate, then it is difficult for the central headquarters to coordinate the behavior of subsidiaries and their employees. Management may have to be more differentiated, semiautonomous, and decentralized units. Expatriates from the home base culture may be more prone to culture shock on assignment in the host culture.

Cultural Interdependence—the degree of sensitivity of the culture in responding to conditions and developments in other cultures. This dimension may range from economic dependence on other nations for raw materials, supplies, and equipment, to adaptation and adoption of new technology and processes from other interacting cultures, to being subject to scrutiny in the host culture for attitudes and actions that occurred on the part of the corporation in another culture.

Thus, all such factors impact the multinational organization's culture, impacting decisions, planning, information systems, and conflict resolution. Terpstra cites a variety of strategies that a transnational corporation can use to cope with the vagaries of international operations—environmental impact assessments, comparative and/or cluster analysis, cultural scanning and intelligence systems, computer simulations, social cost/benefit analysis, systems dynamics and modeling, social indicators/quality-of-life monitoring, risk analysis and scenario writing, trend extrapolation and technological forecasting, and establishment of external affairs units. To be a world-class organization, synergy should occur between the host, base, and international business environments. It requires adaptations within the transnational organization's culture to local factors of language and communication, law and politics, values and beliefs, education and training, technology and material resources, and social organization.

To be a world-class organization, synergy should occur between the host, base, and international business environments.

EXHIBIT 4.7

SUMMARY OF BETTER UNDERSTANDING CULTURAL DIFFERENCES

CLASSIFYING CULTURES

DIMENSIONS	AUTHORS
■ Monochronic or polychronic, high or low context, past or future oriented.	Edward T. Hall
■ Power distance, collectivism/individualism, femininity/masculinity, uncertainty avoidance, long-term/short-term orientation.	Geert Hofstede
■ Civilization divisions: West European, Hindu, Orthodox, Japanese, Sinic, and African.	Samuel Huntington
■ Problem solving in terms of time, person-nature, human nature, form of activity, and relationship to one's fellows.	Florence Kluckhohn
■ Universalist/particularist, individualist/collectivist, specific/diffuse, achievement/ascription oriented, neutral/emotional (affective).	Fons Trompenaars

Source: Lewis, R. D. *Behavioral Scientists Classifications for Cultural Analysis*, The Cultural Imperative (Yarmouth, ME: Intercultural Press, 2003), p. 64.

In the past few decades, anthropologists and management educators have offered a variety of ways, in addition to those already cited in this book, to enable global leaders to better understand cultural differences of both nations and organizations. Exhibit 4.7 attempts to summarize some of this thinking on cultural classifications by leading authors whose works are referenced throughout our volume.

People in Organizational Cultures

The source of greatest cross-cultural difference in organizations throughout the world is probably in the concept of management and human resources. For managers and other professionals, there is much to be gained from mutual exchanges on this issue of organizational culture and leadership. For a high performing organization, there needs to be a fit between its culture and personnel if synergy is to occur. Effective global leaders will direct more effort toward promoting that match.

One strategy is to carefully search and select personnel who will be comfortable in a particular system. Then acculturate them to a strong corporate culture that further ensures commitment to the institution's

One strategy is to carefully search and select personnel who will be comfortable in a particular system.

goals and values. Organizational cultures continually reaffirm the company folklore on watershed events of their past and "how we do things around here." Behavior models among management display the same traits and become mentors to young protégés. To better manage organizational energies, the strong culture offers a consistent set of implicit understandings that help in dealing with ambiguities of business politics and relationships.

Another approach is to adapt the organization to its people, especially in terms of a particular place or time. It is not only plants and equipment that can rust and deteriorate. Within human systems, values and norms, policies and practices, leadership and technologies can also lag or become obsolete. That may call for planned renewal when the people and their productivity are being undermined by outdated or archaic procedures or processes. In the behavioral sciences, technologies have been created for such organization development (OD). Consultants, either internal or external, are used to solve people and structural problems, while facilitating planned change of the organization's culture. More recently, a new type of consultant has emerged who is concerned about promoting organizational transformation (OT). The emphasis is on the impact of transformational leadership or new management, on the organization regarding what it should become in the light of changing times and conditions.

Since organizational culture is dynamic, leaders initiate adaptations necessary for survival by enabling people to:

- Spend their lives on something worthwhile that will outlast them.
- Live a life of consequence without stress and undue cultural restraints.
- Preserve for tomorrow what is useful today.
- Value the work as much as the work ethic.
- Accept differences and appreciate similarities.
- Seize opportunities for personal and professional development, while overcoming the disadvantages to developing one's potential.

Within the emerging knowledge culture, personnel are largely knowledge/technical and service workers of multicultural backgrounds. Because managerial skills for such people will be scarce and in demand, one can envision the development of a cadre of executives and administrators capable of being transferred across the traditional boundaries of nations, industries, and public/private sectors. Argyris[20] believes that the organizational culture of the future will include personnel policies that:

- Encourage employees to be authentic with one another and with management.
- Fully appreciate the value of human resources which so contribute to organization success.

■ Foster individual responsibility for career development.
■ Take a holistic approach to promoting organizational health.

Significantly, management consultants are beginning to appreciate that an organization's *informal culture* has as much influence on corporate effectiveness as the formal structure of jobs, authority, technical and financial procedures. Now the target for planned change is the organizational climate, as well as work attitudes and habits of employees. Organization excellence is attained by maximizing their human energy assets and minimizing their human energy losses. Knowledge organizations capitalize on ad hoc, unstructured relationships among people to cope effectively with uncertainty and accelerating change, and to cooperate in diverse environments.

Efforts to improve the organizational culture based on such premises can be found throughout the world. Managers, consultants, and researchers are cooperating in sharing their findings relative to quality of work life and participation experiments. Convergence of endeavors to "humanize the organizational environment or work culture" is happening on a universal scale and calls for more synergy on the part of corporate and government leaders.

Toward the end of the twentieth century, profound changes became evident within *transitional economies*. Remarkable alterations are going on in nations and organizations formerly under totalitarian, communist rule, as well as in developing countries, where work cultures are moving inevitably toward greater personal freedom and emphasis on human rights. The transition from centralized planning of socialist economies to a free-market economy and political democracy is progressing in Russia and Eastern Europe, Africa, India, and even the People's Republic of China. As the *macroculture* shifts, so does the *microculture* of its institutions. Thus, organizational cultures within these societies are experiencing gradual transformations. Free enterprise within the private sector is being encouraged, while the public sector companies are being sold to investors or cooperatives. The cultural change is evident in eight new members of the European Union, post-communist countries which now are open to foreign trade, and creation of institutions that make capitalism work. . . . One of the most dramatic examples of such change is in Germany, within its Western and Eastern regions. With political unification came slow economic integration—but consider the challenges involved in joining together such disparate cultures, one conditioned by the democratic capitalistic system and the other by a communist, central planning! Imagine the differences in German workers—one group attuned to participation, innovation, and profit motivation, and the other to totalitarianism, bureaucracy, and autocratic management. Yet in 2005, a woman professor of physics from the old East German, Angela Merkel, has been chosen Chancellor and leads the effort to renew the German economy.

MANAGING THE KNOWLEDGE CULTURE

Progress in science and technology are powerful forces in the advancement of knowledge.

The biggest challenge facing twenty-first-century leaders and populations may be learning to function effectively in a *knowledge culture.* This book has amply explained what is involved in the concept of *culture*, but what do we mean when it's coupled with *knowledge*? Among the dictionary definitions, "knowledge is information, ideas, and understandings gained through experience, observation, study, and research." Knowledge by humans is perceived, discovered, and learned—a means to attain erudition and wisdom. Yet Albert Einstein thought *imagination* was even more important than knowledge because it has no boundries!

Progress in science and technology are powerful forces in the advancement of knowledge, as well as in the discovery of new processes, products, and services. In the past hundred and fifty years, science and its by-product technology have produced new knowledge and insights that are transforming our lives in health care, education, and commerce. Exhibit 4.8 may help the reader appreciate the role of science in a knowledge society.

At this opening decade of the twenty-first century, three themes dominate business news and professional literature—information, knowledge, and innovation. Universities and colleges offer courses on these

EXHIBIT 4.8
SCIENCE PRODUCES KNOWLEDGE

Among human activities, science is unique. It is an adventurous exploration of the unknown that affects each of us in many ways. Science is a process that explores every facet of our world in a way meant to uncover and test verifiable truths. The process goes like this: Scientists generate multiple reasonable explanations of what we can observe. Only after testing does that new explanation become the building block of knowledge from which we begin to take the next step. For example, when we appreciate more of the complexity, finiteness, and delicate balance of ecosystems, we can see how crucial it is to preserve them, and why damaging them hurts us later. The controlled creativity of scientific inquiry sometimes can take us in unexpected, often dazzling directions. Science based on the intense, insatiable curiosity and creativity of scientists matters because it is the foundation of new knowledge . . . the foundation for all the benefits we have accumulated as a species.

Source: Apple, M. Why Science Matters, Council of Scientific Society Presidents, December 2002.

subjects. Corporate titles change to include Manager of Information Resources, Director of Innovation and New Products, or Knowledge Officer. Within the field of management, entire curriculums in higher education center on knowledge management; numerous textbooks are being published and professional societies formed around this theme.

McElroy states that the first stage of knowledge management (KM) was driven by information technology, the World Wide Web, and the sharing of best practices and lessons learned. The KM second stage emphasized human factors, systems thinking, and knowledge creation that included both tacit and explicit communications. Now, apparently, a KM third stage is the arrangement and management of content through taxonomy construction and use, especially by means of information technology.[21] Today, there are practitioners of knowledge management who have developed theories, principles, and methods for increasing and managing knowledge in both organizations and society. Essentially, this is a *cultural change* in our values and world views. Capital, now perceived as more than financial, is broadened to include other forms of capital—human, intellectual, structural, customer, organizational, innovation, process, and other intangible assets. For example, knowledge consultants are concerned about *social innovation capital*—that is, the structural manner in which social systems organize themselves and carry out the *production and integration of knowledge*.

Knowledge Is Power

The emphasis today on *knowledge economies, industries, and centers* has caused me to describe the present living and work environment as a *knowledge culture*. Knowledge has become the new currency for economic and career advancement. This focus on information and knowledge in our times is a radical change in the traditional business perspective. The synthesis now requires different patterns of management thought and practice, so as to ensure success in a more complex, global market and workplace. Albee[22] proposes that production, prosperity, and knowledge are created through value networks. Because organizations are living systems, she maintains that we must utilize business webs, communities of practice, knowledge technologies, network analysis, and even biology. Albee maintains that digital, Web-enabled technologies help global leaders weave together a web of knowledge that supports people in their work.

In his many books, Peter Drucker accurately forecasted business and management futures. He predicted the altering of global cultures will force us to change our mind-sets and mental geography.[23] Global leaders would do well to heed his message summarized in Exhibit 4.9.

Knowledge will be the resource, and knowledge workers the dominant group in the workforce. In the future, there will be two workforces made up of the under fifties and the over fifties, respectively. These two workforces are likely to differ markedly in their needs and behaviors, and in the jobs they do. In a transnational company, there is only one economic unit—the world. Selling, servicing, public relations, and legal affairs are local. Social changes may be more important for the success or failure of an organization and its executives than economic events.

Source: Drucker, P. Managing in the Next Society, Oxford, UK: Butterworth–Heinemann/Elsevier Science, 2002.

CONCLUSIONS

Global leaders appreciate and understand the impact of culture on people and their organizations. Furthermore, they influence and manage cultural change within their institutions. When groups of people formulate a company, association, or agency, its culture reflects that of the larger community, impacting behavior both within and without the enterprise. The human and material energy exchanged through the organization is affected by culture, which may foster or undermine productivity and profits. Organizational culture may motivate or obstruct high performance.

Culture is a dynamic concept that changes, as does the way we communicate it. Those with the mind-set and skills of a global manager exercise proactive leadership in altering both the macro- and microlevels of culture. To cope effectively with today's accelerating change, effective leaders continuously revise their images of self, role, and organization and assist their personnel to do the same. Thus, attitudes and behavior are modified to become more relevant.

Although our outlooks on change and leadership are culturally conditioned, we must realize that the new work culture worldwide requires us not only to be open to change, but to build its dynamics into our social systems. We best meet human needs by creating new technologies, markets, processes, products, and services.

Successful leadership styles are dependent to a degree on the people and their cultures at a given point in time. Generally, the contemporary work environment calls for more participative, team-oriented management that responds rapidly and synergistically to changing situations. In the emerging knowledge culture, leadership opportunities

Global leaders appreciate and understand the impact of culture on people and their organizations.

*Global leaders
should be
planned
change makers,
beginning with
one's self.*

are shared with competent knowledge workers, regardless of gender, race, religion, or nationality. The aim is to empower people, so that they will, in turn, develop their own as well as the organization's potential. To meet that challenge, the underlying assumption of this chapter is that global leaders should be planned change makers, beginning with one's self.

We also emphasized that postindustrial society is becoming a knowledge culture, an external driving force for change at work and in our communities. The Information Age requires the transformation of education and training, so that all institutions become learning organizations. When knowledge, like people, is treated as a resource, lifetime continuing self-education helps us to avoid obsolescence.

MIND STRETCHING

1. What are some of the most significant trends and changes that you observe in society and the community, work and the global market? How can you personally deal with such changes?
2. Why is it important to be open-minded and flexible with changes brought on by research, invention, discovery, and innovation? How can you anticipate such changes and stay on the leading edge of your field or discipline?
3. What is different about the emerging knowledge culture? How is it affecting the economy, organizations, and workers?
4. How is the concept and practice of leadership changing? How can you become a global leader?
5. Why is lifetime learning essential in a knowledge culture?

REFERENCES

1. Drucker, P. F. *Managing in the Next Society*. Oxford: Elsevier/Butterworth-Heinemann/Elsevier Science, 2002, pp. 74–75 (www.books@ elsevier.com/management).
2. Human Technology Inc. *The Complete Guide to Managing Change and Transition*. Amherst, MA: Human Resource Development Press, 2001. [For inventories or questionnaires to evaluate oneself regarding change, consult Harris, P. R. *Twenty Reproducible Assessment Instruments for the New Work Culture*; Sanaghan, P., Golstein, L., and Roy, A., *The Change Management Readiness Survey*—both available from www.hrd-press.com]; Johnson, S. *Who Moved My Cheese*. Carlsbad, CA: CRM Learning, 2000—learning package consisting of book, video, audio book, change profile, and support tools (www.cheeseexperience.com).

3. Curley, K. C. and Kivowitz, B. *The Managers Pocket Guide to Knowledge Management.* Amherst, MA: Human Resource Development Press, 2001; also refer to Rao, M. (ed.). *Knowledge Management Tools and Techniques.* Burlington, MA: Elsevier/Butterworth-Heinemann, 2004 (www.books@elsevier.com).

4. Suzuki, L. A., Ponterotto, J. G., and Maller, P. J. (eds.). *Handbook of Multicultural Assessment.* San Francisco, CA: Jossey-Bass Publishing, 2001.

5. Harris, P. R. *The New Work Culture—HRD Transformational Management Strategies.* Amherst, MA: HRD Press, 1998. [Republished as *The Work Culture Handbook.* Mumbai, India: Jaico Publishing House. 2003 (www.jaicobooks.com).]

6. Drucker, P. F. *Managing in the Next Society*, and *Management Challenges for the 21st Century.* Also Bennet, D. and A. Bennet, *Organizational Survival in the New World—The Intelligent, Complex Adaptive System.* Oxford: Elsevier/Butterworth-Heinemann, 1999, 2003.

7. Moran, R. T. and Riesenberger, J. R. *The Global Challenge: Building New Worldwide Enterprises.* London: McGraw-Hill, 1994; Harris, P. R. *Managing the Knowledge Culture.* Amherst, MA: HRD Press, 2005.

8. Abbott, J. D. and Moran, R. T. *Uniting North American Business—NAFTA Best Practices*; Simons, G. D., et al., *Eurodiversity—A Business Guide to Managing Differences.* Oxford: Elsevier/Butterworth-Heinemann, 2002.

9. Grove, A. S. *Only the Paranoid Survive.* New York: Currency/Doubleday, 1996; also refer to Peterson, B. *Cultural Intelligence—A Guide to Working with People from Other Cultures.* Boston: Nicholas Brealey/Intercultural Press, 2004.

10. Symonds, E. "When Companies Connect—How the Internet Will Change Business," *The Economist*, June 26–July 2, 1999, Special Survey Insert, pp. 1–40; also refer to Benson, L. K. *The Power of eCommunication* and Carliner, S. *An Overview of Online Learning.* Amherst, MA: HRD Press, 2004.

11. Bellingham, R. *The Manager's Pocket Guide to Corporate Culture Change.* Amherst, MA: HRD Press, 2001; also refer to Rivard, S., Aubert, A., et al. *Information Technology and Organizational Transformation.* Burlington, MA: Elsevier/Butterworth-Heinemann, 2004.

12. Young, S. "Micro-inequities: The Power of Small," *Workforce Diversity Reader*, Vol. 1:1, Winter 2003, pp. 88–93. [Quarterly published by The Learning Institute of Workforce Diversity, 30095 Persimmon Dr., Cleveland, OH 44145, USA, Tel: 1-800/573-2867; www.workforcediversity.org.]. Kirton, G. and Greene, A-M. *The Dynamics of Managing Diversity.* Burlington, MA: Elsevier/Butterworth-Heinemann, 2004.

13. Beatty, R. W. and Ulrich, D. "Re-Energizing the Mature Organization," *Organizational Dynamics*, New York: American Management Association: 1991, Vol. 20 Summer; Refer to Armstrong, C. and Saint-Onge, H. *The Conducive Organization-Building Sustainability.* Burlington, MA: Elsevier/Butterworth-Heinemann, 2004.

14. Developed by the author's late wife, Dr. Dorothy Lipp Harris, when she was a professor at the School of Business and Management, United States (now Alliant) University in San Diego, California. For update, refer to

Holbeche, L. *Understanding Change—Theory, Implementation, and Success*. Burlington, MA: Elsevier/Butterworth-Heinemann, 2005.

15. Pritchett, P. and Pound, R. *Employee Handbook for Organizational Change*; Pritchett, P. *The Employee Handbook of New Work Habits for a Radically Changing World*, 1994. (Both available from Pritchett and Associates. PO Box 802889, Dallas, TX 75380, USA.) Refer to Hubbard, E. E. *The Manager's Pocket Guide to Diversity Management*. Amherst, MA: Amherst, MA: HRD Press, 2005.

16. "A European Giant Stirs," *The Economist,* February 15–21, 2005, pp. 57–58.

17. "Leadership in a Changed World," *Harvard Business Review,* August 2003 (pp. 38–44; 101–108); Bellingham, R. and O'Brien, W. *The Leadership Lexicon: A Handbook of Leadership Competencies with Skill and Development Actions*. Amherst, MA: HRD Press, 2005.

18. Philip R. Harris, *High Performance Leadership—HRD Strategies for the New Work Culture*. Amherst, MA: Human Resource Development Press, 1994.

19. Terpstra, V. and David, K. *The Cultural Environment of International Business*. Cincinnati, OH: Southwest Publishing, 1985. Also refer to Hofsteade, G. J., Pedersen, P., and Hofsteade, G. *Exploring Culture*. Boston, MA: Nicholas Brealey/Intercultural Press, 2002.

20. Argyris, C. *Knowledge of Action—A Guide to Overcoming Barriers to Organizational Change*. San Francisco, CA: Jossey-Bass Publishing, 1993. Refer to Oakland, J. S. *Total Organizational Excellence*. Burlington, MA: Elsevier/Butterworth-Heinemann, 2001.

21. McElroy, M. W. *The New Knowledge Management—Complexity, Learning and Sustainable Innovation*. Oxford, UK: Elsevier/Butterworth-Heinemann, 2003.

22. Albee, V. *The Future of Knowledge—Increasing Prosperity through Value Networks*. Also refer to Rothberg, H. and Erickson, G. S. *From Knowledge to Intelligence*. Oxford, UK: Elsevier/Butterworth-Heinemann, 2003 and 2004.

23. Drucker, P. F. *Managing in the Next Society*. Oxford, UK: Elsevier/Butterworth-Heinemann, 2002. In 2006, this same publisher will release Peter Drucker's last book before his death, *The Effective Executive in Action* (www.books@elsevier.com). Also check out this web site: www.economist.com/nextsociety.

5

GLOBAL LEADERS LEARN FROM OTHER MANAGEMENT SYSTEMS

Global leaders must first and foremost be learners.
        —A fundamental theme in *Managing Cultural Differences*

The crow imitating the cormorant drowns in the water.
                        —Japanese proverb

LEARNING OBJECTIVES

"Cultural imperialism" in some countries has been irrepressible. History, however, has shown that it is never sustainable in the long term. This chapter presents the idea that global leaders—leaders of enterprises and governments, all leaders—can learn from others. "No one person has truth by the tail" (no "person" is right all the time); "no nation is fully developed in all aspects" are themes in Chapter 5. Cultural aspects in the United States are identified with contrasting values in others.

Learning from Japanese Management Practice, we believe that all persons and organizations can learn from others and adapt aspects of other systems to fit their own. The following example is based on Robert Moran's experiences in Japan.

"Cultural imperialism" in some countries has been irrepressible.

I'd like to tell you how I first learned about Japanese management techniques. Between 1965 and 1968, I was the playing coach of the Seibu Ice Hockey Team, the best team in Japan. The owner of the team and the president of the company, Yoshiaki Tsutsumi (at that time identified by *Fortune* magazine as one of the world's 10 wealthiest people), decided to devote some of his time to developing ice hockey in Japan in preparation for the 1972 Winter Olympics, which had just been awarded to the city of Sapporo in northern Japan. . . .

In October 1968, shortly before leaving with a group of 25 Japanese hockey players for a one-month, 17-game series against Canadian amateur and semiprofessional hockey teams throughout Canada, I was asked to attend a meeting with Mr. Tsutsumi. I was told the purpose of the meeting was to decide on the wardrobe for the players during their tour of Canada, which was to take place in January (Canada's coldest month).

There were six persons at the meeting, including the owner/president, his secretary, three other staff persons, and myself. After exchanging pleasantries, we began the serious business of selecting what would go into each player's luggage bag.

Department managers from the Seibu Department Store were waiting in an adjoining room with samples of the various possibilities. The meeting lasted over four hours. First, we decided on the outerwear—coats, hats, gloves, and overshoes, then the formal and informal suits and sweaters, and finally the *underwear*. Yes, we even decided on the kind and number of undershorts that each player would be allocated. The person making these decisions was the president himself, Mr. Tsutsumi. Of course, many hundreds of hours were spent planning other aspects of the tour.

Of the 17 games played in Canada, the Japanese team won 11, and from both Canadian and Japanese perspectives, the tour was a total success. On several occasions, during the pregame discussion and between-period pep talks, the fact that the company president was concerned about them to the extent of assisting with the selection of their wardrobe was mentioned. He also telephoned before and after each game and spoke to several of the players a number of times. In my opinion, this was an example of Japanese management in its purest form.

What is the moral of this story? Is it that the owners of amateur and professional hockey teams (and perhaps baseball, football, and other teams as well) should select the underwear for their players? No, it isn't. But having worked and conducted communication and team-building workshops for a professional hockey team in the National Hockey League, I certainly believe that a little more care on the part of the owners in understanding the world of the players, in getting to know them, and occasionally working with them might have done wonders for their morale and have had a positive impact on their ability to win hockey games.

Can the crow learn to imitate the cormorant? Can any management system borrow from another—in some cases, yes, and in others, no. Work environments in various countries are culturally different, and management systems and practices are deeply rooted in culture.

GLOBAL STUDY OF MANAGEMENT

Most studies in the management literature are comparative in nature. A book compares, for example, managerial processes and interdepartmental relations in the United States and Germany, or an article compares the career paths of Japanese and American managers. These kinds of cross-cultural studies are useful. However, because our world is becoming more pluralistic and interdependent, it is vital, though difficult, to study *interactions* between managers from more than one country.

Peter F. Drucker, perhaps, the most significant management thinker of the twentieth century died at the age of 95 in 2005. In 1954, he wrote *The Practice of Management*, which helped managers focus on the customer and what value means to organizations. Many of his ideas are universal and are timeless. The questions he asked and discussed in his books helped leaders shift their focus of reference and the categories they considered important. Dr. Drucker stated he wanted to learn from every student he met and subsequently he became a great teacher.

Much of the management literature and textbooks (there are more MBA programs in the United States than most, if not all, countries combined) are produced in the United States, along with much of the organizational and management behavior research. However, researchers in the United States should not assume that U.S. management techniques are necessarily the best even for American managers or for managers of other countries. American management techniques are based on American values and assumptions (for example, that we can influence and control the future to a high degree). Managers from other countries do not necessarily have such values and assumptions—at least they may not place as much emphasis or importance on them.

It is generally accepted by managers that improved individual and organizational performance is the purpose of most organizational change. In attempting to implement such change, one strategy that has not been sufficiently employed in the United States with any degree of consistency is that of studying other nations' management systems and asking what we can learn from them. Many managers feel that there's no need to do this. After all, they ask, "Hasn't the United States developed the most highly sophisticated system of management in the world? Don't the managers of the best foreign companies come to U.S. business schools for MBA degrees and executive management courses?" Yes, it may be true that many foreign managers come to the United States for training, but Americans can still learn from and borrow aspects of foreign management systems.

A word of caution from Hamel and Prahalad[1] who suggest a pitfall in taking aspects of another culture, such as from Japan, and trying to integrate them into one's business philosophy. They cite a survey in which 80% of U.S. managers polled believed that "quality would be

American management techniques are based on American values and assumptions.

a fundamental source of competitive advantage." However, 82% of the Japanese believed "the ability to create fundamentally new products and businesses will be the primary source of competitive advantage."

Today many countries, especially in Europe and Canada, have their own world-class programs in management education. Some of their MBA degree programs have unique features and adaptations worthy of emulation, particularly in cross-cultural management and organizational behavior.

Japanese and American Management

Studying managers solely through comparisons is not enough. One must also consider what happens when differences come together—namely *interactions*. Aspects of North American or European managerial systems are not necessarily appropriate for managers of other geographic areas and may not even be the best for their own managers. Furthermore, management is a dynamic process and is constantly changing. We can learn from the "way it was" by contrasting it with practices current at the end of the century. For example, the following research was conducted over 25 years ago but shows how American and Japanese management styles have influenced one another and caused changes. Recent economic problems in Japan have forced many companies in that country to abandon some traditional customs, like "lifetime employment."

The Type Z Hybrid

Ouchi and Jaeger[2] identify characteristics of typical American organizations (Type A):

1. Short-term employment
2. Individual decision making
3. Individual responsibility
4. Rapid evaluation and promotion
5. Explicit, formalized control
6. Specialized career path
7. Segmented concern

and characteristics of typical Japanese (Type J) organizations:

1. Lifetime employment
2. Consensual decision making
3. Collective responsibility
4. Slow evaluation and promotion
5. Implicit, formal control

6. Nonspecialized career path
7. Holistic concern

They then compare these organizations and relate them to their sociocultural roots. They conclude by presenting a hybrid organizational form (Type Z), which they suggest may be useful in the United States. Each of the two types of organizational structures (American and Japanese) represents a natural outflow and adaptation to the environments to which they belong.

Ouchi and Jaeger suggest the following characteristics for Type Z organization (modified American):

Long-term employment
Consensual decision making
Individual responsibility
Slow evaluation and promotion
Implicit, informal control with explicit formalized measures
Moderately specialized career path
Holistic concern for individuals

One of the most dramatic cases for East-West synergy lies in the interdependent relationship between Japan and the United States. This relationship has been tested many times, but overall it has been mutually beneficial.

Japan's previous success in production, distribution, and marketing has been due to the ability of the Japanese to learn from Western nations and then apply this knowledge to their own business situations. Nowhere is this more evident than in the field of management, where Japanese executives borrowed ideas from the United States and then refined them for increased productivity.

Many American companies have made significant changes in manufacturing techniques, including Kanban manufacturing, quality control circles, and just-in-time (JIT) purchasing that are part of mainstream American/Japanese industrial production. Boosting the morale, knowledge, responsibility, and therefore productivity of a corporation's workforce by using these techniques can only be accomplished if employees realize that they have a growing role in the firm's processes, problems, and profits.

Total Quality Management (TQM)

Who originated the quality initiatives that are a fundamental part of most, if not all organizations? Japan? Germany? the United States? A review of the history of quality initiatives shows that the beginnings were in the United States but the quality concept was taken to Europe and Japan following World War II by Edward Deming and others.

One of the most dramatic cases for East-West synergy lies in the interdependent relationship between Japan and the United States.

Subsequently, after Japan's great reconstruction success, it was reintroduced to the United States. "Total quality management" became a buzzword. Goldman outlines the history of quality initiatives and the present-day quality initiatives used worldwide.[4]

- Customer involvement—customers' requirements are integrated into the product services.
- Company cultural change—everyone's responsibility—labor, and management to instill a quality orientation in any organization.
- Continuous improvement and statistical measurement—measuring changes resulting from a quality process that can always be improved.
- Employee empowerment—the mentality of the employee changes, and the quality becomes the most important objective.
- Teamwork—working together on mutual goals.
- Benchmarking—comparing your organization to the best of your competition.
- Cycle time reduction—reducing the time to deliver a product from the beginning to customer satisfaction.

Six Sigma takes all of the above including ISO (International Standards Organization) which result as a business practice rudely used in many organizations in the financial improvement of an organization.

SKILLS FOR GLOBAL LEADERS

We will now consider the question of being an effective person in an overseas assignment. The cross-cultural management literature does not contain precise statements or criteria concerning the factors related to cross-cultural adaptation and effectiveness.

Cross-cultural communication behaviors or skills can be learned so that a manager can function effectively with host nationals. We are now making important distinctions between cognitive competency or awareness and behavioral competency. Behavioral competency is the ability to demonstrate or use skills; cognitive competency is the intellectual awareness or knowledge base.

Ruben has identified the following skills as being associated with effective transferring of knowledge in a multicultural environment.[5] We shall refer to these skills as abilities. Most of them are common sense skills but often not demonstrated by multinational managers or supervisors of minority employees in one's own culture.

- *Respect.* The ability to express respect for others is an important part of effective relations in every country. All people like to believe and feel that others respect them, their ideas, and their accomplishments.

However, it is difficult to know how to communicate respect to persons from another culture. The following questions should be considered by managers working in another culture with persons from that culture. What is the importance of age in communicating respect? What is the significance of manner of speaking? Do you speak only when spoken to? What gestures express respect? What kind of eye contact expresses respect? What constitutes "personal questions" as an invasion of privacy and a lack of respect? These are only a few of the many questions that could be generated relating to the important question, "How do I demonstrate that I respect the people I am working with?"

- *Tolerating Ambiguity.* This refers to the ability to react to new, different, and at times, unpredictable situations with little visible discomfort or irritation. Excessive discomfort often leads to frustration and hostility, which are not conducive to effective interpersonal relationships with persons from other cultures. Learning to manage the feelings associated with ambiguity is a skill associated with adaptation to a new environment and effectively working with managers who have a different set of values.

- *Relating to People.* Many Western managers, concerned with getting the job done, are overly concerned with the task side of their jobs. Transferring skills and knowledge to persons in another culture requires getting the job done, but in such a way that people feel like they are a part of the completed project and have benefited from being involved. Too much concern for getting the job done and neglect of "people maintenance" can lead to failure in transferring skills.

- *Being Nonjudgmental.* Most people do not like to feel judged by others in what they say and do without the opportunity of fully explaining themselves. The ability to withhold judgment and remain objective until one has enough information requires an understanding of the other's point of view and is an important skill.

- *Personalizing One's Observations.* As previously indicated, different people explain the world around them in different terms. A manager should realize that his or her knowledge and perceptions are valid only for him- or herself and not for the rest of the world. Thus, one would be able to personalize observations, be more tentative in conclusions, and demonstrate a communication competence showing that what is "right" or "true" in one culture is not "right" or "true" in another. As one author said, "this is my way, what is your way? There is no 'the way' way"—it is all relative.

- *Empathy.* This is the ability to "put yourself in another's shoes." In this context, most people are attracted to and work well with managers who seem to be able to understand things from their point of view.

- *Persistence.* The multinational manager may not be successful at getting things done immediately, but with patience and perseverance,

Learning to manage the feelings associated with ambiguity is a skill.

the task can be accomplished. There are many self-learning aids to acquire more synergistic skills for global management.

CHALLENGES IN INTERNATIONAL MANAGEMENT

We invite our readers to analyze the following material[6] and complete the exercise with colleagues from other cultures in light of the chapter messages:

Trivial Pursuit™ is a board game that has sold millions of copies throughout the world. The game requires players to answer questions in a number of categories such as geography, entertainment, history, art and literature, science, and nature and sports. The category of the question is determined by a roll of the dice.

I would like to invite you, the reader, to play this game. You have rolled the dice and drawn the category "Global Management." This is your question: "Which countries produce the most skillful global leaders?"

If the question were in Trivial Pursuit™, it would be in the genius edition—a very difficult question. Two words in the question contribute to the difficulty—skillful and leader. A standard dictionary provides this definition of skillful: "well qualified, capable, fit." "Leader" is a little more murky. The dictionary definition is "someone who acts as a guide." One person I asked suggested Japan.

Japan indeed has a successful track record of best-selling products, including cars, electronic equipment, and steel, among others. This is largely accomplished through Japanese businessmen who work for the nine giant Japanese trading companies—the *sogo shosha*. But the Japanese cheat in trade, he said. They have been found guilty of commercial piracy, bribery, and falsifying documents. They also distort the international value of the yen, my friend said, so that some Japanese goods sell for less in other countries than in Tokyo. Moreover, they have exploited the open-door policy of some countries while vigorously pursuing a closed-door policy for themselves.

A Vote for the United States

Another businessman who was listening to this conversation said he thought the United States produced the most competent internationalists in business. The United States is the biggest economic entity in the history of the world, with dominant positions worldwide in computers, space, medicine, biology, and so on. Its competent internationalists in business make this possible.

This was overheard by a French manager, who said that Americans are naïve internationally. American businessmen, according to him, are the most ethnocentric of all businessmen (the dictionary definition is "one who judges others by using one's own personal or cultural standards").

Besides, he said, American businessmen have their priorities mixed up. They are too materialistic, too work-oriented, too time-motivated, and equate anything "new" with the best. Americans also have the highest attrition rate (dictionary definition—"return early from an international assignment") of any country, said the French manager.

The question is indeed a tough one. At a recent meeting of American managers attending a seminar on international joint ventures, I posed the same question. It evoked considerable discussion but no agreement. One person suggested they vote and most hands were raised when Sweden was proposed. But Sweden, said one person who voted for another country, couldn't be the winning answer. Sweden is too small and the Swedish economy has declined sharply since the late 1970s because Swedish internationalists aren't aggressive enough. At this point, another participant suggested the right answer was the Soviet Union. Most people laughed at this suggestion. I assume that implied some disagreement.

Britain has had foreign operations for centuries. Maybe the British manager is the most competent internationalist. But when business travelers from several countries discussed this possibility while caught in Geneva International Airport recently during a snowstorm, no one thought Britain was the winning answer because Britain has lost so much in the international marketplace. Several businessmen from Britain were among those who participated in the discussion.

Since no agreement could be reached on the correct answer to my first question, I decided to rephrase it: What contribution to a multinational organization is made by managers of various nationalities?

Different Contributions

Hari Bedi, an Indian expatriate working for a large multinational company in Hong Kong, believes that Asian internationals use the 5 Cs of *continuity* (a sense of history and tradition), *commitment* (to the growth of the organization), *connections* (where social skills and social standing count), *compassion* (balancing science and political issues), and *cultural sensitivity* (a respect for other ways).

These qualities are among the contributions made by Asian managers to a multinational organization, he says. Western managers, according to Bedi, use the 5 Es: *expertise* (experience in managerial and technical theory), *ethos* (practical experience), *eagerness* (the enthusiasm of the entrepreneur), *esprit de corps* (a common identity), and *endorsement* (seeks unusual opportunities).

The answer is that managers of every country contribute something to a multinational organization. The usefulness of that contribution depends on the situation. Skilled global leaders are able to recognize the contribution made by managers of various nationalities. They are also able to develop solutions to problems faced by global organizations by using these contributions and cultural diversity as a resource, rather than a barrier to be overcome. They are first and foremost learners.

STRATEGIC COLLABORATIONS AND MERGERS

In 2005, mergers and acquisitions in the oil and gas industry alone tripled in value from 2004 to more than $160 billion.[7]

"Companies are just beginning to learn what nations have always known: in a complex, uncertain world filled with dangerous opponents, it is best not to go it alone."[8] Mergers and acquisitions result. Some thrive, some survive, and some die. Some are perceived as an act of desperation, and others are more strategic. The following points are relevant:

■ Internal growth possibilities are diminished for many organizations and mergers or acquisitions are strategies to survive or grow.
■ Increasing products, markets, and technology lowers risk.
■ Organizational culture clash is a major problem in integrating different companies.
■ Making the deal is easy, making it work is difficult.
■ Ashkenas et al.[9] outline the following lessons learned by GE Capital.
■ Acquisition integration begins with the due diligence studies of all aspects of the organization.
■ Integrating management is a full-time business function like marketing.
■ Decisions on structure, roles, and other important aspects of integration should be announced soon after the merger or acquisition is reported.
■ Integration involves not only technologies and products, but cultures.

Integration involves not only technologies and products, but cultures.

These lessons are relevant when the integrated organizations are from the same national culture. When they are from different national cultures, the challenges are more significant, and the skills required to make them succeed are broader, deeper, and more sophisticated.

Global leaders are required to meet, socialize, and negotiate with foreign business persons and government officials. The manager must be able to communicate and work with persons who have been socialized in a different cultural environment. Customs, values, lifestyles, beliefs, management practices, and other aspects of their personal and professional life are therefore different. For the global leader to be effective, one must be aware of the many beliefs and values that underlie his or her country's business practices, management techniques, and strategies. Awareness of such values and assumptions is critical for managers who wish to transfer technology to another culture or who wish to collaborate with those who hold different values and assumptions.

Exhibit 5.1 identifies several U.S. values with possible alternatives. Examples of how the cultural system might influence management are also indicated in the third column.

EXHIBIT 5.1

U.S. VALUES AND POSSIBLE ALTERNATIVES

Aspects* of U.S. Culture	Alternative Aspect	Examples of Management Function Affected
The individual can influence the future (where there is a will there is a way).	Life follows a preordained course and human action is determined by the will of God.	Planning and scheduling
The individual can change and improve the environment.	People are intended to adjust to the physical environment rather than to alter it.	Organizational environment, morale, and productivity
An individual should be realistic in his aspirations.	Ideals are to be pursued regardless of what is "reasonable."	Goal setting and career development
We must work hard to accomplish our objectives (Puritan ethic).	Hard work is not the only prerequisite for success. Wisdom, luck, and time are also required.	Motivation and reward system
Commitments should be honored (people will do what they say they will do).	A commitment may be superseded by a conflicting request or an agreement may only signify intention and have little or no relationship to the capacity of performance.	Negotiating and bargaining
One should effectively use one's time (time is money, which can be saved or wasted).	Schedules are important but only in relation to other priorities.	Long- and short-range planning
A primary obligation of an employee is to the organization.	The individual employee has a primary obligation to family and friends.	Loyalty, commitment, and motivation
The employer or employee can terminate their relationship	Employment is for a lifetime.	Motivation and commitment to the company
A person can only work for one company at a time (one cannot serve two masters).	Personal contributions to individuals who represent an enterprise are acceptable.	Ethical issues, conflicts of interest

continues

EXHIBIT 5.1

U.S. VALUES AND POSSIBLE ALTERNATIVES (CONTINUED)

Aspects* of U.S. Culture	Alternative Aspect	Examples of Management Function Affected
The best qualified persons should be given the positions available.	Family considerations, friendship, and other considerations should determine employment practices.	Employment, promotions, recruiting, selection, and reward
A person can be removed if he or she does not perform well.	The removal of a person from a position involves a great loss of prestige and will rarely be done.	Promotion
All levels of management are open to qualified individuals (a clerk can rise to become company president).	Education or family ties are the primary vehicles for mobility.	Employment practices and promotion
Intuitive aspects of decision making should be reduced and efforts should be devoted to gathering relevant information.	Decisions are expressions of wisdom by the person in authority, and any questioning would imply a lack of confidence in his or her judgment.	Decision-making process
Data should be accurate.	Accurate data are not as highly valued.	Record keeping
Company information should be available to anyone who needs it within the organization.	Withholding information to gain or maintain power is acceptable.	Organization, communication, managerial style
Each person is expected to have an opinion and to express it freely, even if his or her views do not agree with his or her colleagues.	Deference is to be given to persons in power or authority, and to offer judgment that is not in support of the ideas of one's superiors is unthinkable.	Communications, organizational relations
A decision maker is expected to consult persons who can contribute useful information to the area being considered.	Decisions may be made by those in authority and others need not be consulted.	Decision making, leadership

EXHIBIT 5.1 (CONTINUED)

Aspects* of U.S. Culture	Alternative Aspect	Examples of Management Function Affected
Employees will work hard to improve their position in the company.	Personal ambition is frowned upon.	Selection and promotion
Competition stimulates high performance.	Competition leads to imbalances and to disharmony.	Career development and marketing
A person is expected to do whatever is necessary to get the job done (one must be willing to get one's hands dirty).	Various kinds of work are accorded low or high status and some work may be below one's "dignity" or place in the organization.	Assignment of tasks, performance, and organizational effectiveness
Change is considered an improvement and a dynamic reality.	Tradition is revered and the power of the ruling group is founded on the continuation of a stable structure.	Planning, morale, and organizational development
What works is important.	Symbols and the process are more important than the end point.	Communication, planning, quality control
Persons and systems are evaluated.	Persons are evaluated but in such a way that individuals will not be embarrassed or caused to "lose face."	Rewards and promotion, performance evaluation, and accountability

* Aspect here refers to a belief, value, attitude, or assumption that is a part of culture in that it is shared by a large number of persons in any culture.

The above Exhibit is not only to compare cultural values affecting management practices in culture X with those in culture Y, but also to provide a basis whereby a manager might "synergistically" relate to managers trained in another cultural system and management practices developed in other cultures.

The observations in this section take on added significance when computer networking and the Internet are used to form strategic alliances and partnerships. The *connectivity* of the Internet enables us to create *information partnerships* with personnel, customers, suppliers, contractors, and consultants. The key in such electronic endeavors is to treat them as *collaborators* rather than competitiors.

EXHIBIT 5.2

CULTURAL VARIATIONS: PERFORMANCE APPRAISALS

Dimensions— General	United States— Low Context	Saudi Arabia— High Context	Japan— High Context
Objective of P.A.	Fairness Employee development	Placement	Direction of company/ employee development
Who does appraisal	Supervisor	Manager—may be several layers up—appraiser has to know employee well	Mentor and supervisor Appraiser has to know employee well
Authority of appraiser	Presumed in supervisory role or position	Reputation important (Prestige is determined by nationality, age, gender, family, tribe, title, education)	Respect accorded by employee to supervisor to appraiser
	Supervisor takes slight lead	Authority of appraiser important—don't say "I don't know"	Done equally
How often	Yearly or periodically	Yearly	Developmental appraisal monthly Evaluation appraisal—after first 12 years
Assumptions	Objective appraiser is fair	Subjective appraiser more important than objective Connections are important	Objective and subjective important Japanese can be trained in anything
Manner of communication and feedback	Criticism direct Criticisms may be in writing Objective/ authentic	Criticisms subtle Older more likely to be direct Criticisms not given in writing	Criticisms subtle Criticisms given verbally Observe formalities
Rebuttals	U.S. will rebut appraisal	Saudi Arabians will retreat	Japanese will rarely rebut
Praise/motivators	Given individually Money and position strong motivators Career development	Given individually Loyalty to supervisor strong motivator	Given to entire group Internal excellence strong motivator

Source: Adapted from report of the Association of Cross-Cultural Trainers in Industry, now Pacific Area Communicators of International Affairs, 16331 Underhill Lane, Huntington Beach, CA 92647.

Performance Appraisals

This is a "hot topic" among many human resource professionals. The lingering question underlying most performance appraisal systems is, are these categories of performance measurement universal and of equal importance? Also, do they really measure this individual's contribution to the organization in any meaningful way?

Edwards et al.[10] ask whether employment practices in subsidiaries can be transferred to practices in the country of origin. The descriptions for Saudi Arabia and Japan might provide suggestions for U.S. and European organizations regarding performance appraisals.

Exhibit 5.2 illustrates the cultural variations in performance appraisals between Japanese, Americans and Saudi Arabians.

CONCLUSIONS

In this chapter we have presented the idea that all global leaders, who must be first and foremost learners, can learn from other leaders and other management systems.

In China recently the following conversation was overheard. A visiting executive asked the non Chinese Managing Director of a large global enterprise based in Shanghai this question: "you have been in China 3 years, what have you learned from the Chinese, what has the Chinese way of managing/leading contributed to your company?"

The foreigner paused and said: "well nothing really, the Chinese want to learn from us."

Hopefully readers of this chapter will be increasingly convinced of the importance of learning from others in a global business world.

All global leaders can learn from other leaders and other management systems.

MIND STRETCHING

Trends in the global marketplace have made organizations from various countries more interdependent. Effective leaders in international negotiations and the forming of strategic alliances or partnerships cultivate the mind-set and skills presented in this chapter.

The following questions are important to consider.

1. Is the "Americanization of the world" happening as a function of globalization?
2. Have we lost our "curiosity" about other peoples and nations? Curiosity has been demonstrated to be an important trait of skillful global leaders.

REFERENCES

1. Hamel, G. and Prahalad, C. K. *Competing for the Future*. Boston: Harvard Business School Press, 1994.
2. Ouchi, W. G. and Jaeger, A. M. "Made in America Under Japanese Management," *Harvard Business Review*, Vol. 52, No. 5, pp. 61–69, 1974. See also Chen, M. *Asian Management Systems*. London: Routledge, 1995 and Funakawa, A. *Transcultural Management*. San Francisco: Jossey-Bass, 1997.
3. Hamel, G. and Prahalad, C. K. *Competing for the Future*. Boston: Harvard Business School Press, 1994.
4. Goldman, H. H. "The origins and development of quality initiatives in American business," *The TQM Magazine*, Vol. 17, No. 3, pp. 217–225, 2005.
5. Ruben, B. *Handbook of Intercultural Skills*. Vol. 1, New York: Pergamon Press, 1983. See also Kenton, S. B. and Valentine, D. *Crosstalk: Communicating in a Multicultural Workplace*. Upper Saddle River, NJ: Prentice-Hall, 1997.
6. "Cross-cultural Management," *International Management*, March 1985.
7. www.theaustralian.news.com.au/common/story, M&A gusher: oil and gas deals triple to $225 bn, Carola Hoyos, March 28, 2006.
8. Ohmae, K. "The Global Logic Strategic Alliances," *Harvard Business Review*, March–April 1989.
9. Ashkenas, R. N., DeMonaco, L. J., and Francis, S. C. "Making the Deal Real: How GE Capital Integrates Acquisitions," *Harvard Business Review*, January–February 1998.
10. Edwards, T., Almond, P., Clark, I., and Colling, T., et al. "Reverse Diffusion in US Multinationals: Barriers from the American Business System," *The Journal of Management Studies*, Vol. 42, Issue 6, Oxford: September 2005, pp. 1261–1286.

WOMEN AS LEADERS IN GLOBAL BUSINESS

So often the "problem with no name" is experienced by women as a situation that affects them alone or worse, as a problem with them ... We have seen that when women share their experiences, they recognize that many of the problems they experience as individuals are actually systemic and not unique to them or to their organization. And they realize that promoting change can benefit the organization as well as the men and women in it.[1]

Dear Ms. Moran
Thank you for your email.
We do not carry women's pilot shirts.
I did check online and found a web site that lists this item
www.mypilotstore.com
Please let me know if I can be of further assistance.
Sincerely,
Customer Service

Dear Customer Service:
Thanks for your response, it is appreciated. I was able to do a search and was initially excited to find "girl's are pilots too" websites, only to be disappointed in finding they sell pink tank tops with "I love my pilot" written on them, with a link to "Dog's are pilots too" (selling stuffed animals). After further searching, I was able to find one that sells proper professional women's pilot shirts. The search was a bit of a disappointment (in more ways than one), but if I ever need aviation cookware I know where to find it online now. I guess one has to have a sense of

humor . . . May I suggest you (being one of the most popular pilot supply websites) sell women's pilot shirts?

Thank you,

Rebecca, Pilot in Tanzania, East Africa

Why can't women seem to get ahead in the corporate world? The easy answer is the corporate world is fundamentally sexist . . . There is a second answer that isn't so easy . . . biology . . . there are few women CEOs and a disproportionately small number of women executives because women have babies.[2]

American women can lead European companies successfully if they are sensitive to cultural nuances, says Nancy McKinstry, the chief executive of Wolters Kluwer based in the Netherlands.[3]

In 2005 the total world population equaled approximately 6,463,063,000. About 3,248,080,000 are males, and 3,214,983,000 are females. This means there are roughly 101 males per 100 females.

LEARNING OBJECTIVES

The first objective is to raise some issues regarding women as leaders in organizations. The second objective is to suggest some ideas regarding women as global leaders and specific issues women may be confronted with in managing cultural differences.

As globalization has transformed worldwide organizational culture and the workforce, so too is the case for workforce collaboration and support. Seeing that national corporations have expanded to global corporations, companies have had to account for an increasingly diverse workplace of varying ethnicities, nationalities, and languages. Over the last 50 years, an increasing number of professional women have entered and remain in the global workforce. For workforce professionals to perform to their potential, they need support, training, and mentoring. For women the challenge goes well beyond this. Women must often deal with the subconscious counterforces of corporate cultural practice and micromessages that ensure only members who fit well within the dominant organizational cultural system succeed.

In this chapter we address the opportunities and challenges faced by women as global businesspeople. From an organizational perspective, companies that use and build on an increasingly diverse workforce that includes women will have the competitive advantage. While the number of international businesswomen has grown over the years, the number has not grown at a rate consistent with the number of women in the workforces of their respective countries. Exhibit 6.1 shows female directors as a percentage of the total directors in twelve countries that are economically highly developed. If women are less than 25% of the

Companies that use and build on an increasingly diverse workforce that includes women will have the competitive advantage.

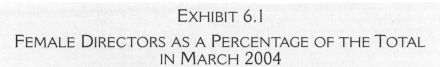

EXHIBIT 6.1
FEMALE DIRECTORS AS A PERCENTAGE OF THE TOTAL IN MARCH 2004

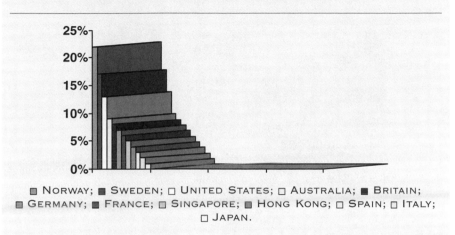

■ NORWAY; ■ SWEDEN; □ UNITED STATES; □ AUSTRALIA; ■ BRITAIN; ■ GERMANY; ■ FRANCE; ■ SINGAPORE; ■ HONG KONG; □ SPAIN; □ ITALY; □ JAPAN.

Source: Adapted from The Conundrum of the Glass Ceiling, *The Economist*, July 23, 2005, p. 64. Original source: Ethical Investment Research Serial.

total directors in highly developed countries, progress for women is still far from accomplished.

CURRENT STATUS OF GLOBAL WOMEN MANAGERS

While women make up about 49% of the world's population, in no country do they represent nearly half of the corporate managers.[4] Although globally women have drastically increased their presence in all industries, Exhibit 6.2 is yet another example that progress is yet to be made.

Meyerson and Fletcher[5] wrote that while outdated, but still prevalent, women are still responsible for the "softer" aspects of work. However, corporate culture still values highly the traits of toughness, aggressiveness, and decisiveness—all stereotypically associated with men. This isn't to say that men are to blame and that all men benefit because corporate culture is primarily male dominated. Many organizations are working hard to leverage workforce diversity and gender equality so that all people can succeed.

The key to making concrete changes in organizations is the leadership, who must have a keen interest in recruiting and *retaining* a diverse workforce while promoting qualified women. Unfortunately, statistics demonstrate that companies are falling short of the goal of gender

While women make up about 49% of the world's population, in no country do they represent nearly half of the corporate managers.

EXHIBIT 6.2[6]
CURRENT STATUS OF GLOBAL WOMEN MANAGERS

Facts	Women	Men
CEOs of *Fortune* 500 companies	6, or 1.2% (Carleton S. Fiorina: former CEO, Hewlett-Packard Company; S. Marce Fuller: Mirant; Andrea Jung: Avon Products Inc.; Anne M. Mulcahy: Xerox; Marion Sandler: Golden West Financial Corporation; Patricia Russo: Lucent)	494
CEOs of *Fortune* 1000 companies	11	989
Number among top corporate officers	2,140, or 15.6%	11,533
Number holding "clout" titles	191, or 7.9%	2,221
Representation among top earners	118, or 5.2%	2,141

equity in the workplace. Meyerson and Fletcher stated that "Women at the highest levels of business are still rare. They comprise only 10% of senior managers in *Fortune* 500 companies; less than 4% of the uppermost ranks of CEO, president, vice president, and COO; and less than 3% of top corporate earners."[7] Likewise, tied to the challenge of leveraging a diverse workforce with equal opportunity and compensation, the statistics for women of minority ethnicities are even worse: "Although women of color make up 23% of the U.S. women's workforce, they account for only 14% of women in managerial roles. African-American women comprise only 6% of the women in managerial roles."[8]

Laura Tyson, head of the London School of Economics, estimates that in the United Kingdom 30% of British managers are females, but largely confined to middle management or executive positions in human resources. In the top FTSE 100 corporations, women account for only 11% of the nonexecutive directors; 8% of the FTSE 250 firms; and fewer than 4% at smaller quoted companies.

According to *The Economist*:

- In Japan, 20 to 30 years ago, it was unacceptable for a woman to stay in the office past 5 P.M. There has been some progress since, with two women being appointed in 2005 as the head of two big Japanese companies:
  - Fumiko Hayashi is now the chairman and the CEO of Daiei.
  - Tomoyo Nonaka has been appointed CEO of Sanyo Electric.

30% of British managers are females, but largely confined to middle management

"Equality in the French workplace ... is a far off dream."

- In France, Corinne Maier, an economist with EDF, a French energy group, said that 5% of French executives are women and that "Equality in the French workplace . . . is a far off dream."
- In Britain, a large research sample of British companies found that 65% had no women on their board at all in 2003. Though 44% of the British workforce is female, no British woman has ever been the head of a large British company.[9]

According to a 2006 report by the BBC, 75% of women work in the five lowest paid sectors; women hold less than 10% of top positions in FTSE 100 companies, the police, the judiciary, and trade unions.[10] Retired women have on average a little over half the income of retired men.

Barriers to women's entry into senior management, otherwise known as the "glass ceiling," exist across the globe, and it is worse in some areas of the world than in others. An article on the most influential women in business highlighted that it is easier to find ethnic British and Chinese women in positions of power but much more difficult to find Korean or German women at the same level.[11] And although women represent 43% of the European workforce, they are still largely under-represented in top management—in the UK, women represent slightly over 30% of managers and senior executives.[12]

Barriers to women's entry into senior management, otherwise known as the "glass ceiling," exist across the globe.

EXHIBIT 6.3[13]

2001 CATALYST CENSUS OF WOMEN ON BOARD OF DIRECTORS OF THE *FORTUNE* 1000 COMPANIES—KEY FINDINGS AND TRENDS

Women Directors

- In 2001, women held 12.4% of board seats of *Fortune* 500 companies, up from 11.7 in 2000 and 11.2% in 1999.
- 87% of the *Fortune* 500 companies have at least one women board director, an increase from 2000 (86%) and 1999 (84%).
- 2.6% of board seats are held by women of color at the 409 *Fortune* 500 companies on which Catalyst compiles data.
- Women hold 8.9% of all seats in the *Fortune* 501–1000, an increase of less than $\frac{1}{2}$ percentage point from 1999.
- 61% of the *Fortune* 501–1000 companies have at least one woman board director, down from 62% in 1999.
- 1.3% of board seats at the 430 *Fortune* 501–1000 companies are held by women of color.
- In all of the *Fortune* 1–1000, women hold 10.9% of all board seats and 74% of the companies have at least one woman director.

Biases or stereotypes often hinder—although women and men are equal in their managerial abilities and overall ability to succeed—the promotion of women to senior positions.

GLOBAL CULTURAL STEREOTYPES ABOUT WOMEN LEADERS

From Asia to the Americas to Europe, some of the unfortunate and disturbing *global stereotypes* include, but are not limited to:

- Women are fundamentally different and too "soft" to handle ruthless managerial decisions. Women cannot be aggressive enough and will therefore lose business or do not have the competitive edge needed to win.
- Women overcompensate when in male environments and become too masculine when managing, alienating employees and often alarming clients.
- Women lack quantitative skills and therefore cannot hold technical positions or understand the numbers required in a profit and loss environment. Women possess "soft" skills such as communication and team building.
- Women are not as dedicated nor as committed as their male counterparts and therefore are not "executive material." Once a woman becomes a mother, her priorities change completely and she can no longer be counted on as before. Women often opt to quit working and become full-time mothers. How can a company promote someone who they know will ultimately leave? Companies cannot afford to have women coming and going whenever they wish.
- Women are not interested in an international career and therefore should not be considered for international positions. In addition, women can't handle the cultural differences that occur outside their home country.
- When companies send women abroad, their image will be less credible in male-dominated societies.
- Other men won't take the woman manager seriously.
- Because of current sexual harassment laws, nothing can be said to women without getting it blown out of proportion and all interaction becomes suspect.
- Women cause problems by looking for love in the workplace, and this will disrupt the workplace and ultimately lead to greater problems.
- There aren't enough qualified women to promote. No matter how hard the company has tried, there just aren't any women with the exact qualifications they are looking for.

STEREOTYPES ABOUT WOMEN

Such stereotypes are extremely counterproductive in the workplace. Blind stereotypes inhibit women and men from working effectively together; inhibit women from working to their potential because they are active in keeping women "in their place." Overall, they inhibit the advancement of women in business around the world, obscuring women's skills. In the end, as in the beginning, these false beliefs lead to behavior that inevitably creates weaker business results.

STEREOTYPES CAN INVARIABLY LEAD TO ORGANIZATIONAL BARRIERS HINDERING THE ADVANCEMENT OF WOMEN

There are a variety of global issues that confront women in the workplace. A few are highlighted to gain a greater understanding of the obstacles women must still overcome.

Women are more likely to be pigeonholed into less challenging positions than men. Women are often tracked into separate, and less promising, career paths. As upper management positions require broad and varied experience among other skills and talents, as well as profit and loss responsibility, many potential executives are "pipelined" through certain high-visibility and high-responsibility areas such as marketing, finance, and production.[14] These are often referred to as "line" positions, in preparation for upper-management promotion. Women "tend to be in supporting, 'staff' function areas—personnel/human resources, communications, public relations, and customer relations. Movement between these positions and 'line' positions is rare in most major companies. Furthermore, career ladders in staff functions are generally shorter than those in line functions, offering fewer possibilities to gain varied experience."[15]

This is a stereotype that can be found across the globe; women are seen as more "human" and therefore better suited for a specific type of job, such as human resources, communications, public relations, and marketing. Management, especially in the areas of finance and information services, continues to often be seen as a job better suited for men.

This stereotype could be linked to the global expectation of a woman's role as mother or primary caretaker in the family. This common stereotype is as follows: if a woman's focus is on bearing children, she would subsequently be taking time off, and could not be considered an effective front-line executive. In Chile, a woman's marital status can be an important consideration during the hiring process; it is generally featured at the top of a resume with other essentials such as name, address, and phone number, along with a photograph. A young, married woman with no children can be considered a "risky

There are a variety of global issues that confront women in the workplace.

investment" because the perception is that she will soon have children, leave her job, and the company will have to pay for pregnancy expenses. Although times may be changing in Chile, it is still generally expected that women will relinquish their career aspirations and stay at home when children arrive. For some women this can begin immediately after marriage.

During the 1980s in the United States the "mommy track" was designed to facilitate having children and maintaining a professional life. Nevertheless, many women who choose to have children still maintain high career aspirations and get stuck in less challenging or demanding jobs. This is also changing as a number of male partners and husbands of working women are staying home to care for children.[16]

Significant pay gaps exist between women and men in the same position. Despite significant progress and a variety of laws designed to prevent wage discrimination, women are still earning less than their male counterparts for the same job. According to Catalyst, in the United States, "The nation's highest-paid female corporate executives earn 68 cents to every dollar earned by the highest paid [male] corporate executives. The median total compensation of men in the study was $765,000; the median for women was $518,696.[17] The BBC reported that according to the Equal Opportunities Commission (EOC) there is a 19% pay gap between men and women in the UK.[18]

Exclusive corporate cultures. One influential factor still affecting women's advancement in business, and this is true in many areas across the globe, is that most of today's existing work environments were designed by men. Women, functioning in sometimes a more male-oriented corporate culture, are under constant pressure to adapt or transform their styles of working. This, however, is slowly changing. In Japan, for example, women face a challenge to adapt to the expectation that management requires mixing work and play, often by drinking and bar-hopping until late hours. Women colleagues are nowadays invited to join in on such social activities, although a married woman with a family might find it very difficult to meet, on a consistent basis, such a time commitment. In some South American countries, strong, unspoken norms exist about what is appropriate or inappropriate for a woman to do, regardless of career position; as such, higher level female executives can be excluded from after-work activities and/or can exclude themselves in fear of the backlash in breaching these norms.

In some American corporate environments, younger generations of women have almost eradicated the "male only" designated corporate culture by joining in, and instigating, happy hours, golf games, and softball tournaments. In some cases, these women have even redefined the culture itself by adding new twists like cultural outings.

Limited access to information, contacts, and high-level networking opportunities. While the term "old boys' network" was coined long ago, in many companies the institution itself is thriving. The "old boys' network" refers primarily to a group of white male executives who have an informal yet somewhat exclusive club that manifests itself in the upper echelons of management. Women and people of color are generally not included. Communication within these exclusive informal networks can perpetuate gender stereotyping and bias through jokes, stories, and slurs. Whether it is on the golf course, hunting, having late night drinks, or in the men's room, women are often excluded from this high-level interaction, when it is often these informal networks that can improve chances of promotion and success. According to *The Economist* few women are able to reach the higher management levels because of exclusion from informal networks, which in Asia and in America can include late-night boozing and a common tradition for sales teams to take potential clients to strip clubs.[19] Executives and upper-level managers like to hire who they know, and the more contact with an individual the better. Unfortunately for women, many of the "bonding" experiences take place in venues that are not necessarily women-friendly, such as strip clubs, or where women are simply not invited out of habit. In Israel, women are almost completely excluded from the senior ranks of the military. This exclusion from what is considered by many in the corporate world as an invaluable learning experience for managing large organizations limits women as choices for future senior executives.[20]

As a result, women often are not informed of advancement opportunities, are not as visible as male colleagues, and are not given additional opportunities to prove their credibility for promotion. According to Wernick,[21] "Managers and executives look for 'signals' from those they will select to advance. Those signals found to be most significant indicate credibility and provide increased access to visibility to decision makers. Access to information, which is critical to advancement, is often limited to selected groups or individuals within the managerial ranks or workplace." This can be exacerbated when the company does not have a formal executive development program or tracking program that explicitly monitors promotions and pay increases for employees.

Fewer women participate in executive development programs, employer-sponsored training programs, or "fast-track" programs. As evidenced through a variety of studies, women are often not given as many opportunities as their male colleagues for education, training, or special high-profile programs. This could emanate from the stereotype that women will eventually leave their jobs to have children, so why invest the money in enhancing their skills when a male would be a better "investment" opportunity? Without proper corporate intervention to increase women's participation in such programs and opportunities, the result would be that women remain in their positions with little to no overall growth.

Fewer women participate in executive development programs, employer-sponsored training programs, or "fast-track" programs.

Fewer women are asked to take on risky positions. One area where this is particularly evident is in expatriate work, where the position and results tend to be highly visible. Fewer women are asked to fill expatriate positions, although just as many women as men request these positions abroad. Adler interviewed many women to determine whether MBAs from seven management schools in the United States, Canada, and Europe would like to pursue an international assignment during their career.[22] The overall response was 84% favorable, with little difference between male and female responses. Adler conducted another survey of 686 Canadian and American firms to determine the number of women sent abroad.[23] Of 13,338 expatriates, only 3% were female when women actually accounted for 37% of domestic management positions. One other obstacle exists for women who would like to hold international assignments; the biases in certain countries against women, both native and foreign, are such that it is very difficult for women to succeed in that particular country.

WOMEN AND OVERSEAS, EXPATRIATE ASSIGNMENTS

Women's representation in the global arena has grown (albeit slowly) to 17 percent of the expatriate population, according to ORC's 2005 Dual Career and International Assignments Survey, though, in some industry sections, the percentage is considerably higher.[24]

Although the percentage of women expatriates is rising, many companies fail to send women overseas on an expatriate assignment in particular areas of the world where the demarcation between male and female roles is clearly defined. Global women managers often talk about the "double-take" or stares they receive in Asia, South America, or the Middle East when they are first introduced. For example, in Latin America, women report having been mistaken for the wife or the secretary during important high-level business meetings and social events. However, most women who were sent abroad say that the first reaction of surprise is quickly replaced by professionalism and respect. Adler interviewed many women who held challenging positions in what are considered nonwomen-friendly countries, and nearly all reported their assignments successful. Nevertheless, when many women have been nominated for an international business assignment in what the company thought would be a hostile culture, most of these women have succeeded with flying colors. Why? Because expatriate women are not expected to behave according to the same social guidelines as natives of that particular culture, and "women are especially adept at cross-cultural management skills because they use behavior patterns empha-

Nevertheless, most of these women have succeeded with flying colors.

sizing sensitivity, communication skills, community, and relationships. This personal orientation is valuable in globalization."[25]

Adler,[26] writes that women are seen as foreigners first, and thus are beholden to different rules of conduct than the local women. She gives some words of advise for women to help lay the groundwork:

1. **Establish credibility**—Have strong support from senior management in the organization and make sure that your expertise is communicated to the destination location.
2. **Have a higher ranking person** who knows the people in the culture with whom you will be working openly talk about your credentials.
3. **Present yourself** as sincere, professional, and confident.
4. **Act reserved** with male colleagues (and formal).
5. **Wear tasteful conservative clothing**, especially in male hierarchical cultures.
6. **Express your opinions** politely, diplomatically, and tactfully.

Adler[27] also emphasizes the following words of advice: If a woman is going to work in a society with culturally based sexism, when asked about your marital status, it is helpful to have pre-prepared answers so that you answer with grace. In more "macho" cultures, be culturally sensitive. Allow men to pay for your drinks, food, and cab. It also helps to include a businessman in your work dinners to ensure the message is sent that the dinner is work only. In hierarchical cultures, respect peoples titles, and introduce your educational background and accomplishments.

The difficulties that women may encounter when working on a foreign assignment depend to a certain extent on the social and economic context of the country in which they are conducting business, and on the individuals with whom they come into contact. Both the woman international manager and the company she represents can take steps to minimize any negative aspects.

Lay the groundwork. Do not surprise a client. Before any meeting, regardless of the gender of the participants, provide adequate information about the agenda and who will be present.

Practice what is preached. If a corporation empowers women managers and treats them equally and seriously in business dealings abroad, it should ensure that women are also treated equally and fairly in the organization. Success begins at home.

Consider women and men for international positions. Do not rely on the assumption that women will not want to accept the position.

Provide proper cross-cultural training and preparation courses. Training is vital to women's success abroad. Specific assistance should include what to expect from male superiors, peers, clients, and subor-

Do not surprise a client.

dinates and how to handle uncomfortable situations, such as discrimination.

Be realistic. Women managers abroad suffer from the same culture shock as men. It is important to keep expectations reasonable, build trust, and create professional relationships.

BALANCING WORK AND FAMILY

Balancing family and the work life is a major concern of most working women.

Balancing family and the work life is a major concern of most working women. Though in the past women were required to make a clear choice as to whether they wanted to have a career or a family, today a professional career and motherhood are no longer considered mutually exclusive. Nevertheless, working mothers tend to have to juggle two full-time jobs. Knight interviewed a series of women who were either middle or senior managers and who had recently become new mothers.[28] All of the women interviewed stated that motherhood had given them a new perspective on their work and that this was, in general, very positive. They also felt that motherhood had given them a new sense of confidence enabling them to let their personalities become apparent in the workplace. Planning was critical to juggle the daily demands of family and work. Nevertheless, many women, particularly in Europe and in Asia, choose to take a break from professional work once they begin a family.

It is certainly a strain to balance one's personal and professional responsibilities. In the United States, for example, there is still a lingering belief that it is the woman's responsibility to take care of children. Some women, having reached a critical point in their career and personal life, are forced to make the choice of one over the other. Conversely, the European Union has made it possible to take time off from work to raise children without even the thought that a career is being put in jeopardy.

Many American businesses are addressing the bottom-line implications of employees' need for affordable and high-quality child and elder care. Wiley Harris of GE Capital Services states that "Every employee is important to our company's health, and when employees are distracted by family issues, we lose productivity."[29] The Family and Medical Leave Act of 1993 was a response to concerns from men and women about being able to care for family members at critical life stages without the risk of job loss. Even with its enactment, the United States continues to compare poorly with other developed countries such as France, Sweden, Canada, and Finland, where family care is institutionalized. Many women, although able to take the time off without the risk of losing their jobs, cannot do so for monetary reasons.

COMPANY INITIATIVES TO BREAK THE GLASS CEILING

Most companies have put into place specific programs to assist in breaking down barriers impeding a woman's progression. Many include a combination of flexible work arrangements, mentoring, women's support groups, and leadership development. Various companies have also developed supports and structures designed to advance women.

A Tracking System

Accenture is the winner of the "2003 Catalyst award for Innovative Programs to Help Women Advance in the Workplace." Accenture developed a global "Great Place to Work for Women" initiative and uses a variety of innovative processes such as geographic scorecards, global surveys, and performance appraisals to guarantee that company leadership remains accountable for the initiative's results. Joe Forehand, Accenture chairman and CEO, states that "empowerment without opportunity is useless. At Accenture, we've focused on fostering a more inclusive work environment. Our Great Place to Work for Women program is one way we're enabling women to take charge of their careers and move into broader leadership roles."

A Support Structure

IBM, Kodak, and 3M have women's networks in place to help promote women's careers. Apparently, one-third of all *Fortune* 100 companies have such networks aimed at developing skills, career building, and supporting women.

Mentoring Programs

Research has demonstrated that mentoring is a critical part of career success. Mentoring is defined as "a cooperative and nurturing relationship between a more experienced businessperson and a less experienced person who wants to learn about a particular business and gain valuable insight into some of the unspoken subtleties of doing business."[30] Many experts claim that it is beneficial to have more than one mentor present within an organization and that these mentors should be at different levels. Mentoring comes into play at crucial points in an individual's career and can be an effective source of advice and encouragement.

Burke and McKeen found, however, that men and women view mentoring in different ways.[31] It is often more difficult for women than men

Research has demonstrated that mentoring is a critical part of career success.

to find appropriate mentors. Many Internet sites have popped up in the past few years offering women the opportunity to network with each other in a nontraditional setting. The U.S. Small Business Administration has set up a specific program, open to all women, specifically focused on helping women entrepreneurs and those considering becoming entrepreneurs.

Work Still to Be Done

Although women have achieved significant advances since entering the workplace, much remains to be done, for women are as qualified and talented as men. Companies need to take more responsibility to fully integrate women into their environments at all levels of the corporate hierarchy. Companies that champion diversity champion women. Some issues to consider include the following.

Increasing the flow of information and educating women about current issues. It is only with concrete facts and information about women's position in the workplace that any calibration of gains can be measured. Catalyst, a nonprofit organization focused on women's issues in the workplace, has taken a wonderful role in initiating this process. When women appreciate where they have been and understand the issues that confront them, they can see and decide where the future lies.

Demonstrating CEO commitment. As the corporate leader, the CEO has the most significant influence on the direction and vision of the firm. It is through her or his direction that a "persistent campaign of incremental changes that discover and destroy the deeply embedded roots of discrimination" will occur.[32]

Closing the pay gap. A true merit system distinguishes individuals based on their effort and skills and rewards each person for their work regardless of gender. Men and women work equally hard in the same positions; their pay should reflect this equality.

Increasing recruitment, providing training opportunities, and placing women in high-profile positions. Companies should step up their efforts to recruit and train qualified women and ensure that more women get access to "line" positions versus being immediately segmented into "staff" positions.

SELECTED WOMEN MANAGERS' VIEWS

How have several specific women succeeded? Are they going about business differently? The August 5, 1996 edition of *Fortune*, ran an article titled "Women, Sex and Power." Contrary to what the title might suggest, the article focused on seven women who are the best of the best in their fields of business. Among the women were Charlotte Beers of Ogilvy & Mather and Jill Barad of Mattel. These women are part of a new female elite who are changing the way women reach the top.

Have confidence in yourself. In the past, many women felt obliged to hide their femininity so as to be seen as managers first and women second. Many women in today's business world no longer view their sexuality as a hindrance. Despite the fact that the office is often still male dominated, they are no longer attempting to become more male-like or androgynous in order to be promoted.

Survive and overcome difficult working conditions. Most women, especially of older generations, have had to face discrimination from men and women alike. Charlotte Beers remembers, saying, "Early in my career, during my first week at J. Walter Thomson in Chicago, I had a secretary who asked the company for a transfer. She told me, 'No offense, but I want to work for a man who's going to move ahead,'" The story goes that two years later, the secretary, impressed by Beers' stellar career path, asked to come back and Beers, who liked her honesty, accepted.[33] Many successful businesswomen have had to overcome adverse working conditions and have been able to build their careers during these tough moments.

Do things differently. Many women are successful by incorporating aspects of their personality into their work or by daring to do things differently. In the end, many of them drastically change the way business in their field is done. Linda Marcelli, of Merrill Lynch, started selling stocks by setting up personal meetings instead of cold calling. Anita Roddick was an international hit with her "Body Shop" that brought environmental consciousness to a new level.

Have your own leadership style—neither "feminine" nor "masculine." Women are often described as having a more "open" approach to management, relying on consensus building as opposed to the old style of command and control. Recent research demonstrates that women and men executives in similar positions demonstrate more similar behaviors than dissimilar. Wajcman discusses her recent research examining current female and male managers' perceptions and attitudes. Her data show that "women who have made it into senior positions are in most respects indistinguishable from the men in equivalent positions. In fact, the similarities between women and men far outweigh the differences between women and men as groups."[34]

Many women are concerned that the debate as to whether men and women exhibit different leadership styles continues to perpetuate typical stereotypes of women as "soft" managers. As Adler and Izraeli point out, managers (male and female) in the United States have tended to identify stereotypically "masculine" (aggressive) characteristics as managerial and stereotypically "feminine" (cooperative and communicative) characteristics as "unmanagerial."[35]

Women are often described as having a more "open" approach to management.

More and more companies are aggressively trying to advance women's issues. "Woman-friendly" companies have been proven to provide a more beneficial environment to *men* and women.[36] In Great Britain, several programs have been created to promote women. Quite a few organizations have created a development program specifically for women to help them attain the necessary qualifications, career development, and guidance within an internal organization.

THE FUTURE OF WOMEN IN LEADERSHIP POSITIONS

The obvious long-term goal is gender equality in the workplace.

The obvious long-term goal is gender equality in the workplace: equal job opportunity, equal pay, equal advancement. Once gender parity and equality are achieved, management can redirect its additional time and energy to further enhance corporate objectives.

Increased emphasis on strategic alliances between women. The May 10, 1999 *Wall Street Journal* reported on a new conference "Women & Co.," designed for high-level, high-powered women executives from across the nation. The conference not only facilitated female-specific networking and alliance-building opportunities, but also educated the women on current hot topics such as crisis management, the media, dealing with investors, risk management, and selecting CEOs and directors.[37] With the steady increase of women in management, female-to-female mentoring systems and extended support networks and associations will gain significant power in lobbying for change and making significant inroads in the boardroom.

More women and men working out of the home. Advances in technology combined with more family-friendly businesses will allow women and men to easily work out of the home and spend quality time with their children or elder relatives. E-mail, fax, and tele- and video-conferencing capabilities are just a few of the high tech conveniences that enable all workers to create an office and work productively for their firm in the home. New advances are surely in the pipeline to further facilitate working out of the home. As a result, both the mother and father will have more time to devote to raising the children and sharing family duties.

More woman-owned businesses. Often, women who get discouraged with the traditional workplace create their own businesses. If companies are slow to respond to women's needs, we can expect more woman-owned businesses that will change the fabric of today's workplace. Woman-owned businesses have already doubled as women are recognizing the value of creating one's own work environment, calling the shots, making the hours, and reaping the monetary rewards. Furthermore, with their comprehensive workplace knowledge, these women will design a workplace that is woman-friendly.

Changed roles within the home. With more and more couples working full-time, duties in the home will become equally divided. Couples will distribute tasks equally, including chores, child rearing, and elder care, and pay more for services such as house cleaning, shopping, laundry, prepared meals, etc. As women continue to make more money, it will be more acceptable and common to see a "house husband" as the couple together decides the payoff with one breadwinner in the family.

Heightened development of family-friendly policies. As companies value their human capital more, policies could include allowing for two-year "sabbaticals" for either parent to raise children, with computerized "update" training and a guaranteed job upon return. "A few employers, including Eli Lilly and IBM, guarantee a job after a three-year leave. Such policies take the heat off parents."[38] Via Internet education, companies could update these employees on current corporate issues or the latest technology in order to ensure that the employee transitions effectively back into the company.

Acceptance of paid paternity leave designed for new fathers. When companies offer paid paternity leave, they are further encouraging the active role of the father in the family unit. While many women get paid time off after the birth of a child, most fathers are left out of the loop, with only evenings and weekends to help out with the child rearing. While some companies offer time off for the new parent, paid paternity leave is rare. Nevertheless, in France, the government recently offered two weeks of paid paternity leave to all new fathers.

Growth of part-time, contract, temporary, or freelance career paths. If companies do not adequately respond to working parents' needs, the part-time, contract, temporary, and freelance career options will boom. These types of careers give parents the flexibility to combine work and family life, yet without the responsibility of a full-fledged, self-owned business. Many intelligent and educated women choose to stay home with their families because they are forced to choose between work and a family; these types of careers can offer a lucrative middle ground. *The Wall Street Journal* reported an increase in the profitable temporary executive business, where an individual is hired to do high-powered work for a short period of time.[39]

New markets will emerge to support the career woman's work/life balance. Changes in the workforce and consumer demographics inevitably lead to increased opportunity for new markets. This could translate into increased opportunities in the service industry, retail, food, health care, child care, and elder care to meet the needs of working women. Convenience, portability, and ease of use will become more vital as people have less and less time for complicated items.

Women who choose to be full-time mothers and homemakers should be respected for their choice. However, we recognize and believe that

In France, the government recently offered two weeks of paid paternity leave to all new fathers.

the role of nurturer within the home is increasingly being seen and acknowledged as a role both men and women fulfill.

CONCLUSIONS

Careful observation reveals a rapidly increasing number of countries and companies moving away, for the first time, from their historical men-only pattern of senior leadership. Of the 47 women who have served in their country's highest political leadership position—either as president or prime minister- more than two-thirds have come into office in just the last decade, and all but seven are the first woman their country has ever selected. Similarly, among the current women CEOs leading major global companies, almost all are the first woman whom their particular company has ever selected. The question is no longer "is the pattern changing?" but rather "Which companies will take advantage of the trend and which will fall behind?" Which companies and countries will lead in recognizing and understanding the talents that women bring to leadership, and which will limit their potential by clinging to historic men-only patterns. . . .[40]

Depending on the country, different societal forces have contributed to increasing female presence in high-level positions within corporations. Women in the United States have benefited from affirmative action and equal opportunity laws that hold employers accountable for promoting women. During the 1980s, French legislation was passed that made unions the "porte-parole" of women's progress.[41] Women in Europe have also benefited from a history of trail blazing with regard to family-friendly laws.[42] In Eastern Europe, quotas were set regarding the number of women in local management.[43] In Germany, women are becoming increasingly present in the political arena. Nevertheless, despite recent progress in most countries, women's advancement in the business arena has been steady but slow. As we move into the twenty-first century, companies will need to increasingly reflect this diversity in all levels of their workforce.

The problem of how to get women in those positions of great importance throughout the enterprise still remains. Numerous barriers still exist for women across the globe. Women have made incredible advances, yet one of their next great challenges will be to assure proportional representation in senior management positions. But it is perhaps no longer in the hands of women to assure that their voices are heard in business. Demographic projections in the United States, for example, show that new workforce entrants over the next 20 years will be 15% white males. The other components of the workforce will be women and members of minority groups.[44] A strong business imperative can be made that companies who do not address the needs of their women employees (as well as employees of minority cultures) in

In Germany, women are becoming increasingly present in the political arena.

terms of recruiting, promotion, and career development will suffer several long-term consequences.

- Not being viewed as an employer of choice.
- Undervaluing top performers, therefore not using employees' full potential.
- Losing a competitive edge.

In today's competitive world, ignoring the potential of the greatest (in number and in potential) component of your workforce is more than just an oversight—it is extremely costly.

MIND STRETCHING

1. What are the cultural expectations of women in your culture?
2. What are the stereotypes of women that are believed and communicated in your culture?
3. What is your personal view of women's role
   - In relationships?
   - In family?
   - In business?
   - In politics?
4. What are the specific issues women may experience in business in specific countries in North America, South America, Europe, Asia, the Middle East, and Africa?

REFERENCES

1. Meyerson, D. E. and Fletcher, J. K. "A Modest Manifesto for Shattering the Glass Ceiling," *Harvard Business Review on Women in Business.* Boston: Harvard Business School Publishing, 2005, p. 94.
2. Welch, J. S. "Ideas the Welch Way," "What's Holding Women Back," *Business Week.* February 13, 2006, p. 100.
3. Holstein, W. J. "An American in Europe Bridges a Cultural Divide," www.nytimes.com/2005/12/04/business/.
4. Adler, N. and Izraeli, D. "Where in the World Are the Women Executives?" *The Business Quarterly*, London, 1994.
5. Meyerson, D. E. and Fletcher, J. K. "A Modest Manifesto for Shattering the Glass Ceiling," *Harvard Business Review on Women in Business,* Harvard Business School Press, 2005, pp. 69–94.
6. *Catalyst 2002 Census of Women Corporate Officers and Top Earners of the Fortune 500.*

7. Meyerson, D. E. and Fletcher, J. K. "A Modest Manifesto for Shattering the Glass Ceiling," *Harvard Business Review on Women in Business*, Harvard Business School Press, 2005, p. 70.
8. Ibid., p. 94.
9. "The Conundrum of the Glass Ceiling," *The Economist*, July 23, 2005, pp. 63–65.
10. BBC NEWS, Briton's "accept" pay sexism, 2/28/06, www.newsvote.bbc.co.uk/1/hi/business/3038394.stm.
11. "Most Powerful Women in Business, The Power 50, Why are some women more successful in some countries than in others?" *Fortune*. September 27, 2002.
12. www.AdvancingWomen2003.org
13. www.charitywire.com
14. Glanton, E. Womenconnect.com. "Pay Gap Endures at Highest Levels," AP News, November 10, 1998.
15. Glass Ceiling Commission. The Glass Ceiling Fact-Finding Report. "Good Business: Making Full Use of the Nation's Human Capital," 1995, p. 15.
16. "She Works, He Doesn't," *Newsweek*, May 12, 2003.
17. *Catalyst 2002 Census of Women Corporate Officers and Top Earners of the Fortune 500.*
18. BBC NEWS, Briton's "accept" pay sexism, 2/28/06. www.newsvote.bbc.co.uk/1/hi/business/3038394.stm.
19. "The Conundrum of the Glass Ceiling," *The Economist*, July 23, 2005, pp. 63–65.
20. Adler, N. and Izraeli, D. "Where in the World Are the Women Executives?" *The Business Quarterly*, London, 1994.
21. Wernick, E. *Preparedness, Career Advancement, and the Glass Ceiling*, Glass Ceiling Commission, May 1994.
22. Adler, N. J. and Izraeli, D. (eds.). "Competitive Frontiers: Women Managing Across Border," *Competitive Frontiers*. Cambridge, MA: Blackwell Publishers, 1994, p. 28.
23. Ibid, p. 27.
24. Solomon, C. M., *Women Managers in the Global Workplace: Success through Intercultural Understanding*, Mobility, January 2006.
25. Adler, N. J. *Organizational Behavior*, Third Edition. Cincinnati, OH: South-Western Publishing, 1997, pp. 308–309.
26. Adler, N. J. *International Dimensions of Organizational Behavior*, 4th Edition. Southwestern, Thomson Learning, Canada, 2002.
27. Op. cit.
28. Tanton, M. *Women in Management: A Developing Presence*. London: Rutledge, 1994, p. 82.
29. http://www.pathfinder.com/ParentTime/workfamily/workcare.html
30. www.sysop@advancingwomen.com
31. Karsten, M. F. *Management and Gender: Issues and Attitudes*. Westport, CT: Praeger Publishers, 1994.
32. Meyerson, D. E. and Fletcher, J. K. "A Modest Manifesto for Shattering the Glass Ceiling," *Harvard Business Review on Women in Business*, Harvard Business School Press, 2005, p. 70.
33. "Women, Sex and Power," *Fortune*, August 5, 1996.

34. Wajcman, J. *Managing Like a Man.* University Park, PA: Pennsylvania State University Press, 1998.

35. Adler, N. J. and Izraeli, D. J. (eds.). *Women in Management Worldwide.* London: M.E. Sharpe, Inc., 1988, pp. 20–24.

36. Wilkof, M. V. "Is Your Company and Its Culture Women-Friendly?" *The Journal for Quality and Participation,* June 1995.

37. Beatty, S. "A Power Confab for Exclusive Businesswomen," *The Wall Street Journal*, May 10, 1999.

38. Shellenberger, A. "Work & Family: The New Pace of Work Makes Taking a Break for Child Care Scarier," *The Wall Street Journal*, May 19, 1999.

39. "Work Week," *The Wall Street Journal*, May 11, 1999.

40. Adler, N. J. International Dimensions of Organizational Behavior, 4th Edition, 2002, Southwestern, Thomson Learning, Canada, pp. 173–174.

41. Adler, N. and Izraeli, D. "Where in the World Are the Women Executives?" *The Business Quarterly*, London, 1994.

42. Ibid.

43. Ibid.

44. Peters, T. *The Circle of Innovation*, New York: Alfred A. Knopf, Inc., 1997, p. 423.

MANAGING DIVERSITY IN THE GLOBAL WORK CULTURE

Modern psychology has demonstrated repeatedly that stimulus-response models are inaccurate representations of human behavior. Insofar as the same stimulus is interpreted differently by different individuals or groups, beliefs matter. The identity of individuals and groups in part shapes how they see the world; the way people see the world shapes how and when they perceive threat, as well as how they formulate their goals, assess constraints, process information, and choose strategies. Individuals are not passive receptors of environmental stimuli, but they actively construct representations of their environment.[1]

Movies . . . television often show people in an overly simplified way. This often takes the form of stereotypes . . . Challenge your children to question so they can develop an eye for sexism, racism and other prejudices.[2]

The globalization of economies and marketplaces including advances in communication technologies are transforming worldwide the workplace culture and the workforce. Workers are moving in greater numbers across borders and national cultures, increasing the diversity within societies and institutions.

Movies . . .

television often

show people in

an overly

simplified way.

LEARNING OBJECTIVES

The effective utilization of the talents of all employees is stated by most executives as the organizations' greatest asset but these executives often do not know how to accomplish this with an increasing multicultural workforce. This chapter will provide a basis and some implementation strategies on effectively managing a diverse workforce.

To unleash the talent and potential of this changing workforce, the public and private sectors are assessing their organizational systems to capitalize on the prevailing benefits of a diverse workforce and clientele. Although there is much controversy over the definitions of diversity and the organizational processes that may result, Thomas states that

> people want to act like diversity is synonymous with differences. They talk about diversity fracturing the country, fracturing the organization. For me diversity refers to both differences and similarities. So diversity, as opposed to fracturing, becomes the context within which you can talk about the ties that bind and also the differences that make us unique. . . . We can be different and still united. . . . Now it remains to be seen if we can come together and move forward in a united way around similarities and still be very different.[3]

The process of leveraging workforce diversity has many applications, and this chapter focuses on a few of them. We do want to stress that the strategy and subsequent actions in managing a diverse workforce are crucial and must be considered from a systemic standpoint. This is critical for a company to attain the end goal of maximizing employee potential, whether the employee belongs to the majority or minority group.

The process of leveraging workforce diversity has many applications.

DEFINING CULTURAL DIVERSITY

By valuing differences, companies are acknowledging the historic shifts in the makeup of the labor market. They realize that it is a business and bottom-line issue, for it involves motivating and communicating with diverse employees so that individual and combined work reflects each employee's highest potential.

Human diversity is popularly understood to refer to differences of color, ethnic origin, gender, sexual or religious preferences, age, and disabilities. Stated definitions of *organizational* diversity recognize a wide range of characteristics. According to American Express Financial Advisors, they include

> race, gender, age, physical ability, physical appearance, nationality, cultural heritage, personal background, functional experience, position in the organization, mental and physical challenges, family responsibilities,

sexual orientation, military experience, educational background, style differences, economic status, thinking patterns, political backgrounds, city/state/region of residence, IQ level, smoking preference, weight, marital status, nontraditional job, religion, white collar, language, blue collar, and height.[4]

Simons explains that diversity is related to the vast range of cultural differences requiring attention to facilitate living and working together effectively. This reality has stimulated strategies and interventions to deal with interactions between people different from one another. In his book, *EuroDiversity*, Simons quotes from the *Declaration of Cultural Diversity* issued by the European Union's Committee of Ministers. Exhibit 7.1 excerpts a portion of that statement which examines this concept from the perspective of national interchanges.

Of course, each human being is unique and our basic differences also stem from our perceptions of one another, influenced by our cultural backgrounds. Though originally we came from the same ancestors, through migration humans over time have uniquely developed physically, linguistically, and culturally. Our diversity is a reflection of how humans have dealt with universal problems of human nature including how humans relate to nature, time, activity, and relationships—something each culture has found their own unique solution.[5] South African Samuel Paul, a victim of apartheid, states, "Differences are not deficits to be changed and corrected, but gifts to be cherished and to enjoyed."[6]

> *"Differences are not deficits to be changed and corrected, but gifts to be cherished and to enjoyed."*

EXHIBIT 7.1[7]

INTER-NATION FRAMEWORK FOR CULTURAL DIVERSITY

1. Cultural diversity is expressed in the coexistence and exchange of culturally different practices and in the provision and consumption of culturally different services and products.
2. Cultural diversity cannot be expressed without the conditions for creative free expression and freedom of information existing in all forms of cultural exchange, notably with respects to audio-visual services.
3. Sustainable development, as defined in relations to cultural diversity, assumes that technological and other developments, which occur to meet the present, will not compromise the ability of future generations to meet their needs with respect to the production, provision, and exchange of cultural diverse services, products, and practices.

PEOPLE ON THE MOVE

It begins in Africa with a group of hunter-gatherers . . . It ends some 200,000 years later with their six and a half billion descendants spread across the Earth, living in peace or at war, believing in a thousand different deities or none at all, their faces aglow in the light of campfires and computer screens. In between is a sprawling saga of survival, movement, isolation, and conquest, most of it unfolding in the silence of prehistory. . . . The human genetic code, or genome, is 99 percent identical throughout the world. What's left is the DNA responsible for our individual differences—in eye color or disease risk. . . .

In the late 1980s Allan Wilson and his colleagues used mtDNA to determine human ancestry. By comparing mtDNA and Y chromosomes from people of diverse populations, they were able to map human migration originating in Africa many years ago.[8] "Migration has helped to create humans, drove us to conquer a planet, shaped our societies and promises to reshape them again. . . . If they [people] had not moved and intermingled as they did, they probably would have evolved into a different species."[9]

The social fabric in the host countries is being reconfigured and strained by massive waves of immigrants, legal or illegal, who come to live and work permanently or temporarily in another country. The demographic changes are often from developing economies to industrialized nations. The mass migrations are usually in pursuit of a better way of life; however, this movement of people from different cultures and backgrounds has frequently caused costly, complex social and financial problems for the host culture struggling to absorb the new arrivals.[10]

In addition to business, government, and global travelers as well as tourists, there are also three other categories of people on the move:[11]

- ■ **Refugees:** People living outside their country of nationality, afraid to return for reasons of race, religion, social affiliation, or political opinion. At the beginning of the twenty-first century, there were an estimated 30 million internationally recognized refugees, many of whom sought asylum from some kind of persecution or discrimination.[12]
- ■ **Internally displaced persons:** People forced to flee their homes because of armed conflict but who have not yet crossed international boundaries. Like refugees, they have generally lost all they own and are not protected by their national governments. Today we estimate 30 million internally displaced people.[13]
- ■ **Migrant workers:** People, both skilled and unskilled, who work outside their home country, including the legally employed migrants without legal permission to work abroad, and undocumented

The human genetic code, or genome, is 99 percent identical throughout the world.

immigrants. It is estimated that there are as many as 50 million migrant workers and their families worldwide, with as many as half of them illegal.

Exhibit 7.2 summarizes the dual impact of the ongoing push and pull of immigration.

The immigrant situation in North America has been highlighted by Dr. Lionel Laroche. He documents that between 1991 and 1996, over 1 million people immigrated to Canada, and another 6 million plus to the United States, but the country of origin differs somewhat in each case. Canada appears to attract new arrivals mainly from Asia, Poland, the United Kingdom, and the United States; while the United States draws newcomers not only from Asia, but also from Latin America (especially Mexico), as well as Haiti and the Caribbean.

These recent arrivals bring new energy, talent, and enthusiasm to the pursuit of freedom and other democratic benefits, while adding both human and financial capital. The mix of citizenry, ethnicity, and tribal backgrounds is like a mosaic. Thus, the global work culture is best characterized by two words—*change* and *diversity*. It is well to remind ourselves that, just as in nature, diversity makes for adaptation.

As the twenty-first century begins, global leaders who understand what is happening to societies and workplaces should also be aware of two other countertrends impacting world development.

The global work culture is best characterized by two words— change and diversity.

■ Resurgence of the world's attention on people's interest in their ethnic identities, religious roots, and ancient affiliations as related to conflict that stems from discontent. "One-sixth, at most, of the world's population identifies with politically active cultural groups. More precisely a survey . . . has identified 268 politically significant national and minority peoples in the larger countries of the world. The outer bound of potential supporters for these ethnopolitical movements is slightly more than one billion, or 17.7 percent of the global population."[14]

■ Emergence of transnational ethnic groups or *global tribes* who have a major influence on international trade and the economy. The latter, whatever their origin, are frequently venture capitalists, financiers, arbitrageurs, and entrepreneurs who benefit by the discipline of their traditions. These commercial tribes are bound together by common heritage, language, and culture.

A third trend to recognize is the desire of migrants everywhere for freedom, democracy, and protection of their human rights, including at work. This means that leadership should always be committed to resolving any conflicts that arise, with full respect toward the rights of all individuals involved. The United Nations has best articulated their aspirations in its Declaration of Human Rights. Those who would

Exhibit 7.2[15]
Root Causes of Immigration

When people leave their homes generally there is a "push" factor from the sending country and a "pull" factor from the receiving country. Of course, individual, religious, political, or economic reasons play a critical role.

Principal "push" factors include:	"Pull" factors in receiving countries include:
■ War and civil strife, including religious conflicts	■ Substantial immigration markets and channels opened up in the West
■ Economic decline and rising poverty	■ Family reunion with workers already living in Europe
■ Rising unemployment	■ Safety
■ Population pressures (more specifically, burgeoning numbers of unemployed youth)	■ Freedom from fear or violence, persecution, hunger, and poverty
■ Political instability	■ Economic opportunity
■ Large-scale natural disasters and ecological degradation	■ Education
■ Human rights violations	■ Maintaining ethnic identity
■ Denial of education and health care for selected minorities, and other kinds of persecution	■ Access to advances in communication and technology
■ Government resettlement policies that threaten ethnic integrity	
■ Resurgent nationalism	

be competent and nondiscriminatory global leaders recognize that both society and the work environment must follow the declaration's guidance.

GLOBALIZATION AND DIVERSITY

Globalization is shaping our world today, and cross-cultural conflict is only one by-product.

Advances in telecommunications, mass transportation, and technology and changes in the global political arena have led to the emergence

Globalization is shaping our world today

of a global, information-oriented culture. With the expansion of globalization, awareness of the global complexities involved in cross-cultural interactions has been expanding. Globalization is at both the macrolevel, exemplified by the expansion of technology through business, and at the microlevel, exemplified by the individual use of laptops, cellular phones, and the Internet, greatly increasing interaction. Though it can be said that at the macrolevel there is a form of global culture around the use of technology, communication, and business; at the microlevel, the experiences, values, perceptions, and behaviors of individuals vary within and across national and ethnic cultures.

These wide-ranging forces of differing languages, customs, beliefs, and values are illustrated through the behavior of individuals of a particular culture and through groups of individuals working together. Cultural behavior is exemplified in many ways: by a culture's legal system, which enforces socially acceptable behavior; how it avoids or resolves conflict; and its social protocols, religious beliefs, international relationships, and business practices.

The shift in the global workforce from homogeneous to heterogenous groups causes workers to form coalitions and alliances on a new basis that moves beyond obvious differences of race, gender, color or clothing. Diversity initiatives facilitate such integration within the work environment by counteracting cross cultural conflict, and racism and prejudice, indicated in Exhibit 7.3.

EXHIBIT 7.3
FORCES UNDERMINING RACISM

Modern genetics has shown the errors of 19th century eugenics. Systematic genetic differences between people from different parts of the world, though they exist, are small when compared to the variations between people from the same place. The visible differences, such as skin color, are the result of a mere handful of genes. Under the skin, humanity is remarkably homogeneous. . . .

Racism, in other words, can be eliminated.

Racism is actually an unfortunate by-product of another phenomenon—a tendency to assign people to "coalition groups," and to use whatever cues are available, be they clothing, accent, or skin color, to slot individuals into such groups or "stereotype" them . . . The good news is that experiments done by researchers suggest such stereotypes are easily dissolved and replaced with others. Racism, in other words, can be eliminated.

Source: "The Origins of Racism—Them." *The Economist*, December 1, 2001, p. 63.

Global Diversity and Conflict

Because our world is interconnected, we are in constant contact with our differences, characterized by varying cultures, ethnicities, religions, fundamental beliefs and values. From the beginning of our existence, humans have lived in alternating states of peace and conflict. When in conflict, it is difficult for individuals to perform to their potential.

Human discord results from many factors. Throughout history, there are examples of forced assimilation of minority cultures into the dominant culture, in both nations and organizations. However, consistently, history has shown that few cultures can be completely assimilated into another. There are consistent global examples of the differential treatment of various ethnic groups in political, social, and economic areas. Statistics[15] best illustrate this example.

"Disadvantages" means socially derived inequalities in material well-being or political access in comparison with other social groups. The Minorities at Risk project gathered information for the 1980s on the political and economic inequalities and discrimination affecting some 220 politically active ethnic groups.

The results illustrate serious and pervasive interethnic inequalities.

- 16 groups (7%) had political advantages relative to the majority.
- 32 groups (14%) were no different from the majority.
- 57 groups (25%) were slightly disadvantaged compared to the majority.
- 59 groups (26%) were substantially disadvantaged compared to the majority.
- 60 groups (27%) were extremely disadvantaged compared to the majority.

In the chaos theory, or "butterfly effect," events in one part of the world can significantly affect the other side of the world. Likewise, events in the political arena spill into the business arena, and political oppression is linked to social and economic oppression. "Traditional concepts, like the balance of power or ideology, are . . . not as useful as they once were in explaining the sources of . . . conflict, particularly when conflicts are rooted in a complex and rich brew of ethno nationalism, religion, socioeconomic grievances, . . . globalized markets, and geopolitical shifts."[16]

Humanity must learn to appreciate the fact that our common survival and the satisfaction of our universal needs and concerns are interdependently linked. Cultures are no longer isolated. All must work toward our common survival through multilateral action that reflects appreciation and acceptance of differences, with mutual respect for each other. In order to do so effectively, learning conflict analysis and resolution skills are necessary in today's world. An example of one

In the chaos theory, or "butterfly effect," events in one part of the world can significantly affect the other side of the world.

organization that seeks to address this need is Stirling University. This school has recently developed a course for leaders, students, writers, and politicians to learn skills in conflict resolution, management and prevention. Course director Vassilis Fouskas states: "Although we would all wish otherwise, there is little likelihood that the world in the 21st century will be a better place to live in, or that it will be without conflict, war, dictatorship, terrorism, genocide or poverty. The least we can do as academics and teachers is to try to produce serious-minded, prospective leaders able to understand the past, intervene in the present and shape a more just, fair and equitable world."[17]

An excellent example of working together for the common good is the European Union.

European Union Diversity and E-Europe

The phenomenon of growing diversity in the work environment is worldwide.

The phenomenon of growing diversity in the work environment is worldwide. But Europe today is a prime example as 27 national cultures now seek to integrate as members of the European Union (EU). Bulgaria and Romania were admitted to the European Union in January 2007. What began as a smaller economic community seeking a greater share of the global market has evolved into a grand plan of sociopolitical and even military association with its own unique constitution. Simons has articulated the challenge of diversity and globalization.

> Our present diversity challenges are being determined by forces shaping the economy and business world generally and cannot be discussed in isolation from them. Diversity is about globalization, organizational learning, and the growing importance of knowledge management, just as much as it is about recruitment, equal opportunity, workforce demographics, and social integration. It concerns the information technology that is almost daily revolutionizing communication. It affects interactive networking and transport. It is perhaps the critical issue in many mergers and acquisitions—and often the least attended to! It is at the root of how organizations transform themselves....
>
> Historically, Europe, or the "Old World" is different from the lands in which European emigrants settled and made their own. Europe has always been very diverse, and Europeans have always been conscious of their diversity. They differ from North Americans in what they do about it. In the best of times, Europeans believe that "good fences make good neighbors." In the worst of times, those who attempt to shape or create or reshape those borders are painted in blood.... Diverse by nature, the European Union got its start in the search for peace and prosperity after history's most devastating war (World War II, 1938–1945)... in Europe, economic cooperation among its diverse peoples was the starting point. Only later did this cooperative enterprise begin to take responsibility for a social and cultural integration whose necessity, utility, and desirability continue to be questioned every step of the way.[18]

The Cultural Diversity Market Study reported that the European Committee for Standardization (CEN) has been focusing its activities on cultural diversity and e-business.[19] "E-Europe feels that global issues increasingly demand global response, and that is the reason that there is a strong need for a collective European approach. Globalisation, enlargement, and internationalisation are keywords in E-Europe. This requires consideration of the cultural and linguistic diversity of Europe, thereby giving equal chances to all businesses and citizens in Europe to benefit from the Information Society." This study[20] related three main conclusions:

1. An identified lack of awareness regarding the importance of cultural diversity was apparent. Diversity was not a high priority of EU industry or its consumers; however, there were many activities handled in a multicultural manner.
2. Issues surrounding cultural diversity are addressed primarily from a technical perspective, with little or no quantitative look at the costs and benefits.
3. The study recognizes the need for cooperation within the international environment and within industry.

The European Union has had to overcome periodic conflicts in the past by working together across cultural differences to build a multinational, multicultural, multilingual powerhouse. In business today, people are the most important source of sustainable competitive advantage. Every person brings a unique combination of background, heritage, gender, religion, education, and experience to the workplace. This diversity represents an enormous source of new ideas and vitality. The subject of increasing immigration, especially in Europe, is also discussed in Chapters 10 and 14.

A MACROSYSTEMIC PERSPECTIVE ON ORGANIZATIONAL DIVERSITY

Global leaders understand the complexity of global business and are always studying it from multiple perspectives. They understand that there are many ways to perceive a particular situation and that each perspective helps create the larger picture.

The talented and systems-oriented global leader oversees an organizational system that enables each employee to reach her or his potential. Synergistic leaders understand that to influence the macrosystem through the interaction of each individual, the microsystemic aspect, the whole organization is efficiently empowered. In the event of an international merger or acquisition, the cultural variance can have enormous negative effects if the differences and systemic discrepancies

Global leaders understand the complexity of global business and are always studying it from multiple perspectives.

are not properly addressed. For example, in 1996 Ericsson bought a company based in California, called Raynet and in taking its usual integration approach, quickly discovered that a majority of the staff whose skills were crucial to Raynet had left. Subsequently, Ericsson took a more hands-off approach in its acquisition, allowing the organizational culture to maintain its system. Taking too much of a hands-off approach after a merger or acquisition can prove to be risky as well. "Such failures of management reflect cultural differences."[21] Culturally synergistic leaders address the cultural organizational systems allowing for the *highest level of competence*, building on diversity reflected at all levels of the organization.

Thomas and Ely conducted a six-year study that researched the process of solving the systemwide challenge of leveraging the full potential of a diverse workforce.[22] From the standpoint of an employee, cultural diversity and the multiplicity of benefits that can be fully engaged, the leader who enforces a simple approach to addressing diversity in an organization was found to be holistically inadequate, which resulted in the opposite outcome. The results of and the recommendations from this study are worth noting in some detail, offering global leadership a framework to understand how to effectively leverage cultural organizational diversity from a systemic perspective.

The simple assumption of increasing number representation of diversity was used to investigate its link to organizational effectiveness. The study found that, in fact, it (i.e., number representation) inhibited organizational effectiveness as employees are unable to bring their "whole" self to the workplace.

Companies use two paradigms, in general, to address workforce diversity. However, they were found to be counterproductive, creating more problems and inferior employee performance. A third paradigm emerged from this study, which portrayed an organization in which leadership plays a fundamental and crucial role through systemic analysis while redefining cultural variance or diversity and its subsequent actions, thus enabling each "individual to work to her or his potential." This organization can actualize its goal of improving organizational processes for the company and cultivating a high level of productivity at all levels of the organization.

A short synopsis of the three paradigms is as follows.

■ The Discrimination-and-Fairness Paradigm, characterized by leadership that values the equality of all employees. These are often bureaucratic, controlled structures that have easily observable culture. Its benefits are demographic diversity and promotion of fair treatment; however, the limitations of this paradigm were significant. Disagreements, wrongly interpreted, often did not generate multiple ways of leading, working, or viewing the market. The result is a workforce unable to work to its potential or to be open about ideas, and the

Culturally synergistic leaders address the cultural organizational systems allowing for the highest level of competence.

inability of the organization to improve its own strategies, procedures, and performances.

■ The Access-and-Legitimacy Paradigm, which emerged between the 1980s and 1990s, is based on the acceptance and the honoring of diversity, with the main push toward a more diverse clientele by matching workplace demographics. The company focuses on matching diversity among its employees with the diversity of its clientele, focusing on difference but without assessing how those differences affect work. Workers are placed in positions, often being pigeonholed.

■ The third emerging paradigm is where the organization makes the most of its diverse employee and customer base. This paradigm surpasses the previous paradigms in promoting equal opportunity and acknowledging cultural differences as a valuable asset. These organizations tended to "*incorporate* employees' perspectives into the main work of the organization and to enhance work by rethinking primary tasks and redefining markets, products, strategies, missions, business practices, and even cultures. Such companies are using the learning-and-effectiveness paradigm for managing diversity and, by doing so, are tapping diversity's true benefits."[23]

There are eight preconditions for making a paradigm shift.

1. Leaders who appreciate the perspectives and approaches of a diverse workforce and who value the diversity of opinions.
2. Leaders who acknowledge that with this diversity of perspective and approaches comes conflict and learning opportunities.
3. The culture of the organization reflects high standards of performance from each employee.
4. With high standards of performance comes the need for the organization to continuously inspire the personal development of all employees, bringing out each employee's full potential.
5. The organizational culture must encourage openness through a high tolerance for differences of opinion. The organization understands the value of organizational learning that comes out of conflict.
6. All workers must feel valued by the organization. Workers must feel empowered and committed to the organization to feel comfortable in taking full advantage of their resourcefulness to enhance their job performance.
7. The mission of the organization must not only be well articulated and widely understood, but it must also be followed by each individual in the organization and enforced by all leadership. This organization understands that hypocrisy has severely negative consequences for employee performance and retention.

All workers must feel valued by the organization.

8. This organization must have a structure that is egalitarian and nonbureaucratic but still gets things done. At the same time, it promotes an exchange of ideas and welcomes constructive challenges to the status quo.

A MICROSYSTEM'S PERSPECTIVE

Synergistic leaders move from the macrosystem to the microsystem easily. They are aware that each works together.

Young wrote about the impact of "small" communicated messages on the entire organization.[24] From a 10-minute conversation, he estimated that two people can send from 40 to 120 micromessages to each other. Though the small isolated message might not have a significant effect, continuously repeated micromessages do. "Negative micromessages, 'micro-inequities,' erode organizations. They are a cumulative pattern of subtle, semi-conscious, devaluing messages, which discourage and impair performance, possibly leading to damaged self-esteem and withdrawal. For example, micro-inequities can occur within a team when a manager or a colleague communicates different messages to team members, often linked to differences between them."[25] Within the organization, one challenge that companies face is encouraging peak performance from every employee.

Cross-Cultural Training and Diversity Training

Leadership must also approach diversity from a macrosystemic perspective.

While the leadership must also approach diversity from a macrosystemic perspective, all employees must be made aware of company-wide efforts to leverage employee potential through the microsystemic efforts of enforced behavior and consistency. One way is through diversity training. Also known as cross-cultural training, pedagogically well-rounded training programs should include the following components:

- A cultural general section
- A section that emphasizes mastering cross-cultural communication
- A section that teaches cultural self-awareness
- A section that has cultural specifics
- A section that focuses on developing cross-cultural skills.[26]

As identified in the research by Moran,[27] if employees are subject to cross-cultural or diversity training that is mere "lip service," while at the same time these employees are experiencing negative micromessages that insinuate subtle discrimination in the workplace, then all training efforts are in vain. If negative micromessages are focused on employees who are of specific ethnic backgrounds and these messages are allowed to fester in the workplace, then the end result is a workplace where certain employees (usually women or people of color) cannot work to their full potential.

Globalization has prompted domestic business to seek diverse partners abroad, sometimes as part of the process of "de-verticalizing" an organization in which manufacturing is left to others.[28] Likewise, international competition is another powerful force behind the diverse work culture. C. K. Prahalad believes that a company's competitiveness comes from its ability to develop unique core competencies that spawn unanticipated products. Thus, the firm must (a) seek workers, regardless of gender, race, or ethnic origin, who possess these core competencies; (b) create a work community in which these high performers freely exchange information and knowledge about optimum work practices, and (c) share collective knowledge to keep ahead of competition.[29]

The challenge lies in establishing a diversity mission that is communicated through employee training, in which leadership attains its goals through systemwide enforced action, both behaviorally and communicatively. Changing the attitudes and behaviors of any workforce is challenging, but changing them in an unreceptive environment is an enormous task requiring a strong visionary blessed not only with persistence and stamina but also with the foresight to realize that it takes consistent enforcement of its policies. It is unrealistic to expect upper management, leadership, and employees to throw off their deeply embedded perceptions and embrace diversity overnight—no matter how charismatic or persuasive the leader. Rethinking diversity and establishing a companywide enforced strategy will positively affect every aspect of organizational culture.

The results of a study that researched the negative effects of organizational communicated messages on team members and on employees' performance follows.

Micro-Organizational Communication—A Study

Moran conducted a study that looked at a *Fortune* 100 company's diversity training from the perspective of expressed employee needs determined from focus group data.[30] It is found that this organization does have some characteristics determined to be within the first two paradigms identified by Thomas and Ely.[31] The study analyzed focus group data from four different ethnic groups regarding their organizational experiences in the company of their managers, mentors, and team members. It also looked at employees' perceived ability to progress and utilize their potential, all as related to organizational diversity. The second aspect of this study was a comparative look at employee expressed needs regarding diversity in the organization (determined through focus groups) and the yearly, strictly-adhered-to diversity training offered to, and required of, employees. Although this company has consistently been ranked in the top 25 of companies that

C. K. Prahalad believes that a company's competitiveness comes from its ability to develop unique core competencies.

value diversity, the results of the study has shown otherwise. The findings were as follows.

■ Employees had specific requests for the company to address precise issues around employee relations, mentor relationships, team leader communications, customer service strategies, and team interaction. Employees believed the company ignored these requests and did not properly address them.

■ This company endorsed a "diversity training" that was rigid in form and practice. Diversity trainers were required to follow word for word, page by page, an eight-hour training session, which employees were required to attend yearly.

■ The content of the training encompassed American legal reasons why diversity is required of this company, why prejudice and stereotypes are "bad," and specific activities that enforced political correctness in the workplace.

■ Employees had the genuine desire to learn concrete strategies to improve their productivity within their culturally diverse teams, and international customer relations, and improving mentor/manager to employee relationships. This was not addressed nor recognized by the diversity training offered by this company.

■ By the same token, the leadership was striving for and had accomplished excellent outside recognition of their diversity efforts. Employees found the training and organizational system practiced by this company to be wholly contradictory to the recognition and rewards endowed on the company for its diversity efforts.

■ As this company operates through the custom of team management, a phenomenon emerged that was found to be explained by focus groups and diversity training. A majority of the focus group members, who were employees of color, expressed an overwhelming experience of being disconnected from their mentors and were unable to succeed to their potential. Likewise, work group and team member relationships were strained as employees were unable to effectively work together, for their differences created more conflict than harmony. Negative microcommunications had a profound effect on these employees, resulting in a communication breakdown cycle that had the likely results of inferior team performance and substandard employee productivity.

In the Industrial Age, much emphasis was placed on loyalty to the organization, and many employees stayed with the same department or work unit throughout their career. As the old system disappears, the new work culture calls for dynamic, flexible, and responsible adults committed to personal and professional excellence.

In the diverse work environment previously described, loyalty is now transferred from the organization to the work team to one's individual career enhancement. It is crucial for leadership to enforce a diversity mission that is consistently acted upon. It must be inescapable for the organizations' leaders, from lower-level managers to the highest-level executive, and all employees must be able to see this enforcement. Leadership and employee productivity are exceptionally different in a liberated workforce, unencumbered by fear, false expectations of promotions, or the distractions of politics, favoritism, and trying to impress the boss.

Capitalizing on People Diversity

As a concept, diversity has different meanings and applications depending on where you are in the world. Within our Information Society, it is important to recognize that increasing *globalism* enormously impacts the workforce worldwide. For leading-edge organizations, globalism means the creation of a culture that embraces diversity to maximize the potential of personnel, especially through cohesive work teams.[32] For global managers, the challenge is to innovate ways to improve human commitment and performance at work. Because so many people achieve their full potential through their work and career, the new work culture fosters values like empowerment and character development, gauging success not in terms of organizational status but in the quality of work life. For metaindustrial workers, Nair suggests that the quest for personal/professional excellence and meaningful business relationships takes precedence over climbing the corporate ladder and the pursuit of external rewards.[33]

If results are to be achieved, readjusting to the demands of today's work realities requires a revision of cultural assumptions about the external global environment, the organization, the manager, and the group, as suggested in Exhibit 7.4, which illustrates the main components influencing the new work culture.[34]

Diversity has different meanings and applications depending on where yu are in the world.

EMPOWERING WORKERS

The concept of empowerment originated in North America. Generally, it refers to altering management style and transforming organizational setups from hierarchical to more participatory, sharing authority and responsibility with workers in a variety of ways. To empower means that leaders, be they heads of organizations, groups, or families, give individual members more freedom to act and therefore have more control over their own lives. Inclusion, rather than exclusion, particularly with regard to women and minorities, becomes the organizational norm based on the competence of the individual. This approach is more open and decentralized. Thus, team management is spreading across Asia and Europe. The Japanese, who are culturally group-oriented,

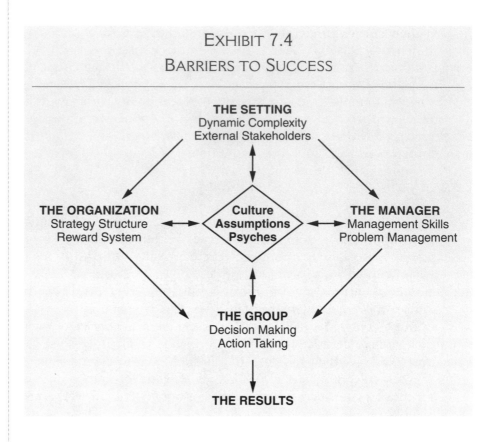

EXHIBIT 7.4
BARRIERS TO SUCCESS

THE SETTING
Dynamic Complexity
External Stakeholders

THE ORGANIZATION
Strategy Structure
Reward System

Culture Assumptions Psyches

THE MANAGER
Management Skills
Problem Management

THE GROUP
Decision Making
Action Taking

THE RESULTS

have been slow to empower women and minorities. Meanwhile, in some countries in Asia and Eastern Europe, empowerment is manifesting itself in political restructuring from authoritarianism to democracy and free enterprise, in which managers are freed from government or party controls and are beginning to involve their coworkers in the process of reshaping factories, cooperatives, and businesses. As globalization bridges the gap between national economies and peoples, empowerment does the same between management and labor.

Kouzes and Posner state that there is one clear and consistent message about empowerment: "feeling powerful—literally feeling 'able'—comes from a deep sense of being in control of our own lives."[35] When we feel we can determine our destiny and we have the assurance that the resources and individuals needed to support us are available, we can persist in our efforts. Conversely, when an individual is controlled by others, he or she may comply but not excel. Leadership is enhancing the individual's self-confidence and personal effectiveness. Kouzes and Posner have identified five fundamental strategies for empowering others.

1. *Ensure self-leadership by putting people in control of their lives.* When leaders share power and control with others, they demonstrate trust and respect in others' abilities. They, in essence, make

There is one clear and consistent message about empowerment.

a covenant with them that is reciprocal and mutually beneficial. Individuals who can affect their leaders are attached to them and committed to the give-and-take of the shared power of their responsibilities.

2. *Provide choice.* Providing individuals with options and discretion in the day-to-day operation of their jobs increases creativity and flexibility as one is freed from the standard set of rules and procedures. Jobs that are broadly designed and defined encourage this. Choice without skill can leave many employees overwhelmed.

3. *Develop competence.* Thus, developing competence is the third essential strategy for empowerment. Leaders must invest in developing individuals' skills and competencies. Giving employees opportunities to grow in their area of expertise, as well as in general business knowledge, enables them to act in the best interest of the corporation and the customer.

4. *Assign critical tasks.* Critical problems in an organization are usually addressed by those who have the most power. However, in innovative corporations like Chaparral Steel, research and development, for example, is brought to the factory floor. Empowerment encourages involvement and responsibility regarding tasks that employees can own and make excellent critical judgments about.

5. *Offer visible support.* Leaders who want to empower are highly visible and make conscientious efforts to have employees gain recognition and validation. Making connections and building strong networks and relationships is empowering. A leader introduces employees to others in the corporation or community who may help them along their career path as well. Individuals take responsibility for their own career development, while leaders create a work environment that encourages others to achieve their human potential.

Making connections and building strong networks and relationships is empowering.

Employees who feel powerless often hoard whatever shreds of power they possess, enforcing the organizational cultures that are often hierarchical and bureaucratic. Leaders, who share power, build profound trust and responsibility. Employees view improvements and communication as a two-way street, with the leader being as influenced by his or her workforce as the workforce is by management. Each is committed to effectively doing its part.

With a multicultural workforce and customer base, leadership must provide the vision, motivation, and reasons for commitment. For contemporary organizations and their workers, knowledge and innovation equal global marketplace power. To that end, the transformation of systems values diverse personnel for their competency rather than establishing barriers based on race, gender, or handicaps.

The popular manifestation of this trend is *worker participation* that involves employees in ongoing organizational change and development. Examples range from putting employees on the corporate board through devolving power to teams on the factory floor or in offices. Avis, the automobile rental company, empowers workers through 150 influential participation groups. The ultimate application is employee ownership where the workers actually become shareholders, often receiving equity by swapping contract concessions, as happened at Northwest and United Airlines. The National Center for Employee Ownership in Oakland, California, reports that 9500 American companies already have employee-shared ownership plans (ESOPs), representing 10% of the nation's workforce, while 5000 other firms have other programs through which personnel share options and ownership. Although in these, workers usually share only 20% or more of equity, research indicates that a combination of worker participation and/or ownership promotes a 10% growth rate in the enterprise. That seems to have happened in the British retailing institution, John Lewis Partnership (JLP), where 38,000 employees in its 22 department stores receive a profit-sharing bonus up to 24% of salary.

Worker Transitional Problems

Becoming a temporary or contract worker also has a positive side—it can improve one's quality of life and permit the individual to decide how much he or she wishes to work. Within companies and agencies that employ large numbers of temporary workers, whole new management policies, styles, and relationships are becoming necessary, further altering the organizational culture.

One reality of the new work culture is that the bond is being broken that once tied workers and employers to long-term contracts. Today job security is only to be found by the individual worker who has marketable skills and the ability to learn new ones. Observers of the contemporary work scene also express concern over what they perceive as the "dehumanization of the workplace." They complain about myopic executives who sacrifice, in the name of "reorganization," long-term worker loyalty to gain short-term profits.

Within work cultures and the reality of changing work dynamics, employee diversity and the overall challenge of empowering the workforce must be managed effectively and innovatively, both by the individual and the institution.

Job security is only to be found by the individual worker who has marketable skills and the ability to learn new ones.

CONCLUSIONS

Diversity of all kinds has always been a significant aspect of society. However diversity has been addressed in the past, today, in our globally interconnected world, diversity cannot be ignored or pushed to the side. In culturally diverse societies and organizations, it is imperative that leadership expect that all individuals learn to value diversity. The challenge that remains is enforcing this expectation through macro- and microsystemic changes into true, consistent action. The following statements about diversity make a good summary:[36]

1. People who are part of the minority culture do not want to be tolerated. Neither do other employees. They want to be valued. If they are valued, they can be effective.[37]
2. The "inventor" of racism is not present in any society or organization, but we all need to learn how to work with one another more effectively.
3. When power is shared, people are able to devote tremendous energy to the work at hand.
4. Human beings are the most important asset of any organization. They are the only sustainable competitive advantage for the future.
5. There is a great deal of information on the subject of human diversity, and much of it is overlapping.
6. There is no simple model for effective cross cultural and diversity training. However, it should address the specific needs of the organization's employees. Pre-written generic training programs are generally ineffective.
7. Diversity initiatives should be systemwide. If effective, they impact positively on an organization's productivity.
8. Diversity initiatives should focus on information, management, processes, and results.
9. Diversity initiatives are not a replacement for Equal Employment Opportunity (EEO) or Affirmative Action (AA).
10. Diversity is to be cherished, for it enriches life and advances the actualization of human potential.

Human beings are the most important asset of any organization.

MIND STRETCHING

1. In what ways does a multicultural workforce impact an organization's productivity?
2. Why is it important to take a systems approach to improving employee performance within multicultural organizations?
3. What cross-cultural organizational experience that you were involved in was difficult for you? How was it difficult, and how would you improve the situation?
4. Do you believe your organization or educational institution values diversity? Why or why not and give specific examples.

REFERENCES

1. Stein, J. G. "Image, Identity, and Conflict Resolution," *Managing Global Chaos; Sources of and Responses to International Conflict.* In Crocker, C. A., Hampson, F. O., and Aall, P. (eds.) Washington, DC: United States Institute of Peace Press, 1999.
2. *The Arizona Republic,* April 27, 2006.
3. Thomas, R. R. "Diversity Is a Business Issue," *Cultural Diversity Fieldbook.* Simons, G., Abramms, B., Hopkins, L. A., and Johnson, D. J. (eds.) Princeton, NJ: Peterson's/Pacesetter Books, 1996.
4. American Express Financial Advisors. "Diversity: Report to Benchmark Partners," *Cultural Diversity Sourcebook.* Abramms, B. and Simons, G. F. (eds.). Amherst, MA: ODT, 1996.
5. Ferraro, G. P. *The International Dimension of International Business,* Fifth Edition. New Jersey: Pearson, Prentice Hall, 2005.
6. *Los Angeles Times,* September 27, 1993, p. B5.
7. Simons, G. *EuroDiversity—A Business Guide to Managing Difference.* "Declaration on Cultural Diversity," Burlington, MA: Butterworth–Heinemann/Elsevier, 2002, Appendix 1, p. 397.
8. Shreeve, J. "The Greatest Journey," *National Geographic,* March 2006, pp. 61–73.
9. Parfit, M. "Human Migration," *National Geographic,* October 1998, pp. 11–14.
10. Stalker, P. "The Work of Strangers: A Survey of International Migration," Bohning, W. R. and Schloeter, M. L. (eds.). *Aids in Place of Migration.* Geneva, Switzerland: International Labour Office, 1994. (Also available from ILO Publications Center, 49 Sheridan Ave., Albany, NY 12210, USA.)
11. "A Global Pursuit of Happiness," World Report, *Los Angeles Times,* October 1, 1991, H13.
12. Gurr, T. R. "Minorities, Nationalists, and Ethnopolitical Conflict," Crocker, C. A., Hampson, F. O., and Aall, P. (eds.). *Managing Global Chaos; Sources of and Responses to International Conflict.* Washington, DC: United States Institute of Peace Press, 1999.
13. Ibid
14. Gurr, T. R. "Minorities, Nationalists, and Ethnopolitical Conflict," Crocker, C. A., Hampson, F. O., and Aall, P. (eds.). *Managing Global Chaos; Sources of and Responses to International Conflict.* Washington, DC: United States Institute of Peace Press, 1999.
15. Op cit. (Gurr).
16. Crocker, C. A., Hampson, F. O., Aall, P. (eds.). *Managing Global Chaos; Sources of and Responses to International Conflict,* Washington, DC: United States Institute of Peace Press, 1999.
17. Course Teaches Conflict Solving, Published: 2006/04/04, http://news.bbc.co.uk/2/hi/uk_news/scotland/4876028.stm
18. Simons, G. *EuroDiversity—A Business Guide to Managing Differences.* Burlington, MA: Butterworth–Heinemann/Elsevier, 2002, pp. xviii, 1, 2.
19. "Cultural Diversity Market Study," Pricewaterhouse Coopers, draft final report, Luxembourg, February 14, 2001.
20. Ibid., p. 2.

21. Willman, J. "In European Countries, There Are Three or Four Competitors. In the US, There Are 10 or 20," *Financial Times*, February 25, 2003.
22. Thomas, D. A. and Ely, R. J. "Making Difference Matter, New Parading for Managing Diversity," *Harvard Business Review on Women in Business*. Boston: Harvard Business School Publishing Corporation, 2005, pp. 125–158; see also Moran, S. "Comprehensive Evaluation of a Diversity Training Initiative in a Global Company," unpublished master's thesis, Arizona State University, May 2000.
23. Ibid., p. 40.
24. Young, S. "Micro-Inequities: The Power of Small," *Workforce Diversity Reader 1, No. 1* (Winter 2003): 88–93.
25. Ibid., p. 89.
26. Ferraro, G. P. *The International Dimension of International Business*, 5th ed. NJ: Pearson, Prentice Hall, 2005.
27. Moran, S. "Comprehensive Evaluation of a Diversity Training Initiative in a Global Company," unpublished master's thesis, Arizona State University, May 2000.
28. Pueik, V., Tichy, N. M., and Barnett, C. K. *Globalizing Management: Creating and Leading the Competitive Organization*. New York: John Wiley & Sons, 1993; see also CPC/Rand Report, *Developing the Global Work Force*. Bethlehem, PA: CPC I., 1994.
29. Prahalad, C. K. and Hamel, G. *Competing for the Future: Breakthrough Strategies for Seizing Control of Your Industry and Creating the Markets of Tomorrow*. Boston: Harvard Business School Press, 1994.
30. Moran, S. "Comprehensive Evaluation of a Diversity Training Initiative in a Global Company," unpublished master's thesis, Arizona State University, May 2000.
31. Thomas, D. A. and Ely, R. J. "Making Difference Matter, a New Parading for Managing Diversity," *Harvard Business Review on Women in Business*. Boston: Harvard Business School Publishing Corporation, 2005, pp. 125–158.
32. Gardenswartz, L. and Rowe, A. *Managing Diversity—A Complete Desk Reference*. San Diego, CA: Pfeiffer & Company, 1993. The same publisher offers numerous diversity games, profiles, and training activities.
33. Nair, K. A. *Higher Standard of Leadership—Lessons from the Life of Gandhi*. San Francisco, CA: Berrett-Koehler Publishers, 1994.
34. Kilmann, R. H. "A Completely Integrated Program for Creating and Maintaining Organizational Success," *Organizational Dynamics* (Summer 1989), pp. 4–19.
35. Kouzes, J. M. and Posner, B. Z. *The Leadership Challenge*. San Francisco, CA: Jossey-Bass, 1995.
36. Moran, R. T. and Stockton, J. L. *Diversity Training, What Works: Training and Development Practices*.
37. Bassi, L. J. and Russ-Eft, D. (eds.), Alexandria, VA: American Society for Training and Development, 1997.

EFFECTIVE PERFORMANCE IN THE GLOBAL MARKETPLACE

Increased global competition, aided and abetted by technology, has meant that organizations in every sector are having to compete on the basis of speed, cost, quality, innovation, flexibility, and customer-responsiveness. If organizations wish to be able to complete successfully in the global marketplace, they need to develop innovative products and services quickly and cost-effectively. That requires high performance organizations and personnel. . . .[1]

LEARNING OBJECTIVES

This chapter reexamines leadership and performance in the context of the global marketplace and the need for cross-cultural skills. Effective performance in an international workplace is advanced through strategic alliances, innovation, and entrepreneurial culture, as well as mentoring and coaching. An analysis of how to advance individual and organizational performance, especially among knowledge workers, follows. Also considered are ethical behavior in a global contract and performance in terms of global change, technology transfer, and in/outsourcing within today's knowledge culture. Global Performance Challenges consider these three quotations.

Fifteen people are seated around the table each representing one of our businesses in Asia-Pacific. . . . The outgoing President of Asia-Pacific formerly ran our business in South Africa. The new president comes from Australia. There are Americans at the table, an Australian, a New Zealander, and a Brit . . . and they're attending this business meeting in Beijing . . . home of one of our most recent joint ventures.[2]

We are considering opening an office in Dubai and none of us know anything about that country.

—A global executive

The most common reason that organizations do not have exceptional global leadership is a lack of commitment to the process of developing it.[3]

The implication of these quotations is that cross-cultural sensitivity and skill, and commitment are essential to effective global leadership. *Leadership* is a hot topic among best-selling books. We discussed some aspects of leadership in Chapter 5. The following world leaders share some insights about such leadership and performance in a political context.

Boutros Boutros Ghali, former secretary general of the United Nations states: "Leadership as a quality may be more innate than acquired, but some qualities and characteristics can be identified . . . vision, eloquence, a cooperative spirit, courage, political intuition."[4]

Jimmy Carter, thirty-ninth president of the United States, commented about leadership in conflict resolution: "All too often, conflicts and wars arise when we fail to consider the views of others or to communicate with them about differences between us."[5] The Carter Center Principles for Peacemakers amplifies their vision of what a global leader should do that provides useful guidance for corporate executives:

■ Strive to have the international community and all sides in any conflict agree to the basic premise that military force should be used only as a last resort.
■ Study the history and causes of the dispute thoroughly.
■ Seek help from other mediators, especially those who know the region and are known and respected there.
■ Be prepared to go back and forth between adversaries who cannot or will not confront each other.
■ Be willing to deal with the key people in any dispute, even if they have been isolated or condemned by other parties or organizations.
■ Insist that human rights be protected, that international law be honored.
■ Tell the truth, even when it may not contribute to a quick agreement.
■ Never despair, even when the situation seems hopeless.

Mikhail Gorbachev, former President of the Soviet Union, observed this on leadership: "The world is becoming ever more integrated. . . . The real leaders of today are capable of integrating the interests of their

All too often, conflicts and wars arise when we fail to consider the views of others.

The good leader

is one who is

affirming of

others, nurturing

their best selves,

coaxing them to

become the best

they are capable

of becoming.

countries and peoples into the interests of the entire world community. . . . [A] leader combines a political and a moral authority."[6]

Desmond Tutu, the South-African Archbishop who received the Nobel Peace Prize in 1984, writes: "The authentic leader has a solidarity with those he or she is leading. . . . The good leader is one who is affirming of others, nurturing their best selves, coaxing them to become the best they are capable of becoming. . . . [has] the capacity to read the signs of the times . . . knows when to make concessions."[7]

L. D. Schaeffer, when CEO of Blue Cross of California, described leadership not as a ". . . state but as a journey, requiring different styles that are determined in part by the demands of the marketplace."[8]

Qualities of Global Leadership

Wilson Learning Corporation[9] has developed a global competency model based on a thorough examination of the literature and interviews with organizations in the airline, high-tech, telecommunications, and consumer goods industries. They identify the following themes related to global leadership:

- Understanding the business from a global perspective
- Assimilating and acting on large amounts of complex or ambiguous information
- Driving change based on global strategy
- Commitment to learning
- Communication in an effective manner cross-culturally
- Establishing personal connections readily across cultural boundaries

On the basis of more than 50 executive surveys and a review of many books and articles on globalization and leadership, Moran and Riesenberger[10] identified these twelve competencies of a global leader:

Attitudinal Core Competencies
    1. Possesses a global mind-set
    2. Works as an equal with persons of diverse backgrounds
    3. Has a long-term orientation
Leadership Core Competencies
    4. Facilitates organizational change
    5. Creates learning systems
    6. Motivates employees to excellence
Interaction Core Competencies
    7. Negotiates and approaches conflict in a collaborative mode
    8. Manages skillfully the foreign deployment cycle
    9. Leads and participates effectively in multicultural teams
Cultural Core Competencies
    10. Understands their own cultural values and assumptions

11. Accurately profiles the organizational and national culture of others
12. Avoids culture mistakes and behaves in an appropriate manner in other countries.

Goldsmith, Greenburg, Robertson, and Hu-Chan[11] state the qualities of effective leadership as "communicating a shared vision, demonstrating integrity, focusing on results, and ensuring customer satisfaction." They identify five critical factors that are important for the future leaders: think globally; appreciate cultural diversity; develop technological savvy; build partnerships and alliances; and share leadership.

Bernie Bass, a professor emeritus at Binghamton University, has written thirteen books on leadership. His research focus for the past 25 years has been on the concept of **transformational leadership,** that is, a type of guidance that changes and develops the organization and its people. Many believe this makeover needs to occur with top management, which too often functions on a crisis model caused by chaos, confusion, or outright corruption, even among key executives.[12]

In 2003, 120 CEOs gathered to examine the problem at the Forum for Corporate Conscience (www.forumforcorporateconscience.com) led by Hugh McColl, former Bank of America Chairman and CEO. The group addressed issues of **corporate stewardship,** that is, leadership that serves both profit and societal goals. The underlying thesis is that corporate executives with a long-term view achieve both goals with success and sustainability. At this forum, the CEOs grappled with issues of work-life balance, health care, education, and executive compensation. Abuses with the latter have undermined both stockholder and public trust—a recent national report gave company executives an approval rating of only 17%, on par with used-car dealers. Thus, much discussion here centered on divergent demands on corporate leaders to respond to social and community needs, while still delivering the quarterly profit results. John Alexander, President of the Center for Creative Leadership, was in attendance and supported the following statement of participants for greater accountability: *We, as business leaders, share these aspirations for sustainability, responsibility, and value for our corporations of the world.*

In a knowledge culture, establishing global alliances requires skills, some of which are discussed in previous chapters. To make these partnerships succeed, many more competencies are essential. But first put these endeavors at forming synergy in a larger context.

Human performance is dependent on culture and the attitudes it engenders, particularly toward work, management, and marketing. The hunting culture, now found only in isolated locations, focused on survival through the skill of the hunter in the pursuit of food. For mainstream civilization, the agricultural work culture followed, and today, in many lands, long hours are still devoted to tilling the soil and herding

In a knowledge culture, establishing global alliances requires skills.

the flocks. With the rise of the industrial culture, humankind advanced to another stage of its development. Over the past several hundred years, machines, factories, and urbanization have influenced the worker's performance and lifestyle. Industrialization brought unions and an emphasis on safety, social legislation and security, equal employment opportunity, and career development. It also provided workers with more time for education, recreation, and actualizing human potential.

According to futurist Alvin Toffler, we entered the Third Revolution in 1956 when white collar and service workers outnumbered factory workers. In this revolution, knowledge is the ultimate factor of production. Now we are creating a new work culture—the *metaindustrial*. It is a knowledge society that emphasizes information processing and servicing others. To exercise leadership in the design of this mainstream work culture, global leaders need to transform and move beyond the dying industrial culture.

In this emerging knowledge culture, electronic communication technologies are converging, uniting, and educating us. This new capacity to share information and knowledge across traditional boundaries is the catalyst for the globalization of trade and markets. Computers, first digital and now neural, are powerful tools to further transcultural communication, aiding in design and manufacturing. Caltech physicist Carver Mead indicates that today's real leaders are those who master ideas and technologies, not land and material resources—they use the global network of telecommunications to liberate human creativity.[13] But to use such technological advances effectively, new global expertise is required, as when innovations in information systems necessitate crossing the borders of functions and departments, as well as disciplines and nations.

So much of today's business is international, requiring collaboration with *foreigners*—those who work outside the home culture and domestic operations. In addition to cross-border mergers and acquisitions, there are joint ventures and partnerships that are formed with manufacturers, suppliers, marketing specialists and various consultants from around the world. The same phenomenon is present in any profession—architects, engineers, lawyers, physicians, and academics form alliances with their counterparts across the planet. Even going off world to build an International Space Station or a lunar base, collaborating agencies from other countries have to work together in alliances to successfully manage the challenges of outer space projects that are so costly and complex. In all such ventures, cross-cultural skills are essential. Exhibit 8.1 illustrates the many facets of global leadership that impact performance and productivity.

Global Entrepreneurs

Furthermore, in knowledge-based economies and industries that cross cultures, creativity is a critical factor for remaining on the leading edge

Electronic communication technologies are converging, uniting, and educating us.

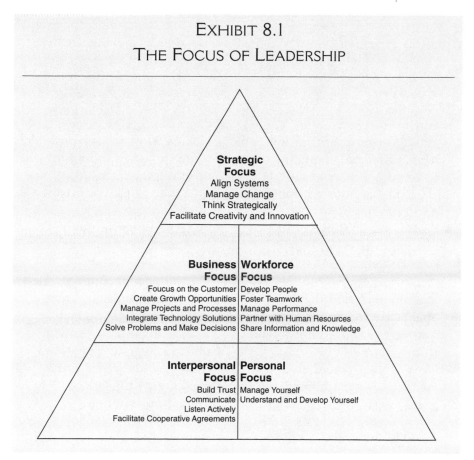

EXHIBIT 8.1
THE FOCUS OF LEADERSHIP

Strategic Focus
Align Systems
Manage Change
Think Strategically
Facilitate Creativity and Innovation

Business Focus
Foucus on the Customer
Create Growth Opportunities
Manage Projects and Processes
Integrate Technology Solutions
Solve Problems and Make Decisions

Workforce Focus
Develop People
Foster Teamwork
Manage Performance
Partner with Human Resources
Share Information and Knowledge

Interpersonal Focus
Build Trust
Communicate
Listen Actively
Facilitate Cooperative Agreements

Personal Focus
Manage Yourself
Understand and Develop Yourself

Source: *Human Resource Development Press 2004 Catalog* (vol. 1, pg. 19). Amherst Massachusetts: HRD Press.

of any business or field. In Chapter 6, we reviewed the matter of innovation, so here we focus on leaders in start-up enterprises that span the global, such as Microsoft and Google. The entrepreneurial spirit can also manifest itself within existing world organizations through *intrapreneurs*. In either case the entrepreneurial personality reflects creativity, risk taking, self-confidence, optimism, venture commitment, high performance, and effective management of both change and resources. Burt Rhutan is such a person—he not only built the light-weight *Voyager* that flew around the world, but went on to lead a privately backed team that flew three orbital flights in 2004 with *SpaceshipOne*. For that feat his company, Scaled Composites in Mojave, California, won the X Prize of $10 million. Now they are busy working on a new *SpaceshipTwo*—a passenger spaceliner created for another global entrepreneur, Kenneth Branson and his Virgin Galactic Airline.

The entrepreneur aims to control his or her own destiny; anticipates people and market needs; avoids excessive expenditures and bureaucracy; seeks greater freedom and rewards. Like innovators,

The entrepreneur aims to control his or her own destiny.

EXHIBIT 8.2
CONTRAST IN ENTREPRENEUR'S MIND-SET

The Promoter	The Trustee
■ Perceives opportunity.	■ Controls current resources.
■ Has short-term orientation.	■ Has an evolutionary outlook.
■ Makes minimal commitment of resources when decisions are made to pursue business opportunities.	■ Makes maximal commitment of resources when decisions are made to pursue business opportunities.
■ Prefers minimal overhead, seeking to borrow, barter, or lease.	■ Prefers to own or control contractually.
■ Is comfortable with a flat, lean organization that emphasizes team management and networking—knows who to call upon.	■ Is comfortable with organized hierarchy, levels of responsibility, and position management; is dependent on staff.
■ Creates high-potential ventures to meet human needs, using varied management systems/styles— manages for ultrastability.	■ Manages for stability and steady growth, seeking annual bottom-line profitability and quantifiable results.

Source: Philip R. Harris, *Managing the Knowledge Culture*. Amherst, MA: HRD Press, 2005, p. 207.

entrepreneurs work for self-fulfillment by high performance. Backed by venture capitalists, such men and women are adventurers, inventors, and discoverers. Their strategic orientation is driven by the perceptions of opportunity which they are committed to seize. To control resources effectively and flexibly, they create a flat management structure with multidisciplinary project teams and multiple informal networks. Exhibit 8.2 contrasts their entrepreneurial mind-set with the more staid manager or *trustee*.

To fully comprehend the significance of this phenomenon, we must understand the connection between the entrepreneurial culture and high performance.

GLOBAL HUMAN PERFORMANCE

As society transitions into a knowledge culture, work and performance are impacted. The traumas are evident in social, economic, and vocational life. Examining the cycles and patterns of economic upswings and downswings, Mensch,[14] a German economist, observed in the 1970s that innovations increase dramatically during periods of transition from one era to another. We live in such a transitional period, witnessing multiple innovations in information, software, silicon, solar, and space technologies that are causing a decline in traditional industries and pointing the way to tomorrow's work culture. Global managers with vision capitalize on the ongoing innovations, especially in technologies. Vaill[15] uses a metaphor to explain the contemporary change, uncertainty, and turbulence that characterize today's organizational life. Vaill states that it is like paddling a canoe in permanent white water, requiring one to shoot the rapids and experience upset and chaos. Leaders, then, learn to read the river, to play in it and even to navigate.

Global leaders track trends that increase human performance in the international marketplace. For example, among MBA programs, those catering to working professionals, about 75% include an international study trip as part of the curriculum. Often this involves a short assignment abroad where graduate students work with a company overseas as a consultant without compensation under faculty supervision, dealing with real problems.[16] Another source of qualified international workers is found among ex-volunteers of the Peace Corps and nongovernmental organizations.

Operating globally involves coping with differing human resource systems. The CPC Foundation/Rand Corporation Report[17] found the following factors important for effective performance: generic cognitive skills; social skills; personal traits; on-the-job training; knowledge acquired from an academic major; prior work experience; firm's recruiting and hiring practices; prior cross-cultural experiences; foreign language competency; and the attributes of educational institution from which the candidate graduated. But the significant findings in this study were that the three highest-rated factors are ones not generally associated with any specific training (generic cognitive skills, social skills, and personal traits); nonacademic training and experience (on-the-job training and prior work experience) are as highly rated as is academic knowledge. The issue is whether such findings like these in one country are valid in another culture?

Psychological Contract

According to Lewis,[18] a *psychological contract* is forged between the individual and the institution which employs that person. This represents unwritten, unexpressed needs and expectations on the part of both parties. For an employee or member, it is a highly subjective perspective, and is the glue that binds that person to the organization. In the disappearing industrial work culture, the psychological contract

Global leaders track trends that increase human performance.

Continued

exposure abroad

to a stressful

environment

may cause

alterations in

sleeping patterns,

high anxiety, and

neurotic defense

mechanisms.

focused on job security in return for loyalty and hard work. Currently, the emphasis is for employees to give their organizational support in return for compensations, plus opportunities to learn and acquire new skills. Employability, rather than stability, is the centerpiece of the contract. And the contract varies somewhat when personnel are posted outside their homelands.

For expatriate workers, the employer has more influence in terms of provisions for housing, education, welfare, recreation, and social events. Because of this, perceived contractual violations may provoke intense reactions from employees overseas. This dissatisfaction may be expressed in a variety of ways from negative communications and damage to company reputation, to misconduct, hostility and even sabotage. Continued exposure abroad to a stressful environment may cause alterations in sleeping patterns, high anxiety, neurotic defense mechanisms, and other manifestations of culture shock.

Exhibit 8.3 illustrates a framework for avoiding this situation, which has been labeled "breakdown" by Lewis because if one or more of its components is violated, dissatisfaction and negative repercussions are likely to increase. The items listed affect both work and home life, and if these expectations are met in the host country, the newcomer is likely

EXHIBIT 8.3

A PROPOSED FRAMEWORK FOR NEGOTIATING AN EXPATRIATE'S PSYCHOLOGICAL CONTRACT AND AVOIDING "BREAKDOWN"

Arrival

Home

Work

Balance time
Reception by employer
External environment
Amicable colleagues
Knowledge of culture
Domestic happiness
Obligations and promises
Work environment
Notable salary

Met?

to settle into the alien culture, creating both a positive experience and impression. Should this psychological contract be violated, then negative results may be expected.

Developing Human Resources

Throughout this book we have underscored the pervasive impact of culture on our lives in general, as well as on management and work practice in particular. Some cultures inhibit people, constrain their creativity and intellectual activities. These cultures exclude whole segments of their populations because they are *different*, whether their prescriptions are against ethnic or religious minorities, youth, or women. In such cultures, females, for example, are not permitted to be free and independent human beings; their minds, voices, and desires are locked inside social prisons; their lives are dedicated to the service of males and their families—women's personal rights are minimal, their contributions to the advancements of society and themselves are aborted.

In some developing countries, human development is further curtailed by the misuse of child labor. Rather than a childhood experience of education and play, youth are abused by being recruited into labor-intensive occupations or into the military as "child soldiers."

Even in developed nations, schooling of the young is undermined by violence and racism on campus, prejudice toward women, minorities, homosexuals, and the disabled. Hate crimes are perpetuated in schools as well as the community. Moreover, such deviant behavior is also found within institutions of higher education, those supposedly dedicated to the pursuit of knowledge and enlightenment. Hence, cross-cultural education at all levels, including elementary, becomes important so that the young are taught *tolerance*, that is to respect each other and accept differences in people. As societies and workplaces become more multicultural or diverse, learning intercultural sensitivity and skills is essential at all levels of human resource development (HRD).

In today's knowledge culture, continuous, lifetime learning is necessary for all people. The scope of such preparation has been outlined somewhat by the American Society for Training and Development in Exhibit 8.4.

Mentoring and Coaching

In previous stages of human development, the apprentice system was used to train craftsmen and workers. In this knowledge culture, such one-to-one guidance by experts to newcomers is done, formally or informally, through mentoring and coaching. A *mentor* is an experienced and wise counselor to a student or new employee for the purpose of personal or professional advancement. The two form a relationship

In today's knowledge culture, continuous, lifetime learning is necessary for all people.

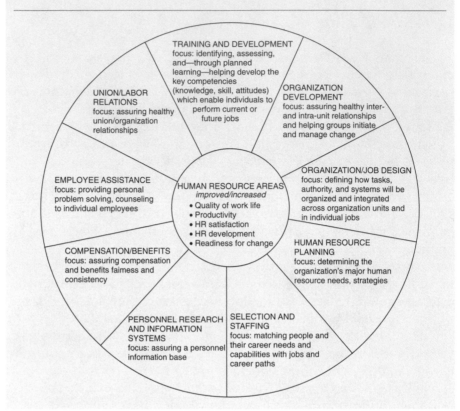

Source: American Society for Training and Development. Washington, D.C. Reprinted with permission.

in which the older person shares knowledge and expertise with the younger individual seeking to learn and advance. This communication may take place in a variety of ways from personal to electronic encounters, from meetings to e-mail, chat rooms, and conference calls.

Another strategy to improve human performance is coaching. A *coach* is a competent and experienced person who trains, tutors, or teaches a beginner, individually or in groups, to improve performance in a specific skill. Sometime the learner is designated an *intern,* staying in that role for a specific time period until a measure of mastery is attained. Teams, whether at work or at sport, may benefit from the coach's guidance.

Contemporary institutions have to become *learning organizations,* establishing knowledge management and HRD systems that ensure continuous growth in member knowledge and skills. That may translate to establishing formal mentoring and/or coaching systems so that new generations of workers benefit from the wisdom gained by their

Contemporary institutions have to become learning organizations

predecessors. When formalized as part of ongoing HRD, consider requiring a written agreement between the learner and the mentor or coach. This clarifies the relationship, especially relative to purposes, processes, resources, and measurement of progress. For global organizations, a mentoring or coaching system abroad might include expatriates assisting locals, or older indigenous personnel helping the newly hired. Whatever approach is adopted, it makes good policy to utilize the brain power and expertise of high performing mature workers or even retired ones, to help the younger members develop their potential.

ETHICAL BEHAVIOR IN THE GLOBAL WORKPLACE

Worldwide issues of character and honesty in human exchanges are critical. Witness what has happened recently in the political, business, religious, and virtually every center of power. One observes lying, cover-ups, lack of integrity, accountability, and stewardship together with unfocused, narrow, and self-serving visions of the future. Cases abound in the newspaper and in business journals. In the Berkshire Hathaway, Inc. 2002 Annual Report, some corporate executives were described as having "behaved badly at the office, fudging numbers and drawing obscene pay for mediocre business achievements." More recently news stories tell "horror tales of accountants who fudge on their audits of companies, and architects in Japan who cut back on required materials to reduce costs on supposedly *earthquake-proof* buildings. Unethical behavior undermines *trust,* an essential ingredient in successful enterprises. Sometimes it may lead to accidents and deaths of innocent people.

CEO of the Vanguard Group, John J. Brennan,[19] stated that the lessons from the recent scandals in U.S. business (Enron, WorldCom, Tyco, etc.) are twofold. One, the people at the top must have integrity; two, the right systems must be in place so people of integrity are not tempted to go astray. *Corporate governance* has suggested that boards be independent, own stock, have experience in the company's core business, and be active.[20] Interestingly, also in 2002 *Time* magazine's *Persons of the Year* were whistle-blowers: Cynthia Cooper of World-Com, Coleen Rowley of the FBI, and Sherron Watkins of Enron. All are women who had the courage to take risks to identify executive behavior that lacked integrity.[21]

Conflict of interest in organizational relationships may lead to unethical behavior and unintended consequences. For example, the City of San Diego got into serious financial difficulties and almost bankruptcy because of its employee pension system. Over years the Pension Commission had been voting for increased benefits without sufficient funds to underwrite these. The problem centered on conflict of interest by

Unethical behavior undermines trust, an essential ingredient in successful enterprises.

some commission members who would personally benefit from the increases they supported.

Bribery and Ethics in a Global Context

Corruption and bribery are present in most, if not all, societies; more so in some cultures than others. Truth and honesty are noble ideals, but they are also relative. As managers operate globally, they must be aware of the *relativism* in each culture regarding acceptance of a tip, bribe, incentive, etc. Different criteria and values between Eastern and Western cultures, for example, determine what is acceptable or appropriate. In developing countries where people struggle to survive, bribes and corruption, especially in the public sector, are endemic to the system, while in industrialized countries, the practice is often more sophisticated, less visible but prevalent. Payoffs to public officials, especially the police, have been reported in the media from Mexico City to the New York Police Department.

Ethical Relativism

As indicated earlier, the perception of bribery is culturally relative and one's *conscience* is "culturally conditioned." In some countries, the same action condemned as *bribery* might be considered a *tip* (to ensure promptness or service), especially when dealing with a bureaucracy. Among government officials in many lands the ethical dilemma has also been labeled "influence peddling." Here there is a fine line between legal and illegal, or even moral and immoral behavior. The spread of questionable and inappropriate behavior in both business and government within so-called advanced countries has led to a demand by the public for more character education in the schools, especially university courses in ethics at business and professional schools. What is ethical or standard in one culture may not be so in another.[22]

Hooker[23] makes three distinctions regarding cross-cultural ethics:

- **Contextualism** which allows for different obligations in different cultural contexts, though they may flow from the same universal principles. *Cronyism and nepotism* may be unacceptable if one's culture is built on transparency and merit, but acceptable in a culture that is relationship-based. People tend to support the cultural system on which they rely.
- **Ethical relativism** claims that fundamentally incompatible ethical principles rule in different cultures. Western individualism leads to ideas such as equality and human rights, while Hindu pantheism recognizes the connectedness of all beings and permits a stratified society based on *karma* (fate or destiny). On the other hand, *ethical universalism* holds that world cultures ultimately agree on basic values.

■ *Metaethical relativism* states that value statements are inherently relational—judgments based on prevailing conditions. Thus, in this analysis ethical assertions, as opposed to normative ethics, mean investigating the circumstances in which decisions or behavior occur. For example, corruption in Western societies is criminal behavior because this is a rule-of-law-based culture that perceives rules as fair and justly enforced; people generally play by those rules. In Chinese culture, *guanxi* or the giving of favors contributes to stable and trusting relationships important in their trade and negotiations.

Corporate Social Responsibility

In today's global marketplace, there is a positive trend toward good corporate citizenship and business ethics. Thus, global leaders at all levels of management are concerned that neither the organization nor its personnel engage in behavior that harms society. The proper goal of business is still maximizing owner value, but within the constraints of ethical conduct. That means leaders recognize that some actions may be legal, but unethical; also that many things required by ethics are not required by law. Owner value, however, implies respect of other's property rights, especially "intellectual property." Edith Sternberg, a business philosopher, maintains that "ordinary decency" excludes behavior in commerce like lying, cheating, coercion, violence, spying, stealing and even killing. Normally, honesty and fairness is good for business, and crime does not pay. Corruption and intimidation, as well as subversion of politics and law enforcement, not only undermines business, but society. "Distributive justice," on the other hand implies performance and promotion are based on merit, not influence; benefits are distributed in return for helping the organization achieve its goals. In too many corporate scandals, managers acted as if they were accountable to nobody.

Thus, the movement toward *corporate social responsibility* (CSR)—that is, good management and accountability for the benefit of stakeholders and society means ethical behavior, like ordinary decency and distributed justice, are adhered to by organizational leaders.[24] It is up to government to be guardians of public interest by reasonable legislation and enforcement, mediating among diverse interests, collecting taxes to provide public goods and services, and when necessary to organize resources in cases of disaster.

CULTURE, MANAGEMENT, AND TECHNOLOGY TRANSFER

Global leaders function within four basic intermeshing systems of management philosophy and practice: the *technical* system, the

Leaders recognize that some actions may be legal, but unethical.

economic system, the *political* system, and the *cultural* system. The first three systems are relatively easy to quantify. For example, the use of government statistics, trade association and industry figures, and other quantifiable items are readily available in most countries. The cultural system has received the least consideration because it tends to be abstract and its influence on management is difficult to specifically describe. The authors hope that this book will provide insight on this latter system.

The Cultural Management System

The *macroenvironmental* approach in cross-cultural management attempts to identify the impact of education, politics, law, etc., on management practices and effectiveness. The assumption is that management practices depend on these external variables, and the differences among organizations in various countries can be explained as a result of differences in environmental conditions. This approach is useful; however, it is incomplete because it seems to imply that the individual passively adapts to his or her environment, and it gives the manager little credit for improving the environment.

Our approach is *behavioral*—in the sense that behavioral differences in managers and organizations are a function of cultural influences. The assumption is that a manager's attitudes, values, beliefs, and needs are determined at least in part by his or her culture. Management practices and theories will, therefore, vary from culture to culture, as was discussed in Chapter 3. Taking the behavioral approach allows us to respond to these questions: What are the determinants of human behavior? Or, how can I understand why a manager is acting in a particular way?

In the global manager's attempt to understand one's self, as well as to comprehend and predict the behavior of others, he or she uses a *multilayered* frame of explanation. If one knows the culture of the other person, then it is possible to make tentative predictions about the person's behavior. Furthermore, if one knows the other person's social roles and personality, one can predict behavior with a greater degree of accuracy.

The *basic personality* of a culture is the personality *configuration* shared by most members of the culture, as a result of the early experiences they have in common. This does not mean that behavior patterns of all members of a culture are similar. There is a wide range of individual differences, but there are many aspects that most of the people share to varying degrees. In Unit 2, unique cultural aspects of several areas of the world are discussed. These local customs and practices can serve as guidelines for managers who must determine appropriate and inappropriate ways of interacting abroad. They illustrate geographic themes and patterns that can be identified to facilitate international business.

Behavioral differences in managers and organizations are a function of cultural influences.

In this volume, only the nontechnical aspects of business are considered. These pragmatic observations, subject to change with time, circumstances, and the personalities involved, are proposed for facilitating international business. As Edward T. Hall states: "Deep cultural undercurrents structure life in subtle but highly consistent ways that are not consciously formulated. Like the invisible jet streams in the skies that determine the course of a storm, these hidden currents shape our lives; yet their influence is only beginning to be identified."[25]

Renewing Diverse Cultures

Worldwide, people are in transition because of rapid social changes and stunning technological advances. One result of modernization is greater diversity within the global workforce. Some cultures have adapted, with progressive social legislation impacting the work environment, while others are still in the midst of social protest and chaos.

In many countries there has been a rise in the "new ethnicity" and a recognition of pluralism. Social philosopher, Michael Novak, explains that this as a movement of *self-knowledge* on the part of members of third and fourth generations of Southern and Eastern European immigrants here.[26] Novak contends that in a broader sense, the new ethnicity includes a renewed self-consciousness on the part of many North American ethnic groups, be they Irish, Norwegian, Swedish, German, Senegalese, Cuban, Chinese, Japanese, or Italian. With Hispanic Americans now constituting a major segment of the U.S. population, it is understandable why those with Mexican, Cuban, Puerto Rican, or some other Latin origin are not only seeking new expressions of identity, but also political-social power in U.S. society. The consciousness-raising pride in heritage and accomplishment has been especially evident among the Native Americans and African Americans during the past half century.

As society becomes more pluralistic and cultures become more open, people become more aware of both dissimilarities and similarities between themselves and others. They also demand the freedom to be themselves, regardless of cultural context. Minorities seek acceptance and tolerance, as well as the elimination of discrimination and prejudice. Becoming more culturally sensitive fosters a living environment in which internal dignity, as well as equity of treatment, can coexist. A sense of one's separateness, one's uniqueness, one's ethnic or racial background need not hamper an individual from becoming a multicultural cosmopolitan. Rather, it may enhance the contribution of a new infusion of diversity toward a *common culture*.

When people are unsure of themselves, uncertain of who they are, and are upset by the transition to a new way of life or work, their performance is affected. Accelerating change threatens our images of self

As society becomes more pluralistic and cultures become more open, people become more aware of both dissimilarities and similarities between themselves and others.

and role. People need assistance in conjuring up new perceptions of themselves, both individually and institutionally. This is where organizational leaders can help personnel bridge the gap between where technology is and where culture, in general, lags, contributing to identity crises for many persons. We thought we knew who we were, but the old absolutes gave way, and we are uncertain. We are people in transition, caught between disappearing industrial and the emerging knowledge cultures. Under such circumstances, *individuals* may experience a crisis of identity.

Similar representations may be made of *organizations*, because human systems—collections of people—also suffer identity crises. Caught between a disappearing bureaucracy and an emerging "adhocracy," the institution may experience downturns in sales, poor morale, membership reductions, bankruptcy threats, obsolescence of product lines and services, and increasing frustration with unresponsive management. Organizations, then, are challenged to go through planned renewal and to redesign their public images. However, before undertaking such changes, wise leaders evaluate their organization's culture, which can facilitate or hinder the process. Since culture underlies every initiative, all organizations periodically need to pursue a cultural assessment, so as to align that culture with the principles of effective and ethical management.

Human response to cultural change and contact with differences, as the late Herman Kahn reminded us, can be constructive or pathological, nonviolent or violent, rational or apocalyptic. Cultural exchange, Octavio Paz observed, requires experiencing the other, and that is the essence of change. It alters our psyche, our outlook, and causes some loss of our own cultural beliefs. The paradox is that it may also stimulate a gain or an enlargement of one's perceptions and performance in the adoption of new cultural patterns. Cultural, like biological, evolution demands adaptations for survival and development. Culture is a human product subject to alteration and improvement. We are, therefore, discovering innovative ways to improve our performance, even within the new realities, such as global communications or outer space developments. As we continue to unravel who we really are and become more comfortable with our "selves," then our performance increases and our potential begins to be realized.

Hospital reminds us that in the last few decades an ever-increasing number of people find themselves moving between and among several cultures within a life span.[27] This dislocation may occur for political, economic, educational, or professional necessity. It may occur through natural disasters, such as the hurricanes of 2005, which forced many to relocate. Thus, the issue of cross-cultural malaise and trauma keeps surfacing in short stories and novels, while the research literature on the subject expands. One cultural anthropologist claims it takes two generations to make the transition from one culture to another and that

Wise leaders evaluate their organization's culture.

those in transit can experience problems after years of apparently successful adaptation.

Managing Technology Transfer

Since culture involves the transmission of both knowledge and experience, the arena of technology is one of its most practical manifestations. Technology represents that branch of knowledge dealing with industrial arts, applied science, and engineering—the material objects and artifacts of civilization. When technology results in concepts, inventions, processes, production methods, and mechanisms that are transferred from its place of origin, it becomes a cross-cultural phenomenon. Seurat,[28] who has written a treatise on technology transfer, describes this human characteristic as "the capacity to store and transmit to people the accumulated experience of others." When it is done properly, human progress and prosperity are advanced; but if done improperly, then human life and property may suffer. A laudable goal is to improve the standard of living for those who are to benefit from the transfer. Consider the advantages that come to us in recent times through information technologies, such as described in Exhibit 8.5.

The account is an excellent example of the impact of technology on global culture. Technology involves much more than the sale of licenses, franchises, and other forms of agreements. It may include the transmission of a scientific theory, an engineering capability, or management system—everything from drawings, plans, software, and manufacturing instructions, to tools and instruments, machines and computers, facilities and training materials. Technology's scope in a research and development project may range from a pilot experiment to finished production, or from human resource development to turnkey factories.

All facets of technology transfer, however, have a cultural dimension. For example, two companies from different countries establish a joint venture for the transfer of unique consumer or industrial products from an industrialized to a developing nation. In the process, their representatives communicate, but with different cultural understandings and systems of law, finance, education, and transportation. One entity may be from the private sector, while the other is from a government-owned company, or combination of both. The technology transfer is best accomplished when it fosters cultural synergy for all parties. Cultural factors influence project success in every phase of the transfer process—from planning (including setting goals and objectives, defining needs and criteria), to systems analysis (including examination and synthesis of alternatives, selecting optimum targets, and writing specifications), to program implementation (including work definition, scheduling, budgeting, procurement, and control systems). Unless global leaders

All facets of technology transfer, however, have a cultural dimension.

cope with these cultural realities, planning is undermined, goals are fuzzy, sequencing and scheduling are unrealistic, incentives are lacking, misunderstandings abound, and corruption may flourish.

High Performing Global Leadership

To ensure top performance, the global leader continually updates and broadens his or her understanding of culture and its impact on our lives. Although there may be few management theories that can be universally applied across all cultures, there are many principles and practices of leadership that can be adapted to various countries. Despite the cultural differences in managerial approaches, it is possible to produce cultural synergy in the pragmatic operations of management.

There are many principles and practices of leadership that can be adapted to various countries.

Elashmawi,[29] in his research into global joint ventures, focused on clashes within multicultural work environments, such as establishing a plant overseas. These offshore enterprises require the hiring, training, and management of local in-country personnel of differing cultural and technical backgrounds. Our late colleague identified cultural clashes arising from language and nonverbal communication, time and space orientation, decision-making and information systems, conduct of meetings and training, as well as motivation. On the other hand, Hampden-Turner and Trompenaars[30] urge transforming conflicting values into complementary values.

Technology transfer in the twenty-first century has seen accelerated growth in *outsourcing/insourcing/nearsourcing*, especially in the fields of information technology and services. Exhibit 8.6 reviews the cross-cultural challenges therein.

Technology transfer in the twenty-first century has seen accelerated growth in outsourcing/ insourcing/ nearsourcing.

EXHIBIT 8.6[31]

MOVING THE WORK ABROAD

To remain competitive in the global workforce, many companies are cutting back on their costly domestic workforce, and contracting the work offshore to a developing country. This is being done increasingly by North American and European companies as they transfer service activities to India, the Caribbean, or even China. By utilizing *outsourcing* as a strategy to lower costs, companies gain access to an educated workforce, often skilled in English, to undertake high-tech and information services, as well as chip making, recordkeeping, insurance claims, telemarketing, and especially answering telephone orders or inquiries. To experience this personally, just telephone technical services at AOL or Microsoft, and you probably will get an operator half a world away. By 2015, Forrester Research forecasts some 3.3 million jobs from the American service industry will be exported overseas. As a result, India, with a surplus of well-trained engineers and a much lower pay/benefits scale, has developed their own modern, high-tech industrial parks. The *outsourcing* process allocates human and financial resources to where they are most productive, while fostering free enterprise, competition, and wealth creation.

Insourcing refers to the current practice of importing skilled workers from abroad, or upgrading the skills of domestic workers by relocation from one part of the nation to another geographic area. For example, Silicon Valley benefits by the number of software engineers from India or China that can be brought over temporarily in occupations having a shortage of qualified personnel. Western

continued

EXHIBIT 8.6[31]

MOVING THE WORK ABROAD (CONTINUED)

Europe also benefits by hiring qualified workers from Central and Eastern Europe. The latter has been dubbed *nearshoring* or *near-sourcing* within the European Union where a willing and educated workforce is available from the new EU/CEE members. Such personnel may relocate from East to West on the continent; or production, research, and business is moved to these "Second World" countries that are relatively nearby and where operations are much cheaper than in the UK, France, or Germany. For instance, Skype, a Scandinavian software company recently bought by eBay, has been employing programmers from small countries formerly under Communist control in the old East Bloc. The trend is accelerated by the spread of *euro* currency, EU human resource legislation, and CEE wages that are typically half the Western European levels. . . . And for the same reasons, corporations outside that continent are also doing business in the CEE region. Progeon, a division of India's Infosys IT group, specializes in business outsourcing and opened a center in Czech city of Brno where 100 people are working in 13 languages. The company admits that its work could not be done from India, but the Czech Republic offers advantages of *cultural affinity* because of a friendly time zone, good political and regulatory environment, and multilingual workers.

WHAT ARE THE IMPLICATIONS OF THESE TRENDS? Obviously, in a global marketplace within a knowledge culture, cross-cultural competency is critical for success!

In a global marketplace within a knowledge culture, cross-cultural competency is critical for success!

Regional Technology Transfer

Pacific Rim Enterprise: New technologies will turn the Pacific Ocean into a lake of commercial exchange. Bounded by Canada, America, and Mexico on the east, and by Australia/New Zealand, Japan, China, Indonesia, and Malaysia on the west, the Pacific's key trading cities will be Hong Kong, Singapore, Tokyo, and possibly Sydney, Manila, Vancouver, Los Angeles, and San Diego. We envision that by 2010, the Pacific Basin will be a vast, powerful, interconnected economic and cultural community of 4.5 billion people, over half the world's population and 60% Pacific Rim Enterprises as its consumers.

Despite present economic turmoil in the nations of the Far East, the Pacific Basin is a major twenty-first century market. With Hong Kong returned to China, it is emerging as a principal financial center, like Singapore and Tokyo. However, with China as the most populated country with rapidly increasing exporting, buying, and spending power, PRC already attracts external investment and continues as an international market target. Today, a common theme is that the Pacific Ocean is becoming a "highway" that links the countries on its rim and that a regional synergy is being forged that is geographical, economic, and cultural in scope.

Atlantic Rim Enterprise: Despite the mania about the Pacific markets, many firms see Europe as their best hope in the near future, especially for technology transfer. That continent has a concentration of some of the most advanced economies and highest living standards in the world. With the growth of the European Union, their economic muscle rivals somewhat that of the United States, with whom they share important cultural and historic ties. The Europeans were the first to invest in the "New World," and that legacy continues, for their financial stake in America dwarfs that of Asia. Geographically, Europe is positioned for increasing trade and commerce with Russia, Turkey, Africa, and the Middle East.

Changing Performance Standards

As cultures change, so do performance management and standards. For example, worldwide there is increasing concern for deterioration of the environment. Political leaders are trying to reach agreements such as the Kyoto Protocol, that would reduce global warming, burning of forests and pollution. Progressive global business anticipates such trends, and positively adjusts to such public and consumer interests. General Electric's CEO, Jeffrey Immelt,[32] has altered the standards by which managerial performance will be judged—in addition to the usual measures, such as return on capital, managers will be held accountable for helping to save the planet. GE's new goal is to cut its overall GHG emissions by 2012 to 1% or below. The company's newfound embrace of *greenery* appears both genuine and substantive. Immelt is convinced that clean technologies will be GE's future, so has adopted as his mantra *ecomagination,* namely that clean energy can become lucrative business. So his strategy is doubling research on such technologies that are environmentally friendly and offer business opportunities. One drawback is GE's organizational culture, which has not been known for innovative product breakthroughs. It remains to be seen whether this global corporation can be nimble enough to implement this new strategy. But the CEO has set forth a growth vision that is backed by hard targets and funding. For his management, it will be a departure from a well-known and successful path, so will GE rise to the challenge?

Clean energy can become lucrative business.

The thrust of this chapter has been on *effective* performance management in the global marketplace. The above example illustrates cultural systems adapting to new circumstances.

CONCLUSIONS

Twenty-first century global leaders can have constructive impact on this new millennium.

Global business is a learning laboratory. Peaceful and cooperative free enterprise on an international basis contributes to world economic development, while reducing disparities in terms of poverty and population. The export/import exchange, particularly of information and new technologies, fosters political and social stability, as well as developing human resources and potential.

The global market and workplace is the forum for satisfying human needs, while building a multicultural environment where high performance and productivity flourish. As Alvin Toffler wisely observed, "Nobody knows the future." However, twenty-first century global leaders can have constructive impact on this new millennium—they can make a difference in achieving human potential. Integrity, courage, cultural sensitivity, and a cosmopolitan mind-set are prerequisites for making a positive difference.

MIND STRETCHING

1. Why are cross-cultural sensitivity and skills so important for the success of global leaders?
2. What other personal and professional qualities should global leaders cultivate?
3. How does the global marketplace benefit from the activities of innovators and entrepreneurs?
4. How is global work performance improved by the practice of HRD management, mentoring and coaching, ethical behavior, and appropriate technology transfer?

REFERENCES

1. Holbreche, L. *The High Performance Organization—Creating Dynamic Stability and Sustainable Success.* Burlington, MA: Elsevier/Butterworth-Heinemann, 2005. (www.books.elsevier.com/human resources).
2. Bonsignore, M., Chairman CEO Honeywell Inc., The Conference Board, 1995, presentation at the Strategic Alliances Conference, March 29, 1995. Also refer to Gundling, E. *Working Global Smart: 12 People Skills for Doing Business Across Borders.* Palo Altos, CA: Davies-Black, 2003.
3. McCall, M. W. and Hollenbeck, G. P. *Developing Global Executives.* Boston, MA: Harvard Business School Press, 2002. Also refer to Pedersen, P. and Connerley, M. *Leadership in Diverse and Multicultural Environments.* Thousand Oaks, CA: Sage Publications, 2005.

4. Ghali, B. B. "Leadership and Conflict," *Essays on Leadership*. Washington, D.C.: Carnegie Commission on Preventing Deadly Conflict, 1998, pp. 1–6.

5. Carter, J. "Searching for Peace," *Essays on Leadership*. Washington, DC: Carnegie Commission on Preventing Deadly Conflict, 1998, pp. 26; 36–36.

6. Gorbachev, M. "On Non-Violent Leadership," *Essays on Leadership*. Washington, DC: Carnegie Commission on Preventing Deadly Conflict, 1998, pp. 64–65.

7. Tutu, D. "Leadership," *Essays on Leadership*. Washington, DC: Carnegie Commission on Preventing Deadly Conflict, 1998, pp. 70–71.

8. Schaeffer, L. D. "The Leadership Journey," *Harvard Business Review*, October 2002.

9. Leimbach, M. and Muller, A. "Winning the War for Talent: Global Leadership Competencies." Wilson Learning Corporation, Version 1.0, 2001.

10. Moran, R. T. and Riesenberger, J. R. *The Global Challenge: Building the New World Enterprise*. New York: McGraw-Hill, 1994. Also refer to Adler, N.J. *International Dimensions of Organizational Behavior*, Fourth Edition. Cincinnati, OH: Southwestern Publishing, 2002.

11. Goldsmith, M., Greenburg C. L., Robertson, A., and Hu-Chan, M. *Global Leadership: The Next Generation*. Upper Saddle River, NJ: Prentice-Hall, 2003, p. 2.

12. Klann, G. *Crisis Leadership*. Greensboro, NC: Center for Creative Leadership, 2003 (www.ccl.org). [This premiere center for leadership research and education sponsors a bimonthly magazine, *Leadership in Action*, with the publisher Jossey-Bass/Wiley—www.jossey-bass.com.]

13. Gilder, G. *Into the Quantum Era of Microcosm: Economics and Technology*. New York: Simon & Schuster, 1989.

14. Mensch, G. and Niehaus, R. J. (eds). *Work, Organization, and Technological Change*. New York: Plenum, 1982. Also refer to Hofstede, G. and Hofstede, G. J., *Culture and Organization*, Second Edition. New York: McGraw-Hill, 2004.

15. Vaill, P. *Managing as a Performing Art*. San Francisco, CA: Jossey-Bass, 1989. Also refer to Stanford, N. *Organizational Design—The Collaborative Approach*. Burlington, MA: Elsevier/Butterworth-Heinemann, 2004.

16. Groves, M. "Multinational Perspective: MBA Programs Are Serious About Giving Students Experience Abroad," *Los Angeles Times*, July 4, 1996, D.4. Also refer to Kirton, G. *The Dynamics of Managing Diversity*. Burlington, MA: Elsevier/Butterworth-Heinemann, 2004.

17. Foundation/Rand Corporation Report. *Developing the Global Work Force*. 1994. Also refer to Laroche, L. *Managing Cultural Diversity in Technical Professions*. Burlington, MA: Elsevier/Butterworth-Heinemann, 2002.

18. Lewis, K. G. "Breakdown—A Psychological Contract for Expatriates," *European Business Review*, Vol. 97:6, 1997, pp. 279–293. Also refer to Rampersad, H. K. *Total Performance Scorecard—Redefining Management to Achieve Performance with Integrity*. Burlington, MA: Elsevier/Butterworth-Heinemann, 2003.

19. Brennan, J. J. "The Market Value of Integrity." Waltham, MA: Center for Business Ethics, October 29, 2002, p. 11. Also refer to Ciulla, J. B. *Ethics of Leadership*. Belmont, CA: Thomson-Wadsworth, 2003.

20. Lavelle, L. "The Best and Worst Boards," *Business Week*, October 7, 2002.
21. Lacayo, R. and Ripley, A. "Persons of the Year, " *Time* magazine, January 6, 2003.
22. Daly, M. "The Ethical Implications of Globalization of the Legal Profession," *Fordham International Law School Journal*. New York: Fordham University, 1998.
23. Hooker, J. *Working Across Cultures*. Standford, CA: Standford University Press, 2003, pp. 314–330.
24. Beniff, M. and Southwick, K. *Compassionate Capitalism: Can Corporations Make Doing Good an Integral Part of Doing Well?* London, UK: Career Press, 2004.
25. Hall, E. R. "Beyond Culture," *The Basic Works of Edward T. Hall*. New York: Bantam/Doubleday, 1989, Vol. 3.
26. Novak, M. *Rise of the Unmeltable Ethnics*. New York: MacMillan, 1972.
27. Hospital, J. T. *Dislocations*. Baton Rouge, LA: Louisiana State University Press, 1989.
28. Standage, T. "Tim Berners the World Wide Web. First he wrote the code for the World Wide Web. Then he gave it away!" *Smithsonian*, November 2005, pp. 76–77 (www.smithsonianmag.com).
29. Elashmawi, F. and Harris, P. R. *Multicultural Management 2000: Essential Skills for Global Business Success*, 1998. Also refer to Elashmawi, F. *Competing Globally—Mastering Multicultural Management and Negotiations*. Burlington, MA: Elsevier/Butterworth-Heinemann, 2001.
30. Hampden-Turner, C. M. and Trompenaars, F. *Building Cross-Cultural Competence: How to Create Wealth from Conflicting Values*. New Haven, CT: Yale University Press, 2002.
31. Harris, P. R. *Managing the Knowledge Culture*. Amherst, MA: HRD Press, 2005, pp. 140–143, 186. Also refer to "Special Report on Eastern Europe," *The Economist*, December 23, 2005, pp. 65–67; Sears W. H. and Tamulionyte, A. *Succeeding in Business in Central and Eastern Europe*. Burlington, MA: Elsevier/Butterworth-Heinemann, 2001.
32. "A Lean, Clean Electric Machine," *The Economist*, December 10, 2004, pp. 77–79.

LEADERSHIP IN CREATING CULTURAL SYNERGY

Multinational organizations have a special role not only in building cross-cultural bridges. But in innovating synergies through their practical knowledge of putting together human and natural resources with the know how of managing both in the most effective ways.[1]

In 2005, I was in China and visited with the foreign manager of a very successful hi-tech operation. I asked him, "You have been in China now over three years and you have over 100 Chinese employees including many senior managers, what management practices or management philosophies have you taken from the Chinese and incorporated into your operations?" He paused for several seconds and said, "I can't think of any."

—Conversation of a co-author of *Managing Cultural Differences*

LEARNING OBJECTIVES

Synergy is a difficult word to understand and even more challenging to implement. It implies a belief that we can learn from others and others can learn from us. Ways to understand synergy and conflict are presented in the chapter, along with ways to create harmony.

If we are able to learn from others (Chapter 5), we have the possibility of creating synergy. Consider the differences that would take place in the quality of life in the twenty-first century if we were to take

Synergy *is a*

difficult word to

understand.

the time to develop the mechanisms of working together on policies, attitudes, and procedures, striving for synergy to create synergy.

Previously, the authors described organizations as energy exchange systems. This description applies equally to nations and governments, as well as to corporations and associations. On one hand, conflict unresolved has many negative consequences and thus undermines performance and productivity. Promoting synergy, on the other hand, contributes to a peaceful work environment and improves the quality of work life; thereby human energy is effectively utilized, and its potential is developed. Hence, global leaders should be concerned with not merely managing cultural differences, but with learning and fostering ways to work through conflicts to thus encourage cultural synergy.

Cultural synergy is a dynamic approach to managing cultural diversity.

Cultural synergy is a dynamic approach to managing cultural diversity in a variety of contexts. Nations and organizations as systems are continuously affected by the dynamics of globalization. Global economic trends have shown increasing enchantment with globalization. The universal proliferation of services and technology opens markets and accelerates global business opportunities. Globalization has also shown that attempts to effect international deregulation and economic integration have elicited strong protectionist measures stemming from economic, ideological, cultural differences and the simple desire to retain autonomy.

The practice of synergy capitalizes on difference through cooperation and collaboration. Because of the complexity and interconnection of today's world, people must thoroughly understand the myriad of global issues through first seeking to learn and subsequently understanding why and how the different cultural perspectives and realities impact global systems. Global leaders who are dedicated to accessing the benefits of globalization know that multilateralism with a commitment to cultural synergy as a tool helps to empower all people of multicultural, diverse backgrounds.

Cultural synergy builds on common ground, transcending mere awareness of difference, to form multifaceted strategic alliances and partnerships. In this manner, people who represent disparate perspectives and needs find ways through working together to seek a solution where all parties are content with the outcome and therefore together succeed. This is the essence of effective cross-cultural management.

UNDERSTANDING SYNERGY'S IMPLICATIONS

Synergy comes from the Greek word meaning *working together*. This powerful concept:

1. Represents a dynamic process.
2. Involves adapting and learning.
3. Involves joint action in which the total effect is greater than the sum of effects when acting independently.
4. Creates an integrated solution.
5. Does not signify compromise, yet in true synergy nothing is given up or lost.
6. Develops the potential of members by facilitating the release of team energies.

Synergy is a cooperative or combined action and occurs when diverse or disparate individuals or groups collaborate for a common cause. The objective is to increase effectiveness by sharing perceptions and experiences, insights, and knowledge.

Synergy begins between colleagues, then extends to their organizations, and finally involves countries. The differences in the world's people can lead to mutual growth and accomplishment that is more than the single contribution of each party. As people, we can go beyond awareness of our own cultural heritage to produce something greater through synergistic actions. The sharing of dissimilar perceptions and cultural backgrounds can be used to enhance problem solving and improve decision making. Using information and technology to promote cooperation among disparate elements in human systems creates something better than existed by separate endeavors.

Since our beginnings as a species, humans have shared information and experience, either formally or informally. As already noted in earlier chapters, culture itself is an attempt, consciously or unconsciously, by a people to transmit to future generations their acquired wisdom and insight relative to their knowledge, beliefs, customs, traditions, morals, law, art, communication, and habits. Peers in a particular career, trade, or profession have long banded together to exchange ideas and pursue common interests and vocational development. Opportunities for the practice of synergy take on more urgency within the global electronic business community as computers and the Internet, and other types of mass media, permit unprecedented possibilities for global, regional, and local collaboration.

Some cultures are synergistic and inclined toward cooperation, while other cultures tend toward individualism and competition. The late anthropologist, Ruth Benedict studied this phenomenon. Her research was amplified by groundbreaking humanistic psychologist Abraham Maslow. A summary of their characterizations of high-synergy and low-synergy societies is presented in Exhibit 9.1. This model analyzes various cultures throughout the world as to their synergistic relations or the lack of the same. Japan and Sweden are two national cultures that are seemingly high synergistically, while Serbia and Iraq would seem less so. While Japan and Sweden are highly synergistic, they are

Synergy begins between colleagues, then extends to their organizations, and finally involves countries.

EXHIBIT 9.1

CHARACTERIZATIONS OF HIGH-SYNERGY AND LOW-SYNERGY SOCIETIES

High-Synergy Society	Low-Synergy Society
Emphasis is on cooperation for mutual advantage.	Uncooperative, very competitive culture; enhances rugged individualistic and "dog-eat-dog" attitudes.
Conspicuous for a nonaggressive social order.	Aggressive and antagonistic behavior toward one another, leading to either psychological or physical violence toward the other.
Social institutions promote individual and group development.	Social arrangements self-centered; collaboration is not reinforced as desired behavior.
Society idealizes win–win.	Society adheres to win–lose approach.
Leadership fosters sharing wealth and advantage for the common good. Cooperatives are encouraged, and poverty is fought.	Leadership encourages private or individual gain and advantage, especially by the power elite; poverty is tolerated, even ignored.
Society seeks to use community resources and talents for the commonwealth and encourages development of human potential of all citizenry.	Society permits exploitation of poor and minorities, and tolerates the siphoning of its wealth by privileged few; develops power elites and leaves undeveloped the powerless.
Open system of secure people who tend to be benevolent, helpful, friendly, and generous; its heroes are altruistic and philanthropic.	Closed system with insecure people who tend toward suspiciousness, ruthlessness, and clannishness; idealizes the "strong man" concerned with greed and acquisition.
Belief system, religion, or philosophy is comforting and life is consoling; emphasis is on the god of love; power is to be used for benefit of whole community; individuals/groups are helped to work out hurt and humiliations.	Belief system is frightening, punishing, terrifying; members are psychologically beaten or humiliated by the strong; power is for personal profit; emphasis is on the god of vengeance; hatreds go deep and "blood feuds" abound; violence is the means for compensation for hurt and humiliation.
Generally, the citizenry is psychologically healthy, and mutual reciprocity is evident in relationships; open to change; low rate of crime and mental illness.	Generally, the citizenry tends to be defensive, jealous; mass paranoia and hostility; fears change and advocates status quo; high rate of crime and mental illness.

Source: Ruth Benedict, Anthropologist; Abraham Maslow, Psychologist.

also highly monocultural. When one group makes up the majority of all peoples within a system, finding common ground is far easier than when multiple groups, who often have different and conflicting beliefs, values, religions, and cultures live in proximity with each other. Iraq and Serbia represent such highly complex and multicultural societies, whose history has shown internal conflict due to fundamental differences and historical grievances.

The most dramatic example of creating synergy among national cultures is occurring within the European Union and Parliament.[2] Sometimes the diverse membership may agree on policies and procedures, such as in working out a common Euro currency, some members, such as the United Kingdom, opted out of the plan. Cultural diversity figures well into this scenario, and though historically members of the European Union have been in conflict with each other, the creation and management of the European Union represents a commitment to cultural synergy.

Obviously, the opposite behavior to synergy is to be unsynergistic or uncooperative. Such an approach at the least leads to isolation, but often to conflict, power struggles, and even violence. Therefore, it is important for global leaders to also build skills in conflict resolution and anger management.[3] Interestingly, the Quakers, known worldwide as peacekeepers, even have a program of conflict resolution for prisoners. They conduct *Hands of Peace Workshops* to provide inmates with an alternative method of dealing with differences. The training includes exercises in listening and empathy, role playing, trust, and team building. Similar efforts are a regular part of any effective human resource development program in leading-edge global organizations. It is viewed as an investment in human or social capital. Individuals increase this capital by improving their human relations or social skills.

Before we discuss methods of fostering cultural synergy in the workplace, we need to appreciate how cross-cultural conflict occurs and sustains itself. Throughout human history, conflict has been a common occurrence. Conflict often results from a need for insufficient basic resources; the desire for power, control, and revenge; the desire to enforce one belief over other beliefs; the belief of the inherent superiority of groups, cultures, religion, and government; the interaction of basic human differences; and the interaction of cultural, societal, and religious differences.

CROSS-CULTURAL CONFLICT AND CULTURAL SYNERGY

What comprises a conflict in one culture is a daily difference of opinion in another. A serious insult in one setting—crossing one's legs

What comprises a conflict in one culture is a daily difference of opinion in another.

or showing the sole of one's foot, for example—is a matter of comfort in another. An arrogant challenge in one culture—putting one's hands on one's hips—is a sign of openness in another. A normal pathway for deescalating a conflict in one society—fleeing the sene of an accident—constitutes a serious offense in another. Human boundaries are cultural creations; social boundaries, legal boundaries, and emotional boundaries are all drawn according to each culture's values, myths, and preferences.[4]

To use an analogy, it is nearly impossible to accurately define competence without also addressing incompetence; to define light, without also discussing darkness; and to define peaceful cultural synergy, without discussing cross-cultural conflict. To develop culturally synergistic organizations, global business leaders must be skilled at understanding and resolving cross-cultural conflict *while* enforcing cooperative cross-cultural organizational behavior in a dynamic, multicultural work environment. In the chapters on Women in Global Business and Managing Diversity in the Global Work Culture, we address the challenges that women and people from the nondominant culture face in global organizations. These challenges are systemwide and help to perpetuate and enforce conflict. If diversity within organizations is managed from a systemwide, culturally synergistic manner, then it is highly likely that overall employee performance, retention, and morale will show significant improvement.

According to Adler,

> Cultural synergy, as an approach to managing the impact of cultural diversity, involves a process in which managers form organizational policies, strategies, structures, and practices based on, but not limited to, the cultural patterns of individual organizational members and clients. . . . This approach recognizes both the similarities and differences among the cultures that compose a global organization and suggest that we neither ignore nor minimize cultural diversity, but rather view it as a resource in designing and developing organizational systems.[5]

We would like to emphasize that there are many pathways to avoiding conflict and creating a form of cross-cultural harmony within multicultural systems and organizations. In the extreme, forcing 100% cultural assimilation of those who fall outside the cultural norm is one path. However, it breeds resentment and ultimate conflict. For although it may work on the surface, as openly expressing one's frustrations is not culturally rewarded, it inevitably creates new conflict. Imagine for a moment the frustration and anger you might feel of being forced to behave completely different from who you are. If a family immigrates from Italy to North America, it is understandable and necessary to adapt to the North American cultural norm. Yet to adapt 100% is extremely difficult and requires a complete reinvention of self to do so. Most people would never consider this option.

To develop culturally synergistic organizations, global business leaders must be skilled at understanding and resolving cross-cultural conflict.

When an employee is asked to immigrate from Saudi Arabia to England, two cultures that are starkly different from each other, even more adaptation is necessary, and the struggle to find a balance between adapting to the new culture and retaining a sense of self is much more difficult. To expect full assimilation implies that one way is the best way. Usually, this can be the expectation placed on others, with the anticipation that they should change and adapt. However, this same belief is almost never required of the individual or society holding the philosophy of full assimilation. This is reflective of an ethnocentric philosophy, where cultural diversity is seen as a problem for organizations and they attempt to select an unicultural workforce.[6]

Another approach is the parochial philosophy, through which cultural diversity is seen as having no impact on the organization, and diversity is effectively ignored.[7] Parochial thinking leads to the marginalization of groups who fall outside the cultural norm. This is another enforced pathway to discourage cross-cultural conflict. And yet, as was seen in France in 2005, with the rioting of French youth who were born in France and whose parents immigrated from Africa, it is only a solution for those who fall into the majority cultural group. Marginalization leads to a lack of opportunity for members of the group. In this example, French youth were expressing pent-up frustration at the lack of opportunity they felt came from their marginalized status. The president of France, Jacques Chirac, stated that "We are all aware of discrimination," and he called for equal opportunities for the young while rejecting the suggestion of a U.S.-style quota system. "How many CVs are thrown in the waste paper basket just because of the name or the address of the applicant?"[8]

We are all aware of discrimination.

From the business and organizational perspective, the marginalization of groups leads to frustration and to lack of productivity and employee retention. When employees are marginalized, not only does team performance suffer, but the poor relationship between management (team leaders) and members of marginalized groups can lead to resentment, diminished productivity, and ultimately, conflict among team members.

The truth is that conflict is a fact of life. When humans interact, whether or not cultural differences are a factor, it is inevitable that conflict will arise and must be resolved. In the workplace, managers must learn how to manage conflict successfully; if it is left unresolved, the negative effects extend far beyond the conflicting parties.[9] "If the executive director of a nonprofit agency and her board cannot get along, employees tend to take sides, fear for their jobs, and, like those above them, wage a campaign discrediting the other group.... Ignoring workplace conflict sets destructive forces in motion that decrease productivity, spread the conflict to others, and lead to lessened morale."[10]

According to Wilmot and Hocker, if employees study organizational conflict, they can learn how to get along with their colleagues, their manager, and the public better; supervisors can learn how to predict the onset of conflict, learn how to utilize a productive response to conflict, and help employees resolve their differences while keeping conflict from spreading to other parts of the organization.[11] In cross-cultural conflict, it is difficult to predict an individual's behavior toward conflict by his or her country of origin. However, here are some guidelines to help you to acquire an approximate idea of likely behavior toward conflict from a dualistic perspective. As noted in an earlier chapter, cultural traits fall along the continuum of individualistic at one end and collectivistic at the other end. The following guidelines have been adapted from Wilmot and Hocker.[12]

Patterns of Behavior toward Conflict from Individualistic Cultures:
- Individualistic cultures tend to emphasize analytic, linear logic and view a difference between the conflict and the conflicting parties involved.
- Conflict tends to ensue when individual expectations are violated.
- People from individualistic cultures are very direct and tend to be confrontational.
- Individualistic cultures tend to enforce the following approaches to dealing with conflict:
  - Solution and action orientation
  - Open and direct communication
  - Linear logic with the use of rational and factual rhetoric

Patterns of Behavior toward Conflict from Collectivistic Cultures:
- Collectivistic cultures tend to emphasize holistic logic with group-oriented, collective normative expectations.
- There is an integration of the conflict and the conflicting parties. No separation is seen.
- Conflict tends to ensue when collective expectations are violated.
- People from collective cultures tend to conceal their conflict and to be indirect, nonconfrontational, and passive aggressive.
- Collective cultures tend to enforce the following approaches to dealing with conflict:
  - Saving face and one's relations as a priority.
  - Intuitive, affective, ambiguous, and indirect rhetoric strategies to resolve conflict.
  - Point-logic styles of communication.

Global Complexity and Cultural Synergy

It is theorized that the flap of one butterfly's wings, flying over the Great Wall of China, has a direct link to the substantial dust storm that forms over Marrakesh, Morocco, some time later, severely disrupting all forms of travel from air traffic to ground travel for a full day.

The Butterfly Effect came out of chaos theory, in which seemingly small local events have the distinct potential to cause systemwide disruptions.[13] The idea behind this theory is that global societies and global, multicultural organizations can be analogous to a living creature that adapts and learns, in which the individual person is influenced by many factors, including governmental policies, religious creeds, societal influences of others around them, and cultural pressures.[14]

Global leaders who are cross culturally effective understand that it is impossible to have a one-to-one predictability of cross-cultural behavior, for in actuality unpredictable multiple factors intervene and alter the immediate outcome.[15] The attempt to make linear that which is unlinear is an inherent challenge to global leaders. Thus, governmental, business, and organizational leadership in general must become well acquainted with all the factors that make up the complex system, including the unintended and unexpected consequences of actions that arise.

Accordingly, for each action there is a reaction and often several diverse reactions. On the human front, from each perspective, there lies a way of seeing the world and reacting to it, which then determines behavior and actions. The following quote illustrates perspective from the standpoint of two people interacting presumably from the same culture. After reading it, imagine the complexity and potential for conflict when different cultural groups interact within the context of organizations.

> *You* can see things behind my back that *I* cannot see and *I* can see things behind *your* back that are denied to your vision. We are both doing essential the same thing, but from different places: although we are in the same event, that event is different for each of us. Our places are different not only because our bodies occupy different positions in the exterior, physical space, but also because we regard each other from different centres.[16]

Information technology and globalization has created a vastly different world from the world of our grandparents. And the reality is that though the connections are there, though the speed of international communication and transportation has advanced exponentially, though the facility of conducting international business has improved dramatically *there always will be cultural differences*—distinctly different perceptions of the "right" way to behave, the "right" way to believe, the "right" way to do business, the "right" way to conduct governmental practice, and the "right" way to address global political, economic, environmental, and religious challenges stemming from conflicting differences.

This right way is a reflection of each nation's culture, and it is also a reflection of each organization's culture. Each nation's culture has

The Butterfly Effect came out of chaos theory, in which seemingly small local events have the distinct potential to cause systemwide disruptions.

values and norms, social nuances, behaviors, beliefs, relationships, languages, work habits, and practices that influence their perception of the right way, continuing on from generation to generation and thus ensuring its very survival. The global leader understands the metaphor of how the movement of the butterfly can lead to the dust storm. In other words, he or she understands that, in turn, this dust storm has the possibility of leading to massive systemic disruptions. In this, she or he should foster the ability to develop other leaders who, like themselves, value (in belief and actions) multilateralism in systems that have cultural diversity, who understand that in the complex world of global interactions, multilateral efforts help with the management and resolution of conflict and the enforcement of culturally synergistic organizational systems.

Two continuous actions that are fundamental to helping leadership resolve cross-cultural conflict and aid in curtailing large problematic systemic disruptions include:

1. Always account for cultural, political, and economic complexities that are involved. This must be done from multiple perspectives and standpoints.
2. Conduct multiple projections of the systemic consequences of a particular action to determine plausible and alternately entirely possible but "unlikely" outcomes.

Errors can easily lead to exacerbated conflict.

In the context of managing cultural differences, the global leader who is unable or unwilling to view reality from the many different perspectives involved is bound to make gross errors in judgments. These gross errors can easily lead to exacerbated conflict and in the global organization create systemwide disorder. Leadership that actively uses these two points can more effectively implement systematic cross-cultural synergy.

SYNERGY IN ORGANIZATIONAL CULTURE

Within the context of global business, namely multinational organizations, their subsidiaries, divisions, and teams, global leaders who promote cultural synergy influence social change in human behavior and improve system effectiveness. Bear in mind that behavioral scientists suggest that while managers may seek efficiency, or *doing things right*, in the work environment, leaders aim to promote effectiveness, or *doing the right things*.

Professor Nancy Adler suggests five strategies to be considered when working in teams or managing groups across cultures.[17] Often, Adler states, a balance is created by using all these options when the appropriate business situation calls for it.

1. *Cultural dominance.* When one organization is in a more powerful position than the other, the more powerful organization will dominate, usually continuing to do things as they are done in the home culture. "On an individual level, managers often choose the cultural dominance approach when they strongly believe their way is the only right way and especially when they perceive the situation to involve a fundamental ethical issue."

2. *Cultural accommodation.* This option is the opposite of cultural dominance. Managers implementing this option tend to imitate the host culture, attempting to blend in. Fear often surfaces at headquarters whether a manager can properly represent the interests of the organization abroad. Examples of cultural accommodation occur when managers learn or become fluent in the native language or construct contracts using the local currency of the host culture instead of that of the home culture.

3. *Cultural compromise.* This approach is a combination of the first two, with both sides conceding something to work together more successfully. Most often the most powerful partner gives up less; however, both sides must make concessions.

4. *Cultural avoidance.* Asian managers often use this approach. Such managers work and manage as if no conflict of cultures exists. This approach emphasizes saving face and is most often used when the unresolved issue is less important than the final outcome of the situation or negotiation.

5. *Cultural synergy.* This option develops new solutions that respect all cultures involved and often increases the choices for working effectively in a transcultural business environment. An example of these options is the choice of language in which to conduct business. When working internationally, businesspeople often do not share the same language and must then decide which language to use. If, for example, a French firm insists that negotiations with the Germans be conducted in French, it is an example of cultural dominance. If the Germans agree at once, it is cultural accommodation. If both sides decide that interpreters are better, their choice reflects cultural compromise. However, if the Germans and French agree to negotiate in a third language, it is a cultural synergy approach, whereby no side will have a language advantage. If both Germans and French negotiators are fluent in several languages, they can agree to speak in any of those languages.

Just as there are high- and low-synergy societies, there are high- and low-synergy organizations. A high-synergy corporation is one in which employees cooperate for mutual advantage because the customs and traditions of the corporation or organization support such behavior. In

Just as there are high- and low-synergy societies, there are high and low-synergy organizations.

*Low-synergy
business is one
that is ruggedly
individualistic.*

this noncompetitive atmosphere the individual works toward his or her betterment as well as that of the group. Employees work to ensure that mutual benefits are derived from their common undertakings. The same high/low synergy dimensions may also be applied to group activities.

A low-synergy business is one that is ruggedly individualistic, insisting on going it alone. It avoids partnerships and agreements with other entities and finds it difficult to adapt quickly to change. Employees are not empowered-often systems and policies are more important than the customer or the people. Managers impose "their way" or organizational culture upon others, often to their mutual detriment. The business focus is on getting ahead at any cost, without regard to the human needs of workers or customers or long-term effective solutions.

In culturally synergistic organizations, the best of each culture is melded together without infringing on the other. This diversity and respect enables leaders to solve problems synergistically. Adler advocates three steps in synergistic problem solving manifested by high-synergy corporations.

> *Describe the situation.* Although it may sound easy, when working across cultures, this is one of the most difficult and critical steps. This process involves describing the situation or problem from the perspective of one's own culture, and then describing, from the perspective of each of the cultures involved, their perceptions of the situation. Each individual's divergent business and cultural values will challenge us to see and describe the situation from another perspective. This may lead to some accommodation in the planning and actions.
> *Culturally interpret the situation.* Global leaders in high-synergy organizations must ask, What historic and cultural assumptions exist in this cross-cultural situation? All behavior is understandable from the perspective of the person who is behaving; our cultural biases often lead us to misinterpret the logic of other cultures' behavioral patterns. Role reversal is an effective tool in identifying the similarities and differences between our own cultural assumptions and actions and those of other cultures.
> *Increase cultural creativity.* Many alternatives are investigated and searched out in high-synergy organizations. Individuals from all cultures involved offer solutions. The resolution should be compatible with all but not imitate any one culture's solution, transcending the behavior and patterns of each culture.

After the problem solving, implementing a culturally synergistic solution should be planned carefully. Employees need to have an awareness of both their own culture and cross-cultural awareness of values, assumptions, and behaviors of others with whom they interact.

Without this cultural understanding, synergy in the implementation may not make sense nor be viable.

Key managers within a corporation, university, association, or agency are challenged to transform their institutional culture so that it encourages both internal and external synergistic relationships. Within the business and with outside entities, personnel can be trained in collaborative and conflict-resolution skills, but also in the acceptance of diversity and the practice of tolerance.[18]

With the increasing number of mergers, acquisitions, strategic alliances, and other forms of partnering, executives need to plan for the melding of different organizational cultures. When two or more systems combine their resources, the whole endeavor may be undermined if issues of organizational culture are not addressed. In essence, a new institutional culture is being forged that should build upon the best of those institutions involved. Thus, a synergistic organizational culture is patiently developed.

SYNERGY IN GLOBAL ORGANIZATIONS

Synergy is a dimension of organizational culture that is more important as international business and government activities become more global in scope, more complex in practice, and more sophisticated in technology. Previous chapters cited the need to create cultural synergy so that the enterprise values cooperation, collaboration, and team management as one of the characteristics of the global leader. Promoting synergy in and through the organization is one of the characteristics of the new work or knowledge culture.

To facilitate understanding of this key concept, imagine the following scenarios, for which we will later provide examples, of how synergistic relations can be fostered in acquisitions, relocation, structural change, personnel change, role change, consortium formation, and global consultation.

- The chief executive officer of a large global corporation visits the facilities of a newly acquired subsidiary to determine which of the parent company's policies, procedures, and personnel should be utilized in the merged firm and which approaches or strategies of the acquisition should be retained.
- A New England plant is being relocated to Alabama. Its Northern employees have been given the opportunity to move to the South, so as to join an enlarged workforce of local Southerners. The plant manager at the Alabama plant is a technocrat from England who immigrated to the United States five years ago.
- A major retailer is in the midst of profound organizational change. A traditional company with branches throughout the country, it is

Synergy is a dimension of organizational culture that is more important as international business and government activities become more global in scope, more complex in practice, and more sophisticated in technology.

proud of its seventy-five years of customer service and long records of faithful employees. Declining sales, fierce competition, and inflation led to the election of a new chairman of the board who has hired some new competent managers. Together they have begun to shake up the corporation to ensure its survival.

■ A European conglomerate has purchased controlling rights of an American steel manufacturer. Key management positions have been filled with French, Italian, and German specialists in downsizing and mergers, though most of the effective American management has been retained. Plans are under way to improve operations and turn the company into a profitable venture.

■ As employees become more sophisticated at computers and information processing, doing business electronically in the global marketplace is critical. Thus, competent Information Technology personnel begin a retraining program in new systems and networking.

■ European partners are successfully involved in producing innovative aircraft at Airbus Industrie. It began with three major companies from three different countries, and eventually a fourth company/country entered into the agreement.

■ A Canadian consulting firm agreed to assist a Mexican corporation in the use of advanced technology. It is part of a larger deal between the governments of both countries in which Mexican energy is to be supplied in return for Canadian expertise and equipment.

■ A Japanese auto manufacturer seeks to penetrate the EU market, so it buys existing automobile plants in England and Poland.

■ Sixteen nations and their space agencies join forces in constructing and maintaining a macroproject, called the International Space Station.

The common element in each of these scenarios is the opportunity to exercise leadership in cultural synergy. In these situations, differences in organizational cultures can either weaken the intended actions or they can be used to enhance goal achievement.

Managers can either impose their corporate policies, procedures, and cultures on others, often to their mutual detriment, or simply be aware of the other's institutional culture, its strengths, and limitations. But a better approach is to objectively evaluate what is of "value" in each of the existing enterprises and build upon such foundations, being sensitive to cultural differences and opportunities for synergy that result in mutual growth and development.

Within transnational systems, there are seven specific situations when synergy in organizational culture is most desirable. They are exemplified by the previous incidents, and they include:

Acquisition. Whenever a corporation acquires or merges with another entity, domestically or internationally, synergy skill is required.

Differences in organizational cultures can either weaken the intended actions or they can be used to enhance goal achievement.

Opportunities for synergy

For organizational effectiveness, there must be a synthesis of two distinct microcultures, not just an imposition by the more powerful company. This is particularly true in the case of a newly acquired subsidiary. The executives from the parent company can do much to facilitate the integration process if they take time to analyze the subsidiary's culture. Furthermore, this merger of two organizational worlds and climates is aided when management from the acquired firm melds its distinct culture with the other, perhaps creating new policy, procedures, and processes, as well as corporate goals, attitudes, and strategies.

Relocation. When a company moves an existing facility and employees to another site, at home or abroad, synergistic efforts must be undertaken. Relocation services offered by the corporation must go beyond moving and new community information, as employees require orientation to the realities and opportunities of the new cultural environment. To facilitate the transition, many firms employ relocation consultants.

Structural/Environmental Change. When there is a major change within the organizational structure, employees should be prepared for the new shift in policy, procedure, product, or service. Planned change strategies can be used to ready personnel for reorganization and renewal without abrupt disruption of the work climate. The quickening of the work pace on understaffed operations can lead to greater resentment, exhaustion, and "burn out." Involving employees in cooperative efforts to regulate and monitor change or growth results in fostering synergy within the work environment.

Personnel Change. Whenever the composition of a workforce shifts, planned endeavors are needed to integrate the new employees. In addition to hiring and retaining large numbers of women and minorities, there are many diverse cultures represented in today's workforce. The global insights and knowledge of international markets that is gained validates the talents of multicultural personnel.

Role Change. The introduction of new technology into an organization usually means that personnel roles and relationships change. In the traditional Industrial Age corporation, work disciplines, units, and departments were fairly stable and separate. But in complex, postindustrial organizations, the divisions between line and staff are more obscure and fluid. New interpersonal skills are required that enable personnel to form quick, intense organizational relations of a cooperative, mission-oriented enterprise. This is evident in today's project/product teams and matrix management.

Consortium. Organizations often move outside their own operational sphere seeking partners who will join together for mutual benefit. Synergy is required for a combination of institutions to pool their talent and capital for a successful operation. Project management, for instance, provides opportunities for diverse departments and activities within a single organization to come together to achieve desired objectives. This

Planned change strategies can be used to ready personnel for reorganization and renewal without abrupt disruption of the work climate.

approach has brought together diverse or similar companies from the same or several industries, from the same or many nations. The very complexities of the global economy demand such collaboration.

Global Consulting. Whenever a group of "experts" enters the client's organizational culture, then synergistic skills are necessary. Knowingly or not, the representatives from a consulting group bring their own national/organizational culture into the client's environment. When such assistance is rendered on an international scale, the intervention may also include two or more national cultures. Consultants should attempt to acculturate into the organizational culture and community of their customers and not impose the mind-set or systems of the consultants upon the client organization. In other words, such external interventions require skillful acculturation to the customer or client's environment.

These seven dimensions can be used as a model for promoting synergy in organizational or group cultures. In such instances, it is vital that global leaders bring about change in a way that gives consideration to human needs as well as the "bottom line." A wise leader appreciates the long-term implications of a synergistic work culture and strives to create an "internal strategic unity within a chaotic external environment."[19] Some global corporations have experienced protests and backlash from activists, especially in the environmental movement, because of their lack of social responsibility.

Today, responsible corporate leadership seeks to foster balance between economic development and environmental preservation. Learning from its disastrous oil tanker spill in Alaska, ExxonMobil now provides a sanctuary for protected birds in the heavily industrialized ship channel off Houston. This global corporation has joined with state regulatory agencies to restore habitat by enlargement of St. Mary Island for ground-nesting birds.

Transforming the Work Culture

High-synergy organizations are essential in a knowledge culture. Promoting synergy in and through the organization is one strategy for transitioning into this twenty-first century work environment. It is impossible to fully describe here this new work culture.

For the past fifty years a wide range of behavioral scientists, in cooperation with executives and other organizational leaders, have been engaged in transforming the work environment from that of the Industrial Age toward the postindustrial directions. Our research has identified 10 general characteristics of this emerging work culture. In the future, workers at all levels will generally manifest:

- Enhanced quality of work life
- More autonomy and control over their work space

Today, responsible corporate leadership seeks to foster balance between economic development and environmental preservation.

- Improved organizational communication and information dissemination
- Participation and involvement in the enterprise and its decision making
- Relevant, creative organizational norms or standards
- High performance and productivity
- Skill in using new communications and robotic technologies
- More research and development activities
- More personal entrepreneurialism and organizational intrapreneurialism
- More utilization of informal and synergistic relationships.

Such should be the goals of global leaders who seek to transform the work culture.

SYNERGISTIC TEAM MANAGEMENT

Traditional organization models and management styles are gradually being replaced or reworked because they are inadequate and unproductive within the knowledge culture. A major transition is under way in social systems from "disappearing bureaucracies" to "emerging ad hocracies." Global leaders facilitate the transition from past to futuristic operations by promoting team management practices. This approach may operate under various designations, such as a project, task force, product, or business systems team, or an ad hoc planning committee. The point is that work is organized around a "temporary" group that involves permanent (functional) and impermanent lines of authority.

Understanding the Team Strategy

The dictionary defines a *team* as a number of persons associated in some joint action, while *teamwork* is described as a cooperative or coordinated effort by persons working together. Teams are collections of people who must rely on group collaboration if each member is to experience the optimum of success and goal achievement.

Changing technology and markets have stimulated the team approach to management because temporary groups can function across organizational divisions and better cope with diversity of membership. Multicultural and multifunctional teams are becoming commonplace. Furthermore, the complexity of society, and the human systems devised to meet new and continuing needs, requires a pooling of resources and talents. Inflation, resource scarcity, reduced personnel levels, budget cuts, and similar constraints have underscored the demands for better coordination and synergy in the use of "brainpower."

Teams are collections of people who must rely on group collaboration.

Synergy through team efforts can occur within a single enterprise or among different organizations that formerly competed or rarely mixed with one another.

In effect, the team management model alters organizational culture. The term used currently is *self-managed teams*, which contribute to employee empowerment and problem solving. Such work units evolve their own unique *team culture*. As noted previously, high technology corporations excel with project teams consisting of a variety of skilled specialists from management information systems, accounting, and new technologies. With the team approach, obsolete business separations give way to synergistic, functional arrangements among those employed in manufacturing, marketing, and administration; line and staff activities overlap and often merge.

Synergy through team efforts can occur within a single enterprise or among different organizations that formerly competed or rarely mixed with one another. The trend is evident among companies, agencies, and associations as well as between the private and public sections. For example, in 2003, the U.S. government set up the Department of Homeland Security made up of many agencies that formerly did not work closely together. To combat terrorism, cross-departmental teams were essential for their efforts to be complementary and synergistic in achieving mission objectives. For decades, the government and military have set up task forces and committees to deal with special problems. The issue is whether the participants have ever been trained to maximize group problem solving.

The computer has been the most powerful tool in making team or project management feasible while fostering a revolution in organizational culture. Other forces propelling this change are *globalism* and *regionalism*. Governments at all levels find that problems of planning, economics, ecology, conservation, and even population control are too big for local solutions. Only by the integration of overlapping jurisdictions and efforts can the public sector meet the challenges of today's business environment. Thus, there is a remarkable growth in the establishment of interagency task forces in planning, training, or criminal justice activities. For effective macro problem solving in complex societies, regional commissions or authorities are sometimes formed, in which local governmental power is delegated to a more comprehensive organization, bringing together a technical support staff with representatives of each local government.

The same trends occur in the private sector to bring together resources more quickly. For example, an interdisciplinary team at the Cleveland Clinic is used to combat brain tumors. Known as CAMIS (computer-assisted minimally invasive surgery), the technique and equipment represents a marriage between aerospace and medical technologies. The high tech health care team is the result of a combined effort among two companies, four hospitals, four universities, the U.S. Air Force, and NASA, facilitated by the Ohio Aerospace Institute. To bring together diverse organizations in a common undertaking is called *levering of resources*. Such synergy transcends organizational boundaries by creating new entities that develop *integrated cultures* of their own.

Increasingly, team management is employed when the organization's activities are less repetitive and predictable. Such an approach increases the need for liaison, management by exception, and sharing of authority and information. All this is contrary to traditional organization cultures. Management in transition today challenges institutions to improve information processing, enhance integration of realistic schedules, and share decision making, subject to continuing revision and change.

Furthermore, there is a fundamental shift in the way power is exercised. Interfunctional product teams, for example, involve a delicate balance of power among peer specialists. Because joint decisions are to be made, each member must be sensitive to the others if the contributions of all are to lead to the team's success. The product manager's task is to facilitate collaboration across functional lines. For many this will necessitate an attitude change. Contemporary management in older companies, for instance, is concerned about organizational renewal or "reengineering," but this requires cooperation rather than confrontation in the triple relationship between business, labor, and government. Even where a traditional approach to business is still in force, labor and management can develop team relations. It is common to have quality-control circles composed of workers and supervisors who meet regularly to discuss how to improve product quality and service.

Team Building for Success and Synergy

Astute HRD executives make provisions for team building or training within their organizations by qualified internal or external consultants. In such human-relations training, leaders seek to cultivate a **team environment** that facilitates the group's performance. However, these guidelines might be questioned in whole or part by readers from other national or cultural backgrounds. In essence, in team building, members learn:

- Tolerance of ambiguity, uncertainty, and seeming lack of structure.
- To take interest in each member's achievement, as well as the group's.
- The ability to give and accept feedback in a nondefensive manner.
- Openness to change, innovation, group consensus, team decision making, and creative problem solving.
- To create a team atmosphere that is informal, relaxed, comfortable, and nonjudgmental.
- The capacity to establish intense, short-term member relations, and to disconnect for the next project.
- To keep group communication on target and schedule, while permitting disagreement and valuing effective listening.

Astute HRD executives make provisions for team building.

■ To urge a spirit of constructive criticism, and authentic, nonevaluative feedback.
■ To encourage members to express feelings and to be concerned about group morale/maintenance.
■ To clarify roles, relationships, assignments, and responsibilities.
■ To share leadership functions within a group and to use total member resources.
■ To pause periodically from task pursuits to reexamine and reevaluate team progress and communications.
■ To foster trust, confidence, and commitment within the group.
■ Sensitivity to the team's linking function with other work units.
■ To foster a norm that members will be supportive and respectful of one another, and realistic in their expectations of each other.
■ To promote an approach that is goal-directed, seeks group participation, divides the labor fairly, and synchronizes effort.
■ To set high performance standards for the group.
■ To cultivate listening skills.

Since each team experience is different, uniqueness and flexibility should be encouraged. Yet at the same time, coordination and integration of team effort with other units and the whole enterprise are essential if the sum is to be greater than its parts. When team cultures contain the elements previously outlined, and are reflective of the whole organizational environment, then they become closely knit and productive. The more team participation is provided and employees are included in team decision making, the healthier and more relevant is that human system.

The teams may be part of the formal organizational structure as in the case of matrix management. However, some traditional hierarchies are slow and difficult to change. Then collateral organizations of informal teams may be formulated as a secondary mode of problem solving. This unofficial, parallel organizational arrangement is a change strategy to use with problems that are intractable in the formal system. In effect, it is a virtual organization.

Team management is suitable for knowledge problems that require high-quality, creative solutions with rapid processing and high output. When complex problems are less structured, quantifiable, definable, and past experience is unreliable, team management is necessary.

Improving Performance through Team Culture

Just like the organization in general, we might have an image of the team as a smaller "energy exchange system." When the group functions well, human psychic and physical energy is used effectively. Team interaction is an energy exchange. As the group seeks to achieve its goals, members energize or motivate themselves and one another by example. Team planning and changes become projections on energy use and its alteration. Every aspect of the group process can be analyzed in terms of this human energy paradigm. The key issue, then, is how the team manages its energies most productively and avoids underutilizing or even wasting the group energies. There are ways that members can analyze their functions and performance in projects, task forces, or product teams.

Team behavior can be examined from the viewpoint of task functions, which initiate, give or seek information, clarify or elaborate on member ideas, and summarize or synthesize. It can also be seen from the angle of group maintenance or morale building, such as encouraging, expressing group feeling, harmonizing, and compromising. It is the last element that builds group cohesion and camaraderie.

Such periodic behavioral review and data-gathering can be useful to improve the group's effectiveness. Not only can the information help a member to change his or her team behavior, but when such findings are combined into a visual profile, they offer a diagnosis of team health from time to time. It is recommended that teams pause on occasion for such self-examination. Sometimes a third-person facilitator, such as an internal or external consultant, can be most helpful in this analysis of team culture and progress. When the group's assessment is summarized, the team can then view its implications for more effective use of member energies.

Teams pause on occasion for such self-examination.

Team participation is an intensive learning experience. When members voluntarily involve themselves and fully participate, personal and professional growth is fostered. The team is like a laboratory of the larger organizational world in which it operates. Although a temporary experience, it is an opportunity for individual and team development. Each participant shares self and insights from the basis of unique life and organizational experiences. Synergy occurs when the members listen to each other and enter into the private worlds of the others. Total team perception and wisdom then become more than the sum of the parts.

If the organization's culture emphasizes employee participation through team management, the group microcultures are likely to reflect that system's macroculture. Thus, collaborative management should be evident not only within an individual team, but in intergroup relations. There is an implicit assumption that the team culture exerts a significant influence on an individual member's behavior. As a team member, one functions beyond the individual level, becoming representative of the group "persona." Those who serve in two or more interlocking groups are expected to act as linking pins in the accomplishment of organizational mission through these separate but interdependent entities.

Everything that anthropologists would examine in the culture of people in a national or organizational group can be analyzed in the miniature environment of the team. That can range from the group's beliefs and attitudes, to procedures and practices, to priorities and technologies. The team atmosphere, task orientation or processes, communication patterns, role clarification or negotiation, conflict resolution, decision making, action planning, intragroup and intergroup relations all can be scrutinized for better diagnosis of the group's dynamics. When a global manager or consultant engages in such analysis, the team can become more effective in the use of its energies.

Whether it is a family group (a permanent work unit) or a special group (temporarily constituted for a particular purpose), each individual contributes uniquely to the team from his or her own experience and talents. The team's resources can be strengthened when intercultural differences are used for synergy, rather than allowed to become a cause for divisiveness. The differences of perception that arise from varied academic or training backgrounds, work expertise and experiences, ethnic and national origins can enrich the group's basis for creative problem solving and achievement. The team's culture can be the means for capitalizing on, so that all members accomplish something together. A strong team culture enhances group communication and permits confrontation, stimulating group growth, and cohesion. Through shared vision, goals, and learning, the combined energy of members can accomplish more than individual effort, enhancing performance. Then, as a team identity is strengthened, bonding, group morale, camaraderie, and "esprit de corps" are also improved.

All education and training should have the purpose of developing human performance and potential.

All education and training should have the purpose of developing human performance and potential. While high performance demonstrates achievement, one's potential is yet to be realized. Just as there are ways to motivate and unleash individual potential, especially through counseling and mentoring, so it would seem possible to use teams to release the full potential of group performance. Dr. Raymond Forbes and his colleagues at Franklin University in Columbus, Ohio, are using a method of *Personal Executive Coaching* in their Graduate School of Business to enable its MBA students to better utilize their untapped potential. This educational strategy primarily uses coaching, as well as emotional intelligence, brain dominance, and strategic development, to unlock the learner's potential.[20] Similarly, it would seem reasonable that such coaching models could be utilized in team building to liberate hidden group performance potential! Surely an HRD team *coach* can facilitate this by helping to identify talent, providing suitable learning experiences, and then linking this to organizational goals. In this way, team development is attuned to the knowledge culture!

Transcultural Teams

Social scientists are conducting research on what people can do in small multinational groups to facilitate a meaningful experience and productive outcome. One exciting example of this occurred at the East-West Center in Honolulu, Hawaii.

At its Culture Learning Institute, Dr. Kathleen K. Wilson spearheaded an investigation with 15 other distinguished colleagues on the factors influencing the management of International Cooperative Research and Development projects. Their ICRD findings still have implications for any professional seeking to improve human performance and collaboration. Although the researchers are examining project team effectiveness among internationals, their insights can be extrapolated to other forms of inter- and intragroup behavior, whether it is a matrix organization, product team, task force, or any work unit.

The contexts in which international cooperative groups operate may vary, but there are similar factors present that affect performance. These external factors affect the environment within the project itself, and include such diverse elements as political, organizational, and cultural aspects, the size and scope of the endeavor, the disciplinary background of team members, and individual characteristics, research, and development policies and problems. A summary of factors that foster or hinder professional synergy follows in Exhibit 9.2 Certainly, the exhaustive list of situations that influence a project's effectiveness points up the need for strategies to manage the many cultural differences existing between and among professionals attempting to work together. Try to apply these insights to real-time group situations, such as teams functioning:

- within the United Nations or UNESCO, the World Health Organization, World Bank, or International Monetary Fund;
- within a global corporation that spans many countries and includes multinational membership;
- within the International Space Station, both on the ground and in orbit, with its sponsorship of some sixteen nations; and
- within the European Union as it moves from 15 members to include 10 more from Central and East Europe.

The East-West research on international cooperation projects offers some criteria that can be used in recruiting, selecting, and assessing professionals. *Team member characteristics* that foster group synergy are also implied in Exhibit 9.2. Such benchmarks can be helpful in interviewing potential team members, choosing collaborators, and setting goals for self-improvement in organizational relations.

Finally, these ICRD researchers offered some indications for ensuring synergy within global teams. First they established these criteria for evaluating international project effectiveness and management competence:

1. Individual team member satisfaction.
2. Group satisfaction and morale.

The contexts in which international cooperative groups operate may vary, but there are similar factors present that affect performance.

EXHIBIT 9.2

HUMAN FACTORS THAT FOSTER OR HINDER PROFESSIONAL SYNERGY WITHIN A PROJECT

- How project business is planned.
- Consideration of other problem-solving viewpoints.
- How the work should be organized.
- Approach to R&D tasks.
- Definition of R&D problems.
- Ambiguity resolution and problem formulation.
- Methods and procedures.
- Decision making relative to recurring problems.
- Allocation of resources to team members.
- Accountability procedures relative to resource use.
- Timing and sequencing approaches.
- Determining objectives for an R&D effort.
- Affiliation and liaison with external groups and degree of formality in their work relations.
- Quantity and type of project human resources.
- Qualifications, recruitment, and selection of new members.
- New member orientation and training on the project.
- Management of responsibilities.
- Underutilization of workers relative to skill competencies.
- Motivating behavior and reward expectations.
- Coordination of long/ short-term members.

- Agreement on degree of innovation required.
- Experience with cooperation especially relative to international R&D tasks.
- Official language(s) to use on project.
- Method of reporting every one's involvement in the project.
- Coping with internal demands and visitors.
- Meeting face-to-face and having to resort to other forms of more impersonal communication.
- Involvement in making viewpoints known.
- Power differences because of institution resources brought to the project.
- Prestige, risk-taking, tolerance of uncertainty, and perceptions.
- Project leadership and/or organizational policies changing unexpectedly.
- Quality of work presented in evaluation methods.
- What constituted success in project work, and what to do when members fail to meet group expectations.
- Clarification of roles on the relationships.

3. Work progress relative to intended goal statements.
4. Social and cultural impact of the endeavor on people.

Second, the East-West Center's researchers also identified interpersonal skills that influence a professional group's situation and accomplishments. These international team competencies and capacities are summarized in Exhibit 9.3.

These insights offer a compendium of the shared leadership skills that professionals should expect to contribute in the course of group collaboration. For organizations that provide project management training or team building for their members, these are the skills to be sought in team development, especially when members represent multicultural backgrounds.

SYNERGY AMONG PROFESSIONALS

To be a professional in the broad sense of the term, one can be an athlete, technician, or programmer, as well as an attorney, physician, or scientist. A professional in any occupation is the person concerned with improved performance and career development. Often the word is used to distinguish between an amateur and a skilled person in a field who makes a livelihood in such endeavors, such as a professional actor, singer, football or baseball player. Today professional relationships with colleagues are often temporary and intense. Peers may come together to share information and learn from one another. This may occur electronically or in person, such as by attendance at a convention of a professional society, or by participation in a project or research team, or in writing jointly a report, article, or handbook. It is a "bridge building process" among specialists or among those with special interests. Often these relationships are formed with persons from a variety of microcultures within disciplines or fields of learning, as well as within the organizations' units. The link-up effort is even more complex when the participants are internationals from diverse cultures.

Professional relationships with colleagues are often temporary and intense.

To promote synergy among professionals in teams and networks, four steps are essential:

1. Bring the new person "on board" quickly by various means of reaching out, briefing, orientation, and inclusion efforts.
2. Foster intense, ad hoc work relationships, as well as possible outside social relations.
3. Disengage rapidly when the task is completed and reassignment occurs or another undertaking is begun.
4. Follow up on the aftermath of the professional activity and maintain limited communication with members of the prior team or consortium.

EXHIBIT 9.3
SELF-MANAGEMENT COMPETENCIES AND EFFECTIVE TEAM MEMBERS

Self-Management Competencies Permit the Project Member to:

- Recognize other members' participation in ways they find rewarding.
- Avoid unnecessary conflicts among other team members, as well as resolve unavoidable ones to mutual satisfaction.
- Integrate different team members' skills to achieve project goals.
- Negotiate acceptable working arrangements with other team members and their organizations.
- Regard others' feelings and exercise tactfulness.
- Develop equitable benefits for other team members.
- Accept suggestions/feedback to improve his or her participation.
- Provide useful specific suggestions and appropriate feedback.
- Facilitate positive interaction among culturally different members, whether in terms of macrodifferences (national/political), or microdifferences (discipline or training).
- Gain acceptance because of empathy expressed and sensitivity to end users.
- Encourage dissemination of project outcomes throughout its life.
- Recognize national/international differences in problem statements and procedures, so as to create appropriate project organizational responses.
- Anticipate and plan for probable difficulties in project implementation.
- Recognize discrete functions, coordinating discrete tasks with overall project goals.
- Coordinate transitions among different kinds of activities within the project.

The Effective Team Member Has the Capacity for:

- Flexibility and openness to change and others' viewpoints.
- Exercising patience, perseverance, and professional security.
- Thinking in multidimensional terms and considering different sides of issues.
- Dealing with ambiguity, role shifts, and differences in personal and professional styles or social and political systems.
- Managing stress and tension well, while scheduling tasks systematically.
- Cross-cultural communication and demonstrating sensitivity to language problems among colleagues.
- Anticipating consequences of one's own behavior.
- Dealing with unfamiliar situations and lifestyle changes.
- Dealing well with different organizational structures and policies.
- Gathering useful information related to future projects.

In the pursuit of our interests and careers, we have numerous opportunities to form professional relationships. They may occur through the Internet by means of electronic mail and chat rooms. Or they may come about by joining a professional association or an organization, such as the Rotary or Kiwanis Club, which have worldwide branches. For those engaged in international business, for example, local *world trade centers* are "passports to opportunity." Usually operating in conjunction with the Chamber of Commerce in major cities, they offer global managers a chance for synergistic networking and career development. Often they sponsor a World Trade Day dealing with such subjects as business opportunities on the Internet, overseas markets, tips for importing/exporting, gathering competitive intelligence, and forming strategic alliances.

Local volunteering also allows one to form cross-disciplinary professional relations. For example, when technical personnel give time to fostering the performing arts in their community, they are exposed to wholly different types of persons and a new cultural experience. Or when bankers, scientists, and professors participate in projects to educate or mentor at-risk or homeless children, they promote enriching, synergistic relationships for both parties. Donating time becomes a *win–win* situation for both the giver and receiver—again, it is a way for professionals to build up their *social capital*, while fostering community trust and mutual benefit.

Local volunteering also allows one to form cross-disciplinary professional relations.

Networking for Synergy

Individuals have always formed linkages and exchanges with each other within a society or field of human endeavor. What is different in recent decades is the escalation of these phenomena on a global scale, across both cultures and disciplines of knowledge. Twentieth-century advances in communication and transportation have accelerated the process on a mass scale. Such interactions counteract professional obsolescence and contribute to continuing career development.

One's vocational peers provide a reference group, against which individual performance can be measured, and which can provide professional motivation or recognition. Thanks to the Internet and international travel, helpful professional colleagues may be contacted around the world, not just within one's own country or one's own field of learning. As more people study abroad, attend professional conferences overseas, and engage in career activities globally, transnational linkages are formed. The potential for enlightening synergy among professionals through such developments is astounding. Frequently, such persons provide the key to problem solution or the means to further one's research and career advancement.

In these new patterns of collaboration, it is important that self-reliance is fostered in the participants and that interdependence is perceived as the basis of networking. Networks, in effect, form a new microculture of people working for more diverse and innovative practices, standards, and perspectives suitable for the twenty-first century.

Computer networking may lead to performance improvement because it creates a system of interrelated people or groups, offices or workstations, linked together personally or electronically, or both, for information exchange and mutual support. Networking is a modern mechanism for coping with complexity and change in the transition to the information society. Furthermore, it is in harmony with many national cultures that are naturally collaborative and group oriented.

For networking to achieve positive contribution to its members and society, these characteristics should be cultivated:

■ Free-forming and adaptive relationship in which the person is the most important feature, the boundaries are unstructured, the power and responsibility are distributed, the participants may play many roles, the balance is maintained between personal integrity and collective purpose, and the sharing of concerns and values is encouraged.
■ Willingness of those linked together to exercise initiative, take risks, be assertive, be autonomous, be informal, and be authentic in communications.
■ Ability to cope with differences, ambiguity, uncertainty, and with lack of closure.

Innovative Cooperation with Colleagues

Now that the concepts and means for promoting synergy in professional activities have been reviewed, it may help to examine some creative approaches to the subject. It takes vision, courage, and risk to innovate. In 1931, Professor Neil Gordon of Johns Hopkins University had a brainchild for transmitting scientific information in a different way. Gordon wanted small groups of scientists to meet for summer seminars in a secluded and relaxed setting for informal, free give-and-take of information and knowledge exchange. Today, this innovative concept yields 100 Gordon conferences annually in seven New Hampshire schools and colleges for 12,000 professionals. Among the participants are Nobel laureates who enjoy the relaxed exchange of data where there is no pressure, no publicity, and no need to publish.

But what is innovation? And are there already some models of it that demonstrate synergy among professionals? *Innovation* has been defined as creative idea generation, or the act of introducing something new into the established order; it is a change or different way of doing things from the traditional pattern. Innovation, for survival and development, should be built into the operating mechanisms or policies of corporate

Innovation has been defined as creative idea generation.

systems. All social institutions, especially government agencies and corporations, have a desperate need to encourage creative deviations from the traditional norms and practices. Only organizations that build innovative performance into their systems will survive.

Drucker's[21] comments about innovation and business can be applied to all human systems:

> Innovation means, first, the systematic sloughing off of yesterday. It means, next, the systematic search for innovative opportunities in the vulnerabilities of a technology, a process, a market, in the lead time of new knowledge; in the needs and wants of a market. It means willingness to organize for entrepreneurship, to creating new businesses. . . . It means, finally, the willingness to set up innovative ventures separately, outside the existing managerial structure, to organize proper accounting concepts for the economics and control of innovation, and appropriate compensation policies for the innovators.

The new work culture values creativity and innovation and manifests this in its support of entrepreneurial activities. Innovative management builds mechanisms for entrepreneurship into organizational systems, such as developing an incentive system to reward risk-taking or creating a people-oriented climate that provides employees with a sense of ownership. Individuals from multiple disciplines and associations can be brought together cooperatively to accomplish something more than any one as an individual could achieve. That is how synergy is created.

TRANSITIONING INTO THE KNOWLEDGE CULTURE

Organizations have to be designed or redesigned to facilitate the exchange of information and the creation of knowledge. Obviously, global leaders can provide their corporations or associations with the information technology (IT) that will expedite this process. Yet if personnel are viewed as important persons—human assets—then management seeks to develop a work atmosphere that stimulates thinking, investigation, and creativity. The wise use of data, the pursuit of knowledge, and the practice of synergy do not occur automatically within institutions—management should be exercising leadership that makes it happen. For this to occur, consider how the following practices foster such behavior.

■ **Synchronize Perception**—endeavor to continually bring management and workers onto the same wavelength in the promotion of new strategies, policies, and attitudes. In an increasingly diverse

Organizations that build innovative performance into their systems will survive.

workforce, it is more productive when executive and employees views on critical issues match one another and reality. For example, the leadership has to truly mean that business practices cultivate, celebrate, and reward ethical, moral behavior. No wonder there is a crisis of conscience when top management at the global corporation Enron issued a viable code of ethics and mouthed support for it, but then acted otherwise—they became behavior models for corporate malfeasance. There was a dissonance of perceptions and behavior.

Effective managers emphasize the positive

■ **Positive Reinforcement**—when individuals or teams act upon the concepts discussed in this book, such as practicing synergy or pursuing knowledge, then leaders should confirm the behavior in some positive way. Effective managers emphasize the positive in worker behavior, instead of harping on negatives.

■ **Support Meritocracy**—actions, not just words, affirm to knowledge workers that management does indeed value competence and promotes on the basis of merit, rather than seniority or connections. Performance recognition comes in many ways—more challenging work assignments and benefits that strengthen family life are helpful, in addition to the usual promotions and pay raises.

■ **Determine Next-Step Skills**—all personnel who expect advancement should determine what is the next level of skills and information required for a new position and then begin to acquire such expertise. An effective strategy is for supervisors to treat people as if they had already attained this next level so that they will be motivated to meet such expectations.

■ **Provide for HRD**—a knowledge culture requires continuous learning, so global leaders have the responsibility to ensure that such opportunities are made available for personal and professional growth. Internally, this may be done through a dynamic Human Resource Development program that takes full advantage of group and electronic training. Externally, encouragement of professional development can include advanced education in the community, financial support for attendance at conventions and leading-edge conferences, or even sabbaticals to pursue further skills and knowledge. High on the HRD priorities should be varied training in synergistic team management.

■ **Capitalizing on Human Assets**—When an organization invests in its people, normally it will have unexpected payback, beyond shareholder value. Humanity benefits, too, by more socially aware, informed, and knowledgeable citizens. Perhaps we could learn from the Quakers of old who founded many British and American firms—in their tradition, regular meetings were held to justify to peers the good the business was doing. Many modern companies do much good for their communities without government regulation or intervention. They build trust and foster synergies that bring profitable returns in myriad ways.

CONCLUSIONS

After explaining the concept of cultural synergy, this chapter provided a contrast of societies that could be characterized as having high or low synergy, as well as organizational culture that reflects high and low synergy. Current affairs demonstrate that building synergistic relationships across starkly different cultures is difficult. It is especially complicated when the process of addressing difference is through conflict as the norm rather than establishing multilateral relationship building procedures.

The contemporary international conflicts reflected in terrorism and the war in Iraq are examples of a very complex dynamic. On one hand, there are deep-seated historical grievances between two groups (Western and Christian, and Eastern and Muslim) whose cultures, values, governments, and beliefs are very different.[22] This conflict is a complex political, economic, cultural, and religious issue that must be approached with both sides using multifaceted, multilateral, and synergistic actions. Building a bridge between the differences through developing culturally synergic pathways that value the "difference" is the first step.

Within organizations, the research insights reported here centered on behaviors and practices that contribute to synergy and success among teams, particularly in terms of international projects. The concluding section described people who are truly "professional," in their attitude toward their career and work and in how they can mutually benefit by synergy. Global leaders actively create a better future through synergistic efforts with fellow professionals. The knowledge work culture favors cooperation, alliances, and partnership, not excessive individualist actions and competition. This trend is evident, as well as necessary, in corporations and industries, in government and academic institutions, in nonprofit agencies and unions, and in trade and professional associations of all types. In an information or knowledge society, sharing ideas and insights is the key to survival, problem solving, and growth. But high-synergy behavior must be cultivated in personnel, so we need to use research findings, such as those outlined in this chapter, to facilitate teamwork and ensure professional synergy. In addition to fostering such learning in our formal education and training systems, we also should take advantage of the increasing capabilities offered to us for both personal and electronic networking.

Contemporary global leaders, then, seek to be effective bridge builders between the cultural realities or worlds of both past and future. Cultivating a synergistic mind-set accelerates this process.

Global leaders, then, seek to be effective bridge builders

MIND STRETCHING

1. Why is it difficult to achieve cultural synergy in multinational organizations?
2. What are some best strategies global business leaders should take to mitigate these difficulties?
3. There are many examples of cross-cultural organizational conflicts and problems. Think of one and determine the root causes of the conflict. Then answer: How would you create a culturally synergistic solution to this challenge?
4. What basic skills must a global leader have to build up a culturally synergistic organization?
5. Why is it insufficient for global leaders to be global-minded thinkers? Why is taking a systems approach also important?

REFERENCES

1. Freeman, O. L. "Foreword" by former president of Business International Corporation, Governor of Minnesota, and U.S. Secretary of Agriculture. In Moran, R. T. and Harris, P. R. *Managing Cultural Synergy*. Houston, TX: Gulf Publishing, 1982.
2. Simons, G. F., et al. *EuroDiversity—A Business Guide to Managing Differences*. Oxford: Butterworth–Heinemann/Elsevier Science, 2002.
3. Hart, L. B. *The Manager's Pocket Guide to Conflict Resolution: Learning from Conflict*. Amherst, MA: HRD Press, 2001, 2 vols.; Gordon, J. *Managing Conflict at Work Security and Development*, a journal published by Carfax/Taylor & Francis (325 Chestnut St., Philadelphia, PA 19106; www.tandf.co.uk).
4. Augsburger, D. W. *Conflict Mediation Across Cultures: Pathways and Patterns*. Louisville, KY: Westminster/JohnKnox Press, 1992, p. 23.
5. Adler, N. J. *International Dimensions of Organizational Behavior*, 4th ed. Canada: South-Western Thomson Learning, 2002, p. 116.
6. Ibid.
7. Ibid.
8. BBC News, *Chirac in new pledge to end riots*, November 15, 2005, (http://news.bbc.co.uk/2/hi/europe/4437206.stm)
9. Wilmot, W. W. and Hocker, J. L. *Interpersonal Conflict*, 7th ed. Boston: McGraw-Hill, 2006.
10. Ibid., p. 6.
11. Ibid. Original source is Gudykunst, W. and Ting-Toomey, S. *Culture and Interpersonal Communication*. Beverly Hills, CA: Sage, 1988, p. 158.
12. Ibid.
13. Crocker, C., Hampson, F. O., and Aall, P. (eds.). *Introduction: Managing Global Chaos*. Washington, DC: United States Institute of Peace Press, 1999.

14. Ormerod, P. *The New General Theory of Social and Economic Behavior: Butterfly Economics*. New York: Pantheon Books, 2000.

15. Falk, R. "World Prisms: The Future of Sovereign States and International Order," *Harvard International Review*, 21, no. 3 (Summer 1999). (http://hir.Harvard.edu/back/article.php3?art_id=falk1213&fulltext=1)

16. Wheatcroft, A. *Infidels, A History of the Conflict between Christendom and Islam*. New York: Random House Trade Paperbacks, 2005, p. 295.

17. Adler, N. *Organizational Behavior*, 3d ed. Cincinnati, OH: South-West Publishing Co., 1997.

18. Gibson, D. and Tulgan, B. *Managing Anger in the Workplace*. Amherst, MA: Human Resource Development Press, 2001; Black, C. H. "Culture Effects on Organizations: The Cross-Cultural Challenge," PhD. Dissertation, Haywood, CA: California State University, 2001; Laroche, L. *Managing Cultural Diversity in Technical Communcations*. Oxford, UK: Butterworth-Heinemann/Elsevier, 2003; Dees, M. Carnes, J. *Teaching Tolerance Magazine,* a project of the Southern Poverty Law Center (400 Washington Ave, Montgomery, AL 35104; www.teachingtolerance.org).

19. Gordon, J. *Building Better Teams*. Indianapolis, IN: Wiley/Pfeifer, 2003; Pope, S. *The Manager's Guide to Team Sponsorship*; Farrell, J. and Weaver, R. *The Practical Guide to Facilitation*. Amherst, MA: HRD Press, 2001.

20. Forbes, R. L. *The Michaelangelo Response: Release Our Hidden Performance Potential*. Columbus, OH: Franklin University, Graduate School of Business, 2003; Auerbach, J. *Personal and Executive Coaching*. Ventura, CA: Executive College Press, 2001; Whitmore, J. *Coaching for Performance*, Third Editon. London, UK: Nicholas Brealey, 2002.

21. Drucker, P. F. *Innovation and Entrepreneurship*. Oxford, UK: Butterworth-Heinemann/Elsevier, 1999.

22. Wheatcroft, A. *Infidels, A History of the Conflict between Christendom and Islam*. New York: Random House Trade Paperbacks, New York, 2005.

MANAGING TRANSITIONS AND RELOCATIONS IN THE GLOBAL WORKPLACE

A hero ventures forth from the world of the common day into a region of supernatural wonder: fabulous forces are there encountered, and a decisive victory is won: the hero comes back from this mysterious adventure with the power to bestow boons on his fellowman.
—Joseph Campbell, The Hero with a Thousand Faces.

Peace and prosperity in the 21st century depend on increasing the capacity of people to think and work on a global and intercultural basis. As technology opens borders, educational and professional exchange opens minds!

We need to throw our hats far away to make retrieving them interesting. (French saying)

LEARNING OBJECTIVES

To appreciate the challenges inherent in transitional experiences and relocations, so as to acquire necessary cross-cultural competencies. To examine ways for fostering acculturation when abroad, especially through customized deployment systems that train expatriates in proper business etiquette and protocols for living and working appropriately in an alien environment.

SAGA OF MY BRAZILIAN ADVENTURE

The adventure was finally started. The airplane landed smoothly in Guarulhos Airport in São Paulo, Brazil, early in the morning on January 2, 2004. This was to be about the last smooth experience I would have for a long while.

Many times, I wondered how I was so lucky to have found my way into the position that I was in. Here I was, a person from the rural midwestern United States, being charged with upgrading the breadth and depth of a major multinational company's corn-breeding organization in Brazil. I was to do this from a base in Central Brazil, right on the frontier of the Cerrados, the vast Brazilian savannah. This must have been what it was like when my grandfather emigrated from Europe to southwest Minnesota about 100 years ago. He was moving to the land of Crazy Horse, the famous Sioux Indian Chief, big sky, and horse races by the pool hall. I was moving to the land of Rondon, Amazonia, bigtime agricultural entrepreneurs, and the best football (soccer) in the world.

At customs, I immediately noticed things were different. People from the United States were being segregated into a separate line. This had never happened before. Fortunately I was at the head of the line since there were only a few people on the flight from the United States and only a very small group of them were U.S. citizens. As I walked up to the tables I noticed they were manned by the Federal Police and the tables were in addition to the customary immigration booths that one passes through to enter the country. It all seemed rather haphazard but very police-like.

I immediately noticed things were different.

As I handed the tall, brasiliera in a Federal Police uniform my passport, I inquired

"What is going on?"
"What do you think of your president?" she growled.
"What is the right response?"

She gave me an attractive smile and eased off. She then explained "that some judge in Mato Grosso" had ordered her to come to the airport and provide the same scrutiny to the incoming people from the United States as the United States was giving to the brasilieros. This was done at the last minute and this guy was doing this only for political reasons.

She then proceeded to fingerprint me, all ten fingers dipped into ink and pressed onto a card. I then had numbers somehow arranged onto a card, maybe it was my passport number, and held this against my chest while the other policeman "photographed" me. Both were a source of amusement as I was the first one for them and they were somewhat shocked at the process once they actually did it, especially for a *ianqui* that they learned enjoyed their country.

Finally I was appropriately documented, and allowed to go to the other line for the normal immigration and behind all the other foreigners in my flight and another much fuller flight. Eventually I passed through immigration and went to retrieve my luggage.

I was coming into the country with only what I was carrying so I was traveling heavy. After filling my luggage cart with the four bags I was carrying, two quite large and heavy, plus my carry-on bag and brief-case, I headed out the door, finally!

No sooner had I passed through the door than a very smartly dressed man with a perfect haircut and smile came up to me and asked me if I was an American. I indicated I was and only then noticed the person with the television camera coming up. He introduced himself as working for a television station in São Paulo and he asked if he could interview me regarding my thoughts on the revised immigration procedure for U.S. citizens.

This is trouble.

My immediate thought was: "This is trouble." I had some experience with the press in the past and had an inherent distrust of their appetite for controversy. I politely responded, "No, but I am sure there are others that would be happy to respond to your questions."

With that I turned away and began to make my way through the crowded airport. Guarulhos is one of the few airports that I travel to that can be crowded on January 2.

I must have looked like a beleagured American with lots of heavy baggage, tired from 18 hours of traveling, needing to change clothes, wanting to brush my teeth, needing a cup of coffee, and working my way through the crowd. Before I went 20 feet, the television reporter again asked for an interview, only this time the man with the camera appeared to have it running. Again I politely declined.

By the time I reached the center of the main hallway in the airport, the crowd thinned, but once again, my shadow, the television news personality was there to ask for an interview. This time I reconsidered. I decided he was not going to go away and I did not want to be cast as the ugly American. The best approach was to give him a brief interview and then I would be able to have some peace.

"How did you feel about the new immigration procedures, finger-printing and photographing of everyone from the U.S.?"
"I like Brazil so much that it is worth the effort."

A noticeably perplexed look began to appear on his face.

"Was the line long and did you have to wait a long time?"
"Yes the line was long but so was the other line."

By this time the interviewer realized this would be a rather boring interview so he stopped asking questions and thanked me for my time.

I was sure I had escaped unscathed and went on to my destination, Brasilia, which required another six hours of travel time.

Two weeks later I traveled back to São Paulo to participate in a week-long Portuguese immersion course. No sooner had I been introduced to my first professor that she recognized me from television. She was shocked.

Apparently, the news program had found a U.S. citizen who was sufficiently angry that they obtained the desired emotion. They ran my interview along with the other one as a measure of the range in response. About this time, widely publicized reports began to appear of an incident involving a pilot of a U.S. commercial airline. Apparently, the pilot became angry with the delays on entering the country; flight crews normally do not have to stand in line with all the passengers and get preferential treatment at immigrations. So he very publically insulted the federal police. He was arrested and fined quite a considerable amount of money.[1]

CROSS-BORDER GLOBAL TRAVEL

Today people move across the planet or beyond in person, or electronically for short or long time periods. Such travel may be for pleasure, professional development and education, or for business and military service. Humans have the capacity to move their bodies and/or their brains. The latter is evident in unmanned, automated space missions to the far corners of the universe. Electronic travel may range from telephone, radio, and television, to computer exchanges via the Internet in the form of mail, Web sites, chat rooms, podcasts, blogs, and wikis. In all cases, cross-cultural sensitivity and skills can facilitate global communications. Perhaps it would be wise to heed the advice of humorist, Mark Twain: "Twenty years from now you will be more disappointed by the things you didn't do, than by the things that you did. So throw off the bowline, sail away from the safe harbor. Catch the trade winds in your sails. Explore, Dream, Discover. . . . Travel is fatal to prejudice, bigotry, and narrow-mindedness."

Travel is also the principal avenue to the *transitional experience*. Ask yourself what is the common factor in each of these real life experiences.

People move across the planet.

- A young woman leaves a small Midwestern town to pursue a drama career in New York City.
- A sick, elderly widower is forced to sell his house of 40 years and enter an assisted-living retirement home.
- A successful manager in London, England, is transferred to Juarez, Texas, on the Mexican border.
- A military reserve officer is called up to duty for assignment to Iraq, leaving behind a spouse, two children, and a lucrative civilian job.

- A Chinese engineering graduate from Beijing receives a Fulbright grant to study for a master's degree at the Massachusetts Institute of Technology.
- A North African worker is smuggled illegally into Europe in the hope of getting a job that will enable him to support his family back in Morocco.
- Two happy kids from Marin County, California, learn they are to leave their friends and school to go to Bolivia, where their parents are to serve in the Peace Corps.
- A 32-year-old housewife is left alone with three children when her husband divorces her for a younger woman and moves out of town.
- A successful 50-year-old accountant retires early, sells his practice, buys a yacht, and sails around the world with a new lady friend.
- When their parents die in a plane crash, three Puerto Rican adolescents are sent to live with their aunt and uncle in Quebec, Canada.
- A dive master and underwater photographer leaves San Diego to accept a desirable position at a resort in the Cayman Islands, West Indies.
- A British oil company manager is transferred to an oil platform in the North Atlantic, leaving his family behind for a six-month assignment.
- A Canadian family relocates to Africa because the mother has been appointed executive director of Oxfarm, a humanitarian organization serving in Kenya.
- A Swedish marketing manager regularly travels the world in pursuit of new business for a global wireless company.
- A wealthy high-tech executive from the United States becomes the first space tourist by buying his way onto a Russian spacecraft going to the International Space Station.

Each situation represents a life turning point that can cause the person to advance or regress.

The common element above is people who are facing the challenge of altering their lifestyles. Each situation represents a *life turning point* that can cause the person to advance or regress. Some are facing a relocation; all are facing a transition. Some will view it as an opportunity, others as a tragedy. In any event, our species has been migrating around this planet since primordial times.

In this regard, historians and cultural anthropologists suggest the instincts for survival and exploration are the major motivators in such situations. In today's global village, the number of people living in another country for lengthy periods is increasing. Virtually everyone comes in contact with individuals who speak a different language or who were reared in another culture. In this twenty-first century, cultural homogeneity and isolation exist in very few places—heterogeneity, or diversity, is the reality everywhere. Within our shrinking world, everyone from executives to entertainers, soldiers to humanitarian volunteers, needs skills in managing both cultural differences and synergy.[2] Furthermore, we are transitioning into an emerging *knowledge culture* that offers new applications for such competencies. Richard Lewis suggests that it is a risk-taking, electronic culture that (1) encourages entrepreneurialism, Western-style individualism, and rapid decision cycles; (2) responds quickly and flexibly to end-user needs; (3) allows for greater customization of brands and services; and (4) communicates interactively for "communities of families and friends."[3]

Embarking on a "hero's journey" is the way the late anthropologist, Joseph Campbell, describes the challenge of living outside one's culture, while Osland reports on adventures abroad as "hero's tales."[4] An expert in mythology, Campbell beautifully describes these challenges.

Furthermore, we have not even to risk the adventure alone, for the heroes of all time have gone before us. The labyrinth is thoroughly known. We have only to follow the thread of the hero path, and where we have thought to find an abomination, we shall find a god. And where we have thought to slay another, we shall slay ourselves. Where we had thought to travel outward, we will come to the center of our own existence. And where we had thought to be alone, we will be one with the world.

COPING WITH TRANSITIONAL CHALLENGES

Early researchers in cross-cultural studies were concerned primarily with what happened when a person transitioned from home culture to a host culture. Today, interdependence between nations has facilitated the cross-border flow of people, ideas, and information. But we have a broader view of *transition trauma* associated with life's turning points, be they a relocation or other personal and professional challenges. The trauma may simply be triggered by multiple career assignments or opportunities, whether experienced domestically or internationally. In addition to the ordinary lifestyle transitions that everyone faces, contemporaries must cope with rapid alterations in their work, environments, and cultures. Consider the implications of the following United Nations report summarized in Exhibit 10.1.

Increasingly we interact with people who are very different from us, or in situations that are unfamiliar. Even when we share a common nationality, we may have to deal with citizens who are indeed "foreign" to us in their thinking, attitudes, vocabulary, and background. Individuals may face challenges within their environment due to their upbringing or local cultural conditioning. These challenges present opportunities either for growth or disruption. Such life turning points may range from married couples who divorce; to families who move from one geographic area to another, whether at home or abroad; to those who have major alterations in careers, jobs, or roles; to personally confronting issues of serious illness or even death.

To get a sense of transitional experience that can cause culture shock, analyze the following six scenarios.

Increasingly we interact with people who are very different from us, or in situations that are unfamiliar.

EXHIBIT 10.1
U.N. STUDY CITES VALUE OF GLOBAL MIGRATION

A recent United Nations study reports a surge in global migration at the turn of this century that is keeping populations from declining in Europe, as well as stimulating economic growth in North America by increased foreign income and workers. The researchers urge governments to re-examine national immigration policies, inasmuch as most countries only seek to control who and how many people immigrate there. To reap the economic and social rewards of new migrations, officials should be considering ways to integrate new arrivals and providing clear rules of transit.

Today more people are living outside their country of origin than ever before in history. According to Hania Zlotnik of the U.N. Populations Division, some 175 million worldwide were living outside their homelands in year 2000, and that number increases every year. Currently, migrants represent about 3% of the world population. The trend takes on even grater significance as the newcomers gain voting rights in their adopted country, as with the Hispanics in the United States. In the latter nation, the number of immigrants increased from 13.5 million in 1910, to 35 million in 2000. In North America, migrants now represent some 43% of the total populations. Whether the issue is legal or illegal entry into a nation, governments want to regulate the number and quality of new émigrés who have socioeconomic impact on both the host and home cultures.

Majority to Minority Culture

Your company transfers you and your family to a section of your country where you feel like an alien. From the Northeast you come to this Sunbelt state that is so different and unique. Your boss suggests you enroll at the local university to take a course entitled "Living Texas" to introduce you to the myths and mannerisms of Texans. The course teaches newcomers how to adapt to this former republic, rather than be considered "people from the outside." Texas is a state of contrasts, from huge ranches and high technology to Bible-belt mentality and laws. The course covers everything from "Talking Texas" and Texas cooking, to the Mexican VIEW of the Texas revolution and Texas folk heroes. If you can adapt, you will probably fall in love with these friendly people, their jalapeno lollipops and chili pepper dishes, and even discover their diverse ethnic mixture and the "Austin country" and "Mariachi" sounds of music.

Transitions in the Global Marketplace

You are a North American marketing consultant worldwide for a high technology company worldwide. Because of your expertise, you are much in demand, traveling beyond your home culture on short assignments. Your professional activities take you to a variety of host cultures. Typically, you are there for one to two weeks, consulting with local executives, many of whom are quite different in their approach to you as a woman. Most of your clients are men from cultures as diverse as Indonesia, Malaysia, Mexico, India, Hungary, and Russia. Their knowledge of English is sometimes limited, usually as a second or third language. You have no foreign language skills and depend on translators or interpreters. In your world travels, you often experience changes in time zones and resultant "jet lag," as well as problems with the native foods, social customs, and the loneliness of the female professional "on the road." You also face gender discrimination and sexual problems in some of these cultures. How to cope better in such circumstances?

Technology Transfer

You are an engineer from a highly industrialized nation. Your overseas assignments are mainly to less-developed countries. You realize that the indigenous population is not ready for sophisticated technologies. To help them in their transition to modern economies, and rather than sell them expensive equipment that they cannot afford or maintain, you prefer to design appropriate machines that pump water, cook food, and meet their real and practical needs. Your company partners with local institutions, scales projects back for maximum benefit, and provides ample training in what is usable, affordable, and appropriate technology. You are patient in your instructions and use bright natives to transmit your expertise to local workers. Furthermore, you encourage your company to underwrite scholarships for intelligent local youth to receive a more advanced technical education. Your attitude is that we are all part of the same human family.

Adjusting to New Immigrants

You live in east San Diego near a local Somali community and have been a leader, helping new arrivals to acculturate. You have been notified that in 2005, some 10,000 more Somali Bantu refugees are being relocated to the United States with your government's assistance. Two hundred of these tribal people, descendants of slaves, are coming to "America's Finest City." As an African American, you volunteer to help with their resettlement. The newcomers are from Tanzania, Malawi, and Mozambique, but have been scattered in United Nations refugee camps since the 1991 Somali civil war. You ask yourself hard questions about these impoverished victims of violence and discrimination. What can be done to facilitate the transition of these bewildered families and their children from a Third World lifestyle, to that of a so-called First World country? You have watched videotapes of their cultural orientation arranged by the U.S. State Department, met with city representatives from the health and education departments about their advanced planning for the Moslem Bantus, and enlisted other volunteers from nearby churches and non-profit organizations. The International Rescue Committee, Catholic Charities, and Alliance for African Assistance are already working on housing, household goods, and transportation. But many of these immigrants are illiterate farmers, denied education and jobs, so how will they ever make it in the West? And how will the locals react to them, especially the African-American minority and the Latino majority. Your friend Mohammed assures you these people are grateful for this humanitarian gesture. He says to expect help from the Somali community who have lived in this urban area for a decade—they are beginning to prosper and pay taxes. There are 11 million refugees in the world today.

Deployment for War and Peacekeeping

As a U.S. Marine sergeant, you are a veteran of the Gulf War with all its brutality and chaos. You were one of those 25,000 Camp Pendleton marines who went off to fight in the last decade and returned forever changed by your brief, intense experience with death and privation. You came back a driven and changed man, worrying if your marriage would also become a casualty. That desert war left some of your buddies depressed and with a variety of emotional, social, and physical problems. You changed into a more mature and determined person, responsible for training green troops for the next big conflict. Now you find yourself back in Iraq. While seemingly confident, all of you face a combination of tedious and funny moments, of comradeship and solitude, of gut-twisting fear and concern, of maiming or death from insurgents. Your wife and kids are frustrated by your long absence again, but send e-mails and packages to keep up your morale.

Death and Beginning Again

You were happily married to a loving and inspiring woman for 30 years. In every sense, you were partners, both personally and professionally. During your heart attacks, surgeries, and recuperations, she lifted your spirits. You shared stimulating life experiences around the world. Just as you both were getting ready to enjoy retirement years together, she suffered an auto fatality. After a year of loss and depression, you eventually marry a creative woman who is ten years younger than you. At 74 years of age, it is hard to change and start again, but you are open to new life possibilities.

All of these above incidents are *real, transitional experiences*. Each is an example of a life challenge that can be perceived as either devastating or a new chance. Having in-depth, intercultural encounters can be stimulating or psychologically disturbing, depending on your preparation and approach to them. Acculturation, or the process of adjustment to new experiences or living environment, takes time, possibly months and even years, while one learns new skills for responding and adapting to the unfamiliar. The extent of the trauma depends on the situation, such as whether one lives abroad among the native population or in a protected compound, be it a military, diplomatic, corporate, or religious enclave. The experience of coping with global diversity can be renewing or debilitating. When we are strangers in a place where the traditions and customs are foreign and unexpected, we may lose our balance and become unsure of ourselves. The same thing can happen within our own society when change happens so rapidly that the old traditions, the cues we live by, are suddenly undermined and irrelevant, threatening our sense of self.

Transitional experiences offer two alternatives—to cope or to "cop out." One can learn to comprehend, survive in, and grow through immersion in a different culture. The positive result can be increased self-development. Whenever we leave home for the unfamiliar, it involves basic changes in habits, relationships, and sources of satisfaction. Inherent in cultural change is the opportunity to leave behind, perhaps temporarily, one set of relationships and living patterns and to enrich one's life by experimenting with new ones. Implicit in the personal conflict and discontinuity produced by such experiences is the possible transcendence from environment or family support to self support. Intercultural situations of psychological, social, or cultural stress also stimulate us to review and redefine our lives—to see our own country and people in a new perspective. Or, we may reject the changes or new culture and lose a possible growth opportunity.[5]

Transitional experiences offer two alternatives.

Culture Impacts Identity

One reason the transitional experience is so significant is that it may alter our sense of identity. Fearn[6] writing on the subject of philosophy makes the point that all humans are faced with three critical questions. One, *who am I?* (mind and body); Two, *what do I know?* (language and knowledge); Three, *what should I do?* (morals and meaning of life). Major turning points in our lives often force us to rethink our answers to these inquiries which affect our self-perception, and the image we project to others.

All transitions influence one's sense of identity—some strengthen this sense of self, while others may threaten that identity or even change it. That is why our colleague, Gary Wederspahn, suggests in Exhibit 10.2 that we deal with this matter before departure overseas. When we go outside our home culture into a foreign culture, we may, for example, experience an identity crisis abroad. As a result, personal development occurs when we redefine our answers to the above questions, thereby expanding our perceptual field.

Perhaps the most important lesson for the cross-cultural sojourner is to understand one's cultural baggage. In addition to the dozen volumes in our own *Managing Cultural Differences* series (listed opposite our

All transitions influence one's sense of identity—some strengthen this sense of self, while others may threaten that identity or even change it.

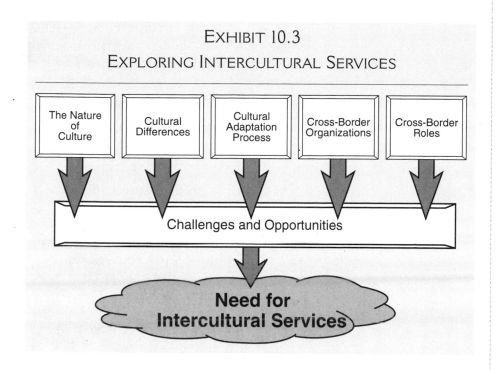

EXHIBIT 10.3
EXPLORING INTERCULTURAL SERVICES

The Nature of Culture | Cultural Differences | Cultural Adaptation Process | Cross-Border Organizations | Cross-Border Roles

Challenges and Opportunities

Need for Intercultural Services

title page), there are many popular books to help travelers going abroad. To assist their workers coping with such transitions, organizations—through their human resource development division—provide their personnel with professional, intercultural services. The rationale for this is summarized in Exhibit 10.3.

RELOCATION CHALLENGES

When we relocate within our own country or abroad, we may be subject to culture shock. Although scholars have only researched this phenomenon during the past 50 years or so, its impact on people has been written about in works of fiction as early as 1862, including Tolstoy in his book *The Cossacks*. Again, Jack London, in a 1900 story, described what it felt like to be a "foreigner," but in a literary, not scientific, way. London describes what a sojourner should expect:

> He must be prepared to forget many of the things he learned, and to acquire such customs as are inherent with existence in the new land; he must abandon the old ideals and the old gods, and oftentimes he must reverse the very code by which his conduct has hitherto been shaped. . . . The pressures of the altered environment are almost unbearable, and they chafe in body and spirit under the new restrictions which are not understood. This chafing is bound to act and react, producing diverse evils and leading to various misfortunes.[7]

He must be prepared to forget many of the things he learned.

Essentially, culture shock, as described by London, is our psychological reaction to a totally unfamiliar or alien environment, which often occurs with any major transitional experience.[8] Culture shock is neither good nor bad, necessary nor unnecessary. It is a reality that many people face when in strange and unexpected situations that make it difficult for automatic coping, as we do in our home culture. Oberg referred to culture shock as a generalized trauma one experiences in a new and different culture because of having to learn and cope with a vast array of new cultural cues and expectations, while discovering that your old ones probably do not fit or work. More precisely, he notes:

> Culture shock is precipitated by the anxiety that results from losing all our familiar signs and symbols of social intercourse. These signs or cues include the thousand and one ways in which we orient ourselves to the situations of daily life—how to give orders, how to make purchases, when and when not to respond. Now these cues, which may be words, gestures, facial expressions, customs, or norms, are acquired by all of us in the course of growing up and are as much a part of our culture as the language we speak, or the beliefs we accept. All of us depend for our peace of mind and efficiency on hundreds of these cues, most of which we are not consciously aware of.[9]

Consider the potential for culture shock that Napoleon Barragan faced when he left his hometown of Yagui, Ecuador, to seek his fortune in New York City. Born in 1941, he is now the CEO of 1-800-Mattress. Exhibit 10.4 tells part of his acculturation story in his own words.

EXHIBIT 10.4
A RELOCATION SUCCESS STORY

I come from a small village in the mountains of Ecuador. When I was five, I moved to the next town where there was a school. I lived then with my grandmother and aunt during the school months. But in the summers, I would go back to my parents who had a little farm. I used to show my mothers maps, saying that one day I will be in some of those places and countries. She would reply, "You can do it if you want."

At 17, before I finished high school, I left for Bogotá, Colombia. I was influenced by the radio programs I had heard from Colombia, especially the music and the news. While I was thinking of a better future for my family and me, it really was about having an adventure. Without friends or relatives in that land, I learned to survive, first with a job there distributing soda and beer on donkeys. My boss, Diomeres Sanabria, treated me like a member of his family. When he found out that I had not told my parents where I had gone, he took me to the airport, bought a plane ticket, and sent me back to

Culture shock is precipitated by the anxiety that results from losing all our familiar signs and symbols of social intercourse.

my family and to finish high school. I did that, eventually going back to Colombia with only 24 pesos in my pocket when I arrived there in Barranquilla. I slept in the park and for three days I did not eat. There are moments like that in your life which help you to appreciate where you come from and where you want to go. When I came to New York City in 1968, my circumstances were similar. By then I was married, had a 2-year-old daughter, and very little money. Even our plane ticket was on credit. We lived with my mother-in-law in her apartment in Jamaica, Queens. She found a second-hand sofa for my wife, my daughter, and myself.

I went from one factory to another, and in three years got a job working in the finance department of a furniture store in Manhattan. Later I went to another furniture store where I ended up the manager. But I knew nothing about business. When a customer asked me something that I did not understand, I usually answered that we did not have it. But my boss proposed opening another store in Jamaica, New York, with me, so my initial contribution was $2000, all our savings. When our partnership ended, I began my own second-hand furniture and mattress store. Then a friend offered me another larger store. I worked long, late hours. One day when reading *The New York Post* newspaper, I came across an advertisement for "Dial-A-Steak." I started thinking and changed the word "steak." Twenty years later, it became the name of the company I founded—1-800-Mattress! My favorite business book is *Discovering the Soul of Service* by Leonard H. Barry.

Source: Adapted from an interview by Eva Tahmincioglu entitled "A Long Road from Ecuador," *The New York Times*, July 3, 2005, p. 8BU.

This is a true story representative of the story of many immigrants from Latin America to North America. What Mr. Barragan left out of his tale are the vision, persistence, and toil it took him to overcome cultural differences and immigration regulations to become a successful executive.

Myriad Forms of Culture Shock

A new form of this trauma, growing exponentially throughout the world, is *future shock*, of which Alvin Toffler warned in his 1970 book by that title and again in a 1980 volume, *The Third Wave*. Essentially, this mass culture shock is being experienced by whole groups and nations because of the inability to transition rapidly from a previous stage of human development (e.g., agricultural or industrial) into our present Information Society, or knowledge culture. The technological, scientific, and knowledge advances have been so large and so accelerated that many people cannot cope with the pace of these changes. They opt out or are bypassed by the mainstream of civilizations; many end

A new form of this trauma, growing exponentially throughout the world, is future shock.

up in an underclass position in modern society. Furthermore, today, countries and institutions—such as religious, educational, and political systems—are resisting modernization, suffering from culture lag, and living in the past, unable to cope with present and future challenges. For institutions, the same phenomenon is referred to as *organization shock*.

According to Klopf[10] there are six stages of culture shock resulting from relocation.

1. The *preliminary stage* involves preparation for the experience. During this stage, anticipation and excitement build as one packs, makes reservations, and plans for departure with many unrealistic expectations.

2. Arrival at the destination marks the *spectator stage*, during which there are many strange sights and different people. All of this newness produces fascination with the culture. This honeymoon stage may last from a few days to six months.

3. The *participation stage* occurs when the individual must do the hard work of living in the culture and learning about it, especially its language—the honeymoon has ended. The sights have been visited and now coping with everyday life must occur.

4. When problems begin to arise that are difficult to handle, usually the *shock stage* sets in. Irritability, lethargy, depression, and loneliness are symptoms. One must find ways to confront and adjust to the differences in culture.

5. If the individual reaches the *adjustment stage*, identification with the host culture has progressed satisfactorily. Relationships with locals develop, along with a sense of belonging and acceptance.

6. For individuals living permanently in a culture, the adjustment stage finishes the transition period—one may assimilate or become bicultural in mind-set. For those who are temporarily living in a host culture, the return to the home culture introduces the *re-entry stage*. Culture shock in reverse may set in with individuals again going through the above five stages, but this time in their native land. A sense of discomfort, disorientation, and even frustration may be experienced, often up to six or more months.

The pace at which one advances through these stages is different for each individual. For those who are experienced in international travel, it may quicken and perhaps lessen the trauma. Obviously, the two global executives described in Exhibit 10.5 no longer are bothered by this phenomenon.

For such managers in the global workplace, like Ghosen and Garner, corporation have to hire consultants, like Cendant Mobility, to design new HR management systems. But what provisions were initially made by employers, so that such personnel might better cope with the cultural factors in their cross-border deployment?

However, for the *long-term expatriate* exposed to a very different culture from one's own, physical and psychological concerns may be

EXHIBIT 10.5[11]

THE TRUE COSMOPOLITAN

Carlos Ghosn is a Brazilian, who next month will be spending 40% of his time in Paris as the new boss of Renault, 35% in Tokyo where he will continue as head of Nissan, and 25% elsewhere—mostly in America. Jean-Pierre Garner is a Frenchman who heads a British drug company (GlaxoSmithKline), but spends up to 70% of his working life outside Britain and France. . . .

The two bosses are the most visible examples of a growing army of mobile workers who are giving human resource (HR) departments a headache: how to track where they are and when, for tax and visa purposes. Brian Friedman, president of Ernest & Young's Institute of Global Mobility, says this is a major challenge for such departments. Gone are the days when working abroad was merely a matter of signing a formal expatriate package—with allowances for differences in cost of living and the quality of life—before waving goodbye for another three years. . . . Today's global business is creating a new sort of worker, termed the *stealth expatriate*.

real or imagined. Those experiencing culture shock manifest obvious symptoms such as excessive anxiety over cleanliness and sanitary conditions, feeling that what is new and strange may be "dirty." This may be seen with reference to water, food, dishes, and bedding, or evident in unreasonable fear of servants and shopkeepers because of disease they might bear. Other indications of such traumatic behavior are feelings of helplessness and confusion, growing dependence on long-term resid of one's own nationality, constant irritations over delays and minor f trations, and undue worry about being cheated, robbed, or inju Some may exhibit symptoms of mild hypochondria, expressing app hension about minor pains, skin eruptions, and other ailments, rea imagined—it may even get to the point of actual psychosomatic illness Often, individuals experiencing culture shock postpone learning local language and customs, dwelling instead on their loneliness a longing for back home, to be with one's own and to talk to people who "make sense." However, persons who seek international assignments as a means of escaping "back-home problems" with career, marriage, or substance abuse, will probably only exacerbate personal problems that would be better resolved in their home culture.

Osland[12] uses the concept of "learning to live with paradox" instead of emphasizing the shock that may come from experiences in an alien society. Such paradox occurs when we have to hold ideas in mind that are seemingly opposite to the home perspectives. Osland calls this the "road of trials" when we are confronted with obstacles and tests on our

Persons who seek international assignments as a means of escaping "back-home problems" only exacerbate personal problems that would be better resolved in their home culture.

way to "normally" perceiving and functioning. To deal with such paradoxes more effectively, she proposes we learn from expatriates who have gone before us, which can begin before departure and continue on-site.

To facilitate acculturation, organizations responsible for sending others abroad should be careful in their recruitment and selection of individuals for international assignments. Surveys have shown that those who adjust and work well outside their own culture are usually well-integrated personalities, with qualities such as *flexibility, personal stability, social maturity, and social inventiveness.* Such candidates for overseas work are not given to unrealistic expectations, irrational concepts of self or others, nor do they have tendencies toward excessive depression, discouragement, criticism, or hostility. Global corporations, government agencies, and international organizations that sponsor people abroad have a responsibility to prevent or reduce culture shock among their representatives. It is not only necessary for individual acculturation, but is more cost effective, while promoting out-of-country productivity and improving client or customer relations with host nationals. This will be discussed further in the section on deployment systems.

One should also be realistic about the difficulties that may be experienced when living abroad.

One should also be realistic about the difficulties that may be experienced when living abroad. Intestinal disorders and exotic diseases are real and may not always be avoided by inoculations or new antibiotics. In some countries water, power, transportation, and housing shortages are facts, and one's physical comfort may be seriously inconvenienced. Political instability, ethnic feuds, and social breakdown may make an assignment unacceptable. Adjustment may also be slowed because of not knowing the local language, or in trying to cope with strange climates and customs. But we are born with the ability to learn, to adapt, to survive, to enjoy. After all, human beings do create culture, so the shocks caused by such differences are not unbearable or without value. The intercultural experience can be more satisfying, contributing much to personal and professional satisfaction. One can discover friends everywhere. The expatriate experience has always meant accepting risk implicit in living and traveling beyond your own borders.

As non-governmental organizations (NGOs) increase in number and influence, *global humanitarians* are more prevalent. But today, their service abroad on behalf of others may often place them in "harm's way." Civil strife may cause them to shut down operations, or they may face kidnapping, bodily harm, and even death. Exhibit 10.6 is one of the many stories of those who do such noble and hazardous work on behalf of others in the human family—namely, Doctors Without Borders most worthy of support.

Role Shock

The phenomenon and process of culture shock have applications to other life crises. For instance, there is also role shock. Each of us

EXHIBIT 10.6[13]
GLOBAL HUMANITARIANS

Envision yourself as director of recruitment and training for the international, nonprofit organization called Doctors without Borders, or "Medecins sans Frontieres" (MSF). All of their members are volunteers from the professional health care fields worldwide. Founded in 1970, its representatives have been so effective as to be awarded the Nobel Peace Prize in 1999. Doctors without Borders has received many recognitions for being one of the best relief and development charities. In 2002, they received an A rating from the American Institute of Philanthropy as well as an "exceptional rating" from "Charity Navigator," which helps donors make informed decisions about their contributions.

With such a distinguished reputation for high performance, your job in MSF human resource development is to ensure that those standards are maintained. You are preparing culturally diverse physicians, nurses, therapists, and social workers for service in over 80 countries. You are training transcultural teams who are mission focused, but who don't venture into areas where they lack expertise. You are to help them to involve local leaders in program design and implementation before moving on. You are to ready dedicated medical volunteers to meet the next emergency wherever and whenever it occurs, be it disease outbreak, natural disaster, or even war. These humanitarians are expected to offer not only emergency medical aid, cope with malnutrition, epidemics, or ethnic cleansing and mutilations, but also to give the deprived victims *hope* to survive and rebound! Yet personally, these dedicated medics have to be able also to cope with culture shock, unbelievable bureaucracy, corruption, manifold traumas, as well as their own fears of personal harm or even kidnapping!

Now design a foreign deployment system for such a group. What recruitment and assessment methods will you employ? What kind of predeparture training will you provide, especially in the matter of cross-cultural relations, teamwork, and changing roles? What type of orientation and support services will you offer overseas for these medical teams? How will you evaluate on-site performance? How will you coach or counsel these professionals for reentry to their home cultures and health careers?

chooses, or is assigned, or is conditioned to a variety of roles in society and its institutions—man or woman, family member, son or daughter, parent or child, husband or wife (single/married/divorced), teacher or engineer, manager or union organizer, amateur or professional. In these positions, people have expectations of us, as we do of their varied positions. These role opportunities or constraints often differ in another culture. A woman, for instance, may do in one culture what is forbidden in another. In some societies, senior citizens are revered and in others, ignored. In some cultures, the youth regard teachers with awe, while others treat them as inferiors or "buddies."

Role perception is subject to change according to time, place, and circumstances.

Role perception is subject to change according to time, place, and circumstances. But for the past 60 years, our defined roles have changed at an accelerating rate. In the past, our roles were fairly stable, clear, and predictable. Today, our roles are fuzzies, more unpredictable, and fluid. The person who has a particular understanding of what a manager is and does may be upset when he or she finally achieves that role, only to discover it to be altered considerably! Our traditional views of such functions are suddenly obsolete. All this role uncertainty can be very disconcerting; the resulting shock to our psyche may be severe and long-lasting. Role shock can lead to an identity crisis, especially if one's sense of self and life are tightly linked to a career or work role. Consider the trauma an older person experiences when suddenly there is a reduction in the workforce, and unemployment lines are long, while jobs are scarce. Furthermore, a cross-cultural assignment can accentuate role shock. Many individuals sent abroad find themselves adjusting to totally different role requirements than back home.

Role shock may be apparent as a result of organizational mergers or acquisition, or of reorganization or redesign of a system. The outcome may cause a person's position to be combined with others, downsized, or even lost. In the past decade, many middle managers were simply eliminated in corporations trying to cope with new economic conditions. Even when one retains his or her post within a newly acquired company, the organization and its culture may perceive "your role" in an entirely different way. Role transformation or elimination may come from new technologies, new research, new markets, or new crises.

Consider the alteration worldwide of the traditional role of spouse, parent, and even son or daughter. Role change may occur without much warning or preparation, as Exhibit 10.7 confirms. So what is the antidote? Part is *personal*, a change in mind-set and attitudes. One can *learn* to be more open-minded, more ready for change, more willing to explore and consider alternatives, more able to take risks. Part is *organizational*—personnel can be educated, trained, counseled, and even conditioned to ensure such perceptual and behavioral change.

CHANGING ROLES REDEFINES WHAT IT MEANS TO BE THE MAN OF THE HOUSE

Dick Dinse, a 54-year-old retired Marine, had no idea how a ballet slipper worked. A self-described "typical male," Doug James worries how to help his daughter through adolescence.

When their military wives shipped out for the war against terrorism, these two dads, and more like them, got a whole new job description: home front duty.

It's a challenge; said Dinse of Oceanside, "You go to bed a lot earlier and wake up a lot quicker." His wife, Betty, is an Army reservist activated for the first time in July. Now she's at Ramstein Air Base in Germany, and he is father and mother to their 4-year-old, Sarah. . . . "Everything associated with running the household, whether it's cleaning, laundry, groceries, shopping, yard work—it all has to be tucked into taking care of a daughter," said Dinse who previously left such duties to his wife. "You really don't give it a second thought until you've got it all to do."

James' wife, Lt. j.g. Candice James, departed on the aircraft carrier Nimitz on March 3. This is her fourth deployment. On the pier before their mother's departure, the three James daughters tearfully embraced her. Then they clustered around Dad, wordlessly clinging to his strong, steady presence as the ship pulled away from the dock.

The switch in traditional gender roles doesn't appear to be an ego buster for these two men, both of whom have served Uncle Sam themselves. About 15% of the U.S. military is female. . . . The Pentagon says about 85,000 of America's 210,000 female warriors are married with children.

Reentry Shock

When expatriates return from foreign deployment, they face another form of reverse culture shock. Having objectively perceived his or her culture from abroad, one can have a more severe and sustained jolt through reentry into a home culture. The intercultural experience widens perceptions and broadens constructs, so the person is less myopic in the homeland and more cosmopolitan. Some returning "expats," or those returning from long service overseas, feel a subtle downgrading and loss of prestige and benefits. Others bemoan the loss of household help and social contacts, as well as other "perks." This is especially evident with members of the military who come home after a lengthy deployment in other parts of the world. Many feel uncomfortable for

When expatriates return from foreign deployment, they face another form of reverse culture shock.

six months or more in their native land, frustrated with their organization and bored with their "narrow-minded" colleagues who never left home. Some returnees seem out of touch with what has happened in their country or corporation during their absence and no longer seem to fit into the domestic organization.

Something similar has been experienced by astronauts and cosmonauts after long off-world missions. Forty years ago, the Apollo astronauts returning from the Moon began to show signs of this *overview effect*. They had seen the "pale blue dot"—our planet from outer space! They had seen our world without borders, so environmentally fragile and interdependent. They had begun to perceive themselves as citizens planet; in fact, the United Nations called them "envoys of mankind." When they came back to Earth, many of them dealt with serious readjustment problems, physical, psychological, and sociological. The perceptual field of spacefarers are altered, so the longer a person is in orbit, the more likely they will experience *reentry* on their return to Earth.

After World War I, a popular song described the reentry problem of the troops very simply, "*How you gonna keep them down on the farm after they've seen Paree* (Paris)?" In those days, many disturbed soldiers were hospitalized for *shell shock*. The issue became more acute with veterans from World War II, and then the Korean Conflict. But Vietnam veterans seemed to have the most difficult time in returning to civilian life, especially those with *post-traumatic stress*. Many "vets" of that era's conflicts in Asia are homeless and emotionally walking wounded, suffering from mental illness and/or substance abuse. In the two more recent Gulf and Iraq wars, troops from many nations experienced severe adjustment problems upon their return. All wars that cause citizens to cross borders or fight overseas produce pain, suffering, and challenges. The affects are felt not only by military service people, but by their families, who are left to cope at home during their absence and after their return.

The coming home phenomenon described here, whether for civilians or military, can be temporary and less intense if the expatriate is helped by a professional reorientation program. For some, culture and reentry shocks may be the catalysts for major choices and transitions, such as a new locale and new relationships, pursuit of additional education or training, a change in job or career, and generally an improved lifestyle. While some expatriates never make the necessary readjustments, living as strangers in their home cultures, for the majority, the intercultural experience is very positive, a turning point toward an enriched quality of life.

FOSTERING ACCULTURATION

After culture shock subsides, with hope, real acculturation settles in. Anyone who has gone from home to live, work, or study in a foreign country must learn about and adapt to another quite distinct cultural environment. As early as the 1930s, *acculturation* was being formally researched by scholars. The definition developed then is just as valid today—when groups of individuals having different cultures come into continuous firsthand contact with subsequent changes in the original cultural patterns of either or both groups.[15]

Most obviously, one must assimilate to fulfill practical needs for survival and accommodation in strange situations, like finding grocery stores, doctors, schools, banks, etc. Integration into a different society produces more personal changes, as one moves beyond the familiar patterns and institutions of the old while attempting to absorb and understand the new. Value systems and attitudes also undergo alteration in this process. Furthermore, there may be biological changes as one adjusts to a different climate, bacteria and viruses, or unknown food and plant life. Also, social changes occur as the visitor seeks to find and form new relationships and friendships. All of these happenings may result in stress or tension.

Sociologists point out that stable, healthy family relationships can make the difference between success and failure in the foreign assignment. Families who interact in mutually supportive ways can be their own resource for acculturation into another environment. As ambassadors of your native culture, do endeavor to establish wholesome intercultural relations with the local people. Such behavior not only contributes to creating a favorable image of your own country, but facilitates your adjustment as well. Extending culture shock can be a hindrance to forming friendships and effective business relations abroad. Travelers abroad have to reach out and create a friendly, positive impression, lest we be perceived as arrogant and imperious. Exhibit 10.8 offers wise counsel in this regard.

Healthy family relationships can make the difference between success and failure.

The following ten recommendations will help to deflate the stress and tension overseas, while advancing successful acculturation:

Be Culturally Prepared. Forewarned is forearmed. Individual or group study and training are necessary to understand cultural factors and cultural specifics. Public libraries and the Internet provide a variety of resource material. Also, the public health service will advise about required inoculations, dietary clues, and other sanitary data. Before departure, the person scheduled for overseas service can experiment with the food in restaurants representative of the second culture. Furthermore, one might establish contact in his or her homeland with foreign émigrés, students or visitors from the area to which he or she is going. A helpful approach is to seek out your own *cultural mentor*— a wise friend or counselor who has lived in the host country, or who is upon arrival. The expatriate's mentor is capable of guidance, encouragement, and help in mastering the intricacies of a new culture. Sometimes your organizational sponsor abroad may link you to such a resource or even provide a *cultural coach* as described in Exhibit 10.9.

*International
assignees and
business travelers
need to make
positive personal
impressions on
their
counterparts
overseas.*

EXHIBIT 10.8[16]
PREVENTING NEGATIVE IMAGES

International assignees and business travelers need to make positive personal impressions on their counterparts overseas. Failure to do so not only defeats their labors and undermines the missions of their organizations, but also cuts them off from potential local allies during times of trouble. In most instances, negative images are created by conflicting values and expectations that lead to misinterpretation of expatriates' behavior or intentions. Rarely are these [negative] images consciously or intentionally caused. Nevertheless, they are far too common and cause much harm. Reactions from people in other countries indicate that more intercultural training of U.S. personnel is required.

EXHIBIT 10.9[17]
TRANSCULTURAL ELECTRONIC COACHING

Intercultural business coaching is on the rise, especially by electronic means through the establishment of corporations' own intranet for internal communications among their global personnel. For example, 15 nationalities participate in a team chat room to share cross-cultural information and insights. Since the network is proprietary, employees must use a code to get into this resource and to dialogue with colleagues from various cultural backgrounds. These *virtual* intercultural teams use electronic bulletin boards for posting notices and materials and exchanging electronic mail within the organization worldwide.

Learn Local Communication Complexities. Study the language of the place to which one is assigned. At least, learn some of the basics that will help in exchanging greetings and shopping. In addition to courses and books on the country, audio or videocassettes and discs can advance your communication skills in the host culture. Published guides can be helpful in learning expected courtesies and customs.

Interact with the Host Nationals. Meeting with people from the country you are going to is helpful. There are many such foreign nationals within your own organization or local community who may provide introductions to relatives and friends abroad as well as useful information regarding their native culture and its unique customs. If one lives overseas within a corporate or military colony, avoid the "compound mentality." Immerse oneself in the host culture. Whenever feasible, join in on the artistic and community functions, the carnivals and rites, the international fraternal or professional associations. Offer to teach students or business people one's language in exchange for knowledge of their language; share skills from skiing to tennis, from the performing to intellectual arts—all means for making friends worldwide.

Be Creative and Experimental. Innovating abroad may mean taking risks to get around barriers of bureaucracy and communication to lessen social distance. This principal extends from experimenting with the local food to keeping a diary as an escape to record one's adventures and frustrations. Tours, hobbies, and a variety of cultural pursuits can produce positive results. One needs to be existential and open to the daily opportunities that will be presented. Consider preparing a newsletter for the "folks back home" in which you share your cross-cultural adventures and insights, either by regular or electronic mail.

Be Culturally Sensitive. Be aware of the special customs and traditions that, if followed by a visitor, will make one more acceptable. Recognize that in some cultures, such as in Asia and the Middle East, saving face and not giving offense is considered quite important. Certainly avoid stereotyping the natives, criticizing their local practices and procedures, while using the standard of one's own country for comparison. Americans are dynamic and pragmatic, generally liking to organize things "better," so it may be a challenge for them to relax and adjust to a different rhythm of the place and people they are visiting.

Recognize Complexities in Host Cultures. Counteract the tendency to make quick, simplistic assessments of situations. Most complex societies comprise different ethnic or religious groups, stratified into social classes or castes, differentiated by regions or geographical factors, separated into rural and urban settlements. Each of these may have distinct subcultural characteristics over which is superimposed an official language, national institutions, and peculiar customs or history that tie a people together. Avoid pat generalizations and quick assumptions. Instead, be tentative when drawing conclusions, realizing one's point of contact is a limited sample within a multifaceted society.

Understand Oneself as a Culture Bearer. When going abroad, each person brings his or her own culture, conditioning, and distortions. Thus, one views everything in the host culture through the unique filter of his or her own cultural background. For example, if one is raised in democratic traditions, it may be unsettling to live in a society that values the authority of the head male in the family and extends this reverence to national leaders. But with locals, quiet conversations

When going abroad, each person brings his or her own culture, conditioning, and distortions.

and behavior may persuade others to appreciate your cultural perspectives.

Be Patient, Understanding, and Accepting of Self and Hosts. In an unfamiliar environment, one must be more tolerant and flexible. An attitude of healthy curiosity, a willingness to bear inconveniences, patience when answers or solutions are not forthcoming or difficult to obtain, are valuable ways to maintain mental balance. Such patience may also extend to other compatriots who struggle with cultural adjustment.

Be Realistic in Expectations. Avoid overestimating oneself, your hosts, or the cross-cultural experience. Disappointments can be lessened if one scales down expectations. This applies to everything from airline schedules to renting rooms. Global managers, especially, must be careful in new cultures not to set unreasonable work expectations for themselves or others until both are acclimated.

Accept the Challenge of Intercultural Experiences. Anticipate, savor, and confront the psychological challenge of adapting and changing as a result of a new cross-cultural opportunity. Be prepared to alter one's habits, attitudes, values, tastes, relationships, or sources of satisfaction. Such flexibility can become a means for personal growth, and the transnational experience can be more fulfilling. Of course, a deep interest and commitment to your work—professionalism—can be marvelous therapy in intercultural situations, counteracting isolation and strangeness when living outside your home culture. Wederspahn describes the intercultural services cycle in the following Exhibit 10.10.

In the last 10,000 years, the human population on Earth has doubled 10 times, from less than 10 million to more than 6 billion now, and an estimated 10 billion by year 2050! Wherever human beings go, the ecosystems are impacted for better or worse. Today, we experience a vast movement of people from the place where they are born to another nation or area to live, study, or work. Furthermore, Homo sapiens is in the process of going *offworld* and spreading into the universe. In this relocation process, some leave home in an orderly fashion to dwell in unfamiliar worlds, while some come and go in an unplanned way, especially if they are refugees from natural or man-made disasters. The issue, then, is how can these ***transcultural exchanges*** be facilitated for the benefit of both the expatriate and the indigenous population?

Deployment Systems

When an organization is sending people out of the country as its representatives, it has an obligation to ensure that such persons are adequately selected, prepared, and supported, as well as assisted when they return to the homeland. The sponsors need to have a *system* for relo-

Be prepared to alter one's habits, attitudes, values, tastes, relationships, or sources of satisfaction.

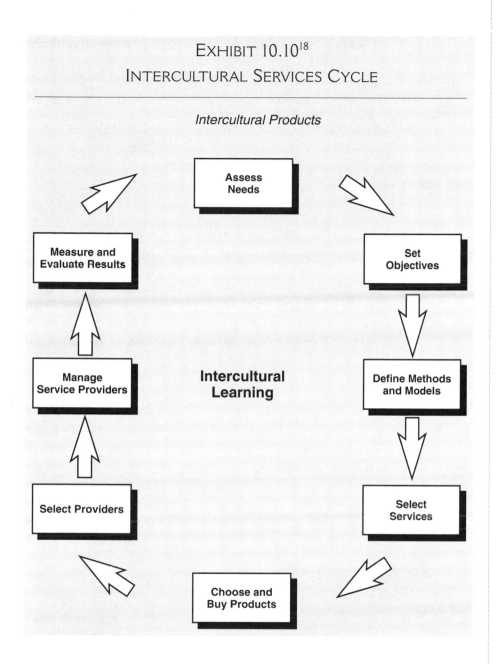

EXHIBIT 10.10[18]

INTERCULTURAL SERVICES CYCLE

Intercultural Products

Assess Needs

Measure and Evaluate Results

Set Objectives

Manage Service Providers

Intercultural Learning

Define Methods and Models

Select Providers

Select Services

Choose and Buy Products

cating their personnel or members. Behavioral scientists have been investigating the whole phenomenon of people exchanges, especially for those who live and work in isolated and confined environments (ICE).[19] The latter experience may range from offshore oil rigs and polar research stations to undersea submarines, orbiting space stations, and a lunar base. The following describes the four major components in a relocation or deployment system, whether terrestrial or in space. The extent to which these guidelines are followed depends on the length of the assignment.

Stage One—PERSONNEL AND PROGRAM ASSESSMENT

The first major component in a relocation or foreign deployment system involves assessing individual candidates for service abroad or in ICE, and later evaluating their on-site performance. In addition, the sponsor should periodically and objectively evaluate its relocation services and training, including transfer and reentry process.

Predeparture Assessment—From the perspective of the sponsoring organization's responsibilities, a complete foreign deployment evaluation system needs to:

■ Ascertain the adaptability of key personnel for foreign service, including their ability to deal with the host nationals effectively.

■ Develop a psychological profile for the candidate—summarize a psychological evaluation of the candidate's skills in human relations within an intercultural context, as well as determine the candidate's ability to cope with changes and differences and the candidate's susceptibility to severe culture shock.

■ Identify specific physical and intellectual barriers to successful adjustment in the foreign environment, if possible, to correct any deficiencies before departure.

■ Highlight any specific technical or management factors that need strengthening before the cross-cultural assignment.

■ Seek out any personal or family problems that would undermine employee effectiveness abroad.

Develop a performance review plan.

■ Develop a performance review plan for the individual when abroad, as well as assessment of the support services to be rendered.

■ Adapt the above evaluation process to foreign nationals brought on assignment into domestic operations.

■ Involve expatriate employees who have returned from foreign sites or host country nationals in predeparture training of émigrés.

■ Provide instruments for data gathering about the candidates' attitudes and competencies regarding change, intercultural knowledge and relations, and communication skills. These may involve commercial or homemade questionnaires, inventories, checklists, and culture shock tests.

■ Use, for both assessment and training, simulations, case studies, and critical incidents that approximate life abroad.

■ Employ a reality check on individual expectations regarding the foreign post, as to living conditions, job requirements, opportunities, and incongruities.

On-site Assessment—When the individual is sent overseas, the continuing performance review might further investigate:

■ The actual tasks or activities the expatriate engages in, and the person's ability to accomplish them.

- The people with whom the individual interacts—his or her ability to deal with the indigenous or local population.
- The extent to which the official posting requires social interactions with host and third country nationals, as well as expatriates from other organizations—capacity of the sojourner to deal with such variety of human relationships.
- The work duties required, whether by an individual or team collaboration, especially with persons outside the company.
- The language skills required (English or a foreign language), and the capacity of that employee to meet them.
- The individual's outlook abroad, whether provincial or cosmopolitan. Has that person demonstrated interest in the local culture and its manifestations? Has the organization's representative made satisfactory progress in the foreign culture?
- The expatriate's self-reporting—his or her sense of how the international experience is affecting personal and family life, including impact of absence from the homeland while on foreign assignment (i.e., influence on personal life and that of dependents, as well as on career development and life plans).
- The overall rating of the individual's performance and adjustment in the foreign assignment and its society.

Continuing System Improvements—Findings and insights obtained from both the pre-departure and on-site assessment programs should be viewed as feedback to further improve the relocation system with the next group of candidates. For example, a survey of employees on foreign assignment or of expatriates who have returned may reveal special needs and problems that the organization's foreign deployment system is, or is not, addressing satisfactorily.

The selection systems of organizations vary, but some use the following techniques:

- Within the HRD division or department, establish an assessment center that has the responsibility for recruitment and selection of overseas personnel.
- Outsource for services by contracting an external relocation resource, such as intercultural consultants and/or an international executive/management/technical search firm.
- Set up a selection review board made up of an organization's own employees or members, qualified volunteers who have served abroad, especially in the target culture; include company specialists in corporate health and personnel services.
- Limit selection for overseas assignments to expatriates who have previously demonstrated their effectiveness abroad, whether within the organization or hired from outside.

Selection Criteria—Overall, seek candidates for overseas service who are capable of empathy, openness, persistence, sensitivity to intercultural factors, respect for others, role flexibility, tolerance for ambiguity, and who possess two-way communication skills. Research indicates that possession of these characteristics is correlated to adaptation and effectiveness outside an individual's home culture. Russell[20] reviewed the literature on what factors are associated with successful international corporate assignments. Although his study was conducted some years ago, his findings are still valid. Exhibit 10.11 summarizes these dimensions of overseas success in industry.

EXHIBIT 10.11
DIMENSIONS OF OVERSEAS SUCCESS IN INDUSTRY

(Asterisks indicate the most desirable characteristics of foreign deployment candidates.)

1. Technical Competence/Resourcefulness
   *Technical skill/competence
   Resourcefulness
   Imagination/creativity
   Demonstrated ability to produce results with limited resources
   Comprehension of complex relationships
2. Adaptability/Emotional Stability
   *Adaptability/flexibility
   Youthfulness
   Maturity
   Patience
   Perseverance
   *Emotional stability
   Variety of outside interests
   Ability to handle responsibility
   Feeling of self-worth/dignity
   Capacity for growth
3. Acceptability of Assignment to Candidate and Family
   *Desire to serve overseas
   Willingness of spouse to live abroad/family status
   Belief in mission/job
   Stable marriage/family life
   *Adaptability of spouse/family
   *Previous experience abroad
   *Motivation
   Willingness to take chances
   Willingness to travel

4. Planning, Organization, and Utilizing Resources
   *Organization ability
   Self-sufficient as a manager
   Ability to build social institutions
   Management skills
   Administrative skills
5. Interpersonal Relationships/Getting Along with Others
   *Diplomacy and tact
   Consideration for others
   Human relations skills
   Commands respect
   *Ability to train others
   Desire to help others
   Ability to get things done through others
   Sense for politics of situations
6. Potential for Growth in the Company/Organization
   *Successful domestic record
   Organizational experience
   Industriousness
   *Educational qualifications
   *Mental alertness
   Intellectual
   Dependability
7. Host Language Ability
   *Language ability in native tongue
8. Cultural Empathy
   *Cultural empathy/sensitivity
   *Interest in host culture
   Respects host nationals
   Understands own culture
   Open-minded
   Area expertise
   *Ability to get along with hosts
   *Tolerant of others' views
   Sensitive to others' attitudes
   Understands host culture
   Not ethnocentric/prejudiced
   Objective
9. Physical Attributes
   "Good health
   Sex gender acceptability
   Physical appearance
10. Miscellaneous
    *Character
    Generalist skills

continues

EXHIBIT 10.11

DIMENSIONS OF OVERSEAS SUCCESS IN INDUSTRY
(CONTINUED)

Independence on job
Social acceptability
*Leadership
Friendliness
Initiative/energy

If a corporation or agency is not using an external consulting group to conduct its relocation services, then internal organizational resources should be developed before the next stage in the deployment process can occur. For example, a corporate computerized data bank or electronic chat room on cultural specifics could be developed for each overseas location. The HRD facilities might include a library with a cross-cultural collection of books, slides, audio/videocassettes, and CD-ROMs, as well as reports and diaries from previous employees who served overseas. In a large global organization, both management and employees would have access to this information. Such data, plus discussions on salary and benefits, housing provisions, and other like realities, might even contribute to the candidate's turning down the assignment abroad. A valuable reference in this regard is Gary Wederspahn's volume, *Intercultural Services—A Worldwide Buyer's Guide and Sourcebook.*

Stage Two—PERSONNEL ORIENTATION AND TRAINING

The second component in a foreign deployment system is some type of self- or group-learning experience or training about culture generally, as well as specifics about the target area's culture. This can be accomplished electronically or in live sessions with *PowerPoint* briefings. The general content can include learning modules on cross-cultural communications and change, understanding culture and its influence on behavior, culture shock and cross-cultural relations, improving organizational relations, and intercultural effectiveness. To increase cultural awareness and skills, several alternative methods are possible. These have amply been reviewed in our accompanying *Instructor's Manual for Managing Cultural Differences.*

Today, an increasingly popular means of cross-cultural learning is electronic, especially by means of the computer and television. To supplement or replace formal group instruction, individualized learning packages can be provided for the employee and his or her family. Such programmed learning and media systems can educate on cultural dif-

The second component in a foreign deployment system is some type of self- or group-learning experience or training about culture generally, as well as specifics about the target area's culture.

ferences in general, as well as on the specific country to be visited. This type of learning can occur in a company learning center or at home with one's family. It might also serve as preparation for classroom instruction.

Culture-specific briefing programs can be developed for a particular geographical region or country, such as is provided in Unit 2 of this volume. For example, the Middle East could be a subject of study, with particular emphasis on Egypt, Saudi Arabia, and Turkey, or even Israel/Palestine, Iraq, and Iran. A learning program of 12 or more hours can be designed with a self-instruction manual for individual study, or the materials used for group training. Obviously, no relocation orientation is complete without adequate language and technical training. However, the focus here is on cultural training and preparation.

Current thinking on this second stage of foreign deployment leads us to these recommendations for dividing the preparation for service abroad into four phases. In other words, the predeparture program would involve the following 18 steps. The time and scope of each activity would again depend on whether it was a long- or short-term assignment out of country:

Phase One—General Culture/Area Orientation

1. Become aware of the factors that make a culture unique and the characteristics of the home culture that most influence employee behavior abroad.
2. Seek local cross-cultural experience and engage in intercultural communication with minority cultures within the homeland so as to sensitize oneself to cultural differences.
3. Foster more global attitudes and tolerance within the candidate family, while counteracting prejudice and ethnocentrism. For example, cook national dishes of other countries, attend cultural weeks or exhibits of foreign or ethnic groups, or invite a foreigner to your home.

Phase Two—Language Orientation

1. Undertake 60 to 80 hours of formal training in the language of the host country.
2. Supplement classroom experience with 132 to 180 hours of self-learning in the language, by listening to the foreign tongue via audio/videocassettes or radio; by watching television or Internet shows and films; by reading newspapers, magazines, or books in the new language; by speaking to others who have this language proficiency.
3. Build a 500-word survival vocabulary in the target language.
4. Develop specialized vocabularies for the job, marketplace, etc.
5. Practice the language at every opportunity, especially with family members.
6. Seek further education in the language upon arrival in the host country.

Current thinking on this second stage of foreign deployment leads us to these recommendations for dividing the preparation for service abroad into four phases.

Culture shock

Phase Three—Culture Specific Orientation
1. Learn and gather data about culture specifics of the host country.
2. Understand and prepare to counteract "culture shock."
3. Check out specific company policies about the assigned country. These policies are related to allowances for transportation, housing, education, expense accounts, and provisions for salaries, taxes, and other fringe benefits, including medical service and emergency leave.
4. Obtain necessary transfer documents (passports, visas, etc.), and learn customs, policies, and regulations, as well as currency restrictions, for entry and exit to host country.
5. Interview, in person or electronically, fellow employees who have returned from the host country. Get practical information about banking, shopping, currency, climate, mail, and law enforcement.
6. Read travel books and other information about the country and culture.

Phase Four—Job Environment/Organization Orientation
1. Obtain information about the overseas job environment and organization.
2. Be aware of the government's customs, restrictions, and attitudes regarding business, and your local corporation or project.
3. Arrange for necessary technical training to assure high performance abroad; seek a local mentor or coach.

Relocation strategies should encompass the staff engaged in recruiting, selecting, and training; the employee and dependents assigned abroad.

Relocation strategies should encompass the staff engaged in recruiting, selecting, and training; the employee and dependents assigned abroad; as well as the host culture managers who are responsible for expatriate personnel in the new environment. The focus should be on the opportunities afforded by the international assignment for personal growth, professional exchange and development, and effective representation of country and corporation.

Stage Three—SUPPORT SERVICE: ON-SITE SUPPORT AND MONITORING

Once employees have been recruited, selected, trained, and transported abroad, the organizational responsibility to personnel should be to:

(a) Facilitate their integration into a different work environment and host culture.
(b) Evaluate their needs and performance abroad.
(c) Encourage morale and career development, especially through homeland communications.

As a follow-up to the predeparture training and after the employee or family arrives in the host country, some type of on-site orientation and briefing should be arranged. Back home there might have been a lack of readiness to listen to details about the job and new community. Now that the expatriates are faced with the daily realities of life abroad, they may have many questions. Periodically, the newcomers should be provided opportunities to come together socially and share as a group.

The in-country orientation should be pragmatic and meet the needs of the expatriate family. It should demonstrate that the organization cares about its people. It should aid the employee and his or her family to resolve immediate living problems; to meet the challenge of the host culture and the opportunities it offers for travel, personal growth, and intercultural exchange; to reduce the culture shock and to grow from that experience; and to provide communication links to the local community and the home organization. Much of this can be accomplished in a systematic, informal, friendly group setting or even electronically.

On-site support services should not just be for the first year abroad. Do not take for granted that the adjustment is satisfactory if the family manifests no overt problems in the first two years of a five-year tour of duty overseas. There must be a continuing follow-up of the foreign deployment program with reinforcement inputs that reduce expatriate stress and strain.

Furthermore, more emphasis should be placed on mental health services in both the selection and support of overseas personnel. Ideally, a total system of transcultural personnel services should offer counseling and community services to expatriate families. Not only is this a preventative approach, but it ensures greater productivity and performance abroad.

At headquarters and on site, the organization's human resource development staff might employ these strategies:

- *An adjustment survey*. Approximately three to six months after arrival, request the employee to supply feedback on the foreign deployment situation. The short survey should be completed with other family members. Greater cooperation and authenticity might be forthcoming if on-site management does not have access to the individual responses. A second administration of the questionnaire might be considered 12 or 18 months after arrival, or just prior to completing the assignment.
- *Data analysis and reporting*. The information is analyzed from two viewpoints: individual need and general foreign deployment policies and practices. The material would be analyzed for the identification of problems and the recommendation of solutions. Reporting enables back-home management to monitor its relocation system,

On-site support services should not just be for the first year abroad.

while on-site management can improve the quality of working life for the expatriate employees. As group data are compiled and stored in a computer, a profile is drawn of overseas employee needs and concerns relative to foreign deployment at a particular location. This collection of significant information is then used in future orientation and training programs for planning. Data stored from deployment groups over a period of years provide insight into the requirements of overseas personnel in a geographic area. The results from such inquiry studies, whether used on a short- or long-term basis, have preventive value relative to problems of cultural adjustment and lead to considerable savings in financial and human terms.

One useful way to foster on-site acculturation is to arrange for a coach or mentor from the host culture to work with the expatriate during his or her stay abroad.

■ *Organizational communications.* To counteract alienation, loneliness, and feelings of being "cut off," an organization must establish communication links with its representatives abroad through electronic bulletins, newsletters, company newsletters and magazines, and video or audiocassettes, which are sent to expatriates and their families. The communications can report the latest developments in the home organizations or reinforce previous learning and ego building at the foreign location. Thus, the employee continues to be "plugged in" to domestic operations. All such efforts and on-site company briefings build morale and confidence that the overseas assignment is important. The Internet is an ideal tool to use for this purpose through electronic mail, chat rooms, and Web sites.

Ideally, at least six months before completion of the foreign assignment, the employee should get assistance with plans for departure, transition, and reintegration into his or her native country and domestic work environment.

Stage Four—REACCULTURATION: REENTRY PROGRAM

The last component in the foreign deployment system involves reintegrating the expatriate into the home society and domestic organization. The person or family who has been abroad for some time will discover when they return that the homeland and the organizational cultures will have changed. The reentry process begins overseas with the psychological withdrawal the expatriate faces with returning home. Upon return, reentry shock may occur for six months or more, as the person struggles to readjust to the lifestyle and tempo of the changed home and organizational cultures. Apart from the challenge of reestablishing home and family life is the issue of reassignment in the parent company or agency.

For many expatriates, the last stage of the culture shock process is a time of crises and trauma. Such personnel may experience mild or severe **reentry shock**. The experience abroad for those who are sensitive and who become involved in the host culture is profound. It causes many people to reexamine their lives, values, attitudes, to assess how they became what they are. It is a turning point, prompting lifestyle changes when they get back. The reentry process becomes the opportunity to carry out these aspirations. Individuals may not be satisfied to return to old neighborhoods, old friends, or the same job or company affiliation. Many wish to apply the new self-insights and to seek new ways of personal growth. The organization that sent them abroad in the first place should be empathetic to this reality and be prepared to deal with it, including by providing severance benefit packages or even outplacement services. The relocation system is incomplete unless it helps returning employees to fit comfortably into their home culture and organization. Closing the deployment loop may involve group counseling with personnel specialists, psychologists, and former expatriates. Always consider expatriates coming back from an overseas assignment as a valuable resource. The corporation can learn much from their cross-cultural experience.

The reentry process becomes the opportunity to carry out these aspirations.

Related Personnel Issues

Tung[21] examined the issue of managing personnel abroad. To bolster the contention that human resource management (HRM) is the key to successful international operations, she surveyed programs at training institutes (UK's Center for International Briefings at Farnham Castle, Japan's Institute for International Assignment, and Japanese American Conversation Institute). In addition, she analyzed the expatriate policies and practices within British, Italian, Swiss, and German multinationals and two transnational corporations (an MNC owned by people of different nationalities with two or more parent headquarters). Tung concluded that European and Japanese multinationals have lower failure rates with "expats" because they are more international, or global, in their selection, orientation, and preparation of people who are more adept at living and working in a foreign environment. Is this still true today? In any event, world-class enterprises provide a cross-cultural component in the human resource development of not only those they send abroad, but also with the company's local host nationals who must learn to work effectively with internationals. More recent surveys also indicate that many global corporations still do not hear the message about the need for comprehensive deployment assistance. The following findings call for immediate improvement in policies and practices for sending personnel abroad:

- Settlers International, a worldwide relocation company, reports that the divorce rate is 40% higher among expatriates compared to their domestic counterparts, while the "expat" children have a 50% higher school dropout rate than children in their home country.
- Cendant International Assignment Services found that of 300 companies contacted, 63% reported failed foreign assignments.
- American Training and Development Society discovered that 70% of the American business people going abroad had *no cultural training or preparation* for employees going on international assignments, while 59% of the HRD executives surveyed responded that their firms offered *no cross-cultural training.*
- 2002 Global Relocation Trends Survey by the Global Relocation Services, National Foreign Trade Council, and SHRM Global Forum revealed that 77% of the expatriates studied were not frightened to live and work overseas and, despite terrorism threats, expected to complete their international assignments; 74% expressed willingness to accept future expatriate positions. Given their risk-taking courage, we wonder if their sponsors are providing the skills and tools that will ensure their safety and security.

Furthermore, there is often a discrepancy between perceptions of key management and the expatriate as to how helpful, or not, the organization's deployment efforts may be. One of the above GRTS findings underscores the problem, as illustrated in Exhibit 10.12.

In the first decade of this twenty-first century, one conclusion is evident—personnel deployment strategies are essential in a global marketplace, but they should be both dynamic and flexible. One relocation program might be designed within the home culture, while another is focused upon the global manager in a host culture. The latter may have two variations:

- for professionals, technicians, and sales representatives who operate abroad on short-term multinational assignments, often with limited time spent in a variety of countries;
- for long-term expatriates assigned to a specific region or country.

In either situation a modular program is preferable, with standard learning content or procedures that are customized to meet differing employee needs. For example, if dependents are included in the transfer, then there should be a family approach to relocation and travel, to identity crises and culture shock, and to reentry challenges. Trauma and dislocation problems can be managed if people are forewarned, trained to interact in a mutually supportive way, and use resources to facilitate adjustment within an alien environment. It is easy to advise in international travel, "Treat people as you would wish to be treated." Better yet, as Milton Bennett said many years ago, "Treat people as they wish to be treated."

Trauma and dislocation problems can be managed if people are forewarned, trained to interact in a mutually supportive way.

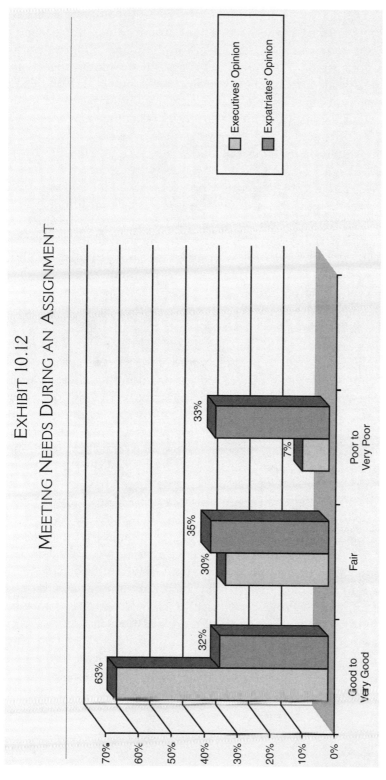

EXHIBIT 10.12

MEETING NEEDS DURING AN ASSIGNMENT

Executives' Opinion
Expatriates' Opinion

70%
60%
50%
40%
30%
20%
10%
0%

Good to
Very Good

63%

32%

Fair

30%

35%

Poor to
Very Poor

7%

33%

Source: Global Relocation Trend Survey 2002, Global Relocation Services.

Further, special consideration needs to be given to the matter of *dependent children*. If they are left at home while the parent goes abroad that requires one type of counseling and support program. If these youngsters accompany the parent overseas, then another approach is needed, including involvement in the regular predeparture and on-site training. For this purpose, we recommend these Nicholas Brealey publications (www.interculturalpress.com): *Uprooted Childhood* by F. Eidse and N. Sichel; *Third Culture Kids* by D. C. Pollack and R. E. Van Raken; *Where in the World Are You Going* by J. M. Blohm; *Moving Your Family Overseas* by R. Kalb and P. Welch; *Host Family Survival Kit* by N. King and K. Huff; *The Aliens—Being a Foreign Student* by Darmouth College's International Office.

The last reference above brings us to a final issue—*students studying abroad*. For these wandering scholars, higher education occurs in a borderless world. It is almost routine for many undergraduates to spend a year studying abroad, or for graduate students to seek exchanges with foreign universities. Today, many people not only seek college degrees, but often with part or all of their studies outside their own culture. The brightest students want to study in the world's best universities, particularly in the United States, Britain, France, Germany, and Australia. And the universities and colleges are actively seeking foreign student tuitions. North America has dominated the market for international students, and the latter contribute $13 billion a year to its GNP. In a knowledge culture, education is becoming an export industry, with many institutions opening programs overseas. Singapore has established close relations with 14 partner schools abroad, including Stanford, Cornell, and Duke. Dubai has established a "knowledge village" with 13 foreign universities, while Qatar has an "educational city" with four foreign universities that cater to Middle Easterners who want a "western education." China not only sends the most students abroad, but is the leading host in Asia of alliances with foreign universities. For example, New York's Fordham University has a Beijing International MBA program that brings Western-style business education which nurtures an international mentality among its Chinese students and alumni. Peking University's China Research Institute is the partner in this venture. Fortunately, there are international associations and programs in both the universities and non-profit sponsors, such as the Institute of International Education, who provide cross-cultural preparation for those involved in their student exchanges.[22]

China not only sends the most students abroad, but is the leading host in Asia of alliances with foreign universities.

BUSINESS ETIQUETTE AND PROTOCOL ABROAD

Cooperation in world trade and commerce is considered by many to be humanity's best chance to maintain global peace and prosperity. The potential for international business synergy is enormous, as was covered in Chapter 6.[23] Training in managing change, interpersonal skills, cultural difference, and creating synergy can improve not only human relations, but the "bottom line."

To perform effectively outside one's native country, companies should be providing employees with:

- *Technical knowledge* for penetrating foreign markets (e.g., introducing new products in foreign markets, licensing patents and dealing with non-tariff barriers abroad, identifying potential export opportunities).
- *Comparative management* for dealing with foreign business and government (e.g., comparison of regional management practices, cross-cultural negotiating skills, current international business issues and trends).
- *International business strategies* for coping with the protocol, etiquette, and ethics of the host culture or region. This applies to communications in person as well as online. Chapters 3 and 7 already discussed some of these matters in greater detail.

The scope of foreign investment in other nations' economies is another reason for concern about observing their business protocols. World corporations invest billions in businesses of other countries. Cross-cultural sensitivity on the part of such investors and their representative not only ensures that the right ventures and projects are chosen, but that trade and business relationships are developed, which can ensure mutual success.

Today, the more- or less-developed countries transfer funds and resources across borders to underwrite projects, purchase stocks, or outsource to fill needs. As a result, consumer goods and services flow more easily among most nations. In this global marketplace, even local or regional stock markets are interdependent in their networking and exchanging with one another. *Cultural faux pas* in such interchanges can undermine ventures and prosperity.

Another cultural dimension requiring caution is the legal system in various countries. U.S. legal practices are rooted in English Common Law, whose premise is "you are innocent until proven guilty." However, some countries, like Mexico, are guided by the Napoleonic Code where if accused, "you are guilty until you prove your innocence." Other regions are governed by Islamic law, while others have underdeveloped legal systems in need of modernization. Some areas lack any written legal system, being governed by traditional tribal observances.

The consequences of transgressing local *law* can be horrendous for the naïve. La Pere[24] wrote of her ordeal caused by a persistent street peddler in Pamukkale, Turkey. To get rid of the pesky salesman, she paid $20 for three dirty marble heads that turned out to be ancient

The consequences of transgressing local law can be horrendous for the naïve.

Roman sculpture from nearby ruins. Detained by customs officials, she was accused of smuggling antiquities and faced Turkish law based on the Napoleonic Code. The harrowing experience ended with an unauthorized escape. One had best know and observe the laws of the foreign country in which one visits or does business.

Webster's dictionary defines protocol as *a code prescribing adherence to correct etiquette and procedures*. While modern management, the Internet, and mass communications are forming new protocols for the global marketplace, we still cannot ignore the local expectations for business and professional activities. Nelson,[25] advises these basic protocols be observed.

1. Remembering and pronouncing people's names correctly.
2. Using appropriate rank and titles when required.
3. Knowing the local variables of time and punctuality.
4. Creating the right impression with suitable dress.
5. Practicing behavior that demonstrates concern for others, tact and discretion, and knowledge of what constitutes good manners and ethics locally.
6. Communicating with intercultural sensitivity, verbally and nonverbally, whether in person, electronically, or in writing or printing.
7. Giving and receiving gifts and favors appropriate to local traditions.
8. Enjoying social events while conscious of local customs relative to food and drink, such as, regarding prohibitions, the use of utensils, dining out and entertaining, and seating arrangements.

Matters of business etiquette refers to all forms of intercultural communications, whether in person, in writing, or electronically.

John Mole's *Mind Your Manners* focuses on the countries and cultures within the expanding European Union. He provides cultural specifics on thirty-three different business cultures (www.interculturalpress.com).

Finally, remember matters of business etiquette refers to all forms of intercultural communications, whether in person, in writing, or electronically. Cultural offense can be given just as easily on the telephone or computer, as in direct conversation. For example, Paramount's DreamWorks Animation now has an improved videoconferencing system to cut down on business travel and boost productivity. Called *Halo*, it is designed to create "as though you were there collaborating." With such technology, one must be careful to observe good manners and proper protocol, as if the actual persons were in your presence.

Relocation into a host culture in person or electronically requires continuous learning, especially about the nuances of local business etiquette. A true cosmopolitan is well informed on such matters, so as not to offend his or her host or international counterpart.

CONCLUSIONS

Life is filled with crises, some of which can be turned into challenges for personal and professional growth.[26] Such transitional experiences occur with major illness, divorce, and death of a beloved. Some happen by going abroad into another culture, or even in making the passage from an industrial to knowledge work environment. The trauma experienced in this adjustment process can take many forms, whether it is called culture or reentry shock, role or organization shock, or even future shock. Essentially, cross-cultural transitions threaten our sense of identity. Such transitions force us to rethink and reevaluate the way we read meaning into our private worlds. They are opportunities to learn and develop, causing a transformation in our behavior and lifestyle, as well as in our management or leadership.

Organizations can reduce such shocks to their personnel by coaching, counseling, and training. The stress and anxiety that may result, need not lead to severe disorientation, depression, and unhealthy behavior. These can be countered by increasing awareness and information that provides more enjoyable intercultural experiences. Knowledge of cultural specifics can facilitate the acclimation and integration into the unfamiliar situation.

When considered in the context of sending employees overseas on assignment, the return on organizational investment in cross-cultural preparation and continuing support services can be considerable. We recommend that sponsoring multinational corporations or agencies institute a foreign deployment *system*. This approach to relocation activities will not only reduce premature return costs and much unhappiness among expatriates and overseas' customers, but it can improve performance, productivity, and profitability in the world market. Furthermore, observing and practicing both national and international protocol facilitates human performance and cooperation, especially in development projects. Such counsel becomes even more meaningful in the context of technology transfer, whether within a nation or across borders.

Organizations can reduce such shocks to their personnel by coaching, counseling, and training.

MIND STRETCHING

1. Explain the concept of the transitional experience and its many manifestations. Apply these insights to the university graduate going into the world of work, or civilian and military personnel assigned overseas.
2. Why are so many workers leaving their culture of origin to work abroad, despite the many difficulties encountered? What

are the responsibilities of communities and organizations in facilitating the acculturation of foreign newcomers?

3. Why does a relocation assignment pose a challenge to one's sense of identity? What are culture and reentry shock? How can these phenomena be avoided or delimited?

4. What is your understanding of being "cosmopolitan"? How can you promote this approach or mind-set in yourself and others?

5. Why should world-class corporations have a foreign deployment system? Overall, what does such a system entail? How can global leaders advance cross-cultural skills among their workers or members?

REFERENCES

1. Shoper, J. April 18, 2006. email.
2. Peterson, B. *Cultural Intelligence—A Guide to Working with People from Other Cultures*, 2004; Comes, A. *Culture from Inside Out—Travel and Meet Yourself*; Storti, C. *Figuring Foreigners Out*. Boston: Nicholas Brealey/Intercultural Press, 1999.
3. Lewis, R. D. *The Cultural Imperative-Global Trends in the 21st Century.* Boston: Nicholas Brealey, 2002, p. 228; Lewis, R. D. *When Cultures Collide—Managing Successfully Across Cultures*. Boston: Nicholas Brealey, 2000.
4. Campbell, J. *Hero with a Thousand Faces*. Princeton, NJ: Princeton University Press, 1968; Osland, J. S. *The Adventure of Working Abroad—Hero Tales from the Global Frontier*. San Francisco, CA: Jossey-Bass, 1995; Hofstede, G. J., Peterson, P. B., and Hofstede, G. *Exploring Culture—Exercises, Stories, and Synthetic Cultures*. Boston: Nicholas Brealey/Intercultural Press, 2002.
5. Spencer, S. A. and Adams, J. D. *Life Changes—Growing through Personal Transition*; Bridges, W. *Transitions—Make Sense of Life's Changes*; Biracress, T. and N. *Over Fifty—Resource Book for the Better Half of Your Life*; Cort-VanArsdale, D. *Transitions—A Woman's Guide to Successful Retirement*. These books on lifestyle transitions are available from Knowledge Systems, Inc. (7777 W. Morris St., Indianapolis, IN 46231).
6. Fearn, N. *Philosophy: The Latest Answers to the Oldest Questions*. New York: Atlanta Books, 2005.
7. Lewis, T. and Jungman, R. (eds.). *On Being Foreign: Culture Shock in Short Fiction*; Kols, L. R., *Survival Kit for Intercultural Living*; Storti, C., *The Art of Coming Home*. Boston: Nicholas Brealey/Intercultural Press, 1986, 2001.

8. Furnham, A. and Bochner, S. *Culture Shock—Psychological Reactions to an Unfamiliar Environment*. New York: Methuen & Co., 1986.

9. Oberg, K. "Culture Shock and the Problem of Adjustment to New Cultural Environments." Washington, DC: Foreign Service Institute, 1958; Storti, C. *The Art of Crossing Cultures*; eds., F. and Sichel, N. *Uprooted Childhoods—Memories of Growing Up Global*. Boston: Nicholas Brealey/Intercultural Press, 2001, 2004.

10. Klopf, D. W. *Intercultural Encounters*, Third Edition. Englewood, CO: Morton Publishing Company, 1995. Also refer to Gundling, E. *Working Global Smart—12 People Skills for Doing Business Across Borders*. Palo Alto, CA: Davies-Black, 2003; Ember, C. R. (ed.). *Cultures of the World*. New York, NY: Macmillan, 1999.

11. "Expatriate Workers—In Search of Stealth," *The Economist*, April 23, 2005, p. 62.

12. Osland, J. S. "The Hero's Adventure: The Overseas Experience of Expatriate Business People," unpublished doctoral dissertation, Case Western University, 1990. Available through University Microfilms International (300 N. Zeeb Road, Ann Arbor, MI 48106); Also refer to Dr. Eileen Sheridan (Wibbeke) more recent doctoral dissertation on this subject in 2005 at the University of Phoenix Online (EM: docwibbeke@gmail.com).

13. Doctors without Borders, P.O. Box 1869, Merrifield, VA 22116, USA (www.doctorswithoutborders.org).

14. Steele, J. "When Mom Gets Her Marching Orders," *The San Diego Union-Tribune*, March 11, 2003, pp. A1/12.

15. Brislin, R. W. (ed.) and Berry, J. W. "Psychology of Acculturation," in *Applied Cross-Cultural Psychology*. Newbury Park, CA: Sage Publications, 1990; Laroche, L. *Managing Cultural Diversity in Technical Professions*. Burlington, MA: Elsevier/Butterworth-Heinemann, 2002.

16. Wederspahn, G. M. "With the Right Training, Expatriates Blend In," *Mobility*, October 2002, publication of the Employee Relocation Council (www.employeerelocationcouncil.org). Also refer to Gary Wederspahn's book, *Intercultural Services* (www.books@elsevier.com/management).

17. Interview with consultant Garry Wederspahn (www.interculturalhelp.com), March 12, 2003. Also refer to Yunker, J. *Beyond Borders—Web Globalization Strategies*. Indianapolis, IN: New Riders Publishers, 2002. Rosinski, P. *Coaching Across Cultures*. Boston, MA: Nicholas Brealey/Intercultural Press, 2003.

18. Reprinted from Gary M. Wederspahn's *Intercultural Services*. Butterworth–Heinemann/Elsevier Science, 2000, Ch. 7, p. 205.

19. Relative to *deployment systems*, refer to Haines, S. G. *The Manager's Pocketguide to Systems and Learning*. Amherst, MA: HRD Press, 2004. Also contact the Society for Human Performance in Extreme Environments for information and publications (e-mail: Society@HPPE.org or Web site www.hpee.org). Relative to a *space deployment system*, Harrison, A. A. *Spacefaring—The Human Dimension*. Berkeley, CA: University of California Press, 2001; Harris, P. R. *Launch Out—A Science-based Novel about Lunar Industrialization*, 2003; Freeman, M. *Challenges of Human Space Exploration*, 2000; Harris, P. R. *Living and Working in Space—Human Behavior, Culture, and Organization*, 1996. These space

books are available from UNIVELT INC., Escondido, CA (www.univelt.com or EM: roberthjacobs@compuserve.com).

20. Russell, P. W., Jr., unpublished paper presented at SIETAR Conference, Phoenix, AZ, 1978; Hampden-Turner, C. M. and Trompenaars, F. *Building Cross-cultural Compentence—How to Create Wealth from Conflicting Values*. New Haven, CT: Yale University Press, 2000; Marquardt, M. J. *The Global Advantage—How World Class Organizations Improve Performance Through Globalization*. Burlington, MA: Butterworth–Heinemann/Elsevier Science, 1998.

21. Tung, R. L. *The New Expatriates—Managing Human Resources Abroad*. Cambridge, MA: Ballinger/Harper & Row, 1988; Pedersen, P. and Connerley, M. *Leadership in Diverse and Multicultural Environments*, Thousand Oaks, CA: Sage Publications, 2005; Koslow, L. E. *Business Abroad—A Quick Guide to International Business Transactions*. Burlington, MA: Butterworth–Heinemann/Elsevier Science, 1998.

22. *The Economist*, September 10, 2005, pp. 16–17.

23. Ward, K., Kakabadse, A., Bowman, C., *Designing World Class Corporate Strategies*; Kenny, G. *Strategic Planning and Performance Management*. Burlington, MA: Elsevier/Butterworth-Heinemann, 2004; Koslow, L. E. *Global Business—308 Tips to Take Your Company Worldwide*. Burlington, MA: Butterworth–Heinemann/Elsevier Science, 1996; Nelson, C. A. *International Business—A Manager's Guide to Strategy in the Age of Globalization*. London: International Thomson Business Press, 1999.

24. La Pere, G. *Never Pass This Way Again*. Bethesda, MD: Adler and Adler, 1987; Heiss, D. *Study Abroad/Learning Abroad*. Boston, MA: Nicholas Brealey/Intercultural Press, 1997.

25. Nelson, C. A. *Protocol for Profit—A Manager's Guide to Competing Worldwide*. London: International Thomas Business Press, 1998; Olafsson, G. *When in Rome or Rio or Riyadh—Cultural Q & As for Successful Business Behavior Around the World*, 2004; Mole, J. *Mind Your Manners—Managing Business Cultures in the New Global Europe*, 2004. Boston, MA: Nicholas Brealey/Intercultural Press.

26. Sheehy, G. *New Passages, Mapping Your Life Across Time*. New York: Random House, 1995.

UNIT 2

REGIONAL CULTURE SPECIFICS

"Culture hides much more than it reveals."

Edward T. Hall

It is 24 hours before you're to be born as a baby and a genie appears. He tells you that he thinks you're a winner and has great confidence in you. So great is his confidence in you that he is going to let you set the rules in the very world that you'll be born into. You can set the social rules, the political rules, the economic rules—whatever you like. And whatever rules you set will apply for your lifetime and your kids' lifetimes too.

You think: This sounds great! What's the catch? And the genie then tells you that you don't know if you'll be born rich or poor, black or white, male or female, sick or healthy, intelligent or slow. The only thing you know is that there's a lottery with 6 billion different lotto balls and what you start life as is represented by one of them.

—Warren Buffet, world's second wealthiest man, in a talk given at the Harvard Business School, October 28, 2004

11

DOING BUSINESS WITH MIDDLE EASTERNERS

Egypt, Saudi Arabia, and Region

The roots of our Western civilization are deepest around the Mediterranean Sea. The Egyptian, Phoenician, Greek, and ultimately Roman civilizations flourished there. The Arab empire that originated there in the seventh century filled the vacuum left by the fall of the Roman Empire. The Arabs expanded and perfected the art, music, science and technology of the Romans and their Mediterranean predecessors. They developed a network of cities that survive today as the "casbahs" of Arab metropolises. . . . The Arab empire was a tremendous force for globalization, implanting Mediterranean musical practices as far away as India, and bringing back what we today call Arabic numerals. Yet this globalization maintained, rather than reduced diversity, as the cultures in this vast empire enriched each other, without one culture dominating or obliterating the other. . . . Metropolitan centers throughout the Middle East attracted many peoples, resulting in a fusion of cultures that varied from center to center.

—Doris Bitter and James Rauch, "Syria and the Roots of Western Civilization," *San Diego Union-Tribune*, May 1, 2003, p. B1

LEARNING OBJECTIVES

This chapter is dedicated to a better understanding of the cultures and complexities of that region of the world known to geographers as the Middle East. We will provide information and insights on Middle

Middle East

Eastern business customs and protocols, as well as the prospects for synergy in the area. Specifics will be shared as to the dominant Arab culture there, plus contrasts in the cultures of Egypt and Saudi Arabia. In addition, cultural capsules of a dozen other nations in the region will offer a more comprehensive overview of the region's peoples and challenges. Our aim is to facilitate appropriate communications with Middle Easterners wherever they are encountered.

The Middle East commonly refers to the lands from the eastern shores of the Mediterranean and Aegean seas to India. Geographically, it encompasses areas of the eastern Mediterranean and Central Asia. To many of its inhabitants, it is known as the Arab homeland (*Al-waton Al-Araby* refers to those areas in which Arabic is spoken). This chapter includes material on these 14 countries: Egypt, Syria, Lebanon, Israel, Jordan, Saudi Arabia, Yemen, Oman, United Arab Emirates, Qatar, Bahrain, Kuwait, Iraq, and Iran. Note that these countries are bounded by six major waterways: the Mediterranean Sea, Red Sea, Gulf of Aden, Arabian Sea, Persian Gulf, and Caspian Sea. Turkey, once the center of the Ottoman Empire that ruled the region, is popularly considered part of the Middle East; but that nation is covered in Chapter 14 on Europe. Although largely Muslim, Turkey is a non-Arab country whose dominant language is Turkish. Its more than 69 million people include ethnic minorities who speak Arabic, Kurdish, and Greek.

The Middle East is a region where geography and ecology are important architects of history; it is where three continents meet and so serves as a focal point in the development of civilization. After the Ice Age, its topography was gradually transformed from a climate that supported grasslands and waterways into vast steppes and desert. In 2000 B.C., a pastoral people called Aryans or Indo-Iranians pushed into India and western and central Asia, including present-day Iran and neighboring countries. This landmass has been considered a strategic location, a crossroad for trade, faith, and conflict.

The Middle East is a region where geography and ecology are important architects of history.

MIDDLE EAST OVERVIEW

The Historical Perspective

In ancient times, the Middle East was referred to as Mesopotamia, the Fertile Crescent from which agriculture and settlements would emerge. In those days, what is today called Libya was rich in olives, wine, and livestock, and Egypt was a marshland teeming with wildlife and reed forests. It was here that farming and irrigation were first developed along the Nile Valley and that the original dwellers of the Tigris-Euphrates Valley brought forth civilization in Sumer, today's southern Iraq. The Sumerians became largely Semites and spoke a Semitic language from which evolved the major languages spoken by Middle Easterners, such as Aramaic, Syriac, Hebrew, and Arabic. Here the first cities were founded and flourished with ancient names like Ur, Babylon, and Gaza. This ancient land became the center of world civilization—its cultures first produced the wheeled vehicles; the pottery wheel and pottery making; written records and codes of law in cuneiform; art, monumental architecture, and urbanization; and multiple religions, along with complex political and trading systems.[1]

From its very beginning, as a site for human settlement, until now, the Middle East has been marked by *diversity*. For thousands of years, the waves of migration into the area have extended from the Sumerians, possibly from central Asia, to the latest Filipino, Korean, or Indian immigrant searching for work. In the latter part of the twentieth century, more than 3 million Asian and Indian laborers were imported into the area to help build a modern infrastructure. Although the majority of Middle Easterners have many things in common, such as the Arab culture, language, and religion, there are also distinct ethnic minorities in every country of the region. Since the seventh century, Islam has been the principal binder among the peoples of this area—it is a *way of life*, not just a religion. *Islam* is an Arabic word that means surrender or submission to Allah or God; a person who so behaves and follows the teachings of Islam is called a Muslim. Non-Arabs, such as the Iranians, are linked to their Muslim brothers and sisters throughout the world through their religion of Islam.[2]

The Middle East has been marked by diversity.

Recall that this is the same place from which the religions of Judaism and Christianity arose; all three faiths revere the prophet Abraham. Islam began later, in A.D. 570, with the birth of Muhammad the Prophet in Mecca on the Arabian Peninsula. This great leader was a combination of general, statesman, social reformer, empire builder, and visionary. Islam as both a religion and a philosophy owes its origin to Muhammad's teachings, which he encapsulated in the Qur'an (Koran), the sacred book of Muslims, as precious to them as the Holy Bible is Christians and the Torahs to Jews Islam, as noted earlier, means the act of giving one's self to Allah or God, and this faith has worldwide followers. The Koran contains the discourses Allah revealed to his prophet Muhammad. Yet, as a religion, Islam is diverse in terms of having different interpretations of its teachings—for instance, by Sunni Muslims in Algeria and Saudi Arabia, or Shi'is Muslims in Iran and Iraq where most believers are Shi'ites. Neither visitor nor businessperson traveling to the Middle East can hope to comprehend its peoples without understanding the powerful religious and cultural force of Islam. Its primary tenets are summarized in Exhibit 11.1.[3]

The teachings in the Koran, like those in the Bible, can be taken out of context and distorted to serve a particular cause—such as when ultramilitants twist the interpretation of *jihad*, a verse prescribing struggle against the enemies of God for spiritual purity and enlightenment.

EXHIBIT 11.1

PILLARS OF ISLAMIC BELIEF

Profession of Faith (Shahadah)—open proclamation of submission that "there is no God but Allah and Muhammad is the messenger of God"—at mosques this is chanted five times a day.

Prayer (Salah)—at prescribed hours, worship or ritual prayer five times daily, individually if not preferably in groups—the bowing or kneeling for this is toward Mecca; the Muslim doing this must be pure, hence newly washed and not dirty; Friday is the traditional day of rest, when the congregational prayers of men at midday should ordinarily be performed in the mosque.

Almsgiving (Zakah)—the Koran teaches that all believers must give to the needy, and today this is normally a personal act ranging from 2 to 10% of one's yearly income.

Fasting (Sawm)—throughout the 30-day lunar month of Ramadan, a Muslim abstains from food and drink, while practicing continence in other respects, from dawn to sunset; in some Muslim countries, such as Saudi Arabia, the obligation is legally enforced.

Pilgrimage (Haj)—at least once in a lifetime, if one is financially and physically able, a Muslim is expected to perform this act of piety by going to Mecca as a pilgrim during the month of Haj; merit is great for those who go there and perform the rites and ceremonies for 8–13 days.

Note: Some Muslims believe in a sixth pillar, *Holy War* or *Al-Jihad*, which offers the reward of salvation. This effort to promote Islamic doctrine among nonbelievers is not necessarily done through actual war as occurred in past ages. All observant Muslims are expected to practice hospitality toward strangers, even "infidels," as well as to enhance family relationships.

Contemporary analysts in books like Oliver Roy's *Globalized Islam*, and Faisal Devji's *Landscapes of the Jihad*, argue that the concept of jihad as practiced today by the al-Qaeda followers is a product of globalization, which transcends conventional politics and represents a radical and subversive departure from traditional Islam.

Having some historical perspective helps when visiting Muslim lands. At its height, Islam's empire was larger than that of Rome at its zenith. Islam produced great civilizations that made enormous contributions to art, architecture, astronomy, literature, mathematics, medicine, and other intellectual pursuits, which we still benefit from today.

Furthermore, to appreciate Islam's Middle Eastern origins, consider the many other countries outside the region to which it spreads. For example, the Muslim culture and way of life is global in scope. Parts of Europe have large Muslim populations, including Albania, Bosnia,

At its height, Islam's empire was larger than that of Rome at its zenith.

France, Spain, and Russia with its neighbors in the Commonwealth of Independent States. In North America, there are large Muslim communities in both the United States and Canada. But in Asia (e.g., Bangladesh, Pakistan, and Indonesia) as well as in Africa (e.g., Gambia, Morocco, and Nigeria) entire nations are Muslim. Thus far in the twenty-first century, Indonesia is the largest Muslim nation. Throughout the world, there are 42 Muslim majority nations, and Iran, Sudan, and Mauritania are officially Islamic states ruled by Islamic law. In Chapter 15 the continent of Africa is discussed, which alone contains 11 countries with majority Muslim populations, only one of which, Egypt, is considered Middle Eastern. Religious diversity is also evident in all Middle Eastern nations because of varied religious minorities, including Christians and Jews of many persuasions or sects, as well as myriad other believers. Islam has more than a billion followers and is growing fast; Exhibit 11.2 helps us to visualize its worldwide influence.

The Modern Middle East

The word "cauldron" describes this region because for a very long time the Middle East has been embroiled in different forms of conflict. The seeds of contemporary turmoil were largely sown in the past, so one should analyze current events in the region within that larger context. When the indigenous tribes and religious sects were not in conflict with one another, their crossroad location became the battleground for warring invaders, some of whom were called Crusaders in medieval times. The Muslims of the Middle East were under the domination of the Ottoman Turks from the sixteenth century until the nineteenth century when the West began to exercise control there. In the twentieth century alone we have witnessed a series of external wars extending to the region, resulting in European colonial occupiers with League of Nations' mandates taking over as "protectors." Many nations were created after World War I, with land divided without respect for tribal differences or for promises made to Arabs for their aid during that war. This resulted in unresolved issues to this day. History has much to tell us about current issues, so take the time to understand the twenty-first-century conditions within the region, in order to comprehend the full complexities. Furthermore the re-creation of the nation of Israel in 1948 convulsed and divided the Arab world, leading to several wars between Israelis and Palestinians, which involved neighboring countries. Unfortunately, that conflict continues 60 years later as these two Semitic peoples still struggle for peaceful coexistence. In recent decades, two American and Allied invasions triggered by controversy between Iraq and Kuwait led to the Gulf War and United Nations' sanctions. In this century, the United States and its allies not only went to war again in Iraq, supposedly searching for weapons of mass destruction,

The word "cauldron" describes this region because for a very long time the Middle East has been embroiled in different forms of conflict.

EXHIBIT 11.2
ISLAM'S INFLUENCE IN THE WORLD

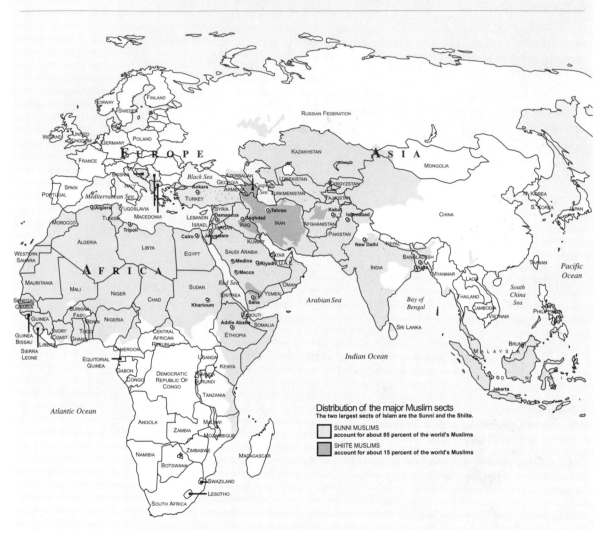

Source: Based on a graphic by M. Mansur and L. E. Craven from *The Kansas City Star,* and reproduced by the *San Diego Union-Tribune*, October 12, 2001, p. E5. Data drawn from *CIA World Fact Book*, *World Almanac*, *The Statesman's Yearbook, DK Illustrated Dictionary of World Religions*, and University of Texas–Austin.

but invaded Afghanistan to replace the Taliban fundamentalists with a more democratic government.

Sometimes the conflicts are within countries where Muslim extremists oppose established governments, as in Algeria, Egypt, and Saudi Arabia. At other times, fighting has occurred because local groups, with outside assistance, oppose the occupiers, as in Palestine's West Bank and Gaza, Kuwait, and Afghanistan. Often there have been outright civil wars, as in Yemen and Somalia, and possibly Iraq in the near future. Currently, the hope for the region is that the battles between Israel and its Muslim neighbors give way to peaceful negotiations, conflict resolution, and economic development, such as happened with Egypt and Jordan. However, some are more concerned about the clash of cultures and civilizations. The largest of the clashes in the area is that of the Western-style modernization and way of life, fueled by interaction with oil-seeking external powers, which is in contention with traditional Muslim values.

To put events in the Middle East in context, an astute observer of Islam today, R. D. Lewis, reminds us that[4]

- A persistent historical characteristic of the Muslim religion has been open tolerance for other faiths.
- Western civilization is indebted to Arabic translations in the Middle Ages of Hellenistic knowledge and tradition, especially in science and medicine.
- A mutually enriching coexistence of Muslims and Westerners has been the rule, rather than the exception, over the centuries.
- Islamic scholars maintain they are not against the West, but fear its power and influence within their own societies, particularly with reference to materialism and cultural imperialism.
- More than half of the world's 1 billion Muslims are not Arab, and most Muslims are moderates who admire piety and devoutness.
- Muslims are divided among themselves with a multiplicity of interests and agendas, especially in their Sunni and Shi'ite communities.
- Many Muslims are concerned about the slowness of democratic reforms and the unequal distribution of wealth in their countries, not about supporting violent Islamic radicalism and its call for jihad in an effort to change the current political structure and in an aggressive manner promote their own worldview.

A watershed event occurred on September 11, 2001, which rudely brought the problems of the Middle East into global consciousness. On that day, a terrorist network under the leadership of wealthy Osama bin Laden crashed three hijacked airliners into New York's World Trade Center and Washington, D.C.'s Pentagon buildings, killing over 3000 people. Fifty-six Muslim states immediately condemned the attack, pointing out that such behavior was against the basic tenets of

More than half of the world's 1 billion Muslims are not Arab.

Islam. These atrocities against humanity generated a global war against terrorism, accompanied by Western invasions, occupations, and reforms in both Afghanistan and Iraq.

In a *Discovery* Channel television broadcast on the root causes of the 9/11 catastrophes (March 26, 2002), commentator Thomas L. Friedman summarized the problems of the contemporary Arab world that might prompt individuals to commit such misguided acts. Primarily, they seemingly result from the frustration of people's needs because of the challenges faced within contemporary Arab civilization, such as the corruption of their leaders, some of whom become dictators; poverty and economic powerlessness of the majority, despite some oil riches; male oppression of women by exclusion and underdevelopment of their potential; radicalization of their youth by fundamentalists and extremists and Friedman emphasized that the younger Arab generation, including those educated abroad, often has a sense of being oppressed and humiliated by Westerners. Some of these disillusioned young people have been recruited into militant, terrorist networks.

Economic factors almost beyond their control are sweeping the Muslim nations and peoples into the global marketplace. In general, the Middle East today can be described as a region in the midst of profound cultural, social, political, and economic transition.[5]

To complete this introduction on the Middle East, we will review several areas or countries in the region. Typically, it is grouped into four geographic regions—North African States, Gulf States, Central Arab States, Iran and Israel—a combined population of more than 250 million people. Despite traditions extending back several millennia, most of the nations are relatively new; with the exception of Egypt and Iran, the others came into being in their present form in the twentieth century, largely since World War I. Depending on the time period, political conditions, and geographic perspective, the number of states in the Middle East varies. Currently, there are 14 nations in this designated area, but the final outcome of the Israel/PLO negotiations, the *Roadmap for Peace*, may hopefully result in Palestinian autonomy, with another state emerging before the end of the decade.

In modern times, leadership in Pan-Arabism was initially manifested by Christian Arabs in Lebanon and Syria. Attempts at the political formation of a "United Arab Republic" have been unsuccessful in the long term. Economic integration of six Persian Gulf countries resulted in the founding of a Gulf Cooperation Council. An Arab League promotes better communication systems for the region using the language of Arabic and the Arab Regional Satellite System (ARABSAT). As oil discovery and development became the dominant economic thrust of the area, Middle Eastern oil-producing nations joined together in the Organization of Petroleum Exporting Countries (OPEC), founding their own Organization of Arab Petroleum Exporting Countries (OAPEC). In the twenty-first century, regional governance has ranged from authoritarianism to democratic experiments, interspersed with Muslim regimes ruled by the *mullahs* or religious leaders, as is currently the case in Iran. Of the 20 countries composing the Arab world, seven consider themselves republics, including Mauritania, which calls itself an Islamic Republic, and Syria, which is known as the Baath Socialist Republic; seven others are monarchies; four have one-party rule or dictatorships; the United Arab Emirates (UAE) is a federation of sheikdoms; and Somalia currently lacks a functioning government. Politically, the Middle East is still in evolutionary transition as a result of modernization, particularly with reference to economic and educational development. Economically, the Middle East has yet to integrate itself through trade pacts and tariff agreements. Since 65% of all the world's petroleum reserves lie beneath the Middle East, oil extraction and refining play a significant role in the region and in global economics, impacting the welfare and politics of many Western countries.

Finally, the effects of Western cultural and military invasions in Middle Eastern societies have caused explosive dislocations. Westernization has brought changes at a high price, including:

- Weakened parental authority and family cohesion.
- Broken homes, sexual promiscuity, and materialism.
- Poverty for the masses and affluence for the elite.
- Urban ills, such as inadequate housing and traffic congestion.

The outcome of this social unrest has been twofold. First, Islamic fundamentalists cry out against what they perceive as Western decadence and immorality. They reject modern democratic values, such as individual freedom, the right to know, the rights of women, and other practices that are standard in industrialized nations. Some traditionalists have established, or seek to form, a government based on ancient Islamic law. Some terrorist networks have organized violent attacks and kidnappings against foreigners. Second, some Middle Eastern governments have responded to activists with harsh and authoritarian security actions, branding all dissidents as terrorists. This happened in Algeria, where attempts by the populace to democratically elect an Islamic government were suppressed by the ruling power.

Many fear that the global bombings, killings, and devastation caused by actual terrorists in the name of Islam may portend a crucial struggle between Muslim societies and the Judeo-Christian order within the secularized West. Others, in spite of differences in religion, culture, and history, hope for reconciliation and understanding between non-Muslims and Muslims. This cultural divide may only be bridged if local government and business leaders are more sensitive and less assertive regarding the Islamic ethos and aspirations. Perhaps the best place to begin efforts toward greater cultural synergy is with the Muslim communities within Western countries. Since the horrific acts of 9/11, hate crimes have surged in North America and Europe against innocent people of the Islamic faith. In the healing process, it might be well to recall the astute words of the chief rabbi for the United Hebrew Congregations of the Commonwealth:

> No one creed has a monopoly on spiritual truth . . . In heaven, there is truth; on earth, there are truths. Therefore, each culture has something to contribute.
>
> —J. Sacks, *The Dignity of Difference*, 2002

CHARACTERISTICS OF ARAB CULTURE

For outsiders, the key to a better comprehension of the contemporary Middle East is understanding Arab culture. We stress the point that not all Middle Easterners are Arab, as Iranians, Turks, and Israelis will remind us. Over 20 Arab countries can be identified as members of the League of Arab States.* Although Arab countries are considered Middle Eastern culturally, not all Middle Eastern countries are Arab. To say that member countries have similar cultural attitudes, behaviors, and communication is very misleading. For example, in the Muslim countries of Sudan, Somalia, and Mauritania, tribal languages, rather than Arabic, are spoken, and there are cultural practices that favor their African heritage.[6]

Not all Arabs believe in Islam, as Christian Arabs will confirm.

Not all Arabs believe in Islam, as Christian Arabs will confirm. But Arab peoples have a Muslim majority. As a rule, *Arab* is an ethnic reference to a Semite, whereas *Muslim* signifies religious belief and grouping. One who is attuned to such cultural differences can create cultural synergy, not only in this region but also in interactions with those throughout the world whose way of life is strongly influenced by Islam or Arab culture.

The connotation "Arab" refers to a group of people whose behavioral pattern is unique because of their culture, language, religion, and even their nationalism. They do not all look or dress alike and should not be stereotyped. Furthermore, Arab is *not* a race, a skin color, a nationality, or even a Muslim. By original definition in the pre-Islamic period, an Arab was an inhabitant of Arabia, a member of the nomadic Bedouin tribes. During the Islamic Expansion Era, Arabs carried their religion, language, and culture throughout the Middle East and beyond, intermarrying with the conquered peoples from Persia to the Pyrenees. Thus, today Arabs are not so much an ethnic group as a community with a state of mind. Arab leaders once explained the concept as, "Whoever lives in our country, speaks our language, is brought up in

* Arab countries: Algeria, Bahrain, Comoros Islands, Djibouti, Egypt, Iraq, Jordan, Kuwait, Lebanon, Libya, Mauritania, Morocco, Oman, Palestine, Qatar, Saudi Arabia, Somalia, Sudan, Syria, Tunisia, United Arab Emirates, and Yemen.

our culture, and takes pride in our glory, is one of us." The confusion about the meaning of this term has meant that Arab often is used interchangeably with Middle East or Muslim.[7]

What are some generalities about this distinctive Arab culture? Simply that it is a varied tapestry of religious and sociopolitical configurations, causing Arabs to constantly recast and revise themselves as circumstances around them also change.

Arab Values

In traditional societies, the paramount virtues are considered to be dignity, honor, and reputation. Foreigners at all costs should avoid causing an Arab to lose face or to be shamed (or, in the case of a woman, to lose her virginity before marriage). Loyalty to family as well as courteous and harmonious communications are emphasized. In tribal and traditional communities, Arab priorities are first to one's self, then kinsman, townsman, or tribesman, and those who share the same religion and country. Yet there is a degree of collectivism, for rapid urbanization has decreased the influence of tribalism, such as in Egypt and Iran. Given the impact of modernization, scholars wonder how long this community can maintain their traditional characteristics of generosity, gallantry, courage, patience, and endurance. Contrast this image of an Arab with the false stereotypes created by the Western media, film, and television industry about such peoples.

Loyalty to family as well as courteous and harmonious communications are emphasized.

Arab Personal Distance

Arabs seek close personal relationships, preferably without great distance or intermediaries. Thus, olfaction is prominent in Arab life. For many Arabs, smells are necessary and a way to be involved with each other. Body and food odors are used to enhance human relationships; the former is even important in the choice of a mate. This cultural difference also extends to an Arab facing or not facing another person; to view another peripherally is impolite, so to sit or stand back to back is rude. Although Arabs may be very involved when interacting with friends, they may not seek a close distance in conversations with strangers or mere acquaintances. On such social occasions, they may sit on opposite sides of a room and talk across to one another. Yet, they are generally a warm and expressive people, both verbally and nonverbally. Arabs are active participants with each other but resist being crowded in enclosed spaces or by boundaries.

Arab Sociability

Cordiality is at the core of this culture and is evident from such occasions as feasting at a lamb banquet to drinking their strong black coffee.

It extends also to business meetings when the first session is devoted to getting acquainted with little regard for schedule or appointments. The communication pattern is both oral and aural—the emphasis on listening also explains why so many prefer to learn from audiocassettes and radio. The traditional greeting is to place one's right hand on the chest near the heart as an indication of sincerity and warmth, though modern Arabs may precede this with a long, limp handshake. The custom is for men to kiss one another on both cheeks. For those Arabs who are Muslims, there are Islamic teachings that affect social relations, such as taboos against eating pork, drinking alcohol, gambling, and prostitution.

Arab Women

Arab patriarchal culture places the male in the dominant role.

The Arab patriarchal culture places the male in the dominant role, while protecting and respecting the female. In an Arab household, for example, the man is overtly the head with a strong role and influence; the mother "behind the scenes" is often the authority on family matters. Publicly, the woman defers to her husband, but privately she may be more assertive. Paradoxically, Islam does not advance the notion of women's inherent inferiority, only her difference; it does not perceive biological inferiority, and it affirms potential equality between the sexes. During an interview, Dr. Fatima Mernissi stated:

> The whole Muslim system is based on the assumption that the woman is a powerful and dangerous being. She argues that Arab rules and customs regarding polygamy, repudiation, sexual segregation, etc., can be perceived as a defense against the disruptive power of female sexuality. Others point out that Arab advocates of women's rights are using Islam and the opinion of enlightened religious scholars to ease restrictions on the role of females in society.[8]

In some Arab countries, women enjoy equality with men, while in others they have a limited role. In more traditional Arab communities where mullahs control marriage laws, men are allowed to marry more than one woman, including the foreign born. Women may marry only one husband, excluding foreigners. Husbands may divorce without stating a cause, whereas a wife must specify grounds to the satisfaction of the court, and in a courtroom, it takes the testimony of two females to equal one male.

The Koran, for instance, does not say that women must be veiled, only that they must be modest in appearance by covering their arms and hair, which are considered very sensual. Scholars see the use of the veil as symbolic with sociological meaning. The veil's use depends on time period and circumstances. Some Arab countries are without dress restrictions for women, so they may wear the latest fashion; whereas others, which are more traditional, may require a long cloak of black gauze or chiffon—an *abaya*—which is to cover from crown to ankle. The cultural contrasts within Arab societies on this matter are considerable. In some Arab countries most females are illiterate, whereas in others they are well educated; in some they are not allowed outside their home alone or permitted to drive an automobile, whereas in other states, women may hold jobs and drive cars. In many Arab states, women are not allowed to vote, whereas in others they have that franchise; in most Arab societies, marriages are arranged, whereas in a growing number, freedom of marital choice is respected. Within an Arab world in turmoil and change, one may observe both resurgent Islamic fundamentalism and an emerging feminist movement. In the traditional societies, such medieval codes of female behavior may be enforced by a Committee to Prevent Vice and Promote Virtue—the *matawa* or religious police. In more conservative Arab communities, when a woman disobeys these rulings, such as not being modestly clocked in the *abaya*, not entering a bus by a separate rear door and sitting in a segregated section, she may be flogged or caned by these religious police. Yet, there is great diversity within the Arab world on the status of women. A Freedom House report in May 2005 rated the exercise of women's social and cultural rights in Arab countries in this order: Tunisia, Lebanon, Palestine, Kuwait, Jordan, Egypt, Syria, UAE, Iraq, and the lowest Saudi Arabia.

Foreign females visiting Arab countries must exercise great sensitivity to what is acceptable or unacceptable in the local situation. Whether traveling as a tourist or on business, women visitors have to attune themselves to what is considered proper behavior and attire for their gender in each locality. Ladies from outside the culture who do not heed this counsel may have unhappy experiences. Whether female or male, those who would engage in successful commercial or professional exchanges within the Arab world should be aware of such proprieties. Further insights on these matters will be presented in sections that follow. But realize that the traditional Arab way of life is undergoing profound alteration worldwide—socially, economically, politically, and even religiously. Practices may vary depending on the degree of secularization and economic progress, as well as the extent of modernization and education. A profile summary of eight Middle East countries is included in Exhibit 11.3.

There is great diversity within the Arab world on the status of women.

CULTURAL ASPECTS OF EGYPT AND SAUDI ARABIA

By focusing on two similar but distinctly different cultural targets, one may gain insight into the cultural dimensions of these and other remarkable peoples in the region. Both Egypt and Saudi Arabia are part of the Arab world, but Egypt originates from an ancient civilization

EXHIBIT 11.3
PROFILES OF EGYPT, IRAN, IRAQ, ISRAEL, JORDAN, KUWAIT, SAUDI ARABIA, AND SYRIA

NATION	Egypt	Iran	Iraq	Israel	Jordan	Kuwait	Saudi Arabia	Syria
AREA (sq km)	1,001,450	1,648,000	437,072	20,770	92,300	17,820	1,960,582	185,180
POPULATION	77,505,756	68,017,860	26,074,906	6,276,883	5,759,732	2,335,648	26,417,599*	18,448,752
CAPITAL	Cairo	Tehran	Baghdad	Jerusalem	Amman	Kuwait	Riyadh	Damacus
RELIGION	Muslim (mostly Sunni), Coptic Christian	Shiite Muslim, Sunni Muslim, Zoroastrian, Jewish, Christian, Baha'i	Shiite Muslim, Sunni Muslim, Christian	Jewish, Muslim, Christian	Sunni Muslim, Christian	Shiite Muslim, Sunni Muslim, Christian, Hindu, Parsi	Muslim	Sunni Muslim, Alawite, Druze, Christian
LANGUAGE	Arabic, English, French	Persian, Turkic, Kurdish	Arabic, Kurdish, Assyrian, Armenian	Hebrew, Arabic, English	Arabic, English	Arabic, English	Arabic	Arabic, Kurdish, Armenian, Aramaic, Circassian
LITERACY	57.7%	79.4%	40.4%	95.4%	91.3%	83.5%	78.8%	76.9%
LIFE EXPECTANCY	71 years	69.96 years	68.7 years	79.32 years	78.24 years	77.03 years	75.46 years	70.03 years
GDP PER CAPITA	$4400	$8100	$3400	$22,000	$4800	$22,100	$12,900	$3500
GOVERNMENT	Republic	Theocratic republic	Iraqi Transitional Government (Democracy in progress)	Parliamentary democracy	Constitutional monarchy	Nominal constitutional monarchy	Monarchy	Republic (under authoritarian regime)

* Includes 5,576,076 nonnationals.

and is more liberal, whereas Saudi Arabia is a traditional nation created in the last century propelled by vast oil discoveries. Review Exhibit 11.3 for a basis of comparison of these two target countries with six profiles of their key Middle Eastern neighbors. Note that geographically, Egypt lies on the continent of Africa, but we include it here as culturally part of the Middle East.

EGYPT

Modern archaeological studies continually provide insights into Egypt's Old Kingdom as the findings eventually translate into museum exhibits and popular media presentations. This is the civilization that built the first great nation-state, flourishing for five and a half centuries before its collapse. It is a culture that produced *hieroglyphics*—one of the world's first written languages—and humanity's first macroprojects—construction of monumental pyramids dating from 2630 to 2250 B.C. Whether tombs of predynastic kings or later Pharaohs, these magnificent structures reveal a culture whose leaders and builders were dedicated with preparing for the afterlife. In the mineral-rich eastern desert of Upper Egypt, the hub was Thebes with its awesome funerary temples and rock-cut tombs. The building of pyramids and tombs became a central force for the organization and mobilization of townspeople, a means for creating a national state, and a magnet for early Middle Eastern trade. Then, as now, the Nile River with its network of hand-dug canals ties the country together geographically. By 2200 B.C. climatic crises arose when Nile flooding became undependable and drought seized the land.

This is the civilization that built the first great nation-state, flourishing for five and a half centuries before its collapse.

The People and Their Homeland

Most of Egypt is high dry plains, rugged hills, and mountains, stretching along the Red Sea Coast to the valley of the Nile. The population of the Old Kingdom was less than 2 million, while today's Egypt has more than 77 million inhabitants. This most populous of Arab states has one of the highest population densities in the world. Cairo, for instance, has approximately 11 million people for a city originally designed for 3 million. Its citizens are mostly a Hamitic people practicing the Sunni form of the Muslim religion.

Northern Egypt has a mixture of peoples from the Mediterranean and other Arab countries, whereas the south consists mainly of black African Nubians. In addition to thousands of the latter, this region also includes two other minorities—a few million Coptic Christians and more than 50,000 nomadic Bedouins. The major language spoken is Arabic, with some French and English, reflecting the heritage of previous European colonialists. Immigrants from all over the Middle East also live and work in this country.

Although upward of 44 million Egyptians are literate (68% male and 47% female), 32 million are illiterate. Despite the government provision of free education through university, only some 6 million benefit from this learning opportunity at some level. Egypt's educated people are sought by other Arab nations as professors and teachers, scientists and technicians, managers and engineers, and specialists and craftsmen.

Geographic Features and Cities

Although Egypt is a Middle Eastern nation, it is located on the African continent at a crossroads for the Mediterranean Basin, Africa, and Asia. Less than 5% of the country is cultivated, with the climate permitting several crops a year, but the potential exists for increased agricultural production. Beside its great north-south Nile River, the following are other notable geographic features:

The Suez Canal linking the Mediterranean Sea on the north with the Gulf of Suez and Red Sea on the southeast divides the Eastern or Arabian Desert from the Western or Libyan Desert (the Great Sand Sea).

The northeastern Sinai Peninsula, a desert area that abuts Israel and the Gulf of Aqaba.

The Aswan High Dam in the southeast with its Lake Nasser extending down into the Nubian Desert and the southern border with Sudan.

Egypt has 10 major cities, which besides the capital Cairo, are Alexandria, Giza, Shoubra, El-Kheima, El-Mahalla, El Koubra, Tanta, Port Said, and El Mansoura. There are new projects to develop new urban areas, such as Sadat City on the road between Cairo and Alexandria, and Nasser City in the desert near the International Airport. To better disperse the population now concentrated in 5% of its territory, Egypt has undertaken a massive opening and reclamation of new lands along its Mediterranean coast and in the Sinai. With the assistance of UN and U.S. aid, a master plan to reconstruct the Suez Canal area within the inner/outer regions is under way. The capital, Cairo, is Africa's and the Middle East's most populous city, blending the cultures of both ancient and modern, East and West, Islam and Christianity. Its origins can be traced to nearby El Fustai, founded by Arabs in A.D. 641.

Political and Social Conditions

The foundations of governance were laid by 20 dynasties when pharaohs and kings reigned from 3000 to 715 B.C., extending their rule as far as Lower Nubia, Palestine, and Syria. Invasions in that period brought in temporary rulers and settlers from Asian Hyksos, Libya,

Persia, and Nubia. Since 333 B.C., Egypt's heritage has reflected the presence of a series of conquerors—from Alexander the Great and the Roman Empire to Arabs and the Turkish Ottoman Empire, to the establishment of a British presence (1882–1952) during which a monarchy was formed in 1922 under King Fouad I. Because of dire economic and social conditions, military officers staged a coup d'état on July 23, 1952 under the leadership of Lieutenant. Colonel Gamel Abdel Nasser—that date is now celebrated in Egypt as National Day. On June 18, 1953, this junta declared Egypt a republic. This became a turning point for modern Egyptians, who then felt more independent, spearheading a resurgence of Arab nationalism throughout the Middle East. In 1971, a new constitution was adopted for the Arab Republic of Egypt that guarantees the individual rights of its citizens. Subsequently, two more presidents have led the country—former General Anwar Sadat who was assassinated, and, currently, former General Hosni Mubarak, recently reelected to that post. There is a National Assembly with four political parties.

During the closing four decades of the twentieth century, Egypt struggled internally to restructure its socioeconomic system, including reapportioning wealth and some land reform. Moving away from earlier experiments with socialism, contemporary Egypt espouses democracy and a market economy, providing incentives for both domestic and foreign investment. Yet, this is a developing economy, plagued by uncontrolled population growth, poverty, and insufficient food. With 94% of its people Muslim adherents, it is understandable that civil law is influenced by Shariah or Islamic law. But it is economic degradation among the masses that fuels Islamic militants seeking to establish a Muslim government, often leading to terrorist acts against both the leadership and foreigners.

Many external pressures explain why Egypt has used its limited resources on military expansion and regional conflicts. Supposedly, the leader of the Arab world was expected to provide the primary opposition to the establishment of Israel as a state. Since the late President Sadat signed and put into effect a peace treaty with Israel (March 25, 1979), Egypt for many years was both the target of Arab economic reprisals and the recipient of significant foreign aid from the United States. Reconciliation and synergy are increasingly its goals with its neighbors. Jordan and the Palestine Liberation Organization have also signed agreements with Israel, and Syria/Lebanon consider the prospects. To curb attacks of Islamic militants in the area, President Mubarak hosted a summit in Cairo at the beginning of Ramadan in 1995. Prime Minister Yitzhak Rabin of Israel, PLO leader Yasser Arafat, and the King Hussein of Jordan joined him in the elusive pursuit of peace and prosperity for the Middle East. In a collective communiqué, "the four parties condemned all outbreaks of bloodshed, terror, and violence in the region and reaffirmed their intentions to stand

Egypt struggled internally to restructure its socioeconomic system.

staunchly against and put an end to all such acts."[9] Ironically, Rabin was assassinated by a Jewish fundamentalist in 1995. But Egypt continues to cooperate as a peace broker in a region where nations have more to gain by peaceful cooperation than from continuing conflict.

The governance and political system have undergone some liberalization in recent times. The constitution provides for a strong president, vice president, prime minister, cabinet, and governors for 26 provinces. The single legislature is the People's Assembly with 444 elected delegates and 10 appointed by the president; 50% reserved for farmers and workers. The *Shura* is a consultative council for advising on public policy but with little legislative power. The governing National Democratic Party (NDP) dominates politics. Today, Egyptians are intensely nationalistic and Arab sensitive. Though a secular state and somewhat Westernized, especially with reference to international business, traditional Arab patterns are also present.

The Economy and Business

Europe, followed by the United States, is a growing importer of Egypt's exports.

The change and diversification under way in Egypt are evident in its exports—a shift from the traditional cultivation of cotton and rice to the rising production of petroleum, cotton textiles, and metal products, as well as increasing tourism, construction, and mining. Europe, followed by the United States, is a growing importer of Egypt's exports. With the gradual dismantling of bureaucratic regulations, foreign investment increases, as do reclamation projects. The currency is the Egyptian pound divided into 100 piasters or 1000 millimes. Seeking to maintain parity with the U.S. dollar, the Central Bank weekly sets the premium exchange rate.

In addition to the general business protocols for the region discussed above, local customs for doing business include:

Investments—Law 43 and subsequent amendments liberalize foreign investment, providing incentives, particularly with reference to new technologies, and exemptions (from nationalization, custom duties, some regulations and taxes, etc.), plus guarantees for repatriation of capital. For potential traders and investors, the most significant developments have been in the banking system that now allows joint ventures with foreign banks and improvements in transportation, hotels, and resorts.

Workforce—Since 1974 there have been significant changes in the business environment, encouraging the private sector in an economy still dominated by the public sector. The 10 million plus people that comprise the available workforce are well trained. Egyptian skilled labor and entrepreneurial talent is sought by other nations in the area. Basic Labor Law 91 protects workers' rights and sets work policy; foreign firms may be exempt from some of these regulations.

Social Life—This is oriented toward extended families and public gatherings, with a close sense of distance. Prepare for a slower way of life, including decision making, and a lack of punctuality in keeping appointments. People follow the Islamic calendar with a 28-day lunar month or 354 days a year. Five national holiday dates are fixed, whereas Ramadan and Islamic New Year are approximate depending on lunar observations.

Work Practices—The workweek is from Saturday through Wednesday, with no business conducted on Thursday and Friday (Muslim Holy Day). Business hours vary, but typically in summer are 8 A.M. to 2 P.M.; in winter, 9 A.M. to 1 P.M. and 5 to 7 P.M. Paperwork includes two dates—Gregorian or Western and Hijrah or Arabic (Coptic Christians have a different calendar).

As in all Muslin societies, the *hajj* is an important annual event, as Exhibit 11.4 explains.

SAUDI ARABIA

The Arabian Peninsula is the heartland of Islamic culture, which is 14 centuries old, originating in Mecca. Arabia's inhabitants were the primary source of Arab expansion throughout the Middle East and Europe from A.D. 570–1258, the Golden Age of the Arab empire. But Saudi Arabia as a nation is a product of the twentieth century, particularly because of oil discoveries and development. In decades, its citizens have transitioned from a Bedouin tribal culture to a modern urban culture. After hundreds of years of subsistence living, a nomadic, patriarchal, and impoverished society has suddenly been transformed into a more prosperous, educated, and internationally oriented one. Within this whirlwind clash between tradition and modernization, the affluent kingdom founded on Islamic principles has experienced cataclysmic change. Popular magazines have described the nation as a desert superstate—a rich, vulnerable, feudal monarchy progressing into the modern age.

Its citizens have transitioned from a Bedouin tribal culture to a modern urban culture.

The People and Their Homeland

Approximately 90% of the Saudi people are Arabs, with a 10% minority of Afro-Asians. The kingdom's population has risen rapidly to almost 26 million and is growing. The country occupies four-fifths of the Arabian Peninsula, a landmass of 850,000 square miles, making it geographically one of the largest countries in the region. Geographically, it is a harsh, rugged plateau reaching from the Red Sea on the west toward the Gulf on the east (called Arabian by the Saudis and

EXHIBIT 11. 4

THE HAJJ—JOURNEY OF FATIH

This is the annual holy pilgrimage to the heart of Islam, Mecca in Saudi Arabia. Called Makkah in Arabic, this is the "City of God" where the Prophet Muhammad is buried. Considered the fifth pillar of Islamic belief, performing it at least once in a lifetime is required of every Muslim who is able. A deeply spiritual undertaking, it underscores the historical continuity of Islam's 14 centuries. By returning to the site of *Kabah* to pray and commemorate Abraham's willingness to sacrifice his son to God's command, the rites of *Id al-Adha,* Muslims reenforce the links that bind them to each other, to the Prophet Muhammad, and to the beginnings of monotheism.

As a result, these pilgrims have opened up trade routes across the world, developing in the process an Afro-European free trade zone. In the name of charity, other Muslims facilitate their travels by building rest sites or caravanserais, supplying water and providing protection, and giving them pious donations to assist with expenses. The Hajj has also become important as a social phenomenon, contributing to the forging of Islamic culture worldwide, while bridging differences of nationality, ethnicity, and custom. Hajj is the heartbeat of the Earth's first genuinely transcontinental culture, nurturing and expanding science, commerce, politics, and religion. Millions of pilgrims learn of their commonality during prayer fives times each day facing Makkah, fasting together during Ramadan, observing the injunctions of the Qur'an, and sharing hospitality. Over centuries, the desire to assist pilgrim travel spurred Muslim advances in mathematics, optics, astronomy, navigation, transportation, geography, education, medicine, finance, culture, and even politics. Despite the arduous journey and multiple risks, the constant flows of these pilgrims are channels of cultural and intellectual ferment.

[Editor's note: while camel caravans have been replaced by modern transportation, today the Kingdom of Saudi Arabia continues to prepare for and welcome every year masses of Hajj pilgrims, despite setbacks caused by terrorists, fire, and stampedes.]

Source: Adapted from David W. Tschnaz's "Journeys of Faith, Roads of Civilization," *Saudi Aramco World*, September/October 2004, pp. 2–5.

Persian by the Iranians on the opposite side). Other Gulf states sharing that peninsula from north to south are Kuwait, Bahrain, Qatar, and the United Arab Emirates. The Saudi's northern frontier abuts Jordan, Iraq, and Kuwait, and in the south, Yemen and Oman. There is wide variation in the Saudi citizens, ranging from desert dwellers to, increasingly, city dwellers. Bedouin tribesmen in origin, they are a keen, alert, astute people, never to be underestimated. Saudi Arabians live in an entirely Muslim country with oil reserves of 261.8 billion barrels.

Today the country has 300 modern hospitals, as well as 5 million students enrolled in 24,000 schools, 8 universities, and numerous colleges and training centers. But too many Saudi youths in higher education are not being realistically prepared for the present-day job market because their studies are not in line with market realities. Thus one of every five workers in the kingdom is foreign born. Approximately 1 million immigrants and technicians are in Saudi Arabia to help build the infrastructure and defense, as well as to provide new technologies and services. This influx includes Americans, Europeans, Japanese, and Third World laborers and servants, such as Filipinos, Africans, and other Middle Easterners.

With a literacy rate of over 78%, rapid Saudi modernization and affluence has brought increased educational opportunities both at home and abroad for males and some females. Throughout history, Arabic has been a source of a great literary communication. Although this language with its three forms (classic, standard, and dialects) is principally used by Saudis, English is widely spoken or understood among the educated commercial class. The citizens' three most common symbols are the date palm emblematic of growth and vitality, the unsheathed sword of strength rooted in faith, and the Muslim reed. Although the unique, flowing robes and headdress of the Arabs are preferred, cosmopolitan Saudis are equally at home in Western dress when appropriate.

The kingdom follows a form of strict Islamic conservatism called *Hanabalism* (or *Wahhabism* by detractors). It is among the most restrictive of Sunni Muslim jurisprudence. Although it has been criticized by outsiders as rigid, uncompromising and self-righteous, most Saudi people follow a hybrid that mixes local traditions with modern developments. The ordinary Saudi is known for exercising generosity and hospitality.

Geographic and Economic Features

Saudi Arabia is three and a half times larger than the state of Texas and has four major topographical regions:

- Asir, a relatively fertile strip of coastal mountains in the southwest with peaks up to 10,000 feet and terraced farming.
- Hijaz, a mountain chain encompassing the rest of the west coast along the Red Sea.
- Nejd, the arid peninsula plateau with the Rub-al Khali or Empty Quarter, the largest continuous sand desert in the world, a place of oases in the north as well as shifting sand dunes and untapped oil

Saudi Arabia is three and a half times larger than the state of Texas.

fields—the capital city of Al-Riyadh at its center is a "garden" because of springs and well water.

■ Al Hasa, the eastern province where the principal oil and gas production occurs, along with agriculture in numerous oases, such as Haradh and Hofuf.

Saudi Arabia has 14 principal population centers and 4 major cities. Riyadh, the royal capital of some 4.2 million, is a modern desert city with new freeways, hospitals, schools, shopping malls, and the largest airport in the world. The Red Sea port city of Jeddah is the nation's leading commercial center and hub of the country's 8000-mile highway system. Jeddah's huge, $10 billion airport handles the 2 million Muslim guests annually en route to its holy places. Assembling on the Plains of Arafat, the *hajj*, or pilgrim caravan, moves to Mecca some 50 miles away. Then the pilgrim traffic heads for Medina, the sacred city of the prophet Muhammad, also a growing commercial center with the nearby new port of Yanbu. On the east coast, two additional important commercial hubs are Al-Khubar and its nearby port city of Dammam, the Arabian rail terminus to Riyadh. Also nearby are the two oil cities of Dhahran with its Aramco compound of American-style homes, and Ras Tannurah, the world's largest petroleum port. Fifty miles north up the coast is the new industrial city of Jubail with its giant new port and naval base. Jubail and Yanbu are the two largest public works projects in history. Since the 1970s, when they were built virtually from nothing, they now account for 10% of the world's petrochemical production.[10]

Political and Social Conditions

The nation's history parallels the House of Saud, founded in the eighteenth century, which recaptured the traditional family seat of Riyadh in 1902 and then extended their control over what is modern Saudi Arabia. This was accomplished under the leadership of Abdul Aziz ibn-Abd ar-Rahman. Called ibn-Saud, he was proclaimed king of the entire region in 1927; the new nation was named the Kingdom of Saudi Arabia in 1932 and by 1945 was a founding member of the United Nations and the Arab League. With the help of American petroleum engineers, King Abdul Aziz in 1939 launched the country and the Aramco company's future by opening the valves for oil production at 4 million barrels a day. Over time hundreds of billions of barrels have been extracted, and it is still flowing. Aramco is now entirely state owned under Saudi control and management and produces 95% of the nation's oil. In the year 2005, the country was admitted as a member of the World Trade Organization.

The sixth king, Abdullah bin Abdul Aziz al-Saud rules today with assistance from a royal family of some 30,000, of whom 7000 are "princes." About 500 princes are in government service, but only 60 are thought to be involved in decision making. Since his days as crown prince, Abdullah, now in his mid-80s, has promoted some consultation, consent, and liberal reforms. Like its kingly predecessors, his administration encourages economic, medical, educational, and technological progress and friendly Western relationships, while maintaining orthodox Islamic teachings and supporting Arab world ambitions. Tribal connections are maintained through the Saudi National Guard. The combined wealth of the Al Saud family is estimated to be in the hundreds of billions of dollars.

In Saudi Arabia, the Shariah governs national life and behavior. A judiciary interprets and advises the king on this law and in other matters not stated. The Shariah courts consist of 700 judges, the backbone of the legal system, but the bane of reformers. The ruler is also assisted by a council of ministers chaired by the crown prince acting as deputy prime minister. The *Majlis al-Shura* is a consultative council of 150 appointed members, broadly representative of the kingdom's diversity, except it excludes women. Although there are no elections or legislature, the king and his governors of provinces, as well as the royal princes, govern by consensus but with absolute authority. In a system based on trust, they hold regular *majlis* or audiences where citizen petitioners may approach in open court to make requests, to lodge complaints, or to adjudicate grievances. Internationally, the king opposes Western democracy and its institutions, while gently nudging his country forward on social matters without unduly offending conservatives. A step toward democracy occurred in 2005 with elections for municipal councils, but for only half the seats. The country spends approximately $15 billion annually for a defense force to protect the kingdom from external enemies.

Islam permeates Saudi life—Allah is always present, controls everything, and is frequently referred to in conversation; that name appears in Arabic script on the nation's flag. Everything written in the preceding sections on Islam and Arab culture is fervently present in this traditional society, now on the verge of even greater change. Islamic tenets enhance the status of women by limiting the number of wives a man may have, by imposing restrictions on divorce, and by ensuring a woman's rights to property and inheritance from husband or father. Men may divorce their wives with a simple oath, while women must plead before an all-male Wahhabist judiciary, and mothers have no right to custody of the children. Further, husbands may deny wives the right to travel, work, or study at university. Following the impact of the first Gulf War with Iraq, women began a quiet revolution. For centuries, women in Saudi Arabia lived in extreme privacy, wore the long veil or *abaya*, and were protected by the males. Today, Saudi women are still socially segregated, constrained in their movements and dress, and very much dominated by the husband or male family head. The

In Saudi Arabia, the Shariah governs national life and behavior.

many successful female entrepreneurs resent having to have a male agent to represent them. Yet with advanced education, Saudi women have begun to enter the business world and the professions, especially teaching along with social and public services. The so-called invisible women are said now to control as much as 40% of private wealth, much of it inherited under the law. Despite social limitations on women, as well as bans on their driving, travel, and political activity—all enforced by the *mutawa* or religious police—cosmopolitan female Saudis slowly forge ahead. Their growing economic assets are increasingly used to invest in property and to engage in business ownership—2000 of the latter are registered with the Riyadh Chamber of Commerce. Another hopeful sign is that 55% of university enrollments are women.

The kingdom was jarred on November 20, 1979, when 350 armed religious zealots invaded Mecca's Sacred Mosque. The siege and intense fighting lasted two weeks before Saudi troops killed or captured these "renegades of Islam," as the *ulama* or theologians called them. At the same time in the city of Qatif, minority Shia Muslims, representing 5% to 10% of the population, rioted. The whole affair was thought to have been orchestrated by Iranian Shia pilgrims, followers of Ayatollah Khomeini who had overthrown the monarchy in Iran. Since then, Saudi rulers have sought both to limit non-Islamic influences and reestablish policies closer to the fundamentalist form of the majority Sunni Muslims.

The royal family, controlling the top government positions and a large share of the nation's wealth, struggles to maintain some balance between modern global influences, and insular, ultraconservative, clerics of Wahhabism who seek to return Islamic practices to the seventh- and eighth-century versions. But in the twenty-first century, they face a time bomb, with 70% of its population under 21, incomes falling, unemployment rising, and external Middle Eastern conflicts impacting their society. Their inherited power and absolute monarchy include neither free elections and media nor political parties and human rights protections. The House of Saud fears not only accelerating social and political change, but a possible revolt comparable to that which overturned the Shah in Iran in 1979. Islamic radicalism and extremism appeals to disheartened and struggling youth. Some children of the elite have been inspired by the rhetoric of Osama bin Laden, whose father built the BinLaden Group into a $5 billion construction empire. The son's radical followers, including many young Saudis educated in fundamentalist religious schools, have been responsible for a network of terrorist attacks against the United States, Europe, Africa, Asia, and the Middle East, which destroyed thousands of innocent lives and disrupted national economies.

The second watershed event was the May 2003 attack against three Riyadh residential compounds that killed 34 persons, including 7 Saudis, along with diplomatic and businesspeople and their families from America, Australia, Britain, Jordan, Ireland, Lebanon, Philippines, and Switzerland; 190 were injured and hospitalized. Having been negligent in providing adequate security, the government is alarmed and is cracking down on terrorists. The then Crown Prince Abdullah warned that anyone who tried to justify such crimes in the name of religion "would be considered a full partner to the terrorists and share their fate."

The Saudi government is under great pressure to change faster because of events such as the following in the opening of the twenty-first century:

■ The global war on terrorism and attacks by Islamic militants on Western targets, such as New York City and Washington, D.C.; Madrid, Spain; and London, England. Many of the youths involved had been born and raised in Saudi Arabia, often from affluent families. They had become radicalized in fundamentalist Mosque schools at home or abroad funded by wealthy Saudis and taught by fiery mullahs who were narrow-minded, religious zealots. Furthermore, some of the Islamic charities supported by Saudi funding were found to be the source of financial support for extremist groups. Yet many Saudi donors claim they did not know their contributions were being so misdirected. In any event, this internal terrorism has prompted intense introspection and debate.

■ Their ally, the United States, undertook a preemptive invasion of Muslim Iraq and this resulted in a greater destabilization in the Middle East. While many American troops have since been removed from Saudi Arabia, the fellow Muslim nations criticize Saudi Arabia for its close ties for eight decades to the United States, supporter of the Israeli enemy and interloper in Muslim countries.

■ Human rights abuses seemingly exist, especially among foreign workers who face petty discrimination and have little recourse to justice. There is apparently some persecution of religious minorities, such as non-Wahhabi Muslims and visiting Christians.

■ Increasing quiet agitation by an affluent middle class for political reforms, liberalization of strict religious constraints, especially on women, and for more democratic institutions. The *Islahi* or reformist movement performed best in the first municipal elections. A progressive elite has a strong voice in the local Saudi press and on satellite television channels. Thus, the Al Saud family, representing a broad spectrum of opinion, strives to preserve a balance between liberal demands and strident preachers among the *mutawa*.

The Economy and Business

During the twentieth century, Saudi Arabia's financial situation skyrocketed from the subsistence level based on herding and farming to

The Saudi government is under great pressure to change faster.

A series of five-year development plans and over $91 billion in government expenditures on ports and roads have spurred commerce.

wealth from oil and gas development. Over the past 90 years, this developing economy has been transformed from a desert backwater with nomadic trade and barter to a rich, complex, global system. By the mid-1970s, energy production accounted for 74.5% of gross domestic product ($44 billion, 8 million barrels of oil per day), thus enabling the country to become the world's largest exporter of petroleum. Large-scale diversification into hydrocarbon-based industries is vigorously pursued. Provision of new infrastructure also spurred the growth of the nonoil economic sector, expanding private enterprise as well. A series of five-year development plans and over $91 billion in government expenditures on ports and roads have spurred commerce.

Sheep, goats, and camels have given way to automobiles, jets, and supertankers, making for a new mobility for both the populace and their products. By the 1980s, with a proven oil reserve for the next 60 years, the country was producing 9.5 million barrels of oil per day, contributing significantly to the economic well-being of both the West and Japan. Yet by the 1990s the GNP was down to almost half of what it had risen to in the previous decade. Saudi Arabia became a member of the World Trade Organization in 2000 accepting WTO policies, including removal of some protectionist regulations. Two sectors of the economy that may be privatized are telecommunications and electricity. As the world's largest producer and exporter of oil, Saudi Arabia benefits economically from high oil prices. But when crude oil prices are very low, the Saudi economy experiences problems with international cash flows. The country has also sought to reduce its dependence on Western technology and military protection and to curb anti-Western fanaticism, which fostered a climate of ideological extremism.

To appreciate this $300 billion economy, consider that SABIC alone, a maker of petrochemicals and steel, is the largest industrial group in the Middle East, and its stock market value is a whopping $175 billion! Stereotypes about this country constantly need changing. For example, although there is much desert, the Saudis have been turning 200 acres of it into farmland. Green circles, each with a deep well, pump water for irrigation from as deep as 4000 feet underground. Wheat and animal feed are grown some 250 miles from the Red Sea because of large investment in roads, wells, irrigation equipment, power, seeds, and fertilizer. Desalination plants treat hot, mineralized water before it is sprayed on the crops. The number of farms continues to grow, and Saudi Arabia is the only Middle Eastern country with surplus food.

Officially, unemployment is rated at 9.6%, but outside estimates are as high as 20%. Nine out of ten women are not actively seeking jobs. There has been a cutback on the dependence on foreign workers, and more emphasis put on young Saudis learning the skills necessary to operate the new economy. Yet, foreigners still make up 60% of the 8.5 million workforce and work 30% cheaper than Saudi manpower. Not only are many locals averse to taking orders, but they find much of the work demeaning. Despite a recent law that requires 75% "Sauisation" of workers, many of the schools are not producing employable people, partially due to the emphasis on rote learning, inefficient separation of the sexes, and excessive religious instruction.

Other trends within the kingdom are the following:

- A foreign investment law in 2000 permitting 100% ownership of in-country projects and reduced corporate taxes to 30%; agreements signed with eight international companies to invest in three integrated natural gas development ventures.
- Encouraging privatization within a state-run economy, establishing a public stock market, and building of the futuristic Al Faisalah complex with modern stores, hotel, and apartments.
- In the past 10 years, the appendage of 40 laws to streamline commerce. The country's regulatory bodies are well regarded in their governance of capital markets, telecoms, and industrial standards, while the patent office is under reform. SAGIA, the government's business-promotion entity, is competent and seeks foreign investment.
- Active support, loans ($14 billion), and contributions to numerous international and humanitarian organizations and causes, especially to Middle Eastern peace and development. The King Faisal Foundation alone has contributed millions of dollars to global philanthropic projects promoting Islamic values. It also assists the world's 1.2 billion Muslims in making global religious pilgrimages to the holy sites of Mecca and Medina, with the government providing support to the needy making the *hajj*.
- Reduction of income polarization, so that 3 million Saudis now hold local equities. With 23 million people and rising, the market for trade is promising. This population growth necessitates huge investments in infrastructure. Thus in 2005, the World Bank ranked Saudi Arabia as the best place in the region to do business!

To balance such positive development, consider these observations of Madawi al-Rasheed, a Saudi scholar, who says that the family that unified the kingdom some 80 years ago now has become a "headless tribe" with at least five factions. "Supposedly, this gerontocracy sits atop a society in stress, where money, in the absence of constitutional tools or intellectual freedom, has been the only buffer against wrenching and rapid change."[11]

Before arriving in Saudi Arabia, expatriate business and professional people are advised to learn about its customs and traditions, some of which are discussed in the separate section to follow on business protocol.

Yet, foreigners still make up 60% of the 8.5 million workforce and work 30% cheaper than Saudi manpower.

CULTURAL CAPSULES OF OTHER MIDDLE EAST COUNTRIES

In addition to the profile of Middle East countries provided in Exhibit 11.3, we offer cultural observations for thirteen other states:*

BAHRAIN. An archipelago of some 33 islands, only one of which is large, Bahrain is home to some 670,000 people. With a per capita GDP of $13,000, it is an outpost of many multinational firms because it is the most liberal state in the Persian Gulf and is popular with tourists. In the 2004 elections, it voted for a constitutional monarchy.

IRAN. Inheritor of the ancient Persian empire and culture, this country is a Shiite giant of over 65 million people. In 1979, an Islamic revolution overthrew the Shah to install a government called the Islamic Republic. Ruled by religious clerics, it engaged in a brutal war with Iraq in the 1980s, which cost a million lives. In 1979, it permitted the takeover and closure of the American embassy by radicalized students, who then took the staff as hostages. A sworn enemy of Israel, it has sponsored Hamas and Hezbollah terrorism in that country and Lebanon, and has encouraged Shiite extremists in Iraq. An important player in the region, it faces UN sanctions for its development of nuclear power, and possibly weapons. Its educated population wish for social, economic, and economic reform in their elections, but with little success.

IRAQ. The land of ancient Mesopotamia between the Tigris and at Euphrates rivers, and the luxurious city of Babylon. With a population estimated at 27 million, plus the second largest oil reserve in the world, this state is strategically placed for Western interference. The British established its monarchy with a figurehead king; then an army coup installed the dictator Saddam Hussein, who fought a war with the Iranians, practiced genocide on his own citizens, and invaded Kuwait in 1990. This provoked United Nations sanctions, and two invasions by the United States and its coalition partners—first the Gulf War in 1991 and again in 2003 in which the regime and its large armed forces were quickly defeated both times. Although the present occupation by U.S. and allied troops failed to uncover "weapons of mass destruction" as expected, it did trigger a serious insurgency by locals and foreign terrorists, resulting in much loss of life and property which may lead to civil war. Hussein was captured and put on trial, and efforts are underway to formulate a more democratic form of government. Elections have been held for the first time in the country's history to pass a constitution and install a parliament. Under the previous Baath Party's totalitarian rule, Sunni

*Adapted from "Middle East—Crossroad of Faith and Conflict," map supplement of the National Geographic Society, October 2002.

Muslims, a minority, dominated the government, so they are resisting participation in the new regime. Thus, the majority Shiite Muslims and the minority Kurdish Islamist parties have the power at this time, governing along ethnic and sectarian lines. Whether these three factions can ever cooperate in establishing a balanced government of national unity is an open question.

U.S. officials predict that the economy will grow in 2006 by 4% or more as sales of consumer and durable goods soar. Reconstruction and rehabilitation projects have been hampered by security problems. The people fear for their safety, complain about electricity failures and high unemployment, and are struggling to create a democratic market economy.

The Kurds in Iraq have gained a measure of autonomy and peace for their mountainous northern region and are currently cooperating with the central government in Baghdad. Their goal is to control some 9 billion barrels of crude oil in Iraqi Kurdistan and eventually gain independence to form a new state with the Kurds living within the borders of Syria, Turkey, and Iran in a plan vehemently opposed by those three nations. Having 100,000 of their people killed under Saddam's administration and having tasted freedom for the last 15 years, the Iraqi Kurds will not give it up without a fight. With foreign aid and smuggling, these fierce warriors and builders are now experiencing a measure of prosperity, despite their lack of a native industry.[12]

ISRAEL. Although the Hebrews lived on this ancient land during biblical times, they did not regain a state until 1948 with the help of the United Nations when the British left Palestine. Since then Israel has turned these 20,277 square miles into a prosperous garden, economy, and refuge for over 6 million Jews from all over the world. But its successes with agriculture, industry, technology, trade, and tourism have been eclipsed by conflicts in the region. There have been numerous incursions and reprisals by Israel and its neighbors, along with ongoing peace negotiations involving the United Nations and many countries. Peace and synergy continue to elude these two Semite peoples.

JORDAN. Created as a buffer state and wedged among Saudi Arabia, Iraq, Syria, and Israel, Jordan made peace with Israel in 1994. The skilled statecraft of the late King Hussein and his son King Abdullah II have kept this constitutional monarchy on a steady course. Meager resources, regional trade, and international aid have enabled Jordan to maintain some balance in the region. With a population of over 5 million, more than half of whom are Palestinian refugees, continuing military conflicts in surrounding nations—including the two invasions of Iraq by Western powers—have made it very difficult for this small country to function.

KUWAIT. With crude oil reserves of 95.6 billion barrels, this tiny city-state has made a remarkable recovery from the Iraq invasion and sabotage of its oil fields in 1991. Its 2.3 million residents enjoy a GDP per capita of some US $15,500. A monarchy led by an emir, it has instituted a legislative council, but denies the vote to women, or reentry to guest workers who fled the war—including hundreds of thousands of Palestinians.

LEBANON. A land of great natural beauty overlooking the Mediterranean Sea, this is a popular vacation location when there is peace. Known as Phoenicia in ancient times, this maritime country is home today to some 4.3 million people with a per capita GDP of approximately $3200. Its population is 70% Muslim and 30% Christian, a religious division that has been reflected in how the government is constituted and is the source of fighting among local militias, resulting in much destruction. After suffering 16 years of civil wars, the Lebanese requested Syrian troops to maintain order, and the Syrians reluctantly withdrew in 2005. The little nation has been invaded twice by Israel in retaliation for terrorist acts by Hamas and Hezbollah elements within its borders; in 2000, Israel withdrew its army from occupying a "security zone" in south Lebanon for 22 years. In 2006, as a response to Hezbollah's rocket fire into Israel and the kidnapping of soldiers, Israel bombed many parts of Lebanon and occupied the southern part of the country. International negotiations with Lebanon and Israel have led the cease fire, Israel's withdrawal, and the introduction of Lebanese and United Nations peacekeeping forces along the southern border.

OMAN. In the past 35 years, Oman has transformed itself from a closed society to a progressive sultanate that enjoys good relations with both Arab nations and the West. Its 2.6 million inhabitants have a per capita GDP of $8200 and crude oil reserves of 5.5 billion barrels. Home to mostly Ibadhi Muslims, a conservative but tolerant sect, Oman sweeps along the Arabian Sea to the Persian Gulf. It is thus strategically important to the U.S. military which has basing privileges there.

PALESTINIAN AUTHORITY. The West Bank and Gaza Strip are governed by this Authority, which hopes to negotiate an independent state recognized by its neighbor, Israel. The West Bank area adjoining Jordan has some 2.2 million inhabitants, while the separate Gaza Strip has a population of 1.1 million located in the southeast corner of Israel on the Mediterranean Sea. Since 1967, these original inhabitants of Palestine have been locked in mortal combat with Israelis whom they view as occupiers of their land. Kindled by the 1993 Oslo peace accord, continuing negotiations for a settlement have unraveled as the result of reciprocal attacks between Palestinians HAMAS and Israeli soldiers. Apart from the issue of illegal Jewish settlements in both entities, in 2005 Israel withdrew its troops and settlers from the Gaza Strip. The combined per capita GDP for both areas is only about $1500, and prospects for economic development are grim unless a cooperative accord is reached with Israel.

QATAR. Ruled by one of the region's most progressive monarchs, Sheikh Hamad, this state has modernized at breathtaking speed, funded by oil and the world's largest natural gas fields. With a population of only 618,000, its per capita GDP is $21,000, and it has a crude oil reserve of 15.3 billion. A key coalition ally in the Persian Gulf War, Qatar hosts both the U.S. military and *Al Jazeera*, the global Arabic language television news network.

SYRIA. An ancient land currently ruled by the Baath Party and its president, Bashar al-Assad and patronized by the former USSR it has supported terrorist groups like Hamas and Hezbollah, while assisting the U.S.-led fight against al Qaeda. An ally of Iraq, it considers Israel its mortal enemy as Israel captured its Golan Heights in the 1967 war and still occupies this strategic position. Having been accused of plotting the assassination of Lebanon's prime minister, UN and international pressure encourage Syria to remove its troops from that neighboring country.

UNITED ARAB EMIRATES (UAE). A federation of seven sheikdoms on the Persian Gulf, the UAE was under the protection of the British until 1971. Since then, it has skyrocketed from rural and poor to urban and oil-rich. Its most progressive and futuristic city is Dubai as described in Exhibit 11.5. With a total population of 3.5 million, the federation's per capita GDP is $21,100 and rising, while its crude oil reserves are estimated to be 97.8 billion. On the Arabian Peninsula, it's a favorite destination for tourists, businesspersons, and the military on leave. The UAE also has a large number of guest workers, mainly from India and Pakistan, as well as a more equal attitude toward women.

YEMEN. Located on the southern tip of the Arabian Penisula where the Red Sea and the Gulf of Aden join, Yemen has established its ancient capital as Sanaa. In 1990 the traditional north united with the Marxist south, and then plunged into civil war four years later until peace was restored. Its population of 18.6 million only has a per capita GDP of $820—the region's lowest. It is a poor, very traditional people, and its recent past has been marked by kidnappings, oil pipeline attacks, and the bombing of the U.S.S. *Cole* at Aden. There is popular sympathy in Yemen for the terrorist, Osama bin Laden, whose clan originated in southern Yemen.

MIDDLE EAST BUSINESS CUSTOMS AND PROTOCOL

Consider this case in point:

A midwestern banker is invited by an Arab sheik to meet him at the Dorchester Hotel in London. A friend of both arranges the get-together and facilitates the introduction. Dark sweet coffee is served. No business of consequence is discussed, but there is a sociable exchange. . . . Subsequently, the American is invited to a series of meetings in Riyadh. The Saudi greets the banker with "There is no god but Allah, and Muhammad is his messenger." More strong coffee is served and sometimes others are present in the meeting room. In time, a mutually beneficial business relationship is established.

EXHIBIT 11.5
DUBAI—A FUTURISTIC CITY

This is a zany, ambitious, and modernistic boomtown on the Persian Gulf. Salem Moosa is developing skyscrapers and other marvels built on man-made islands in the shape of palm trees. He is creating replicas of great monuments, such as the Eiffel Tower, the Pyramids, the Taj Mahal, and the Lost City of Atlantis. Dubai also boasts an indoor ski resort, an underwater hotel, the world's largest shopping mall, and largest skyscraper. Suffering from construction fever, it is afloat in fantasy, ambition, and rivers of cash. This city is at the forefront of the Emirates' push to the sky, as it reinvents a once sleepy port of pearl traders and pirates. Perched at the crossroads of Europe, Africa, and India, the sheikdom has relatively little oil while becoming a global trading hub and a center of Arab investment. Dubai is also a bewildering stew of nationalities, a place where natives are less than 20% of the 1 million population, politics are played down, and spending is played up. Among its many development projects are Internet City which five years ago was only sand; a tall encased ski run; the world's most treasured diving sites recreating the Maldives, the Barrier Reef, the Caymans, and the Red Sea. The man-made islands were the vision of Crown Prince Sheik Mohammed ibn Rashid al Maktum, who started the innovation process in Dubai.

Source: Adapted from Megan K. Stack's "In Dubai, the Sky's No Limit," *Los Angeles Times,* October 13, 2005, pp. A1 & 6.

This short episode encapsulates several important points for succeeding in Middle Eastern business ventures. First, nothing happens quickly and patience is a virtue. Second, trust is paramount, and it is cultivated over a period of time, often with the assistance of a third-party acquaintance. Although business customs will vary somewhat in the region, by trying to understand Islam and Arab culture, an individual is in a better position to be effective. In this section insights from Saudi Arabia may be adapted and selectively applied elsewhere in the Middle East but are subject to change.

Among the modern institutions of higher education recently established within Saudi Arabia, King Fahd University of Petroleum and Minerals is among the best. There Dr. Mohammad I. At-Twaijri has conducted and published studies comparing Saudi and American managers, purchasing agents, and negotiators. Some of his research findings and comments are offered for consideration here.[13]

- There is a trend toward Westernization of Middle East managers and Saudi managers are becoming less paternalistic.
- There are significant differences in the way Arab managers respond to questionnaire items in their native Arabic language as opposed to the English version of the same instrument.
- In negotiations, the Saudis have two dominant styles, competitive and collaborative, both of which are expressed within the Arab cultural context.
- For the hundreds of joint ventures under way between the United States and Saudi Arabia, foreigners are required to build extensive training programs for the locals into the project management which is increasingly the trend in most Middle Eastern countries.

Apart from what has already been described about Middle Easterners and the Arab culture, Arabs are a people of great emotion and sentimentality—and sometimes of excess and extremes. They hold in high regard friendship, loyalty, and justice, and, when events and behavior go against that sense of justice, they will likely be morally outraged and indignant. Arabs tend to be warm, hospitable, generous, and courteous. Like many Middle Eastern persons in commerce, the stereotype is that they are either very sincere and trustworthy, or, the opposite, insincere and sly. It is dangerous to make generalizations about any culture, so one is advised to deal with each Middle Easterner individually as a person and to treat him or her with respect and dignity. Semites, whether Arab, Christian, or Jew, also have reputations as effective traders and salespeople.

Arab society places great emphasis on honor.

Furthermore, Arab society places great emphasis on honor. Its concept of shame is somewhat alien to Western mind-sets. Shame must be feared, avoided, or hidden, so one prays to Allah for protection from others (public exposure). Thus, foreigners should avoid embarassing Arabs. Because of the society's powerful identification between the individual and the group, shame means a loss of power and influence, particularly for the family. In addition, the tribal heritage influences and values a high degree of deference and conformity, often expressed in a somewhat authoritarian tone. In return, the individual has a strong sense of place and shares in the group's social prestige. That is why Arabs typically worry about how their decisions, acts, and behavior reflect on their family, clan, tribe, and then country. In a traditional society, honor is important, and to admit "I don't know" may be shameful for some; constructive criticism can be taken for an insult.

For an Arab, the "self" is buried deep within the individual. This relates to the previously explained sense of distance because the "self" is personal and private in public touching, and jostling among males is quite evident.

Business Tips

Business and trade are highly respected.

To an Arab, commerce is a most blessed career—the prophet Muhammad, after all, was a man of commerce who also married a lady of commerce. Thus, business and trade are highly respected, so one is expected to be sound, shrewd, and knowledgeable. Some Middle Eastern business practices of note are as follows.

- *Business relationships* are facilitated by establishing personal rapport, mutual respect, and trust—business is conducted between people, not merely with a company or for a contract.
- *Connections* and *networking* are most important—vital to gaining access to both private and public decision makers—so it is important to maintain good relations with people of influence.
- *Negotiating* and *bargaining* are commonplace processes, and somewhat of an art in these ancient lands, so one can expect some old-fashioned haggling.[14]
- *Decision making* is traditionally done in person, thus requiring an organization's representative of suitable rank; decisions are usually made by the top person in the government agency or corporation and normally are not accomplished by correspondence, fax, or telephone.
- *Time is flexible*, according to the concept of *Bukra inshae Allah*, meaning "tomorrow if God wills"; it is an expression of the cultural pattern of fatalism. One should avoid imposing Western time frames and schedules, though as such modern business practices become customary, appointments may be set and kept. Arabs may be prompt, or not, and appointments will likely not be exact or may start late. Their day is divided into five prayer times, and meetings are scheduled accordingly.
- *Marketing* should be focused on specific customer–client segments. Because centralized governments in many Arab countries hold the economic power and are the principal buyers, one must learn the public sector development plans for obtaining goods and services and then develop contacts and relationships with senior officials in appropriate ministries.
- *Socialization* in business is traditional, and social gestures, courtesies, and invitations are commonplace, but deals are not usually concluded under such circumstances. Traditionally, Arab women are not part of this scene, but mixed social gatherings in private are becom-

ing more common. Foreign women in Saudi Arabia, as spouses or on business, will not only have to call upon inner resources, but also take advantage of local support networks and female clubs (particularly in the expatriate communities).

■ *Communication* is especially complex in the Middle East, and outsiders should show harmony and agreement, following the host's lead. Arabic as a language is high context, manifested with raised voices and much nonverbal body language (wide gestures, animated facial expressions, eyebrow raising, tongue clicking, standing close, eye contact, and, except with strangers on first meeting, a side nod of the head is often given as affirmation). Hyperbole is normal, and a *yes* may really mean *maybe* or even *probably not*.

■ *Taboos* are many, so caution is advised in unfamiliar circumstances. Exhibit 11.6 offers some further insights for appropriate business behavior in the region.

In light of the advice given here, it is interesting to note that among U.S. troops in Iraq, the Marine Corps Intelligence Activity issued *Iraq Culture Smart Cards* with cultural tips to help American military stay out of trouble in that Arab country. It contains pointers on gestures to use (right hand over the heart as a sign of respect; right hand palm up, fingers touching to mean slow down or be patient; quick upward head

---

EXHIBIT 11.6
IN THE MIDDLE EAST AVOID—

■ Bringing up business subjects until you get to know your host, or you will be considered rude.

■ Commenting on a man's wife or female children over 12 years of age.

■ Raising colloquial questions that may be common in your country but possibly misunderstood here as an invasion of privacy.

■ Using disparaging or swear words and off-color or obscene attempts at humor.

■ Engaging in conversations about religion, politics, or Israel.

■ Bringing gifts of alcohol or using alcohol, which is prohibited in some countries, such as Saudi Arabia.

■ Requesting favors from those in authority or esteem, for it is considered impolite for Arabs to say "no."

■ Shaking hands too firmly or pumping—gentle or limp handshakes are preferred.

■ Pointing your finger at someone or showing the soles of your feet when seated.

snap with tongue click to signify "no"). They are to avoid using the left hand in contacting others; showing women attention by touching or staring; or slouching as a sign of indifference.

Global Managers Alert

Nineteen states in the Middle East share the common Arab culture and practice of Islam.

Nineteen states in the Middle East share the common Arab culture and practice of Islam, but there are differences in interpretations and practices. Saudi Arabia is stricter in this regard as the Gulf's elder statesmen and protector of Muslim traditions, especially as perceived by the Wahhabi sect. Elsewhere social and business life may be more relaxed as in Bahrain or somewhere on the continuum between a country like Iran, now under a fundamentalist religious regime, and Jordan, which is under a progressive monarchy greatly influenced by the British presence and customs. Business ethos in one country may frown upon *baksheesh* or payments for favors received, whereas elsewhere it may be tolerated, even encouraged. In some Arab countries, a local sponsor or partner is essential for a successful joint venture, whereas in others it is not.

- ■ It is helpful to develop a small vocabulary of Arabic words or phrases to be used properly for greetings and introductions, as well as to observe the protocol of names (e.g., *ibn* meaning son of) and titles (e.g., Your Excellency).
- ■ Middle Eastern food, while tasty and carefully prepared, may affect Westerners not familiar with the diet. Be cautious to drink bottled water, not tap water, and if cooking with nonbottled water, one must purify it; peeling fruits and vegetables is advised.
- ■ The future of the region may be shaped by its oil-rich nations, and other Arab states without such wealth generally are more populous and economically dependent on the oil-rich states. At the moment, the Middle East is unstable and violent in places, so make security provisions and observe your government's travel advisories. In some locations, a bodyguard is advisable.
- ■ Think twice about renting and driving a car yourself in the Middle East, versus hiring a careful driver and vehicle. The region has a high automobile accident rate, with reckless drivers and speeders blamed for 3000 traffic deaths a month. This is a leading public health problem and the second highest cause of death in Arab nations.
- ■ Avoid misreading the holding of hands among Arab men. A recent photo showing the president of the United States and the King of Saudi Arabia holding hands surprised many. However, the holding of hands in the Arab world is considered an expression of warm affection between men, a sign of solidarity and kinship. It has no

sexual connotation, and not to touch is a sign of disdain. Kissing cheeks, long handshakes, and clutching hands are meant to reflect amity, devotion, and equality of status. Strangers, do not kiss or hold hands, and the strong do not kiss the weak. Because the sexes are separated, males rarely have a chance to touch or show affection toward women, especially in public. Men spend a lot of time together, and these customs grew out of that tradition.

Middle Eastern Reactions to Westerners

Peoples from ancient civilizations, like Egypt, Persia, Turkey, and Arabia, are proud of their past—their history, art, poetry, literature, and cultural accomplishments. Unfortunately, many Westerners and Asians carry distorted cultural images or stereotypes about Middle Easterners and their contributions to human development. North American and European media has been particularly inept, slanted, and at times false in their presentations about the Middle East and Arabs.

The Middle East has a deep underlying suspicion of former European colonial powers, especially the British and French who once ruled much of the area. But insensitive American behavior and racism toward Middle Eastern peoples and their religion explain, in part, reactive "anti-American" campaigns abroad that undermine both political and business relationships. That happened in Iran, a non-Arab country, in 1979 when American influence and actions threatened the Persian identity and culture to the point of a violent takeover of and hostage taking at the U.S. Embassy. Currently, resentment centers on America as the only superpower capable of military intervention in their region, especially the U.S. coalitions that went to war twice in Iraq and against the Taliban in Afghanistan. Arabs and Westerners are both given to distorting each other's actions, behavior and beliefs, thus promoting mutual xenophobia. Remember that the global terrorist movement among Islamic militants arose partially out of fear that Western culture and values would destroy or undermine traditional Arab culture.

The Middle East has a deep underlying suspicion of former European colonial powers.

The middle East has 70% of the world's oil reserves. This results in an influx of Europeans, Americans, and even Asians into the region, bringing repercussions from the indigenous peoples about these guests who come to engage in business and development. Here is a summary of the feedback about foreigners from the Arab perspective:

■ Many foreigners express superiority and arrogance; they know the answers to everything.
■ Many do not want to share the credit for what is accomplished by joint efforts.

- Many are frequently unable or unwilling to respect and adjust to local customs and culture.
- Some fail to innovate to meet the needs of local culture, preferring to seek easy solutions based on the situation in their homeland.
- Some individuals refuse to work through the normal administrative channels of the country and do not respect local legal and contractual procedures.
- Some tend to lose their democratic ways when on foreign assignments, becoming instead more autocratic and managing by instilling fear in subordinates.
- Westerners are often too imposing, aggressive, pushy, and rude.
- Americans and Europeans have provided much more support and aid for Israel than for the Palestinian cause and human rights.

So it is all a matter of perception that we have to endeavor to change. Beauty and ugliness is in the eye of the beholder.

SYNERGY: MIDDLE EAST HOPE

Slowly and painfully, a new cooperative relationship is emerging among the states and inhabitants of the Middle East. In addition to Arab unity efforts among themselves, peace accords have included neighbors in the area, such as between Egypt and Israel. Peaceful negotiations, mediation, and problem-solving skills are needed to resolve long-standing conflicts, instead of using weapons and violence. Gradually, this approach led to agreements between Israelis and Jordanians, while the search continues for comparable accords with the Palestinians, Syrians, and Lebanese.

Middle Easterners of all types are beginning to prefer collaboration with one another.

Middle Easterners of all types are beginning to prefer collaboration with one another, even former enemies, to realize the economic potential of the region. Since they are only a short jet hop away from Europe, the interchange with peoples on both continents has increased. Arabs fly regularly to EU countries for study, investment, commerce, medical assistance, vacations, or even to reside. Europeans in greater numbers go to the Middle East seeking new markets and as tourists. In place of former colonial dominance, the present and future offer opportunities for more synergistic relationships if Europeans, Americans, and Arabs learn to appreciate each other's cultural heritages and differences, while seeking mutual benefits from interchanges. Practicing synergy is the key to peace and prosperity in the twenty-first century both for that region and the world.

Efforts promoting cultural synergy need to be widely extended at all levels of education as well as through churches, mosques, synagogues, and community forums. Indeed, knowledge of foreign languages and culture are keys to successful interaction and security in today's globally interconnected world—cultural skills are necessary to help peoples comprehend what is actually meant when they communicate with or about one another. If bridges are to be built across cultural divides, all must reach out to learn about other religions and countries. Only in such peaceful cooperation can the world community, especially through the United Nations, contribute to solutions of current Middle Eastern challenges, such as these:

The reconstruction of Afghanistan and Iraq, so that their peoples may meet basic human needs in freedom and dignity.[15]

The resolution of conflict and violence between Israel and the Palestinian Authority and the internal dispute between Fatah and Hamas.[16]

The restoration of harmony in Iran's internal struggle between the elected representatives of the people and the elected representative of God.[17]

The modernization of socio-political-economic systems in the region.

Through the practice of cultural synergy, the Middle East has prospects for security, prosperity, and peace for its inhabitants.

CONCLUSIONS

Although the business boom is declining somewhat in the Middle East, global organizations will continue to seek commercial opportunities and relationships there. Thus, we have offered an introduction to the area in terms of its ancient glories, diversity, and current difficulties. Particular attention was devoted to increasing understanding of both Islam and Arab culture, the dominant factors in the vast majority of populace in the area. Because it was not feasible for us to cover all of the national conditions within the Middle East, we chose two target cultures that are more representative of the majority while acknowledging the presence of Jewish and Christian minorities in the area. Thus, in the context of doing business in Egypt and Saudi Arabia we reviewed the people and their homeland, the geographic features and cities, political and social conditions, and the economy and business.

Because each country in the Middle East is unique and different, we provided an overview of business customs and protocols. We concluded with a call for cultural synergy not only within the region, but also between the Middle East and Europe, Africa, America, and Asia, because so many of its former inhabitants now live and work in these other areas.

Each country in the Middle East is unique and different.

MIND STRETCHING

1. Have you ever read the Koran, eaten Middle Eastern foods, or made friends with an Arab whether Muslim or Christian?
2. What do you know about the Islamic contributions in the Middle Ages and thereafter to science and medicine, art and architecture, trade and travel?
3. How has traditional, nomadic Arab tribalism adapted to accelerating social and economic changes of the last century?
4. What major differences do you perceive between Egypt and Saudi Arabia?
5. How could the implementation of synergistic relationships benefit Iran, Iraq, Lebanon, Syria, Palestine, and Israel?
6. What are your reactions to this quote from Reza Aslan in his book, *No God but God: The Origins, Evolution and Future of Islam* (New York: Random House, 2005):

   "What is taking place now in the Muslim world is an internal conflict between Muslims, not an external battle between Islam and the West. . . . The centuries-old struggle is between the traditonalists and the rationalists over proper" interpretation of the Quran, and the outcome is in doubt. . . . The fact is that the vast majority of one billion Muslims in the world are committed to genuine Islamic values, like pluralism, freedom, justice, human rights, and above all, democracy.

REFERENCES

1. Fisk, R. *The Great War for Civilization—The Conquest of the Middle East.* New York: Knopf, 2005; Norwich, J. J. *Byzantium: Decline and Fall.* New York: Knopf, 1996; Roaf, M. *Cultural Atlas of Mesopotamia and the Ancient Near East.* New York: Facts on File, 1990; *Atlas of the Middle East.* Washington, DC: National Geographic, 2005; Nawwab, I. I., Speers, P. C., and Hoye, P. F. (eds.). *Aramco and Its World—Arabia and the Middle East.* Houston, TX: Aramco Services Company, 1981. (For information on Middle Eastern publications, visual aids, and exhibits, contact *Saudi Aramco World*, Box 2160, Houston, Texas 77252, USA. www.aramcoservices.com.)
2. Esposito, J. L. *The Oxford History of Islam.* Oxford: Oxford University Press, 2000; Armstrong, K. *Islam: A Short History.* New York: Modern Library, 2000; Lunde, P. *Islam: Faith, Culture, and History.* Fremont, CA: DK Publishing/Rumi Bookstore, 2002.
3. Roy, O. *Globalized Islam: The Search for a New Umah.* New York: Columbia University Press, 2005; Kepel, G. *The War for Muslim Minds: Islam and the West.* London: Belnap Press, 2005; Zaytuna Institute and

Al-Qalam Institute. *Islam in the Balance: Toward a Better Understanding of Islam and Its Followers.* Fremont, CA: Rumi Bookstore, 2001. (For further information, visit these Web sites: www.rumibookstore.com; www.islaminthebalance.org.)

4. Lewis, R. D. "Epilogue: After September 11," in *The Cultural Imperative—Global Trends of the 21st Century.* Boston: Nicholas Brealey/Intercultural Press, 2003.

5. Devji, F. *Landscapes of Jihad: Militancy, Morality, Modernity.* Ithaca, NY: Cornell University Press, 2005; Little, D. *American Orientalism: The United States and the Middle East Since 1945.* Chapel Hill: University of North Carolina Press, 2002; Reeves, M. *Muhammad in Europe: A Thousand Tears in Western Myth-Making.* New York: New York University Press, 2000; Lewis, B. *The Crisis of Islam: Holy War and Unholy Terror.* New York: Modern Library, 2003; Lewis, R. D. *When Cultures Collide: Managing Successfully Across Cultures.* Boston: Nicolas Brealey Publishing, 2000.

6. Kristof, N. D., "Looking for Delam's Luther," New York Times, October 15, 2006.

7. Aslan, R. *No God But God: The Origins, Evolution, and Future of Islam.* New York: Random House, 2005.

8. Mernissi, F. *Los Angeles Times*, June 8, 1990, p. VII/25.

9. *San Diego Union Tribune*, February 3, 1995, pp. A1 & 12.

10. Pampanini, A. H. *Cities from the Arabian Desert: The Building of Jubail and Yanbu.* New York: Praeger, 1997.

11. *The Economist,* November 19, 2005, p. 88.

12. www.ngm.com/0601

13. At-Twaijri, M. I. "The Negotiating Style of Saudi Industrial Buyers," *International Journal of Value-Based Management*, 5, No. 1 (1992); "Language Effects in Cross-cultural Management Research," *International Journal of Value-Based Management*, 3, No. 1 (1990); "A Cross-cultural Comparison of American-Saudi Managerial Values," *International Studies of Management & Organization*, 19, No. 2 (1989); "Empirical Analysis of the Effects of Environmental Interdependence and Uncertainty on Purchasing: A Cross-Cultural Study," *Industrial Marketing Purchasing*, 3, No. 1 (1988); "The Impact of Context and Choice on Boundary-Spanning Process," *Human Relations*, 40, No. 12 (1987). (For reprints, write to Dr. Mohammad I. At-Twaijri, Dean, College of Industrial Management, King Fahd University of Petroleum & Minerals, Dhahran 31261, Saudi Arabia.)

14. Moran, R. T. and Stripp, W. G. *Dynamics of Successful International Business Negotiations*, 1991; Elashmawi, F. and Harris, P. R. "Managing Intercultural Business Negotiations," in *Multicultural Management*, 1993; Elashmawi, F. *Competing Globally-Mastering Multicultural Management and Negotiations*, 2. Burlington, MA: Elsevier/Butterworth-Heinemann, 2001.

15. Braude, J. *The New Iraq: Rebuilding the Country for Its People, the Middle East, and the World.* New York: Basic Books/Perseus Group, 2003 (www.newiraq.com).

16. Cockburn, A. "Lines in the Sand—Deadly Times in the West Bank and Gaza," *National Geographic—In Focus*, October 2002, pp. 102–111 (www.nationalgeographic.com/0210).

17. Grimond, J. "God's Rule or Man?—A Survey of Iran," *The Economist*, January 18, 2003, p. 16. Among other periodic surveys from *The Economist* on vital topics or regions of the world, note Rodenbeck, M. "A Long Walk—A Survey of Saudi Arabia," January 7, 2006, 12 pp. (www.economist.com/surveys).

DOING BUSINESS WITH LATIN AMERICANS

Mexico and Brazil

The debate over the causes of Latin America's failures relative to the success of Canada and the United States has been a recurrent focus of Latin American intellectuals, and there are enough explanations to suit anyone. At the beginning of the nineteenth century, they put the blame on the Iberian inheritance with its intolerant Catholicism. Around the middle of that century, the shortcomings were attributed to the demographic weight of an apparently indolent native population opposed to progress. At the beginning of the twentieth century, and particularly with the Mexican Revolution in 1910, it was said that poverty and underdevelopment were caused by an unfair distribution of wealth, above all by the peasants' lack of access to land. Starting in the twenties and accelerating thereafter, "exploitative imperialism," mainly "Yankee imperialism," was blamed. During the thirties and forties, the view was espoused that Latin America's weakness was a consequence of the weakness of its governments. . . . All these diagnoses and proposals reached the crisis point in the eighties—"the lost decade"—when experience demonstrated that all of the arguments were false, although each may have contained a grain of truth. . . . Who is responsible? One possible, although partial, answer is "the elites": the groups that lead and manage the principal sectors of a society; those who act in the name of certain values, attitudes, and ideologies which, in the Latin American case, do not favor collective progress.[1]

Latin America

MEXICO

BELIZE

HONDURAS

NICARAGUA

GUATEMALA

EL SALVADOR

PANAMA

CENTRAL
AMERICA

COSTA RICA

VENEZUELA

COLOMBIA

ECUADOR

GUYANA

SURINAME

FR. GUIANA

ATLANTIC
OCEAN

BRAZIL

PERU

BOLIVIA

PARAGUAY

CHILE

SOUTH AMERICA

ARGENTINA

URUGUAY

PACIFIC
OCEAN

ATLANTIC
OCEAN

LEARNING OBJECTIVES

This chapter provides an overview of Latin America, along with specifics on Mexico in North America and Brazil in South America to foster an appreciation of the unique, complex, and diverse Latin American peoples and their cultures. Coverage will also include some of the other countries in both Central and South America. In addition, information will be presented on the principal themes of Latin American cultures to facilitate doing business in or visiting this region. Finally, we examine some of the challenges for Pan American cooperation in the decades ahead.

LATIN AMERICAN OVERVIEW

The map will help you visualize the geographic area of those people designated as Latin Americans. The term refers to those countries from Mexico to Puerto Rico, Cuba, and the Dominican Republic which are within North America, through Central America, and on to that huge continent called South America.

Many countries in Latin America differ widely in history, socioeconomic status, education, governance, society, and the behavior and values of the people. Nevertheless, there are commonalities and overlapping cultural themes in Latin American countries such as the influence of the Catholic Church, the value of the family, the separate but distinct male and female roles, and, for many inhabitants, the Spanish language.

Countries in Latin America differ widely in history.

The Latin American region has been inhabited for thousands of years. Archaeologists are unsure of the origin of the early inhabitants. However, we will begin our examination of the diverse cultures in the southern parts of Pan America with their aboriginal descendants, the so-called Indians. Many are descendants of ancient, highly developed peoples and civilizations, such as Aztec, Inca, and Maya. Native peoples, commonly called Amerindians today, make up a high proportion of the populations of many Latin countries, including Mexico and Bolivia. In some parts of the Southern Hemisphere Indians have integrated into modern civilization. In other localities they have chosen to remain more traditional.

Global and local developers frequently impinge on the rights and lands of such peoples in the name of economic development, often with destructive results. Agencies like the World Bank are now demanding inclusion of programs that protect the rights of 200,000 aborigines before they will fund economic development projects in the Amazon region. In Central America, Indians try to survive the ravages and clutches of civil and guerrilla warfare. The Hispano-Indians are caught in conflicts between the forces of both left and right. Sometimes the rebels seek haven or recruits among the Indians, while the government troops destroy the Indian villages. The "Amerindians" are often caught in the middle of various sociopolitical revolutionary struggles currently taking place throughout Latin America.

As the original European colonies of the last five centuries were gradually replaced by the contemporary nation-states, these southern countries of the Americas failed to keep up with their rich neighbors to the north, the United States and Canada. Despite their natural beauty and resources, the Latin countries have been plagued by poverty, despotic governments, bloody revolutions, and profound social unrest. Part of this has been caused by financial mismanagement of enormous natural and human resources, and part by the unequal distribution of wealth and power that is concentrated among less than 5% of the total population—the upper class educated "elites." In the last century, some progress was made in the growth of a middle class, the adoption of democracy and free enterprise—especially because of NAFTA, the Andean Group, and all regional trade and border agreements among neighboring countries seeking to promote free enterprise markets and greater prosperity.

We begin this section with a profile (Exhibit 12.1) of Latin America with its diverse people and culture. Then our in-depth coverage of

EXHIBIT 12.1
LATIN AMERICA—PROFILE

Population	Land Mass
393,300,021 people	8 million square miles

National Cultures

- Twenty countries
- One commonwealth (PR)
- Twelve island countries of West Indies
- Many Indian cultures

Major Cultural Inputs

- Native Indians—descended from ancient, highly developed civilization that flourished prior to European arrival (Mayan, Incas, Aztecs)
- European—in most countries largely Spanish with lesser influences of Germans and Italians, except in Brazil where dominant influence was Portuguese
- African

EXHIBIT 12.1

LATIN AMERICA—PROFILE (CONTINUED)

Sociopolitical Developments

- Asian—ancient Polynesian influence and some Japanese influence, particularly in Brazil
- Napoleonic Code of Laws
- Feudalistic societies of Spain/Portugal imposed by conquerors on developed Indian civilizations
- French/Austrian royalty/empire imposed on Mexico, the latter being the center of revolutions in 1821, 1824, and 1838 that impacted South America
- Family oriented with authority centered in the father and often extended to the "father of the nation"
- Universities and republics from the nineteenth century with great dependence on military institutions controls
- Problems of social class integration—although there was much intermarriage of the races, the powerful elites from an economical/social/political standpoint control and dominate the poor, often peasants of Indian heritage. The disenfranchised have moved beyond political/military protest for social justice to terrorism as a means of changing the status quo.
- Economically and technically developing, and in the process of moving from the agricultural through the industrial stage of development; energy discoveries and development in Mexico can dramatically forge a new relationship with its neighbors.
- Despite significant growth in spiritualism and Protestantism, the Roman Catholic tradition is still dominant, but undergoing a profound role change—instead of traditional support for the oligarchy many clergy provide some leadership in a revolution for social justice.

Roman Catholic tradition is still dominant.

Education

In the European tradition, especially Spain/Portugal/France, ancient and traditional university education with emphasizes the humanities, especially studies in law, medicine, and engineering. *Colegios* are more numerous than American secondary schools and offer the equivalent of junior college. Upper classes tend to send their off spring to private schools and universities, often conducted by the orders of the Catholic Church. Although literacy is increasing, many in the population overall do not receive more than a very few years of primary education; notable exceptions are found in the larger countries that provide more education. There is rigorous examination competition for university entrance. Technical education also is on the increase as well as use of mass media.

Hispanic cultural specifics will feature Mexico, part of the big three nations of North America.

In summary, the Latin American peoples are transitioning in this twentieth-first century, caught between their pasts and possible futures. They are in the process of modernizing their economies, social institutions, and infrastructures. Because of their cultural heritage and architecture, many of these countries are popular as tourist destinations where visitors may view a wide spectrum of human development—from ancient cities like Machu Picchu in the Peruvian Andes to Galapagos Islands off the coast of Ecuador to space programs in Mexico and Brazil.

MEXICO

Mexico is a land of contrast and promise. The vagaries of politicians and economics in the last century brought the country from relative prosperity to economic collapse in 1994 caused by a botched devaluation and the global investment market. This also contributed to a change in government, as well as a slow revival in the twentieth-first century, partially fueled by the North American Free Trade Agreement.[2]

Over 761,000 square miles in landmass, this country has an expanding population of more than 100 million. The burgeoning population lives in the central highlands, which constitutes half of the country's total farmland. Within the nation's 31 states, 20 million people are concentrated in the Federal District capital of Mexico City. Like many developing countries, the young greatly outnumber the old. Other interesting population trends are as follows:

- 13% of Indian pure-blood ancestry, 10% of European heritage, 75% mixed
- Increasing urbanization and immigration north to the United States
- Decreasing infant mortality, but still a death rate of 21 per 1000
- Rising literacy rate—now 92% of the population—plus a rising educational level
- Rising income per capita, but 18 million underprivileged people, largely in rural areas
- Inadequate diet, medical care, housing, and social security
- Increased social unrest due to increased drug trafficking, some of which is caused by neighboring countries to the south; kidnappings for ransom around Mexico City
- Increased tourism and high-tech industries, plus oil exports, contributing to an improving economy

Further insights on this fascinating and developing nation can be viewed in Exhibit 12.2.

EXHIBIT 12.2

MEXICO—PROFILE

Population	106,202,903 (July 2005 est.)
Land	1,923,040 sq. km
Education	92.2% literacy rate
Ethnic Groups	Mesitzo (Amerindian-Spanish), 60%; Amerindian or predominantly Amerindian, 30%; White, 9%; Other, 1
Religions	Roman Catholic, 89%; Protestant, 6%; Other, 5%
Government	Federal republic
Political Parties	CD, Convergence for Democracy; PRIT, Institutional Revolutionary Party; PAN, National Action Party; PVEM, Mexican Green Ecological Party; PRD, Party of the Democratic Revolution; PT, Workers Party
Per capita income	$10,000 (2005 est.)
Exports to U.S.	Total exports = $213.7 billion U.S. accounts for 87.6% Total exports to U.S. = $187.2 billion (2005 est.)
Imports from U.S.	Total imports = $223.7 billion U.S. accounts for 55.1% Total imports from U.S. = $123.3 billion (2005 est.)

One-fourth the size of the United States, Mexico has a topography that features desert, tropical, mountainous, and temperate regions with equal parts divided by the Tropic of Cancer. The lofty central plains are the main agricultural region, but only 24 million hectares of the agricultural land are cultivated. Although predominantly an agricultural nation, Mexico is rapidly industrializing and is a leading exporter of metals, especially silver. In addition to growth in manufacturing and tourism, Mexico's hope for a better economic future lies in its recent discoveries and developments in oil and gas. Its energy supplies may rival those of Saudi Arabia. Mexico has a proven oil reserve of 40 billion barrels and a potential of 220 billion barrels.

With the implementation of NAFTA, Mexico's relationship with the United States is changing, although it has been stormy since the Americans invaded the country in 1846. After the war, Mexico ceded almost half of its original territory to the United States by the Treaty of Guadeloupe (this included Texas, California, Arizona, New Mexico, and parts of Utah and Colorado). No national border on earth separates two more widely divergent standards of living. Despite conflicts over illegal immigration, trade, and drug smuggling, the American and Mexican peoples are generally friendly, and the prospects for Mexican and American synergy are promising.

Doing Business in Mexico

From a business perspective, global managers should understand the following facts.

■ The nineteenth century in Mexico was marked by political unrest, the twentieth century by economic progress, and in the twenty-first century, this nation may come into its promise and potential. Discovered by European Hernán Cortéz in 1519, Mexico subsequently revolted against Spanish rule and achieved independence in 1821. It defeated French influence and interference by 1876 and survived a series of revolutions, achieving political and economic stability by 1940. One political party has been dominant since 1930. The federal government consists of an executive, legislative, and judicial branch, and the military does not play a significant role in governance. Government seized and nationalized all Roman Catholic Church properties and reduced the power of that religious institution by anticlerical laws, but culturally, the people are still influenced by Roman Catholic morality and spirituality, despite the inroads of Evangelical Protestant Christianity in this country.

■ The structure of capital and labor is somewhat different here from that of other countries in Latin America. The old, landed oligarchy has lost a major share of its property and power. A large rural bourgeoisie has grown among a large group of small landowners, who today provide the capital for industrial and financial development. There is a growing salaried middle class, some of whom also cultivate their own land. An agrarian revolution has created a new type of peasant class, one benefiting from government land distribution policies or becoming a major source of U.S. agricultural manpower, as well as the Mexican industrialized workforce. Relative to returns for capital and labor, two-thirds go to the corporation and only one-third to the employees.

■ In the 1970s, multinational corporations in Mexico (95% American controlled) provided 93% of the payments for imports of technology, and in the 1980s, 80% of the technology employed was still foreign. Multinational corporations occasionally obtain slightly lower, but safer, profits on their investments in Mexico than they do in other Latin American countries. Trade balances, employment, family planning, consumer price index, worker wages, and other indicators of economic well-being all continue to be troubling issues for Mexico. Frequent devaluation of the peso, problems with inflation, and declining oil prices cause much hardship there. However, NAFTA is the first trade agreement entered into by two industrial-

Mexico subsequently revolted against Spanish rule and achieved independence in 1821.

ized nations and a developing one. The trade agreement is also the first to cover intellectual property, labor rights, and the environment.

■ In the 1990s, corruption among politicians, drug trafficking and questionable elections, and a fiscal crisis of major proportions affected all Mexicans negatively. Yet, in the early twenty-first century, many Mexicans are experiencing a better quality of life. Perhaps Earl Shorts best summed up the challenges in his recent book, *The Life and Times of Mexico* (New York: Norton, 2004):

> "Why has a nation with such a wealth of history and culture, a country with the world's ninth largest economy, failed to confer greater opportunities on its 100 million citizens?" Seemingly for this author, this is a country at odds with itself, fighting the powerful domination of its northern neighbor founded much later than Mexico, a country held hostage by its past.

Noble Nation in Transition

Mexico, too, is a country in major transition, seeking to broaden its social and democratic basis, to control tensions between the evolving middle class and the disadvantaged masses, and to contain radical and revolutionary forces within the society.

Mexicans are a relaxed, hospitable, and warm people who may relate more to their Indian than Spanish heritage. They are proud, patriotic, family oriented, and hard working. Emotional, with a leisurely sense of time, they are generally comfortable with themselves and others, and are very person oriented. It is wise for visitors to take time for conversation and socializing. Subsequent sections in this chapter will deal with the cultural dimensions and challenges of doing business in Latin America that generally are applicable to Mexico.

Relative to communications, specifically, between Mexicans and their immediate northern neighbors, their former president, Porfirio Diaz, made this classic observation: "Poor Mexico, so far from God and so near the United States."

Condon has provided these insights to avoid culture-based misunderstandings:[3]

■ Mexican images and ideals are not only drawn from their Indian heritage, but from Europe (e.g., concepts of freedom and democracy come from France); their views and approach to their Latin neighbors are quite different from those of North Americans.

■ Although the uniqueness of the individual is valued and provides inner dignity, it is not necessarily evident through actions or achievements; slights against personal dignity are regarded as a grave provocation (e.g., Mexicans are comfortable talking about inner qualities like soul or spirit and may look at North Americans as insensitive because they avoid such subjects).

Mexicans are a relaxed, hospitable, and warm people.

- Respect (*respeto*) in Mexico is an emotionally charged word bound up with values of equality, fair play, and democratic spirit.
- In conversations, Mexicans tend to maximize differences between persons due to gender, status, or age in contrast to North Americans who often minimize them. Mexicans generally defer to one of higher authority by using such titles as "señor" or "don" to note social standing. Indigenous people will address whites as "señor" as a sign of respect due them for their race.
- Mexicans live with a sense of death, and celebrate it in their holidays or feast days, even with disguises, toys, confections, song and dance.

Exhibit 12.3 may be helpful in contrasting perceptions between Americans and their neighbors to the south.[4]

EXHIBIT 12.3
HISTORICAL STEREOTYPES[4]

Value Affected	Mexican View of N. American	Mexican View of Self	N. American View of Mexican	N. American View of Self
Self-Control	Cold, insensitive, emotionless	Deal passively with stress, saying "*ni modo*" when something doesn't go to plan	Emotional, volatile, feminine, undisciplined	Rational, calm, masculine, deals actively with stress through discipline in life
Type of Civilization	Condescending, contradictory, not credible	Traditional, technically inferior, morally superior	Primitive, in need of instruction on "how to do things"	Advanced, responsible for showing others how to have democracy and free trade
Racial Attitude	Indiscriminate racism. Can't distinguish high-class Mexican from Indian	Social classes have subtle shades; whiter is better; the masses cannot be elevated anyway. North Americans should be able to distinguish between high and low classes and accept high-class individuals as equals	Indigenous people are inferior, and mestizos combine the worst features of both races. The treatment of the lower classes is unjust, and therefore higher classes deserve no respect	Racially superior. Culturally heterogeneous, but racially homogeneous; racial intermixing not acceptable

Exhibit 12.3

Historical Stereotypes (continued)

Value Affected	Mexican View of N. American	Mexican View of Self	N. American View of Mexican	N. American View of Self
Honesty and Trustworthiness (High- and Low-Context)	Manipulative, tactless, have ulterior motives against Mexico; can't be trusted	More important to be nice than objective; OK to bend truth or retain information if people's feelings are preserved (high context)	Dishonest, indirect, sneaky, not trustworthy	Honest, direct, principled, literal (low context)
Character	Aggressive, at times brutal and abusive	Brave, but overpowered like "niños heroes"	Submissive, weak	Dominant, strong
Time Orientation	Obsessively future oriented. Doesn't know how to relax. Unrealistically believes time can be mastered	Lives in and enjoys present, respects past, awaits a future to be determined by god's will: "si Dios quiere"	Lives too much in present, while dwelling on past; surrenders own will and ambition to chance. Procrastinating	The present is the birthplace of the future; planning, action oriented. "All the flowers of all the tomorrows are in the seeds we plant today."
Social Classes	Although morally corrupted, economically and perhaps racially superior	Exclusive, but more cultured and civilized at top levels; money not only determinant of status for "gente decente" (decent people)	Chaotic, inefficient, unjust; high classes lack character and low classes lack potential	Orderly, efficient, fair; upward mobility is possible to anyone who has money to enter
Religion	Profess a false religion	Repository of higher moral values	Passive Christianity (Catholicism) God's faithful servant	Active Christianity (Protestantism) God's appointed steward
Orientation to Nature	Destructive, futilely trying to control what only God can master	Nature merely "is," a creation of God that man can ultimately neither influence nor control	Man cannot control nature; fatalism seen in failing to try. Evidence is economic underdevelopment	Man can and should manage perfect nature; optimistic due to results of economic progress

EXHIBIT 12.3

HISTORICAL STEREOTYPES (CONTINUED)

Value Affected	Mexican View of N. American	Mexican View of Self	N. American View of Mexican	N. American View of Self
National Intent	Intervention, imperialism, subversion	Sovereignty, respect, recognition	Lacking vision, discipline; needs help to reform flawed political and economic systems	Good natured, missionary, helpful, showing others "the way"
Work Ethic	Obsessive materialism, don't know how or when to relax	Work not inherently redeeming; something that must be done	Lazy, work is bad. As seen in Mexican sayings: "Do not do today what you can do tomorrow" and "work is sacred; don't touch it."	Work is the measure of a man. As seen in sayings "never put off until tomorrow what can be done today" and "an idle mind is the devil's workshop."

Tips for Doing Business and Negotiating with Mexicans

Mexican culture is high context.

Mexican culture is high context, valuing beliefs in the divine, the family, personal relations, and individual respect for dignity. In Spanish, Mexicans customize the language by speaking metaphorically through anecdotes, sayings, and jokes. Among Latin Americans, Mexicans are the most status conscious—status is related to family, school, wealth, position, and authority. Mexican managers are very individualistic; delegation and teamwork do not come naturally but must be learned.[5]

The following from Abbott and Moran offers a profile of Mexican negotiators.[6]

Negotiating Guidelines in Mexico

Negotiating in Mexico is a complex and long procedure, covering several stages. First, the parties involved must determine if they, as individuals or organizations, can do business together. Establishing a warm working relationship with one's counterparts is essential to the process and facilitates the negotiation. The stage of getting to know one another is crucial as a foundation for business; Mexicans will do business with people for who they are, not who they represent. Talking business in the initial stages of a relationship should be avoided.

Many Mexicans resent what they see as a long history of unfair treatment by North Americans, and personal honor or dignity may be a factor within the Mexican negotiating team.

In Mexico, connections are very important, and the government has significant influence in private business matters. Permits are required for just about every business transaction. As a result, a government official might elicit a bit of *mordida* (the bite) to complete the transaction.

Selection of Negotiators

Negotiators are selected primarily on the basis of status. Family connections, personal or political influence, and education are critical. Hence, the importance of *ubicación* (where one is plugged into the system) becomes evident. Mexican negotiators tend to be high level, male, and well connected. They expect their counterparts to recognize that and send only corresponding levels of negotiators.

Role of Individual Aspirations

Whether Mexicans are individualists or collectivists seems to depend on the social arena. In business, and with other men, Mexicans tend to be competitive, set on pursuing individual goals and needs for their personal recognition. Often they feel they owe loyalty to their *patron*, but they seek to project a public image of significance and power.

Concern for Protocol

Mexican culture is dominated by courtesy, dignity, tact, and diplomacy. Protocol is important and social competence is as critical as technical competence. Vigorous handshakes, even pats on the back, are important signs of respect.

Significance of Type of Issue

For Mexicans, relationship-based and personal/internal issues tend to predominate and affect the negotiations. Mexicans emphasize the social and personal aspects of their relationships with the people they encounter, including business people.

Complexity of the Language and Space

Communicative context is formed by body language and emotional cues, not just the words spoken. Mexicans communicate with hand movements, physical contact, and emotional expressions, making them high-context communicators.

All Latin American cultures embrace closeness. People stand close to each other, sit close to each other, and often touch each other.

Nature of Persuasive Argument

Emotional arguments that are overly dramatic and patriotic are considered persuasive. Along these lines, there is the concept of *proyectismo* (constructing plans without critical analysis and assuming in time all will be accomplished). Perhaps much of this stems from the twin origins of Mexican culture: the Indian, based on magic and superstition, and the Spanish, based on imposition, dogma, and faith.

Mexican culture is dominated by courtesy, dignity, tact, and diplomacy.

Value of Time

There is a relaxed polychronic attitude toward time. Although time is a concern, Mexicans do not allow schedules to interfere with experiences involving their family or friends. The culture is more people oriented than task oriented. It is important to be on time for appointments, but one should always expect to wait, as a meeting may not end because the next scheduled appointment has arrived.

Bases of Trust

Evaluations of trustworthiness are based initially on intuition and then later on one's past record. Negotiations should take place within a generally trusting atmosphere. Trust must develop through a series of frequent and warm interpersonal transactions, either social or business oriented. It is not uncommon to invite business partners to family events as part of developing a more intimate relationship.

Risk Taking Propensity

Mexicans tend to be risk-avoidant. They will work to avoid risk as much as possible. Mexicans tend to be very pessimistic in any situation where there is some amount of risk.

Internal Decision-Making System

Decision making is highly centralized.

Decision making is highly centralized in government, companies, and within negotiating teams. Mexican leaders tend to make decisions without concern for consensus. Individuals with *palanca* (leverage) tend to be well positioned, expressive, and forceful with their opinions and decisions.

Form of Satisfactory Agreement

The only way to be certain that a business agreement has been reached in Mexico is with a written document. Agreements in Mexico fall under the Civil Code, the Commercial Code, or the Law of Commercial Companies. Many of the above negotiating tips are applicable with other Latin American Peoples.

Other Mexican Business Insights

Kras covers many important and specific management issues faced by U.S. and Mexican managers as they work together.[7] For example, the popular Latin perception of Americans is as Yankees or "gringos." Most Latins seems to be neutral about Canadians because they are so far north. Many Latin Americans have a love-hate relationship with the United States. They admire its sense of equality and economic progress, and at the personal level may like many Americans. Many seek to live in the United States because of its opportunities. But many Latins also distrust, envy, and fear Americans. Too many North

Americans ignore the needs and possibilities in Latin America, and do not pursue collaboration with these neighboring states and peoples. Europe and Asia are more common partners in economic exchanges.

Finally, foreigners engaged in commerce in Mexico should be aware that the family business model survives and prospers there. "You trust your blood" is their motto, which promotes family-owned business. Exhibit 12.4 examines this Latin country tendency within Mexico.

EXHIBIT 12.4

MEXICAN FAMILY BUSINESS

It is estimated that up to 95% of Mexian businesses are still family owned and run. Indeed, 43% of the Mexican stock market is in firms controlled by just one family, that of Carlos Slim. Though typical of Latin America, only 80% of firms in Europe are family owned. Despite the popularity of the family-owned model in Mexico, they have been greatly outperformed by other forms of business organizations there. Research by McKinsey indicates that in terms of revenues, there was a drop in Mexican family-owned firms from 71 to 57%. Compared to modern, professional, publicly traded companies, family businesses are often overcautious and prone to destabilizing family quarrels. As the old adage puts it: the first generation builds the company, the second lets it stagnate, and the third squanders it.

Yet Antonio Grhèdraui, family owner of Groupo Tony in Veracruz, asserts, "We are Latins, we don't trust anyone." He argues that they have to work in an environment in which every institution proves to be corrupt. By these standards, the family remains a relatively safe place in which to work and invest. Besides giving a sense of stability amidst crisis, the family businesses have long-term vision; do not have to deliver improving quarterly reports to public shareholders; grow slowly but more solidly; close to local markets, they have innate knowledge of local tastes and customs; and as many become more professional and successful, they are expanding into overseas markets. Today Mexican business schools are offering courses focusing on problems and challenges of family-owned business, and the younger generation of the family are enrolling in such.

Source: Adapted from "Business in Mexico—Still Keeping It in the Family," *The Economist*, March 20, 2005, pp. 63–64.

Mahoney makes the following comment on U.S., Canadian, and Mexican relations:[8]

The New World came about from the fracture of three empires. The North American Free Trade Agreement now anticipates a new trade and capital communion between Mexico, Canada, and the United States—one that hopes to transcend two centuries of division and, in the Mexican-American case, deep suspicion. . . . America and Mexico lived within a labyrinth of solitude, lost not only to each other, but to the chance of casting off their traditional roles of the dominant and the dependent. The reawakening at hand is not just with Canada and Mexico, it is with ourselves.[8]

CENTRAL AMERICAN STATES

On the western side of the Caribbean Sea is a land bridge between the northern and southern continents of the Americas that also fronts on the Pacific Ocean. The seven nations located between Mexico and Colombia are usually referred to as Central America—all but Belize are primarily Latin in culture.

If ever there was a need and case for synergy, it is in these Central American states. The nineteenth-century federation called the United Provinces of Central America may have been premature, but it provided a cooperative model for the future—if not politically, at least economically. Only by collaboration can this block of countries overcome their chronic poverty, illiteracy, and violence. Perhaps where political and military power types have failed, local business leaders and global managers may succeed in raising the standards and quality of living for the populace. According to Paige, the only way to understand Central American politics is by focusing on the coffee-growing elites that have long dominated the region.[9] Sandwiched between North and South America, this area cries out for new solutions and contributions from both the Anglo and Latin cultures.

Central America is an area where turmoil imperils hopes for reform. Unfortunately, too often in the past these "banana republics" became comic-opera fiefdoms of U.S. commerce. Despite bustling capitals, millions of people in this strife-torn and suffering region are, for the most part, gentle peasants who have been exploited too long. This strategic landmass is a glaring challenge to the affluent in the Americas. The challenge for Pan-American countries includes educational technology used to provide mass education and literacy; cooperatives on a massive scale to improve the peasants' way of life; scientific and technological know-how shared to improve the economies, the health services, and the development of the region; and social justice brought to all levels of society.

Panama, which has never considered itself part of Central America, has been spared the regional strife and might become a laboratory, along with Costa Rica, for the creation of models that would influence

Central America is an area where turmoil imperils hopes for reform.

the other states to join in a regional entity for self-improvement. Application of new techniques to promote social peace and reduce internal political violence, as in El Salvador and Guatemala, should become the concern of Pan American social scientists. Simplistic, anticommunist, and military approaches will not solve the region's problems or tap its vast undeveloped human and natural resources. Exhibit 12.5 is an overview of six countries in Central America.

In analyzing the above data, look first at the per capita income, then compare that figure with figures for population, literacy, and life expectancy. Obviously, Costa Rica and Panama come out on top. Also note that the six nations all call themselves "republics" but in terms of a functioning democracy Costa Rica is the most viable and progressive government, while Guatemala has been the most oppressive, especially toward its Amerindians. Many of the others have been ruined by right-wing elites/military and civil strife; Panama had to have a recent U.S. invasion to topple its military dictator. Obviously, these poor small states have yet to share the vision of Simon Bolívar for united governance and synergy.

Apart from Puerto Rico, which is a U.S. Commonwealth, there are two other Latin American states in the Greater Antilles. Both are island nations in the Caribbean seas that share the Spanish language and culture. Cuba is 110,861 square kilometers with a population of

EXHIBIT 12.5
PROFILES OF COSTA RICA, EL SALVADOR, GUTEMALA, HONDURAS, NICARAGUA, PANAMA

NATION	Costa Rica	El Salvador	Guatemala	Honduras	Nicaragua	Panama
AREA (sq km)	51,000	21,041	108,889	112,088	129,999	72,082
POPULATION	4,016,173	6,704,932	14,655,189	6,975,204	5,465,100	3,039,150
CAPITAL	San José	San Salvador	Guatemala City	Tegucigalpa	Managua	Panama City
RELIGION	RC, EP	RC, EP	RC, P, Indigenous Mayan	RC, P	RC, P	RC, P
LANGUAGE	Spanish, English	Spanish, Nahua	Spanish, Amerindian	Spanish, Amerindian	Spanish, English, Indigenous	Spanish, English
LITERACY	96%	80.2%	70.6%	76.2%	67.5%	92.6%
LIFE EXPECTANCY	76.84 years	71.22 years	69.06 years	69.3 years	70.33 years	75.25 years
GDP PER CAPITA	$10,000	$5,100	$4,300	$2,900	$2,800	$7,300
GOVERNMENT	Republic	Republic	Republic	Republic	Republic	Republic

11,347,000, but is a communist dictatorship. It has a literacy rate of 97%, a life expectancy of 77 years, and a GDP per capita of $3300.

The Dominican Republic shares with strife-torn Haiti, the island of Hispaniola, which consists of 48,734 square kilometers. This relatively peaceful country, largely Roman Catholic has a literacy rate of 85%, a 71-year life expectancy, and $6500 annual per capita income. Though Latin in culture, its neighbor Haiti is influenced by the French culture and language, as well as African.

Two other recent developments in Central America should be mentioned. One is rapid growth of Latin music throughout the Americas. For example, Colombia's pop star, Shakira, through her record company, Sony BMG, has topped the global charts with her album, *Laundry Service*. All her previous albums were in Spanish, but this one entered the lucrative market when Shakira composed and sang it in English. But her Spanish music reaches beyond Latin America to the United States where Hispanics are 14% of the population and to Spain itself. She reminds us that "globalization made the frontiers between cultures very blurry, I wanted to integrate two audiences." To prove her point, her Spanish album, *Fijacion Oral*, is selling well in nontraditional Latin markets, such as in Germany, Finland, and France.[10]

The other Central American trend is toward greater integration of the nation-states there. The region is finally moving toward some form of federal get-together, à la the dream of Simon Bolivar. The isthmus five current free market governments are planning a Central American Free Trade Agreement. CAFTA would include Costa Rica, Nicaragua, Honduras, El Salvador, and possibly Panama with the United States and perhaps Canada as participants. Since 1821, the isthmus seven small countries with a total population now of 36 million have been trying to become more unified. What is different at this time is the unstoppable trend toward economic integration from the bottom up, along with regional business consolidation. The area's growth in financial services and tourism is stimulating modernization of infrastructure, such as joint national projects like the new container port of La Unión in El Salvador. Regional law enforcement is improving in its battle against the *maras*, dangerous, well-organized regional gangs.[11]

SOUTH AMERICAN CULTURAL DEVELOPMENT

As the global manager flies over the 12 countries that compose the southern continent of the Americas, he or she is struck by the immensity of this landmass and the potential resources down below, especially in Brazil and Argentina. Nine of these Latin peoples have, in addition to their ancient Indian heritages, a Spanish cultural base (besides African, French, British, or Dutch cultural inputs), while one nation,

Brazil, has both the Portuguese and African languages and cultural influences. All share the impact of European immigration. Centered between the Atlantic and Pacific Oceans, South America has been a multicultural cauldron for mixing Asian, East Indian, European, and African cultures in a curious synergy.

South America is a place where we can simultaneously be amazed at the beauty of the pre-Columbian art and civilization, or the very modern and colorful art works and high-rise architecture, and yet be appalled by the poverty of the masses and the great wealth of the few, by the violence and terrorism, and by the dominance of a powerful military or dictator. But outsiders are also encouraged by the progress in education and literacy, improvements in health services and population control, changing images and aspirations of South Americans.

Despite the great diversity in Latin America, there are common themes and patterns. After the development of fairly sophisticated Indian civilizations, there was a period of European colonization and exploitation from the fifteenth through eighteenth centuries, followed by wars of independence and attempts at federation during the nineteenth century. Since the early twentieth century, Latin American nations have been engaged in internal and external conflicts. Yet, the last half of the twentieth century saw relative peace between the nations of Central and South America, and significant economic progress.

With the exception of Suriname in South America's northeast, these countries also share another factor—a Roman Catholic cultural tradition that pervades not only their history, but also their ways of life and thinking. The Spanish and Portuguese explorers and conquerors brought the missionaries with them to convert and "civilize" the pagan inhabitants—ancient, sophisticated indigenous civilizations. Accompanying the military from South America up through North America were Franciscans, Dominicans, and Jesuits. At first, the clergy protected the Indians and through their missions helped to educate the indigenous populations. Their agricultural and trading centers became the great cities of South, Central, and North America. With the passage of time and increase in wealth, the Church became part of the establishment, despite the notable successes of priest revolutionaries, like Father Miguel Hidalgo, who espoused the causes of nationalism of the peasants. As a major landowner itself, the Church has not only supported the oligarchy, but opposed population control, divorce, and social change.

The growth of militant theology and activities in the Latin American Church caused the late Pope John Paul II during his visits to the Western Hemisphere to protest social inequities, yet warn the clergy of the need to concentrate on their spiritual mission. In any event, no modern manager operating in Latin America can afford to ignore the Church as a cultural force. Cooperation and collaboration for social improvement in Latin America can be significantly advanced when business cooperates with all institutions for human development.

Despite the great diversity in Latin America, there are common themes and patterns.

There is also growing global interest in the Latin American market, for both exports and imports.

Rodriquez examined the conversions underway in Latin America from Catholic to Protestant beliefs.[12] The new brand of Christianity on the rise is "Evangelico," principally Pentecostal, with a fundamentalist view of scriptural teachings. In the twenty-first century, Protestants have now risen to 50 million on that continent. With a conversion rate of 400 per hour, demographers predict Latin U.S. will be evangelical before the end of the twenty-first century. The "born again" movement matches the transition toward industrialization and urbanization. The religious cultural shift is away from the more tolerant, feminine orientation with its tragic sense of life and death, toward self-reform, spiritual empowerment, and taking responsibility for improving your own life now, not just in the hereafter. Rodriquez reports that a powerful tool for this religious revolution is satellite television beamed southward from what is left of Protestant America's "Bible Belt." Four hundred years of authoritarian Christianity may be overturned in a single generation, and Latin American peoples will never be the same again.

There is also growing global interest in the Latin American market, for both exports and imports. Exhibit 12.6 is one indicator of this trend.

EXHIBIT 12.6

CHINA'S ROLE IN LATIN AMERICA

While the United States is losing its influence in Latin America, former outsiders, such as China, are assuming a greater role in hemispheric affairs. The economy there grew at a reasonably healthy rate in 2005—4.3 percent, compared to China's 9 percent. The same year the U.S. Presidential Administration, opposed by Venezuela and Boliva, failed again to get a majority for its candidates in the Organization of American States, a 34-country entity. While Washington did succeed in signing a free-trade deal with Central America and the Dominican Republic at the Mar del Plata Summit, the presidents of both Argentina and Venezuela made speeches against the United States, blaming it for the region's ills.

Meantime, China is emerging as one of the largest trading partners of South American countries. Press reports claim the People's Republic of China (PRC) intends to invest $100 billion in Latin America, while its imports of raw materials alone from the region will reach that figure by the end of the decade. Although the region's forecasts are for modest economic growth, the United States is expected to seek its investment opportunities in Asia and Central Europe. On the other hand, Brazil and other Latin countries are becoming successful players in the global economy, thereby reducing the region's poverty somewhat.

Source: Adapted from Andres Oppenheimer's "China Toppping U.S. in Latin America," *Miami Herald* reproduced in the *San Diego Union-Tribune*, December 30, 2005, p. B8.

There are 14 different nations on this continent. Before examining South America's giants, Brazil and Argentina, we offer a profile of its six largest populations in Exhibit 12.7.

EXHIBIT 12.7
PROFILES OF BOLIVIA, CHILE, COLOMBIA, ECUADOR, PERU, AND VENEZUELA

NATION	Bolivia	Chile	Colombia	Ecuador	Peru	Venezuela
AREA (sq km)	1,098,581	756,626	1,138,914	283,561	1,285,217	912,050
POPULATION	8,857,870	15,980,912	42,954,279	13,363,593	27,925,628	25,375,281
CAPITAL	La Paz (admin)	Santiago	Bogotá	Quito	Lima	Caracas, Sucre (legal)
RELIGION	RC	RC	RC	RC	RC	RC
LANGUAGE	Spanish, Quechua, Aymara	Spanish	Spanish	Spanish, Quechua	Spanish, Quechua, Aymara	Spanish
LITERACY	87.2%	96.2%	92.5%	92.5%	87.7%	93.4%
LIFE EXPECTANCY	65.5 years	76.58 years	71.72 years	76.21 years	69.53 years	74.31 years
GDP PER CAPITA	$2700	$11,300	$7100	$3900	$6000	$6400
GOVERNMENT	Republic	Republic	Republic	Republic	Republic	Republic

BRAZIL*

Since it is impossible to cover all countries in South America, we have selected the largest in terms of population, landmass, and economy, Brazil,[13] for in-depth analysis.

> I want people from other parties in my cabinet. I want to combine technical ability with political and social sensitivity.
> —Luiz Ignácio "Lula" da Silva

> He (Lula) never had a maid and washes his own socks and underwear.[14]
> —Frei Belto

---

* Brazil section written by Kristine Elaine Menn (MIM, American Graduate School of International Management). She has lived in São Paulo, Brazil, since 1992, where she works as a consultant and teacher of cross-cultural communication and English.

Historical/Political Overview

To this day, there remain some unanswered questions regarding the European discovery and subsequent colonization of Brazil. One of these subjects of controversy concerns who actually saw Brazil first. While the French claim that their explorer, Jean Cousin, arrived in Brazil in 1488, the Spanish argue that Christopher Columbus probably landed on the northern coast of Brazil during his third journey in 1498. However, it is the Portuguese nobleman and commander of a fleet of more than a dozen ships, Pedro Alvares Cabral, while trying to sail in a southwesterly direction off the coast of Portugal in order to travel around the tip of Africa and then on to India, who is given the credit for the discovery in 1500. Apparently making the mistake of sailing too far to the west, Cabral came in contact with the eastern part of Brazil in the present-day state of Bahia and established a claim in the newly found continent. Little did the Portuguese know at the time that the discovered land was not an insignificant tropical island, but instead, a vast, rich land full of various forms of treasure.

Hence the Portuguese began ruling their colony from Portugal, much as England ruled the new colonies in America. However, unlike the pilgrims in America who fled England in order to start a new life and practice their religion freely, the main objective of the Portuguese explorers was to take full advantage of the numerous riches that the newly discovered territory offered. The name "Brazil" comes from a hardwood tree that was referred to by its Latin name, *brasile*. This tree, which produced a red-colored dye, was found in abundance along the eastern coastline of the new land, and the Portuguese brought shiploads of it back to Europe. Thus started the tradition of exploitation that can still be seen in modern-day Brazil. The brazilwood tree would be the first in a series of products to be exploited. After the cycle of the brazilwood tree came sugarcane, followed by gold and diamonds, rubber, cotton, tobacco, leather, and coffee, among others. The gold, diamonds, and other precious stones that were shipped back to Portugal from the 1690s to the 1760s made the Portuguese monarchy the richest in all of Europe, and very little of the profit was left in Brazil.

Land was distributed in a way that differed greatly from the system used by the settlers in America. Instead of selling small plots of land to individuals so that everyone could share in the wealth of Brazil's resources, the Portuguese monarchy decided to divide their colony into 12 strips of land, which extended east to west, from the Atlantic Ocean to the western hinterlands. Control of this land was granted to nobles. For their part, these nobles were charged with developing and protecting their land from invading countries such as England, France, Spain, and the Netherlands. One example of the need for this protection was when, in order to try to gain control over the sugarcane trade,

Thus started the tradition of exploitation that can still be seen in modern-day Brazil.

the Dutch attacked Rio de Janeiro, Salvador, and Recife in the 1620s and stayed in Recife until they were forced out in the 1650s. Of course, a strong, large labor force was necessary to work on the plantations and in the mines, so the Portuguese eventually solved this problem by bringing 3 to 4 million slaves from Africa during the 300 years from 1550 to 1850. So continued governance of Brazil from afar by the Portuguese for more than three centuries, until a twist of fate would bring about forced change.

It was the occupation of Portugal by Napoleon in 1807 that would induce a change in the way Brazil was governed. In that year, the Portuguese royal family decided to flee to Brazil; when they arrived in the colony in 1808, a new historical era began. Brazil would no longer be just another one of Portugal's colonies ruled from afar but would become the seat of the entire Portuguese Empire. In fact, in 1815, Brazil would be elevated to the status of "kingdom," which put it on an equal footing with Portugal. This was the first step leading to independence. In 1822, in order not to lose his status as king of Portugal, Emperor João returned to Portugal, but his son, Pedro I, decided to stay in Brazil. It was on September 7, 1822 that Pedro I declared Brazil's independence from Portugal with the cry, "Independence or death! We have separated from Portugal!" with almost no resistance from the mother country in Europe. As a newly independent country, the Brazilian Empire experienced instability for many years. Finally in 1831, partly due to great unpopularity in Brazil, Pedro I returned to Portugal, and like his father before him he left his son, five-year-old Pedro II, in Brazil. A council of regents appointed by the parliament ruled the country until 1840, when Pedro II came of age. It was in that year that Pedro II would begin his 49-year reign and that the country would really experience a true transformation from colonial to modern Brazil. Also during the reign of Pedro II, the slaves were freed in 1888. After almost 50 years of monarchical rule, the military overthrew Pedro II in 1889 and proclaimed Brazil a republic.

During the twentieth century, Brazil witnessed a succession of experiments with democracy, dictatorships, and military rule. Getúlio Vargas, one of the greatest Brazilian leaders, led Brazil, as both a democratically elected president during some years and a dictator during others, from 1930 to 1945 and again from 1951 to 1954. From an elite southern ranching family, Vargas is famous for his populist ways. Much like Franklin Delano Roosevelt, Vargas promoted social welfare programs, while at the same time, much like the dictators Franco and Salazar, he engaged in repressive tactics. Another Brazilian leader, considered to be the greatest president of all time by many, was Jucelino Kubitcheck. "Fifty years in five" was his campaign slogan, and indeed, he is famous for the extraordinary works that were accomplished during his short term from 1955 to 1960. Among the most famous of his projects was the construction and inauguration in 1960 of a new

"Independence or death! We have separated from Portugal!"

national capital, Brasília, located in the center of the country. Also during his presidency, heavy industry flourished in Brazil, including the iron, steel, and automotive industries.

Another important phase in Brazil's history is that of the most recent military regime, which lasted from 1964 to 1985. Brazil was one of the first countries in Latin America that came under military rule in the 1960s and early 1970s, and it would be one of the last ones to free itself from this domination. Taking place at a time when the United States was afraid of the spread of communism in the Western Hemisphere, the coup that overtook the Brazilian government had the approval of the United States; American military ships were stationed in the region in case they were needed. After the takeover, Brazil underwent a great transformation. Throughout the late 1960s and early 1970s, the country experienced extraordinary growth. With the implementation of state-intervention methods, the economy grew by as much as 11% a year, faster than any other world economy at this time. Consequently, this period came to be known as the "Brazilian Miracle." However, there was also a sinister side to this remarkable growth. Anyone even suspected of being against the regime was arrested and imprisoned, and the use of torture was widespread. Many consider the period from 1968 to 1974 to be the darkest years of Brazilian history. During this time, many artists and academics went into exile in Europe, the United States, and other Latin American countries.

The oil crises of the 1970s had a big effect on Brazil.

As quickly as the Brazilian economy had shot up, it began its descent. The oil crises of the 1970s had a big effect on Brazil, which depended as much as 80% on imported oil. The huge international debt was also a problem. Furthermore, there were splits in the regime over whether or how to gradually give control back to civilians. Owing to these negative circumstances, as well as pressure from the public, the practice of censorship slowly began to be reversed, and those in exile were allowed to return home during the late 1970s. In the early 1980s, enormous public protests took place, inflation shot up to 100% and higher, and payments on the national debt were stopped. In 1984, the masses took to the streets and demanded immediate direct presidential elections (*diretas já*!). Instead of direct elections, a carefully selected electoral college was chosen by the government. Nevertheless, the opposition candidate won due to the severely divided regime.

Although there are "ghosts" from the military regime that still haunt many Brazilians today (and some of these "ghosts" are alive and involved in present-day politics), during the years since the military regime Brazil has been undergoing a gradual process of opening markets and removing the state's control in the economy. With the first direct presidential elections in 29 years, President Collor de Mello took office in 1990. During his first two years in office, the country experienced some of the biggest changes in its modern history. However, it soon became obvious that the administration was corrupt; subsequently, Collor was impeached in 1992. From 1995 until 2001, Fernando Henrique Cardoso, a sociologist and former Brazilian minister of economy who had gone into political exile during the military regime, served as president. Many positive steps to improve Brazil were taken during his administration in both economic and social areas. During his first term, President Lula has been veering away from his campaign rhetoric involving a complete overhaul of the system and, instead, is sticking to the programs set up under the Cardoso administration. Of course, some very fundamental and urgent changes must be made involving the way things are run in Brazil, but these changes will not come easily due to the characteristics of the country's political system.

As the third largest democracy in the world after the United States and India, Brazil's political system is similar to that of the United States in many ways, but at the same time, there are many differences between the two. The head of state is the president, who is chosen through direct elections every four years and can serve a total of eight years. Voting is voluntary for people 16 to 18 years old and older than 70 years old, but it is compulsory for all others. This has big implications for a country in which the majority of the population doesn't have a fundamental education. Roman Codes are the basis of the Brazilian legal system. The legislative branch consists of a bicameral national congress, much like the one in the United States. The Federal Senate is composed of 81 seats with three elected members from each state and three from the federal district. The senators serve eight-year terms. The Chamber of Deputies is composed of 513 seats. Members are selected by proportional representation to serve four-year terms. The judicial branch consists of a Supreme Federal Tribunal made up of 11 members who are appointed by the president and confirmed by the Senate, the Higher Tribunal of Justice, and Regional Federal Tribunals. Judges are appointed for life.

Although lobbying is not officially legal in Brazil, still many interest groups exert pressure on the congress. Some of the most powerful include the left wing of the Catholic Church, the Landless Workers' Movement (MST), and labor unions that are allied to the leftist Workers' Party (PT).

Since there are so many political parties in Brazil, it is necessary to form coalitions and make concessions in order to win elections or produce any modifications in the law. In fact, one of the great challenges today is to make the necessary changes so that Brazil's economic health can be restored. President Cardoso tried unsuccessfully to alter the provisions in pension and retirement benefit packages; he did not succeed because his party did not hold the majority of the seats in congress. President Lula had a great opportunity to make these changes reality since he possesses much more power in Congress than his predecessor did. Unfortunately, only minimal changes were accomplished

Brazil is the third largest democracy in the world after the United States and India.

before Lula's Workers' Party got tangled up in severe corruption scandals, unlike any seen before in Brazil's history.

Brazil has political relationships with many countries through various international organizations. Some examples of these are the United Nations, the World Trade Organization, the World Bank, and the Group of 77. One of Brazil's most important economic partnerships may be the common market known as MERCOSUR. MERCOSUR is composed of Argentina, Uruguay, Chile, and Brazil. Another significant economic organization being formed is the Free Trade Area of the Americas (FTAA). These trading blocks offer great economic growth potential for the member countries.

The People

Social Structure, Race, Values, and Religion

Brazil is a spectacular country in both social contrasts and geographical size. It is in this fascinating country that you can find the richest of the rich and the poorest of the poor. First World living conditions are seen in upper-class neighborhoods; across the street from the massive, electronically operated skyscrapers you will see people living in favelas (shantytowns) with not even the most basic of public services. It is estimated that more than 4 million people live in these shantytowns in the cities of Rio de Janeiro and São Paulo alone. A 1995 World Bank study found that Brazil has the most unequal wealth distribution worldwide in spite of the fact that it grew faster than any other country in the world between 1960 and 1990. One Brazilian economist in the 1970s proposed changing the name of Brazil to "Belinda" because Brazil's industrial base can be compared to Belgium, but its social situation looks more like that of India.

Another contrast is in the people's skin tone. Here you will notice a complete spectrum of skin colors, from the blackest of black to the whitest of white, and all skin tones in between. Although 54% of the people consider themselves to be "white" (primarily descendants of the Portuguese, German, Italian, Spanish, and Polish) and only 6% consider themselves to be "black," it is estimated that at least 45% of the population has some degree of African ancestry. Furthermore, with 50% of its total population under 20 years of age, Brazil is a very "young" country.

Brazil is a very "young" country.

A prevalent cultural generalization concerning the people of Brazil is that they are a warm, friendly, and emotionally sensitive people who are generous and receptive to foreigners. Brazilians pride themselves as not being prejudiced against anyone because of skin color or nationality. Of course, a type of economic prejudice does exist, as is evidenced by the fact that a black person is much more likely to be poor than a white person. Despite this inequality, it is true that people of all colors do mingle more than is customary in the United States. One explanation could be that the races come into close contact with each other on a daily basis owing to the widespread use of servants in households and offices. Through this contact, not only is a relationship formed, but also a type of experiencing the lives of the other races and classes is present. This coexistence leads to better understanding and tolerance among social strata.

The Brazilian class structure is based on economics. As mentioned earlier, Brazil has the most unequal distribution of wealth in the world. While the highest 10% of the population enjoys 47% of the country's consumption share, the lowest 10% only has 1%. The rich class in Brazil consists of both the traditional wealthy class and a new rich class, which is made up mainly of the descendants of poor immigrants who built up empires of riches.

Brazilians in general espouse the traditional religious values held dear by the Roman Catholic Church. One of the most important of these values is the family. Perhaps more influential in Brazil than in any other Latin American country, the family has been the single most significant institution in the formation of Brazilian society. The meaning of "family" in Brazil is not limited to the immediate family, but instead includes the entire parentela, or extended family, from both the mother's and father's side. This group can consist of hundreds of people, and it supplies the foundation for the individual's social structure. It is not unusual to see many generations living together under one roof, or at least in the same neighborhood or city. It is customary for children to live with their parents until they marry, even though this has been changing recently, especially in the big cities. Loyalty to one's family is the individual's highest-ranking obligation. The traditional family is male-dominated, although today, for economic reasons, many women work outside the home, and single-parent families are common. Other traditional dominant values in the Brazilian society include community, collectivism, procreation, and a hierarchical society. As anthropologist Roberto DaMatta has commented, in Brazil the attitude is one of, "Don't you know who you're talking to?" while in the United States it is more along the lines of, "Who do you think you are?" This depicts the difference between the egalitarian society in the United States versus the hierarchical society in Brazil.

Another traditional value that has its basis in the Catholic Church is one of fatalism. Evidence can be found in expressions that are very common in everyday conversations, such as "Se Deus quiser" ("the Lord willing"). Although this expression is also used in the United States, the typical American attitude is more along the lines of "I can accomplish whatever I want to if I just put my mind to it and work hard." The Brazilian attitude is the result of a history full of unpredictable changes and circumstances over which the individual has had little control. Some examples of more recent circumstances of this type

The Brazilian class structure is based on economics.

include electricity and water shortages that have resulted in periods of blackouts and lack of water supplies. These situations have helped make the Brazilians a very patient people.

Even though the Catholic Church has had a profound effect on the formation of dominant values found in Brazil, a large percentage of Brazilians are only nominally Catholic. This may be due in part to the fact that, unlike other Latin American countries, the royal Portuguese family did not grant the Catholic Church significant power during Brazil's earlier history. As a result, other religions are widely accepted and have become increasingly popular in recent years, especially evangelical religions. Some Brazilians even practice more than one type of religion. Furthermore, although 85 to 90% of the Brazilian people profess to have at least some alliance to the Catholic Church, Brazilian Catholics have adopted many traditions of Afro-Brazilian religions as well. For example, according to one African religion, Iemanjá is the goddess of the sea. On New Year's Eve, one can find many offerings of white flowers, perfume, mirrors, wine, and other items that a vain woman would find pleasing, strewn along the beaches by her admirers, which certainly include Catholics. These are gifts offered to the goddess, traditionally given in exchange for a prosperous new year. Many people draw parallels between this goddess and the Virgin Mary. One can also see offerings made at intersections, even on the busiest of streets in the largest cities. It is estimated that one in three Brazilians participates in some form of Afro-Brazilian religion. Brazilians are also very tolerant of other religions practiced in the country.

Cultural Characteristics of Business in Brazil

Doing business in Brazil can be a challenging experience owing to economic uncertainties involving inflation, currency exchange rates, and interest rates, among other things. At the same time, working in Brazil can be enjoyable and exciting because of all the immense economic opportunities that the country offers. Brazil's economy is as diverse as its geography and people are. The country produces everything from automobiles and airplanes to shoes and orange juice. The service industry is also prevalent and rapidly growing. In addition, Brazil is rich in both natural and human resources.

As in any other country, in order to be successful it is important to learn about the customs and courtesies involved in doing business in Brazil. By understanding the culture better, it is easier to avoid committing blunders that could potentially lead to disastrous results in business and social situations. One of the biggest mistakes that can be made is to consider Brazil to be just another country in Latin America and to assume that what works in Chile or Mexico or Panama will also work in Brazil. Brazil differs from all other Latin American countries

The country produces everything from automobiles and airplanes to shoes and orange juice.

not only in historical aspects, but also in cultural factors. One of the largest differences is that Brazil is the only country in Latin America in which Portuguese is the official language. In addition to this example, there are innumerable subtler cultural differences, some of which will be discussed in the remainder of this chapter.

Greetings

Handshakes are the appropriate form of greeting between men and women in a business setting. However, because Brazilians are warm and friendly people who feel free to show their affection in public, greeting with kisses on one or both cheeks is common between a man and a woman as well as between two women. Women sometimes will kiss three times if one of the women is not married. This is said to bring good luck in finding a husband. Men do not kiss, but it is normal for acquaintances to pat each other on the back or on the arm while shaking hands. It is usual for men and women who are friends to hug each other when they meet. Don't be surprised to see two women walking down the street hand in hand or arm in arm. Brazilians touch each other more and for longer periods of time than is acceptable in some other cultures. Upon arriving and before leaving, it is important to greet and say goodbye to each individual, and to refrain from using the American form of "Hi/Bye everyone!," which Brazilians regard as impersonal.

Names and Titles

Most Brazilians are less formal than people in the other Latin American countries; consequently, titles are not always used. First names are used routinely, but it is a good idea to wait until the Brazilian asks you to call him by his first name before doing so. Often, a title is used with a first name, such as Dona (Lady) Maria or Senhor (Mister) John. Doutor or Doutora (Doctor) may also be put before a first name and is commonly used to express respect even if the person is not a doctor or Ph.D. (especially with older folks). First and last names may be made up of two or more names. Take the example Luís Henrique Meirelles Reis. In this case, it appears that Henrique is the middle name, but friends and family might call him Luís Henrique. Furthermore, a first name may be a combination of the mother's and father's first names. An example of this is Carlene, which is a combination of Carlos and Marlene. A person's compound last name may be a combination of the mother's maiden name followed by the father's last name. This order is different from the order used in Spanish-speaking countries. It is not uncommon for a person's full name to be made up of five or six separate names! Another interesting point is that in the Portuguese language there are two words for the English word you. The use of *o senhor* or *a senhora* denotes more respect than the use of the casual *você*.

Hospitality and Entertaining

Brazilians are well known for their courtesy and hospitality. They will do anything to make visitors feel welcomed and comfortable. Expect to be offered endless cups of very small but very strong coffee (called cafezinho) both in the office or when visiting someone's home. While accepting the coffee is always appropriate, it is not considered rude to politely refuse it either. Brazilians will often keep offering more even if they think that you don't want anymore. Therefore, don't feel that it is necessary to keep accepting more food or drinks just because your host continues offering! It is just his way of being polite. It is also usual for a person who is about to begin eating to offer some of his food to others. This is only done to show consideration to those around him, and the person offering the food probably has no intention of sharing but expects a polite "no thank you" in return.

Toasts are common in Brazil.

Although Brazilians do entertain in their home, among coworkers it is more common to go out for lunch, drinks, or dinner. It is normal for the person who does the inviting to pay the bill, but it is just as normal for the check to be split equally among all present, regardless of who ate what. Toasts are common in Brazil, but they are usually not an elaborate ceremony as they are in some cultures. To make a toast, simply lift your glass and say, "Saúde!" ("Health!"). Never tap your glass with a piece of silverware to get your group's attention before making a toast. Although this may be done in the United States, it is considered very rude in Brazil. Another form of behavior that is not considered polite is to snap your fingers or hiss to get a waiter's attention. Even though this action might be seen in some restaurants, it is not acceptable behavior.

Appearance, Hygiene, and Dress

Considered by many to be very beautiful people, Brazilians in general are extremely concerned about their appearance. They go to great pains to keep in good physical shape by working out in clubs, running in parks or along the beaches, and even undergoing plastic surgery. It is usual for both women and men to keep their fingernails and toenails neatly manicured, and a visitor doing business in Brazil should do the same. Due to the typically hot weather, it is not uncommon for Brazilians to take two or more showers a day. Brazilians always like to brush their teeth after eating, so it is not unusual to see people brushing their teeth in the restrooms of restaurants or companies, which could be considered strange or rude in some cultures.

Dressing for work in Brazil depends on the company, of course, but the standard dress for men is a dark or light-colored two-piece suit, shirt, and tie. Many companies have adopted the casual Friday concept, and some have casual day every day. While men in the Brazilian workplace dress in much the same way as their American counterparts do in general, the same may not be true for the Brazilian women. Many Brazilian businesswomen do wear suits, but others may dress in a variety of other ways. For example, it is not unusual to see women dressed in low-cut, tight, transparent tops, even with spaghetti straps (or no straps) in the office. Sundresses are also common. Often, women will wear sandals without pantyhose. One important point to remember is that a woman's purse and shoes should always match. Brazilian women in general prefer a more natural look and wear little if any makeup. It is also not uncommon to see a woman come to work without drying her hair. Having said this, it is probably in the best interest of a businesswoman visiting Brazil to dress more conservatively than in the manner described here.

Outside the workplace, dressing is usually casual. During the weekends, even at some fine restaurants in São Paulo and Rio de Janeiro, men wear khaki shorts (mainly at lunchtime), slacks, or jeans, and either a button-down or polo-type shirt. Of course, this depends on the restaurant and situation. Keep in mind when traveling to Brazil that the seasons are opposite, so when it is freezing cold in the Northern Hemisphere, it could be steamy hot in Brazil.

Gifts and Bribes

Doing business in Brazil does not require gift-giving, but since Brazilians regard business relationships as personal relationships, they value all acts of generosity, including receiving presents from their visitors. It's a good idea to try to personalize the gift as much as possible: Brazilians appreciate the attention and thought that goes into selecting the right present. Some appropriate gifts include calendars, chocolate, wine, top-quality scotch whiskey, name-brand perfume, or anything unique from the visitor's country that may not be available in Brazil.

When does a "gift" become a "bribe"? This is a difficult line to determine, and although it is traditionally true that bribes are sometimes given in Brazil, things are changing. Therefore, it is best for a visitor to err on the safe side and not to participate in this practice. If one is not familiar with the culture's subtleties, one could get into trouble either by offending someone by offering a bribe or by not offering the right thing. For this and other reasons, it may be beneficial to hire a despachante to help in certain situations. *Despachantes* are specialists in cutting through the endless bureaucracy that can be found at any level of government. A tool that is very useful in Brazil is the *jeitinho*, which is a term that means "getting around obstacles in order to obtain

Despachantes are specialists in cutting through the endless bureaucracy.

what you want." The despachante knows exactly which jeitinho is necessary for each particular situation. Another Brazilian tradition is the *cafezinho*, literally meaning "little coffee." This is a small tip or amount of money that is given to someone when they help out. If a person offers to pay another for doing a favor, and the person who did the favor answers by saying that a cafezinho would be fine, he really isn't asking for coffee!

Time

Brazilians have a more flexible idea of time than some other cultures. Although in the workplace punctuality is considered important in theory, in reality it is common for meetings to start 5 to 20 minutes late (or more!). One reason for this, or maybe more of an excuse, is the unpredictable traffic found in the big cities. Once the meeting does start, it is important to spend some time with small talk. Some topics appropriate for small talk include family (only if one has met the family previously), current events, the weather, or any positive topic. Sometimes discussing soccer is appropriate, depending on the person one is talking to and which team he roots for. In general, negative and controversial subjects should be avoided because they could lead to feelings of embarrassment and an uncomfortable situation. Expect to spend a long time in meetings before any results are produced. Brazilians do not always get down to business right away; in their opinion, it is important to establish personal relationships and a sense of trust before doing business with someone.

Time is viewed differently in social situations.

Time is viewed differently in social situations. Parties always start later than the time shown on the invitation. If offered an invitation for dinner at someone's home, it's a good idea to arrive no more than 15 minutes late even though others may show up later. Even worse, don't come early or exactly on time because the host may not be ready.

Communication: Verbal and Nonverbal

Portuguese is the official language of Brazil, but due to the enormous size of the country, it has many distinct dialects. Accents and even the meaning given to words vary from region to region. Moreover, many subcultures in Brazil still use the language of their ancestors. It is common to hear German and Polish spoken in the South, Italian and Japanese in São Paulo, and Spanish along the borders of neighboring countries. Among the members of the "international business subculture," English is definitely the official language. It is more the exception than the rule for people in managerial positions at multinational companies not to speak some degree of English.

The Brazilian speaking communication style is very expressive and animated. The norm is to speak fast, without much time between the words. Due to variations in the pitch and volume of the voices, a dialogue may resemble a song more than a conversation. Moreover, depending on the topic, it may even appear that a fight is about to break out, but, more often than not, it is just an emotionally friendly discourse. Furthermore, Brazilians like to say one thing, give examples or details, and then rephrase their point many times, repeating the same idea over and over again. Members of some cultures may find this style of communication to be confusing, unorganized, or misleading.

The Brazilian writing communication style shares many characteristics with the speaking communication style. Comma splices and run-on sentences, considered incorrect in English, are common in Portuguese writing. Brazilians also use the indirect style of digression more than other cultures do. This sometimes can make it difficult to understand the writer's line of thought.

The concept of low- and high-context communication styles involves both verbal and nonverbal communication aspects. While Brazilians generally are more low-context than people from Asia and Middle Eastern countries, they are usually more high-context than people of the United States and Northern Europe. Although Brazilians use words profusely, at times they can be very indirect in expressing their feelings. Therefore, it is imperative that the visitor be aware of the possible underlying meanings in communicative exchanges in order to avoid serious misunderstandings.

While it has been said that nonverbal communication accounts for about 70% of all communication, this percentage can be even higher when members of different cultures try to exchange information (as high as 100% if they don't speak a common language!). At times, the nonverbal forms of communication carry more weight in a conversation than the actual words do. One important form of nonverbal communication is eye contact. Brazilians in general, and especially individuals who hold the same status level, look each other in the eye when speaking. However, it is also common for a person from a lower class to look down when speaking to someone he considers his superior. This is a form of showing respect and should not be looked upon with suspicion. In public places, it is not unusual for people to stare at others for lengths of time, which may make members of different cultures uncomfortable.

There is no room whatsoever for silence in Brazilian communication, and the use of interruptions in discussions is common. While this may be considered rude in some cultures and even in Brazil, a person might use interruptions to show his enthusiasm and interest in the conversation in some situations.

In this country, close physical contact is the norm. An individual's personal space is small, and touching during a conversation happens all the time. It is common for pedestrians walking on crowded city

Interruptions in discussions is common.

streets to brush against or even bump into each other without stopping to apologize.

Brazilians like to talk with their hands; it is almost impossible for them to have a conversation without moving their hands to help express themselves. This is even true during phone conversations. Consequently, the use of hand gestures is widespread. The following describes some of the most common gestures in Brazil.

"OK" sign used in the United States is considered extremely vulgar.

- The "OK" sign used in the United States is considered extremely vulgar, especially when the three extended fingers are held parallel to the ground, close to the chest, with the palm up.
- Extending the middle finger upward is also vulgar.
- Hitting an open palm into a clenched fist sends the same message as the two examples above.
- Extending the index and little finger upward while making a fist with the other fingers means, "Your wife/girlfriend is cheating on you."
- Opening and closing all fingers together many times with the palm up means that a place is crowded or full.
- Pulling the lower eyelid down with the index finger means "pay attention!," "watch out!," or "I am watching and paying attention."
- Brushing the fingertips of one hand under the chin and continuing to move the hand out in an outward direction, palm facing inward and then up, means "I don't know."
- Snapping all fingers on each other while moving the hand up and down quickly adds emphasis to what is being said.
- Snapping the thumb and middle finger, palm facing sideways while moving the hand from the chest to the shoulder at ear height means "a long time ago."
- Wiping the fingers of one hand with the fingers of the other hand, in a downward direction in front of the chest with palms facing upward means "it doesn't matter."

Women's Role in Business

Though traditionally Brazil has shared the machismo characteristic with other countries throughout Latin America, the reality in Brazil today is changing, especially in the big cities. In many situations, women need to work outside the home in order to help support the family. Furthermore, in today's business world, women are achieving upper management positions, and even directorships. However, it is still rare to see women presidents in large companies, both domestic and international. Women are also gaining greater roles in political areas. The former mayor of São Paulo is a woman, as is the governor of Rio de Janeiro state. Women also are presently serving at the national level of government as cabinet and supreme court members.

Negotiating in Brazil

Although a sense of fatalism exists in Brazil due to a feeling of lack of control over one's own future, and the "get rich quick while you have the chance, and then get out quick" philosophy can still be found, the general rule for doing business and negotiating in Brazil is more one of "take your time." Negotiations cannot be rushed in this country. Business is usually done with friends and acquaintances, and these types of relationships take a long time to build. Because personal relationships form the basis of trust in business deals, nepotism and giving preference to friends is common in both companies and government.

The following are some characteristics of attitudes and negotiating styles in Brazil.

- *Particular over Universal.* When making decisions, Brazilians like to look at the details involved in each particular situation, instead of applying universal rules or patterns of behavior to all situations.
- *Relationship over Task.* Brazilians feel that a good relationship must be in place before anything can be accomplished, and it is never a good idea to damage a relationship that is intact even if it means not completing a task.
- *Polychronic over Monochronic.* Brazilians tend to view the concept of time in a polychronic way, often discussing the details of a proposal in a random order instead of in a sequential manner.
- *Indirect over Direct.* Seemingly a contradiction, Brazilians are a very emotional, affective, and talkative people, but their style in both personal and business affairs is very indirect. Brazilians are usually nonconfrontational and believe in saving face.
- *Group over Individual.* Although this depends on the circumstances, in general Brazilians feel the group and relationships within the group are more important than individual aspirations. This has implications concerning methods of motivation. Sometimes an individual manager would prefer to share a bonus with his subordinates or coworkers instead of keeping it all for himself.
- *Flexible over Inflexible.* Due to constant changes in Brazilian laws, as well as the uncertainty brought by fluctuations in exchange rates, interest rates, and inflation rates, Brazilians have become very skillful at making adaptations to their plans and "rolling with the flow." They consider people who always follow standard procedures to be unimaginative and to be lacking in intelligence.

Brazilians are a very emotional, affective, and talkative people.

ARGENTINA

The second largest nation on the continent of South America is Argentina, in terms of population, landmass, and economy.

Geographically, it is bounded by five other Latin countries—Bolivia and Paraguay to the north, Uruguay and Brazil to the east, and Chile to the west. This most southern country extends with its neighbor Chile to the tip of Cape Horn where the Atlantic and Pacific Oceans converge. It is the eighth largest national state in the world, and its people dance to the *tango* and the tune of free market enterprise. It is a founding member of a trading group known as MERCOSUR, along with the other members Brazil, Uruguay, Paraguay, and soon Venezuela—a combined market of over 200 million consumers and gross domestic product of over $700 million (see Exhibits 12.8 and 12.9). Chile is an associate member of this free market group, and Bolivia is expected eventually to sign this economic agreement.

Although Spanish is the principal language, the upper classes are also English speakers because of historical British influences there. With the shift from military to civilian political leadership, recent government reforms have not only fostered free enterprise and deregulation, but control of a volatile economy and inflation so as to encourage external investment in this resource-rich land (oil, natural gas, hydroelectricity, ranching, grain, oil seeds, etc.). Exhibit 12.9 provides a profile of this future regional pacesetter.

Cultural Influences

The People

About 20% of the population descend from the original "Indian" peoples who now live largely in remote areas. The remaining 80% are of European stock, largely Spanish and Italian ancestry. Argentina's cosmopolitan and progressive citizens express intensive opinion about world affairs, their government, its police, politics, and taxes, but usually avoid personal public criticism, except among trusted friends. Gregarious by nature, Argentineans are noted for their respect of the individual, acceptance of failure, and lack of punctuality.

Argentineans are noted for their respect of the individual.

Geography

Argentina, containing over a million square miles, has a large plain that rises above the Atlantic Ocean and extends to the towering Andes Mountains to the west. The northwest is home to *chaco* or swamp land and the great rivers of the *Plata* system. The rolling *pampas* or prairies are in the central part, featuring ranches, cowboys, and famous for wheat growing and cattle raising. Sheep raising occurs in the southern tableland of Patagonia. Although its climate is generally temperate, the *Chicao* region is sub-tropical, while in southern Patagonia, the winters are quite cold. The country's expansive capital is the largest in Latin

EXHIBIT 12.8

COUNTRY PROFILE—THE FEDERATIVE REPUBLIC OF BRAZIL

Population (July 2006 est.)	188 million
Landmass	8,511,965 sq km (3.3 million sq miles)
Literacy Rate (July 2006 est.)	86.4% of people 15 years and older
Ethnic Groups (July 2006 est.)	54% white, 39% mulatto (mixed white and black), 6% black, 1% unspecified and other (including Japanese, Arab, Amerindian)
Religions (July 2006 est.)	74% Catholic (nominal), 15% Protestant, 7% none; others including Bantu/Voodoo, Jewish, Spiritualist, Buddhist
Language (Official)	Portuguese
Government	Federative Republic
Political Parties	Brazilian Democratic Movement Party
	Brazilian Labor Party
	Brazilian Social Democracy Party
	Brazilian Progressive Party
	Communist Party of Brazil
	Democratic Labor Party
	Liberal Front Party
	Liberal Party
	Popular Socialist Party
	Workers' Party
Currency	Real
GDP (2005 est. in PPP*)	$1.57 trillion ($619.7 billion official rate)
Per Capita Income (2005 est. in PPP*)	$8400
Exports (2005 est.—21% to U.S.)	$115.1 billion f.o.b. transport equipment, iron ore, soybeans, footwear, coffee, autos
Imports (2005 est.—18% from U.S.)	$78.02 billion f.o.b. machinery, electrical and transport equipment, chemical products, oil
GDP Real Growth Rate (2005 est.)	2.4%
Unemployment Rate (2005 est.)	10%
Population Living Below Poverty Line (2005 est.)	22%

* PPP—Purchasing Power Parity. According to the CIA Web site, due to dramatic fluctuations in the exchange rate (dollar to real), this method "provides the best available starting point for comparisons of economic strength and well-being between countries."

EXHIBIT 12.9
PROFILE OF ARGENTINE REPUBLIC

AREA	2,766,889 sq km (1,068,302 sq miles)
POPULATION	36,518,000
CAPITAL	12,106,000 in Buenos Aires
LITERACY	96%
LIFE EXPECTANCY	75 years
LANGUAGES	*Spanish*, English, Italian, German, and French
GDP PER CAPITA	$12,900; GDP gross = $280 billion
ECONOMY	*Industrial*—food processing, motor vehicles manufacturing, consumer durables, textiles, and metallurgy. *Agricultural*—sunflower seeds, lemons, soybeans, grapes, livestock. Exports—edible oils, fuels and energy, cereals, feed.
GOVERNMENT	Federal Republic

Source: *Family Reference Atlas of the World*. Washington, DC: National Geographic, 2002, p. 125.

America, with the world's largest boulevard, elegant retail shops, and 150 parks!

History

After the Amerindian civilizations flourished, the Europeans entered this land's Rio de la Plata area by way of the Spanish in 1516. By 1580, they had established Buenos Aires as the center of their government on the central east coast adjoining Uruguay on the Atlantic Ocean, it still serves as this modern nation's most beautiful capital. In 1810 a tradition of revolutionary revolts and military *juntas* began as a continuing struggle for governmental control. By 1816, Argentina gained independence from Spanish colonial rule under the leadership of its national hero, Gen. José de San Martín. The economy prospered because of rubber plantations and beef production until the end of World War II when Argentina's unique position of neutrality ended. After decades of instability, Colonel Juan Peron became president in 1946. Under his dictatorship and the help of his wife Evita, the poor supposedly benefited, while the unions, military, and the economy declined. So much so that Peron was forced into exile in 1955. When a provisional military government fared no better, he managed to return to rule with the assistance of the Peronist party which still has influence there—Peron was elected president along with his second wife, Maria, as vice president. Within a year he was dead from natural causes, and his widow became the first woman to head a national government in the Western Hemisphere. In 1976, her administration ended with a bloodless coup and the establishment of martial law.

By 1816, Argentina gained independence from Spanish colonial rule.

Then the ruling military *juntas* were responsible for a campaign supposedly against terrorism, which itself resulted in thousands of kidnappings, arrests, assassinations, and executions. The military's loss of war against the British over possession of the Falkland Islands, brought a return to civilian rule and democracy in 1983 with the election of President Carlos Menem. Sweeping economic reforms and various international agreements brought a measure of prosperity. But in 2001, defaults on $95 billion in bonds, led the subsequent administration of President Nestor Kirchner into conflict with the International Monetary Fund over international loans and repayment of a $14.8 billion debt with the IMF. As industrial production shrunk in 2003, Argentina has been forced to restructure debt and promote economic reforms, despite its $12.3 billion in foreign reserves. Yet, today the economy is relatively robust, boosting tax revenues. In 2005, Kirchner felt confident enough to expand his influence over the judicial system and the media—although freedom of expression is guaranteed by law, the President is getting a more favorable press by incentives and veiled threats to journalists.

In the twenty-first century, Argentina is still a land of promise with enormous potential.

Argentina is still a land of promise with enormous potential.

Religious and Social Life

The observations made elsewhere in this chapter on Latin America also apply, for the most part. For example, 95% of the people are nominally Roman Catholic, but only a fourth are regular practitioners while the remaining limit their participation to special occasions. Foreigners and minorities are free to practice their preferred religions.

Again, Latin social customs are prevalent here, such as described in the next section. . . . The *Senors* (men), *Senoritas* (unmarried, usually younger women), and the *Senoras* (married, usually older females) typically shake hands while nodding to show respect. Close friends among males may embrace, while females will kiss one another on the cheeks and shake with both hands. First names are only used with close acquaintances. Ordinarily females do not speak to strange males without an introduction. Normally, Argentineans do not yell at one another from a distance, but simply raise a hand and smile.

Upper class Argentineans are somewhat proper, with reserved manners, yet friendly. Social etiquette in this country requires one not to open a conversation with a question, but to start with a greeting.

Wait for an invitation to be seated in an office or home. The locals appreciate compliments about their children, décor, and gardens.

They also eat in the European style, with knife in the right hand, and fork in the left. It is considered bad manners at the dinner table to place your hands in the lap, to use a toothpick, to clear your throat, or blow your nose—rather you should excuse yourself and go outside the dining area for such purposes. Beef is a favorite dish. Waiters will respond if you raise your hand and index finger. Dress is elegant but conservative—men's hats are removed when in buildings, elevators, or in the presence of women. In families, the elderly are respected, the wife is the household manager, and deference is shown to father as head.

Generally, in Argentina, business hours are 8 A.M. until noon; then 3 to 9 P.M. Retail stores usually are closed on Sundays. Soccer is a favorite sport, followed by racing, boating, basketball, and horseback riding.

LATIN AMERICAN CULTURAL THEMES

Central and South America are made up of many nations and cultures. In addition to the Amerindian cultures and languages, the Spanish heritage and language dominates, except as has been noted, in Brazil, where the Portuguese language and culture is prevalent. Other European cultural inputs are German, Irish, Italian, as well as African and some Asian influences evident across the Americas. Some countries, such as Mexico, Bolivia, Colombia, and Brazil, have strong manifestations of ancient Indian cultures. The latter people are growing in influences with improved education and economic opportunities. For example, in 2005, the newly elected president of Boliva, Evo Morales, had a powerful mandate because of his indigenous origins. He gained political support from the poor, the Andean Indians, and the *meztizos* (mixed race).

Generalizations regarding Latin America are dangerous.

Global managers realize that all the countries and peoples south of the U.S. border are not basically the same. Communication and business practice has to be adapted to local circumstances.

Generalizations regarding Latin America are dangerous. Many of the countries differ greatly in socioeconomic status, educational levels, governance, and composition of the population. A review of Exhibit 12.2 at the beginning of the chapter underscores this observation. However, the following insights from the late Alison Lanier about Latin America may prove helpful.[16]

Social Customs

Shaking Hands

This is the same as in Europe. If there are several people in the room, enter with a little bow and then go around to each person and shake hands. The "hi, everybody" is considered rude and brash. "So long; see you tomorrow" is equally poor. The *abrazo* (embrace) is a greeting used with individuals one knows well.

Pleasantries

Nobody rushes into business. As a foreign businessperson take your time and ask about your colleague's family's health, or the weather, or perhaps the local sports team.

Expressing Gratitude

Send "thank you" notes promptly after any courtesy. Flowers are often presented as an expression of appreciation.

Time

Latin Americans may often appear to be late for appointments, according to North American standards, but they expect North Americans to be on time. Business hours normally begin about 8 or 9 A.M., depending on local custom. A lunch break or *siesta* may extend from 12 to 3 P.M. Their offices usually close about 6 to 8 P.M. Dinner may begin at 8 to 9 P.M. As a guest, arrive about a half hour late, never exactly on time.

Party Traditions

Traditionally, women congregate on one side of the room and men on the other, but that is changing. For large formal affairs, invitations are written by hand. Flowers are often sent before a large affair. At a smaller party you should take them to your host or hostess.

Privacy

There are often closed doors, fences, and high walls around homes, especially of the more affluent. Knock and wait to be invited in. Don't drop in on neighbors. This is not a custom. Personal security is very important, so the more affluent may have bodyguards and security systems.

Questioning

Some North Americans get to know people by asking questions. However, in Latin America it is safer to talk about local issues of interest. Questions are often interpreted as prying.

Space

Latin speaking distance is closer than North American speaking distance. Instead of handshakes men often embrace.

Class and Status

People may not be served on a first come, first served basis. Their place in society may determine the order of preference as to serving and seating.

Business Practices

The pace in Latin America is traditionally slow, relaxed, and less frenetic.

The pace in Latin America is traditionally slow, relaxed, and less frenetic, especially when negotiations are under way. Normally, decisions are made at the top. Brazilians, for example, do not like quick, infrequent visits. They like relationships that continue. This implies a long-term commitment in Brazil. Deals are usually concluded in person, not finalized over the telephone or by letter or electronic mail. Again, do not call anyone by his or her first name unless the person has invited you to do so. When in doubt, be formal. Dress conservatively and use business cards of good quality and in the local language.

Cultural Themes and Patterns

Themes—basic orientations shared by many or most of the people in the region—are beginning points for understanding, and they sometimes form a pattern of behavior.

Personalismo

For the most part, a Latin's concerns are family, personal friends, hobbies, political party, and possibly athletics such as the local bullfight. But transcending all these is the concern for oneself. So to reach a Latin, relate everything to him or her in personalized terms.

Machismo

Machismo means "maleness" and is an attitude that men have toward women. The macho is aggressive and sometimes insensitive, and machismo represents power. It is made up of virility, zest for action, daring, competitiveness, and the will to conquer. How is it translated into daily business life? A man must demonstrate forcefulness, self-confidence, visible courage, and leadership with a flourish. The machismo concept is implanted early in childhood and varies from country to country. Saving face and honor are important concepts for men. Never criticize family or friends.

Femaleness

Traditionally, women were "out on a pedestal" and carefully protected by the male who was in charge. Yet, the female may actually control the home, children, and husband. As women in Latin America get better educated and pursue careers, their historical role in the family and society as wife and mother is changing. For example, in 2005, Michelle Bachelet was elected president of Chile, only the third woman to be elected to a top job in Latin America and the first who was not the widow of an illustrious husband. Instead, this moderate socialist was a twice separated mother of three children. In a socially conservative country, she previously served in the national government as minister of health and defense. Another consideration relative to femaleness is that in some countries, such as Venezuela, there is the "public" wife who runs the home and its finances, as well as raises the children; and the "private" wife or mistress who is outside the home.

Desires to Get Rich Quick—Fatalism

Many Latin American economies are unstable, and as a result there is a boom or bust attitude. Many desire to make it rich by speculation, manipulation, or gambling. As a result, Latin businesspeople are not as interested in stable growth as U.S. businesspersons. Related to this is the Latin American tendency to let chance guide their destiny. Most are convinced that outside forces govern their lives. They are willing to "accept the inevitable." Don Quixote who followed his quest, whether or not it appeared hopeless, seems like a foolish man to many Americans; to most Latin Americans he is heroic. He was "bowing to fate," "taking what comes," "resigned to the inevitable." Their attitude is "what will be, will be, God willing."

Good Manners, Dignity, and Hospitality

Latin Americans are much like Europeans in this respect. They are more formal and more elaborate. They shake hands on meeting and departing. In Latin America, the work one does is directly related to the social class one is in, "high" or "low." Latin Americans are by and large stratified societies. They are born with a sense of place, but the two classes, very rich and very poor, are giving way to a growing and more affluent middle class.

Latin peoples have enriched cultures because of their skills in music, art, and architecture. At the same time, Latin Americans are warm, friendly, and hospitable. They like to talk, and want to know about a visitor's family and interests.

Human Resources—Authoritarianism/Egalitarianism

Aristocratic values, late industrialization, and strong central governments have combined to create an imbalance in employee needs of South America and the supply. Large numbers of South American

There is a boom or bust attitude.

workers have no industrial skills, while there is an oversupply of professional and white-collar workers, but an acute shortage of managers. Part of the problem lies in a centuries-old university curriculum with an overemphasis on lawyers and engineers; it is very much in need of modernization. The global market, foreign investments, and increases in high technologies are facilitating the emergence of a knowledge culture.

Signs of respect can be determined in both tone of voice and manner, denoting grades of inferiority and superiority in a hierarchical society. The *patron* is the man of power or wealth who sustains loyalty from those of lesser status. He can be the employer, the politico, the landowner, and in other cases the money lender or merchant. Authoritarianism does not allow for questioning. The *patron* knows everything and is all powerful. To play these roles, one has to be respectful in a subservient position. As the middle class continues to grow in size and strength, authoritarianism is less prevalent. Exhibit 12.10 describes the powerful man in business.

EXHIBIT 12.10
LATIN AMERICAN COMMERCIAL POWER BROKER

Carlos Slim is moving closer to dominating Latin America's telecom industry. The $360 million deal to buy a controlling stake in Embratel, Brazil's biggest long-distance provider, is an important step for the Americas' richest tycoon. Slim, owner of Mexico's main telecom firm, and of American Movil, its cellular operator, has plenty of cash and yearning to expand beyond a stagnant home market. In extending across Pan America, his Telemex recently bought AT&T Latin America for $207 million, allowing Slim to penetrate the Chilean, Peruvian, and Colombian telecom markets. Now with the acquisition of Embratel in Brazil, his revenues there will be $4 billion, making him a leading share owner of long-distance telephone and data markets. There has been speculation that this deal maker's next move will be to acquire Telemar, one of their big three fixed-line operators.

Slim is living up to his reputation for "buying assets on the cheap." With his acquisitions, this canny business leader is able not only to push up profits, but to offer corporate customers better mobile telephone services. This is a story of how mergers and acquisitions *within* the Americas are altering the traditional ways of commerce in the region. Obviously, the same thing is happening with foreign investors from outside Latin America.

Source: Adapted from "A Deal in Brazil—Slim Pickings," *The Economist*, March 20, 2004, p. 64.

Latin America is going through a social revolution in which agricultural and traditional societies are giving way to modern industrial and technological economies. The impact of Roman Catholicism is strong in the Latin cultures but lessening as a force in the daily lives of people, especially in the urban areas. The profound social and economic and political changes underway are altering many of the above customs and influences, especially among the younger generation. Democratization, world communications, international exchanges, and contemporary realities are transforming Latin America. Its global managers are sophisticated in the ways of international business and may not illustrate, at least on the surface, the typical social or cultural characteristics of the region.

Cross-cultural Communications in Latin America

Luiguiptre divinity is present throughout Latin America and Gordon has done extensive research to improve cross-cultural communications throughout the Americas, as the following excerpt emphasizes.

> The real difficulties in cross-cultural communications may be occurring because value systems are in conflict. While North and South Americans at a Pan-American conference, for instance, may be in agreement on general goals, the conflict might be anticipated in the means to achieve such goals. That is, the time, place, division of labor, sequence of actions, and other factors. When one is not open to consideration of the other's values, then emotions may rise and disagreements increase.[17]

For successful Pan American exchanges and collaboration, Gordon's research indicates that each party in the cross-cultural encounter must learn (a) to recognize symptoms of miscommunication in oneself and the other; (b) to separate fact, interpretation, and conclusion; (c) to derive silent assumptions about major premises in the interpretive process from the foreigner's minor premises and conclusions; and (d) to request information from the host-country citizen in such a way as not to bias or inhibit the response.

CHALLENGES FOR PAN AMERICAN COOPERATION

The prospects for Pan American synergy in the twenty-first century are encouraging. Inflation is still a major problem, coordination of economic policies is distant, but barriers to trade are being reduced and governments are committed to cutting fiscal deficits. There has also been relative peace between the nations of the Western Hemisphere, despite internal upheavals within various Latin American states.

The prospects for Pan American synergy in the twenty-first century are encouraging.

There have also been some noble efforts toward economic cooperation that lay the groundwork for real collaboration in the future. It takes time for such diverse cultures to learn the value and skills of joint endeavors. But the ground for synergy has been broken in such undertakings as the Organization of American States, the former Alliance for Progress, the North Atlantic Treaty Organization, the Central American Common Market, the Andean Pact, the North American Free Trade Agreement, and similar organizations. Now even the Central American states are exploring a regional trade agreement. In the global marketplace of the twenty-first century, emerging business opportunities will be found in Latin America. A strong synergistic indicator is MERCOSUR (Mercado Comun del Sur). MERCOSUR is a common market made up of Argentina, Brazil, Paraguay, Uruguay, Venzuela, with Chile as an associate member and Bolivia as a potential member. NAFTA is an open market of almost 400 million people, while MERCOSUR seeks to do something similar for its 240 million inhabitants. Meanwhile a revival is under way in the older ANDEAN Group composed of Venezuela, Colombia, Ecuador, and Peru. All such cooperative arrangements seek to collaborate in common economic nd trade policies that are more market friendly while reducing protectionism.[18]

A hopeful economic sign is the shift away from unilateral foreign aid to sharing of resources through multilateral institutions, such as the World Bank and the Inter-American Development Bank. Lately, the concerns of the various American nations have shifted more to the social arena with the establishment of such entities as the Inter-American Commission on Human Rights. Those with vision will set goals to close the Pan American poverty gap within the next 50 years.

Underlying all of Latin America's difficulties is the need for integral development in the areas of education, health care, and opportunities for self-development. The interdependence of North and Latin America and the need of one part of the hemisphere for the other are obvious. Economic development is now more horizontal in the Americas, and not just vertical.

Another reason for optimism about the future of relationships in the Americas is the accomplishments and prospects of the Pan American Development Foundation (PADF). Its objective is to help the lowest income people in Latin America and the Caribbean to participate productively in the socioeconomic and cultural development of their societies. PADF activates the local private sector, especially the business community, through the formation of national development foundations in the various countries.

"Synergizing" the Pan American potential presents a macromanagement challenge:

- To better manage the national resources of all states in the hemisphere by more effective collaboration of public and private sectors in each country, and between north/south regional relations.
- To manage the transfer of technology and information for mutual development of North and Latin American peoples.
- To contribute to the economic and social development of Latin America through the exercise of corporate social responsibility by multinational enterprises on both continents.

These days people in the United States, Canada, and Latin America are worrying about the same thing—each other. One mutual challenge is to build a better, fairer North and South America.[19] To be successful in the global marketplace, the Americas will have to trade effectively together with the nations of the European Union, the African Union, and ASEAN.

CONCLUSIONS

This chapter sought to give global managers an overview of the Western Hemisphere in terms of its diverse national cultures and their development, as well as present some problems and opportunities for synergy. Our review here underscores both the differences and similarities in the peoples and cultures of Mexico, Central America, and South America. (Chapter 16 on North America completes this hemispheric perspective.) To improve the quality of life for all of the Americas' inhabitants, effective and ecologically controlled utilization of resources on these twin continents is a major management challenge. Trained and experienced managers in transnational enterprises throughout Pan America may be able to accomplish in the decades ahead what politicians, dictators, revolutionaries, and soldiers have failed to accomplish in the past centuries—cooperation and collaboration for the common good. The potential of Latin America is finally beginning to be actualized.

The potential of Latin America is finally beginning to be actualized.

MIND STRETCHING

1. What is most striking to you about the contemporary development of Mexico?
2. Why do the Central American states need to finalize their negotiations for regional economic trade and development?

3. What is the significance of Portuguese culture and language in Brazil, in contrast to Spanish culture and language elsewhere in Latin America?
4. How do you envision the future of indigenous peoples or Amerindians in Latin America?
5. Why are North America, Europe, China, and Japan so interested in Latin America?

REFERENCES

1. Montaner, C. A. "Culture and the Behavior of Elites in Latin America," in Harrison, L. E. and Huntington, S. P. (eds.), *Culture Matters*. New York: Basic Books, 2000, pp. 57–58. Also refer to N. Chong and F. Baez, *Latino Culture—A Dynamic Force in the Changing American Workplace*. Boston: Nicholas Brealey/Intercultural Press, 2005.
2. Abbott, J. and Moran, R. T. *Uniting North American Business—NAFTA Best Practice*. Burlington, MA: Elsevier/Butterworth-Heinemann, 2002.
3. Condon, J. *Good Neighbors: Communicating with Mexicans*, 2d ed. Boston: Nicholas Brealey/Intercultural Press 1997; *Mexicans & Americans—Cracking the Cultural Code*. Boston: Nicholas Brealey/Intercultural Press, 2004.
4. Table based on selected observations from *Good Neighbors* by John Condon; *Distant Neighbors* by Alan Riding; *The United States and Latin America: Myths and Stereotypes of Civilization and Nature* by B. Pike; *Occupied America* by Rodolfo Acuña; *The Labyrinth of Solitude* by Octavio Paz; and *The Psychology of the Mexicans* by Rodolfo Diaz-Guerrero.
5. Elashmawi, F. and Harris, P. R. *Multicultural Management 2000*, 2d ed. Burlington, MA: Elsevier/Butterworth-Heinemann/Gulf Publishing, 1998.
6. Abbott and Moran, *Uniting North American Business*.
7. Kras, E. *Management in Two Cultures*. Boston: Nicholas Brealey/Intercultural Press, 1995; *Understanding Spanish-Speaking South Americans: Bridging Hemispheres*. Boston: Nicholas Brealey/Intercultural Press, 2003.
8. Moran and Abbott, *Uniting North American Business*. Butterworth: Heinemann.
9. Paige, J. *Democracy in Central America*. Cambridge, MA: Harvard University Press, 1998.
10. "The Crossover Queen," *The Economist*, July 23, 2005, p. 62.
11. "Together Again, After all These Years?," *The Economist*, May 14, 2005, p. 41.
12. Rodriguez, R. *Los Angeles Times*, Improving Latin American Relations, August 13, 1989.

13. Axtell, Roger E. *Do's and Taboos around the World*, 3d ed. White Plains, NY: Benjamin Company, 1993; Axtell, Roger E. *Gestures: The Do's and Taboo's of Body Language Around the World*. Hoboken NY: John Wiley & Sons, 1998; Burns, Bradford. *A History of Brazil*, 2d ed. New York: Columbia University Press, 1980; Collins, Peter. "Make or Break: A Survey of Brazil," *The Economist*, February 22, 2003, pp. 1–14; Copeland, Lennie and Lewis Griggs. *Going International: How to Make Friends and Deal Effectively in the Global Marketplace*. New York: Random House, 1985; Eakin, Marshall. *Brazil: The Once and Future Country*. New York: St. Martin's Griffin, 1998; Morrison, Terri, Wayne A. Conaway, and George A. Borden, Ph.D. *Kiss, Bow, or Shake Hands: How to Do Business in Sixty Countries*. Holbrook, MA: Adams Media Corporation, 1994; Page, Joseph A. *The Brazilians*. Reading, MA: Perseus Books, 1995.
14. Colott, R. and Lapper, R. "Long Road to Power That Began in the Back of a Truck," *Financial Times*, September 28, 2002, p. 22.
15. Adapted from Harris, P. R. and Elashmawi, F. *Multicultural Management 2000—Essential Cultural Insights for Business Success.* "The Case for Argentina," Burlington, MA: Elsevier/Butterworth/Heinemann/Gulf Publishing, 1998, pp. 281–284.
16. Lanier, A. *Living in Latin America*. Boston: Nicholas Brealey/Intercultural Press, 1988.
17. Gordon, R. *Living in Latin America*. Skokie, IL: National Textbook, 1976.
18. Elashmawi, F. and Harris, P. R. *Multicultural Management 2000*, 2d ed. Burlington, MA: Elsevier/Butterworth-Heinemann, 1998. Refer to Elashmawi, F. *Competing Globally*, 2001, by the same publisher.
19. Stephenson, S. *Understanding Spanish-Speaking South Americans*. Boston: Nicholas Brealey/Intercultural Press, 2003.

USEFUL INTERNET WEB SITES

After http:// and or www.
Tradeport.org/ts/ (enter name of Latin American country for trade information)
mera.com (country business guides)
eiu.com (country name)
living.abroad.com/ (country profiles)
businessculture.com/
expatexchange.com/
cia.gov/LatinAmerica/
ibge.gov.br
lanic.utexas.edu
google.com/ (enter name of Latin American country)

DOING BUSINESS WITH ASIANS AND AUSTRALIANS

Australia, China, India, Indonesia, Japan, Malaysia, Singapore, Pakistan, Philippines, South Korea, Taiwan, Thailand, and Vietnam

Home to nearly two-fifths of humanity, two neighboring countries, India and China, are two of the world's fastest growing economies. The world is taking notice. . . . But India and China, always different, have followed different paths to growth.[1]

LEARNING OBJECTIVES

This chapter focuses on the scope, diversity, and opportunities within the Asian or Pacific Rim region. It begins with an overview of Pacific Basin countries and presents demographics on six Central Asian nations of growing economic importance. Then it examines in some depth, a dozen cultures and business climates of the principal Asia "players" within the global marketplace, especially China, India, and Japan.

Many Asian countries over the past several decades have increasingly experienced the benefits of a market economy over ideology. For some, such as China and Vietnam, this change is new; for others, like Australia and Japan, it is not.

Asia is a continent bounded by Europe, and the Arctic, Pacific, and Indian Oceans. Sometimes referred to as the Far East, its almost 2

Asia/Australia

billion inhabitants are dispersed over 16 million square miles. Exhibit 13.1 provides a visual overview of the area under consideration. It is a place of increasing importance to global managers as a trade shift occurs from the Atlantic to the Pacific. One world leader referred to the next century as "The Century of the Pacific"; if that forecast is valid, then the information in this chapter takes on increasing importance. For example, at the end of the twentieth century, China and India were classified as developing countries and economies. By the end of the twenty-first century, China may be a new superpower with India not far beyond. One indicator is that by the year 2020, China's GNP is expected to exceed the United States' GNP by 40%.[2] Another prediction is that in the emerging world economy, the balance of power will shift to the East, as the economies of China and India grow.

Before such optimistic scenarios can be realized, however, there are regional realities to be confronted. In the early 1990s, many Asian countries achieved spectacular economic growth as their affluence and middle-class population increased. By 1998, many of these same nations were facing social instability as a result of an "economic meltdown" caused by an undermining of their financial, banking, and even political systems. In the opening of the twenty-first century, there are again positive economic signs in most Asian countries, but political uncertainty remains between North and South Korea, and between India and Pakistan. Matlock states:

> The claim that Asia's recent economic success resulted from a specific Asian virtue has suffered a severe blow since the monetary and economic setbacks. . . . What brought rapid economic development to the "Asian tigers" was the same thing that brought it to countries elsewhere: capitalism, hard work, frugality, and limited government. There was no Asian miracle; if economic development was more rapid in some Asian countries than it had been in the West, that was because modern technology and communication have accelerated the process of change and because these countries were playing catch-up. It takes longer for pioneers to clear the way than for late starters to follow a well-marked trail.[3]

To appreciate the general cultural differences between most Asian countries and America, consider Exhibit 13.1. Schnitzer, Liebranz, and Kubin[4] have assembled an introduction to our main topic, contrasting the principal cultural differences of Asians in general with those of Americans. Readers are encouraged to expand this listing based on their experience, readings, Internet search.

EXHIBIT 13.1
ASIAN AND AMERICAN CULTURAL CONTRASTS

Asian Countries

- Equity is more important than wealth.
- Saving and conserving resources is highly valued.
- Group is the most important part of society and is emphasized for motivation.
- Cohesive and strong families, and ties often extend to distant relatives—even the nation and its leaders. Relationship society with strong network of social ties.
- Highly disciplined and motivated workforce/societies.
- Education is an investment in the prestige and economic well-being of the family.
- Protocol, rank, and status are important.
- Personal conflicts are to be avoided (e.g., few lawyers).
- Public service is a moral responsibility.

The United States

- Wealth is more important than equity.
- Consumption is highly valued; awareness of conservation is growing.
- Individual is the most important part of society and the person is emphasized for motivation; although team emphasis is growing.
- Nuclear and mobile family. Experimentation with new home/housing/commune living communities of nonrelatives. Fluid society that de-emphasizes strong social ties.
- Decline in the "Protestant work ethic" and hierarchy.
- Education is an investment in personal development/success.
- Informality and competence is important.
- Conflict is energy to be managed—many lawyers.
- Distrust of big government and bureaucracy.

CENTRAL AND SOUTH ASIAN COUNTRIES

The Far East has a diversity of peoples and cultures in various stages of economic and technological development. For example, approximately half of the human race inhabits Asia, while one-fourth of the world's population alone lives in the People's Republic of China. Asia is so large in terms of geography and human and natural resources, and has such disparate business practices, that total coverage for all the cultures in the region is impossible here. Before beginning our in-depth cultural analysis of the principal nations targeted for this chapter, we

The Far East has a diversity of peoples and cultures in various stages of economic and technological development.

begin with an introduction of six selected neighboring countries in Central and South Asia. Some of the countries were formerly part of the old Soviet Empire (USSR) and are now independent. All of them have important natural resources that Western and other Asian businesspersons are beginning to discover. They will become more prominent on the world stage later in the twenty-first century and the next. Exhibit 13.2 offers a quick overview of these peoples and their homeland. They have been arranged alphabetically, starting with war-ravaged Afghanistan, which is in the process of being rebuilt as a society, so statistics are approximate. Bordering on India are Pakistan and then Bangladesh, which was once part of that country—both will be covered later. Again, note the populations and landmass of each and compare literacy, life expectancy, and per capita income.

To underscore the importance of this region and prevent it from falling again into geopolitical oblivion, *The Economist* (July 27, 2003) published a survey on Central Asia in which it stated:

> **Bumpy Silk Road**—Central Asia is strategically placed at the crossroads between Europe and China, Russia and Iran. Throughout its history, this has been both a blessing and a curse. Trade between West and East moved through Central Asia along the famed Silk Road, bringing development and prosperity. But the region was also repeatedly

EXHIBIT 13.2

PROFILES OF AFGHANISTAN, KAZAKHSTAN, KYRGYZSTAN, TAJIKISTAN, TURKMENISTAN, UZBEKISTAN

NATION	Afghanistan	Kazakhstan	Kyrgyzstan	Tajikistan	Turkmenistan	Uzbekistan
AREA (sq km)	647,500	2,716,998	198,999	143,100	488,000	447,400
POPULATION	29,928,987	15,185,844	5,146,281	7,163,506	4,952,081	26,851,195
CAPITAL	Kabul	Astana	Bishkek	Dushanbe	Ashgabat	Tashkent
RELIGION	Sunni/Shite Muslim	Muslim, Russian Orthodox, Protestant	Muslim, Russian Orthodox	Sunni/Shite Muslim	Muslim, Eastern Orthodox	Muslim, Eastern Orthodox
LANGUAGE	Afghan, Persian, Dari, Pashtu, Uzbek, Turkmen, 30 minor	Kazakh, Russian	Kyrgyz, Russian	Tajik, Russian	Turkmen, Russian, Uzbek	Uzbek, Russian, Tajik
LITERACY	36%	98.4%	98.7%	99.4%	98.8%	99.3%
LIFE EXPECTANCY	42.9 years	66.55 years	68.16 years	64.56 years	61.39 years	64.19 years
GDP PER CAPITA	$800	$8,700	$1,800	$1,200	$5,900	$1,900
GOVERNMENT	Islamic Republic	Republic	Republic	Republic	Republic	Republic

invaded by powerful conquerors with imperial ambitions, from the Scythes and Mongols to the Russians. . . .

Although Central Asia shares a common history and culture, there are plenty of differences among the constituent parts. . . . The cultural split in the region is between nomads from the steppes and mountains, mainly Kirgizs, Kasakhs, and Turkmens, and the sedentary, mainly urban Uzbeks and Tajiks who settled in the river basins of Transoxania. The split was responsible for distinct cultural, religious, and political identities that survive to this day. The split ignores borders. Today's Central Asian states were Soviet creations which, before 1991, had no history as separate independent countries. . . . They were also saddled with large ethnic minorities. Today because of their oil resources, this group of nations have very important strategic value. In this post-Soviet era, they are struggling to become more democratic and less totalitarian.

AUSTRALIA

EXHIBIT 13.3

AUSTRALIA—PROFILE

Population	20,090,437 (July 2005 est.)
Ethnic groups	Caucasian, 92%; Asian, 7%; Aboriginal and other, 1%
Religions	Catholic, 26.4%; Anglican, 20.5%; other Christian, 20.5%; Buddhist, 1.9%; Muslim, 1.5%; other, 1.2%; unspecified, 12.7%; none, 15.3% (2001 Census)
Education	100% literacy rate
Land	7,686,850 sq km
Government	Commonwealth of Australia
Political Parties	Australian Democrats, Australian Labor Party, Australian Progressive Alliance, Australian Greens, Liberal Party, The Nationals, One Nation Party, Family First Party
Exports to U.S.	Total exports = $103 billion U.S. accounts for 8.1% Total exports to U.S. = $8.3 billion (2005 est.)
Imports from U.S.	Total imports = $119.6 billion U.S. accounts for 14.8% Total imports from U.S. = $17.7 billion (2005 est.)

While Australia is its own continent and not a predominantly Asian nation, it is frequently associated with the economies of the Asia/Pacific Basin region.[5]

Australia is both the largest island and the smallest continent in the world, located in the Pacific Ocean. It is surrounded by smaller islands and seas—Timor and Arafura in the north, Coral on the east, and the Indian Ocean in the south. Its landmass is millions of years old,

Australia is both the largest island and the smallest continent in the world.

relatively arid with varied climatic zones and diverse ecology. Off the northeast of Queensland lies the Great Barrier Reef, the world's largest coral reef. The country is part of Oceania, all the islands of Central and South Pacific. The nation's capital is Canberra, and its major cities are Sydney, Melbourne, Brisbane, Perth, and Adelaid.

Historical Perspective

The original inhabitants of Australia were the Aborigines.

The original inhabitants of Australia were the Aborigines, who arrived some 50,000 years ago by raft across the waters separating the continent from the Indonesia archipelago. Portuguese, Spanish, Dutch, and English explorers observed the land throughout the 1600s, but it remained undisturbed for the most part until the next century. In 1770, Captain James Cook explored the east coast and claimed the entire continent for the British Empire, naming it "New South Wales." The first fleet of British settlers arrived in Sydney in 1778 under the command of Captain Arthur Philip, who founded penal colonies in Sydney, Brisbane, and Hobart. Thus, the first European settlers in Australia were solely convicts or soldiers, usually of British or Irish origin. Systematic colonization was sustained by sheep ranching and grain farming.

With the discovery of gold in 1851, the number of immigrants increased dramatically, generating high growth and trade. This environment resulted in unprecedented wealth and stability into the twentieth century. In 1901, the six established colonies—New South Wales, Tasmania, Western Australia, South Australia, Victoria, and Queensland—agreed to federate as the Commonwealth of Australia, under British law. The first federal parliament was opened at Melbourne in May 1901. The seat of government was later transferred to Canberra, a city designed by American Walter Burley Griffin in May 1927. Australia gained complete autonomy from Britain in both internal and external affairs when the Statute of Westminster Adoption Act passed in 1942.

Australia strengthened its ties with the United States during World War II. Since that conflict, Australia has played an active role in world politics and maintained friendly relations with the United States, including sending troops to assist the Americans fighting in Vietnam and Iraq. The ANZUS security treaty, signed in 1952 between Australia, New Zealand, and the United States, continues to be supported despite opposition from New Zealand on nuclear issues.

Australia dominates economically all of Oceania and is a supplier of raw materials to other Pacific Rim countries, as well as an importer of finished products. Increased trading with Asian nations, especially Japan, has resulted in a high standard of living for this industrialized country. Exports have been constrained only by inadequate infrastructure, such as rail systems and port loaders. In 2005, this nation celebrated 15 successive years of continuous economic growth, enjoying low inflation and unemployment, as well as a budget surplus. In 2006, a rail line was opened to connect the continent's northern and southern cities. No longer a captive to the "tyranny of isolation," today Australia has a booming tourist industry, especially for Chinese and other foreign visitors to its Great Barrier Reef. It is also a business hub for the Asia-Pacific region, and target for foreign investment.

Australian Governance

Australia is the sixth largest country in the world, and it is only a little smaller than the continental United States. It is also the only country in the world to make up an entire continent surrounded by water—the Indian and Pacific Oceans, as well as the Southern Ocean and the Coral Tasman Sea. Known until recently as the Commonwealth of Australia, it was subject to the British monarchy, which had formal executive power exercised by a governor-general. It is now an independent federation with an elected prime minister and federal Parliament. The Parliament consists of a House of Representatives, which has 147 members, and a Senate, which has 76 members. Australia includes six federal states, Canberra the national capital, and three territories. Each state has a governor and its own legislative, judicial, and executive system. Although the states enjoy great autonomy, national law overrides all state laws where they conflict. This is a successful democracy with political stability, a good legal system, and a most resilient economy.

Cultural Guidelines for Doing Business in Australia

The current population of Australia is approximately 20 million and is growing at a rate of 1% a year. More than 85% of all households live in urban areas, mostly along the coastal regions. Sydney, Australia's largest city, accounts for approximately 4 million people. Close to 40% of all people live in Sydney or Melbourne. Approximately one-third of all Australians are younger than 20 years, accounting for a very young population. One in four Australians was born outside the continent, making it a polyglot country.

More than 92% of all Australians descend from European ancestry, including Dutch, Estonian, French, German, Greek, Italian, Latvian, Lithuanian, Polish, and Yugoslavian. Increasingly, people from Asian origins immigrate here and compose 7% of the population, including Polynesian, Vietnamese, and Cambodian nationalities. The remaining 1% of Australians are the Aborigines, the original inhabitants of Australia. The country seems more at ease with new arrivals than with its first inhabitants.

Aborigines have a very distinct culture, which, at one time, was almost completely destroyed by Caucasian Australians. However, these

More than 92% of all Australians descend from European ancestry.

Aborigines hold a distinct spiritual link to the land on which they live.

people are an important part of Australian history, and many attempts are being made to preserve and cultivate this culture. The Aborigines hold a distinct spiritual link to the land on which they live. This relationship guides their entire lives as they remain in harmony with the land. The family is the center of Aborigine society, which is a very complex one. However, ceremonies, traditions, and social obligations help the Aborigines feel like they are one with each other and the land. Australians accept that a terrible injustice was done to the Aborigines but still have not worked out the type of restitution beyond granting certain rights to "native title," a groundbreaking legal decision in 1992 by the Australian High Court. Meanwhile, the indigenous people themselves are moving toward "mainstream" life, electing their members to state and federal parliaments. Many celebrities in the performing arts are also Aborigines.

Although Australia is known as a peaceful, multicultural society, in 1998, an unknown retailer, Pauline Hanson, won a seat in the federal Parliament and founded a political party, One Nation, which complained that government was favoring Aborigines over white people and the country was being swamped by Asians. This movement faded, and in 2005, Australia admitted 120,000 immigrants, a third from Asia, and 12,000 refugees. These newcomers helped to relieve a rising labor shortage. With minimal racism, the city of Melbourne has become a showcase of multiculturalism with a lord mayor, John So, born in Hong Kong. With the culture constantly shifting, the Australian Ministry of Immigration, Multicultural and Indigenous Affairs is promoting diversity research. For example, it presently has a study under way on "The Effectiveness of Cross-cultural Training" (contact project manager EM: rsbean@bigpond.com). Population forecasts are for 100 million by midcentury.

Education, free to all, is compulsory from age 6 to 15. Children who live in the Outback can receive schooling via two-way radio. About one-fourth of all Australian children attend private schools. All states have public universities. The school year has four quarters, with three vacation breaks in April, July, and October. Most Australians have completed 11 years of schooling, indicating that they have finished compulsory education and high school. The literacy rate is 99%.

English is the official language of Australia, but many immigrant groups continue to speak their native tongues at home. The Aborigines, who once spoke over 250 working languages, teach only the remaining 50 or so that survived. Because of this loss, the government has started placing greater emphasis on the revival of Aborigine languages. The Aborigine culture stress is learning the Aborigine language first and the English language second. They also have their own radio system, which broadcasts programs and music in many Aborigine languages. As a result, many Aborigine families are now beginning to speak traditional languages at home.

The English that Australians speak is quite similar to the Queen's English and many expressions are British origin English; however, many Australian expressions sprinkle the vocabulary, resulting in a very unique language. For example, the following phrases and words are commonly heard: no worries, mate (no problem, guy); rubbish (trash or garbage); over the road (across the street); rubber (eraser); mate (male friend); biscuits (cookies); chemist (drugstore); and bonnet (the hood of a car). Furthermore, colloquialisms dot the language, including the following: spot on (right on); bingle ("fender-bender"); dinky-di (something genuine); and like a possum up a gum tree (to say someone is moving fast). It is also typically Australian to shorten words, such as uni (university), kindi (kindergarten), and teli (television), or to add an ie to the end; for example, barbecue is barbie, and mosquito is mozzie. Since some Australian slang might insult other non-Australian English speakers and vice versa, it is important to speak Standard English (without using expressions and colloquialisms). The Australians also tend to be very direct in their statements, which results in many strangers, including Americans, feeling attacked when told, for example, "you don't know what you're talking about." The inhabitants call themselves "Aussies." The foreigner will gain much respect, however, if he or she counterattacks but does not try to seek approval or run from the argument.

Customs and Courtesies

Australians are generally easygoing and friendly. Most Australians greet friends with either a firm, friendly handshake or a "G'day," but do not appreciate zealous visitors who constantly overuse the latter. More formal greetings might include a simple "hello, how are you?" style of greeting, but do not have the formal British reserve of their ancestors. It is customary for men to shake hands at the beginning and end of a meeting, but women are not required to do so; instead, they are more inclined to give each other a kiss on the cheek in greeting and leaving. It is quite acceptable for visitors to introduce themselves in social environments without waiting to be introduced by someone else. If friends see each other from a distance, the customary greeting is a wave, not yelling, as this type of behavior is considered impolite.

In an Australian business setting, it is appropriate to offer your business card, but do not be surprised if you do not receive one in return, since many Australian businesspeople do not carry them. When introduced in initial greetings, Australians may address someone with their full name or say "sir" as a sign of respect. However, Australians are quick to switch to an informal first-name basis, and visitors may do so if an Australian initiates this cue. . . . There are some basic rules of etiquette in Australia, which include the following:

Australians are generally easygoing and friendly.

- Men should not wink at a woman, even if they are friends, as this is considered inappropriate behavior.
- Yawning in public is considered rude.
- Men should not behave too physically with each other as this may imply unmanliness.
- The American gesture for "2," forming a "v" with the index and middle finger of one hand is considered vulgar.
- Another rude gesture is the "OK" or hitchhiking sign used frequently in the United States.
- You should avoid using the term *stuffed* or *rooting* (for the home team), since both of these terms have vulgar connotations.
- Like the British, respect is given for lines of people, or queues; therefore, never cut in line. Instead go politely to the end, and wait your turn.
- Sportsmanlike gestures of any kind are appreciated since good sportsmanship is highly respected.
- Guests of honor usually sit next to the host on the right side.
- In some Australian pubs, finishing a drink, turning the glass upside down, and setting it on the pub counter is a sign that you can out-drink anyone else in the house.
- When addressing audiences, one should stand erect and use modest body language.

Australians stated on p. 407 have a good sense of humor, even in tense situations. Most use their hands and nonverbal gestures to emphasize and clarify their speech. They are quite open about expressing their feelings, although men still are not very emotional due to the stigma of appearing feminine.

Australians speak frankly and directly; they dislike pretensions of any kind and will not shy away from disagreement. They generally dislike class structure and differences, which may result in someone sitting next to a cab driver if alone. Close friendships are valued highly and have a somewhat different connotation than friendship in the United States. Australia is a clean country and the citizens respect these standards. Fines are quite high if one is caught littering.

Business attire, however, is very conservative.

Australians tend to dress like Americans and Europeans (i.e., quite informally). Business attire, however, is very conservative. Men typically wear a dark suit and tie, while women wear a dress or skirt and blouse. Regardless of occasion, clothing is never tattered or sloppy and is respectable in public. Wearing clothes with holes or in the wrong size is considered inappropriate. Women tend to wear pants much less frequently than in the United States, and many people wear hats in the summer as protection from the sun. Since Australia is located in the

Southern Hemisphere, the seasons are the exact opposite of North America.

Australia is a land of warm, cordial people, who enjoy life and "work to live," not "live to work." There is a close Australian-U.S. relationship, which covers the spectrum of commercial and cultural contacts to political and defense cooperation. Companies wishing to conduct business in Australia will find relatively few obstacles, especially since the successful conclusion of the General Agreement on Tariffs and Trade Uruguay Round of trade liberalization. However, it is important to remember that while Australians speak English and seem to behave like Americans, differences in language and culture do exist, and should be both respected and appreciated. This respect will result in cementing an already friendly relationship with Australians, as well as lead to success in business.

Overall, Australia is rated as having a desirable business environment with a bright outlook for economic growth. It is attractive to foreign investors because of its robust legal system, transparent and effective government, and well-educated, multilingual workforce.

Australian territory extends south to the large island of Tasmania; southwest New Zealand and northeast Papua New Guineas are its nearest neighbors.

NEW ZEALAND

This beautiful country consists of two large North and South Islands of some 835 square miles, located between the Tasman Sea and the Pacific Ocean. Its population of nearly 4 million is largely Christian, and the people call themselves "Kiwis" after their national bird. While they share many cultural similarities with Australians (e.g., British origins and settlers who share English as the principal language), there are many differences. New Zealanders tend to be more conservative, industrious, and rural. The indigenous people are the Maori who have their own official language. Their largest city and capital is Wellington with about 350,000 inhabitants. With a 99% literacy rate and life expectancy averaging 79 years, as well as spectacular scenery, it is an attractive site for tourists, and for the film industry. Its per capita income is approximately $18,000, in contrast to Australia's $23,000 a year. A stable government stimulates an expanding economy featuring food processing, wood and paper products, textiles, and machinery manufacturing, as well as agriculture centered on sheep and wool, plus wheat, barley, potatoes, dairy products, and fish.

New Zealanders tend to be more conservative, industrious, and rural.

EXHIBIT 13.4
PEOPLE'S REPUBLIC OF CHINA—PROFILE

Population	1,306,313,812 (July 2005 est.)
Ethnic groups	Han Chinese, 91.9%; Zhuang, Uygur, Hui, Yi, Tibetan, Miao, Manchu, Mongol, Buyi, Korean, and other nationalities, 8.1%
Religions	Daoist (Taoist), Buddhist, Muslim 1%–2%; Christian 3%–4% *note*: officially atheist (2002 est.)
Education	90.9% literacy rate
Land	9,326,410 sq km
Government	Communist state
Political Parties	Chinese Communist Party (CCP), 8 registered minor parties controlled by CCP
Per capita income	$6,200 (2005 est.)
Exports to U.S.	Total exports = $752.2 billion U.S. accounts for 21.1% Total exports to U.S. = $158.7 billion (2005 est.)
Imports from U.S.	Total imports = $631.8 billion U.S. accounts for 8% Total imports from U.S. = $50.5 billion (2005 est.)

Those responsible for managing China's industry have had their world turned upside down. Old certainties have been eroded, and new challenges have emerged.[6] China's accession to the World Trade Organization in December 2001, a milestone in its reintegration with the global economy, is beginning to change the economic landscape of East Asia and to have a profound impact not only on China and East Asia, but the rest of the world.[7]

China and India—rarely has the ascent of two relatively poor nations been watched with such a mixture of awe, opportunism, and trepidation. They possess the weight and dynamism to transform the twenty-first-century global economy.[8]

China is on the western seaboard of the Pacific Ocean, south of Russia, with the Himalayan Mountains separating it from India. Almost 10 million square kilometers in landmass, the country is dominated by mountain ranges, broad plains, expansive deserts, and numerous rivers—Huang He (Yellow River) in the north, Yangtze in the central area, and Xijiang River in the south. Beijing is the capital, and other major cities are Shanghai, Tianjin, Guangzhou, and Shenzhen.

For millennia, the Chinese have had high self-esteem and pride in their society and history. Appropriately, the name of their ancient

Chinese have had high self-esteem and pride in their society and history.

country translates as "center of the world"—their image of themselves, their country, and culture is as the center of human civilization. For centuries, they have expected all other peoples and nations to pay tribute to them and their unique culture, which has been so influenced by Confucianism, Taoism, and Buddhism.

Throughout the history of this civilization, Chinese agriculture and handicrafts have been renowned for their high level of development, producing notable thinkers, scientists, inventors, statesmen, authors, and artists. There the art of papermaking was discovered 1800 years ago; printing was invented over 1300 years ago; and movable type 800 years ago. The Chinese writing system, which has lasted for more than 3000 years, spanning generations, has helped unify China, its culture and tradition. Not only has China one of the oldest civilizations in the world, but it has influenced countless others, including Japan, Korea, and Vietnam. People of Chinese descent live all over the planet and are now moving into outer space. They represent a culture that transcends the individual and favors group initiative.

Within this context, foreigners do business within a modern and changing China. For example, its 2001 entry into the World Trade Organization expanded business opportunities and increased trade volume. Progress can be seen in major projects like the Three Gorges Dam on the Yangtze River; the world's largest bridge (36 kilometers), across the Gulf of Hangzhou from Ningbo to Shanghai; very modern industrial parks; and affluent home developments around its major cities. In 2008, Beijing will host the Olympic Games, which will redefine the country's international image. The capital city is spending $13 billion on its transformation to "wow the world." In 2010, ambitious Shanghai will be the site of the World Expo; its futuristic plans can be seen in the Urban Planning Exhibition Hall, including nine planned communities, each of which will house 800,000 residents. That dynamic urban area hopes to "become a global mecca of knowledge workers."

Historical Perspective

China's history can be traced to many centuries B.C., beginning with the first emperor, Fu Xi. The history that followed included feudalism, which hindered China's economic and political development. Once a leader in oceangoing exploration and trade, Zheng Ho, a Muslim of Mongolian ancestry, had led the largest fleet ever assembled on seven expeditions from 1405 to 1433 throughout the Indian Ocean. With some 317 huge ships with up to 30,000 diplomats and troops, he projected China's power, wealth, and influence for political and trade purposes as far as India until a new emperor, Hung-shi, put an end to these voyages. For more than 2300 years, China generally isolated itself behind the Great Wall, forcing most traders and merchants to remain

China's history can be traced to many centuries B.C.

outside. From the Ming Dynasty (fourteenth century) until the 1950s, it sought to close itself to the rest of the world, despite incursions by Western and Japanese imperialism—sources of great humiliation for the Chinese.

In 1949, following the revolution and the establishment of the People's Republic of China (PRC), the Communist Party attempted to change the basic attitudes, values, and behavior of the Chinese people, including both verbal and written language. Its chairman Mao Zedong and his reformers gave the country a new direction, transforming a traditional feudalistic society into a modern socialistic one. With his death in 1976, China's new leader Deng Xiaoping realized that economic progress required infusions of Western technology and skills, opening possibilities for investors who would move China economically forward. On January 1, 1979, full diplomatic relations between the People's Republic of China and the United States of America were established; soon embassies of the United States and the PRC opened in Beijing and Washington, respectively. Since that time a great deal of water has flowed along the Yangtze River, while the number of businesspeople and others visiting mainland China has steadily increased.

Since 1949, two major negative events in Chinese history occurred: the Great Leap Forward in the late 1950s and the Cultural Revolution in the late 1960s. During these two periods, economic efficiency and social order were forsaken as the country embarked on major new programs that were designed to eliminate "revisionist" elements and to illustrate to the people the importance of their role.[9] By mid-1985, Deng Xiaoping had inaugurated campaigns for modernization and economic reform, even encouraging entrepreneurialism and replacing senior party leaders with younger officials. To deter democratization, sad and traumatic events of suppression occurred in 1989, including the riots in Tiananmen Square that have been described as the "great leap backward." In the twenty-first century, the Chinese leadership is moving quickly toward a market economy where individual enterprise is becoming a norm. Necessary legal supports and financial reforms are following very slowly, inhibiting economic development.

The political and military leadership seemingly operates by consensus, especially to ensure economic reform and political stability. In practice, however, the CCP officials make the major decisions. Ministries and/or standing committees of the National People's Congress, the legislature, formulate policy on both long-term and daily issues. Some provincial governors, especially in fast-growing coastal regions, may adopt policy variations. Despite a strong president who is also head of the party, it would appear that China is moving toward collective leadership rather than leadership under one predominant figure. Economically, the country's huge domestic market and tolerance of entrepreneurship gives China global bargaining power that attracts foreign investment.

In the twenty-first century, the Chinese leadership is moving quickly toward a market economy where individual enterprise is becoming a norm.

Sociopolitical Insights

Presently, the People's Republic of China is governed under a constitution formally adopted in 1982. Under its provisions, the highest order of state power is the National People's Congress (NPC). Deputies are elected from every region in China for five-year terms. The NPC then elects the head of state, the president of China. They also elect the State Council that administers the country. The State Council comprises the premier, two vice premiers, ministers, and heads of various state agencies. The Chinese Communist Party controls all government functions. Recently, the people have been permitted to elect local town officials. Although the country's political leaders call themselves communists, they are increasingly acting like capitalists, as Exhibit 13.5 indicates.

Today, China's priority is to restructure state-owned enterprises (SOE) established in the 1960s. Many SOEs have reorganized as commercial, stockholding companies. However, because of this change, SOE employees have dropped by 20 million and overall unemployment has increased. Because China's economic future is so dependent on SOE reform, the government is giving this top priority for the next five years, as state business entities seek to make a mark on world commerce. The aim is to ensure the state's more effective control over the economy, so political, not management, skills are more important in these undertakings. Thus, only 11 such Chinese organizations have made it into the *Forbes 500* list of top global firms measured in terms of revenues produced. Within an intensively political culture, Chinese banks are an appendage to government, seen as massive, bureaucratic and more supportive of state companies (half of their loans go to them). Therefore, the SOEs virtually crowd out the private business sector, threatening the entire financial system. But within that business climate, entrepreneurial activities emerge and expand.

Eleven such Chinese organizations have made it into the Forbes *500 list.*

While the northeast is home to hulking state industries and socialism, the south along the coast is a capitalist heartland, especially Zhejiang where the per capita annual income is the third highest in the country and its inhabitants earn twice as much as those in the north. Sixty-two of China's wealthiest citizens have homes there. Ninety-one percent of its 240,000 enterprises are privately owned with annual revenues of 700 billion yuan. There an entrepreneurial trading heritage combines with family-controlled businesses, which are taking the global markets by storm. The city of Wenzhou alone is home to 3000 small firms that club together in flexible production and create real wealth. People here believe in Chairman Deng's exhortation—*to get rich is glorious, and to be a wealth creator is morally uplifting*! No wonder this is a culture that rarely transcends the individual. Exhibit 13.5 tells one story of Chinese entrepreneurs.

EXHIBIT 13.5

PIONEERING ENTREPRENEUR AND CAPITALIST

The 2005 obituary of Rong Yiren was a unique account of a Chinese anomaly about the scion of a family commercial empire founded in 1902. His death at 69 raised the question of how this Chinese billionaire who was not a known member of the Communist Party ever became vice president of the People's Republic and twice chairman of the National People's Congress. More intriguing is how he managed to regain his wealth after ceding his family's business holdings after the 1949 revolution and losing the rest during the Cultural Revolution of 1966–1976. Yet, within a decade or so, he arose as one of the 50 most charismatic businessmen in the world and one of its richest by a 1999 reckoning of *Fortune* Magazine. All this despite his family fleeing to Taiwan and the United States, leaving him in midcentury to run 24 flour mills, textile, and printing plants employing 80,000.

Mr. Rong presented himself as a "patriotic" capitalist who remained to help China end its poverty by shifting to a market economy. When he gave the party what it wanted, he subtly asked for a favor in return. The astute and handsome executive not only survived, but along the way became vice mayor of Shanghai, in 1959, vice minister for the textile industry. Through *guanxi* or personal connections, he positioned himself to creatively help Deng Xiaoping open windows to the capitalist world. Educated under the British system at Shanghai's St. John's University, this graduate became Deng's symbol of the new Chinese entrepreneur.

In 1979 at the party's behest, he founded CITIC as an investment arm of the state to acquire telecoms, utilities, and highways. When a Special Economic Zone was established in southern China for foreign investments, CITIC was there to exploit the property boom. Rong, roving extensively, found the foreign concerns willing to invest in China and lured them to the Zone. This handsome, sophisticated executive did well for his country and himself. In year 2000, *Forbes* estimated the wealth of Rong and his son, Larry Yung now head of CITC-Pacific, to be $1.9 billion. Their conglomerate boasts global assets of $6.3 billion and includes 200 affiliated enterprises. And in the process China has been moving steadily toward a free-enterprise system!

Source: Adapted from "Obituary—Rong Yiren," *The Economist*, November 15, 2005, p. 94.

There is a big income disparity between rural and urban areas, which the government is trying hard to address. Several coastal cities have a GDP per capita of almost US$5000 per year, while the interior of China, which is more underdeveloped, remains below US$400 per year. The government agreed in 2001 to strict World Trade Organization entry terms and is also encouraging private companies to compete with state-owned enterprises for markets and resources. China's main exporters are the United States, Hong Kong, and Japan, and their leading suppliers are Japan, South Korea, and Taiwan.

The country boasts of stability and potential while developing the fastest growing economy in the world. China's major cities are highly desirable target markets densely populated by consumers with large disposable incomes. The country has 170 cities with populations exceeding 1 million. Cities that are especially promising are Beijing, Shanghai, and Guangzhou.[10]

There has been some progress in modernization and economic liberalization along with some economic setbacks. Yet the gross domestic product has expanded at an average of 9% a year. Within two decades it is forecast that the mass of Chinese will become consumers in the international sense as the middle class emerges.

Chinese manufacturers suck up imports, dictating global prices in everything from steel to microchips. While the central government would like to lower trade barriers and increase competition, provincial leaders resist for fear of local unemployment and instability. In addition to the power struggle between the center and the provinces, Chinese bureaucracy often gets in the way in sensitive industries, such as through directives forcing foreign corporations into partnership with officially designated local companies. Since this bureaucratic system is subject to the *rule of man* rather than the *rule of law*, it is difficult to do business in a society where rights are derived from political power of *guanxi* or personal connections. Although there has been a flood of new legislation in the past 20 years, their laws are full of ambiguities and their enforcement is weak.

Despite rapid and miraculous growth, China faces many challenges ranging from a broken financial system and inadequate stock market to political upheaval and conflict with Taiwan. The burgeoning tourism industry has been somewhat undermined by massive health crises there. Acute Respiratory System (SARS) started in China, and bird flu in the country could lead to a pandemic. Exhibit 13.6 provides insight into another of China's increasing number of entrepreneurs, but this one is a rags to riches story.

Cultural Guidelines for Business in China[11]

China is a hierarchical society, which often makes it difficult to practice Western management theories of empowerment and delegation.

China faces many challenges ranging from a broken financial system and inadequate stock market to political upheaval and conflict with Taiwan.

EXHIBIT 13.6
YOUNGER GENERATION OF CHINESE ENTREPRENEURS

Shantou, a once poor district in southern China, is the birthplace of one of the mainland's richest men. As a deprived boy, Wong Kwong Wu recycled bottles after school to supplement his family's income. At 16, he and his elder brother left to seek their fortunes, ending up in Beijing where they opened a clothing store called Gnome. At 17, Mr. Wong switched its emphasis to home appliances and consumer electronics. In 1992, the brothers split the business—the elder went into commercial real estate and the younger kept the retail store. Now in 2005, they are both rich and jointly own the skyscraper *Eagle Plaza* and the building that houses it in North Beijing. Today Gnome is a prosperous electrical appliance retailer with 437 stores in 132 cities with $3 billion in revenues. A clear leader in the 500 billion yuan electrical appliance market, the company now seeks foreign partners for further expansion. At 36, Wong himself is presently worth some $1.7 billion. Having acquired this wealth within socialist China, the young billionaire has become one of Beijing's biggest residential developers. *The beauty of property over retailing*, he smiles, *is that you don't have to deal with so many people*!

Yet Wong lives frugally; he, his wife, and children live in a commonplace apartment. Although he is driven around in a stretch Mercedes for meetings on the move, personally he is a workaholic given to self-denial. Like many young Chinese entrepreneurs, Wong is sensitive to a regime still ambivalent about private property and the rapid rise in private wealth. Conspicuous consumption is still to be indulged in cautiously!

Source: Adapted from "Face Value—China's Uneasy Billionaire," *The Economist*, February 4, 2006, p. 60.

Chinese tend to think in terms of "role fulfillment": "give me a role or title and I will perform the job." However, the Western assumption is "prove that you can do your job well and more responsibility will be added." Western managers can misconstrue this difference as a lack of initiative on the part of the Chinese. Chinese usually have a "role expectation" for their bosses and maintain a certain distance with them. The leadership traits they admire are determination, calm, strength, intelligence, honor, and reserve.

China is a group-oriented high-context culture. Chinese are not comfortable making recommendations or suggestions publicly. By using

China is a group-oriented high-context culture.

one-on-one communication and understanding nonverbal signals, one can usually determine the true meaning in conversation.

Personal development and growth, as well as monetary reward, are important motivators for Chinese employees. Good training programs are very attractive to them, and often they are willing to take less pay for development opportunities. In any bonus plan or performance award system, consider the individual performance as well as the group. A detailed and clear reward system is important for guidance in these areas.

Experienced China traders advise that when it comes to doing business in this enigmatic country, *throw away the rule book, and expect the Chinese to be one step ahead of you*! The local business environment is eccentric and nonrational, causing managers and negotiators from abroad to make false assessments of the situation. Foreigners are further puzzled by the cultural challenge in the Chinese game to *save face*, so that deception with an opponent is acceptable. Appearance and scoring points often seem more important than substance or making a good deal. Emotion often seems to guide decisions rather than business logic. Furthermore, many Chinese managers suffer from "short termism"—they are not yet interested in taking time to develop sophisticated products and quality control, like the Japanese, so that their home-grown brands will become internationally sought. Too many managers, especially in SOEs, act like "kings" who reward workers on the basis of party loyalty, not on human resource and market standards.

Despite reforms in China, foreign investors and managers are still concerned about inadequate protection of intellectual property and human rights, rapid price inflation, and corruption. They have to act defensively; for example, they avoid joint ventures with government entities and carefully monitor the native who hires staff. Some outsiders play the role of the "dumb foreigner" by asking detailed questions supposedly to better understand the system. The reality is that many Chinese government officials live in fear of being criticized for not upholding the state's interests. Avoid being overanxious and giving too many concessions, lest an unfair deal is forced on you in the local expectation that foreigners will give anything in order to operate in China.

Managing in China requires the introduction of effective human resource programs. Too many Chinese workers prefer not to think creatively and avoid taking responsibility for decisions. The rote education received needs to be countered by training that increases the power of analysis and leadership.

Foreign investors and managers are still concerned about inadequate protection of intellectual property.

Corruption

Some outsiders who have lived and worked within China claim it is among the most corrupt countries in the world. The lack of a legal structure, plus group-oriented and relationship-based interpersonal interactions, make it challenging for Western managers to practice their ethical standards in China. In 1993, China officially began an anticorruption campaign. Although some progress has been made, corruption is endemic to a system that McGregor claims is incompatible with honesty.[12]

Corruption when dealing with import taxes and kickbacks to get contracts are examples. Often, to avoid bribery and corruption, many MNCs use creative ways to build relationships. One example is partnering with top business schools to launch special executive education programs, inviting local businesses to participate. The expatriate executive confronts a culture in which business is about survival—someone has to win or lose!

Negotiating in China

China is a group-oriented society, and any negotiation must cover the interests of many different parties. In meetings, Chinese will examine a counterpart's attitude and speech and apply it to that problem solving. Technical competence is critical, and some negotiators have requested that more seasoned technical people join their negotiating team midway through negotiations.

The Chinese rank among the toughest negotiators in the world, but they are normally reputable and honorable. In addition, China is probably one of the most difficult countries to understand and adapt to. Lucian Pye makes the following points regarding Chinese negotiators from discussions with U.S. negotiators.[13] These points are valid today for anyone interested in negotiating with Chinese:

Emphasis is placed on trust and mutual connections.

- Emphasis is placed on trust and mutual connections.
- Chinese usually stick to their word.
- Long-range benefits are preferred.
- They respond well to foreign representatives who "specialize" in the PRC.
- They are sensitive to national slights and still addicted to propagandistic slogans and codes.

So as not to lose face, Chinese often prefer to negotiate through an intermediary. Initially, a business meeting is devoted to pleasantries—serving tea, chit chat, mental fencing—waiting for the right opening to begin serious discussions. An early key signal of the intensity of Chinese interest in doing business with you is the caliber of the Chinese assigned to the sessions. Chinese posture becomes rigid whenever they feel their goals are seemingly being compromised.

Many outsiders are convinced that the Chinese consciously use slowdown techniques as bargaining ploys (e.g., they exploit a natural

American tendency for impatience to get things done quickly). During first encounters, the Chinese usually seem to be bound by their traditional nonlegalistic practices. Businesspersons soon appreciate that they operate only at the tolerance of the Chinese.

Chinese seem to have a compelling need to dwell on the subject of friendship, convincing foreigners that reciprocity in this spirit was a prerequisite for doing business with China. However, once Chinese decide who and what is the best, they show great steadfastness. Sometimes their strategy is to put pressure on visitors when discussing final arrangements for an agreement. For example, they will suggest that the spirit of friendship in which the business relationship was originally established has been undermined or broken. Remember in negotiations with Chinese that nothing should be considered *final* or *complete* until it has been actually realized. Chinese do not treat the signing of a contract as a completed agreement. They conceive of the relationship in longer and more continuous terms and will not hesitate to suggest modifications immediately on the heels of an agreement. For this purpose, it is wise not to inform people of your departure date. Recognize that China has an inadequate system for dispute resolution.

Business Courtesies

Without a business card, a visitor on business is a nonperson—so one should have an ample supply with information on one side in English and in Mandarin Chinese on the other side. Remember when using colors that gold is considered prestigious, while red is considered lucky. Since Confucianism gives rank to everyone in society, deference to those in higher rank is expected, so at a business conference, the highest in authority leads the delegation. Take time with these people and be patient, so anticipate long speeches. Despite official disapproval, expect locals to resort to traditional beliefs, even in making a business deal (e.g., astrology and geomancy).

When a foreign visitor has an appointment with a Chinese official, one will generally be introduced and offered some tea and cigarettes. The offering of a cigarette in the PRC has become a common expression of hospitality. Prior to your entrance, your Chinese host will be briefed on who you are and why you are there. Polite questions about your trip and about the United States may be intiated, generally in the area of pleasantries, and perhaps even about your family. If your call is merely a courtesy call, it may not go beyond this. If this is more than a courtesy call, it is appropriate to begin discussion of a business nature at this time. The Chinese host will generally indicate when it is time for a person to leave.

Seating arrangements during formal meetings are a critical issue. Guests are seated according to their business or social status. The head of the meeting will be seated at the "master table," in the "master seat."

Seating arrangements during formal meetings are a critical issue. Guests are seated according to their business or social status.

The most important counterparts will be seated at the master table to the right and left of the head. Generally, there will be a key Chinese member at each table to facilitate discussion.

It is also important to reciprocate invitations if they are given by the PRC. For example, if a banquet is given in the honor of the foreign team, they should reciprocate by giving a banquet for the Chinese team. Small company souvenirs or picture books often make good presents, but expensive gifts should not be given. Also, if one is invited to a Chinese home for dinner, it is appropriate to bring a small gift or souvenir perhaps from your country. Often your Chinese host will present you with a gift. Gifts should not be opened when presented but after one leaves.

Some Business Cautions

The Chinese are sensitive about foreigners' comments on Chinese politics. Even a joke about the late Chairman Mao, or any of their other political leaders, is extremely inappropriate. It is best to listen, ask questions related to your particular business reason for being in the PRC, and leave it at that.

The Chinese are punctual, and you should arrive promptly on time for each meeting. They do not like to be touched or slapped on the back, or at times even to shake hands. A slight bow and a brief shake of the hands is more appropriate.

In business meetings, the Chinese expect businesspeople to dress formally. In addressing another, the family name is always mentioned first. For example, Teng Hsiao-ping should be addressed as Mr. Teng.

During one's stay in the PRC, a visitor may be invited to a dinner in a restaurant by the organization that is sponsoring the visit. The guest should arrive on time or even perhaps a little early. The host normally toasts the guest at an early stage of the meal, with the guest reciprocating after a short interval. During the meal, alcoholic beverages should not be consumed until a toast has been made. It is a custom to toast other persons at the table throughout the meal. At the end of the dinner, the guest of honor makes the initial move to depart. The usual procedure is to leave shortly after the meal is finished. Most dinner parties usually end by 8:30 or 9:00 in the evening.

The Chinese generally believe that foreign businesspersons will be highly qualified technically in their specific areas of expertise. The Chinese businessperson does not need to show his or her intellectual expertise or to make an impression on the foreign guest. The foreign businessperson who is a true professional will have discreet but lavish attention showered on him or her while in China. Remember, your Chinese counterpart may be well qualified in engineering, science, and mathematics but less astute in Western business and management practices.

The Chinese businessperson traditionally places much emphasis on proper etiquette. It is recommended that the foreign businessperson seat to the PRC possess dignity, reserve, patience, persistence, and a sensitivity to and respect for Chinese customs and temperament. Cultural and basic language preparation is essential.

The Chinese generally give preference to companies with long-standing relationships with state trading companies or large companies with financial strength and/or political clout. Newcomers and new business organizations have to adjust to the Chinese style of arranging and negotiating contracts. Very often, several visits to the PRC are necessary to consummate any business transaction, so one should be prepared for long-term follow-up.

Traders coming to sell products in China must be prepared to spend a much longer time than buyers and may find themselves waiting for appointments day after day. This is when one must exhibit patience and perseverance, as well as sensitivity to Chinese customs and ways of doing business.

China has a fragmented market due to regional governmental protection. Do not expect to build a factory in one province and think this will automatically give you access to the entire Chinese market.

China has a fragmented market.

Privacy is not highly regarded due to the Chinese strong emphasis on personal relationships and living together in extended families. Personal information that Westerners consider private, like salary, is openly discussed in China since in most state-owned companies what individuals earn is common knowledge. Yet with economic development, the concept of privacy is growing, and modern Chinese are beginning to resent intrusions of nosy employers, data-gathering marketers, ubiquitous security, and officious government inquiries into personal and family life. Generally, better educated people are taking charge of their own lives as central planning yields to the market system. Although Orwellian controls over politics, news media, religion, and free expression remain in place, and legal protections for privacy are limited, times are changing and the trends support the concept of personal privacy.

Facilitating Cross-cultural Communications

Usually foreigners should not focus on the individual Chinese person, but rather on the group of individuals who are working for a particular goal. If a Chinese individual is singled out as possessing unique qualities, this could very well embarrass the person. The visitor should also behave in a noncondescending manner. The people from the PRC have had abundant negative experiences with Western imperialism and superiority.

Generally, the Chinese are somewhat more reticent, retiring, reserved, or shy than North Americans. But like the North Americans they are not a touching society; however, they do not appreciate loud, boisterous behavior, as in the West. They also avoid open displays of affection, and the speaking distance between two people in nonintimate relationships is greater than in the West. Telephone calls, fax machines, and the Internet are becoming a vital part of business, but Chinese think that important business is only conducted face to face.

The insights shared in this section also have some applications to (1) territories over which the PRC has gained national control, such as the former European colonies of Macao (Portuguese) and Hong Kong (British), as well as the Buddhist kingdom of Tibet; and (2) overseas Chinese communities around the world—more so cultural and business practices than political. (Since Hong Kong is such an important international and financial center in Asia, the next section presents additional information on this prosperous and more democratic entity.)

Business savvy and cultural sensitivity are needed for success.

Finally, it is wise for global managers to remember that in all developing nations—from Asia to Africa—Westerners should never denigrate traditional beliefs and practices that are still essential to the culture. As Frankenstein wisely observed: "Business savvy and cultural sensitivity are needed for success and preparing a manager adequately, for his stay in China could make the difference between merely servicing and succeeding."[14]

Hong Kong

Hong Kong is composed of three distinct areas (Hong Kong Island, Kowloon, and the New Territories) each of which became British territory as a result of different historical events. Hong Kong Island and the Kowloon Peninsula were ceded to the British in 1842 and 1860, respectively, as a result of China's losses in the Opium Wars. The new territories were leased from China for 99 years, beginning in 1898. Following the Sino-British agreement, the whole of Hong Kong was handed back to China on July 1, 1997, as a Special Administrative Region (SAR). Hong Kong was granted a high degree of autonomy for the next 50 years and runs a separate constitution. Hung Chee, nominated by the PRC, was selected in 1997 by a 400-member Selection Committee as the first chief executive. In 1998, the Legislative Council held new elections, which was the first government process since the handover to China. The second election took place in September 2000, and in both elections only half of the voting population turned out. The Democratic Party won the majority of the votes; however, the Democratic Alliance for Betterment of Hong Kong was close behind. Used to democracy and freedom, many citizens of Hong Kong continuously protest and struggle for more rights and privileges from the central PRC government. The one-country, two-system policy for Hong Kong continues to evolve.

The population of Hong Kong is estimated at over 6.8 million. Large population increases resulted from refugee inflows from China during the Communist Revolution (1949–1950), the Cultural Revolution (1967–1968), and the Vietnam War. Chinese make up 95% of Hong Kong's population, that group being of Cantonese origin. Other substantial ethnic Chinese groups are Fukkien, Shanghainese, and the Hakka.

Hong Kong exports a majority of its goods to China (44%) and the United States (17%). Clothing and accessories make up the majority of Hong Kong's exports at 47%, with electric machinery second at 13.2%. There are more than 1100 U.S. firms in Hong Kong and approximately 50,000 U.S. citizens living there. Hong Kong is the fifteenth largest trading partner with the United States, and two-way trade now surpasses US$20 billion there. Hong Kong has become a key port for the PRC to do finance and business with Asia, the West, and even Africa. After the PRC took control of this former crown colony, its last British governor, Patten, made these observations on the transition underway:

> If China is able to master the daunting problems now facing it (failing state industries, the social pressures of rising expectations, pell-mell urbanization), it will need more than Hong Kong's wealth; it will also need to heed Hong Kong's experience. . . . Hong Kong is at one and the same time China's window on the world, bridge to the world, shop front for the world, and paradigm for the world of what the whole of China could become.[15]

INDIA

EXHIBIT 13.7

INDIA—PROFILE

Population	1,080,264,388 (July 2005 est.)
Ethnic groups	Indo-Aryan, 72%; Dravidian, 25%; Mongoloid and other, 3%
Religions	Hindu, 80.5%; Muslim, 13.4%; Christian, 2.3%; Sikh, 1.9%; other, 1.8%; unspecified, 0.1%
Languages	15 major languages with English as link
Education	59.5% literacy rate
Land	2,973,190 sq km
Government	Federal republic
Political Parties	India has dozens of national and regional political parties; only parties with four or more

EXHIBIT 13.7

INDIA—PROFILE (CONTINUED)

seats in the People's Assembly are listed: Bahujan Samaj Party (BSP), Bharatiya Janata Party (BJP), Biju Janata Dal (BJD), Communist Party of India (CPI), Communist Party of India (Marxist) (CPIM), Dravida Munnetra Kazagham (DMK), Eqtedar-e-Melli-Eslami (National Islamic Empowerment), Indian National Congress (INC), Janata Dal (United) (JDU), Jharkhand Mukti Morcha (JMM), Lok Jan Shakti Party (LJSP), Marumalarchi Dravida Munnetra Kazhagam (MDMK), Nahzat-e-Faragir-e-Democracy Wa Taraqi-e-Afghanistan (Afghanistan's Democracy and Progress Movement), Nationalist Congress Party (NCP), Pattali Makkal Katchi (PMK), Rashtriya Janata Dal (RJD), Samajwadi Party (SP), Shiromani Akali Dal (SAD), Shiv Sena (SS), Telangana Rashtra Samithi (TRS), Telugu Desam Party (TDP)

Per capita income $3400 (2005 est.)

Exports to U.S. Total exports = $76.23 billion
U.S. accounts for 17%
Total exports to U.S. = $13 billion (2005 est.)

Imports from U.S. Total imports = $113.1 billion
U.S. accounts for 6%
Total imports from U.S. = $6.8 billion (2005 est.)

We are all prisoners of our own time and place, and we inevitably judge the new and strange in terms of the old and familiar. . . . For millennia, humans in the West have sought passage to the East, especially to obtain its spices and precious metals. Herodotus, a Greek who lived 484–425 B.C. and known as the "father of history," regarded India as the richest and most populous place in the world. From 580–480 B.C., these fabled riches first attracted the Persians, Carthaginians, and Egyptians; the latter originally found a way around Africa, as well as to Europe, to facilitate voyages of exploration. India became the destination of the monsoon trading system that took classical form in Islamic times, 750–1500 A.D. The Indian Ocean defines a region of great linguistic, ethnic, cultural and religious variety, with a single unifying factor—the monsoon winds of Southeast Asia. With the epochal voyage around the Cape of Good Hope by the Portuguese, Vasco de Gama, in 1498, Europeans finally broke out of their Mediterranean prison by sailing on the Indian Ocean to the Indian port of Calicut. As the Occident reached out to the Orient, a wide variety of countries benefited from this ocean-going trading network. The seas of the ancient trade routes lead to wealth and invasions, in what was almost a forerunner of today's global economy.[16]

The Indian economy is sometimes likened to an elephant, which is not capable of running as swiftly as some of the smaller "tiger like" Asian countries, but has the advantage of being stable and less affected by shocks and disturbances. These elephantine qualities were severely tested during the recent years when political and economic problems were aplenty. These included the global economic slowdown (exacerbated by the terrorist attacks of September 11), increased political tension with neighboring Pakistan (especially after the terrorist attack on the Indian Parliament), a poorly performing industrial sector, stagnant exports, and a capital market that remained in the doldrums . . . But today India is suddenly an emerging superpower, a center of high and information technology, as of global off-shore business activities.[17]

India is suddenly an emerging superpower.

Historical Perspective

The ancient land of India began in prehistoric times. Around 500 B.C., Aryans descended from the north and integrated with the native Dravidians to form the basis of classical Indian society. The earliest inhabitants settled along the banks of great rivers. Archaeological discoveries reveal that some 500 years ago a high-level civilization flourished in the western and northwestern parts of India.

As in Asia, the sixteenth century saw the Western European nations establishing trading posts in India. The Portuguese efforts were focused on Goa/Cochin on the west coast, and the French in Pondicherry on the east coast. However, the British were the most successful and expanded their influence and power throughout the subcontinent. They built a colonial infrastructure that largely remains intact today, including the heritage of English as a link language in a *land of many tongues*. After World War I, nationalism grew in India. Mahatma Gandhi organized a series of passive resistance campaigns and civil disobedience to British rule. His activities were successful when the peninsula was divided into Hindu India and Muslim Pakistan, amid much rioting and bloodshed. The British reign ended on August 15, 1947. On January 26, 1950, the Indian constitution was promulgated, and the country became a sovereign republic and the world's largest democracy.

The hostile situation between India and Pakistan over Kashmir is a continuing struggle. In July 2000, negotiations began between the government and militants, but the biggest militant group, Hizbul Mujahidein, refused to continue the negotiations because the Indian

Hinduism,

which holds that

birth is destiny,

perpetuates the

caste system.

government would not involve Pakistan. However, after having gone to war with one another over Kashmir, by 2006 peaceful negotiations between the leaders of Pakistan and India have progressed, in partially due to the impact of tsunami disaster of 2005.

Hinduism, which holds that birth is destiny, perpetuates the caste system, which separates the social classes by occupations, so that privileges or disadvantages are transmitted by inheritance. For over 5000 years, the caste system with its thousands of subsystems has divided people into four classes: priests, warriors, traders, and workers. Then there are the untouchables or *dalits*, excluded because of the nature of their crafts, such as working with leather. However, when industrialization began in twentieth-century India, many members of this underclass were recruited by foreign investors to learn new skills for factory work. An example of how this injustice is breaking down for some 200 million so classified is the late K. R. Narayans. Born of a poor southern Indian family and educated by Christian missionaries, he won scholarships to college and proved to be a very talented student, even at the London School of Economics. Upon his return, India's first prime minister, Jawaharial Nehru, a Muslim, found Narayanan a job in the diplomatic service where he ended up an ambassador to Thailand, Turkey, China, and the United States. In 1984, he was elected to Parliament from his native Kerla. To the surprise of the elite, he subsequently was elected vice president and then president, saying: "My life encapsulates the ability of the democratic system to accommodate and empower marginalized sections of society." Today discrimination on the grounds of caste is illegal, and a huge affirmative action program is under way. But India still wastes its human resources because of those in a hierarchical society who still adhere to this obsolete classification; haughty taboos forbid intermarriage among castes, or consign outcasts to "manual scavengers" (e.g., working with corpses and excrement). The rapid growth of information technology and services is further undermining this ancient system.

Since there is not enough work for all the people, poverty is prevalent. Currently, 15% of the population falls below the poverty line. India has implemented intensive population control programs, but none have been successful. The high birth rate (approximately 20.71 births/1000 population) has been attributed to early marriage, the emphasis placed on bearing sons by the Hindu religion, the security of having children to take care of parents in old age, and the low level of education achieved by the rural masses. The literacy rate is 59.5%. However, in some cities in India the population is highly educated.

India's major exports include gems and jewelry, textiles and garments, and the agricultural products. Its leading export markets are the United States (12.3%), Japan (22.3%), Singapore (8.4%), and South Korea (6.8%). Fifteen years ago 50% of the country's national income was derived from agriculture and allied activities. Today the agricultural sector accounts for 25% of GDP, the industrial sector 25%, and the services sector 50%.

Cultural Guidelines for Business in India

Governance

The government of India is based on the British parliamentary system with a bicameral legislature and executive and judicial branches. India is governed by a council of ministers led by the prime minister (appointed by the president). The ministers and prime minister are responsible to the House of People, the Lok Sabha, which is elected by universal adult franchise. There is an upper house called the Rajya Sabha (i.e., the Senate). Bills submitted by the prime minister have to be passed by both the Lok Sabha and the Rajya Sabha before being signed by the president. The bills become law only upon the president's signature. The president may return the bills to the legislature for changes that he or she may suggest.

The government of India is based on the British parliamentary system.

The powers of the government are, in fact, vested in the prime minister, who is generally the leader of the majority party in Parliament and usually the lower house, Lok Sabha. Nevertheless, the president is the commander-in-chief of the armed forces and also has the right to fire the prime minister in cases of national emergency or lack of confidence. The president has very little executive power.

The government owns and runs many enterprises, such as the airlines, railroads, insurance industry, power facilities, and irrigation projects, but privatization efforts continue. However, since 1990 the government has embarked on a program of liberalization. The country has made a move from an import substitution-oriented economy to an export-oriented economy. The government also has controlling power in the production of metals, steel, chemicals, and engineering equipment.

Economics

Money supply is managed by the Reserve Bank of India, which is the country's central bank. The unit of currency is the rupee. The Reserve Bank acts as banker to the government, the commercial banks, and some of the financial institutions. The banking system is deeply involved in the industrialization of the country through financing of both fixed assets and working capital.

Eighty-five percent of the nation's banking assets are government controlled. In terms of business, the public sector banks, namely, the State Bank of India and nationalized banks, occupy a dominating position. The State Bank of India is the largest commercial bank in the country, and it also carries out some of the functions of the Reserve

Bank of India. Some of the larger banks also provide merchant banking service.

The industrial economy of India has a public sector and a private sector. The public sector companies are government-run industrial and commercial undertakings, while the private sector is composed of profit-oriented business organizations run increasingly by professional managers. The country has experienced rapid industrial growth in recent years with capabilities increasing in almost every sphere of industry, especially information technologies. Exports have become much more diversified from just agricultural products to textiles, tea, iron ore, spices, and light engineering products. Exhibit 13.8 indicates why India is becoming an "economic tiger."

Foreign trade has become an important part of the Indian economy. Imports include fuel, petroleum, fertilizers, iron and steel, chemicals, machinery, transportation equipment, paper, and gemstones.

Human and Capital Resources

India has a large pool of managerial, skilled, and semiskilled labor.

India has a large pool of managerial, skilled, and semiskilled labor. It also has a well-developed capital market and a large domestic market. Over the past 10 years, Bangalore, a beautiful city in south central India has emerged as the Silicon Valley of India. In fact, two-thirds of all custom software programming for the United States is done in India.

India is rich in coal, hydroelectric power potential, industrial raw materials (iron and manganese), and manpower. Like their resources, economic development has occurred in only a few isolated sectors of the economy, which many attribute to the constraints of tradition and culture.

EXHIBIT 13.8

THE HIGH TECH REVOLUTION

Bangalore is the center of India's booming information technology industry (IT). Yet it is something of a paradox—inside its modern industrial parks, business and living conditions operate at a higher level, while outside its surrounding urban area suffers from deteriorating infrastructure and attempts at renewal. But this city is a global and national hub of sophisticated software and remote services, such as business processing outsourcing (BPOs or call centers). But the old city and local government are straining to keep up with the demands of its economic drivers, companies like Wipro and Infosys. These high-tech endeavors employ some 260,000 workers, and

EXHIBIT 13.8

THE HIGH TECH REVOLUTION (CONTINUED)

leading firms are hiring 1000 new staff per month; foreign firms are arriving to set up business at the rate of three a week. No wonder when the economic forecasts for this dynamic ecosystem are for 25% or more annually. However, this city, known for its beauty, lush parks, greenery, and mild climate, struggles to cope with a population that has grown from 800,000 in 1951 to 7 million today!

This muncipality has also become a knowledge center that attracts technical and scientific institutes. Their leaders are the Indian Institute of Science, a world-class university known for the excellence, plus Karnaataka whose 77 engineering colleges alone produce 29,000 graduates per year and spearhead India's space program. A few miles out of town is "Electronics City," a cosmopolitan oasis with amenities to suit the needs of these knowledge workers—from "state-of-the-art" remote network management systems and cappucinno bars, to lively nightlife.

With urban chaos and commuter nightmares in major cities, like Bangalore, Delhi, and Mumbai, second-tier cities are growing fast as postindustrial corporations are attracted to Gurgaib and Noida on the edges of New Delhi; Mumbai's new town; Chennai, formerly Madras; Hyderabad in the south; Pune in the west; Mohali in the north. Even old Calcutta, now called Kolkata, is trying to woo investments for its IT and BPO firms. As successful companies expand aggressively, many move out to less congested areas of the country.

Within attractive IT and BPO campuses, the R&D is either outsourced or extended to new global market niches—for example, processing insurance claims; desktop publishing; remote management and maintenance; backup navigation systems; compiling audits and completing tax returns; transcribing medical records; financial research and analysis. Predictions are that in a few years, many multinationals will have up to 25% of their staff in India. Also security and data protection at these advanced facilities are tight! Forecasts for 2008 are that IT and its enabling services will employ some 4 million people who will earn up to $65 billion from exports, accounting for 7% of GDP.

Part of this success is attributed to keeping government out of this new business. Also, India has a big competitive edge in its annual production of 2 million English-speaking graduates, many of whom benefit from a quality education.

Source: Adapted from "Special Report on Outsourcing and IT in India—the Bangalore Paradox," *The Economist*, April 23, 2005, pp. 67–69.

Communications

India has a great variety of languages, customs, beliefs, and cultures, almost all of which are difficult for a Westerner to comprehend. There are 15 official languages including English, plus more than 1400 dialects. Because of a lack of internal transportation, the resulting isolation of people has facilitated the growth of separate cultural regions. Language reflects these regional differences and is a problem in achieving national unity. Most languages find their origin in an ancient Indian language called Sanskrit.

Fortunately, India has an expanding space program that has concentrated on satellites that have not only united the country, especially via television, but has also enabled government professionals to bring health care and education to the most remote villages.

Religions

Hinduism is not only the principal religion of India.

Hinduism is not only the principal religion of India, but its philosophy dominates the entire culture and relationships. Sometimes it is a source of serious ethnic conflict with Muslims and Christians, particularly as manifested in politics. It determines a woman's role in society. Although the Hindu woman's legal position has greatly improved over the years, she is still bound by ancient traditions of behavior that emphasize her absolute dedication, submission, and obedience to her husband and his wishes. This may not be so strictly adhered to in the big cities and Westernized circles where Indian women are increasing in the workforce, especially in the professions (doctors, engineers, lawyers) and in government. Her status in the household is low until she has given birth to a male child. Female children are seen as a burden and future debt because of the dowry paid at marriage to the husband's family.

Only some 12% of the population are Muslim, and two small religious minorities have an influence beyond their numbers—Christians in the fields of private education and health care; and Parsis, followers of prophet Zoroaster, an ancient Persian religion, who are very successful in commerce.

Corruption

While honesty is esteemed in this vast and poor country, corruption and fraud are endemic in all levels of society. Corruption, bribes, or payments for "fixing" exist in everyday life and are something that must be dealt with and accepted to get things accomplished. In India, business is based on personal contacts, and it is crucial to know the right person in order to get contracts.

Social Customs

The people of India are very friendly, hard working, diverse, and somewhat an enigma to outsiders. Family and friends have an importance far beyond that found in the West. Extended family living is the norm and somewhat hierarchical. A friend's role is to "sense" a person's need and to do something about it. To speak one's mind is a sign of friendship. Young, educated urban youth have more modern clothing and attitudes that are far different from those of their counterparts in rural villages.

Astrologers still play an important role in India: the people believe that nothing is accidental and that the universe and all living components have a fundamental order.

Two types of managers are likely to be encountered in India—the more traditional and bureaucratic, loyal to British traditions and systems, and modern, progressive, entrepreneurial business leaders, technologically sophisticated and attuned to the global market.

Social amenities and practices vary in this huge country, depending on location. Those of the Braham elite are in urban areas, as compared to village peasants or Christian communities in Goa or Kerla. Generally, the following guidelines may prove helpful in India.

Astrologers still play an important role in India.

- Social freedom between the sexes is not appreciated very much, except within more progressive communities; normally among traditionalists, a stranger should not speak to a woman if he is not acquainted with her or her family. A stranger will not be expected to help a woman out of a car, boat, as soon as her husband might resent it. For a young woman to take the hand of a man who is not her husband is usually objectionable Bold, emancipated women may dare to indulge in dancing with their husbands, but to dance with anyone who is not her husband would be improper.
- Use of first name for address should be avoided. It is customary to add to the names of the Hindus the affix "ji" as a mark of respect. For instance, Ravi in polite speech becomes Raviji. Here Ravi is the first name, but, by adding affix "ji," you are calling the person with respect and, in this instance, use of first name will not be improper. In Bengal, mister is replaced by "Babu." Thus, Ravi Babu means Mr. Ravi. In much of India, in correspondence or invitation cards, the classic Sanskrit prefixes "Shriman" for men and "Shrimati" for women are used.
- The method of greeting depends on the social status of the person one is meeting. A son greets his father usually by bowing down and touching his feet. A foreign businessperson will be considered an equal, so among equals the usual method used will be to press one's palms together in front of the chest and say *namaste*, meaning,

"greetings to you." Among the other classes of people, educated in Western style, shaking hands is acceptable. Hindu women who have been educated usually would not mind shaking hands with men when introduced. However, it is safer not to extend one's hand to a Hindu woman until she takes the initiative and extends her hand first.

■ Indian food varies from province to province; it is usually spicy because of the curry used in preparation. Fish and Tandoori chicken from the north are popular dishes. Hindus are normally vegetarians, and beef is prohibited for them, while for Muslims and Jews pork is forbidden. Among respectable Hindus, the drinking of alcoholic beverages of any kind is considered most degrading, and in some states prohibition is legally enforced. Traditionally, Hindus are a nation of water drinkers. While entertaining at home, it is purely with nonalcoholic beverages like tea or coffee. However, in upper-middle-class and upper-class homes alcoholic drinks are not uncommon. A variety of desserts made out of fruits or milk are also available. Betel leaf (*paan* in Hindi) is usually taken after a meal to aid digestion and freshen one's mouth. International cuisine is available in all the major hotels and select restaurants. Unless a visitor's body has adjusted to food in India, or special medication has been taken to prevent dysentery, it is safer for foreigners to use bottled water and avoid salads.

■ Hospitality is universal in India, and Indians are tolerant of the social *faux pas* of a foreigner. The duty of entertaining guests is laid down in religion as of prime importance. A well-mannered Hindu will not eat without asking his guest to join him. It is said that satisfaction of a guest will assuredly bring the housekeeper wealth, reputation, long life, and a place in heaven. One is not required to take any gift if invited for supper, but, if one did, it would be accepted graciously. Do not be surprised if you have your meal only with your business partner and not the whole family; wives and children usually help from the kitchen to make sure that the guest is treated well. At Indian homes, eating without knives, forks, and spoons is not uncommon. People eat with their hands at home. If dining with the whole family, wait until everybody is at the table before you start eating. Let the host start eating first before you do or start when you are asked to go ahead. Do not get upset if your host asks you several times to have some more food. Simply refuse politely if you don't want more. It is Indian custom to ask repeatedly to make sure their guest does not get up hungry from the table.

■ For the businessperson visiting India, shirt, trousers, tie, and suit will be proper attire, but should be lightweight in fabric and white or light tan color. The Indian climate is hot; therefore, a very light suit in winter is recommended. If a person is in the north during winter, he or she will find it a little cooler, and, again, a light sweater and a jacket will be sufficient. In public places, women visitors avoid wearing shorts or revealing dresses, as it draws unneeded attention.

Although Western business dress is commonplace, in this climate, coats are often eliminated and hats are worn to protect from the sun. Indian businessmen, in many situations, wear *dhotis*. The dhoti is a single piece of white cloth about five yards long and three to four feet broad. It is passed round the waist up to half its length, and the other half is drawn between the legs and tucked at the waist. For the upper part of the body they wear long shirts. Sikhs from Punjab wear turbans, which have a religious significance. Well-to-do Hindus who wish to appear aristocratic wear long coats like the Rajahs. The long coat, known as *sherwani*, has been standardized and is the dress recognized by the government of India for official and ceremonial wear. Many modernized Hindu males have adopted the European costume in their outdoor life and Indian dress at home. The Hindu lady is extremely loyal to her sari, while female dress may vary in ethnic communities (e.g., Punjabi women may feature scarves and shawls, with loose-fitting blouse and bellowing pants). The modern sari compares favorably with fashionable clothes of Western women.

- The customs and manners of the Hindu majority are strongly influenced by religion. Hinduism involves a variety of beliefs and practices. Its rules may be interpreted in many ways, depending on the community. While Hinduism for thousands of years had a rigid caste system, where class determined what a person did in his or her life, caste taboos, as indicated earlier, are changing in an information society. India is a land of contrasts—from ancient practices, like sacred cows and bullock carts for transportation, to modern lifestyles, such as Air India jets and cosmopolitan shopping malls. Yet the remnants of the past influence the present.

- The noble teachings of Mahatma Gandhi on nonviolence and tolerance are frequently ignored today. India is a place of contradictions and progress: Hindu nationalism dominates the government, often to the exclusion of Muslims; the subcontinent is divided into three antagonistic countries; war threatens intermittently with Pakistan over Kashmir; India is moving ahead with guided missiles, atomic weapons, and a space program; globalization has led to increased foreign investment into Indian enterprises. It is difficult for the visitor to understand such contradictions, no less the myriad cultures and languages to be encountered in India.

The customs and manners of the Hindu majority are strongly influenced by religion.

Nonverbal Communication and Social Tips

To succeed in both business and social situations, here are a few do's and don'ts for India:

- Grasping one's own ears expresses repentance or sincerity.
- Beckoning is done with the palm turned down; pointing is often done with the chin.

- Backslapping is not a sign of affection.
- The *namaste* gesture can be used to signal you've had enough food.
- Foreign men should not touch women in public or talk to a lone woman in public.
- The left hand is considered unclean. Use the right hand for eating with the fingers, for giving or accepting things, and for handshakes.
- Do not lick postage stamps.
- Eat willingly with your hand if the occasion calls for it.
- Don't ask personal questions until you are friends with someone.
- Use titles such as doctor and professor.
- Whistling is considered impolite.
- Public displays of affection are inappropriate.
- Bargain for goods and services.
- Gift-giving is important, but such gifts are not opened in the presence of the giver.
- Business relationships are based on personal relationships.

Eat willingly with your hand if the occasion calls for it.

There is one important thing to remember when going to India: the Indians are very tolerant and will completely accept the fact that you are unfamiliar with their customs and procedures. There is no need to conform to Indian behavior. For example, the body gestures (shaking of the head) for "yes" and "no" are just the opposite for North Americans and Indians.

Finally, when doing business in India, keep in mind that (1) two-thirds of the people live in the countryside and have yet to experience some of the economic boom going on in the cities; (2) the economy in this emerging superpower grew in 2006 to more than 7%; (3) the nation prefers to be nonaligned with international power blocs; and (4) India is an attractive foreign market because of stability, democracy, and demography.[18] India is also developing a vigorous outer space program:

INDONESIA

EXHIBIT 13.9

INDONESIA—PROFILE

Population	241,973,879 (July 2005 est.)
Ethnic groups	Javanese, 45%; Sundanese, 14%; Madurese, 7.5%; Coastal Malays, 7.5%; Other, 26%
Religions	Muslim, 88%; Protestant, 5%; Roman Catholic, 3%; Hindu, 2%; Buddhist, 1%; Other, 1%
Education	87.9% literacy rate

EXHIBIT 13.9
INDONESIA—PROFILE (CONTINUED)

Land	1,826,440 sq km
Government	Republic
Political Parties	Crescent Moon and Star Party (PBB), Democratic Party (PD), Functional Groups Party or Golkar, Indonesia Democratic Party-Struggle (PDI-P), National Awakening Party (PKB), National Mandate Party (PAN), Prosperous Justice Party (PKS), United Development Party (PPP)
Per capita income	$3700 (2005 est.)
Exports to U.S.	Total exports = $83.64 billion U.S. accounts for 12.3% Total exports to U.S. = $10.3 billion (2005 est.)
Imports from U.S.	Total imports = $62.02 billion U.S. accounts for 7% Total imports from U.S. = $4.3 billion (2005 est.)

Straddling the equator and drenched in rain, Indonesia is a treasure house of natural diversity. Its vast stretches of rain forest—the largest outside the Amazon—contain perhaps the richest and most unusual collection of plants and animals on earth, from elephants to tree kangaroos. But the world's fourth most populous nation with 200 million people has crammed 60% of them into the Java area. Yet, this tropical crossroads is replete with natural resources still to be fully utilized. For example, with almost two-thirds of its land covered with forest, the country has become the world's largest exporter of plywood. But logging and farming strip 4700 square miles annually, adding to fire and pollution problems. While oil and gas exports have driven economic growth, the nation is a major exporter also of zinc, nickel and copper. Poor infrastructure has limited resource exploitation.[19]

Historical Perspective Overview

"Bkinncka tunggal Ika," translated "unity through diversity," is the national motto of Indonesia. This nation of islands represents a rich variety of local customs and traditions found among its diverse people. Indonesia is an archipelago situated across the equator between the continents of Asia and Australia. It is the largest archipelago in the world, with 13,677 islands of which 6044 are inhabited. It stretches 3330 miles from east to west and 1300 miles from north to south.

"Unity through diversity," is the national motto of Indonesia.

There are four main island groups in Indonesia: the Greater Sunda Islands, composed of Java, which has a population of 80 million; Sumatra, which is the sixth largest island in the world; and two other large islands. The other three groups of islands include the Lesser Sunda Islands, the Malukus, and West Iran.

Formerly known as the Dutch East Indies, Indonesia remained the territory of the Netherlands until 1942, when it was occupied by the Japanese. Although Indonesia gained its independence in 1945, it continued to struggle with intermittent guerrilla warfare until 1949 in order to gain total independence from the Dutch. In 1949, the Dutch transferred sovereignty of nearly all of the land of the Dutch East Indies except West Iran, which is now known as the Netherlands New Guinea. The new country became known as the Republic of Indonesia in 1950, and by 1963 West Iran also became part of the nation. General Suharto, a leader of the countercoup, was formally made president of Indonesia in 1966. In 1998, because of social unrest, corruption, and financial deterioration, Suharto's 32-year despotic rule ended when a disillusioned populace, led by young students, forced him out of the presidential office. Abdurrahman Wahid was elected to office soon after, but after only 21 months he was impeached due to incompetence. His vice president, Megawati Sukarnoputri, the daughter of Sukarno, took office in July 2001.

In August 2002, the People's Consultative Assembly decided that the president and vice president are to be directly elected. This new procedure began in 2004, whereby the MPR (Upper House of Representatives) now holds the 500 members of the lower House of Representatives (DPR) and 200 members of a newly created Regional Representatives Council (DPD). Currently, the army and police hold 38 seats in the DPR; however, beginning in 2004, they have not had a formal role. Parliaments also exist at the provincial and district levels. Changes are being made to Indonesia's political system to try to restore structure and a free market economy, as well as to improve human rights and inequities in income levels. Although Australia fought the country in the 1960s over Borneo, the economically interdependent neighbors signed a security agreement in 1995 that resulted in Australia recognizing Indonesian sovereignty over East Timor.

During the 1980s, there was apparent economic progress in Indonesia. However, as the decade of the 1990s closed, the Indonesian economy was in ruins with pervasive corruption, millions sinking back into poverty and hunger, exceptional natural disasters, chaos in the explosion of long-suppressed pluralistic politics, and a society threatening to fragment along ethnic and religious lines. While many politicians sought to curb the grip of the Chinese minority over the country's commercial life, the price of rice rose because of global warming and the people starved. So it is that "hunger breeds racial bigotry, a search for scapegoats, and fear of authoritarian backlash."[20]

Today, Indonesia faces several challenges: to maintain political stability; to restructure Indonesia's banking system; to ensure peace in Banda Aceh after the people's recent revolt; to rebuild after the death and destruction of the 2005 tsunami; and to effectively combat global terrorism, especially from Islamic militants.

Cultural Guidelines for Business in Indonesia

Although Indonesia is the largest Islamic nation in the world, Islam has not been declared its official religion. Instead the country calls itself *monotheistic*, so that people do not strictly adhere to the rules of the Koran. Rather the village law, or *Adat*, prevails in Indonesian rural and urban areas. The government's official policy is *Pancasila*: belief in (a) one supreme being; (b) a just and civilized humanity; (c) the unity of Indonesia; (d) democracy; and (e) social justice for all. Even though Indonesia is a Muslim country, women have never been veiled, nor have they been secluded like other Muslim women in the Middle East. On many of the islands, women vote and hold leadership positions, because they have been guaranteed full and complete rights. Although Indonesia is a male-dominated country, education of females is inadequate. Women compose only 30% of the students at the university or college level. With this disparity, the Indonesian woman's position is behind that of her male counterpart.

The family is the basic unit of Indonesian life. It is a highly complex system with many interlocking relationships in the vast network of an extended family system. For most Indonesians, the family is the first priority. There are many young people in Indonesia, with nearly 70% of the total population under 30 years of age. The customary law, or *Adat*, permits polygamy, but it is not practiced by many. In December 1973, a bill was passed requiring free consent for girls, with the minimum age of 16, and for boys, with the minimum age of 19, in the sharing of property acquired in marriage. In the case of divorce, the children are often assigned to the custody of both parents.

A basic concept in Indonesian daily life in both a social and a business context is the importance of avoiding making someone feel *malu*. The word literally means ashamed, insulted, or embarrassed. Criticizing or contradicting a person in front of others will cause you to lose face, and the person will feel *malu* as a result of your action.

Also important to Indonesians are the concepts of unity and conformity. They do not strive, as many Americans do, to become individualistic.

Behavior Modes

A common courtesy that should be respected is not raising one's voice or demonstrating externally intense emotions. Head-on confrontations are embarrassing to most Indonesians. Thus, they prefer to talk indi-

The village law, or Adat, prevails in Indonesian rural and urban areas.

rectly and ambiguously about areas of difference until common ground can be found. *Sembah* or *hormat* is the art of paying respect to one's superiors who are generally persons of higher rank or position either by birth, economic status, or age. One form of demonstrating *sembah* or *hormat* is by not questioning one's superiors.

In Indonesia, there is a subtle but very hierarchical approach to interpersonal relationships that is related not only to family and to the village, but also to the larger community and to the government. Leadership is very paternalistic, and consensus is the mode followed by all persons. Young persons defer to old people, though in the cities this is changing somewhat. Indonesians are known for their friendly hospitality.

It is suggested that foreigners working in Indonesia never refuse an offer of food or drink, but at the same time they should not appear greedy; it is customary not to finish the food or drink completely.

Gestures and Greetings

Certain gestures should be avoided while in Indonesia. For example, never touch the head of an older Indonesian, as it is thought to be the place where the spirit resides. Kissing and embracing in public should also be avoided because it is considered rude and coarse. In addition, personal questions should not be asked, as this may be interpreted by Indonesians as an invasion of privacy. The use of the left hand for eating or for passing of gifts should be avoided because it is considered the unclean hand. Pointing is also considered rude in Indonesia and therefore should be avoided. Handshakes are becoming customary in Jakarta among Westernized Indonesians, but use the right hand softly. In general, however, there is no physical contact, especially for different genders and ages. The traditional greeting is a nodding of the head and a gracious smile. With Indonesian introductions, the locals want to know where exactly is the visitor from and whom do they know in their land. So foreigners should attempt to learn what area of Indonesia the local comes from and anything distinctive about that microculture—for example, Java, Batak (North Sumatra), Sudanese (West Java), Pandang (West Sumatra), Manado (North Sulawesi), or Ache (North Sumatra).

The traditional greeting is a nodding of the head and a gracious smile.

Managing in Indonesia

Indonesians are extremely indirect in business contexts. Therefore, it is very important to circumvent a subject before the critical issues are mentioned. Everything is negotiated in Indonesia, and the people love to bargain. With the exception of department stores, there are few fixed prices. Once a person is respected as a bargainer, a merchant will offer far more reasonable prices.

Indonesians do not like to be pressured or hurried, whereas time in the United States can be wasted, spent, utilized, and saved. There is a phrase in Indonesia describing this concept that translates as "rubber time," meaning that time stretches or shrinks and is therefore very flexible. Since promptness is not considered a virtue, only foreigners are expected to be punctual, not the locals. Furthermore, making people wait can be an expression of social structure—deference is shown the higher ranking person who does so. Also, three calendars are observed: the Western or Gregorian is the official one; the Arabic calendar dates Islamic holidays and fasting periods, like Ramadan; and the Javanese or Hindu-influenced calendar is selectively observed (Javanese have only a five-day week). When holidays on these different calendars coincide, the day is considered lucky and auspicious. The work week is four days, followed by two half days on Friday and Saturday. Business hours are generally 8 A.M. to 4 P.M., and 8 A.M. to 12 noon on half days, though retail shops may maintain a different schedule.

The national language of Indonesia, Bahasa Indonesia, was officially adopted in 1928. At the time of this decision, Bahasa Indonesia was a regional language spoken by only 5% of the total population of Indonesia. To achieve the higher ideal of unity, the major subcultures such as Javanese (14%) and Sundanese (14%), and others pushed aside their regional feelings and adopted the idea of a common language.

Our late co-author in the MCD Series, Dr. Farid Elashmawi, was a Muslim who did extensive consulting work in Indonesia. When doing business in that island nation, his research confirmed the importance of establishing good relationships and connections, so that through such persons outsiders could go to the top manager of any enterprise. When introducing yourself, mention one's personal references, educational attainments, organizational position, and hobbies. During his work with key management in Indonesia, he inquired about their five values that receive priority and asked them to share their perceptions of what they thought were comparable value systems of Americans and Arabs. Exhibit 13.10 summarizes his findings. The two other nation-

The national language of Indonesia, Bahasa Indonesia, was officially adopted in 1928.

EXHIBIT 13.10
COMPARISON OF VALUE PERCEPTIONS

Indonesians	Americans	Arabs
Relationships	Equality	Seniority
Group Harmony	Freedom	Spirituality
Seniority	Openness	Reputation
Family	Self-reliance	Family
Cooperation	Cooperation	Authority

Source: Elashmanwi, F. *Competing Globally—Mastering Multicultural Management and Negotiations.* Burlington, MA: Elsevier/Butterworth–Heinemann, 2001, p. 107. (www.books@elsevier.com/management).

alities can decide for themselves whether the Indonesian assessment of their cultural values was valid.

JAPAN

No country in modern history has moved so swiftly from worldwide adulation to dismissal or contempt as did Japan. . . . In the past 15 years, amid crushing stock and property markets, mountains of dud debt, scores of corruption scandals, vast government deficits, and stagnant economic growth, Japan mutated from a giver of lessons to a recipient of lectures, all of which offers recipes for its reform and revival. . . . Now, however, the time for lectures is over. Japan is back. It is being reformed. It is revising. Really?[21]

Contemporary Japanese culture is considerably different from previous, traditional notions of it and from most people's current stereotypes, including those of the Japanese themselves. Japan is commonly and stereotypically known as a land of nobility and chivalry with values such as honor, pride, and perseverance. These form a moral code of everyday living that has permeated Japanese society for generations, even centuries. Yet contemporary Japanese culture (especially for younger Japanese) seems to operate from different values, attitudes, beliefs, norms and behaviors. In short, Japan is evolving into a society with a different culture.[22]

Asia is a potpourri of nations and cultures, so it is difficult to generalize about its diverse peoples and their mind-sets. To many, Japanese behavior may seem puzzling and a source of both confusion and wonderment. For North Americans, perched on the Pacific Rim, Japan is the epitome of the Far East and its enigmas. While Exhibit 13.11 provides readers with a quick overview of Japanese demographics, the two quotations above indicate the social changes underway in that relatively homogeneous land. Because Japan is going through profound economic and social transformation within a generation or so, its cultural specifics must be viewed in that context.[23] Realities of their participation in the global market and media are only two of the driving forces altering cultural preferences in that traditional society, especially among the new generation.

Japanese markets are indeed hard to crack but not impossible, as McDonald's, Coca-Cola, IBM, and many others have demonstrated. Informal protection in the form of close linkages between supplier and customer is a handicap to outsiders.

Japanese markets are indeed hard to crack.

EXHIBIT 13.11

PROFILE OF JAPAN

Population	127,417,244 (July 2005 est.)
Ethnic groups	Japanese, 99%; Others, 1% (Korean 511,262, Chinese 244,241, Brazilian 182,232, Filipino 89,851, Other 237,914)
Religions	Shinto and Buddhist, 84%; Other, 16% (including Christian 0.7%)
Education	99% literacy rate
Land	374,744 sq km
Government	Constitutional monarchy
Political Parties	Democratic Party of Japan (DPJ), Japan Communist Party (JCP), Komeito, Liberal Democratic Party (LDP), Social Democratic Party (SDP)
Per capita income	$30,400 (2005 est.)
Exports to U.S.	Total exports = $550.5 billion
	U.S. accounts for 22.7%
	Total exports to U.S. = $125 billion (2005 est.)
Imports from U.S.	Total imports = $451.1 billion
	U.S. accounts for 14%
	Total imports from U.S. = $63.2 billion (2005 est.)

Historical Perspective Overview

Geographically, the Japanese archipelago in located on Asia's east coast, consisting of four large islands (Honshu, Hokkaido, Kyushu, and Shikoku) as well as approximately 4000 small islands. Honshu, the largest island and cultural center, has about 50% of the population, including five major cities, the capital of Tokyo, as well as Yokohama, Osaka, Nagoya, and Kyoto (its ancient capital). This relatively small landmass has contributed to a collective mind-set paradox—insularity and expansionism.

Indeed Japan is an ancient society. Myth holds its founding to be in 660 B.C. by Emperor Jimmu, but records on this country do not appear until A.D. 3. Seemingly, the majority of its people are descendants of migrating Mongolians from the northeast; its minority population of *Ainu* inhabitants concentrated in the north supposedly descended from Caucasoid types from northern Asia. Only in the twenty-first century has foreign presence increased in the homeland.

Japan is an ancient society.

Since its beginnings, Japan has been influenced by Chinese and Korean cultures, as well as by Shinto, a dominant philosophy entwined with the state. This "way of the gods" details rituals and customs, which foreigners perceive as religious ceremonies. From the fifth century onward, there is evidence of development of a clan-based society on the Yamato plains. It is here that the myth originated of the clan leaders' divine descent from the sun goddess, continued through the imperial line over the centuries until Emperor Hirohito in 1946 denied his divinity, a traumatic experience for his subjects.

The clan system of governance gave way in A.D. 1192 to military overlord rule and establishment of the feudal system. Emperors were relegated to ceremonial roles, power shifted to powerful noble family control holding the title of *shogun*. This was the period of family lineage and honor, self-discipline, and bravery epitomized in the warrior retainer or *samurai*. Various shogunal dynasties rose to rule. This agrarian economy changed slowly following encounters with Westerners, starting with the Portuguese in 1542. By the mid-1600s, foreign missionaries were expelled and Japan cut itself off from the world for 200 years. For most of its modern history, Japanese were influenced by feudalistic concepts of absolute obedience and loyalty to their superiors.

Japanese feudal society lasted until the nineteenth century, when Commodore Perry's voyage forced Japan to open to the West. Typically a series of changing images about the Japanese people and culture emerged and can be grouped around stages. The first is pre-World War II, when the Japanese were admired for their ambitious effort to catch up to European and American industrialization. At this stage and the next, many viewed Japanese diplomatic endeavors as devious and were threatened by Japan's assertions of hegemony over Korea, annexation of Taiwan, and war with Russia (1904–05) which it won, gaining control not only of Korea, but also of the southern tip of Manchuria until it had total control there by 1931. As Japan sought further modernization, it became a major colonial power, invading even China in this process. Aligned in East Asia with Nazi Germany and Fascist Italy, the nation exhibited an imperialism that compelled the United States to impose limited economic sanctions in 1940. America and its allies were shocked by the daring and destructive Japanese attack on Pearl Harbor in 1941 that forced the United States to declare war on Japan. During World War II, Japan continued to expand in China, Vietnam, and elsewhere in Asia until Allied military successfully forced a retreat. The use of the atomic bomb finally caused the Japanese government to surrender and accept American occupation of their homeland. The victors then proceeded to demilitarize the nation, democratize the government, and reform the Japanese society and economy. The Allied peace terms stripped Japan of all territories acquired since 1894 in East Asia. During the postwar period, the foundations were laid for today's economic and political society, and the occupation ended in 1952 when Japan was declared an independent state.

Since then Japan has transformed itself into an industrial superpower. By 1960, it had the third largest economy in the world. Although it has eight political parties, the Liberal Democratic Party (LDP) has dominated the government since its founding in 1955, despite corruption, other scandals, and economic reverses. Now Japan is a strong democracy where human rights are respected and militarization is avoided. Under the new constitution, the parliamentary form of government has been retained and the emperor's role is symbolic. The head of government, the prime minister, is elected by the Parliament or National Diet. The upper and lower houses are elected by the public. Despite its economic "miracles" and leadership in the global marketplace, Japan is still a highly insular culture with an entrenched bureaucracy and protectionist trade policies.

Cultural Guidelines for Business in Japan

Japan is a "high context" culture that thrives on subtlety and consensus. Its people manifest high educational abilities, formidable technological skills, and powerful social coordination.[24] In all they undertake, they are usually meticulous and methodical. The following general insights may prove helpful when dealing with the Japanese, whether at home or abroad.

Language and Communication

The Japanese language is complex, subtle, and predictable. By the time a native speaker is halfway through a statement, a Japanese will translate simultaneously and likely know how the sentence will end, whereas that same person interpreting from English will wait until the foreigner has finished before beginning the translation into Japanese. Communications in Japan are usually marked by the following characteristics.

- Indirect and vague references are more acceptable than direct and specific references—ambiguous terminology is preferred.
- Sentences frequently are left unfinished so that another may make a conclusion.
- Conversation transpires within an ill-defined and shadowy context, never quite definite, so as not to preclude personal interpretation.
- Language is capable of delicate nuances regarding states of mind and relationships—while rich in imagination, it can be clumsy for science and business.
- There are layers of soft language with various degrees of courtesy and respect. The female is especially affected by this; "plain" or "coarse" language is considered improper for her.

The Japanese language is complex, subtle, and predictable.

■ The listener makes little noises of tentative suggestion, understanding, and encouragement. "*Hai*" may mean more than "yes" and imply, "I'm listening" or "I understand."
■ Nonverbal communications are subtle, and Japanese are disconcerted by broad expressions and gestures of Americans.

In Elashwami's research, he asked Japanese managers to describe their system of business communication in contrast to that of Americans. He reported the findings summarized in Exhibit 13.12.

EXHIBIT 13.12
CULTURAL CONTRASTS IN BUSINESS COMMUNICATIONS

	Japanese	Americans
Objective	Seek information and formulate a proposal.	Provide information and seek commitments and actions.
Opening	Thanking; apologizing; assessing.	Move directly to meeting purpose agenda.
Content	Specific questions; solicit details and data.	Seek facts and develop a plan of action.
Persuasion Tools	Waiting; patience.	Immediate gain or loss of opportunity.
Non-verbal	Modesty; minimize position.	Urgency signified by body gestures.
Closing	Maintain harmony for future relationships.	Seek affirmation; ascertain specific requests to move ahead.
Cultural Values	Politeness; indirectness; Develop relationship.	Efficiency; directness; action.

Source: F. Elashwami and P. R. Harris, *Multicultural Management—New Skills for Global Success*. Burlington, MA: Elsevier/Butterworth–Heinmann Gulf, 1993, p. 124.

Frequently, while entertaining, the real business and political deals are concluded.

Japan has a formal politeness for official negotiation and ordinary business communication, while an informal approach may be used while socializing. Frequently, while entertaining, the real business and political deals are concluded.

The Japanese require more information about the person with whom they interact, so as to determine which form to use in their complex language. Thus, they are given to asking questions about your job, title, responsibilities, and so on. When a business meeting is scheduled, they prefer advance information in the form of electronic mail, brochures, and even proposals.

They appreciate it when outsiders seek to learn more about their unique culture and language, even if it is only a few phrases or expressions in Japanese.

Dress and Appearance

Neat, orderly, and conservative attire is recommended for managers. Ordinary workers and students frequently wear a distinctive uniform and even a company pin, which managers also may sport (a holdover from feudal days when a kimono carried a lord's symbol). The ancient, classical dress, the kimono, is becoming less common even in the privacy of the home and is retained for ceremonial events. Western formal dress is used for important state occasions. Traditional native dress is sexless, although the shape of the garment is different for the two sexes. The colors are often neutral, with women sometimes tending toward flowery patterns.

Japanese youth prefer to wear contemporary clothes and hairstyles; they want to look like teenagers seen elsewhere. Also with changes in diet, the young appear to be physically larger than their parents, and obesity is a growing problem with this affluent generation.

Colors have different significance in Japanese culture (e.g., white for sorrow, black for joy).

Food and Eating Habits

Eating in Japan is ritualistic, communal, and time consuming. The interaction is considered as important as the food. While the traditional diet emphasizes rice, noodles, and fish, youths tend toward popular Western foods. The alcoholic beverage of *sake* often accompanies the main or ceremonial meal so as to facilitate conversation.

Tokyo is said to have a restaurant, bar, or cabaret for every 110 members of the population, with many international foods represented. Fast-food establishments are everywhere and popular.

Time, Age, and Rewards

Japanese are punctual and need time for connections to make proper contacts. Yet they expect you to wait for group decisions that also take time to arrive at consensus.

Traditionally, they respect seniority and the elderly. There is a sense of order, propriety, and appropriate behavior between inferiors and superiors.

Young managers, recruited from the universities after stiff examinations, are expected to stay with a company until they are 60 years of age, conforming, doing what is expected of them, and showing respect

Japanese are punctual.

and deference to senior or older employees. Then the crucial decision is made as to whether the 60-year-old manager is to become a company director; if he or she makes it, he or she can stay beyond the normal Western retirement age and may work into the 80s. The remainder of the managerial group not so selected become department or subsidiary directors and are expected to retire between 55 and 60, though even then they can be retained in a temporary capacity. These customs are now changing, however.

The tendency is to reward and recognize the group or organization rather than the individual in Japanese organizations. One achieves and is recognized through the group in ever-widening circles: family, team, department, division, company, nation.

Great emphasis is placed on security and the social need for "belonging." When traveling abroad, Japanese stay within their own group, generally avoiding individual contact with the locals.

Relationships

Japan is cohesive and crowded.

A nation the size of California, Japan is cohesive and crowded, which accounts for its rituals of bowing and politeness in crowded urban areas. Japanese relationships are familial and group oriented, instead of individualistic; Japanese value group relations and harmony. Group leadership is more highly regarded than individual initiative. There is a tendency toward clannishness based on family or group connections—know your place and be comfortable with it. Thus, the drive is toward agglomeration, combines, and clustering of organizational relationships.

Since personal relationships score high with Japanese and future relationships depend on how you respond in the first encounter, cut-and-dried relationships with business contacts are inadequate and must be supplemented by a social relationship for maximum effect. This usually means entertaining the client with a "night on the town" and not at one's home. Part of the Japanese manager's reward is a generous budget for entertaining. When away from home on business, the Japanese businessperson expects to be entertained lavishly (meals, theater tickets, etc.), but repays this kindness manifold.

With regard to international relationships, Japan has close emotional and economic ties to the United States but is suspicious of aggressive Americans. The Japanese fear China, yet they are emotionally allied and identify with the Chinese.

In business relationships, there are two Japans: officialdom and the intellectuals (e.g., politicians and businesspersons). In both, decisions tend to be group mulling for consensus, give-and-take inconclusiveness, and the traditional authority pyramid. There is a symbiotic relationship between government and business—cozy but not constricting. This is still an unsolved issue.

In the context of social relations, Japanese tend to be clean, polite, and disciplined; but publicly, with strangers, they can be pushy and inconsiderate (e.g., the tourist). Social and self-control disguise a highly emotional quality of the Japanese character and relationships; the mesh of binding social relationships is weakening and hard to comprehend. While the Japanese are sensitive to what others think or expect of them and have a sharp sense of right and wrong, they find it difficult to deal with the unexpected and strange, and so they may laugh inappropriately.

Again, youth epitomize the culture in transition. They are energetic and productive, yet anxious for change, gaining a new sense of "I/my/me-ness," while the pattern for their elders is "we-ness." The general gap between the generations is very wide. For example, younger university graduates are more open to entrepreneurship, especially information technologies.

Youth epitomize the culture in transition.

In business organization, the "bridge" for the young manager is an elder, upper middle manager assigned as a guide or facilitator. This senior person is rarely the direct superior of the young manager but is expected to know him or her, meet regularly, and be available for advice and counsel, and to assist in transfers and discipline, when necessary. This respected elder manager is always consulted on promotions and other personnel matters concerning that young person's career. He or she is the human contact for the organization with the young manager, the listener and guide who provides a significant human relationship.

Attitudes and Beliefs

The typical Japanese character is diverse, with a sense of poetry and of the ephemeral. There is a concern for the transitory, inconclusive qualities of life, for nature, and its observation. It is actively curious, energetic, and quick, with a sense of delicacy and wistfulness. One manifestation is in the art of flower arrangements.

Although many Japanese will not admit to being religious, two philosophies of life are pervasive in Japan and influence their behavior: Confucianism introduced in the sixth century A.D. and Shintoism which is native to this island people. Shinto teaches respect for nature and counsels harmony between human and nature. Shinto minor deities are found in shrines (*jinja* distinguished by red wooden archways, and in nature itself (e.g., mountains and rivers)). The dominant religious thrust is the convergence of Shintoism and Buddhism (married Shinto, buried Buddhist). Buddhism is the largest conventional religion in Japan, while Christianity has made limited impact (except with Christmas celebrations and decorations in retail stores). The crusading Soka Gakkai sect is also a political party that fights inequalities of the social structure, while enshrining the idealistic, self-denial, and the underdog.

Values and Standards

The Japanese personality generally is self-confident and flexible, demonstrating a sense of order, propriety, and appropriate behavior. There is a tendency toward diligence and thrift, balanced by a fun-loving approach, which, at times, seems almost frivolous and extravagant. In outlook, the Japanese are cautious and given to stalling tactics. They are also insular, which is manifested by the in-group tendency. The rigid, ossified Japanese class system, by which each person has his or her place as superior or inferior, is disappearing.

Japanese value peace and economic progress, ensured somewhat by the fact that only 1% of the nation's gross national product is devoted to defense spending. This culture highly regards new ideas and technologies, swallowing them up until they are Japanized (internalized) after careful, detailed examination. The success of Japanese communications and automotive industries confirms this value. Today there is a subtle shift in emphasis under way from copying others to creating one's own by innovation.

Japanese society also values training and education, especially of the young. It also esteems a spirit of intensity and craftsmanship manifested by a quality of deep penetration and pride in work no matter how humble.

A basic standard of Japanese life is work and play hard.

Japanese prefer congenial, known surroundings and seek to create an atmosphere of well-focused energy and disciplined good cheer. A basic standard of Japanese life is work and play hard—work particularly for the good of the family or company family, and maintain controlled competition and cooperation in the process. Then play hard—modern Japanese devote more time to leisure and recreational activities.

Postwar Japanese fear foreign military involvement, but they are willing to engage in humanitarian endeavors sponsored by the United Nations and sent a small contingent to Iraq.

The younger generation seeks more control over their lives. A minority of radical, revolutionary Japanese youth have an entirely different set of values from the majority. Some can be vicious and violent, yet espouse a spirit of self-denial, self-correction, and self-dedication to what they consider a higher cause. Even criminal gangs will publicly apologize in press conferences to the public when they cause too much violence and disruption in society.

Essentially, in the twenty-first century, this is a society concerned about national economic welfare, market penetration; and humanitarian endeavors. Increasingly, Japanese companies are giving a percentage of profits to promote education, social welfare, culture, and protection of the environment.

Management in Japan

Japanese continue to pursue the acquisition of Western management skills, not simply technical, knowledge of products, or manufacturing, but sophisticated management theory and concepts transferred to the Japanese environment. This is forcing changes in the way of dealing with foreigners. A more competitive climate is developing for foreigners or *gaijin* that permits more direct investment in Japanese enterprises. Furthermore, when expatriate managers return from working in Japanese operations abroad, they introduce some of their new learning from that experience into local management.

In their organizations, the goals are product quality and superiority; teamwork and consensus; corporate growth and social responsibility. Here are some observations about this unique business culture:

- Japanese will try to achieve sales and profits without harming face and harmony or creating a poor standing in the business community.
- Third-party or indirect introductions are important for creating trust between individuals who come together through a mutual friend, go-between, or arbitrator. This person may be involved until the conclusion of the negotiation.
- Whomever you approach in the organization, do so at the highest level; the first person contacted is also involved throughout the negotiation.
- Avoid direct communication on money; leave this to the go-between or lower echelon staff. Money, if passed to a Japanese businessperson, should be in an envelope.
- For social visiting, a guest is frequently given a present or small gift, such as a hand towel beautifully wrapped; however, on the next exchange of visit, you are expected to offer a gift in kind.
- Do not publicly put a Japanese in a position where he or she must admit failure.
- Play down praise of your product or services; let your literature or go-between do that.
- Use business cards with your titles in both Japanese and English.
- A logical, cognitive, or intellectual approach is insufficient; the emotional level of communication is considered important (e.g., as in dealing with a known business associate versus a stranger).
- Formality prevails in senior staff meetings with interpreters present. The more important the meeting, the more senior executives present.
- Wait patiently for meetings to move beyond preliminary tea and sometimes long formalities.

Decision Making

Again, the Japanese value decision by consensus. Before action is taken, much time is spent on defining the question. They decide first if

A guest is frequently given a present or small gift.

there is a need for a decision and what it is all about. The focus is on what the decision is really about, not what it should be; once agreement is reached, then the Japanese move with great speed to the action stage. The question is referred to the appropriate people, in effect indicating top management's answer to the question. The system forces the Japanese to make big decisions and to avoid the Western tendency toward small decisions that are easy to make (minutiae). For example, instead of making a decision on a particular joint venture, the Japanese might consider the direction in which the business should go, and this joint venture is then only a small aspect of the larger issue.

Terms of Employment

The traditional corporate policy of long-term or life-time employments is changing. First, not all workers are considered permanent. A substantial body of employees (perhaps 20%) is not subject to this job security. Some positions are hired and paid for by the hour; women are generally considered in the temporary work category, and some who retire at 55 may be kept on in that temporary capacity; adjustments in the workforce can be readily made among these "temporaries."

For full-time employees, pay as a rule is on the basis of seniority and doubles every 15 years. Retirement is a two-year salary, severance bonus, usually at 55. Western pension plans are beginning to come into companies slowly and are low in benefits. In the past, permanent employees who left an employer would have a very difficult time being permanent again for another employer. The practice of lifetime employment is being undermined in the new work environment.

Another standard of Japanese work life seems to be continuous training.

Another standard of Japanese work life seems to be *continuous training*. The work life has a performance focus in contrast to a promotion focus; in scope, it involves training not only in one's own job, but in all jobs at one's level. The emphasis is on productivity, and the real burden of training is on the learner—"What have we learned to help us do the job better?"

On the whole, Japanese believe that the older worker is more productive and that output per man-hour is invariably higher in a plant with an older work population. With the new knowledge workers, that attitude is also being altered. Recognize also that the Japanese labor force is both aging and diminishing today. This has promoted the trend toward more women in the workforce, and they are being given a greater role; increased use of robots is also in evidence. Birth rates have plummeted: the population is shrinking drastically—possibly from 128 million (in 2006) and to 100 million by 2050.

This will affect the nation's GDP which is also on the decline. Japan in the near future can be expected to become a major leader in pan-Asian cooperation, while remaining a close ally of the United States.

The Japanese are a remarkable and unique people. Their subtle, complex culture in particular illustrates the differences and diversity of Asian cultures in general. The Japanese have also learned and successfully applied many lessons from other countries, and other nations are learning from them, especially in terms of management and organizational behavior.

MALAYSIA

The country of Malaysia consists of 127,317 square miles divided into two geographically separate parts—Peninsular Malaysia and East Malaysia. Peninsular Malaysia is a long strip of land below Thailand, and at its tip is the Republic of Singapore, across the Strait of Malacca. East Malaysia is located on the north of the island of Borneo and consists of two states—Sarawak and Sabah. (Indonesia occupies the southern part of this island, while Brunei lies to the north of Sarawak.) Peninsular Malaysia contains dense jungles and steep mountain ranges in the north and fertile coastal plains to the west.

Historical Perspective Overview

Some 40,000 years ago Stone Age Malaysians lived here, and the aboriginal *Oran Asli* likely came from southwest China. Some 4500 years ago, Proto Malays supplanted them and are the ancestors of its modern inhabitants. Ethnically, they may be related to the peoples of Java, Sumatra, and the Philippines. For six centuries A.D., the Malay Peninsula has been controlled by outsiders from the kingdom of Funan (today Cambodia); in the seventh century A.D., the Sumatran Srivijaya Empire took over until the thirteenth century when the Java-based, Hindu Majaphahit Empire assumed governance. Various local states, especially Malacca, have ruled the area until 1511, when the Portuguese came, only to be overthrown by the Dutch in 1641. For 180 years they successfully occupied the region until 1795 when the British took over, and established a trading post in Singapore. The British attempted to join the various territories administratively, while developing local industries. In December 1941, the Japanese conquered the Malay Peninsula and ruled until their World War II defeat in August 1945 when the British again resumed control and attempted to unify the various entities. In 1955, the British agreed to permit full independence for Malaya, so elections were held and a federal government formed.

In 1963, the Federation of Malaysia became fully independent, consisting of 13 states, 11 of which are part of Peninsular Malaysia, plus the 2 states of Sabah and Sarawak. With a stable economy but

In 1963, the Federation of Malaysia became fully independent.

unstable politics, the new nation prospered in the 1990s by focusing on material gain rather than government accountability and corruption. Opposition parties are more concerned about political freedom, human rights, and improving race relations. Further information is contained in Exhibit 13.13.

EXHIBIT 13.13

MALAYSIA—PROFILE

Population	23,953,136 (July 2005 est.)
Ethnic groups	Malay, 50.4%; Chinese, 23.7%; Indigenous, 11%; Indian, 7.1%; Others, 7.8%
Religions	Muslim, Buddhist, Daoist, Hindu, Christian, Sikh; note—in addition, Shamanism is practiced in East Malaysia
Education	88.7% literacy rate
Land	328,550 sq km
Government	Constitutional monarchy
Political Parties	National Front or Barisan Nasional (BN), Alternative Front or Barisan Alternatif (BA) (includes PAS and PKR)
Per capita income	$10,400 (2005 est.)
Exports to U.S.	Total exports = $147.1 bilion
	U.S. accounts for 18.8%
	Total exports to U.S. = $27.7 billion (2005 est.)
Imports from U.S.	Total imports = $118.7 billion
	U.S. accounts for 14.6%
	Total imports from U.S. = $17.3 billion (2005 est.)

Today, the government is a parliamentary democracy under a constitutional monarchy with a king as head of state. Kuala Lumpur is the capital of Malaysia and is the location of the federal parliament and the prime minister. In addition, each of the 13 state governments has parliaments and prime ministers, except for 9 headed by sultans. The constitution provides for a strong federal government, restricts the power of the monarchy, and provides for an independent judiciary. The present government policy promotes Malay participation in business and the dispersal of industry to less developed areas. Malaysia's major exports are rubber, tin, palm oil, timber, and petroleum, textiles and apparels, chemicals, electronic components, transport equipment, manufactured and wood products; the major imports are machinery, transportation equipment, and consumer goods.

Cultural Guidelines in Malaysia

The fundamental concept of *Budi* surrounds the ethical system of the Malay people. *Budi* illustrates the ideal behavior expected of a Malay. Its basic rules are respect and courtesy, especially toward elders; affection and love for one's parents; and a pleasant disposition and harmony in the family, the neighborhood, and in the society. There are two forms of *Budi*: *Adab*, which means that the individual has a responsibility to show courtesy at all times; and *Rukun*, which means that the individual must act to obtain harmony either in a family or in society. Malays place the utmost importance on relationships with relatives, friends, and colleagues.

Malays do not seem to value the pursuit of wealth for its own sake. They do, however, believe in hard work and self-reliance. Life is viewed as a passing thing, and family and friends take precedence over self-centered interests, such as the accumulation of profit and materialism. The Malays' love for children is reflected in the gentle and tender manner in which they raise them.

Budi illustrates the ideal behavior expected of a Malay.

Gestures and Greetings

In this multicultural society, you should determine first what ethnic group representative you are communicating with—Malay, Indian, Chinese. The Malays or *Bumiputeraten* tend to dominate government positions and speak the official language—*Bahasa Malaysia*. Indians may speak one of several Indian languages and are prevalent in professions, such as lawyers and journalists, as well as laborers. Chinese usually speak a southern dialect of their language and make up the majority of affluent businesspeople. The last two groups are largely immigrants and culturally reflect the practices of their homelands, previously described. Chinese migrated in the fifteenth century, while the Indians mainly relocated in the twentieth century, they trace their presence here over 400 years ago when they came as traders and brought their Islamic religion. Generally, the educated in all three groupings speak English.

There are several forms of nonverbal communication in Malaysia. Familiarity with greetings and knowledge of which gestures to avoid will lead to a more successful business trip. The following are a few examples:

■ When meeting a Malay, the elder person should be mentioned before the younger, the more important before the less important, and the woman before the man.
■ In rural areas, it is customary for men and women to shake hands with each other. When meeting a man, a Malay woman may *salaam*,

which is bowing very low while placing the right palm on the fore-head, and then covering the hands if a person is believed to be unaware of the social etiquette pertaining to handshaking. The traditional Malay greeting resembles a handshake with both hands but without the grasp. The man offers both hands to his friend, lightly touches his friend's outstretched hands, and then brings his hands to his breast. This simply means, "I greet you from my heart."

- In Malaysia, instead of pointing to a place, object, or person with the right index finger, which is considered impolite, it is more common to point with the thumb of the right hand with the fingers folded under.
- In calling for a taxi, one uses the fingers of the right hand, moving them together with the palm facing down in a waving or "come here" gesture, which is opposite of the typical American beckoning of a taxi.
- A gesture to avoid is patting a child on the head. The head is considered to be the center of the intellectual and sacred power; it is therefore holy and should not be touched.

Religion, Nature, and Human Nature

Islam is the state religion of Malaysia.

Islam is the state religion of Malaysia, exerting a great influence not only on the method of worship but also on the Malay's way of life. Foreign business representatives hoping to function effectively in Malaysia must understand Islam to comprehend the culture. (Refer back to observations about Islam in Chapter 11.) Such religious practices are an integral part of daily life.

A Muslim is guided by the prescriptions of the Koran, which details the rules of behavior, including all social and business activities. Muslims are expected to recite the creed, "There is no God but Allah, and Muhammad is his Prophet." They must pray five times a day and worship Allah as the only true God. Providing charity, helping the needy, fasting during the month of Ramadan, and, if possible, making a trip to Mecca are additional practices that the Muslim Malays are expected to perform. They should also refrain from eating pork and drinking alcoholic beverages. In the main portion of the mosque, the Muslim place of worship, Malay women sit apart from the men and are not allowed at any time to mix casually or to eat with them. Thus, foreigners respect their taboos—greet and eat only with the right hand; never show the soles of your shoes; never touch anyone on the head.

Malays deeply respect traditional customs, even those of the religious minorities. These traditional practices and beliefs are called *Adat*, meaning custom. The importance of *Adat* is illustrated by their proverb, "Let the child perish but not the *Adat*."

In some Western cultures, an underlying belief exists that humanity can overcome nature. In the Islamic faith, the Malay position concerning the human relationship to nature is one of being subject to or living in harmony with nature. At times, a Malay feels subject to the elements because of a fatalistic attitude and belief in the supremacy of God's will. A Malay also believes that he or she is part of the natural world that reflects his or her belief in animism—the notion that plants and animals have a spiritual dimension.

A Malay pays little attention to what has happened in the past and regards the future as both vague and unpredictable. Planning for the future or hoping that the future will be better than either the present or the past is simply not their way of life, although the government seemingly favors long-range planning.

From the perspective of the Islamic faith, there is a strong sense of fatalism, as indicated by common expressions such as "God willing" or "if God wants me to be something I will, if not, God's will be done." These factors favor a lack of motivation for worldly success, which is replaced by a motivation to develop deep and lasting relationships with friends and relatives. Traditionally, Malays have felt that in receiving material success, they might lose the highly valued respect of their family and friends. Most of the Chinese inhabitants call themselves Buddhists but may follow other religious traditions simultaneously.

Trust, Respect, and Leadership

Trust for a Malay is fundamental to a successful interpersonal relationship. An individual's capability for loyalty, commitment, and companionship are the key characteristics on which the Malay generally bases trust. The process for developing trust is internal and personal. In some Western cultures, the basis for trust is external and professional, centered on a level of expertise and performance.

Initially in a relationship, Malays show respect through formalities. However, as a relationship progresses, formalities are slowly dropped until an informal atmosphere is reached. This slow transformation can confuse some businesspersons. Malays respect a compromising person who is willing "to give and take." In Malay negotiations, the person who compromises is the most respected person and will often receive more than anticipated.

In Western organizations and institutions, status is usually attributed to someone demonstrating leadership capabilities. In Malaysia, the process is somewhat reversed. Malays are born into a certain social position or status, and if the status is very high or important, then they are expected to demonstrate leadership capabilities. For a Malay, the most important quality of a leader is confidence and the ability to understand people. A leader in Malaysia is also expected to be religiously devout, humble, sincere, and tactful. Even if a person is not worthy of respect, the position might demand that he or she receive it. A Malay feels most comfortable in a hierarchal structure with a clearly

A leader in Malaysia is also expected to be religiously devout, humble, sincere, and tactful.

defined role and emphasis on room for growth in interpersonal relationships.

Work Ethic

In Malaysia, work is viewed as one of many activities. A large percentage of time in a Malay's life is spent developing deeper relationships with family and friends in ways that would appear as idle time to many. An example of this perspective is the treatment of the elderly. An elderly person in Malaysia is regarded as a wise counselor who plays an important role in society. To get ahead, however, both connections and merit are necessary. Education and training are considered key components for economic and social advancement.

For some Muslims, the work week in five states is normally Saturday through Wednesday; this pattern allows for Friday as a holy day, or at least two hours off to attend mosque. The "weekend" starts on Thursday. Elsewhere, business hours are generally 8 A.M. to 5 P.M., Monday through Friday, with variations in government offices, banks, and retail shops. Check out local customs in regard to workdays and hours.

Politics and Power

Malaysia is a nation in rapid transition.

Malaysia is a nation in rapid transition to a modern industrialized society, so many of the old traditions are disappearing. Of fundamental importance to anyone working here is an understanding of the sensitive pluralism. To succeed in this country, one must understand some of the differences, similarities, and difficulties between the Malays and other Bumiputra, Chinese, and Indians.

After much ethnic tension and rioting, a 20-year development plan favoring the Malays was initiated in 1970 between Malaysia and China. The plan contained two principal economic objectives: (1) to check the dominance of Chinese economic control by requiring a definite percentage of the labor force to be Malay; and (2) to reduce the foreign share of the Malay market from 60 to 30% by 1990. In spite of the modernization and education efforts, results have not been completely satisfactory. Even though there has been a decrease in the Malay market allocated to foreign investors, there is still room for expansion of the present foreign-controlled market.

The near balance of power that exists between Malays and Chinese requires close cooperation between the two cultures. However, due to differences in customs, culture, and values, there has been a great deal of tension between them, at times producing unstable environments. The unpleasant relationship between the Malays and the Chinese appears ongoing, perhaps due to the strong cultural differences between the Chinese Buddhist and Islamic practices of the Malays.

Economically, growth averages 7 to 8% per annum, and the country has become a regional economic powerhouse in the last decade. Most sectors are open to international trade. Foreign businesspersons in Malaysia are challenged to facilitate synergistic skills to their relationships with this people. This will foster not only cooperation between and among the locals, but will also contribute to collaboration with the country's diverse inhabitants. Also one should be aware that the government policy is against drug addiction and that draconian sentences are given to those so arrested and sent for rehabilitation.

PAKISTAN

Modern Pakistan has the Arabian Sea to its southwest, India to the southeast, Afghanistan to the north (which adjoins Turkmenistan, Tajikistan, and Kyrgyzstan), and China to the east.

Historical Perspective Overview

The recorded history of the people now living in this land goes back to 3000 B.C. Here in the Indu Valley, the Indo-Aryan civilizations developed a mixed culture resulting from numerous invasions of nomadic tribes from the west, including Persians. Located on a number of major trade routes, the region also attracted Arabs, Mongols, and Europeans; more recently, Afghan refugees have arrived in great numbers. Today, the inhabitants are primarily Punjabis, but the other four groups include Pathan, Sindhi, Mujhair, and the Balucchi—all named after provinces from which they originated. Given such ethnic divisions, the society is split along tribal, caste, and economic lines, although 97% are Muslim—77% Sunni and 20% Shiite.

The Islamic Republic of Pakistan was founded in 1947.

The Islamic Republic of Pakistan was founded in 1947, when Britain divided into two nations. Religion was the main divider, as the Hindus were predominantly in India and the Muslims in Pakistan. At that time, Pakistan was also divided, whereby Muslim districts were in West Pakistan, and East Pakistan consisted of a single province. In 1971, East Pakistan gained independence and is known today as Bangladesh. Since its founding, India and Pakistan have not been able to come to an agreement about the states of Jammu and Kashmir. The status of Kashmir is in dispute still and the cause of much hostility with India.

In the twenty-first century Pakistan has assumed a strategic role in the war on terrorism, especially with the Talaban and al Qaeda in Afghanistan. Many members of al Qaeda are in hiding from the United States and allied forces in the mountains of Pakistan. In 2005, the country also suffered from massive volcanic eruptions that prompted significant international aid to flow into this poor country.

Today, Pakistan is a federal republic with the prime minister as head. In October 1999 there was a military coup which suspended the existing constitution. The new President General Pervy Musharraf, oversees the county as head of the eight member military. He has been able to bring some social and economic stability to this volatile diverse country.

Cultural Guidelines for Business in Pakistan

The official language of Pakistan is Urdu, but it is only spoken by 9% of the population; 48% speak Punjabi, 12% Sindhi, and 27% speak other languages, including Pushtu, Saraiki, Baloch, and Brahui. English is used by the government and military. The state religion is Islam, which 97% follow (refer back to Chapter 11 for further insights on Muslims). Minority religions include Christianity, Hinduism, and Parsi. Ethnically, Pakistan is composed of Punjabis, Sindhis, Pashtuns, Afghans, Balochs, and Muhajirs. As indicated in Exhibit 13.14, life expectancy and literacy rates have increased, while infant and maternal mortality has dropped.

Pakistan is still behind many countries with similar per capita income. There is also a big gender discrepancy, whereby boys will usually complete five years of school and girls only 2.5. Similarly, 62% of males and only 35% of females are literate. Muslim fundamentalism is partially responsible for women failing to achieve their full potential in this traditional society, but gender restrictions are lessening. In urban areas women have moved ahead in government and the professions.

Pakistan faces another development problem: 32% of the population fall below the poverty line. GDP growth in 2002 was only 2.6%.

The state religion is Islam.

EXHIBIT 13.14

PROFILE OF PAKISTAN

Population	165,803,500
Languages	Punjabi, Sindhi, Siraiki, Pashtu, Urdu, English
Religions	Sunni & Shiite Muslim, Christian, Hindu
Education	48% literacy rate
Life expectancy	63 years
Land	796,095 sq km (307,374 sq. miles)
Government	Islamic Republic
Capital	Islamabad (755,935 population)
GDP per capita	$2400

Agriculture accounts for 21.6% of GDP. Pakistan is one of the world's largest producers of raw cotton, and in 2001, 59% of its total exports was cotton. The United States is Pakistan's biggest export market, representing 24%. The UAE is second at 7.9%. The two biggest suppliers to Pakistan are the UAE (10%) and Saudi Arabia (11.6%).

In the late 1990s, the United States imposed sanctions on Pakistan following nuclear tests conducted in 1998. However, following the terrorist attacks on September 11, 2001, the United States needed Pakistan's help to achieve military action in Afghanistan. The situation changed overnight for Pakistan with over a billion dollars in loans coming from the United States. Pakistan ended ties with the Taliban in December 2002 and has cooperated with the West in seeking out terrorists, even within its own borders.

Recently, Pakistan indicated that it would eliminate its nuclear weapons if India would do so as well. Pakistan has also been implementing a strategy to end its conflict with India, especially over Kashmir. Better relations and negotiations between these two great nations of the subcontinent are proceeding.

Exhibit 13.15 provides additional insights for business, humanitarian, and military personnel working in this country.

EXHIBIT 13.15
TIPS FOR DOING BUSINESS IN PAKISTAN

The family and the clan is the basis of this culture and such connections influence business and political relationships. Unfortunately, economic gains have benefited the few wealthy families who control commerce and government; some large landowners have become regional officials in the public sector. Two-thirds of the masses live in rural villages with limited opportunities. There is some social mobility, particularly in urban areas. After family, friends are important. Pakistanis are straightforward, honest, hospitable, and tolerant of foreigners.

Work Practices—During winter, business and government offices normally operate from 9 A.M. to 5 P.M.; during summer (April 15–October 15) from 8:30 A.M. to 5 P.M. Hours differ for retail shops and banks and for Ramadan when normal work is from 8:30 A.M. to 11:30 A.M. The work week is Sunday to Thursday, with time off on Friday for the Islamic holy day of rest; some businesses open on Saturday morning. Prayer time is 1 P.M.

Business Relationships—Foreigners are well advised to have an introduction to key persons they seek to contact. They should verify references and anticipate boasting about capabilities. Maintaining

EXHIBIT 13.15

TIPS FOR DOING BUSINESS IN PAKISTAN (CONTINUED)

personal honor is critical. The government has two investment agencies that produce helpful publications for the company and exporting. To facilitate export, 57 industrial estates have been established throughout the country to provide infrastructure and various concessions that encourage investment. Expect handshakes, business cards, and tardiness. This people have a relaxed sense of time and deadlines.

Social Customs—Since this is a strict Muslim society, act accordingly; the locals do not eat pork or drink alcohol. The left hand is unclean so do not touch food with it. The culture is very protective of women so their head is covered or veiled and many wear the *burqah*, the dark tent-like garb. Business entertaining is usually done with dinner in a restaurant or by an invitation to a home. If so invited, remove shoes before entering and bring a small gift. Pakistanis are generous, hospitable, and will ensure you have plenty of food to eat.

THE PHILIPPINES

*The Philippines'
7000 islands
cover
approximately
116,000 square
miles.*

The Philippines' 7000 islands cover approximately 116,000 square miles in the South China Sea. The largest islands comprise over 95% of the total land area and population, with Luzon being the largest island and Mindanao the second largest. Although Quezon City was declared the capital in 1948, most government activity still remains in Manila on the island of Luzon. See exhibit 13.16.

Historical Perspective Overview

In this island chain, prehistoric evidence of humans goes back 22,000 years. By the ninth century A.D., trade with China was vigorously under way and continues to this day. In the twelfth century, traders and clergy from Indonesia brought Islam to the Philippines. In 1521, Ferdinand Magellan became the first European to visit in Cebu, claiming the lands for the king of Spain. In 1565, the Spanish began to settle and named the archipelago *Philippines* in honor of their king, Philip II. Spain was so successful in converting the natives to Christianity that it remains the majority religion even today. Their missionaries in religious orders impacted the culture, especially education, social life, art, and architecture. By the eighteenth century, these orders were the largest landowners. However, Muslims in the southern islands resisted these conversion efforts. Many of the nation's modern problems stem from its colonial past.

EXHIBIT 13.16

THE PHILIPPINES—PROFILE

Population	87,857,473 (July 2005 est.)
Ethnic groups	Tagalog, 28.1%; Cebuano, 13.1%; Ilocano, 9%; Bisaya/Binisaya, 7.6%; Hiligaynon Ilonggo, 7.5%; Bikol, 6%; Waray, 3.4%; Other, 25.3%
Religions	Roman Catholic, 80.9%; Evangelical, 2.8%; Iglesia ni Kristo, 2.3%; Aglipayan, 2%; Other Christian, 4.5%; Muslim, 5%; Other 1.8%; unspecified, 0.6%; none 0.1%
Education	92.6% literacy rate
Land	298,170 sq km
Government	Republic
Political Parties	Kabalikat Ng Malayang Pilipino (Kampi), Laban Ng Demokratikong Pilipino (Struggle of Filipino Democrats or LDP), Lakas Ng Edsa (National Union of Christian Democrats or Lakas), Liberal Party (LP), Nacionalista, National People's Coalition (NPC), PDP-Laban, People's Reform Party, PROMDI, Pwersa ng Masang Pilipino (Party of the Philippine Masses or PMP), Reporma
Per capita income	$5100 (2005 est.)
Exports to U.S.	Total exports = $41.25 billion. U.S. accounts for 18.2%. Total exports to U.S. = $7.5 billion (2005 est.)
Imports from U.S.	Total imports = $42.66 billion. U.S. accounts for 18.8%. Total imports from U.S. = $8.02 billion (2005 est.)

Spain exploited the country's wealth, ruling through Mexico where its galleons shipped cargo to the motherland. Yet they were economically surpassed by overseas Chinese engaged in inter-Asian trade. Spanish prestige was further undermined when the British won the Seven Years' War and captured the Philippines. Though returned in 1764, from then on English and American influence emerged. By the nineteenth century, many Filipino elite had visited Europe, and nationalists began to advocate independence. When the United States won a war with Spain over Cuba in 1898, it took over the Philippines. This foreign regime was subject to wars and sporadic fighting with the nationalists, until the Japanese occupation from 1942 to 1945. The Americans had established a new political structure in 1935, known as the Commonwealth of the Philippines. After the Japanese surrender, the United States granted the country independence on July 4, 1946, partially in appreciation for Filipino help during the war. The Americans retained military bases; these were a source of contention with the locals until Clark Air Force Base was closed in 1991 and Subic Bay Naval Base in 1992.

The basic problem for the people for centuries was that the Filipino landlords pocketed most of the wealth, leaving the masses in poverty. This contributed to a communist Huk insurgency in 1946 that lasted decades. Although Ferdinand Marcos was elected president in 1965, by 1972 he declared martial law and ruled as a dictator until overthrown in 1986. Cronyism has always permitted the well-connected to profit illegitimately. A series of unstable governments have further weakened the government, even under two women presidents.

Historically, power in this land belongs to an oligarchy of powerful landed gentry and extended families as will be seen in Exhibit 13.17. In 1987 a new constitution was adopted, modeled on that of the United States, and the nation returned to a constitutional democracy with the election of a president and vice president by popular vote, along with a bicameral legislature, plus an independent judiciary headed by a Supreme Court. For governance, the country is divided into three geographic regions—Luzon, Visayas, and Mindanao—in addition to 15 administrative regions.

EXHIBIT 13.17
CONFRONTING POWER AND WEALTH

A crippled woman is leading the way to greater democracy in the Philippines. "My weakness is my strength," declared Grace Padaca, the recently elected governor of Isabela, a poor northern province. She referred not only to a childhood bout with polio that requires her to use crutches, but also her lack of political connections and financial muscle. To promote reforms that benefit the average poor citizen, she confronts influential political clans. Despite their elections previously as president, both Corazon Aquino and Gloria Arroyo came from the elite class and had such family connections. The reality, especially at the national level, is that Philippine politics is more dynastic now.

Province Isabela is a case in point. When Ms. Padaca won the election against a rival, she ended the Dy family's 41-year monopoly as local governors and mayors, representatives in Congress. Such wealthy families perpetuate themselves in power by a patronage network which functions as political parties elsewhere. Those in public office use their positions to channel money, jobs, and other benefits to their supporters. In this province, Chinese-Filipinos dominate business, as with the Dy clan's heritage. Padaca, a popular radio crusader, was able to counter such alliances to get elected, but as she tries to promote necessary social change, her efforts are frustrated by the Dys, one of whom was the former governor who left the public treasury heavily in debt. Padaca's three-year term is threatened by a recall election engineered by the Dy opposition. Sheila Coronel of the Philippine Center for Investigative Journalism argues that it is almost impossible for independent candidates to break the political dynasties' lock on high office. But democracy is fighting back in mayoral and local elections. Joel Rocamora of the Institute for Popular Democracy maintains that there are more first-generation candidates emerging and winning lower offices. The hope is that political dynasties will be undermined as the people move to the cities where they become better educated and more independent-minded in their voting.

Source: "Asia—The Philippines, Limping Forward," *The Journalist*, March 19, 2005, pp. 47–48.

Cultural Guidelines for Business in the Philippines[25]

While its neighbors became bywords for economic dynamism, the Philippines became famous for the excess of its rulers and for the poverty in major cities. The government's budget is on course with a surplus, and the infrastructure bottlenecks that throttled growth for so long are gradually being tackled. At last, the Philippines seems ready to emulate sustained rapid growth, enjoyed by much of the region until recently.[26]

In this multicultural society, Filipino, or Philipino, is the principal language, but English is also spoken as well as Chinese. Hospitality, friendliness, and sincerity are prominent aspects of the Filipino culture. An ambience filled with gaiety is the result of over 300 years of the Spanish influence. Filipinos are predominantly of Malay stock, with Chinese and American cultural influences.

The Philippines presents great contrasts in terrain and climate. Northern Luzon is mountainous, the southern islands are comparatively dry, while other parts are dense jungle areas. In addition,

Hospitality, friendliness, and sincerity are prominent aspects of the Filipino culture.

throughout the islands there are a number of volcanoes. The Philippines are located within the tropic zone with the low areas having a warm, humid climate and only slight variations from the average temperature of 80°F. The monsoon season lasts from June to November, and periodic typhoons pass over the island causing immense floods and damage to crops and homes.

The foreign policy of the Philippines is based on a close alliance with many other Asian countries. The major alliance is ASEAN—the Association of South East Asia Nations. Contacts in high places of government are essential in cutting through the bureaucratic red tape. The people basically work on the "mañana" system, since they seldom complete things on time despite deadlines. However, in their own fashion, things do get done. "Almost, but not quite" is the foreigner's conclusion.

Utang na loob, literally meaning "debt on the inside," is another trait of some Filipinos. A Filipino remains indebted for a favor for a long period of time, perhaps several generations. One may be asked to respond to a favor that was bestowed upon an ancestor many years ago.

The nation's economy is based on agriculture, forestry, and fishing, which employ more than half of the total labor force and account for more than 50% of all exports. The agricultural sector consists of the production of food crops essentially for domestic consumption (rice and corn) and cash crops for export. The country's major exports are sugar, copra, copra meal, coconut oil, pineapple, tobacco, and abaca. The Philippines is also one of the world's leading producers of wood and wood products. Although fishing contributes to the economy, the fertile fishing area has not been developed to its full potential. The Philippines are rich in mineral resources with nickel, copper, and other mineral deposits among the largest in the world. However, only a small portion of these have been surveyed and exploited. Government programs have recently been initiated to strengthen the industrial development and have included protective import duties and taxes. The United States has been a leading trading partner of the Philippines, purchasing about 18.2% of the country's exports, Japan purchasing approximately 20.1%, and the EU about 7%. Imports consist mainly of fuel and manufactured goods, particularly machinery. Of the 32 million people in the labor force, nearly 12% are unemployed or underemployed. Over the past three years, the Philippines has been recovering from an economic slowdown, but unemployment still remains high. The current president is trying to restore confidence both domestically and internationally in an attempt to regain economic stability.

The Philippines' population has more than doubled since independence was obtained some 60 years ago and contributes to the poverty of the masses. With a population numbering approximately 87 million, the Philippines has one of the highest birth rates in the world. Fur-

A Filipino remains indebted for a favor for a long period of time.

thermore, émigrés have come to the Philippines from many Southeast Asian countries, such as Indonesia, Malaysia, and China. The blend of these cultures has formed the Filipino culture. The most significant alien ethnic group residing in the Philippines are the Chinese who have played an important role in commerce since their arrival in the fourteenth century.

The present culture strongly reflects all of these influences, especially Hispanic. The education system was impacted by the presence and relationship here of the United States from 1898 to 1946. Education is highly valued, and there is free, though not compulsory, education through the secondary level. The literacy rate is approximately 93%, with a large portion of the nation's budget being spent on education. The Philippines prides itself on its educational system, and many of its graduates become professionals who work overseas, particularly in health care.

The standard of living in the Philippines varies, with only a few families owning a large percentage of the rural and urban real estate. These wealthy few control profitable businesses and the universities, as they live in luxury. Reform, especially in land ownership, progresses very slowly.

Business and Social Tips with Filipinos

Harmony

Filipinos believe in *pakiksama*, which literally means the ability to get along with people, emphasizing their attitude of conceding with the majority rather than strongly standing up for one's personal opinion. Confrontation is usually avoided. The consequence of an insult or a crime is quick, often violent, retaliation. The true feelings of the Filipinos are often subtle, behind an agreeing facade; the foreign businessperson in the Philippines should attempt to read hidden signals.

Social Forces

Hiya, or shame, is important for Filipinos, and the idea is instilled in their children at an early age. To accuse a person of not having this *hiya* trait is a gross insult because it indicates that a person is unable to feel shame as well as all other emotions. Therefore, in this society, avoid criticizing another person in public or in front of his friends because it shames him or her and is thus the greatest of insults.

The negative ramifications of *hiya* are that the Filipinos avoid change, innovation, or competition simply because if the result is failure, it would cause him to shame his family. Consequently, the Filipino family and the Filipino businessperson will "save face" at any cost.

Filipinos believe in pakiksama, *which literally means the ability to get along with people.*

Fatalism

Success for the Filipino is often a function of fate rather than individual merit, therefore, most people are content in their social position only because they feel fate has placed them there. Expressions such as "never mind," "it doesn't matter," or "it was my fate" are common reactions to problems such as typhoons, epidemics, and crop failures. Another demonstration of their belief in fate is that the Filipinos frequently gamble and play games of chance.

Sensitivity

Owing to their heritage, Filipinos are a somewhat emotional people and very sensitive. They are loyal friends and demand the same kind of loyalty in return. This aspect is reflected in social situations as well as business interactions. They are reluctant to share or to do business with a person unless there is a mutual sincerity. This has been a great obstacle in the past, as Filipinos have described American businesspeople as being overly aggressive and insensitive to feelings.

Hospitality

Filipinos enjoy entertaining others.

Filipinos enjoy entertaining others. When accepting invitations, one should inquire if the starting time is "American time" or "Filipino time." In the case of American time, one should arrive at the hour requested. However, if the arrival time is on Filipino time, it is not necessary to arrive until an hour or two later than requested. However, for sit-down dinners with a limited number of guests, one is expected to be on time. Filipino food may be eaten the *kamayan* way, or with the hands.

Individualism

The Filipinos much value individualism. If a foreign businessperson fails to treat a Filipino as an individual, the visitor may be refused help. It is important to take time to talk with adults and children, and to avoid being judgmental. The Filipinos will make every effort to maintain their reputation as being a hospitable people. In return, foreign businesspeople should be mutually polite and respectful toward them, avoiding superiority.

Female Roles

Although a moral double standard for males and females is still prevalent in the Philippines, the country prides itself on being one of the few Asian countries with a large percentage of women in government and politics. Women as well as men inherit property here, in contrast to other Asian countries.

Nonverbal Communication

Nonverbal techniques used in the Philippines include raising of the eyebrows indicating an affirmative reply, namely, a "yes." A jerk of the head downward means "I don't know," while a jerk upward means "yes." Like the Japanese, the Filipinos rarely say "no" like Americans do. They resist confrontation and may say "yes" verbally while putting their head downward, namely, a nonverbal signal for "I don't know." To indicate "come here" one would extend the hand out with the palm down, moving the fingers in and out as in a scratching motion.

Religion

The Philippines is the only predominantly Christian country in the Far East, primarily because of the Spanish influence. Over 80% of all Filipinos are Roman Catholic, which affects their culture and daily activities. The second largest church in the country is the Protestant *Iglesia ni Cristo*, or Church of Christ. There is a growing revival of fundamentalism in the country. A significant minority striving for human and religious rights is the one and a half million Filipinos who are Muslims. In southern areas of the islands, Islamic practices and militants dominate, and violence, kidnapping, and clashes with the government continue.

Morality and Ethics

"Correct" behavior is more likely to be defined by tradition and to be related to the family and other reciprocal obligations. Failure to measure up in terms of family expectations and traditions produces feelings of shame. As in most developing nations, including the Philippines, corruption is prevalent in the public services, government, and business. It is not uncommon for many complications in business and government bureaucracy to be speedily resolved by the payment of a favor. Such practices are the result of long historical and cultural development, rooted in the Spanish tradition. Also, as in the case of many developing countries, a foreign businessperson should be aware that an informal business sector operates underground, parallel to the formal sector.

Family Corporations

Family corporations are numerous, with management composed of the nuclear family and all the stockholders are relatives. Trust is not

Family corporations are numerous,

easily given to those who do not belong. The *palakasan* system refers to going through connections instead of through the proper channels. Having the right connections can facilitate a deal or employment. Note that Filipinos have produced an extraordinary synergy among their diverse cultural groups, and so are open to cooperation and collaboration.

Work Relations

Filipinos see no reason why conflict should be courted when silence or evasive speech will preserve peace. Filipinos' excessive attention to recognition sometimes results in preoccupation with form over substance, and people tend to say what they do not mean to maintain appearances. The business card, as far as Filipinos are concerned, is a handy reference and could be exchanged at the end of a meeting. In a business negotiation, every detail, however insignificant, should be negotiated to avoid misunderstanding and renegotiation. A Filipino business partner has to be cultivated and then this development may result in a reliable business relationship. Greater importance is given to personal relations than to written contracts.

A Filipino business partner has to be cultivated.

SINGAPORE

EXHIBIT 13.18
PROFILE OF REPUBLIC OF SINGAPORE

Area	618 sq km (239 sq miles)
Population	4,492,150
Religions	Buddhist, Muslim, Christian, Hindu, Sikh, Taoist, Confucian
Languages	Mandarin Chinese, Malay, Tamil, English
Education	94% literacy rate
Life Expectancy	81 years
GDP per capita	$26,500
Major cities	Singapore, the capital (4,108,000)

Singapore is located at the southern tip of Malaysia and is linked by the causeway over the Johor Straits. Essentially a city-state, it consists of 1 main island and 59 islets. The mainland, at 26 miles long and 14 miles wide, is smaller than New York City and the smallest nation in the world. At its center, the topography is small hills; the west has low but steep ridges; the east is generally flat with streams flowing into the South China Sea. Its nearest neighbors are Malaysia, Indonesia, and the Philippines.

Historical Perspective Overview

Traders between India and China have traveled to this island since the third century A.D. By the seventh century, it was part of the maritime Srivijays Empire, including Sumatra, Java, and the Malay Peninsula. As a result of commerce, the Malay Archipelago became a mix of culture and languages, including Chinese, Indian, Arab, Thai, Malay, and Javanese. In 1229, a trading city was established here as *Singapura* or "Lion City." Controlled for the next three centuries by Asian rulers, this major trading port was burned down by the Portuguese in 1613 and abandoned for a time. In 1818, Malay officials settled on the island, sharing it with indigenous tribes and Chinese. Later migrants came from India as merchants or detainees of the English, becoming today the second largest ethnic group on the island. This island society has long struggled with ethnic conflicts and violence but has emerged in modern era as a cosmopolitan environment.

In 1826, the British organized the Straits Settlements including Singapore, and eventually these were delegated as a Crown Colony. Under their administration, Singapore became a premier trading center and port of call between Europe and Asia. During World War II, the Japanese occupied the area until their surrender to the Allies in 1945. The city then became a hub for the British military in the region, and its infrastructure was renewed. In 1959 after the British allowed internal self-government, elections were held on the island for its own prime minister. By September 1963, the city was merged with Malaya and other territories, but the Malaysian Parliament forced Singapore to separate, so the city became an independent nation in August 1965. The new government concentrated on building a multiracial and multilingual society with a united "Singaporean identity." Focused also on economic development, the city-state attracted investors, international business, and tourists. Under the regime of the People's Action Party (PAP) political party and its prime minister Lee Kuan Yew, Singapore maintained political stability and prosperity until 1990 when the second prime minister, Goh Chock Tong, took over. By 1997, he pursued a policy of strong control in which society's rights were put ahead of individual freedom. Recently, Singapore was designated one of the Asian Tiger countries because of significant economic growth and prosperity. Considered by outsiders as the booming entrepôt of Southeast Asian capitalism, this community is known for its cleanliness, and its laws against littering, chewing gum, jaywalking, illegal drugs, weapons, pornography, spitting, and smoking in most public places.

The city became an independent nation in August 1965.

Cultural Guidelines for Business in Singapore

Singapore is a modern trading and industrial country and the major financial center of Southeast Asia. There are currently over 3000 multinational corporations headquartered in Singapore. It has achieved success partially because of its strategic geographic position and its natural harbor. At the beginning of the twentieth century, Singapore became a center for processing imports of rubber and tin from the Malay Peninsula, later developing into a center of distribution for European manufactured goods throughout the Asian region.

The ethnic composition of its population is 76.8% Chinese, 13.9% Malay, 7.9% Indian, and other small ethnic groups. The prevalent languages of Singapore are Chinese, Malay, Tamil, and English; English is the main language for business as well as the primary language in school. The literacy rate is 97% of males and 90% of females over the age of 15.

Singapore's major trading partners are the United States, Malaysia, and Hong Kong. Its major export is in electronics, representing 25%. Its manufacturing sector performed very well during the investment boom of 1999 and 2000. However, because the economy is not diversified, it took a dive during the Asian financial crisis in 1997. The government is currently considering various bilateral free-trade agreements to encourage foreign investment. The dominant People's Action Party (PAP) tends toward a social democratic stance and has been in power since 1959. In 1991, the constitution called for the president to be elected by the people rather than by parliamentary election.

SOUTH KOREA

Today's South Korea's business landscape stands radically transformed.

Today's South Korea's business landscape stands radically transformed. Of the 30 biggest *chaebol*, 16 have been shut down or radically downsized. The survivors—companies such as Samsung Group and LG—barely resemble their former selves. Of the 2100 financial institutions cluttering the banking industry in 1998, just 1600 are now standing. Of 24 major city banks, only half remain. Imagine such ruthless restructuring in Japan.[27]

The Korean Peninsula lies south of China, with the Yellow Sea to the west, and the Sea of Japan to the east. Manchuria and Russia border on the north. The total landmass for this peninsula, including islands, is 220 square kilometers (85,265 square miles). Today the communists in North Korea occupy about 55% of this land, while the democratic Republic of Korea in the south controls the remaining 45%. North and South Korea are separated by the Demilitarized Zone, an outcome of the end of the Korean War in 1953. This DMZ is a 4-kilometer-wide strip of land that runs along the 38th parallel for 243 kilometers (150 miles). Our focus in this section is South Korea with its capital of Seoul, just 56 kilometers (35 miles) south of this Demarcation Line. Other major cities in the Republic include Pusan, Taegu, Inch'on, and Taejon.

Historical Perspective Overview

In the prehistory period of 5000–1000 B.C., a Paleo-Asiatic people, Netolithic descendants, established settlements on this peninsula. According to myth, "Tangun" founded the Korean nation in 2333 B.C. By 57 B.C., three kingdoms were dominant on this landmass: Koguryo in the north, Paekche in the southwest, and Silla in the southeast. In A.D. 688 Silla conquered the other two kingdoms to found a state that was the foundation of modern Korea. Over their long history, Korcans clashed with many neighbors until the Monguls conquered them in 1259 to set up a reign that lasted a hundred years. In 1392, the Korean throne was seized by General Yi-Song-gye whose Choson Dynasty ruled until 1910. Previously, the country, afraid of Christian missionaries, isolated itself from the rest of the world and was known as the "Hermit Kingdom" until it opened itself to trading with the West in the 1860s. In the nineteenth century, both Japan and China vied for control of Korea, so the king turned to Russia for assistance, but Russia sought to control the nation's warm-water ports. When Koreans staged protests for independence, it led to the Sino-Japanese War of 1894–1895, which resulted in Japan assuming control on the peninsula, something confirmed again when Japan won a war with Russia in 1905. By 1910, the Japanese abolished the Korean monarchy and treated the country as a dependent colony, ruling ruthlessly. When Japan again went to war with China, from 1937 to 1945, it mobilized the country as a military base, while reorganizing its industries and economy. The locals were forced to adopt the Japanese language and names, as well as belief in Shintoism and the divinity of the Japanese emperor.

By 1910, the Japanese abolished the Korean monarchy.

Korea and its sufferings were virtually ignored by the rest of the world until the end of World War II, and the defeat of Japan by the Allies. Then Russia assumed control of the peninsula north of the 38th parallel, while Americans occupied the rest of Korea in the south. In 1948, the Soviets established a communist state in their zone and withdrew from the country. This Democratic Republic of Korea (DPRK) in the north is still the center of international tension in the twenty-first century (see Exhibit 13.19). The next year, the Americans also withdrew, leaving in place the Republic of Korea (RFK), known today as South Korea. United Nations efforts to reunite the two entities were blocked by communist nations. At that time, Korea became a focus of world attention in a clash between the East and the West: a battleground of communist and democratic ideologies. When

Exhibit 13.19
South Korea—Profile

Population	48,422,644 (July 2005 est.)
Ethnic groups	Homogenous, except for approximately 20,000 Chinese
Religions	No affiliation, 46%; Christian, 26%; Buddhist, 26%; Confucianist, 1%; Other 1%
Education	97.9% literacy rate
Land	98,190 sq km
Government	Republic
Political Parties	Democratic Labor Party (DLP), Democratic Party (DP), Grand National Party (GNP), People-Centered Party (PCP), United Liberal Democrats (ULD), Uri Party
Per capita income	$20,300 (2005 est.)
Exports to U.S.	Total exports = $277.6 billion U.S. accounts for 17% Total exports to U.S. = $47.2 billion (2005 est.)
Imports from U.S.	Total imports = $248.4 billion U.S. accounts for 12.9% Total imports from U.S. = $32 billion (2005 est.)

North Korea invaded South Korea in 1950.

North Korea invaded South Korea in 1950, it led to war with both the United Nations, led by the Americans, and China's intervention. With a stalemate in this conflict, an armistice was signed in 1953, leaving Korea divided by the DMZ in two states of suspended hostilities.

Syngman Rhee was elected the first president of South Korea, serving in that role from 1948 to 1960. After a period of political disorganization and rule by military junta led by Park Chung Hee, a new constitution obtained widespread public support. When Park was officially elected president in 1963, his authoritarian regime was successful in promoting the country's development. South Korea's economic transformation is the wonder of the world.[28] It took South Korea only three decades to transition from a farming nation to an industrial giant. Its quality products and energetic workers are exported around the globe, along with eager-to-learn technicians. South Korea has begun to open its market in a bid to join the big league of global competition, but some say it is difficult to shed its protectionist ways.[29]

South Korea has renewed its cities and built satellite cities around Seoul, as well as renewing the country's west coast. While northern relatives have stagnated under totalitarianism, this dynamic society produced first-class Olympic Games and facilities in 1988. It has experienced relatively peaceful elections and a more democratic government. Its population is restless for more freedom, improved working conditions and benefits, plus progress toward national reunification with the North. The Korea Development Institute reports that the country, like Taiwan, is being restructured toward a domestic-driven economy, especially with citizens having more disposable income. There is a growing demand for domestic goods and services, along with the desire for improved housing and tourism abroad. Yet, most South Koreans feel they have sacrificed too long; they live in relative poverty and complain of inequities. The workforce is no longer docile and cheap. Doing business there requires great care and sensitivity. The Korean people are responding to the economic crisis of the late 1990s with "disciplined determination and entrepreneurship."[30]

And to the north, a ruthless regime abuses the inhabitants, denying its people freedom and food, while undermining international relations as Exhibit 13.20 and the following quote underscore:

Most South Koreans feel they have sacrificed too long.

EXHIBIT 13.20
NORTH KOREAN NIGHTMARE

In the twenty-first century, the international community has been concerned about North Korea's ability to create nuclear power and weapons. Numerous six-party negotiations by America, South Korea, Japan, China, and Russia with this rogue regime have ended in discord. Despite promises of food and other aid, Kim Jong II and his militarists have resisted attempts to coax better behavior. But that is not the only problem neighbors have with this wily and cruel administration which permits its own population to starve. There are a range of other complaints about its criminal activities, ranging from kidnappings of other nationals and production of fake drugs, to money counterfeiting and laundering, to illegal trade in endangered species, missiles, and other weapons. This racketeering state, responsible for tons of illicit goods and fake currency, throughout Asia, has seen its diplomats expelled from a variety of countries. Last year the United States slapped sanctions on North Korea for illicit weapons proliferation. Up to 40% of the state's exports result from its criminal sector, earning up to $1 billion in ill gotten gains. Meanwhile, South Korea has quietly negotiated with northern officials to provide material assistance, while lessening restrictions on the exchange of citizens throughout the peninsula.

Source: "Asia—North Korea and Those Six-party Talks: A Frustrating Game of Carrots and Stichs," *The Journalist*, February 11, 2006, pp. 39–40.

Kim Jong II is pushing the world towards a showdown over his nuclear weapons program. As a result, there is a general anxiety experienced in Korea with many younger Koreans favoring some kind of detente with the north and the majority of elder Koreans, who remember the Korean War, are opposed.[31]

Cultural Guidelines for Business in South Korea

Religion and Spirituality

The underlying ethic of Korea is Shamanism, but the people have also been strongly influenced by Buddhism and Confucianism. Shamanism, the religion of ancient Koreans, venerates the spirit and ancestors, and considers elements of earth, mountains, rivers, and so on as sacred. Buddhism was introduced in Korea in the fourth century and has the longest history among the organized religions in Korea; 27% identify themselves as Buddhists. Confucianism also has been a strong force and the reason behind this people's appreciation of knowledge and education. The most influential of the newer native Korean religions is *Ch-ondo-gyo*, which was founded in the mid-nineteenth century on the belief that every person represents heaven.

Koreans are proud that Christianity was not introduced there by missionaries. Instead, in 1777, a Korean scholar in Peking had himself baptized as Catholic and introduced his new religion to his homeland. Protestantism gained a foothold in 1984 through a Korean doctor who became a royal physician diplomatic and spread this religious version. Today Christianity has the second largest constituency (about 24%), of which the majority adhere to Protestant denominations.

Koreans in all walks of life consult fortune tellers, called a *mudang*. Even executives resort to their forecasts, and a bad report may undermine a business undertaking.

National Characteristics[32]

If one were seeking a national characteristic for this people, one would choose resiliency to describe the ability to survive hardship and to sacrifice. A vital concept to understand in Korea is *kibun*, which is one of the most important factors influencing the conduct and the relationship with others. The word literally means *inner feelings*. If one's *kibun* is good, then one functions smoothly and with ease. If one's *kibun* is upset or bad, then things may come to a complete halt, and one feels depressed. The word has no true English equivalent, but "mood" is close. In interpersonal relationships, keeping the *kibun* in good order often takes precedence over all other considerations.

In business situations, individuals try to operate in a manner that will enhance the *kibun* of both persons. To damage the *kibun* may effectively cut off relationships and create an enemy. One does not tend to do business with a person who has damaged one's *kibun*. Much of the disturbance of *kibun* in interpersonal relationships has to do with lower-class persons disturbing higher-class persons. Thus, for example, a teacher can scold a student in the class and no individual feels hurt, so no one's *kibun* is especially disturbed.

Proper interpersonal relationships are all important among Koreans, and there is little concept of equality in relationships. Relationships tend to be vertical rather than horizontal, and each person is in a relatively higher or lower position. It is essential for one to know the levels of society and to know one's place in the scheme of things. In relationships, it is often necessary to appear to lower oneself in selfless humility and to give honor to other people. To put oneself forward is considered arrogance and worthy of scorn.

Confucianism's emphasis on hierarchy has also influenced relationships. Confucianism teaches that one should rank the public higher than the private; one's business or government duties come before one's personal consideration. Protocol is also important to Koreans. When meeting others, if you do not appreciate a person's actual position and give it due recognition, then one might as well withdraw on some pretext and try to avoid future contacts. A representative of another person or group at a meeting is treated with great care because the substitute may be sensitive to slights, either real or imagined, and report it back to his or her colleagues. This is very difficult for Westerners to understand, but a Korean who fails to observe the basic rules of social exchange is considered by other Koreans to not even be a person. He or she is an "unperson" or "unable." Koreans show very little concern for an unperson's feelings or comfort, and in short, such an unperson is not worthy of much consideration. However, every effort must be made to remain within the framework of polite relation.

Deference and Respect for Elders

Elders in Korean society are always honored, respected, pampered, and appeased. To engender the anger of an elder means serious damage, because age allows an older person to influence the opinions of others, regardless of the right or wrong of the situation. Like children, elders must be given special delicacies at meals, and their every wish and desire is catered to whenever possible. The custom and manner in which elderly people are sometimes sent to elder-care facilities in the United States is extremely barbarous and shocking to the Koreans. Every home in Korea, no matter how poor, allocates the best room in the house to the honored grandfather or grandmother. Like Japan, one wonders how long this admirable tradition will survive in the twenty-first century.

Elders in Korean society are always honored.

Etiquette

Koreans avoid touching another person.

Koreans are considered to be among the most naturally polite people in the world when the proper rules of etiquette are followed. In personal relationships with strangers or associates, Koreans avoid touching another person. This is considered an affront to his or her person, unless there is a well-established bond of close friendship or childhood ties.

In modern Korean society many businesspersons now shake hands. However, they will very often bow at the same time that they shake a person's hand. To slap someone on the back or to put one's arms around a casual acquaintance or to be too familiar with someone in public is a serious breach that may effectively cool future relations.

To embarrass someone by making a joke at his or her expense is highly resented, even if done by a foreigner who does not understand the customs. After a few drinks, businessmen often become very affectionate but at the same time apologize for being a bit drunk. The next day they will tell their colleagues that they are sorry for imposing on one's good nature while being a little tipsy.

When appearing in public to speak, one bows first toward the audience and then toward the chairman of the meeting. Businesspeople should learn the proper bowing procedures and etiquette expected here. Korean businesspersons do not seem to worry about keeping time, being on time, beginning on time, or leaving on time to the same extent that Western businesspersons do. However, this is changing now, and the tendency is to follow the same time schedule as in the West.

Introductions

Koreans do not customarily introduce one person to another. Instead, one would say to another, "I have never seen you before" or "I am seeing you for the first time." The other person repeats the same thing, and then usually the elder of the two persons in age or rank says, "Let us introduce ourselves." Each person then steps back a little, bows from the waist, states his or her own name, or the elder initiates a handshake. They are then formally introduced. Names are stated in a low, humble voice, and then calling cards are exchanged. One may learn the new person's name and position at leisure. Do not say, "Sorry, I did not get your name. Would you tell me again?" Business cards are very necessary in Korea and should be used by foreign or Western businesspeople at all times, beginning with the first visit.

The use of names has an entirely different connotation in Korea than in most Western cultures. To the Confucian, using a name is presumptuous and impolite, as a name is something to be honored and respected and it should not be used casually. In Shamanism, to write a name calls up the spirit world and is considered bad luck. One's name, whether it is written or spoken, has its own special meaning and is that person's personal property. To call someone directly by his name is an affront in most social circumstances.

In Korea there are approximately 300 surnames, but more than half are Kims, Lees, and Parks. When a Western businessperson uses a Korean's name to his face, one can usually observe a slight wince around the eyes of the Korean. It is almost always there. A Korean is addressed by his title, position, trade, profession, or some other honorific title such as teacher. As opposed to our U.S. training of saying, "Good morning, Mr. Kim," a polite good morning is better, or "Good morning, teacher" is acceptable. Many Koreans live next to each other for years without even knowing their full names. A Korean's name is usually made up of three characters—the family's surname is placed first, and then the given name, which is made up of one character. It is used by all members of the same generation. By knowing this name, a person's generation in the family tree can be recognized.

Privacy and Propriety

South Korea has one of the most densely populated, crowded nations on Earth, so personal space is limited. On the street, this may result in standing or sitting close together, unintentionally bumping into one another or treading on another's foot without apology. Privacy is a luxury that few can afford in Korea, so the people have learned to make imaginary walls about themselves. A visitor calling on a hot day may find this person with his feet on the desk, fanning himself. The visitor coughs to announce his arrival, but he does not knock. This person does not "see" the person he has come to visit, nor does this indiviual "see" the visitor until he has risen. Then they "see" each other and begin the formality of greeting. To have privacy, a Korean withdraws behind an imaginary curtain, or does what he or she has to do, not seeing or being seen by those who, by the literal Western eye, are in plain view. It is considered discourteous to violate this screen of privacy once it is drawn about a person. A discreet cough is intended to notify the person behind the screen that an interruption is impending.

Table manners are based on making the guest feel comfortable. The attitude of a servant is proper for a host with his guest. Traditionally, at meals, the hostess is at the lowest place, the farthest from the place of honor, and often will not even eat in the presence of a guest. Before beginning to eat, the host will often make a formal welcome speech stating the purpose of the gathering and paying his respects to his guest. Often food is served on small individual tables, each with many side dishes of food, a bowl of soup, and a bowl of rice. Korean food tends to be highly seasoned with red pepper; thus, a careful sip of the soups is advisable before taking a large mouthful. To lay the chopsticks or spoon on the table is to indicate that you have finished eating; to put

Table manners are based on making the guest feel comfortable.

them on top of a dish or bowl means that you are merely resting. A guest may show his appreciation for the meal by slurping soup or smacking one's lips. The host will continue to urge his guest to eat more, but a courteous refusal can be accepted. A good healthy belch after a meal is a sign that one has eaten well and enjoyed it.

Avoid writing or printing a Korean's name in red ink; this is the color that Buddhists reserve to announce death or its anniversary.

Gift-Giving

Koreans give gifts on many occasions, and the appropriate etiquette surrounding the giving of gifts is often a problem to Western business-people. In this context, every gift expects something in return, and one rarely gives an expensive gift without a purpose. The purpose may be to establish an obligation, to gain a certain advantage, or merely to create an atmosphere in which the recipient will be more pliable to the donor's request. To return a gift is considered an affront, but in some instances it may be better to return the gift than to accept it with no intention of doing a favor in return. Some Koreans have a special ability to work their way into the affection of foreigners and form personal relationships that may later prove embarrassing and/or difficult to handle when some impossible or very often illegal and unlawful request is made. In Korean, "yes" may merely mean "I heard you," and not agreement or intention of complying. To say "no" is an affront and could hurt the feelings and thus is poor etiquette. Many Koreans often say "yes" to each other and to foreigners and then go their own way doing quite the opposite, with little sense of breaking a promise or agreement.

Business and Managerial Orientation

In business, praise is a way of life.

In business, praise is a way of life, and without subtle praise, business would come to a halt. One must begin on the periphery in business relationships and gradually zero in on the main business in narrowing circles. To directly begin a discussion of some delicate business matter or new business venture is considered by Koreans to be the height of stupidity and dooms the project to almost certain failure. Impatience to a Korean is a major fault. A highly skilled businessperson moves with deliberation, dignity, and studied motions, and senses the impressions and nuances being sent by the other businesspeople.

To Korean businessmen, Western businesspersons often appear to make contracts on the assumptions that all the factors will remain indefinitely the same. In Korea, a written contract is becoming as important as in the West. A change in the economy, the political situation, or personal reasons among one of the contractors may invalidate the completion of the contract without any sense of misdeed.

The economy and corporate structure here is still dominated by *chaebols* or large business conglomerates, which are closely related to the governement. Some of these entities are family owned and managed, and employees tend to stay a long time with one employer. To navigate business here, an outsider needs a Korean intermediary, as well as the help of the chamber of commerce and embassy.

Korea is a male-oriented society, and a man rules at work and at home. The "boss" is all important in this hierarchical culture and all is deferred to him. The "supervisor" is therefore treated with much respect. This trait is reflected in eye contact—persons of lower rank will avert their eyes during conversation with a higher ranking individual. Foreigners should avoid extended eye contact with Koreans, for this is often associated with anger or aggression. Korean managers are also very territorial about their desks; visitors never would put information or sales literature on that desk, but give it to a lower intermediary for transfer upward. Korean society accepts centralized control and makes a clear distinction between the ruler and subordinates.

Gradually, educated women are moving into middle management within business. Family household, financial, and child management are the female's responsibility. In public, this gender may appear quiet and submissive, but behind the scenes, women may exert great power. Public displays of her power or affection are unacceptable.

Because there are similarities between Korean and other Asian cultures, cross-cultural skills that are effective in this society have application elsewhere. For example, there is a large minority population of Koreans in Los Angeles and their native language is the third largest spoken in that California city. In many ways Korean is also a synergistic culture, except for the political division of the peninsula. Fortunately, North and South Korea have begun a positive dialogue to permit further exchanges among the divided families. This may eventually lead to improvement in their political and economic relationships. Remember, modern Koreans, especially among the young, may not fully practice the traditions and taboos described above.

Educated women are moving into middle management within business.

TAIWAN

EXHIBIT 13.21
PROFILE OF TAIWAN

Population	23,036,087
Literacy rate	96%
Life expectancy	77 years
GDP	$26,700

Taiwan is an island just 240 miles long and 85 miles wide at its maximum point. It is 80 miles east of mainland China and separated by the Taiwan Straits in the South China Sea. It lies 700 miles south of Japan and 200 miles north of the Philippines. The population is approximately 23 million. The people are predominantly Chinese, most of whom are descendants of immigrants from southeast China or mainlanders who retreated to Taiwan in 1949. The original inhabitants numbered only about 150,000. The principal religions are Buddhism and Taoism, with over 75% of the population practicing these two religions. Christianity has also been growing, and there are currently 600,000 believers. Education is compulsory until the age of 16, and the literacy rate is approximately 94%.

Historical Perspective Overview

The island's early history is relatively unknown. About 10,000 years ago, it is believed that the first known inhabitants migrated here, possibly from Indonesia or Malaysia. In 500–1000 A.D., the *Hakkas*, a persecuted minority originally from the Henen Province in China, arrived. During the fourteenth century, Han Chinese, mainly from the southern Chinese province of Fujian, sailed here to trade and escape the Mongols.

Portuguese sailors in the sixteenth century discovered the island which they named *Ilha Formosa* or "beautiful island." Over time, the island has been occupied by the Dutch, Spanish, French, and Japanese invaders. The Dutch colonists were ousted by the Chinese in 1661, and in 1684 Taiwan was made a prefecture of China's Fukien Province. The island was ceded to Japan following the Sino-Japanese War of 1895, remaining under Japanese control until the end of World War II, thus having a major cultural impact here. In 1949, the successes of Mao Zedong's communist forces on the mainland ousted Generalissimo Chiang Kai-shek's nationalist government, which then retreated to the island of Taiwan. Mao's plans to invade Taiwan in the 1950s were thwarted by the Taiwanese army, which was assisted by the U.S. Seventh Fleet. Although the government in Taiwan claimed to represent all of China, calling itself the Republic of China, few other nations have established diplomatic relations. The People's Republic of China was admitted into the United Nations in Taiwan's place in 1971. Official diplomatic relations with the United States were severed in 1979 as a result of normalized relations between Washington and Beijing. For more than a half century now, there has been tension, posturing, and threats as the PRC tries to regain control of its "lost province." At the same time, the Taiwanese have moved steadily toward a more democratic and independent state, much to the embarrassment of the mainland communists.

In 1684 Taiwan was made a prefecture of China's Fukien Province.

Cultural Guidelines for Business in Taiwan

There are four main ethnic groups on this island: Taiwanese (70%); Hakkas (10% or more); recent mainland Chinese émigrés since 1949 (14%); and aborigines (1.5%). The cultural insights provided above on the Chinese basically apply to the people on this island. However, this is a more open, free enterprise society. There is also a generation gap; the older people identify with their original homeland of China, and are more industrious and competitive. The younger are more global minded and materialistic, proud of the island's economic progress, and identify themselves as Taiwanese, speaking a local dialect. For them, education is the key to social and economic progress. Confucianism provides a common philosophy of life and code of ethics, encouraging hard work, success in business, and accumulation of wealth. Taiwan has no official religion, but Buddhism and Taoism are prominent, while Christianity and Islam are minority religions. Belief in folk religion and ancestor worship is widespread.

In general, public harmony is more important than factual truth. However, the Taiwanese are more expressive of their feelings than the typical Asian and are prone to emotional outbursts and vindictiveness with their own kind. Initially, the locals tend to be suspicious of foreigners, but they eventually accept outsiders. Family connections are important in business. The work ethic is adequate, but not exceptional—be persistent with procrastination there. A common attitude is that one can only get ahead by stepping on someone else. The Taiwanese tend to be individualistic and entrepreneurial, but seemingly have difficulty working in teams. They are also not very service oriented. This is a male-dominated society in which females are still considered socially inferior. Yet women are making progress, moving beyond "office ladies" into positions of authority, as well as achieving success in the professions and academia. It is also a place where family loyalty is a basic tenet (thus, avoid nepotism and having more than one family member working for you).

Taiwanese tend to be individualistic and entrepreneurial.

Foreigners are well advised to learn the intricacies of the island's culture and business. Punctuality, connections, and local agents, for example, are important. Meetings may be scheduled in offices, as well as over lunch or dinner, but wait for your host to initiate business talk. At first encounter, shake hands, offer a greeting (*Ni hoa ma*, or "How are you?"), and be prepared to exchange business cards (use both Chinese and English). Status and titles are considered important. Although Taiwanese do not normally use first names, they may adopt Western names or words that seem odd to outsiders. They smile often, even when nervous, uncomfortable, or in a negative situation. Avoid telling jokes; winking, blinking, or pointing at someone, or touching the head, which is considered a spiritual part of the person. Beckoning is down with palm down. The islanders like to gamble but are reluctant to discuss illness and death.

Taiwan is a high-energy society, and people are always busy and going somewhere, except during a brief nap after lunch (so no appointments between 1 and 1:30 P.M. when the natives recharge their energy). Traffic is heavy, streets are jammed and noisy, nightlife is lively. Physically, these people tend to be smaller and slender than Westerners, so try not to intimidate by your presence (e.g., compensate your tall position so as to be at eye level with a native person). Males tend to be clean shaven and are usually garbed in conservative business dress.

Sociopolitical Insights

Today, the president and vice president in Taiwan are elected by popular vote. There are also five branches of government, known as *yuans*: the executive, legislative, judicial, control, and examination *yuans*. The Democratic Progressive Party (DPP) in the 2000 elections gained control of the national government. The two largest opposition parties are the Nationalist Party (KMT) and the People's First Party (PFP). The DPP has been trying to push for Taiwan's independence, while the KMT and PFP are in favor of unification with China. However, despite these opposing views, recent economic progress has brought China and Taiwan closer together in peaceful pursuits. In November 2001, Taiwan abolished a 50-year ban on direct trade and investment with China. Under this new policy, businesses can invest in China without going through a third country. However, Taiwan cannot invest in high-tech industries or in projects worth over US$50 million. Taiwan became a member of the World Trade Organization in January 2002, just weeks after China joined. Taiwan is not recognized by any OECD country and is not a member of the UN, so a main goal for Taiwan is to gain higher international recognition.

Foreign trade is vital to Taiwan's economy.

Foreign trade is vital to Taiwan's economy. Taiwan is economically connected to China; it is China's second largest export market. Taiwan is also a leader in computer hardware and manufactures about 50% of all laptop computers. Two major export partners of Taiwan are Hong Kong (23.6% of total exports) and the United States (20.5%). Machinery and electrical equipment make up 55% of Taiwan's exports. Taiwan did not suffer as much as its neighbors in the 1997 Asian financial crisis. However, due to its strong IT dependency, the economy was vulnerable during the depression of 2000 and 2001. Unemployment reached an all-time high in 2002 at 5.4%, and GDP growth is slowly increasing (2.9% and upward). In 2006, Taiwan is moving to establish greater economic ties to India, a principal competitor of China.

THAILAND

Once known as Siam, the Kingdom of Thailand is in Southeast Asia.

Once known as Siam, the Kingdom of Thailand is in Southeast Asia and shares its southern border with Malaysia. In the northeast is Laos, to the east is Cambodia, and to the northwest, Myanmar, formerly designated as Burma. Its total land area is 514,000 square kilometers (198,455 square miles), an area the size of France. Tropical rain forests dominate the southern peninsular, with mountains to the north and plains in the central region. Bangkok, its capital and largest city, lies in the center on the Gulf of Thailand. Chiang Mai, the country's second largest city, lies inland to the north.

Historical Perspective Overview[33]

Archaeology indicates that this land has been occupied by humans for over 5000 years. Southern Chinese are known to have migrated here around 700 A.D. When southern Chinese migrated here in 700 A.D., they found this area populated by Mons, a people who extended up to Burma and Cambodia, and as far as India. These people were Buddhists and Khmers Hindu, religions that still influence the Thai belief system.

Modern Thailand's history emerged in the thirteenth century with the foundation of two states: *Sukhothai* in 1220 and *Chang Mai* in 1296. The former's third king, Ramkhamhaeng (1278–1318) is still revered as "The Father of Thailand," especially for his fusing of Mon and Khmer traditions in Thai society. In 1378, the country was absorbed into the larger Kingdom of Ayutthaya which extended beyond present-day borders. In 1569, the Burmese overran Ayutthaya but were displaced by the Thai King, Naresuan, who initiated a golden age of arts and architecture. By 1782, the Chakrai Dynasty was inaugurated by Ram I, and this *Rattanakosin* continues to the present. Subsequently, these monarchs expanded into Cambodia over which they established a protectorate.

In the nineteenth century, the Thai royalty used diplomacy to deter European incursions. To keep its independence, Siam ceded a portion of Malysia to Britain and a little of what is Cambodia and Laos to France. During this period, an enlightened king, Mongkut or Rama IV (1851–1858), introduced Western-style reforms to modernize the country. He is the character popularized in the story, musical, and film, *The King and I*. His son, Chulalongkorn or Rama V (1868–1910), then transformed the nation from a medieval kingdom into a modern state. As a result of a military coup, in 1939, the nation was renamed "Thailand or Land of the Free." In 1941, the Japanese occupied the land until the end of World War II. While the king is still a focus of loyalty and cohesion, the country's generals are the power brokers, involved in a series of administrative turnovers. For the past half century, the Thai government, fearful of communist attacks, has aligned itself with the United States who established military bases there during the Vietnam War. This has aided the democratic process and economic expansion.

Cultural Guidelines for Business in Thailand

Thailand's population of some 59 million is relatively homogeneous: 82% are ethnically Thais, divided into four dialects of their language. Among many minority groups, the Chinese are the largest—12% prominent among the ruling elite. The primary religion, Theravada Buddhism, is practiced by about 95% of the people, while some 2 million Malays there are Muslim. Ancestor worship is prevalent, along with some adherents to Hinduism, Sikhism, and Christianity.

In Thai society, each person has a specific place: people should fulfill their roles with a minimum of fuss and stress, or else one will "lose face." Thai culture values harmony, respect, the dignity of others, tolerance, and whether things are pleasurable. Anger and rude behavior are frowned upon, for differences are to be settled quietly and politely. Problems and setbacks are accepted with an attitude of "Never mind—it doesn't matter." Social ranking depends on a combination of lineage, education, and economic status. The monarchy is respected, and slander against royalty is offensive. Foreigners are expected to use polite speech, and their presence has contributed to the growth of materialism among the locals. The Thais are known for their devotion to family, but traditional males consider females inferior and extramarital affairs are common. Females manage the household and its finances, and increasingly they seek higher education as well as professional and executive positions. The literacy rate there is 94%, and education is valued for future advancement and wealth.

Although Thais smile often, this connotes various things depending on the circumstances. The natives are genuinely friendly and polite, but watch out for "con artists" and aggressive drivers—be cautious

Social ranking depends on a combination of lineage, education, and economic status.

crossing streets. Traffic in Bangkok is so bad that many businesspersons operate out of their cars with mobile phones and faxes. Others commute by boat. Executives usually speak English, and translators are available, and have directions written in the Thai language with taxi drivers. Thais also value enjoyment, so business entertainment is expected as a means of developing relationships. Both natives and visitors avoid embarrassment through laughter. Giving gifts is acceptable, but never open them in the presence of the giver.

In this "land of the free," Thais are proud that they have never been under Western domination; in contrast, all the surrounding nations have at one time or another been colonized. This can be attributed to both the resourcefulness of the Thai people and their willingness to accommodate outsiders within the political structure. In twenty-first-century Asia, Thailand has a fast-growing market, attractive to both investors and exporters.

Thais are proud that they have never been under Western domination.

Sociopolitical Insights

Modern government in Thailand has extensive connections with the military. A number of politicians are also military officers. Government coups often occur because of internal struggles with the military for power. Since 1932, when absolute monarchy was established, there have been seventeen coups, the last being in 1991.

Thailand is a constitutional monarchy in which the king has increasingly become a key political figure, being the only person able to break the impasse between opposing interest groups. Practical politics are handled by the most powerful politician, the prime minister, who serves a four-year term. The National Assembly is divided into a Senate and a House of Representatives. Traditionally, the National Assembly has played a secondary role in government, often serving as a rubber stamp for the prime minister and his council of ministers. In January 2001, the Thai Rak Thai (TRT) Party won the majority of the votes. This election is said to be the most democratic yet, with a low level of fraud.

Since the Asian financial crisis of 1997, economic progress has slowly been made, and GDP in 2002 grew by 5%. Thailand's biggest export and import partners are the United States, Japan, and Singapore. Agriculture is still an important sector, as 49% of the labor force works in agriculture and 9.3% of the GDP is from agriculture. However, Thailand has successfully diversified its economy, and today a majority of its exports are in machinery, mechanical appliances, and computers. Currently, the government faces three social and economic issues. Recent droughts affected half the country's provinces, causing problems for rice planting, Thailand's major food export. In addition, the government faces a rise of AIDS and an increase in drug addiction. The continuing instability of central governance continues to hinder democratic and economic growth. For example, as this is written in 2006, yet another massive, but peaceful, public protest is taking place outside the royal palace to demand the resignation of the current prime minister, Thaksin Shinawatra, reelected a year ago with a sweeping 19 million votes. Along with cabinet resignations and parliamentary censure resolutions, the popular discontent is over supposed corruption in the Prime Minister's family business deals. And the saga of modern Thailand continues.

A coup in September 19, 2006, resulted in the appointment of Swrayird Chulanont as Prime Minister by the military council. Election's are experted to take place in October of 2007.

VIETNAM

EXHIBIT 13.23
PROFILE OF VIETNAM

Population	83,535,576 (July 2005 est.)
Ethnic groups	Kinh (Viet), 86.2%; Tay, 1.9%; Thai, 1.7%; Muong, 1.5%; Khome, 1.4%; Hoa, 1.1%; Nun, 1.1%; Hmong, 1%; Other, 4.1%
Religions	Buddhist, 9.3%; Catholic, 6.7%; Hoa Hao, 1.5%; Cao Dai, 1.1%; Protestant, 0.5%; Muslim, 0.1%; None, 80.8%
Education	90.3% literacy rate
Land	325,360 sq km
Government	Communist state
Political Parties	Communist Party of Vietnam (CPV)
Per capita income	$3000 (2005 est.)
Exports to U.S.	Total exports = $31.34 billion U.S. accounts for 20.2% Total exports to U.S. = $6.3 billion (2005 est.)
Imports from U.S.	Total imports = $34.44 billion *Updated data for U.S. not listed*

Vietnam[34] is located in Southeast Asia, bordered by Laos and Cambodia to the west, China to the north, and the South China Sea to the east and south. It lies on the eastern side of the Indonesian peninsula of the Gulf of Thailand. The landmass is 331,688 square kilometers (128,065 square miles). This long, narrow country has a coastline of over 2000 miles, plus sovereignty over numerous islands. Divided into three main geographical regions, the north is mountainous with its Red River Delta, central highlands in the center, the coastal highlands and Mekong River Delta in the south. The capital of Hanoi is located in the north, while its commercial center, Ho Chi Min City (old Saigon) is in the south. The climate is humid in both the summer and winter seasons, with temperatures in Hanoi ranging between 13°C (55°F) and 33°C (91°F). Monsoon rains are present throughout the year, contributing to the average rainfall of 60 to 80 inches.

Historical Perspective Overview

The earliest known inhabitants of this land lived in the north some 500,000 years ago. In the thirteen century B.C., Bronze Age Don Son culture appeared, and the descendants of modern Vietnamese can be traced to Red River Delta settlers, 500–200 B.C. Always a crossroads for migrants, these ancestors were a mix of Australoid, Austronesian, and Mongoloid peoples. For over a thousand years, from 111 B.C. to A.D. 939, Vietnam was ruled by the Chinese as a province called Giao Chia. Even after throwing out the Chinese, inhabitants had to resist numerous Chinese attacks, and so they allied themselves with their neighbors with whom they maintained close political and military ties. As the population expanded southward, Vietnam came into conflict with a number of ruling dynasties from Cambodia and India. From the first to sixth century A.D., the southern part was under the control of Hindu kingdom of Funan, which influenced art and architecture as well as religious beliefs. However, the people succeeded in overthrowing the Hindu Kingdom, Khmer Empire, and Le Dynasty. While the first Europeans landed here in A.D. 166, it was not until 1516 that their influence became significant with the arrival of the Portuguese. By 1630, Spanish missionaries from the Philippines had perfected a romanized system for writing the Vietnamese language. In 1637, the Dutch were among the many traders from abroad.

By the eighteenth century, the ruling Vietnamese families were beset by a number of peasant rebellions demanding better distribution of wealth from rich to poor. Meanwhile, French missionaries in the north were lobbying their own government for a greater political and military presence in Vietnam. A combination of Vietnamese and French forces defeated the Tay Son rebels, and the Nguyen Dynasty took over the whole country in 1802, becoming the first to rule Vietnam until 1945. But back in 1867 France had brought Vietnam directly under its rule, dividing the country into three parts: protectorates in Tonkin and Annam in the north; the central area of Vietnam; and then directly administering "Cochinchina" in the south. Thus, the French dominated Vietnam until World War II, when the Japanese occupied parts of the country. After Japan was defeated, the Allies divided the country into two parts: the North and the South. France gained power in the South,

The French dominated Vietnam until World War II.

while China chose a new emperor in the North, Boa Dai, who stepped down in favor of Ho Chi Minh, founder of Vietnam's Communist Party. By September 2, 1945, this astute and powerful leader proclaimed the independence of the Provisional Democratic Republic of Vietnam (DRV). Then this political and military genius proceeded to lead an invasion of the French-ruled South, ultimately winning this war in 1954 with the defeat of the French at Dien Bien Phu.

After terms for an agreement were signed in Geneva in 1954, Ngo Dinh Diem became the prime minister of the South, and following a referendum in 1955, he proclaimed himself president of the Republic of Vietnam. He refused to hold 1956 elections under the new peace agreement. Therefore, the North approved a strategy for the communist-based National Liberation Front (NLF) to oppose Diem and move to control South Vietnam. This prompted the United States to expand military support for Diem and his government in 1961. The struggle turned into an American war following an incident involving U.S. warships. American troops and supplies were sent in to fight against the Viet Cong guerrillas (southern communists fighting the South Vietnamese government) and North Vietnamese troops (Viet Minh). The war spread to Laos and Cambodia and eventually to North Vietnam itself. The Americans increased troop deployment to 500,000, bombing extensively areas held by the Viet Cong. When the communists launched the Tet Offensive in 1968, U.S. public opinion diminished support for a war that could not be won. Peace talks in January 1973 included a cease-fire in the South and the withdrawal of U.S. forces by the beginning of 1975. In that year, the peaceful reunification of Vietnam began when the PRG (Provisional Revolutionary Government, formed by the NLF in the South), combined with North Vietnamese troops, attacked the South, ultimately leading to the fall of Saigon in April.

Effective control of Vietnam was placed in the hands of Hanoi.

Effective control of Vietnam was placed in the hands of Hanoi, which renamed Saigon Ho Chi Minh City in 1976. In an attempt to neutralize opposition, thousands of officials were summoned to "reeducation" camps. All three Indochinese countries—Vietnam, Laos, and Cambodia—came under the communist governance. Thousands of families fled these countries at that time, becoming refugees in numerous countries, including North America. In 1976, the reunited country's name was changed to the Socialist Republic of Vietnam, while the ruling party adopted the designation of Communist Party of Vietnam (CPV). The United States refused to acknowledge the new government and severed all diplomatic relations. After the war, troops under Cambodia's Pol Pot government attacked southern Vietnam. This led to an all-out Vietnamese invasion of Cambodia in December 1978, installing a new government loyal to Hanoi. In the same period, the Chinese launched an unsuccessful attack against the Vietnamese and ultimately withdrew from Vietnam.

Since then, Vietnam has focused on internal matters. In 1986, Nguyen Van Linh, the Communist Party general secretary, introduced the concept of *doi moi*, or renovation. This term includes private enterprise and the approval of 100% foreign ownership of firms and joint ventures, openness to overseas Vietnamese, an interest in tourism, and greater individual freedoms. It took three years, however, for the South to start implementing these reforms, along with the withdrawal of Vietnamese troops from Cambodia in 1989. Since then, the government has been fully committed to the idea of *doi moi*, as is evidenced by new investors from Japan, Taiwan, Hong Kong, and Australia. These countries already know they won't have to wait long for the emerging, thriving Vietnamese economy. Australia has targeted Vietnam as its "Asian Business Success Program," while billboards with ads for Minolta and Hitachi dominate intersections in Hanoi and Ho Chi Minh City. For the rest of the non-Asian countries who didn't jump at the early opportunities, competition will be even stiffer now.

It was also the 1989 peace treaty with Cambodia that opened up diplomatic talks with the United States and Western Europe. In fact, the treaty was the turning point for Vietnam. Within months diplomatic ties had been fully reestablished with China and the above-mentioned countries. Washington opened a diplomatic office in Hanoi in 1991 to coordinate the search for American MIAs (soldiers missing in action). After cooperation from the Vietnamese in this search, the United States lifted some economic sanctions in 1992 and 1993. President Clinton then lifted the trade and investment embargo in February 1994, and since then the United States has established itself as a significant investor in Vietnam. The Vietnamese people heralded the removal of the trade embargo as the end of the "American War," rejoicing in total independence from foreign invaders for the first time in centuries.

The year 2000 was significant for Vietnam as it marked 55 years of independence and 25 years since the end of the Vietnam War. The main changes now are more openness than before; founding of the first stock exchange center in Ho Chi Minh City; membership in the World Trade Organization; and reduction of the poverty level to below 10%. Under the administration of technocrats, a top priority of Vietnam is to fix the corruption that has been widespread in government. Inventory in coal, cement, steel, and paper has increased due to foreign competition. Near the end of 2001, the U.S.-Vietnam Bilateral Trade Agreement was launched in an effort to increase Vietnam's exports. Currently, Japan receives about 13.6% of Vietnam's exports, and the United States receives some 20.2%.

Cultural Guidelines for Business in Vietnam

Vietnam has a population of 83 million, of which 87% are ethnic Vietnamese. The largest minority group is Chinese. There are also

The year 2000 was significant for Vietnam as it marked 55 years of independence and 25 years since the end of the Vietnam War.

approximately 50 small ethnic groups who live primarily in the mountain areas. After independence in 1945, Vietnam gradually began to use Vietnamese, which is the official language today and is taught in schools. However, there exist distinct northern, central, and southern dialects. Furthermore, many minority groups speak their own language at home. The most popular foreign languages to study are English, Russian, and French. Most government officials understand some English.

Sociopolitical-Economic Context

Although the new constitution adopted on April 15, 1992, confirmed the omnipotence of the Communist Party, the spirit and practice of free enterprise have expanded rapidly. The National Assembly, consisting of 400 members and elected to five-year terms by universal adult suffrage, holds all legislative powers. The president, elected by the Ninth National Assembly, is also the head of state and commander-in-chief of the armed forces. The president then appoints a prime minister with the approval of the National Assembly, who in turn forms a government consisting of a vice president and a council of ministers. The National Assembly must approve all appointments. The country is divided into provinces, which are under tight control of the central government. On a local level, citizens are elected to a People's Council, which runs the local government.

The Vietnamese economy is based on the agriculture, forestry, and fishing industries, which employ 73% of the workforce and account for 60% of all exports. The agricultural sector consists of a staple crop of rice, which provides about 15% of export earnings as well as other cash crops of rubber, coffee, tea, cotton, and soybeans. A ban was imposed on logs and timber in 1992, in order to preserve the heavily depleted forests. Fishing is also very important: seafood, including shrimp, crabs, and cuttle fish, is exported along with petroleum and coal. Vietnam's principal trading partner is Singapore; others include France, Germany, Japan, and Hong Kong.

Education, which is free to all, begins at age 6 and continues to age 18.

Education, which is free to all, begins at age 6 and continues to age 18. University education is also free, but there is tough competition for admittance. The literacy rate is 94%, and approximately 10% of the nation's budget is spent on education.

The state operates a system of social security, in which health care is provided to everyone, free of cost. However, in 1991 there was one practicing doctor for 3140 inhabitants, and facilities are often inadequate, especially in rural areas. Infant mortality is 26 per 1000; life expectancy ranges from 68 to 74 years.

As reported earlier, the Vietnamese have lived 1000 years under Chinese domination; French colonialism from 1867 to 1954; and a civil war ensued for 30 years, which included the war against the United

States. This has left the Vietnamese people with a strong sense of national pride. They are more future oriented than past oriented. Because the *American War* was relatively short compared to Vietnam's past conflicts, and since two wars have been fought thereafter against China and Cambodia, the Vietnamese today do not harbor animosity toward Americans. They view that conflict already as past history, and they are very curious about all Americans, anxious to conduct business and tourism with their former enemy.

Great change is taking place now in Vietnam, accompanied by struggles to get ahead. People in the urban areas are generally happy, due to improved basic services and a more open political and cultural environment. However, people in rural areas, where 75% of the Vietnamese population lives, are currently very unhappy and frustrated. This malaise is due to a dearth of cultural opportunities, lack of electricity and other basic services, and neglect of the poor. Party officials still take advantage of the peasants, who do not hold much weight in voting matters. For Vietnam to obtain prosperity, the inequalities that exist between urban and rural citizens must disappear.

Customs and Courtesies

In Vietnam, people shake hands when greeting and when saying good-bye to someone. Also common is the use of both hands, which indicates respect. A slight bow of the head also shows respect. Elderly people in rural areas may also nod their head upon greeting someone, and women are more inclined to bow their head than to shake hands.

Names begin with the family name followed by the given name. For example, in the name Nguyen Van Duc, Nguyen is the family name and Van Duc is the given name. Although they address each other by given name, the Vietnamese add titles that show their relationship to the other person. These titles tend to be used more personally, in one's family, rather than professionally. Among coworkers, the younger of the two might call the other *ahn*, or older brother. To say hello to someone using the given name and title, they would say "Xin chao," or hello. However, "Xin chao" could have one of six other meanings, since Vietnamese is a tonal language. Therefore, it is important to stress the proper syllable. International visitors who can properly say "Xin chao" are met with delight by the Vietnamese. In business settings, business cards may be exchanged in greetings, and should be in both Vietnamese and English.

The following gestures should be noted when in the company of the Vietnamese:

- Do not touch the head of a young child as it is considered a sensitive spiritual point.

Do not touch the head of a young child.

- Do not use your index finger to call someone over; it is considered rude.
- When calling someone, wave all four fingers with the palm down.
- Men and women do not show affection in public.
- Members of the same sex may hold hands in public. This is normal.
- Vietnamese use both hands to give an object to another person.

The Vietnamese give a great deal of importance to visiting people. Therefore, one should not just "drop by" someone's house without first being invited. They also show a strong sense of hospitality and prepare well in advance of the guest's arrival. Gifts for the hostess are not required but greatly appreciated. A small gift for the children or elderly parent is also much appreciated. Acceptable gifts include flowers, tea, or incense.

The traditional Vietnamese family is an extended one.

The traditional Vietnamese family is an extended one, including parents, unmarried children, and married sons with their families. The extended family still predominates in rural regions; however, there is a trend toward single-family homes in urban locations. Families maintain strong ties with each other and provide financial and emotional support as needed.

As the world's thirteenth largest country, Vietnam has shown a strong interest in becoming a market economy and opening itself to outsiders. Furthermore, with the reestablishment of diplomatic relations with the United States and other major economic players, business opportunities have increased dramatically over the past years. Those companies that take advantage of conducting business in Vietnam will be rewarded with a high-growth market of consumers estimated to reach 600 million by 2010.

CONCLUSIONS

Asia is a demonstration model of the complex and multidimensional aspects of culture. Although we have provided cultural specifics on only a dozen countries, perhaps it is enough to convince global managers of the important distinctions that exist between the people of this region and Westerners in critical matters like physical appearance, language, religion, family, social attitudes, and other assumptions that influence business practice and relationships. The new market opportunities and diversity in the Pacific Basin alone should motivate us to seek further cultural information, whether we are dealing with Australians who are seemingly similar or with Vietnamese who are so obviously different.

The social situation in Asia is normally peaceful but also very dynamic, often volatile. Traditional societies are in transition to a technological and knowledge culture. Unfortunately, Asia, like the world, is now being threatened by global terrorism and insurgencies, some of which is coming from the Middle East.[35] It is also the scene of home-grown or imported health crises, such as SARS, bird flu, and HIV/AIDS diseases. However, in these ancient lands and cultures, peaceful exchange and trade have always been the way to promote well-being, commerce, and prosperity. International trade is already transforming Asian societies, such as in the emerging superpowers of China and India. The area also benefits from the global cooperation of nations to curb negative behaviors endangering the world community, such as coping with natural disasters, limiting drug trafficking, and containing infectious disease, unequal distribution of wealth and opportunity for the planet's inhabitants!

MIND STRETCHING

1. What is involved as a traditional Asian society transitions into a modern one?
2. What advantages do overseas Chinese have in many Pacific Basin countries?
3. What cross-border commonalities have you observed in this study of Asian cultures?
4. Why is it important for you to increase your knowledge and skill in Asian languages, negotiation styles, and business practices?
5. With the expansion of global terrorism and insurgencies in Asia, as well as disease epidemics, what cautions should you observe in travel to the region?

REFERENCES

1. Long, S. "The Tiger in Front—A Survey of India and China," *The Economist*, March 2, 2005, p. 6 insert (www.economist.com/surveys).
2. *The Economist*, October 1, 1994; Engardio, P. "A New World Economy," *Business Week*, August 28/29, 2005, p. 52.
3. Matlock, J. W. "Chinese Checkers." *The New York Times Book Review*, September 13, 1998.
4. Schnitzer, M. C., Liebranz, M. L., and Kubin, K. K. *International Business*. Cincinnati, OH: South-Western Publishing, 1985; Kleveman, L. *The New Great Game: Blood and Oil in Central Asia*. New York: Atlantic Monthly Press, 2003; Dungung, S. P. *Doing Business in Asia*. San Francisco, CA: Jossey-Bass, 1998.
5. This section on Australia was originally written by Laurel Cool, when a graduate student at Thunderbird, The Gavin School of International

Management, Phoenix, Arizona, but subsequently was updated by the authors. The following references were used.

The Europa World Yearbook, 1994, Vol. 1. London: Europa Publications, Ltd., 1994; "Passport System—A Guide to Communicating in the Global Marketplace," *Getting Through Customs, Australia*, 1993; "Background Notes—Australia," U.S. Department of State, Bureau of Public Affairs, Office of Public Education, February 1994; "EIU Country Profile—Australia," *The Economist Intelligence Unit*. Kent, England: 1994–1995; Morrison, T., Conawaym W. A., and Douress, J. J. *Dun & Bradstreet Doing Business Around the World*. Upper Saddle River, NJ: Prentice Hall, 1997, Australia pp. 11–22. See also Renwick, G. W., Smart, R., and Henderson, D. I. *A Fair Go for A—Australian and American Interactions*. Boston: Nicholas Brealey/Intercultural Press, 1991; *A Survey of Australia*. London: *The Economist*, September 7, 2000. (www.economist.com/surveys).

6. Tang, J. and Ward, A. *The Changing Face of Chinese Management*. London: Routledge, 2003.

7. Ghosal, A. "Some Implications of China Joining the WTO," *INSIGHT*, 3, no. 1 (2003).

8. Engardio, O., "A New Mold Economy," p. 54 (www.businessweek.com/go/china-india).

9. On January 1, 1979, China officially adopted the *pinyin* system of writing Chinese characters in the Latin alphabet. This is a system of romanization invented by the Chinese that has been widely used for years in China on street signs as well as in elementary Chinese textbooks. *Pinyin* has replaced the familiar Wade-Giles romanization system. The following are examples of the differences in these systems:

Wade-Giles	Pinyin
Kwangchow/Canton	Guangzhou
Peking	Beijing
Mao Tse-tung	Mao Zedong
Chou En-lai	Zhou Enlai

10. United States Postal Service, "Focus on . . . The People's Republic of China," *Passport*, 3, no. 1 (1997) 3. Refer to Pomeranz K. *China, Europe, and the Making of the Modern World Economy*. Princeton: NJ: Princeton University Press, 2001.

11. Originally this section was written by Donny Huang, President, 4 Stones Cross-Cultural Development Co. Ltd. Beijing, PRC, but was subsequently updated by the authors. Refer also to Fishman, T. C. *China Inc.: How the Rise of the Next Superpower Challenges America and the World*. New York: Scribner/Simon & Schuster, 2005.

12. McGregor, J. *One Billion Customers: Lessons from the Front Lines of Doing Business in China*. New York: Free Press, 2005.

13. Pye, L. *Chinese Commercial Negotiating Style*. Cambridge, MA: Oelgeschlager, Gunn & Hain Publishers, 1982. Refer also to Zinzius, B. *Doing Business in China—A Handbook and Guide*. New York: Praeger, 2004. DeWoskin, R. *Foreign Babes in Beijing: Behind the Scenes of the New China*. New York: Norton, 2005.

14. Frankenstein, J. *Asian Wall Street Journal*, August 26, 1995. See also Shenkar, O. *The Chinese Century: The Rising Chinese Economy and Its Impact on the Global Economy, the Balance of Power, and Your Job.* Upper Saddle River, NJ: Prentice Hall/Wharton, 2005.

15. Patten, C. *East and West—China, Power and the Future of Asia.* New York: Times Books/Random House, 1998.

16. Adapted from Paul Lunde, "The Indian Ocean and Global Trade," *Saudi Aramco World*, July/August 2000 (www.saudiaramco world.com).

17. Adapted with permission from Moran, R. T. *Venturing Abroad in Asia.* London: McGraw-Hill, 1988; Hutchings, G. *Modern China—A Guide to a Century of Change.* Cambridge, MA: Harvard University Press, 2003; Ahmad, S. "Behind the Mask—A Survey of Business in China," *The Economist.* March 20, 2004, p. 19 insert; Long, S. "The Tiger in Front—A Survey India and China," March 5, 2005, *The Economist* (www.economist.com/surverys). Also, a special issue of *Business Week*, a collection of pertinent articles by multiple authors on "China & India," April 22/29, 2005 (www.businessweek.com/go/china-india); Davies, P. *What's This India Business? Offshoring, Outsourcing, and the Global Services Revolution.* Boston: Nicholas Brealey/Intercultural Press, 2004.

18. "The Great Indian Hope Trick," *The Economist*, February 25, 2005, pp. 29–31.

19. "Indonesia," *National Geographic*, February 1996. Also refer to Dunung, S. P. *Doing Business in Asia.* San Francisco, CA: Jossey-Bass, 1998, pp. 188–221.

20. "Indonesia's Agony and the Price of Rice," *The Economist*, September 19, 1998.

21. Emmott, W. "The Sun Also Rises—A Survey of Japan," *The Economist*, October 8, 2005, p. 18 insert (www.economist/surveys).

22. Matsumoto, D. *The New Japan.* Boston: Nicholas Brealey/Intercultural Press, 2002. For contrast from the same source, read Condon, J. *With Respect to the Japanese—A Guide for Americans*, 1984. Boston, MA.

23. Hall, E. T. and Hall, M. R. *Hidden Differences—Doing Business with the Japanese.* Garden City, NJ: Anchor/Doubleday, 1987.

24. Emmott, W. "The Sun Also Rises—A Survey of Japan," *The Economist*, October 8, 2005, p. 18 insert (www.economist/surveys).

25. Verluyten, S. P. "Doing Business in the Philippines." Preliminary version of paper shared with the authors. University of Antwerp RUCA-TEW, Belgium, November 1992, Dunung, S. P., "The Philippines," pp. 246–270.

26. "Staying Ahead in the Philippines," *The Economist*, November 16, 1996, p. 18/33.

27. "Cool Korea," *Business Week*, June 10, 2002.

28. Amsden, A. *Asia's Next Giant: Late Industrialization in South Korea.* Cambridge: UK: Oxford University Press, 1989. See also Kang, T. P. *Is Korea the Next Japan?* New York: Free Press, 1989; Dunung, S. P. "Korea," pp. 48–80.

29. Wantanabe, T. "Old Habits Die Hard in Hermit Kingdom," *Los Angeles Times*, February 14, 1997, p. 1.

30. Ungoon, G. R., Sters, R. M., and Park, S. *Korean Enterprise: The Quest for Globalization.* Boston: Harvard Business Press, 1997.

31. "How Dangerous Is Korea," *Time*, January 13, 2003.

32. Much of the culture-specific material on Korea originally was excerpted with permission from Dr. Paul S. Crane's excellent book, *Korean Patterns*, © 1974, by the Royal Asiatic Society. Subsequently, the authors have updated the material in this section.

33. The authors acknowledge the help received in this section, particularly with the geography and history of various Asian countries, from Sanjyot P. Dunung's *Doing Business in Asia*, 2nd ed., published in 1998 by Jossey-Bass Books of San Francisco, California, USA.

34. Updated by authors, but originally researched and written by Laurel Cool based on the following references:

    "Socialist Republic of Vietnam," *Culturgram*. Provo, UT: Brigham Young University, 1995; *The Europa World Yearbook*. Vol. 2. London: Europa Publications, 1994; "EIU Country Report, Third Quarter, Vietnam," *The Economist Intelligence Unit*. Kent, England, 1994; Haub, C. "After Decades of War, A New Economy Is Emerging," *Consumers of Southeast Asia Market: Asia Pacific*. Ithaca, NY: W-Two Publications, 1994; Walsh, D. "Another Tiger?" *Consumers of Southeast Asia*. Ithaca, NY: W-Two Publications, 1994.

35. Benjamin, D. and Simon, S. *The Next Attack: The Failure of the War on Terror and a Strategy for Getting It Right*. New York: Times Books, 2005; Kleveman, L. *The New Great Game: Blood and Oil in Central Asia*. New York: Atlantic Monthly Press, 2003; Shadid, A. *Night Draws Near—Iraq's People in the Shadow of America's War*. New York: Henry Holt, 2005; Hashim, A. S. *Insurgency and Counter-insurgency in Iraq*. Ithaca, NY: Cornell University Press, 2006; Nevins, J. *A Not-so-Distant Horror: Mass Violence in East Timor*. Ithaca, NY: Cornell University Press, 2005.

INTERNET WEB SITES

After http:// and/or www. add:
cia.com/ (insert name of a specific country)
economist.com/countries/ (insert name of a country, city, or surveys for briefing)
investaustralia.com
hup.harvard.edu
nationalgeographic.com.

HELPFUL RESOURCES: The Intercultural Press division of Nicholas Brealey Publishing (100 City Hall Plaza, Ste, 501, Boston, MA 02108, USA) has many cross-cultural book titles and simulation games that supplement the cultural specifics of our Unit 2. For example with reference to Chapter 13, Tom Party's *Thumbs Up, Australia* (2006); Paul Davies' *What's This India Business* (2004); Mark Ashwall and Thai Diep's *Vietnam Today's* (2004); *Learning to Think Korean* (2001); Hu Wenzhong and Cornelius Grove's *Encountering the Chinese* (1999), etc. (www.interculturalpress.com).

DOING BUSINESS WITH EUROPEANS

European Union: Principally Great Britain, Ireland, France, Spain, Germany, Poland, Italy, East Europe/Eurasia, Russia and Turkey

Those fusty old Europeans are engaged in a radical experiment to reinvent themselves—a bid to create a "New Europe" that is more than a collection of countries, but less than a unified state. The Maastricht treaty is not yet a teenager, the common currency is barely out of its nappies, a new constitution is being debated.[1]

LEARNING OBJECTIVES

This chapter seeks to enhance an understanding of the cultures and diversity of members and candidates for the European Union, so that we can be more effective in doing business there and visiting as a tourist. Specifically, 14 European countries will be examined in some depth, providing historical perspective and cultural guidelines. Combined profiles will be presented for 18 other nations. So as to appreciate the continent's differences and prospects, this treatment is divided into five geographical areas—western, central, northern, southeastern, eastern, including Eurasia.

Europe is the world's second smallest continent, bounded to the west by the Atlantic Ocean, to its east by Russia, and to the southeast by Turkey. It ambles from Iceland to Gibraltar. In the north, this landmass is set apart by the Arctic Ocean, and in the south by the Mediterranean, Black and Caspian seas. Amidst its landmass, peninsulas, and islands,

Europe is the world's second smallest continent.

Pan Europe

* **Member of the European Union**

it is home to more than 40 countries. Between two major mountain systems, a rolling, fertile plain stretches from the Pyrenees to the Urals. Herein are located some of the world's greatest urban centers, such as London, Paris, Berlin, and Moscow. The continent is home to some 728 million people, three-fourths of whom live in these urban areas. Although set in a northern location, thanks to the influence of the Gulf Stream, Europe generally enjoys a mild climate except for occasional winter and ice storms.[2]

Historical Perspective Overview

The latest scientific research shows that human migration from Africa to what is known today as Europe likely occurred 50,000 to 35,000 years ago. Of course, these people were preceded by the Neanderthals with whom they shared the continent for several thousand years until their prehistoric ancestors were replaced. Recently, hominid fossils, a species of our ancestors, were uncovered in the Atapuerca hills of northern Spain. Carbon dating indicates they were living there some 800,000 years ago; they may be the last common ancestor of both the Neanderthals and Homo sapiens. The first known civilization in the region dates back to 2000 B.C. in Crete where Minoans produced an impressive culture, trading with Egypt and Asia Minor. In the eighth century B.C., classical Greeks enriched the world, especially future European civilizations, through philosophy, mathematics, natural sciences, political thought, the arts, and architecture. This legacy was bequeathed to the Romans, who became masters of architecture, engineering, law, and military strategy. Their empire was the first attempt to unit the continent's peoples, even extending beyond its borders into the Middle East. Though lasting only 500 years, their Latin language, infrastructure, and heritage continues to influence humankind.

As the Roman Empire declined, Christianity, coming out of western Asia, entered Europe and became a binding force in Europe until modern times. Throughout the Middle Ages, monasteries were centers of learning, spirituality, and agriculture. The first major religious split on this continent occurred in the eleventh century. As a result, Roman Catholicism under the popes dominated the West, whereas Orthodox Christianity under the patriarchs reigned in the East. European religious unity was further undermined in the fourteenth and fifteenth centuries with the introduction of Islam by the Ottoman Turks into the Balkans, and later into Spain via North Africa. Both religious and political power were further fractured in the fifteenth and sixteenth centuries with the Protestant Reformation. As feudalism diminished, powerful kings and nations arose, especially in Western Europe.

By the eighteenth century, modern Europe arose in the aftermath of two revolutions in the British colonies of the New World and in France. The powers of aristocracy and royalty diminished, while for the next two centuries, nationalism, socialism, and democracy flourished. Beginning in England some 400 years ago, the impact of the Industrial Revolution extended throughout the planet until present times. In the twentieth century, after two world wars and a Cold War, Europe was divided into two geopolitical spheres between Western Europe and the East Bloc countries under Soviet control. Business practices varied according to whether the capitalist or socialist system was used. The demise of communism blurred that demarcation but complicated the situation. Despite their totalitarian conditioning for 70 years or less, nations from Central and Eastern Europe began to seek entry into the free enterprise system established in 1952 as the European Common Market. In this twentieth-first century, Europe is a dynamic and very exciting place to do business, although it is undergoing a profound transition. The winds of economic, social, and political change are sweeping throughout the entire continent, both in its western and eastern portions. Since 1957, the member nations of the European community, now called *union*, have striven together to improve their standard of living and to foster closer relations among their countries. Their collaboration has facilitated more unified continental activities, while attempting to preserve local cultures and languages.

Europeans today have a long cultural history.

Thus, Europeans today have a long cultural history, representing a highly diverse mixture of peoples and their governance, making generalizations difficult. The next section will provide further context for better European understanding.

EUROPEAN DIVERSITY AND SYNERGY

Late in the twentieth century, the multinational entities of Europe sought ways to unify their economic efforts through the formation of a European Common Market. As the scope of cooperation increased among the participants (e.g., European Space Agency), the term *European Community* (EC) came into use. In 1991, member countries signed the Maastricht Treaty, a road map for establishing an economic and monetary union. The EC was renamed the European Union (EU), and three key institutions were created—a European Council, Commission, and Parliament. By 2002, a common currency called the *euro* was put into circulation and originally adopted by 11 member states (Denmark, Great Britain, Greece, and Sweden have yet to use it officially). The EU member bloc speaks some 230 indigenous languages. About half of the Europeans now speak English. The EU spends more than a billion dollars a year to maintain language equality by translating documents into 20 official documents.[3]

These synergistic endeavors toward a European community resulted in formal agreements that allow goods, people, services, information, and capital to move freely among member countries. The EU membership has now expanded to 25 nations. The older members are Austria, Belgium, Denmark, Finland, France, Germany, Greece, Ireland, Italy, Luxembourg, the Netherlands, Portugal, Spain, Sweden, and the United Kingdom. The 10 new members are Cyprus, Czech Republic, Estonia, Hungary, Latvia, Lithuania, Malta, Poland, Slovakia, and Solvenia. Upon the nearest admissions, President Jacques Chirac of France observed, "For nearly fifty years, the heart of our continent was split between democracy and dictatorship in a balance of terror. The fracture that started in Europe spread across the planet."[4] Now the forces for unity and inclusion on this continent are spreading. Yet, Turkey, while a member of NATO and a leading EU applicant, is not likely to be immediately admitted. Russia has not sought membership but has developed special working relationships with both NATO and the EU. (These two countries are located in Eurasia and will be discussed in the last section of this chapter.)

Currently, the European Union encompasses 457 million people and has an annual GDP of some $13.8 trillion. The 10 new member countries it added in 2004 are principally from Central and Eastern Europe, including some former communist nations who were once part of the old Soviet Bloc. Now central EU themes are (1) a single-market economy of consumers that offers peaceful stability and wealth, as well as political and economic clout; and (2) respect for differences that they live with and not fight about within this voluntary union. Although Europeans still cherish their diversity, not all is smooth sailing as different and competing visions emerge. The EU's rapid expansion has raised tensions over ethnic, religious, and cultural identity.[5]

Many of the following issues have been solved or are in the process of resolution.

- Technical—differing national standards and regulations, conflicting business laws, and protected public procurements.
- Free flow of goods, once they have cleared customs in the EU, as if national boundaries did not exist.
- Free movement of workers, so that citizens of one state may seek employment in another without discrimination relative to type of job, remunerations, or other employment conditions.
- Freedom of establishment, so that a citizen or business from one state has the right to locate and conduct business elsewhere in the EU.
- Freedom to provide services to persons throughout the EU.

European efforts to achieve integration and standardization have successfully led to greater economic and currency unification. Some of the benefits of the new EU policies are intended to accomplish the following:

The European Union encompasses 457 million people and has an annual GDP of some $13.8 trillion.

- Ensure cost savings by removing internal border controls.
- Increase competition and consumer demand.
- Facilitate economies of scale in production.
- Foster greater expenditures on combined research and development.
- Promote more efficient use of continental human resources.
- Decrease unemployment.
- Lower prices while increasing economic growth throughout the EU.

To take advantage of the single-market opportunities, global corporations are establishing EU-based companies; the Japanese are most prominent in this strategy. Many foreign enterprises are acquiring or merging with European industrial units, increasing the cross-cultural challenges at both the national and corporate levels. In addition to knowing about EU policies and regulations, global managers assigned to Europe will have to be more competitive, as well as better trained and more culturally sensitive. They also must deal with various economies and monetary systems, particularly the euro currency. But they face new consumer opportunities, for Europeans increasingly buy beyond national borders, whether it is for insurance policies, bank accounts, mutual funds, or euro bonds. Europe's efforts toward synergy are not without other problems and challenges because of its very diversity, as the next section demonstrates.

The European Union Today

In the opening decade of the new millennium, the optimist would declare the EU a great success in achieving many of the above goals. Leonard argues that the EU is now the world's biggest market, exporter, and foreign investor. He points out that Europe is now home to many of the largest and most successful companies. Some member countries, such as Finland and Ireland, rank at the top of global competitiveness, while new Central Europe members are mainly fast-growing economies. For the past 60 years, Europe has experienced relative peace after rising from economic ruins in 1945. But Rachman in his 2004 survey of the European Union, cites critics who say that far from promoting peace, prosperity, and freedom, it now threatens these achievements. Many of the unnecessary laws and regulations emanating from EU institutions in Brussels weaken some members' self-government and democracy, while engulfing the European economy. Eurosceptics fear that EU enlargement distracts from the formation of an effective federation by increasing the diversity of political interests and views. Furthermore Europe still lacks a common language, national media, and national identity. Half of the people in the EU still speak only their mother tongue, and only one-sixth live in a country other than their homeland. Some contend that further European integration undermines their country's nationalism, for citizens interact mainly with their own

Half of the people in the EU still speak only their mother tongue.

governments, not the EU. The recent failure to ratify the proposed constitution deterred the development of a multitiered union.[6]

Yet the EU has emerged at the heart of the continent's economic life and increasingly impacts social and foreign policy. The candidates for membership, like the Balkan countries, find the benefits of EU membership so attractive that they are even willing to make peace and introduce democratic reforms, Croatia being a case in point. Negotiations are under way to admit Turkey, a large Muslim nation. Euronationalists think there is a distinctive European approach to global needs, such as support for multilateral institutions and antiwar demonstrations. A half-century after its birth, the EU has yet to obtain genuine popular support for "ever closer union" that contributes to the gradual emergence of a Euroculture. What may result is a more diverse EU that allows members and their inhabitants to adopt different levels of integration that are more attuned to their national preferences. This very diversity may stimulate competition between different economic and social models within Europe.[7]

Cultural Guidelines for Doing Business in Europe

As Europe moves beyond national borders and national cultures toward regional cooperation, a new European identity is developing. EU youth, for example those in Ireland, envision themselves as the *new Europeans*. While assimilation takes place within the Union, the cultural identity of each member country needs to be preserved, as the basis for a diverse and enriched European cultural future. Latin verve and British pragmatism, for example, are viewed as strengths within the EU rather than as divisive elements. However, the distinct cultures and enormous differences in values and outlooks among member countries must be addressed to overcome impediments to deeper unity. That being said, among the EU's burgeoning bureaucracy of approximately 26,000 personnel, no organized research is ongoing to study the impact of cultural diversity and ways to promote more cultural synergy.

Nowhere is the latter collaboration more evident than in the field of management. Managers readily cross national boundaries not only on mutual business, but for professional development together. The three great management learning centers have multicultural participants: INSEAD (Fontainebleau, France); International Management Institute (Geneva, Switzerland), and Management Centre Europe (Brussels, Belgium). Furthermore, European managers attend courses and workshops at each other's universities, and read one another's management journals and business publications. Perhaps the transnational aspects of European management is best demonstrated in matters of partnerships, joint ventures, and acquisitions. For example, the Republic of Ireland not only boasts of its more than 200 British industries, and

A new European identity is developing.

many new American and European firms, but of the young, well-educated workforce available for service throughout the EU.

The internationalization of the European workforce has been progressing for at least five decades, accelerated by the multinational corporation. Since World War II, more than 30 million workers—mostly from countries in Southern Europe and North Africa—have flowed into Northern Europe. European businesspeople have always excelled at multilingual skills. These trends are some of the reasons that cross-cultural management training is increasing within Europe.

So who is European? It is no longer the typical inhabitants of the last two centuries on that continent. The enlargement of the EU has changed demographic factors, such as affluence, poverty, and fertility. Also, there is ongoing mass immigration into Europe that is altering the composition and culture of its peoples. Many of the new arrivals face not only discrimination but civil disorder caused by anti-immigrationists. The European Union estimates that 500,000 illegals are being absorbed yearly. Add to that the 400,000 refugees claiming political asylum, and harmony in Europe is threatened. At present, there is no common EU policy on asylum, and refugees are subject to the national regulations of member regimes. And while this influx goes on, the EU is still debating about establishing a policy on Pan-European border policing to replace national frontier controls. Furthermore, there is not a consensus in Europe as to *who is an immigrant*? The EU has not adopted the UN definition—a short-term migrant is anyone who moves to a new country and stays for 3 to 12 months; long term is considered a year or more. The EU member states not only have differing policies regarding those who immigrate to their countries, but also record the numbers differently. In Switzerland, for instance, one may receive "temporary" resident permits of a year or more, whereas in Britain, acceptance or rejection of those seeking entry may take years. In Germany, automatic citizenship is bestowed on children born to foreign parents in that country. Because there may be 500,000 migrants in Italy alone, their parliament is working on proposed legislation for controlling immigration, which may include the deportation of illegals. The country's extensive coastline has large landings of Albanians, Kurds, Africans, and some Asians. The new law, if passed, would require legal immigrants from non-EU nations to have job contracts before leaving their homelands and to be fingerprinted upon arrival.

With the increasing activities of global terrorism networks, EU states have new concerns about foreign visitors and migrants. Furthermore, Europe's Muslim minorities feel stigmatized because of the actions of Osama bin Laden or other criminal Islamic fundamentalists. Although many Muslims assimilate into European cultures, others choose self-segregation, and many are forced, for economic reasons, to live in impoverished "ghettos." Often, they experience cultural chauvinism and discrimination, ranging from unemployment to outright racism

The enlargement of the EU has changed demographic factors, such as affluence, poverty, and fertility.

EXHIBIT 14.1

THE MUSLIM DIASPORA

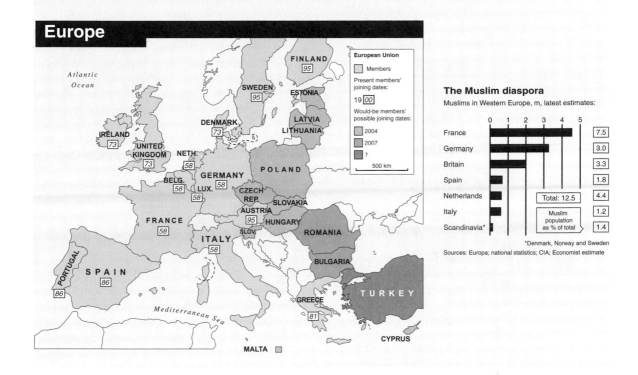

and violence against their person and property. In Britain, for example, there are 1500 mosques, but only two such institutions have been found to be extremist. Most Muslims have come to Europe seeking the opportunity to improve their lives. The scope of challenges for just this one minority can be appreciated from the display in Exhibit 14.1, with a distribution sampling of the 12.5 million Muslim population within the European Union.

European Languages and Demographics

Visitors to Europe often do not comprehend the complexities of its multiple languages; linguistically, Europe is almost like the biblical "Tower of Babel." For example, the Basques in Spain and France have continuously struggled to keep their language, customs, and institutions. Europe also has less well-known language issues:

Europe is almost like the biblical "Tower of Babel."

■ In France, Radio Kerne broadcasts in Breton, a Celtic language spoken for more than 2000 years. This is part of a movement to save Brittany's culture by preserving the language of the Druids, which now has its own Internet Web site. Since 1997, other minority languages, once banned by the French government in the name of equality, may now be taught, such as Occitan, Corsican, and Alsatian. Add to this Gallic mix over 700,000 people who speak Arabic, with French as a second language. Other European countries indicate similar trends.

- In Spain, Catalan is the official government language of Catalonia, and road signs now appear in Arabic to accommodate over a million Moroccan summer vacationers.
- In Germany, a large segment of the population speaks Turkish.
- Gaelic has returned not only to Ireland, but also to Scotland and Wales.
- Broadcasts in Frisian and Limburgs may be heard in northern Italy and the Netherlands, while in Finland, the news can now be heard in Saami.
- In the United Kingdom, twice as many Britons now speak Urdu, Punjabi, or Gujarati as speak Welsh, the native language of Wales in England.
- The 41 nation Council of Europe has created a Bureau of Lesser-used Languages that finances projects such as an Internet browser in Welsh, cartoon books in Alsatian, and the like. Concerned about democracy and human rights, the council's position is that this revival movement has economic benefits as it stimulates local food, dress, music, and crafts, as well as language courses and networks, both personal and electronic.

Until this century, the overwhelming population of Europe was Caucasian and generally spoke three Indo-European language groups—Germanic, Romance, or Slavic. Today, in this densely populated continent, over 40 different languages are spoken among its national and ethnic groups. This number constantly changes in the west with the mass influx of immigrants, both legal and illegal, from former Soviet Republics, Turkey, Africa, and even Asia.

Within the United Nations, there are six official languages. But in the European Parliament today, when one of the 628 members from 15 nations speaks, it is immediately translated into 11 official languages. As new members are added, it is likely more languages will be accommodated. The regulations say that each member language is a working language in all European Union institutions. The $1 million spent daily by the EU on translations is likely to grow, along with the enormous cost of 4000 interpreters and translators to maintain a multilingual Union. English is the EU's dominant working language. A recent survey confirms that 92% of Europe's secondary students in non-English countries are studying English, while 33% learn French and only 13% acquire German.

European Perceptions

When we analyze Europe, it is not easy to define a cultural set of beliefs, customs, values, practices, and feelings. While each country therein has its own distinctive culture, there are still commonalities that distinguish the "old world" from other regions. Below is an overview of principal themes on that continent that may alter outsiders' perceptions.

■ Europeans have an inherent interest in the quality of life, at all levels of society. There is a predominant humanist belief that people are to be served by progress and not the reverse. They enjoy socialization with family and friends over beverage and meals.

■ Europeans generally have an inordinate sense of reality. When one reflects on the wars and disruptions in Europe in the twentieth century alone, one can understand how Europeans know that tragedy can be just a breath away and that perhaps only this moment is real.

■ Europeans have endured. They have survived plagues, atrocities, great wars, border changes, and government upheavals. They have lived through many ambiguities and have the threads of ancient customs and traditions in the fabric of their cultures. They know the fragility of their civilization. On the one hand it is the sense of survival, but on the other hand it is that disaster is often not far off.

Europeans have

endured.

Such perspectives may have a disadvantage in that Europeans may be less willing to take a risk on a new idea or venture with a possibly good future. For them, the concept of simply making money is not the foundation of a company; the long-term survival of the business is as important. According to Bloom et al.,[8] the following characteristics are representative of the overall European cultural outlook.

■ An almost cynical realism schooled by history.
■ A belief that individuals should be at the center of life.
■ A sense of social responsibility.
■ A mistrust of authority.
■ A feeling that all people have weaknesses and sometimes one has to "muddle through" life.
■ A desire for security and continuity.
■ A belief that maximum profit is not the primary aim of business.

It has also been observed that relationships between the individual and authority in Europe are accented by differences in educational and political attitudes within the continent. The reports below would seem to substantiate this observation.

Education/Schooling

Educational systems in Europe tend to be very traditional, somewhat rigid in offerings and organization, and resistant to change. While strong in science, engineering, literature, and languages, courses in business, management, and entrepreneurship were only recently and slowly introduced. Here is a sampling of some trends in schooling.

- Teachers in the Netherlands and Scandinavia have far less "distance" between themselves and their pupils than their counterparts in Mediterranean countries.
- In one of the world's most egalitarian societies, Dutch children are taught to keep low profiles and are told that being "first" at something is not necessarily a virtue, whereas in Mediterranean countries, such as Greece and Italy, children tend to be nurtured as special, unique, and implicitly superior individuals. In Britain it is acceptable to finish first, but only if one can do it without seeming to work harder.
- In some European countries educational systems suffer from culture lag and need an updating of their instructional systems for an "information society" and a "knowledge culture."

Politics/Economics

While there is diversity within Europe's political and economic systems, the EU is a force for standardization. Very gradually, the European Union is fostering political integration, as demonstrated by the euro currency. Examples of trends to follow.

- Countries like Britain and Denmark, with long traditions of relatively nonintrusive government but with respect for the law, have tended to resist proposals for new regulations from EU administrators in Brussels. Yet, once agreement is reached, they have the best record of implementation. But the 10 newest EU members are less resistive and more cooperative, so as to retain EU benefits.
- On the other hand, Belgium, where bureaucracy is oppressive and evading law/regulations are widespread, ranks among the quickest to propose new EU rules but has the worst record for implementing adopted regulations.
- In France, over 700,000 Arab citizens are now eligible to vote in presidential elections, thus influencing the outcome of future governmental policies.
- While some complain that there are too many national entities in Europe, it is also home to many supranational organizations, such as NATO, UNESCO, OECD, and the European Court of Human Rights.

In France, over 700,000 Arab citizens are now eligible to vote in presidential elections.

Kagan argues that Europe is trying to find a "posthistorical paradise"—a self-contained world built on transnational rules and negotiations.[9] His point is that the fundamental cleavage is all about power. The Americans believe that world order ultimately rests on military power, whereas the Europeans envision an orderly world based on international law and multilateral institutions. The New Europe seemingly wants a more independent relationship from America, drawing on the wisdom of the old continent, while forging ahead with a more united destiny of its own creation.

Currently, Europeans are divided in their viewpoint of their world role. With regard to transatlantic relations, France believes that the European Union must balance and sometimes confront American power. Britain maintains that Europe and the United States must work closely together in international affairs, as is done in the North Atlantic Treaty Organization (NATO). This perspective is shared by governments in Spain, Portugal, Italy, the Netherlands, Denmark, and applicants for EU membership. Perhaps this explains, in part, some European opposition to and support of the Anglo-American coalition's assault on Iraq in 2003. Supposedly, its purpose was to remove an evil dictator and liberate Iraq's people, as the United States did twice in Europe during the twentieth century.

Currently, the European Union's main weakness, according to Brittan, lies in inflexible political and economic structures that make it less capable of responding adequately to both globalization and its own enlargement challenges.[10] Yet the EU leaders announced at the turn of this century their goals to create *the most competitive and dynamic knowledge-driven economy in the world by 2010*. With its expansion in membership, the EU's gross domestic product is $13.8 trillion, better than the United States at $11.7 trillion. Exhibit 14.2 offers one insight into the growing Pan European commercial activities and their impact on the environment. For example, readers who watched the 2006 Olympic Winter Games in Turino, Italy, were informed of insufficient snow and its negative impact on athletes.

Immigration and Labor Exchange

The new EU immigration regulations and job opportunities have attracted a host of *external migrants*, legal and illegal, to the continent. They come largely from Africa, the Middle East, and Turkey. Destination Europe now accounts for over 33 million immigrants from abroad. Although the new arrivals ease labor shortages, they increase the anxieties of Europeans about cultural identities and values. EU countries have dealt with the challenge in various ways—from integrating them into society to legal containment or expulsion. For example, Austria will fine and expel immigrants who fail to attend mandated classes in the German language; Britain requires those seeking citizenship to pass

The New Europe seemingly wants a more independent relationship from America.

EXHIBIT 14.2
CROSS-BORDER ALPINE BUSINESS

A recent magazine feature bewailed how the Alps mountain chain is under pressure from the heavy toll of tourism, commerce, pollution, and global warming on Europe's winter playground. Along with artificial snow-making machines, synthetic blankets which reflect solar radiation are being used to slow summer melting. If current temperature trends hold, 50 to 80% of the remaining Alpine glacier ice could vanish by 2100! The whole Tyrolean culture and way of life is under threat. Arrayed across the heart of Europe, the Alps have been intensely used for centuries, but only 17% of its 74,000 square miles are protected. Fourteen million people live there, but usable space in Alpine valleys is limited. Yet there is an orgy of multitasks underway there by humans—factories, train tracks, hotels, houses, churches, ski-lifts, farms, parking lots, stores, boutiques and restaurants, all bounded together by concrete roads. Everyday 4000 tractor trailers thunder through the Mount Blanc tunnel connecting France and Italy. Along with the cars and buses for thousands of tourists, the small village roads are clogged and pollution results from all that traffic. The Alps are big business, a sort of factory producing 1.6 million gallons of liquid water; millions of cubic meters of lumber; tons of iron and salt; spectacular cheese, wines, apples; amusements, athletics challenges, and artistic inspiration, plus mining and fishing. Seventy-seven million tons of cargo move through these mountains in an average year, and trans-Alpine commercial transport is likely to double by 2020!

The Alps stretch 650 miles across eight European nations, housing some 650 ski resorts. Scientists predict that as the permanent snow line rises along with temperatures, half of these resorts will go out of business. Furthermore, less snow and ice cover means less runoff to feed Europe's major rivers; melting permafrost destabilizes steep slopes and the structures built upon them. The mountains also concentrate fumes and noise from all the vehicle traffic, and their carbon dioxide contributes to the global warming, while the valley walls carry the maddening noise upward. Moderns are negatively impacting this unique environment and culture. Alpine people, known for their stoicism and individualism, crafted for a world of isolation and avalanches, are now coping with a host of modern problems. Since the awesome mountains with their beauty and tranquility are the central reality of Alpine life, humanity should cherish and protect them.

Source: E. Zuringle, "Meltdrun—The Alps under Pressure," *National Geographic*, 209, no. 2 (February 2006): 96–115.

a test. As émigrés swarm into Western Europe, the nations there are tightening their immigration laws. Many of these "visitors" live together in ghettos, forming new ethnic minorities. So far European policy has been inadequate, not facilitating integration into their societies and not encouraging assimilation. On the other hand, some of the new arrivals have resisted acculturation, refusing to learn the language and culture of the host country, and not letting their children marry the locals or anyone outside their religious faith. When second- and third-generation children of immigrants are unable to enter the mainstream society, they often resort to protests and riots. Unemployment among such youths is usually higher than average, and obstacles are often in place against home ownership.

Under the EU policies, *internal migrants* seeking work outside their own country in other member nations are free to do so. But such labor exchange, especially from the East, finds an open market that is curtailed, except in Britain, Ireland, and Sweden which only delimit benefit-seekers. Most of the other original 12 members impose transitional arrangements to curb "freedom of movement," which is supposedly a right of all EU citizens. Their governments fear that Eastern Europeans will steal jobs from the locals, but in actuality, more often they take work that the locals shun. Germany and Austria are most cautious of opening their labor market, because their countries are on the border of former communist countries whose workers go west for higher wages (e.g., Austria's wages are five times higher than Slovakia). Globalization and an aging workforce in Europe will eventually cause greater labor mobility that will prove beneficial, forcing more workforce flexibility among the EU15 members who will have to lift restrictions upon employees from the EU10 or elsewhere.

Multiculturalism

Another EU challenge is to promote multiculturalism among its 25 members, developing a continent-wide application and understanding of Article 9 of the European Convention on Human Rights. While secularism is on the rise in Europe, and church attendance falls, new mosques are opening everywhere on the continent—the UK alone has over a thousand. The problem centers on some 20 million Muslims in the midst of the EU. This Islamic community now represents about 25% of the European populations, and so the term *Eurabia* arose.[11] In several member countries, violence has erupted between a swelling Muslim minority and the majority populations. Mosque and Muslim gravesites have been vandalized, and complaints have risen about discrimination against them, particularly identifying them as terrorists. Ordinary devout Muslims are being stigmatized with fanatical Islamic extremists. The Muslim global backlash, as seen in the 2006 riots and burnings because of what they perceive as blasphemous, hurtful car-

Internal migrants seeking work outside their own country in other member nations are free to do so.

toons against their founder and beliefs originating in a Danish newspaper and reprinted elsewhere, is a case in point. The growing Muslim presence is changing the "face" of Europe more than the military invasions of the Ottoman Empire in previous centuries.

In the following sections, we examine select nations within the context of five geographic areas within Europe: western, central, northern, southern, and eastern. Special attention has been directed to three EU target cultures that are the union's largest markets: Great Britain, France, and Germany. The first mentioned is the *mother country* of all English-speaking nations and is considered by many as the EU financial capital; the second is the center of the continental cultural influence and many international agencies; and the third is the economic powerhouse within the EU. The country profiles provide helpful demographics and details that can be supplemented by going to the Internet Web sites of any European country which interests our readers.

WESTERN EUROPE

In Western Europe, depicted visually in Exhibit 14.1, there are three major nations which we will discuss in some detail here: Great Britain, France, and Spain. There are eight other smaller countries in the area, a few of which we will be able to profile briefly: Andorra, Belgium, Gibraltar, Ireland, Luxembourg, Monaco, Netherlands, and Portugal. Most are members of the European Union.

GREAT BRITAIN

The United Kingdom of Great Britain (UK) constitutes the main island consisting of England, Wales, and Scotland. At present, it also includes six counties of Northern Ireland known as Ulster. Other outer islands within the UK include the Hebrides, Orkney, and Shetlands. Although English is the principal language, secondary languages or dialects such as Welsh, Scottish, and Irish are spoken in various regions. Apart from many immigrants from British Commonwealth nations, the principal inhabitants are known as English, Welsh, Scots, and Irish. See the profile in Exhibit 14.3 for further details.

Historical Perspective Overview

Naturally, the British prefer to do business in English, for their language has almost become a universal means of communication, especially in business and international travel, as well as within the European Union. It is a tribute to the hearty race of Anglo-Saxon-Celts living on a few small islands off the eastern coast of Europe who

Western Europe

ATLANTIC OCEAN

IRELAND*
Dublin ✪

UNITED
KINGDOM*

LONDON ✪

ENGLISH CHANNEL

Amsterdam ✪ NETHERLANDS*

Brussels
✪
BELGIUM*

✪ Luxembourg*

✪ PARIS

FRANCE*

ANDORRA ✪

CORSICA

P O R T U G A L *

Lisbon ✪

MADRID ✪

S P A I N *

MEDITERRANEAN SEA

EXHIBIT 14.3
PROFILE OF GREAT BRITAIN

Area	244,820 sq km
Population	60,441,457 (July 2005 est.)
Capital	London (7.5 million population)
Religion	Christian (Anglican, Roman Catholic, Presbyterian, Methodist), 71.6%; Muslim, 2.7%; Hindu, 1%; Other, 1.6%; unspecified or none, 23.1%
Language/Ethnic groups	English, Welsh, Scottish (Gaelic), among Anglo-Saxon native born; plus diverse languages of émigrés (principally from West Indies, India, Pakistan, Middle East, Asia, and Africa)
Literacy	99% literacy rate
Life expectancy	78.38 years
GDP per capita	$30,900
Government	Constitutional monarchy

The sun has set on the British Empire.

managed to create an empire, spanning continents, influencing millions of peoples, and lasting centuries. Even though the sun has set on the British Empire, their global impact in the past, and to some extent in the present, is staggering to conceive. Not only their language, but their customs, laws, and lifestyles penetrated remote corners of the world and held sway over continents from North America and Asia to the Middle East and Africa. It is still evident in the many member states of the British Commonwealth of Nations.

Although the United States is indebted to many nations for its cultural heritage, the English-Irish-Scotch combination provided the main thrust to its society at home and abroad. Through the unique format of the British Commonwealth organization, this island kingdom with its royal family and social institutions has affected many ethnicities and cultures. For example, during their 800 years of control in Ireland, British rulers were the catalyst for exporting millions of Irish immigrants, missionaries, politicians, and prisoners throughout the world. There are leaders today in Australia and Argentina, as well as Africa and the Americas, of Irish heritage whose ancestors were compelled to leave their native "Hibernia" because of past English policies.

The British have been forced to retreat, in many ways, to the confines of their island kingdom and a few remaining small territories, such as the Falkland Islands.[12] And they have been followed home by the multicultural inhabitants of their Commonwealth who used their privilege of British connections to resettle in the "mother country." Added to this influx from the "colonies" are the transfers of many affluent Middle Easterners to England seeking property, education, health services, and recreation. This reverse migration from the British West Indies, Africa, Asia, and the Indian subcontinent is transforming what was once a largely white, homogeneous, class-conscious society into one that is more heterogeneous, egalitarian, and cosmopolitan.

The exception is Ulster, which has been racked by armed struggles (economic, political, social) between its Catholic and Protestant (Orangemen) communities. Paramilitary operations by extremists from both sides have been the source of conflict, violence, and transgressions of human rights. Northern Ireland terrorism has been exported to the very heart of England itself. Currently, the British government is still in negotiations, seeking to promote some form of agreement and reconciliation with all parties, including the radical Protestant paramilitary organizations, the branches of the Irish Republican Party (IRA), and the Republic of Ireland in the south.

Despite recent bombings from Islamic terrorists, the British still go about business in a very civilized, unflappable way. After all, this courageous people did withstand the Nazi bombings and blitz over 60 years ago. But there are new challenges and strains that could undermine the social fabric of the United Kingdom. The government has made commitments to observe the European Convention on Human Rights, but there are problems as the reports in Exhibit 14.4 underscore.

Since the article in Exhibit 14.4 was written, related problems have arisen which are more complicated. Here are some indicators of racial strife within Britain:

The British still go about business in a very civilized, unflappable way.

- Increased tensions between Caucasians and people of color, as when white mobs attacked immigrants in Sydney's blighted, beachfront neighborhoods (December 2005); violence between Afro-Caribbeans and South Asians in Birmingham (October 2005); conflicts in Leicester between minority cultural groups over the growing political assertiveness of Muslims (11% of the city's population), plus Afro-Caribbeans against newly arrived Somalis; atrocities like the blowing up of London trains, straining relations with Muslims and spilling over toward Sikhs (September 2001 and onward).
- Part of the reason for this growing racial tension in Britain can be traced to the changing geography of the inner city and obsolete social policies that lag behind contemporary realities. And yet, progress is being made in the assimilation of ethnic minorities. For example, the annual fair in Middle England has expanded to meet the interests of Muslims, such as hosting a Festival of Living Islam with their food and music, exhibit stalls for Islamic finances, travel packages to Mecca, and speeches.

EXHIBIT 14.4

ASYLUM, MARRIAGE, AND MULTICULTURALISM

Worries about Britain's clogged and scandal ridden asylum systems, particularly its abuse by terrorists, are shifting the immigration debate into new areas. The furor combines three separate issues. One is a serious question about the nature and extent of mass migration into Britain. Although not huge by European Union standards, the new inflow from non-EU countries is estimated at upward of 250,000, high by historical standards. Immigration does bring potential pluses (new skills, cultural diversity, cheap labor) and minuses (poverty, disease, social tensions). This leads to the second issue—the asylum system, which by accident and not design, is the main way people from poor countries move to Britain. The international rules of asylum were drafted in a different age and migration was easier. They did not foresee a situation when thousands of people would turn up having destroyed their identity documents, making unverifiable claims of persecution, whose cases would be processed by a very slow and toothless bureaucracy, with multiple layers of appeals, often aided by determined, publicly financed lawyers. In the past ten years, the number of asylum seekers has shot up to more than 83,000 last year. Stories abound, often exaggerated, of grants, about loans, and other help provided asylum seekers, and with discontent about fraying of services, such as health and education, the result is considerable public crossness. This is tightened by the third worry: terrorism. Some of the people caught this past month were asylum seekers, mostly from Algeria. British people are understandably bothered by the idea that they are paying to shelter people who want to kill them.

Since September 11, 2001, it has become harder and more urgent to inculcate British values into immigrants. One problem is the custom of arranged and forced marriages among the new arrivals. Potential victims are forced to travel home, mainly to the Indian subcontinent, to marry unwanted relatives, so more of the extended family can enter the UK. More young women are resisting coercion, because the British education that makes them more eligible also makes them less docile. Liberal societies sometimes have to adjudicate between individual rights and cultural traditions. And so the government is beginning to challenge violation of personal autonomy for conjugal misery among the immigrant populations. Arranged marriages are also the biggest problem with the ways Britain manages diversity. Most immigrant groups over time become less insular as their children marry locals. The government now wants to move beyond multiculturalism to foster core national values among the newcomers.

Source: "Asylum—Bordering on Panic," *The Economist*, February 11, 2003, p. 47; "Marriage and Multiculturalism—Commercial Wrongs," *The Economist*, November 10, 2002, p. 51.

■ Antisocial behavior is on the rise in the UK. The educated Briton was known for civility, patience, politeness, and generosity, with an instinct to compromise. Today the inhabitants increasingly suffer from incivilities like graffiti, spitting, verbal abuse, and worse. Since the Labour Party came to power in 1997, they have honed legal weapons against such uncivil behavior. The most potent is the Anti-Social Behaviour Order (ASBO), which can be handed out for conduct that causes or contributes to "harassment, alarm, distress" of other citizens—breach the order and the culprit can be subject to five years in prison. Along with curfews and dispersal orders, these regulations to promote good behavior now allow police to evict people from "disorderly households." Children who publicaly mis-behave and are continuously troublesome may cause their parents to attend classes in a "parenting academy," as one means of discour-aging antisocial activities in a more diverse British society.

Cultural Guidelines for Doing Business in Britain

Commercial policies and practices vary slightly in the UK's four major regions: England, Wales, Scotland, and Northern Ireland. Gen-erally, punctuality is highly regarded and people expect you to be on time for appointments. Typically, the British observe a five-day work-week, Monday through Friday at 9 A.M. to 5 P.M., except for govern-ment offices which are closed between 1 and 2 P.M., but open until 5:30 P.M. Introductions, especially by third parties, are important; once the contact is made, the third-party responsibilities are over. During business presentations and negotiations, one should present objective facts, emphasize product safety, and prepare for market flexibility.[13]

In behavior, the British are normally private and traditional, expect-ing visitors to observe conventions, and maintain decorum. So initially be businesslike; it is not wise to get too personal. Their reserve causes them to avoid direct conflict and to hesitate to complain or report inad-equate service. British people tend to be unemotional and to downplay situations that might cause problems. Their sophistication and polite-ness may be punctuated with apologies and self-deprecating humor. There are also some differences in English terminology (e.g., the ground floor in the UK is the first floor in the United States, and the UK's first floor would be designated the second floor in America), as well as in driving habits (the British drive on the left side of the road but have right-handed motor vehicles).

Depending on where you are in the island kingdom, there are regional behavioral differences, especially among the Scots, Welsh, and ethnic groups. Although largely a Christian nation, Muslims make up 11% of the population, and Sikhs, Hindus, and Jews are smaller minorities. There is less class consciousness among the elite, while the average person in the UK is more egalitarian. The "pub" and tabloid

The British are normally private and traditional.

newspapers, along with soccer and cricket, are most popular among the masses. Although the queen is held in respect, royalty garners less affection and has diminishing influence.

Britain shares a unique cultural heritage with and affinity for America, its former colony and frequent ally in many wars. It leads in EU market penetration of the United States. Its economic approach is based on free enterprise, commitment, and encouragement of international trade. The nation has a low-risk reputation because it normally meets its obligations and liabilities, while protecting intellectual property rights. Although an EU member state, the country successfully seeks exceptions, like postponing adoption of the euro currency and retaining the pound sterling as its monetary unit. The UK maintains itself as both a global and EU financial and investment center. Although a strong Anglo-American economic and military partnership exists, the nation is being drawn ever more into the European Union. There the British exercise considerable influence and leadership in economic, trade, and political matters.

With a largely unwritten constitution going back to the Magna Carta, English common law and traditions are observed. Though a democratic, constitutional monarchy, the monarch is nominal head of state, but the influence of the subsidized royal family is largely confined to ritual, ceremony, charity, and tourism. Political power resides in one chamber of a bicameral Parliament, the House of Commons (651 elected members); the scope of the House of Lords is currently under revision. The prime minister heads up the national government, acting through his cabinet and ministers in charge of various governmental departments; the latter appointments depend on which political party or coalitions can command a majority in the Commons. Although a centralized state, a process of devolution is under way, giving more autonomy to regional and government entities. Among some 14 political parties, the Labour Party and the Conservative (Tory) Party are dominant, although the Social Democrats are growing in influence.

For the past decade, Britain has had a strong economy and a relatively crisis-free prosperity. Its work environment is productive and competitive, slightly ahead of its free-trading partners. The country struggles with its increasing diversity of population and devolution of central governmental powers, along with its role in an expanding European Union. Today London is a world-class city, while the nation and its regions are emerging as major artistic and cultural centers.

Businesspeople who form partnerships with the British should be aware of these tips:

■ While often sophisticated and civilized, British leaders are more formal, value privacy, and are somewhat touchy. (Do not initiate conversation about family or work; stick to safe subjects like the weather, sports, or English cultural life.)

- Within the UK's controlled business environment, maintain decorum and avoid casualness in dress and conversation; loudness and shouting are taboo.
- Family names and titles, along with "sir," are used, and deference is given to the superior or the affluent, including maintaining an appropriate distance.
- Negotiators seek to understand the other's position and are marked by tolerance, compromise, and problem resolution by committees.
- Typically, those in the professions and in business find discussion about money or finances distasteful, especially haggling over fees.
- During business days, two breaks are observed, usually for morning coffee or afternoon tea ("high tea" consists of pastries and small sandwiches); lunch or dinner may involve gin and tonic or sherry, with coffee after the meal.
- Fine manners and good etiquette are expected at all social occasions (e.g., holding doors for women, standing when ladies enter a room, not talking business if invited to a club).

To put this in perspective, remember that the younger generation is quite different, breaking with traditions and conventions. Recall that Britain, always known for its literature and performing arts, today is also the home of rock music, pop stars, and mod fashions, superb actors, fine theater, and classic films! Just pick up a British tabloid to get the other side of British lives.

Finally, realize that as a result of globalization, many foreign executives live and work in Britain, heading up some of the top companies there. Of the 50 largest British firms, 17 are run by foreigners, plus more in middle management. Foreign management also find the UK an attractive place to work, with the pay relatively high and lower taxes. The British business culture is also easier to fit into, whether in its capital London or other major cities—Birmingham, Bradford, Bristol, Edinburgh, Glasgow, Liverpool, Leeds, Manchester, and Sheffield.

Next we venture west across the Irish Sea to the island of the Celts and then eastward crossing the English Channel, or possibly through the modern Chunnel (tunnel), to visit France. This country is the UK's closest geographic neighbor on the European continent proper. Many centuries ago, British monarchs and lords ruled in Normandy and surrounding areas.

IRELAND

The Emerald Isle has the Irish and Celtic Seas to the east, and juts out west into the Atlantic Ocean. The green color for which the country is known results from heavy precipitation on its west and south coasts

Within the UK's controlled business environment, maintain decorum.

(60–80 inches annually) and less on its west coast (29–30 inches). The rain which keeps its hills so green is quaintly referred to by the Irish optimists as simply a "heavy dew." The nearby Gulf Stream not only causes the weather to be mild, but myth says tempers the fiery Celtic personality. Exhibit 14.5 offers further details about this small, fascinating country which has sent so many of its sons and daughters across the world (the United States alone has 25 million citizens of Irish descent). The profile focuses on the 26 counties of *Eire* and does not include the six northern counties, still under British sovereignty.

EXHIBIT 14.5
PROFILE OF THE REPUBLIC OF IRELAND

Area	70, 280 sq km (27,137 sq miles)
Population	4,062,235
Capital	Dublin (995,000 population)
Religion	Majority Roman Catholic; minorities Protestants, Jews, Druids, Muslims
Language	English; officially Irish or Gaelic
Literacy	99%
Life expectancy	77 years
GDP per capita	$34,100
Government	Parliamentry Democracy

Ireland now has the second largest per capita income in the world.

Once one of the poorest nations in Europe, Ireland now has the second largest per capita income in the world. After 800 years of English occupation, the Republic gained its freedom in 1921, joined the European Community in 1973, and is one of the wealthiest nations in that union. EU trade took the country out from under British control, and it prospered, starting with EU loans and assistance. South Ireland has become the European headquarters of numerous multinational corporations because of the educated labor pool and location. EU labor exchange policy has turned a homogeneous society into a more heterogeneous one, including workers from Eastern Europe and Africa. The EU influence has transformed a male-dominated society into one that offers equal opportunities for women, including politics (two women have become the nation's president). Irish youth now perceive themselves as the *new Europeans*, so the diaspora is over—many overseas Irish businesspersons and professionals are returning to their homeland. Institutions of higher education include the University of Dublin (Trinity College founded in 1590), National University (headquartered in Dublin, with branches in Cork and Galway), and Maynooth Seminary.

Historical Perspective Overview

Centuries ago, the ancient Celts swarmed out of central Europe, settling finally in Gaul, Scotland, Wales, and Ireland. Irish tribes were eventually formed into kingdoms, suffering occasional sea invasions from the Vikings who founded Dublin. With the coming of a Breton missionary, known today as St. Patrick, the inhabitants were converted to Christianity, replacing the Druids, priests, prophets, and sorcerers who practiced the Celtic religion of Gaul and Britain. The Irish church and monasteries were famous for learning, producing wondrous illustrated volumes, such as the Book of Kells now housed in Trinity College, Dublin. The glory days for the Irish were after the fall of the Roman Empire and the rise of Charlemagne when Western scholarship and literacy were isolated from Ireland. Thus, in these "Dark Ages," Ireland became known as the *land of saints and scholars*, which preserved the knowledge from the Greek and Roman traditions. When the new emperor established stability in Europe, Irish scholars spread throughout that continent, reviving educational and artistic traditions. In fact this early Irish church was quite liberal and advanced, permitting women into "holy orders" to become lawyers, priests, abbesses, and even bishops. Gradually, as this unique form of Christianity was brought under the rule of the pope in Rome, all that changed as the Catholic Church in Ireland became more bureaucratic and rigid in its administration. Over the centuries, monks, friars, and nuns were the humanitarians who cared for the peasants during famine and disasters. Often, the only educated persons in a village were the clergy and the physicians who became figures of authority. The Roman Catholic Church was a major cultural and educational force, as guardians of the national identity. In contemporary times this influence is lessening, and its dogmatism is questioned by the people, including religious prohibitions on contraception, divorce, and abortion.[14]

For the last thousand years, the Gaels have been fighting for freedom and independence. Thus, the second seminal force in Irish history is the British Empire. After Henry VIII changed England's religion from Catholicism to Protestantism, Ireland was invaded many times by English kings who subjugated the people to their rule. Henry VIII became head of the Church in England, eventually introducing the Anglican religion into this country as the "Church of Ireland." Wealthy monasteries became military targets, the Irish were dispossessed of their property, and Protestant aristocrats took over plantations and estates. In the 1650s, Oliver Cromwell's confiscation of property led to a situation whereby in the eighteenth century the native populations owned less than 15% of their own land. The locals' hatred of their oppressors increased when the English failed to help the starving Irish during the potato famines of 1842/1846, 1 million died, and another million

The Roman Catholic Church was a major cultural and educational force.

emigrated, principally to North America and Australia. Matters worsened when the natives were generally denied educational opportunity and illegal schools were secretly established. Essentially what happened was that a more advanced industrial society took over a rural country suffering from culture lag. Since the sixteenth century, the English gentry have invested heavily in Ireland, transforming the north from an agricultural to an industrial society by bringing in new technologies and Presbyterian factory workers from Scotland, known even today as the "Orangemen."

The Irish never accepted British rule.

The Irish never accepted British rule, fighting over and over for their independence under the leadership of numerous patriots. Their pressure for reform, often aided by both English and Irish Protestants, first resulted in Home Rule granted by the English Parliament early in the twentieth century. This became an impetus to Irish investments and protectionism, while World War I brought agricultural and industrial prosperity, even between the years 1915 and 1921 known as the "troubles." Armed rebellion in 1916 under nationalists like Eamon De Valera and Michael Collins resulted in a treaty that established the Irish Free State in 1921. In contrast to the new republic in the Catholic south, the six counties in the industrialized north were dominated by the majority Protestant Orangemen, who sought to remain as a part of Britain. After 1968, their prejudice and exclusionary tactics against minority Catholics led to serious violence between both sides under the cloak of religious differences. Today the British army and the Protestant paramilitary forces have been contained somewhat as a result of a recent disarmament agreement with extremist factions of the old Irish Republican Army.

Today, the Republic of Ireland is a parliamentary democracy, with a president serving seven years largely in a ceremonial role. The bicameral legislature is composed of the *Seanad* (Senate) with 60 members (49 elected, 11 nominated by the PM and elected by local universities) who serve five-year terms; and the *Dail* (House of Representatives) with 166 elected by universal suffrage (proportional representation) for a maximum of five years. The *Taoiseach* (prime minister) is the government leader, and there is an independent Supreme Court. Irish representatives are also playing significant roles in the European Union, in both its administration and parliament.

Ireland is considered the gateway to the European market. Currently, its economy performs strongly, despite high levels of taxation to support an extensive social welfare system in the southern counties. International corporations enjoy significant tax breaks as an incentive for investing and relocating here. The Industrial Development Authority (IDA) and Industrial Training Authority (AnCo) assist foreign and domestic companies in this regard. A stable, conservative, educated, English-speaking, cosmopolitan society that boasts a satisfactory infrastructure is attractive to global investors and businesses.

Cultural Guidelines for Business in Ireland

Ireland's inhabitants have been impacted by the Gaelic culture, language, literature, and music. Worldwide, the Irish are known to be loquacious and sentimental, family oriented and combative, politically astute and active in law enforcement, skilled in arts and crafts, horse breeders and farmers. Their land offers many natural resources, such as, zinc, lead, natural gas, crude oil, barite, copper, gypsum, limestone, dolomite, peat, and silver. Vocationally, the Irish have moved from being primarily farmers, fishermen, soldiers, scholars, and missionaries to bankers and high-technology university, as well as leaders in fashion, cuisine and the culinary arts, glass-making, and the performing arts.

The Irish personality is complex and at times contradictory. While generally conservative and sociable, they can at times be caustic and sarcastic about authority, as well as rebellious. The people also are known for their fighting spirit, hospitality, friendliness, and generosity. Their humanitarian zeal is reflected in their foreign missionaries and rock stars, who raise funds for global needs. Having gone from being a poor to affluent country in just decades, the Irish are ambivalent about wealth and moneymaking. Ostentation is frowned upon, except in giving to charity. When meeting strangers, a favorite pastime is to reveal as little about oneself as possible, while finding out as much as possible about the other person. Given the changeable climate, weather is a favorite topic of conversation, as is the environment. Leisure time is highly valued and structured only in sports.

The Irish personality is complex and at times contradictory.

Socially, the first name is commonly used, while in business the preference is to use the surname. While promptness is expected at work, socially the Irish are more flexible about time. Attitudes toward deadlines are relaxed, unless one emphasizes why a delivery date is important. The 39-hour, five-day workweek is normally 9 A.M. to 5:30 P.M., with lunch usually from 1–2 or 2:30 P.M. There are nine national holidays with special attention given to Christmas, Easter, St. Patrick's Day, and St. Stephen's Day. Vacations tend to be in July and August, not a good time to schedule key appointments and meetings.

Remember that Ireland is a society going through profound transition. The mind-set of the younger generation today is quite different from that of the older population who experienced want and deprivation. The culture is being transformed into a knowledge center with increasingly diverse participants who come not only from the EU but around the world.

FRANCE

France is geographically the largest country in Western Europe. It lies south of Great Britain, separated by the English Channel but connected now by an underwater tunnel or "chunnel." This channel gives the nation access to the North Sea, the Celtic Sea, and the Atlantic Ocean on its western coast, while to the southeast it is bounded by the Mediterranean Sea. On its northeastern border are Belgium, Luxembourg, and Germany; Switzerland and Italy to the east; and Spain in the South, separated by the Pyrenees of which Mount Blanc is the high point. Its natural resources include coal, iron ore, bauxite, fish, timber, zinc, and potash. Beautiful Paris is its capital, while other major cities include Marseilles, Lyon, Toulouse, Strasbourg, Nice, and Bordeaux. Apart from its advanced postindustrial economy, France is also known for its farms and vineyards.

In medieval times, French royalty and troops moved back and forth from Normandy to the British Isles, exchanging feudal domains. In the late eighteenth and early nineteenth centuries under Napoleon Bonaparte, the *grande armée* extended its control across Europe to Russia. The empire's remnants reveal the scope of France's colonial power and help us appreciate the glory that was France. Begin by looking today at what was once French East Africa and where the French language is still spoken (Burundi, Central African Republic, Congo, Djibouti, and to a lesser extent Rwanda). The same cultural impact is still evident in Northern Africa (Algeria, Chad, Egypt, Mali, Mauritania, Morocco, Niger, Tunisia, and Senegal); West Central Africa (Benin, Burkina Faso, Cameroon, Congo, Cote d'Ivoire, Gabon, Guinea, Togo); and even in Southern Africa (Madagascar). Recall too, the influence of French culture and cuisine in such widely separated locations as India (Pondicherry) and Indochina (Vietnam). Today, the Overseas Department of France governs somewhat the Caribbean islands, such as Guadeloupe and Martinique; and far into the Pacific Oceania on the French New Caledonia and Loyalty Islands, Iles-de-Horne and Wallis. In addition, there are other French Polynesian islands (Bora-Bora, Gambier, Hiva Oa, Huahine, Manihi, Moorea, Raiatea/Tahaa, Rurutu, Society Islands, Tahiti, Tuamotu Archipelago, and Ua Huka). All in all, an impressive sphere of global influence lasting for centuries into the present. For another view of France, consider the demographics in Exhibit 14.6.

Historical Perspective Overview

Many history books have been written on the glorious history of France.

Many history books have been written on the glorious history of France—from when it was known as Gaul under the Roman Empire, through the Middle Ages when France was gradually united under its own king, and then its expansion across Europe under Emperor Napoleon. Perhaps its greatest contribution toward the establishment of democracy came from its support of the American Revolution, and then through its own French Revolution. Space limitations permit us only to review France and its people in modern times, after it had

EXHIBIT 14.6
PROFILE OF THE FRENCH REPUBLIC

Area	547,030 sq km
Population	60,656,178 (July 2005 est.)
Capital	Paris (2,144,700 population)
Religion	Roman Catholic, 83%–88%; Protestant, 2%; Jewish, 1%; Muslim, 5%–10%; unaffiliated, 4%
Languages	French, 100%; rapidly declining regional dialects and languages (Provencal, Breton, Alsatian, Corsican, Catalan, Basque, Flemish)
Literacy	99% literacy rate
Life expectancy	79.6 years
GDP per capita	$29,900
Government	Republic

suffered invasion and defeat, instigated by Germany in World Wars I and II. Since then France has had a resurgence, helping to found both the European Common Market and Union, but with a diminished role in the world today.

The current Fifth Republic of France came into being in 1958 and has been governing by "cohabitation"—a sharing of power between the president with a seven-year term and the bicameral parliament of the National Assembly and Senate. The president appoints the prime minister who runs the country on a daily basis; presides over the cabinet; commands the armed forces and concludes treaties. He has the power to dissolve the National Assembly and assume full power. Two-fifths of members in that National Assembly are on leave from civil service. Fifty-seven percent of the adult population are either civil servants or their dependents. The various ministries of government employ some 2,180,240 in public service. Confidence is eroding in the nation's lackluster economic formula of higher taxes and higher social charges, especially during the current slowdown in economic growth. Excessive spending on health care, continuing widespread strikes, and the country's diminishing role in world affairs have disillusioned the public.

France's entrancing countryside consists of vineyards and cornfields, pastures and picturesque villages, superb cuisine and wines. But the country folk have dwindled by 37% in the past decade, as urbanization and industrialized agriculture spread along with fields and rivers polluted from pesticides, hypermarkets, and car lots. Strasbourg is home to the European Parliament, high-tech industrial parks, and the International Space University. Having experienced bitter defeat in

The current Fifth Republic of France came into being in 1958.

three devastating wars (one in Indochina and two on its own soil) produced a strong antiwar sentiment, plus a desire for peaceful cooperation with Germany, especially through the European Union. Despite long positive relations with the United States going back to the eighteenth century, its Gaullist independence prompts French politicians to often disagree publicly with American policies, particularly those regarding the Middle East. Yet France has the world's sixth largest economy and is the tenth largest trading partner of the United States.

Living in the Elyse Palace, French presidents, like the late François Mitterrand, have used public monies for grand schemes. The modern nobility, elite graduates of *grand ecoles* or universities, dominate civil service and business—all supposedly based on meritocracy. But the public sector mistrusts the private sector because it often hampers initiative, creativity, and entrepreneurialism. The French market is mature and sophisticated, open to global suppliers, especially those from within the EU community. The commercial environment is dynamic and reflects consumer trends within a world marketplace. Foreign companies generally face no major obstacles, except in television broadcasting. Consider these other comments on French culture in Exhibit 14.7.

EXHIBIT 14.7
PERCEPTIONS OF FRANCE

- The French constitute the most brilliant and the most dangerous nation in Europe, and the best qualified to become an object of admiration, hatred, pity, or terror, but never of indifference!
  —Alexis de Tocqueville
- The average Frenchmen is concerned about an elite of bureaucrats, businessmen, and politicians who seemingly run the country to benefit themselves amidst corruption and public scandals.
  —*New York Times*, August 1, 1999
- The French themselves are horribly muddled over France's place in Europe, over the impact of globalization, and at root, over what it means to be French. . . . France has an identity problem. It needs the courage to redefine itself.
  —J. Andres, "A Divided Self—A Survey of France, *The Economist*, November 16, 2002
- The French have a passion for engineering and technology, for research and solutions that push back the boundries. The Ecole Polytechnique is one of the best engineering schools in the world, and French technology tends to be very sophisticated.
  —Nani Becalli, CEO, GE Europe (www.thenewfrance.com)

The French have a passion for engineering and technology.

EXHIBIT 14.7

PERCEPTIONS OF FRANCE (CONTINUED)

■ As an American living in France, I personally find the quality of day-to-day life far superior to anything I could afford back home in the USA.

—Richard Chessnoff, Author, *The Arrogance of the French*

■ The biggest lesson of the French riots is that more jobs are needed. In the deprived suburbs, a kind of soft terror rules. When too many young people see nothing ahead but unemployment after they leave school, they end up rebelling. Thus, one rational analysis of the forces that lie behind the riots, car-burning and street battles that have broken out, first in the banlieues of Paris and then right across France for two weeks. It points to a pressing case for action to build a greater sense of identity with French society among the rioters, most of whom are second-generation Muslims of north or west African origin. . . . There are arguments over why 5–6 m Muslims there feel alienated—one-third the total in the European Union and one-tenth of the country's population. But the answer surely lies in the toxic mix of poor housing, bad schools, inadequate transport, social exclusion, disaffection over discrimination, and above all high unemployment. . . . French unemployment has hovered around 10%; the average rate among youth is over 20%, one of the highest in Europe; among young Muslims in the banlieues, it has been twice as high again. . . . Most of the French elite, on the left as well as the right, have simply ignored the festering problem. There are no black or brown mainland members of the National Assembly; hardly any on television. The yawning gap between the French elite and the ordinary people was a big cause of government's loss of the referendum on the European constitution.

The unrest in French cities shows that social and policing policy has failed. . . . France needs to acknowledge its multiracial complexion by adapting its vocabulary, rather than hiding behind "the myth of republican equality."

—"French Failure," *The Economist*, November 12, 2005, pp. 11–12, 24–26

■ France spends 30% of its budget on "social protection," and makes it possible for even an illiterate immigrant to live fairly well without having worked a day in his life. Yet shying away from reality by France's ruling class does not change the reality that one of the most civilized nations in Europe is sliding into barbarism. . . . None of the violence was either surprising or unexpected. Indeed, it was easily predictable denouement of the gradual transformation of hundreds of Muslim enclaves into crime-ridden, self-isolated, anti-societies that have de facto seceded from French

France spends 30% of its budget on "social protection."

EXHIBIT 14.7

PERCEPTIONS OF FRANCE (CONTINUED)

society in virtually every aspect except for continuing to depend upon the welfare state.

This is not merely a local situation, but has implications for much of Europe, in terms of socio-political and economic context. There seems to be three seemingly unstoppable trends: the implosion of the European social-market economy; an unprecedented demographic collapse of the native European populations; and the takeover of the burgeoning Muslim communities in Western Europe by radical Islam. . . . The French and European socio-economic model had much to do with the rise of the Muslim ghetto and its ongoing implosion will dramatically exacerbate its conflicts with society at large. . . . The new tougher economic climate, combined with ever present French xenophobia and racism, lead to the high unemployment and progressive ghettoization of the second generation Muslims. . . . With a fertility rate twice that of the natives, the Muslim community in France and Western Europe is growing at 50% every decade . . . The European Union will lose nearly half its native population by 2050, while its Muslim community increases five-fold to 100 million . . . What is needed is a cultural revolution.

—Alex Alexiev, "France at the Brink," *The San Diego Union-Tribune*, pp. G3/5

Cultural Guidelines Doing Business in France

Practicalities

The French time sense is casual.

Generally, except for lunch, the French time sense is casual, so people are often late and no offense is normally taken. Although the person in the subservient position is usually prompt, the executive is free to be late. Anticipate a reluctance to make commitments, leading to scheduling at the last minute. Also expect frequent rescheduling of meetings and appointments.

The French enjoy leisure and socialization, as can be seen in their two-hour luncheons, seven official holidays (www.getcustoms.com), and four or five weeks of vacations (usually in August when the nation virtually shuts down). Although a land of great medieval cathedrals, over 75% of citizens who call themselves Roman Catholic do not see religion as playing a large part in their lives, and even may be slightly anticlerical. While giving lip service to religious toleration, the over 5 million Muslims in France are treated with mistrust and often only tolerated. Realistically, the country's far-right white extremists, influenced by a colonial past, are xenophobic and hostile toward Arabs. The intensely competitive French educational system puts immigrant children of non-French-speaking backgrounds at a real disadvantage, marooning them between two cultures, even when born in France. French education does impact business—schools are rigorous and value linguistic capability.

French society is stratified with sharply defined and competing classes, where diversity is just beginning to be appreciated. Despite some female prominence in public offices and the professions, women's rights have come late, and sexual harassment only became illegal in the past decade. Foreigners complain of inadequate customer service. Managers and employees are "family" who often unite against outsiders.*

Idealism

The French tend to believe that the basic truths on which life is based derive from principles and immutable or universal laws. They are concerned with the essence of values. The motto of the French Republic is "Liberty, Equality and Fraternity." To the French, values such as these should transcend everything else in life. They behave in an individualistic manner. "*Chacun defend son beef-steak*" (everyone protects his own steak). Sometimes they are frustrated and find it difficult to live by these ideals in everyday life, yet the hunger for these altruistic ideals is still present and deeply ingrained in most French people. For example, contrast the French and the American view on sex and money. The French are not easily embarrassed by sex or nudity. But they are embarrassed talking about money, how you get it, or vocational positions and salaries. To them, your job, your income, and such are personal and not the business of others.

Social Structure and Status

The French are very status conscious. Social status in France depends on one's social origins. Outward signs of social status are the level of education, a beautiful house with a well-designed, tasteful facade (not a gaudy one), knowledge of literature and fine arts, and the social origins of one's ancestors.

Social standing and class are also very important in France. The French social classes are the aristocracy, the upper bourgeoisie, the upper-middle bourgeoisie, the middle, the lower-middle, and lower classes (blue-collar workers, peasants). Social classes categorize people according to their professional activities (teachers, doctors, lawyers, craftsmen, foremen, and peasants), as well as their political opinions (conservative, left oriented). The mass influx of immigrants, an underclass, into a relatively homogeneous society is altering the situation.

*For the insights that follow, the authors express appreciation to Gerd-Peter E. Lotao who first wrote on "Doing Business in France" in the World Trade Notes of *Credit and Financial Management Magazine* (June 1987, p. 10).

Social status in France depends on one's social origins.

Social interactions are thus affected by these social stereotypes. It is extremely hard for a French individual to be rid of social stereotypes. They affect personal identity. Unlike an American who can theoretically attain the highest levels of social consideration by working hard and being professionally successful, the French find it difficult to do so. If professionally successful, the French can expect to climb one or two stages of the social ladder in a lifetime, but often nothing more.

Cooperation and Competition

The French are not basically oriented toward competition. To them, the word *competition* has a very narrow meaning—practicing a sport at the highest level of international excellence. For example, the French consider superstar professional athletes as involved in competition. The average French person does not feel affected by competition, which can be dangerous to the country's economic welfare. A few years ago during a New Year's Eve television speech, then-President Giscard d'Estaing tried to educate the French and make them face the fact that competition really should affect their lives. He said competition is not just what the French soccer team experiences during the World Cup. The economic welfare of the French people actually depends on how competitive French goods are on international markets. He tried to awaken the French to the notion of competition, so that they would motivate themselves to work harder and be more productive.

When confronted with individuals with a competitive drive, the French may interpret them as being antagonistic, ruthless, and power hungry. They may feel threatened and overreact or withdraw from the discussion. Yet, the pyramidal structure of the French educational system exposes French children and adolescents to competition very early.

Personal Characteristics

French people are friendly, humorous, and sardonic.

French people are friendly, humorous, and sardonic. The French wish to be admired. French people are more likely to be interested in a person who disagrees with them. Because they want to be liked, the French are very hard to impress and impatient with those who try. A French person, when trying to get a sense of another, looks for qualities within the person and for personality. French people tend to gain recognition and to develop their identity by thinking and acting against others. French people are more inner oriented and base behavior and evaluations on feelings, preferences, and expectations.

Trust and Respect

Personal honor and integrity are valued in France. A French person trusts an individual according to an inner evaluation of the subject's personality and character. Because social stereotypes are so vivid, an average French person cannot earn respect from members of other social classes merely through work accomplishments and performance.

Carroll reports on a foreign student living with a French family who closed the door to his bedroom after dinner.[15] The student did not understand that closed doors are considered rude and that the visitor was expected to socialize with the family. Furthermore, when shutters to the outside are closed, this is not a sign of distrustfulness by the French, but a desire for privacy from the passer-by.

Style of Conversation

French speakers seldom put themselves forward or try to make themselves look good in conversations. If they accidentally do, they will usually add, "Je ne cherche pas a me vanter mais . . ." ("I do not want to boast but . . ."). Boasting is often considered a weakness, a sign of self-satisfaction and immaturity. In conversations with the French, some may ask their French counterparts questions about themselves. The French will probably shun such questions and orient the conversation toward more general subjects. To them, it is not proper to show characteristics of self-centeredness.

Boasting is often considered a weakness.

Furthermore, the French are so proud of their language that they expect everyone to be able to speak it—visitors not fluent in that language are advised to apologize for lack of that knowledge and to learn a few key phrases and pronounce the words correctly. Be sure to smile when you use them. Remember that for centuries all Western diplomats spoke French, and it was the language of the Russian Czar's royal court. The French are very sensitive about the disappearance of their language in the global market and the introduction of English words.

The French, who may seem contentious, often criticize institutions, conditions, and people they live with. A disagreement can be considered stimulating to a French person. It is not uncommon to see two French people arguing with each other, their faces reddened with what seems to be anger, exchanging lively, heated, and irreconcilable arguments. Then later, they shake hands and comment, "That was a good discussion. We should do it again sometime!" The French tend to think that such arguments are interesting and stimulating. It is also a meaningful outlet for tension.

The French enjoy and appreciate humor. They also often add a touch of cynicism to their humor and may not hesitate to make fun of institutions and people.

Consistency and Contradictions

The French abound in contradictions and are not overly disturbed by them; instead, they relish their complexity. They profess lofty ideals of fraternity and equality but at times show characteristics of utmost individualism and selfish materialism. On the political scene, they seem continuously restless, verbally criticizing the government and capitalism, yet they are basically conservative.

Attitudes Toward Work

Typically, French attitudes toward work depend on whether they are employed in the public sector or in the private sector. In the French bureaucracy and in state-owned concerns, there is little incentive to be productive. Quotas are rarely assigned, and it is virtually impossible to lay off or dismiss employees on the basis of job performance. Massive strikes have caused difficulties when companies have attempted to reform or modernize, or when government tries to pass policies and legislation that many oppose. Strikes by university students have actually brought down the government in power.

In the private sector, the situation is different. It is true that French workers do not respect the work ethic. They are usually not motivated by competition or by the desire to emulate fellow workers. They frown on working overtime and have four to five weeks of vacation a year. However, they usually work hard in their allotted working time. French workers have the reputation of being productive. Part of the explanation for such productiveness may lie in the French tradition of craftsmanship. A large proportion of the French workforce has been traditionally employed in small, independent businesses where there is widespread respect for a job well done, and many French people take pride in such work. This may also be true as many have not been employed in huge, impersonal industrial concerns, where craftsmanship may not be as valued. Rather, they often have a direct stake in the work they are doing and are usually concerned with quality.

Massive strikes have caused difficulties.

Attitude Toward Authority

French companies contain many social reference groups that are mutually exclusive. Tight reins of authority are needed to ensure adequate job performance. The lesser emphasis on delegation of responsibility limits accountability and contributes to a more rigid organizational structure. As a consequence, decision making is more centralized in French companies, and it may take longer before decisions are reached and applied. This may be a source of frustration for foreign executives (especially lower- and middle-management executives) who are working with French executives from a comparable management level. The flow of communication is improved if American executives have direct access to two or three top executives of a French company. This is where the actual decision-making power is.

French subordinates tend to view an attempt to track personal progress as an infringement on their territory. d'Iribane writes, "Factual data can play two roles: it can give an overview on how things are working and it can provide a means to evaluate workers. In the French system, the confusion between these two roles is a source of resistance" (translated from the French).[16]

The following actual example illustrates this point. A consultant on a project in the south of France reported the following:

> The main objective of our project was to increase sales of a high-tech product. One of the ideas to accelerate sales was to introduce the use of a daily chart to track each individual's sales progress. The goal was to focus management and subordinates' attention on specific areas for improvement as well as ask those who were doing well to share tips to help their colleague's progress. Although management thought this idea was great, and many of the salespersons agreed that in theory it was a good idea, nine out of ten salespersons loudly objected. The reason? They did not want management—or their colleagues—to be able to track their sales. This idea was never put into practice.

The highest executives of large French companies also have "different" management styles, as the French are judged on personal attributes, as well as on performance. It takes poor performance for them to be challenged in their functions by a board of directors or by subordinates. Patterns of authority are stable in French industry. Therefore, because they do not need to justify their actions to the same extent, the very top French executives tend to be more autocratic in their managerial style. Executive functions also have more overtones of social leadership.

It is interesting to compare French and American business-magazine interviews of executives. Along with professional experiences and activities, top French executives usually mention details concerning their personal lives such as former professors who had an impact on them, enriching social and personal experiences, books that influenced their outlook on life, and what their convictions on political and social issues are. On the other hand, top American executives will more likely emphasize the progression of their career in terms of professional achievements. But in this arena of exercising power and authority, French management is also changing because of their involvement in the global marketplace and the foreign acquisition, mergers, and alliances of French corporations. Obviously, there are considerable differences in the French management style as compared to managers from other countries.

French management is also changing.

Organizational Structure and Decision Making

The organizational structure of French companies tends to be rigid; the French put less emphasis on control of individual performance. The decision-making process is more centralized in French companies. Important decisions are made only by the top executives, but slowly there is a trend toward team management because of consortia formed with businesses outside the country (e.g., Airbus, a multination partnership).

Motivation

Although the French appreciate American industriousness and devotion to their work, they do not believe it is worthwhile. To the French the *qualité de la vie* (quality of life) is what matters. The French attach a great importance to free time and vacations, and so are seldom willing to sacrifice the enjoyment of life out of dedication to work.

Conflict

French have been aptly described as combative libertarians.

The mentally vigorous French have been aptly described as *combative libertarians*; that is, they appreciate strong argument and contradiction. The French, partly because they live in a more closed society with relatively little social mobility, are used to conflict. They are aware that some positions are irreconcilable and that people must live with these irreconcilable opinions. They, therefore, tend not to mind conflict and sometimes enjoy it. They even respect others who carry it off with style and get results. The French are also less concerned about negative reactions from those with whom they are in conflict.

Mesbache discovered that French managers reported difficulties in adjusting to life in other countries.[17] In a study of 31 French managers from 16 French companies, he reported problems caused by emphasis in the French culture on pride in their past cultural heritage, causing them to be too critical of people who do not benefit from that same cultural tradition. In their self-descriptions, the French managers felt handicapped by their conditioning to a formal way of thinking and by lack of actual knowledge of other cultures.

BUSINESS TIPS WITH THE FRENCH

1. French handshake is FIRM, brief handclasp accompanied by short span of eye contact. When French employees arrive at work, they usually greet their colleagues with a quick handshake, and repeat the process when they leave. Some may kiss their friends of both genders on the cheeks, but this is the exception in a business setting. A French woman offers her hand first. It is considered vulgar to snap one's fingers.

Business Tips with the French (continued)

2. French conversation is not linear, and frequent interruption of each other may occur. Conversation is meant to entertain, not just inform, so expect many references to art and argument, as every possibility is explored and articulated, opinions are expressed, and need not be refuted. The French complain that Americans lecture, not converse.

3. Food is important in France, so expect to share meals enthusiastically while doing business with the locals. Whoever initiates the meal is expected to pay, and to make restaurant reservations, except in hotels and brasseries. With an invitation to a person's home for a social occasion, it is polite to bring a gift of wine or flowers (not roses or chrysanthemums which are more appropriate for funerals).

4. Respect privacy—close doors after you and knock on them before entering.

5. Be attentive to voices—the French expect you to recognize the person over a telephone by voice alone. As a sign of closeness avoid saying, "Who is this?" Regulate voice volume, lest you offend with loud or boisterous talk and braying laughter.

6. Neatness and good taste are important in this culture.

Source: *Dun & Bradstreet Guide to Doing Business Around the World*, Upper Saddle River, NJ: Prentice-Hall, 1997.

Respect privacy.

SPAIN

Situated off the Atlantic, just southwest of France, Spain's continental landmass is supplemented by its Canary Islands to the southwest and the Balearic Islands to the southeast in the Mediterranean Sea (Ibiza, Mallorca, and Menorca). Besides its capital, other major cities are Barcelona, Bilbao, Malaga, Seville, Valencia, and Zaragoza. For over 4000 years, Spain has produced beautiful, world-class art and architecture, writers, performers and musicians—all the product of myriad cultures. As a case in point, consider Barcelona, its first industrial city and the seat of the autonomous government of Catalonia: from time immemorial, this municipal eastern port has reached overseas for riches and opportunity as both a trading and tourist center, while basking in monumental gems from cathedrals and monasteries to palaces and museums. In the south is Granada, the ancient Moorish kingdom, with its splendid Islamic art and architecture; today it is a center for manufacturing. Further details and demographics are offered in Exhibit 14.8.

EXHIBIT 14.8

PROFILE OF SPAIN

Area	504,782 sq km
Population	40,341,462 (July 2005 est.)
Capital	Madrid (3 million population)
Religion	Roman Catholic, 94%; Other, 6%
Language	Castilian Spanish, 74%; Catalan, 17%; Galician, 7%; Basque, 2%; note—Castilian is the official language nationwide; the other languages are official regionally
Literacy	97.9% literacy rate
Life expectancy	79.52 years
GDP per capita	$25,100
Government	Constitutional monarchy

Historical Perspective Overview

Spaniards are very proud of their country, which once was the greatest power in Europe with the grandest overseas empire in the world. As a result, even today the Spanish culture dominates Latin America, parts of the United States, and even the Philippines to some extent. For 150 years, the nation slipped behind the rest of Europe, largely because of coups and civil wars, especially during the reign of the fascist dictator Francisco Franco that ended in 1975. The onset of the twenty-first century finds Spain has adopted constitutional monarchy with an energetic leader, King Juan Carlos. It is a transformed society in terms of political, economic, and social life, and has prospered since joining the European Union in 1986. Contemporary Spain has reclaimed its place internationally, and its economy is forging ahead within a global market. Unfortunately, it has also become a target of international terrorism. In 2004, Islamic militants of North African descent launched a series of bombings against a commuter train in Madrid, killing many in the process. This has led the shocked government to strengthen security across the country, against the Basque revolutionaries as well as the Muslim terrorists.

Contemporary Spain has reclaimed its place internationally.

Cultural Insights for Doing Business in Spain

The culture of Spain is manifest somewhat in the cultures of Mexico and Central and South America (see Chapter 12). The family is central, and it is estimated that 200 families control much of the country's wealth. Personal connections are vital, and nepotism is widespread in all spheres of society. For 1000 years the Roman Catholic Church was the enduring, molding force among its people; today with modernization this religious influence has diminished. In a recent survey only 25% admitted to being practicing Catholics. The exception is the more devout, especially Basques, among one-fifth of the peasant workers still on the land in an agricultural stage of development. Successive governments—led first by the Socialist Party of Felipe Gonzalez who brought the nation into NATO and the EU and later by the People's Party under Jose Maria Aznar—have renewed the economy and work environment. Outdated philosophies and policies have changed, and minds and markets have opened.

Working Environment

Spaniards take an enormous delight in life, which is manifested in their festivals. Time is more leisurely in Spain where people do not feel ruled by the clock, though they expect foreigners to be punctual. Deadlines are objectives to be achieved if possible, though not compulsively.

Usually, the Spanish work a 40-hour week, Monday through Friday. But their workday differs from that of North America's. Typically, business operates between 9 A.M. and 1:30 P.M. and from 3 to 6 P.M., allowing an hour and a half for a leisurely lunch or siesta. Government offices are only open weekly from 9 A.M. to 1 P.M. Banks, on the other hand, open at 9 A.M. and close at 1 or 2 P.M. on weekdays, but on Saturdays, the hours are from 9 A.M. to 3 P.M. Check on arrival in Spain as to observance of the eight national as well as local holidays or feast days.

Since eating helps in establishing business relationships, breakfast meetings are normally scheduled no earlier than 8:30 A.M.; lunch, the main meal, starts around 2 P.M., but many go home for lunch; afternoon snack or *tapas* is usually around 5 or 6 P.M. (often by walking from one bar to another); dinner usually starts at 9 P.M. and may extend to 11 P.M. or later with much socialization.

Social Customs

Although the birth rate has been falling since 1970, children are revered, even pampered, so expect them even at expensive restaurants. Sex roles are sharply delineated, and males are expected to be aggressive and dominant. In the tradition of the Romance language cultures, men often do not observe fidelity in marriage and may have mistresses, whereas women today demand equal freedom and respect. *Machismo* or manliness still lingers, defining an expected male code of conduct and honor. Males tend to be more physical with one another, as seen in the *abrazo* or embrace, touching, or the linking of arms, common with many Southern European men.

Spaniards take an enormous delight in life.

The influence of Catholic religious and monastic orders is diminishing, except for *Opus Dei* (Work of God), a very conservative lay and clerical organization whose members may be found in government, business, and the professions. Religious traditionalists also celebrate their saint's namesake or feast day like a second birthday.

To the Spanish, the circumstances of a person's life are what gives it meaning. Although fiercely independent and at times seemingly arrogant, these people are also friendly and treat guests with the utmost hospitality.

Economy

Since entering the EU, Spain has had steady economic growth. Although it operates an open trading system, in which U.S. products and technologies are in demand, some duty disadvantages are evident on imports from non-EU countries. Privatization is moving forward in telecommunications, power, and energy sectors. Exhibit 14.9 offers additional clues on how to facilitate business in this distinctive country.

EXHIBIT 14.9
BUSINESS TIPS WITH THE SPANISH

1. Though English is spoken widely in business, print proposals and other documents are in Spanish. Business cards are printed in Spanish with that side up at presentations, while the reverse side is in English.
2. Business relies on taking time to establish personal relationships, frequently in connection with eating. Also take care in selecting a Spanish representative of your organization.
3. Business discussion is lively, often chaotic, and negotiations are something extended and laborious.
4. Business dress is usually conservative and formal, though getting more relaxed in recent years. Projecting positive image by bearing and attire are important.
5. Renting and leasing office or homes is subject to the "Law of Horizontal Property"—meaning that anything in a building from utilities, sewers, road frontages, et al. are shared by tenants, and you may end up paying a neighbor's fee to get electric or sewer service.
6. Nomenclatures—first names are used only among friends and young people, and wait for your Spanish counterpart to use same (tu is the familiar form, while *usted* is more formal. In business, most people are addressed by their title and surname. Typically, in Latin cultures there are two surnames—one from the father

EXHIBIT 14.9

BUSINESS TIPS WITH THE SPANISH (CONTINUED)

which is listed first and the other from the mother listed second. Verbally, only the paternal name is used. With marriage, a woman usually adds the husband's family name and goes by that designation in regular conversation. The full Spanish name of both husband and wife is reserved for formal occasions or in written materials. Normally, use titles in addressing individuals, such as *Professor* or *Ingenerio*.

Source: T. Morrison, Conaway, W.A., and Douress. J. *Dun & Bradstreet's Guide to Doing Business Around the World*. Upper Saddle River, NJ: Prentice-Hall, 1997, pp. 371–381.

OTHER WESTERN EUROPEAN CULTURES

In addition to the three major nations covered above in Western Europe, there are eight other smaller countries and principalities—Andorra, Belgium, Gibraltar, Ireland, Luxembourg, Monaco, Portugal, and the Netherlands. The principalities, dependent on the economies of their geographic neighbor, feature tourism and tax havens. The three principal entities are featured in Exhibit 14.10.

Portugal lies off the Atlantic coast to the west of Spain, and though it has some Iberian cultural similarity with its bigger neighbor, it has a different language. In centuries past, this tiny nation also had a powerful empire, extending from Macau in China to Angola in western Africa to Cochin in southwestern India. However, it is in Brazil where the Portuguese culture and language had the biggest impact. Realize that Brazil with its Portuguese heritage has a population today that is the equal of all of South America combined, and a land area bigger than the 25 EU countries.

During World War II, Portugal's capital Lisbon became a center of neutrality and intrigue for both the Allies and the Fascists. Since joining the EU, Portugal, a relatively poor country with pockets of wealth, has cut in half the gap in living standards with the rest of Europe. Today it is a tourist center because of its attractive beachfront coastline, its religious shrine of Our Lady of Fatima, its stately buildings and monuments, and its special music—the flamingo. Its sovereignty now extends only to the islands of the Azores and Madeira.

Belgium is a mixture of French (Walloons), Dutch, and German cultures and languages and a source of many internal confrontations. Its capital, Brussels, is the center of the North Atlantic Treaty Organization, as well as the administration of the European Union. The multilingual Belgians, with an impressive history of colonial expansion, art,

EXHIBIT 14.10
PROFILES OF PORTUGAL, BELGIUM, AND THE NETHERLANDS

NATION	Portugal	Belgium	The Netherlands
Area (sq km)	92,392	30,528	41,526
Population	10,566,212	10,364,388	16,407,491
Capital	Lisbon	Brussels	Amsterdam
Religion	Roman Catholic	Roman Catholic, Protestant	Roman Catholic, Dutch Reformed, Calvinist, Muslim
Language	Portuguese	Dutch, French, German	Dutch, Frisian
Literacy	93.3%	98%	99%
Life Expectancy	77.53 years	78.62 years	78.81 years
Gdp per Capita	$18,400	$31,800	$30,500

and culture, have largely a service economy today, often used for European test marketing by foreigners. Because of its strategic location, this small country suffered invasion and occupation in both world wars of the twentieth century.

The Netherlands, including Holland, also has a rich colonial history that ranged from Indonesia to New York in America. The Dutch, who speak English widely, are good businesspeople and are among the top dozen trading countries in the world. In this egalitarian and open society, which values diversity and tolerance, the emphasis is on clockwork punctuality and data collection. This key NATO/EU country has a capital in Amsterdam, with a seat of government in The Hague, also home to an international court. Because of rising crime and substance abuse among immigrants, there has been a backlash among normally tolerant Dutch citizens. The push is toward better screening and regulation of new arrivals, education for them in citizenship and language, and other assistance facilitating acculturation, especially among the mass of Muslims. A progressive and liberal society, in 2005, along with France, it defeated the adoption of the EU constitution.

The Dutch, who speak English widely, are good businesspeople.

CENTRAL EUROPE

Among the 11 nations in this geographic area we will provide a cultural analysis of the two largest: Germany and Poland and profile selectively some of the remaining nine nations. Bear in mind that with the exception of Switzerland and the western part of Germany, all the others in this region were considered Eastern Bloc nations for the past half century or more. Thus, the majority of them were under the polit-

Central Europe

NORTH SEA

BALTIC SEA

Minsk ⊛

BELARUS

Berlin ⊛

GERMANY*

⊛ Warsaw

P O L A N D

⊛ Kiev

⊛ Prague

CZECH REPUBLIC

U K R A I N E

S L O V A K I A

Vienna ⊛   ⊛ Bratislava

⊛ Bern

SWITZERLAND   **A U S T R I A***

MOLDOVA

⊛ Budapest

Chisinau ⊛

SLOVENIA   **H U N G A R Y**

Ljubljana ⊛

BLACK   SEA

* Member of the European Union

ical and economic domination of the former USSR, meaning cultural conditioning in totalitarian communism and central planning. Though ravaged by war and occupations, Central Europe has a history of high culture, democratic leanings, and relative prosperity now.

GERMANY

Germany has access to the North Sea and thus to the Atlantic Ocean, as well as the Norwegian Sea. On the northeast, Germany connects with the Baltic Sea. Geographically, this nation borders the Netherlands on the west, Belgium and France on the southwest, Switzerland and Austria on the south, and the Czech Republic and Poland on the east. Hemmed in somewhat, it has had to use other countries as corridors for expansion.

Located in a northern climate, Germany is relatively flat in the north, but the elevation rises gradually in the south. Because of its temperate climate, its agriculture includes the raising of wheat, potatoes, sugar beets, fruit, and cattle. Germany's natural resources have led to the production of iron, steel, coal, natural gas, cement, potash, timber, copper and salt. Long famous for its manufacturing and technical skills, its economic emphasis is on vehicles, metals, chemicals and optics. With Berlin reinstated as its capital, other major cities include Bonn, Cologne, Dresden, Frankfurt, Hamburg, Leipzig, and Munich. Further details regarding Germany are in Exhibit 14.11.

Historical Perspective Overview

The forerunner of today's Germans were the Saxons.

The forerunner of today's Germans were the Saxons whose trade and military excursions took them west into England (Anglo-Saxons) and

EXHIBIT 14.11
PROFILE OF GERMANY

Area	357,021 sq km
Population	82,431,390 (July 2005 est.)
Capital	Berlin (3,426,000 population)
Religion	Protestant, 34%; Roman Catholic, 34%; Muslim, 3.7%; unaffiliated or other, 28.3%
Language	German
Literacy	99%
Life Expectancy	78.65 years
Gdp per Capita	$29,700
Government	Federal republic

south into what is now Romania. The foundation of Germany was laid by Teutonic feudal lords. From its Indo-European origins, the Germanic language was not only spoken in Germany, Austria, and Switzerland, but impacted English, Dutch, Flemish, Scandinavian, and other languages. The culture became renowned for excelling in mathematics, natural science, and military science, as well as in the arts and music. Like most European powers in the sixteenth through nineteenth centuries, the Germans were late in becoming empire builders, eventually acquiring overseas colonies that spanned from the South Pacific to West Africa. Its former Kaiser was related to the British royal family. Prussian militarism led the emerging nation into a series of conflicts beginning with the Franco-Prussian War, which it won, followed by World Wars I and II, which it lost. After temporary glories, the attempts at cross-border expansionism in the twentieth century resulted in much misery and deprivation for its people. The rise and fall of Adolf Hitler and his fascist Nazi Party (1933–1945) negatively affected not only Germany, but millions of humans, both Jews and Christians, caught up in the fighting and purges, concentration camps, and the Holocaust. These horrible calamities laid waste to the continent and led to the Soviet invasion of East Germany and the establishment of a puppet state (German Democratic Republic) under the influence of the USSR. The former capital, Berlin, was divided temporarily among the occupying armies of the American, British, and Russian Allies. In 1949, the west became the multiparty Federal Republic of Germany, adopting the *Grundgesetz* as its basic law, with Bonn as its capital.

In time, the communist GDR government in the east built barriers to protect its German inhabitants from contamination by Western democracies and free enterprise. On November 9, 1989, irate Germans tore down the Berlin Wall, and its elimination marked the end of an era. On October 3, 1990, after 41 years of political division, most of Germany was reunified, and the process of reintegration between its western and eastern populations began. The unified Federal Republic of Germany (FRG) has evolved into a democratic, market-oriented system. Over their 40-year separation, the two Germanys had developed differing cultural values, mind-sets, and customs, in addition to opposing economic and political systems. Many in the former West Germany (weiss) complained that those in East Germany (ossis) lived too long in their socialist world, thus were naive and unsophisticated. Because of totalitarian central planning, those in the west thought that their counterparts in the east were not good as managers or entrepreneurs because they had no experience in a market economy, nor were the easterners grateful for the benefits unity brought. On the other hand, the *ossis* observed that the *weiss* were arrogant and materialistic, for relentless competition made them "hard as nails." Furthermore, they resented westerners securing the best jobs in the east, while unemployment hit women workers disproportionately.

The ossis observed that the weiss were arrogant and materialistic.

Although these attitudes linger among some, the healing and integration process of the past decade built bridges over this cultural divide. Recent studies reveal the following:

- Since 1990, more than 200,000 eastern German women have started their own businesses.
- Western managers who have worked with easterners say they show more enthusiasm and flexibility than their counterparts in the west.
- Easterners attach more importance to work than they do to leisure.
- Easterners consider themselves to be more independent, interested, and warmhearted than western Germans.[18]

At the beginning of the twenty-first century, the united Germany, with Berlin again as its capital, has become the largest economy in Europe and the sixth largest export market for U.S. products worldwide. After spending 3 million euros on the unification process, a physics professor, born in East Germany was elected the first woman chancellor in 2006. Dr. Angela Merkel now leads a left-right political alliance trying to recharge the national economy and image. She is encouraging her country to develop a more positive image as a world-class exporter, with plenty of competitive global corporations and improving investments. Although the German market is still wealthy, and the prospect for the future in the eastern states much brighter, the nation's economy has experienced some decline and there are calls for bold reforms. Within the European Union, Germany accounts for almost 25% of its GDP.

The priorities of the German government appear to center on the following goals:

- Maintaining economic growth and competitiveness, especially by facilitating the growth of eastern Germany.
- Promoting peaceful security and commercial relationships with its neighbors, particularly those in the EU and NATO, as well as with Russia and its Commonwealth of Independent States.
- Fostering international relations, both outside the continent and within, such as in Central Europe.

There are two main governing bodies in Germany.

As a parliamentary democracy with a bicameral legislature, there are two main governing bodies in Germany. The larger *Bundestag* (Parliament) consists of 672 deputies elected for four-year terms from the states and possesses legislative power. The upper house, the *Bundersrat*, is composed of delegations from the 16 states that function under the *Laender* (state constitutions). Its 68 votes are based on the proportion of populations, and power is limited, except in exercising vetoes over proposed legislation. Germany has a president, but the position is one of honor and a formality, not one of real power, which lies in the office of the chancellor (*Bundeskanzler*). The chancellor is either the leading representative of the party with a majority of seats in the *Bundestag* or the leader of the largest party in a coalition government.

There are presently five political parties, though the most influential have been the Christian Democratic Union (CDU) and the Christian Socialist Union (CSU). Although each party maintains its own structure, the two leading parties may form a common caucus in the *Bundestag* and do not run opposing campaigns. The CDU/CSU are generally conservative on economic and social policy. The Social Democratic Party (SDP) is the second major party, emphasizing social programs, strong ties with the Atlantic alliance, and improved relations with central and eastern Europe.

Three critical challenges facing Germany today are reform of its educational, health-care, and corporate governance systems. The present school system fails to make the most of its human capital by an inadequate three-tier infrastructure. Furthermore, university curriculum suffers from culture lag and lack of modernization. The health-care system is counterproductive, favoring private insurers, while leaving the public sector with the risks. Large public corporations are unresponsive to stockholder wishes about expenditures and strategies. The two-tier board system is often wasteful and slow. The practice of codetermination is a hindrance to effective company governance, despite strong union support for the worker representation concept. Few German cities are like Jena, whose economic dynamism supports an entrepreneurial ecosystem and diverse educational systems.

Germany is losing its homogeneity; it has some 6.7 million immigrants, 8% of whom are naturalized citizens. The third generation of Turks is increasingly being marginalized by a complicated school system and unresponsive labor market. Frankfurt is innovating with a city government Office of Multicultural Affairs that offers new arrivals language training and translation services, as well as guidance on the educational and health-care systems. Stuttgart assists foreign students through the thickets of German bureaucracy. Germany has to compete in a global war for talent and a knowledge culture requiring skilled and competent individuals. The new German environment will feature greater diversity and flexibility.

Germany is losing its homogeneity.

Cultural Insights for Doing Business in Germany

Germans today are a more diverse people as a result of heavy immigration. Traditionally, they have a reputation for being industrious, hard working, reserved, and perhaps even cold in behavior. Generally they are perceived as meticulous and methodical, and sometimes militaristic in the preciseness of their actions (linear thinking). At the same time, they have a reputation for quality and exactness—their buses, trains, and planes usually run on time. Detail in planning and project implementation is valued. Some of the world's greatest composers, writers, and philosophers are products of the German heritage.

It Most Germans are not a spontaneous people. Their attitude is to organize the time allotted to its greatest efficiency, rather than wait and see what happens. Nor are the Germans normally an outward people; they tend to be very private. They maintain a slightly larger personal space around themselves, usually standing back six inches further than do North Americans. The German language is a key to understanding their national personality. The Germans make a strong distinction between an acquaintance (*bekannte*) and a friend (*freund*). Germans will only use *freund* when they really mean it; otherwise it is a *bekannte*. Close family ties are also cherished.

Business Context

Three things that heavily impact the structure of business in Germany today are the European Union (EU), co-determination, and government involvement. Germany is one of the original members of what was once known as the European Community. Much of German business practices and laws are directly tied to the regulations and directives from that community or union in Brussels. The principle of collective good is important in the idea of codetermination (*mitbestimmung*). Codetermination allows for worker input into the management of the firm. Any firm with more than five employees should have a worker's council (*Betriebsrat*) that represents the employees and helps them solve various grievances with the firm's management. Any coal or steel firm of more than 2000 workers is required to have 50% of the company's supervisory board composed of workers. There is also a specially chosen labor representative on the management board of the company. This all illustrates an attempt to include a most important part of the economic structure, the worker.

German unions are very strong.

German unions are very strong and provide workers with many more rights than some foreign counterparts. For example, they can become involved in decisions on dismissal. The process of codetermination gives management and workers the opportunity to work together to shape or define the firm's goals, objectives, and responsibilities. Employees are represented in five trade unions of professional organizations: German Trades Union Federation, German Salaried Staff Union, Christian Trade Union Federation, German Civil Servant's Federation, and the Union of Executive Employees.

The Germans are among the highest paid workers in the world and enjoy a high standard of living. They are able to afford the luxuries and extras of life. An important part of this concept is the vast welfare state that supports the German worker. This includes liberal pensions, bonuses, medical and dental care, and five to six weeks of annual paid vacation. Though taxes are heavy, this system has relieved the typical

German from many financial worries. But the above factors also contribute to driving up the costs of business and making Germany's products and services less competitive. Currently, Germany is known for its high quality of life and protection benefits for its citizens. But its current weak financial growth has been attributed not just to a downturn in the world's economy, but also to the need for restructuring what has become an overburdened welfare state. German politicians, given to compromise and consensus, are struggling with issues of federalism and decentralization. Without some radical changes, the driving economy of the past will not be regained.[19]

Germany is committed to a free enterprise economy. Government and business work very closely together, as can be seen in the extent of government control/participation in industry. The state holds control or equity participation in hundreds of firms. In the public service arena, the railroads and postal system are now privatized, with the state owning most of the shares. The state also owns a trade monopoly in alcohol. An area that is perhaps the fastest growing in Germany, as well as throughout Europe, is joint government and private business ventures. This means a partnership between private businesses and firms controlled by the government. With denationalization ongoing, this increase in joint partnership ventures is another indication of "collective interest" being an important part of the German business and economic community.

Trade plays a very important role in the German economy for sustaining growth and the standard of living because sufficient natural resources are very limited.

Work Practices

The German sense of time requires punctuality for both business and social engagements but does not seem to extend to delivery dates. Goods and services may be delivered late without explanation or apologies. There are 13 national, plus regional, holidays (see www.getcustoms.com). People take long vacations during July, August, and December. Little work is accomplished during regional festivals, such as Oktoberfest or Carnival prior to Lent. The workweek is Monday to Friday, 8 or 9 A.M. to 4 or 5 P.M., but check on banking hours, which normally are 8:30 A.M. to 1 P.M. and 2 to 4 P.M., sometimes extended to 5:30 P.M. On Saturday, shops may close by 2 P.M. except for once a month when they may be open in the evening. The preferred time for business appointments is late morning or late afternoon, and these should be scheduled several weeks in advance.

Social Customs

Germans are very knowledgeable and capable businesspeople. They pride themselves on having quality products to offer on the world

The German sense of time requires punctuality.

markets. They are formal in their business dealings, not only with foreigners, but among themselves as well. For the foreigner, it is best to be conservative and subdued, unless you are given the indication to be more informal. The Germans do not like loud people, especially in business, and have little respect for the pushy or brassy businessperson. To them such behavior reflects a weakness in the person or company. In this culture, business is taken seriously. Germans tend to be exact in their dealings and somewhat more distant in their business relationships.

The handshake is an important part of the German greeting. They shake hands often. The woman extends her hand first. Firm handshakes are preferred. If one is entering a room filled with many people, the person should proceed around the room shaking everyone's hands. Again, a friendly "good morning" or "good day" is appropriate.

In the German language, there are two forms of address, the polite and the familiar. The familiar form *du*, similar to "thou" in English, is used only for relatives, very close friends, children, and animals. The polite form *sie* is used on all other occasions, including in the business environment. Any foreigner addressing a German should use the polite form. Many Germans have known each other for years and still use the polite form. A German may initiate the usage of the *du* form, although this is not routine. Not only should you use the polite form of speech, but you should also refrain from using first names; *Herr* and *Frau* are more appropriate. In addition, women should always be called *Frau* regardless of their marital status.

Germans are

title conscious.

The Germans are title conscious, and proper etiquette requires addressing them by their title. Also, those who have attained their Ph.D. are addressed by the term *doktor* (i.e., "Herr Doktor Schmidt" or "Frau Doktor Braun"). Women are called by their first names. The wife of Georg Meyer will not be Frau Georg Meyer, but rather Frau Ursula Meyer. A friend or associate should introduce the newcomer to the group, as Germans prefer third-party introductions.

In some countries, it is quite common to entertain a client for dinner at a fashionable restaurant. In Germany, particularly with large corporations dealing in multimillion-dollar contracts, the superiors will not allow their subordinates to accept the invitation. Many German firms would consider this to be a conflict of interest and one could easily lose his objectivity, *verpflichtungen*. A good rule to follow is to conduct business during business hours.

The Germans like to discuss things and enjoy a good discussion on the topics of the day. Religion, politics, and nuclear power are freely discussed, but conversations relating to one's private life are only among friends. Bragging about personal achievements and finances should be avoided.

Communications

Gestures

The Germans are generally restrained in their body movements. They do not wave their arms and hands a lot as in other cultures. It is impolite to talk to someone with your hands in your pockets. It is also considered rude to sit with the bottom of your shoes facing another person. For this reason, German men cross their legs at the knees, rather than with an ankle on the other knee. Most body movements could best be characterized as conservative. Whether sitting or standing, it is generally in a more upright and rigid position.

Language

German is the official language in Germany, although in border areas, other languages are spoken more often. There are hundreds of dialects and local variations spoken throughout the countryside, although dialects are generally only spoken in less formal situations with friends. *Hochdeutsch*, or the "high" German, is found in all magazines, newspapers, television, and the like. In a business context, your counterpart will avoid the usage of dialects. English is the major foreign language taught in Germany, and most businesspeople are conversant in it. With the influx of Turkish workers during the past decade, Turkish is also spoken in some circles.

Exhibit 14.12 provides five concluding suggestions for business success in Germany.

Germans are generally restrained in their body movements.

EXHIBIT 14.12

BUSINESS TIPS WITH GERMANS

1. Guests usually stand until a host enters the room, then remain standing until offered a seat.
2. Avoid chewing gum in public, conversing with hands in pocket, or propping legs on desks or tables.
3. Germans are free thinkers and have a wide variety of interests to discuss on social occasions, such as current events, politics, religion, sex, but avoid talking about work, private life, personal achievements, or American sports.
4. Be formal in business deals, and avoid haggling or price discounting.
5. Be aware that business responsibility is first to society and the environment, and then to maximize profitability.

Because of its location almost in the center of Europe, geography has seriously impacted the history of Poland. Its borders have changed many times by contraction or expansion into neighboring states. A review of the map will help to illustrate the problem. The country's only water access is the North Sea. Otherwise, it is hemmed in my Germany on its western border, with Kaliningrad, Lithuania, and Belarus to the northeast, the Ukraine on the southeast, and Czech Republic and Slovakia in the south. Thus, for the past 60 years, Poland has had to cope with Nazi fascism and East Germany communism to the west, while all the other surrounding neighbors were part of the Eastern Bloc, satellites of the Soviet Union until 1991.[20]

But geography has also favored the Polish economy in terms of agricultural production (wheat, vegetables, and fruits). The economy also has been favored with regard to mineral resources (copper, iron ore, lead, silver, sulfur, salt, and zinc) that favored coal mining, and to the production of chemicals, natural gas, iron, and steel. As a result, the nation specializes in manufactured goods, machinery, and transport systems. Besides its capital in Warsaw, other major cities include Gdansk, Krakow, Lodz, Pozan, and Wroclaw.

Historical Perspective Overview

Poland was a sophisticated and civilized society when Russian city-states were fighting off Asians. This country and its people have a long, proud, but sad history since its inception in A.D. 963. Polish kings were selected from various European royal houses by their nobility (*szlachta*). At times the kingdom spread beyond present-day borders but more often was a target of invasions because of its geographic position as a crossroad between east and west. Early in the twentieth century, the then great powers of Prussia, Austria, and Russia portioned the country. Following World War I the first Polish Republic came into being but degenerated into a military dictatorship. After occupation by Nazi Germany during World War II, the nation was liberated by Allied forces, including communist Russia. As a result of the Potsdam Treaty, Poland ended under Soviet Union domination with its totalitarian regimes and central planning. The puppet Polish government that was formed under the Soviets was finally ousted through a rebellion led by the trade unions and union chief Lech Walesa, who later was elected president.

In the twenty-first century, the Republic of Poland is the most democratic in its history, with a Constitution adopted by the electorate. The bicameral Parliament is composed of a lower house (*Sejm*) of 450 elected delegates, who exercise most of the power, and an upper house

In the twenty-first century, the Republic of Poland is the most democratic in its history.

(Senate), which may suggest amendments to legislation or delay proposals of the *Sejm*. The terms of office are normally four years, unless the president dissolves Parliament and calls for new national elections (e.g., when the government fails a vote of confidence or does not pass a budget). The president as head of state serves a five-year term, nominates the prime minister (subject to *Sejm* confirmation), and chairs the Council of Ministers (18 cabinet ministers). The president is also the armed forces commander and may veto legislation passed by Parliament; however, these vetoes can be overturned by the Parliament with a two-thirds vote.

Poland has 49 provinces (*voivodships*), each headed by a governor appointed by the central government. In addition, independent, local city and village governments are elected by the locals. There are six principal political parties and several smaller ones.

Cultural Insights for Doing Business with Poland

Warsaw is not only Poland's largest city, but also the main economic, cultural, and educational center of the country—the home of some of the world's most famous composers and musicians, artists and writers. Roman Catholicism is a forceful influence within the country. People are proud that their beloved Pope John Paul II who was not only born, educated, and worked there was also a playwright.

Religion

Over centuries, the Roman Catholic Church has played a pivotal role in Polish history and the lives of its people. The Church and its adherents kept the national spirit alive during foreign domination, staving off cultural adsorption by Lutheran Prussia and Orthodox Russia, and more recently by Soviet Union's ideology. The first Polish pope, John Paul II, enhanced the nation's pride, especially through his continuing endeavors resulting in the defeat of both fascism and communism in his homeland.

Gender

Poland is a traditional, male dominated society, but equality for females is slowly emerging. International businesswomen face a challenge to be recognized for their competence and taken seriously. For over a decade, Poles have enjoyed free speech, press, and assembly, with other commonly accepted human rights. The long-held view of woman as wife and mother is being changed by a new generation of educated and career-oriented women professionals.

Poland is a traditional, male-dominated society.

Time

Although Poles may be tardy, the foreign businessperson is expected to be on time. The casual attitude toward punctuality is changing as Poland enters the EU. Normally, there are four national holidays, though, if they fall on weekends, business may be closed on the preceding Friday or following Monday. The five-day work week usually starts at 8 or 9 A.M. and goes to 2 to 3 P.M., but on Saturdays, 8 A.M. to 1:30 P.M.

Human Relations

Like other Slavic societies, Poles have a tradition of hospitality, beneficence, and gracious living, which is manifested in their folk music and dancing. They are normally a friendly, happy, and hard-working people. They revere their past heritage and love history, so evident in their restoration of historic districts. However, they are generally wary of Russians.

OTHER CENTRAL EUROPEAN CULTURES

Nine other countries are geographically located in Central Europe. In terms of the largest populations, we have selected five to profile in Exhibit 14.13: Austria, Czech Republic, Hungary, and the Ukraine which are members of the European Union, plus Belarus and Ukraine which are not yet members. Other nations in the region are seeking EU membership and Romania and Bulgaria have signed accession treaties for admission in January 2007. Other Balkan countries like Albania, Bosnia, Macedonia, Serbia, and Montenegro hope to become part of the EU when they meet its entrance standards.[21]

EXHIBIT 14.13

PROFILES OF AUSTRIA, BELARUS, CZECH REPUBLIC, HUNGARY, AND UKRAINE

NATION	Austria	Belarus	Czech Republic	Hungary	Ukraine
AREA (sq km)	83,870	207,600	78,866	93,030	603,700
POPULATION	8,184,691	10,300,483	10,241,138	10,006,835	47,425,336
CAPITAL	Vienna	Minsk	Prague	Budapest	Kiev
RELIGION	RC/P/M	EO/RC/P/J/M	RC/P	RC/P (C&L)	UO/UC/P/J
LANGUAGE	German	Belarusian, Russian	Czech	Hungarian	Ukrainian, Russian
LITERACY	98%	99.6%	99.9%	99.4%	99.7%
LIFE EXPECTANCY	78.92 years	68.72 years	76.02 years	72.4 years	69.68 years
GDP PER CAPITA	$32,900	$7,600	$18,100	$15,900	$6,800
GOVERNMENT	Republic	Republic	Republic	Republic	Republic

Perspectives

What is striking in the comparisons shown in the Exhibit are the financial differences of the GDP per capita. Compare those figures with their individual populations and land areas. All the above countries, like Poland, with the exception of Austria and Switzerland, had been under the control of the USSR for 50 or more years. Communist conditioning affected many of the above profile categories for the worse—land area, population, religion, language, literacy, life expectancy, GDP per capita, and form of government. It also had a negative impact on human rights, the economy, morale, and productivity of the captive inhabitants. Furthermore, Austria has been impacted by the German culture and languages especially during the World War II period.

For all the money and attention devoted to the ex-communist countries, no one has yet worked out where they are. That is to say, dropping the whole lot into an area called Eastern Europe is an inaccurate leftover from the designation used with former Soviets as "East Bloc nations." But that disregards geography, reason, and fairness. Geographically, these nations are located within Central Europe. But this disguises the reality that contemporary national borders do not reflect their historical boundaries, having been altered so often in this region.

Among the Soviet-era institutions now defunct are the East Bloc alliances (economic, called COMECON, and military, the Warsaw Pact), which the Soviet Union had with its satellite nations. Freed of the communist yoke, the nearly 380 million plus people formerly behind the Iron Curtain, victims of the Cold War, have turned westward for capital, resources, management styles, and training. Although the newly liberated nations of Eastern and Central Europe look to develop markets in Western Europe, North and South America, Asia and Africa, their principal trading partners are likely to be each other, the European Union, and possibly the emerging Commonwealth of Independent States (CIS), of which the Russian Federation is the most prominent member.

After decades under rigid totalitarian control of a now failed socialist system, all of the countries such as the former Yugoslavia, Albania, Bulgaria, Lithuania, Romania, and the CIS are in the midst of slow, painful, traumatic changes toward greater democratic reforms and market economies. In the process, all these sufferers of centralized planning are left with exhausted labor reserves, high unemployment, and ill-prepared and subsequently unproductive workers, using out-of-date machinery and plants. In addition to severe shortages of food and consumer goods, these nations have been devastated by a frightful legacy of environmental pollution, ecological and economic ruins, and obsolete infrastructure. The collapse of the Soviet utopia and ideology left them, especially Russia, a damaged citizenry on the verge of social collapse. Although the empire called the USSR has passed, it produced more deaths than any other country through purges, exile, mass deportation, genocide, and state terrorism. No wonder its citizens became cynical and rejected the "dictatorship of the proletariat." During the past eight decades, marked by a system of "top-down" control over society's entire structure by a single bureaucratized party, the mind-set produced still lives on in many.

Representatives from free-enterprise nations and companies are welcome there to assist in economic and management development and help improve the quality of life. The pace of change in these lands differs, but Hungary and Poland are in the vanguard of recovery, aided by their admittance to the European Union and NATO. EU membership is the one positive hope for Central and East Europe to rejoin Europe on an equal basis and to make life better for their citizens under more democratic, free-enterprise governments. The Czechs, Solvakians, and Hungarians are a few examples of countries beginning to prosper. Reforms are under way to achieve this coveted membership within a few years by Albania, Bosnia, Croatia, Macedonia, Moldova, Montenegro, Serbia, and Solvenia. It is conceivable that within a decade, Belarus and the Ukraine may also join the EU.

Exhibit 14.14 may help readers to appreciate the alterations and the opportunities for Central Europeans.

The pace of change in these lands differs.

EXHIBIT 14.14
WHY WESTERN BUSINESS IS TURNING EAST

Trnava, a tiny town in western Slovakia, is the new face of the European car manufacturing. On January, Peugeot Citroen chose it as the site for a new €700 million assembly plant that will start turning out 300,000 passenger cars a year in 2006. The French company's investment comes on the heels of a joint venture with Japan's Toyota to build a €1.5 billion plant in the Czech Republic. Meanwhile, Britain's MG Rover is poised to make a big investment in Poland; and Renault is preparing to launch a new budget model at its factory in Romania.

The appeal of Central Europe is obvious: cheapest labor cost (roughly one-fifth of those in the European Union); improving infrastructure; and a prized location at the heart of a soon enlarged EU. . . . The investment rush is being encouraged by the fact that Central European countries will no longer be able to offer investors such generous tax breaks once they join the EU in 2004. . . . The Czechs, who boast the region's highest foreign direct investment per head, win praise from multinationals for setting up CzechInvest, an inward investment agency that cuts across bureaucratic rules that can stymie deals.

Source: "European Carmakers Heading East," *The Economist*, March 20, 2003, p. 58.

Northern Europe

Geographically, Northern Europe encompasses nine countries. By far the largest in influence, landmass, and population is Sweden. Four more are grouped together under the nomenclature of Scandinavia: Denmark, Finland, Iceland, and Norway. The three new EU members are commonly referred to as the Baltics: Estonia, Latvia, and Lithuania. Formerly controlled by the USSR, the trio form a peninsula that juts out into the Baltic Sea and Gulf of Finland, attached to the Kaliningrad (Russia) and Poland to their southern borders, Russia to the east, and Belarus to the southeast. Since shifting from Soviet captivity in 1989, the stable, orderly, and undeveloped Baltic nations have been transforming themselves economically into prosperous states, especially through their NATO and EU membership. Each of these countries is creating market niches and attempting to develop high-tech, knowledge-based industries. Within this northern region, the smallest entity, the Faroe Islands, has a population of only 47,000 centered in Tórshavn and associated with Denmark, thus speaking Danish.

Historical Perspective Overview

Since medieval times, the inhabitants of this whole region have had a rich heritage manifested in sea power, exploration, and even conquest. These peoples, then known as the Vikings, roamed far and wide across both Western and Eastern Europe, as well as beyond to North America (Greenland, Finland), North Africa, and even the Middle East. The Franks (French) called the Norse, or Northmen, Normans (men from the North). The many islands and fjords of Sweden and Scandinavia forged a hearty race of shipbuilders, navigators, and seamen who sailed fleets of sleek open boats across the known world. They spoke a similar language and began as farmers who were forced by politics, poverty, and overcrowding to travel abroad as warriors, traders, and pioneers. These fierce fighters, merchants, and colonizers created Normandy in present-day France, settled in England and Scotland, and founded the city of Dublin in Ireland. Their culture, reflected in symbols, sagas, and artifacts, produced sophisticated laws and craftsmanship; excavations have unearthed their handmade tools, beautiful ornaments, and coins from all parts of civilization. Centuries ago, these persons, known today as Scandinavians, had communities without national boundaries, societies divided by class based on wealth and property, and venerated women and children. To confirm all this, one has only to visit Viking ruins and museums, especially at their headquarters on the island of Gotland off the East Coast of Sweden.[22]

Since medieval times, the inhabitants of this whole region have had a rich heritage manifested in sea power.

Northern Europe

* Member of the European Union

Exhibit 14.15 provides a profile of the five largest nations within Northern Europe.

EXHIBIT 14.15
PROFILES OF DENMARK, FINLAND, LITHUANIA, NORWAY, AND SWEDEN

NATION	Denmark	Finland	Lithuania	Norway	Sweden
AREA (sq km)	43,094	338,145	65,200	324,220	449,964
POPULATION	5,432,335	5,223,442	3,596,617	4,593,041	9,001,774
CAPITAL	Copenhagen	Helsinki	Vilnius	Oslo	Stockholm
RELIGION	Evangel. Lutheran	Evangel. Lutheran	RC, Russian Orthodox, Protestant	Evangel. Lutheran	Lutheran
LANGUAGE	Danish, Faroese	Finnish, Swedish	Lithuanian, Russian, Polish	Norwegian	Swedish
LITERACY	100%	100%	99.6%	100%	99%
LIFE EXPECTANCY	77.62 years	78.35 years	73.97 years	79.4 years	80.4 years
GDP PER CAPITA	$33,500	$30,300	$13,700	$42,400	$29,600
GOVERNMENT	Constitutional monarchy	Republic	Parliamentary Democracy	Constitutional monarchy	Constitutional monarchy

Cultural Insights for Doing Business in Northern Europe

Each of the countries within this region has cultural similarities and differences. Foreigners would be well advised to inquire about some of the unique aspects of conducting business locally within each nation. With membership in the European Union, Northern European countries generally follow EU policies and practices. The following culture contrasts emphasize the unity and diversity in the region.

Danes are fiercely independent and egalitarian, and express their opinions freely. The culture is highly nurturing, concerned about quality of life and social welfare. Provision for generous child care and paternity enable a large proportion of women to pursue careers at all levels of business or government, including in the EU. Although the majority is Evangelical Lutheran, religion does not play a central role in the average life. At work, these people resist authority and do not like to be told what to do; managers are perceived more as coaches and

Danes are fiercely independent and egalitarian.

facilitators. Meritocracy is the norm, and nepotism is frowned upon. They prefer well-organized meetings with specific stated agendas and sessions that open and close on time. Participants prepare carefully, expect all to be heard, and then lend support to adopted decisions. Consensus building is important. Except on the five holidays, business hours within Denmark vary from an 8 to 9 A.M. opening to a 4:30 to 5:30 P.M. closing during the five-day workweek; banks usually stay open until 6 P.M. on Thursdays. Danes like to take their time and will not be rushed. Most of their companies are small with less than 200 employees. Work and family life are kept separate, and it is an honor to be invited to a Danish home to share a meal. This society values truthfulness, modesty, and competency, avoiding ostentation, displays of wealth, and the "hard sell."

Finns are a gregarious people.

Finns are a gregarious people who have kept their cultural identity, despite centuries of foreign invasion, domination, and rule. Hardened by nature and climate, they are also egalitarian, homogeneous, and basically middle class. Thus, ethnic strife is minimal. In 1906, this was the first European country to grant women the right to vote, today about 40% of 200 seats in the Parliament (*Eduskunta*) are held by women, one of whom became defense minister. A strong social welfare state with strong humanitarian and environmental concerns, they hold values that emphasize individual responsibility, family stability, and security, and minimalization of social differences. Since the Finnish believe they have what they need, they do not easily accept information or help from others. Since 1923, freedom of religion has been guaranteed, and almost 84% of the people are affiliated with the Evangelical Lutheran Church, which is supported by state taxes. Finns are multilingual (Finnish, Swedish, and English or Russian). Though stylish dressers, they wear conservative business attire, with men using suit coats on all occasions. They are given to business entertaining, for either casual lunch or dinner out. The successful closing of a business deal may include an invitation to an expensive meal and sauna. (Sauna is segregated by gender, for it is in the nude, unless afterward there is public bathing, which requires a bathing suit.) Dancing is quite popular, especially the tango. Allowing for weather problems, generally people are punctual. Business appointments are made several weeks in advance. The five-day workweek is from 8 A.M. to 4 P.M., except during the winter (September to May) when some businesses operate from 9 A.M. to 5 P.M. With their four- to five-week vacations, avoid serious commercial pursuits during July, August, and early September. The Finns are now shaping a special relationship with the Russians as bridge builders between west and east, especially on behalf of the European Union.

Swedes tend to be somewhat serious and dour. Excessive emotion in public is to be avoided, along with discussion of sensitive topics. Rather than small talk, Swedes prefer to get to the point and down to business. Women are accepted as equals. Although the official church is Lutheran and receives tax support, the connection between church and state is dissolving because such a small percentage now attend religious services. Sweden has a social welfare system with generous provisions relative to the aged and unemployed, health care, and educational opportunities. Both socially and at business, punctuality is expected. Except for the 13 national holidays, business is transacted between 8:30 A.M. and 5 P.M., but for a lunch from 11:30 A.M. to 1:30 P.M. (often taken at home). Banks usually start at 9:30 A.M. and close at 3 P.M., except when open in the evenings from 4:30 to 6 P.M. Swedish workers normally get five weeks per year of vacation and usually take it in July. Thus, it is difficult to schedule business during midsummer and the long Christmas holiday.

Scandinavians like food, especially smorgasbord buffets, and many are heavy drinkers at mealtime, so their drunk-driving laws are strict. There is great natural beauty and endless possibilities to be experienced in these north countries, including Sweden.

In the twenty-first century, Scandinavian countries that were relatively homogeneous have become more heterogeneous with increased immigration by Muslims and workers from other parts of the EU.

SOUTHEASTERN EUROPE

Geographically, this region encompasses some 13 national entities, some of which are bounded by seas with exotic names like the Mediterranean, Tyrrhenian, Ionian, Adriatic, Crete, Aegean, and Black. This southern area of Europe includes some of its most ancient cultures, such as Italy (Roman) and Greece, the two focal points of our analysis.

Within Southeastern Europe, Romania is the second largest in population. But it is underdeveloped because of inept communist rulers in the twentieth century, who also held back the Balkan peoples of Albania, Bulgaria, Croatia, Macedonia, and Slovenia. For centuries, despite cultural, agricultural, and industrial advances, the locale has been the scene of invasions, conflicts, and violence up until contemporary times. In just the past decade, both NATO and the EU had to intervene in the civil war and ethnic cleansing provoked by the Serbs within Bosnia-Herzegovina, as well as in the province of Kosovo, now temporarily under UN administration. Unfortunately, the naturally beautiful Balkans off the Adriatic Sea have been a center of political turmoil, infighting, and uncooperativeness for too long.

The smallest states in the area are Malta, San Marino, and Vatican City. Although the island of Corsica lies off the Italian Peninsula, it is now part of France. Recall also, that there is a strong Muslim population in some of these lands as a result of continued influences from the

Southeastern Europe

* Member of the European Union

Exhibit 14.16

Profile of Italy

Official name	Republica Italian (Italian Republic)
Population	58,103,033 (July 2005 est.)
Age structure	0–14 years: 13.9% (male 4,166,213/female 3,919,288)
	15–64 years: 66.7% (male 19,554,416/female 19,174,629)
	65 years and over: 19.4% (male 4,698,441/female 6,590,046) (2005 est.)
Ethnic groups	Italian (includes small clusters of German-, French-, and Slovene-Italians in the north and Albanian-Italians and Greek-Italians in the south)
Religion	Predominately Roman Catholic with mature Protestant and Jewish communities and a growing Muslim immigrant community
Education	98.6% literacy rate
Land	294,020 sq km
Government	Republic
Political parties	Center-right coalition (Forza Italia and others), center-left coalition; (Margherita and others) totaling more than 14 parties. According to the CIA Area Handbook, there are at least 50 parties.
Per capita income	$28,300
Exports to U.S.	Total exports = $371.9 billion
	U.S. accounts for 8%
	Total exports to U.S. = $29.8 billion (2005 est.)
Imports from U.S.	Total imports from U.S. = $11,512.2 million (2005)

Turkish Ottoman Empire that extended there until the twentieth century.

To help readers appreciate the cultural contrasts within this territory, we have selected five countries within Southeastern Europe to profile in Exhibit 14.17.

ITALY[23]

This portion of Europe has always been geographically distinctive because it is seemingly shaped like a human boot. In Southeastern Europe, the country lies south of France, Switzerland, and Austria, with Slovenia and Croatia on its eastern borders. Apart from many small islands, on its eastern coastline, the two largest are Sardinia and Sicily to the south. Generally temperate in climate, Italy's northern borders are separated from its neighbors by the snowcapped Alps, thus enabling its city of Torino to host the 2006 Winter Olympic Games. The rest of the peninsula is surrounded by water—to the east by the Adriatic Sea, while in the southeast, the Gulf of Taranto and the Ionian Sea. To the west there is the Ligurian and Tyrrhenian Seas and in the south, the Mediterranean Sea. Mary Ellen Toffle, MIM wrote the section on Italy. She works in Genova, Italy.

Introductory Comments

What can one say about Italy? Thousands of books have been written about it. Anyone who visits falls in love with its picturesque villages and cities, its musical language, its incredible food and wine. It is the land of art, science, and passion, the land of "saints, scholars and navigators" (Italian proverb). Most people would agree that Italian fashion, food, and sports cars are the best in the world. There we find "La Dolce Vita," the ability to enjoy everything with art and style. But loving Italy and doing business there are two very different things.

One important thing to realize about Italy is that it has two faces, like the two-faced Roman god Janus, one looking forward and one looking backward. Italy is the vestige of the eternal Roman Empire, and it is on the cutting edge of modern scientific research and many types of technology. It looks backward to its age-old traditions, and it looks forward (painfully sometimes) to its position as a strong member of the European Community. Italy is currently in a state of rapid social and economic change. It is facing the major challenges of immigration, European integration, globalization, and family breakdown.

One of the greatest problems facing Italy today is the graying of Italy. It is soon to become the "oldest country." The Italian government must find a way to encourage an increase in the birth rate.[24] The number of retired persons will soon outnumber those in the workforce, causing grave problems to the social security system.

The history of Italy dates back more than 3000 years. Because of Italy's geographical location and extensive coastline, it was historically a target for conquerors. The Etruscans, and afterward the Greeks and Romans, left their indelible footprints on the face of Italy. The contributions of Greco-Roman civilization include law, architecture, Latin, and philosophy, to mention a few. Italy was part of the Holy Roman Empire in the Middle Ages. When that disintegrated, the Italian city-state was born. The Renaissance, which began in Florence and spread throughout Italy and Europe, brought with it a revival of Greco-Roman culture and a new emphasis on art, science, literature, and philosophy. The modern concept of banking was developed at that time in Italy. Later, different countries, including Spain, France, and Austria, controlled many areas of Italy. This foreign domination, in addition to geo-

Loving Italy and doing business there are two very different things.

Italy is currently in a state of rapid social and economic change.

graphical differences, contributed to the development of the diverse regions that are still a part of Italy today.

Contributions of Italy to the Modern World

Immense volumes have been written on the Italian contributions to Western civilization. The West owes its essence and structure to Italy in many areas: science, economics, navigation, art, architecture, politics, and literature, to mention a few. In every area of study stand many Italian geniuses, including Dante, Galileo, Michelangelo, and Marconi. Remember that Christopher Columbus (a Genovese navigator) discovered America, and don't forget that the name "America" comes from the Florentine cartographer Amerigo Vespucci. Italians are very proud of their heritage, and it is advisable for businesspeople to know, appreciate, and respect it.

Ancient as the Italian legacies are, the actual nation of Italy is very young. It was formed as a constitutional monarchy in 1861 and then became a republic in 1946. Thus, Italy as a concept has existed much longer than Italy as a country.

Cultural Values for Doing Business in Italy

Campanilismo

Historically, Italy was divided into independent city-states, each having its own autonomous government, ruling families, dialect (or language, depending on who you talk to), history, cuisine, and traditions. In order to understand the Italy of today, you must realize that Italy is made up of these former city-states, all of which are unique in many ways and in some ways do share some common cultural values. By means of the mass media and the education system, Italy has grown closer together into a more unified country, but it is still rare to find an Italian who will say he is Italian, and not Roman, or Florentine, or Genovese. This tendency demonstrates the strong cultural value of *campanilismo*. The notion derives from the campanile, or bell tower, that can be found in every village in Italy. An Italian feels best when he can see the campanile of his own town. The implication is that Italians prefer to stay in their city of origin and will always consider the interests of their "campanile" in business situations.

Cultural Identity

In a recent survey, the Italians evaluated themselves in terms of their national character. They identified the top three characteristics: the art of *arrangiarsi*, creativity in art and the economy, and connection to the family. Interestingly enough, the characteristic that they identified as the least present was that of civic duty.[25]

The Art of *Arrangiarsi*

Arrangiarsi means to be able to make do, to get by, to work oneself out of any situation. This activity has been elevated to an art in Italy because most systems do not function as expected. The cause of this has historical roots, going back to the numerous invaders, conquerors, and imposed systems of foreign government. In business terms, this could be called "creative problem solving." The Italians have learned to make do as a reaction to the formidable system of government, laws, and taxes. It is hard for Americans to understand this idea because they are used to having systems that actually work as expected. Instead, Italians have developed ways to get around the system and to accomplish what needs to be done in a creative way, via connections and family ties.

Relationships: Family and Friends

Family ties, connections, and relationships are the bastions against the insecurities of life. Over the centuries, the system of family and connections evolved as a solution to problems imposed by foreign occupation. Today family is still the number one cultural value, and friendship is in the top ten. Perhaps the key word in Italy is *relationship*. Today, everything flows from the relationship. From getting a job to opening a bank account, everything depends on connections. The successful foreign businessman makes it a point to understand the connections and use them.

Raccomandazione

Raccomandazione literally means "recommendation," but it is what American business would define as nepotism. In fact, the word "nepotism" is related to the Italian word *nipote* which means nephew/niece or grandson/granddaughter. The implication is that people take care of their families and familial interests first. It is very difficult for people to get their first job in Italy if they don't have some sort of *raccomandazione*. One of the biggest problems facing Italy today is the "brain drain" of highly skilled researchers to other countries in Western Europe or the United States, all because without *raccomandazione* it is almost impossible to land a very desirable position.[26]

La Cordata

La cordata literally means "rope" or "cord" and refers to the practice of pulling along friends and family in the climb up the "corporate

Italians have developed ways to get around the system. Family ties, connections, and relationships are the bastions against the insecurities of life.

ladder." It is an outgrowth of the relationship/family value explained above. People who find work in a company or government office immediately seek to be part of a *cordata*, or network. And they also start their own, with which they gradually bring in their friends or relatives, as the case may be. It also includes the practice of forming alliances between companies for buying materials or products.

Bella Figura

Bella figura literally means "beautiful figure," but it can make or break a business negotiation. It deals with the desire to make a good impression, give a good appearance, and convey a certain image. It is somewhat like the Asian value of "saving face" but encompasses appearance as well as behavior. It is responsible for the fact that Italian fashion, art, and architecture are world renowned and sought-after. Italians seek to make a *bella figura* through their appearance, both physical and economic, and their behavior. It is important for managers to remember this in all areas of interaction. Proposals and presentations must look good. Image is the key in all areas, including dress and behavior. Status and prestige also enter in. The foreign businessperson is advised to imitate the Italians on this one. And be careful not to present a *brutta figura* (ugly figure)—that can mean being obviously drunk, looking slovenly, arriving late, being unprepared, giving an unattractive presentation.

Furbo

Furbo is a word that is very hard to translate. It can have negative or positive connotations. It has evolved as a concept that describes how to outsmart one's adversary or beat the system. A funny example of this is that of the seatbelt law. Seatbelts are now required everywhere in Italy, and the police will fine motorists if they aren't wearing them. Someone in Naples started producing a sweater that was made with a black diagonal stripe from the neck to the stomach, so that when you wear it, it appears that you are wearing a seatbelt. So you outsmart the police. This is being *furbo*. In business, it is very important to be on your guard because often someone will try to outsmart you in some way. Beware of the well-developed *furbo*, because he is waiting to rip you off.

The Two Italys

In addition to having two faces, Italy also has two halves. This is due in part to the historical occupations of the areas. The North is a well-developed industrial powerhouse and one of the richest areas of Europe. In contrast, the South (known as the *Mezzogiorno*), which is the southern half of Italy starting just below Rome, is one of the poorest areas of Europe. (For discussion purposes, this article includes Rome as part of the South, since culturally it tends to be more similar to the South than to the North.) The South is economically depressed and primarily agricultural. It is perhaps the greatest economic problem that Italy has, as well as being a social problem. The South embodies the stereotypes that foreigners have of Italy—chaotic streets, violently honking horns with drivers shouting at each other, Mafia, and so on, whereas the North exemplifies the best rendition of "Italy as a modern industrial power."

North Americans and Northern Europeans will find the business environment in the South (Rome and below) to be less time conscious, even more relationship oriented, and more relaxed.

Economy

The biggest economic problems facing Italy are its high unemployment rate, its heavy business tax burden, and its unwieldy government bureaucracy. One of the main causes of unemployment is the fact that employer taxes are very high—basically double what the employee receives. Employers tend to avoid hiring full-time personnel. Many people are hired as independent consultants to avoid employment taxes. Also, high business taxes and red tape discourage foreign investment. So economic growth is limited by the system itself. The new government is facing a massive challenge. There is also a very strong black market, whose dimension is really not known. This means that the Italian economy is probably a lot stronger than it appears on paper because of the size of the *mercato nero*. Italian industry is also being replaced by Chinese industry, from the garment sector to heavy industry to technological production (computer software, fiber-optics, etc.). Foreign companies that once produced in Italy and also Italian companies are moving out of Italy because of the high costs of production.

There is significantly less foreign investment in Italy than in other European countries, for several reasons. First, communism exerted a strong influence on the government after World War II. This discouraged American business, even though Italian communism was never like Russian communism. Second, Italy's distribution system has a long way to go before it can compete effectively with other European countries. And third, the practice of delayed payment discourages business in all areas. Italian companies usually pay on a 60- to 120-day basis, which ends up frequently translating into 120 to 160 days. This can cause a significant cash flow problem for U.S. companies which are waiting for payment and must finance the delay. As can well be imagined, there is an ensuing snowball effect. Delayed payment is rampant in Italy. Currently, the government is trying to solve the problem, but it is unlikely that a solution will be found very soon.

Sociopolitical Forces

The Catholic Church continues to be a significant political and cultural force in Italy, even though it has declined in power in the last years. Italy is primarily Catholic, but a great percentage of the population does not actually practice. However, the Catholic Church is a powerful presence in the formation of government policy, especially in the moral and ethical areas.

Government and Political Forces

Mussolini perhaps said it best: "It is not impossible to govern Italians. It is merely useless." Italy is a multiparty parliamentary republic. Because of the large number of political parties (last count was around 50), Italy is basically governed by coalitions formed by various parties. One can only imagine the challenge of developing policies with so many parties. There is both a president and a prime minister (called President of the Council). Government and labor unions play a heavy role in business. American managers must be very aware of this added dimension when doing business in Italy.

Italy is a multiparty parliamentary republic.

Legal System

It has been estimated that there are over 500,000 laws in Italy, many of which have never been canceled since Roman and medieval times, as well as the hundreds of new ones that are made every year.[27] This makes the law profession quite attractive and makes it necessary for every business to have a competent lawyer on call. "Such a high number of laws," laughed one Italian businessman, "And nobody follows any of them!" Thus, the cultural value of *arrangiarsi* flourishes in response to an overloaded system.

Nature of Business-Family Capitalism

A great number of businesses in Italy are family-owned. That means that many businesses are not managed by management professionals. The head of the family wants to maintain control over the business. This widespread phenomenon weakens Italy because these businesses do not want to be publicly traded. Because they finance through debt, and because they want to maintain control at all costs, they limit their growth and subsequently cannot compete in the global market.[28]

Determinism

Italians are basically fatalistic: *che sarà, sarà*. Due to their long history of natural and political disasters, and the influence of Catholi-

Italians are basically fatalistic: che sarà, sarà.

cism, they tend to believe that nothing can be done to prevent things from happening according to destiny. Insecurity is viewed as a fact of life. This belief may explain why they tend to live in the moment: remember that the famous Latin quote *carpe diem* came from Italy. So they will seize the moment without really believing that they have control over their success. One source of frustration in business stems from this fatalism. Foreign managers will find it difficult to extract detailed objectives and plans from their Italian counterparts. The practice of setting precise objectives doesn't fly in Italy for the reason stated above. Besides not believing that they don't control their destiny, they also hate to make mistakes (that causes *brutta figura*), so they don't like to pin themselves down too tightly to objectives they aren't sure that they can meet.

Time Orientation

Italians are usually multitasking. It is quite common for them to conduct a meeting, take a phone call, and sign papers all at the same time. Americans may find it stressful to be in a meeting that is constantly being interrupted with phone calls. The mobile telephone is a constant source of interruption that Italians usually allow to take precedence in a face-to-face meeting.

As far as punctuality is concerned, the North is much closer to Northern Europe in its adherence to meeting times and time allocation. In the South, time flows at a slower pace, and people tend to be much more relaxed with appointments and schedules. Whether it be North or South, it is common to have many changes of schedule, shifting, canceling, reinstating, and so forth. Many foreign managers complain that their appointment times and schedules are continually being changed. The best way to handle this is to be flexible and patient. Expect schedule changes as a matter of course.

Action Orientation

Italians tend more towards *being* than doing because of their long past, their traditions, and their propensity to form relationships. They identify themselves more with their region, their family, friends, or soccer team than with their job. Italians also define themselves by their network of relationships and the connections they enjoy.

Again there is a pronounced difference between North and South. The North has a greater focus on activity, and the South has an even greater focus on relationships. The key difference between Americans and any kind of Italian is that individuals do not value themselves by what they do per se but by how well they, their families, and their friends can live based on their financial and professional successes.

Communication

Italian culture is high context, although the North is somewhat less than the South. The Italian language is very colorful and musical. One of the Italians' favorite pastimes is talking and engaging in polemic discussions (Americans may call it arguing). For an outsider, they tend to waste a lot of time talking. They usually speak in high volume, and all at the same time, in very heated discussions. They are known for their flamboyant style, which combines emotion, gestures, and volume that creates an overall impression of a theatrical presentation. One of the most admired abilities is to be able to put on a spectacle or show. They tend to keep one eye on the other members of the group so that they can gauge their performance. They are very expressive; in fact, the best way to describe them is with their own word, *esternazione*, which is difficult to translate. It means "expressing" or venting, or "letting it all out." *Esternazione* is reflected in every communication situation. In politics and the media, it means press releases and shouting matches. In private life, it means "telling it all." There is no word for "privacy" in the Italian language. For some companies, this can pose a problem because "secret" policies are never "secret" and are often discussed at the local cappuccino bar, with the family, and even the press.[29] However, it must never be assumed that the Italian businessman will tell you everything. There is also another Italian quality, *omertà*, which means silence. And there is also the cultural tendency to tell you what you want to hear, or what they hope will come of what you do hear.

Italian culture is high context.

■ *Indirect vs. Direct*
In spite of *esternazione*, personal and business relationships can be quite indirect, based on unspoken (high-context) values that everyone is supposed to know (Italians, that is). Third parties are often used to communicate important messages, especially unpleasant ones. A foreign businessperson must be aware of the hidden cultural assumptions. The best solution for this is to have a bilingual, bicultural person to advise you.

■ *Expressive*
Everyone can agree that Italians are very expressive. Their system of gestures is a language all of its own. They also have an uncanny ability to yell at each other simultaneously and at the same time understand each other.

■ *Formal*
In spite of whatever stereotypes Americans may have about the informality of Italians (i.e., drivers screaming and gesturing at each other in traffic jams), the Italians are initially quite formal in both personal and business relationships. They adore the spectacle of form and

Italians are initially quite formal in both personal and business relationships.

ritual even in business situations. Appropriate titles are always used, such as *Dottore/Dottoressa* (person with a university degree). The businessperson must be sure to know in advance the appropriate titles. When speaking in Italian, the *lei* form denotes respect and formality and is always used unless otherwise specified.

Physical Contact

Italians are very warm, and it is quite normal to see men hugging each other or sitting or leaning close. Women greet each other with a kiss on both cheeks, usually after the first time they meet. Men shake hands with men and will kiss women they know on both cheeks. Italians have a smaller spatial radius than many foreigners. Part of this is due to the nature of the culture, which is very relationship oriented, but also because in many areas space is actually very limited.

Power Distance

Italians tend to follow more traditional roles of hierarchy. They seem to be very egalitarian in their communication style, but they respect hierarchical structure. Status and titles are important. Foreign managers who are more informal must remember to project themselves in terms of their perceived status.

Individualism

Italians pride themselves on being highly individualistic. This comes out repeatedly as being a very important cultural value. But individualistic does not mean independent. They are very social and prefer to be in groups, as long as they are viewed as unique individuals. Most of them hate to be alone. In negotiating, it often happens that each individual wants to speak and basically repeats everything that has already been said. If the individuals are denied the opportunity to speak, they go away feeling resentful and undervalued. The result of this individualism is the fact that Italians find it difficult to truly work on a team. Any foreign manager who must manage a team of Italian employees must be ready to provide extensive team-building activities for successful productivity.

Competitiveness

Italians are competitive.

Italians are competitive, even though they put a high stress on relationships. Probably the biggest areas of competition are physical appearance and lifestyle. But Italian business does not have the same drive toward competition that the United States has. This is probably because business is based on relationships, which means that client relationships take precedence. In terms of long-term vs. short-term business relationships, Italians prefer to build up long-lasting, mutually beneficial business relationships. They want to do business with people they know and trust. It is not common practice in Italian business to give individual awards or to single out one individual for commendation.

Structure

Italian life is highly chaotic, in part because of the bureaucracy, the lack of overall communication between government offices, and the Italian national character: creativity. Thousands of laws are made in the hope of imposing some sort of control. But as one writer said succinctly—the Italians are unpredictable, but they love routine. They are highly risk aversive, but they go out of their way to circumvent regulations.[30]

Thinking

Italians are *deductive* in academic situations, but pragmatic in business negotiations. They tend to decide based on separate situations, and they often refer back to other similar situations and results.

Risk

Italian companies do not like to take risks. However, experience has shown that if a company is willing to take a risk, it will do very well in Italy.

Women in Business

Italy was traditionally a male-dominated society. That of course was always reflected in the business world. In the past few years women have been challenging that position.

"The position of women in Italy has drastically changed in the past twenty years. Women in high managerial positions are respected, although their salaries are not up to par with that of their male counterparts."[31] "It is important to be strong and determined but not try to imitate men. It is important for women to conduct business using a woman's style. The key is to know your own personalized management style."[32]

The position of women in Italy has drastically changed in the past twenty years.

Tips for Doing Business in Italy

- Start up: be aware of possible problems involving laws and taxes.
- Learn Italian.
- Try to find an Italian counterpart to help you through the bureaucracy.
- For the initial contact, a third-party introduction is very helpful; if you can't get that, write directly in Italian.
- Print materials in Italian.
- Meeting: Try to build a relationship. This is a relationship-oriented country and if you form a relationship, you have a better chance. You do that by taking time, finding out about the other person, and building trust. It is perfectly acceptable to ask questions about the family and expect to answer questions about yours. Dress code—look your best.
- Forms of address—be formal until the other person indicates that you may speak in the familiar (that is, if you are speaking in Italian).
- Access the *cordata*.
- Get a good lawyer and a good *commercialista*.
- Be flexible.
- Make connections.
- Be patient (things go along at what seems to be a standstill and suddenly the ball starts rolling).

Exhibit 13.17 profiles important demographic information other countries in the region.

EXHIBIT 14.17

PROFILES OF BULGARIA, CROATIA, GREECE, ITALY, AND ROMANIA

NATION	Bulgaria	Croatia	Greece	Italy	Romania
AREA (sq km)	110,910	56,542	131,940	301,230	237,500
POPULATION	7,450,349	4,495,904	10,668,354	58,103,033	22,329,977
CAPITAL	Sofia	Zagreb	Athens	Rome	Bucharest
RELIGION	Bulgarian Orthodox, Muslim	RC/Orthodox	Greek Orthodox	RC	Eastern Orthodox, Protestant, RC
LANGUAGE	Bulgarian Turkish	Croatian	Greek	Italian, German	Romanian, Hungarian, German
LITERACY	98.6%	98.5%	97.5%	98.6%	98.4%
LIFE EXPECTANCY	72.03 years	74.45 years	79.09 years	79.68 years	71.35 years
GDP PER CAPITA	$9,000	$11,600	$22,800	$28,300	$8,300

GREECE

The mainland and adjoining islands of modern Greece are located south of Albania, Macedonia, and Bulgaria. The country juts into the Mediterranean Sea with the Aegean Sea to the east, the Sea of Crete in the south, bounded on the west by the Ionian Sea. From the fourth through the sixth centuries B.C., the ancient seafaring Greeks dominated Asia Minor, almost treating the Mediterranean as their own "private lake" as the established trading posts and colonies on what is today Turkey in the east and Italy, France, and Spain, to the west. With its temperate climate, this is a place that attracts tourists, along with the Olympic games since they were founded in 60 B.C. For centuries the land has been used for farming, wine making, raising goats, and beef for export. More recently, the economy has been driven by the processing of tobacco, chemicals and textiles, as well as the manufacturing of goods and petroleum products. Exhibit 14.18 provides some context on the history and culture of the ancient Greeks.

Ancient Historical Perspective

The wonder of ancient Greece is that it shone so brightly for so long. Known originally as Hellas, it was a small land of isolated city-states scattered across mountains, coastal plains, and islands. These avidly independent states, with their own laws, armies, colonies, and coins, never gelled as one nation. Locked in fierce rivalries, they were formidable and often brutal foes to foreigners and fellow Greeks alike. But the Greeks shared immense vitality and sowed their culture and language across the then known Mediterranean world, becoming a gleaming and improbable pillar of modern civilizations.

The wonder of ancient Greece is that it shone so brightly for so long.

EXHIBIT 14.18
THE GLORY THAT WAS GREECE

Profile of Greece—Hellenic Republic	
Area	131,990 sq km
Population	10,968,000
Capital	Athens (3,120,000 population)
Religion	Greek Orthodox 98%
Language	Greek
Literacy	95%
Life expectancy	79 years
GDP per capita	22,200
Government	Democratic Republic

Source: Adapted from "Beagles of the Past," a map from *National Geographic*, Washington, DC, 1999 (www.nationalgeographic.com).

In their heroic Mycenaean Age (1600–1100 B.C.) Greece's earliest chiefdoms built thick-walled citadels that amassed great wealth. Homer's *Iliad* glorifies its great warriors like Achilles and Hector. Then Greece declined for several centuries. Emerging from their dark age into a period called Archaic Greece (750–500 B.C.), the Greeks' desire for land spurred colonization abroad. By 600 B.C. the city-states had hundreds of independent colonies spread around the Mediterranean and Black Seas. Far-flung trading brought wealth and an affluent middle class seeking political power that fostered innovations in government and growth of democracy. Gradually, a Penhellenic culture arose with unique art and architecture, religious festivals to honor their gods, athletic games, and tragic or comedic plays.

The barbarians or *Bararoi*, tested Greek power during the Age of Persian Conflicts (499–479 B.C.). Greek cities in Asia Minor, Athens, and Ereteria rebelled against Persia's King Darius I who squashed the revolt and sacked Miletos. Though outnumbered, Athenian troops defeated the Persian army at the famous battle of Marathon. With Persia's withdrawal, the Athenians then built a navy of wooden battleships. In 480, Darius's son, Xeres, invaded, burning the Acropolis in the process, but the Greeks destroyed his fleet of 200 ships. After several other victories against impossible odds led by Sparta and Athens, the latter embarked on a path of brilliance that changed the Western world. Called the Golden Age (478–404 B.C.), Athenian democracy allowed free male citizens to debate laws in the assembly, exercise the power of persuasion, and vote for their leaders annually. Athens also became leader of Delian League, an alliance of states that paid Athens for naval protection from Persians and pirates. Pericles diverted that money to beautifying the city, including building the Parthenon and other sculptured buildings. This income not only provided jobs for citizens, but enabled him to institute pay for public service. The city then produced a series of creative geniuses like playwrights Aeschylus, Sophocles, and Aristophanes; philosophers such as Socrates; historians Herodotus and Thucydides. All this progress of the Sophists in the arts of reasoning and rhetoric angered the militarists of Sparta. The latter with its allies in Corinth and Thebes launched the Peloponnesian Wars in 431 against so-called Athenian tyranny.

When these Greek cities were deeply divided, Philip II transformed a cluster of independent Macedonian tribes and cities in the north into a united kingdom. He then led his army south and by 338 B.C. he ruled Greece. This inaugurated the Age of Alexander the Great (336–323 B.C.) when Philip's son, tutored by Aristotle, succeeded his father at 20 years of age. Two years later, Alexander led 30,000 troops into Persia winning a series of battles that included the burning of Persepolis, the royal palaces of King Darius III. The further conquests of this "lord of Asia" from Egypt to Hindu Kish (India) ended when his war-weary army rebelled. Having minted new cities in vanquished lands where

Greek language and learning thrived, Alexander died of fever at Babylon at the age of 32. His empire split into three successor kingdoms that perpetuated Hellenistic culture and its Greek legacy for the next 300 years. Rome, which admired and emulated Grecian culture, won the last of these successor kingdoms, Egypt, when it defeated Anthony and Cleopatra in 31 B.C. With Greece "made a slave," her subduer, Rome, secured Greece's arts and learning for all ages.

Contemporary Historical Perspective

In this cradle of Western civilization, democracy was born within Greek city-states. Unfortunately, its history of fractious conflict, violence, and border alterations has also lingered even into modern times. For example, ancient Macedonia once included today's Bulgaria, Greece, and the Balkans, including what is now the former Yugoslavia. The latter has a province called Macedonia, but Greeks object to any use of that historic name except in the real "Greek Macedonia" where today separatists struggle to make a state independent of Greece.

Having suffered occupation for many centuries by the Romans and Turks, Greece in the twentieth century faced further brutalization from Nazi Germans and Italian Fascists during World War II. The turbulence continued under communist guerrillas and governments. A coup d'etat in 1967 replaced the constitutional monarchy with an authoritarian military regime and a Greek Republic was declared. A constitution adopted with a president, Parliament, and advisory council resulted. The prime minister now leads the 300-seat Chamber of Deputies.

Greece today is juxtaposed between the ancient and the modern. Amidst its antiquities, such as the Parthenon and exquisite Byzantine churches, Greece has moved ahead with new airports, metro lines, highways, and bridges. In 2004, the originator of the Olympics successfully hosted these international games again. The contrast is also evident in self-serving bureaucrats with stifling regulations versus exuberant yuppie entrepreneurs. Perhaps the insights from a recent survey summarized in Exhibit 14.19 will help readers appreciate the ongoing changes in Greek life.

With a Greek alphabet that goes back to 1000 B.C., this land has been remarkable for its relative homogeneity. But the past century increasingly saw an influx of migrant laborers—Macedonians and Albanians from the north, Turks from the east; in the past decade, the newcomers include Pakistani traders, Polish builders/decorators, Filipino domestics/nurses, and even unskilled African workers. Now with 1.2 million immigrants and 5 million tourists annually, Greece is becoming more heterogeneous, with minorities grudgingly being tolerated. Greek ethnicity and religious orthodoxy are being challenged to be more tolerant by its growing diversity. The modest-rate socialist

Greece today is juxtaposed between the ancient and the modern.

EXHIBIT 14.19
HARNESSING THE GREEK PEOPLE'S FLAIR AND ENERGY

"For a country that stagnated throughout the 1980s and spent the 1990s fretting about the effects of war on its northern borders, Greece is enjoying much greater economic success than seemed likely five years ago. This is both a cause and a reflection of its enhanced status in the European Union. Having shaken off its reputation as a laggard in the EU, it is now setting a new role as a locomotive for the Balkans."

Twenty-first century Greece also benefits from the break-up of the ultra-radical November 17 terrorist group; improving relations with its old rival, Turkey, especially over divided Cyprus; an economy growing twice the EU average; vast private investment in preparations for the Olympics. On the downside, inflation is well above the euro average, and EU funding will run out in 2006; unemployment is still high as public and private sectors modernize; the urgent need to reform arcane company law, complex tax codes, and pension systems. Yet as Greece pursues better commercial relations with its Balkan neighbors, its Promachonas border crossing has become one of the busiest entry points to the EU, as well as an expanding commercial emporium. Instead of the old cross-border passions and conflict, the emphasis is on shopping trips, business deals, oil flows, and working together for mutual prosperity. The entrance of the Greek portion of Cyprus into the EU is also a positive development until the Turkish-Cypriots can also join that union. There is promise also in the passing of the old guard in politics, business, and the professions, to a new, more dynamic generation of leaders—gerontocracy's tyranny and despotism is giving way to bright, career-minded youngsters. Because of culture lag in higher education, Greece now sends more students abroad (30,000) to universities than most other countries in the world.

Among Hellenes today fertility is down, but abortion and new immigrants are up. People are abandoning old ideologies and associations to pursue new peaceful affiliations and social movements. The challenge is for mature European Greeks to use the public sector for community service, rather than personal bounty.

Source: B. Clark, "Prometheus Unbound—A Survey of Greece," *The Economist*, October 12, 2002, p. 20.

government is trying to tackle these contemporary realities and consequences, ranging from rising crime to demands for greater separation of church and state.

Cultural Insights for Doing Business in Greece

Greeks have been engaged in trade and commerce for eons, especially in shipping, and so are quite savvy in business. They have an instinctive sense of trends and opportunities for enterprises in the Balkans, as well as where to best invest venture capital in these postcommunist economies. Currently, they have been leading cross-border cooperation in the region, advocating the use of soft power by "making money, not war."

The usual workweek in Greece is from Monday to Friday, normally 8 A.M. to 1:30 P.M.; and after lunch, from 4:00 P.M. until 7:30 P.M. To be effective as a foreigner with Greeks, cultivate interpersonal and social relations—show authentic willingness to learn more about Hellenistic history and culture. In negotiations, emphasize the subjective and associative aspects more than objective and abstract data. Realistically, face up to ethnocentrism and social distinctions in this traditional society that is now very much in transition—some bias will be expressed toward other classes, ethnic groups, and strangers.

Yet, Greeks are generous by nature; they compliment, but not lavishly, their children, flowers, or food. Greeks are people oriented and value the extended family, as well as meaningful friendships and associations. Trust and respect for the elderly, as well as concern for quality of life and the environment, are important. Among males, machismo is very evident, but women are slowly being liberated to move beyond home care to further education and career development. Although the Greeks appear laid back, there is a strong work ethic in the country. Exhibit 14.20 offers further insights into successful business relations in Greece.

Greeks are generous by nature.

EAST EUROPE/EURASIA

From the ashes of the geopolitical USSR, the Russian Federation has emerged in the past decade, along with its neighbors in the Commonwealth of Independent States (CIS). The CIS has sought to (1) repeal all Soviet laws and assume the powers of that former regime; (2) launch radical economic reforms, including the freeing of most prices; (3) retain the ruble, while allowing new currencies to be adopted in some countries; (4) establish a European-style free trade zone; (5) create joint control of all nuclear weapons; and (6) fulfill all foreign treaties and other obligations of the former regime.

Eurasia

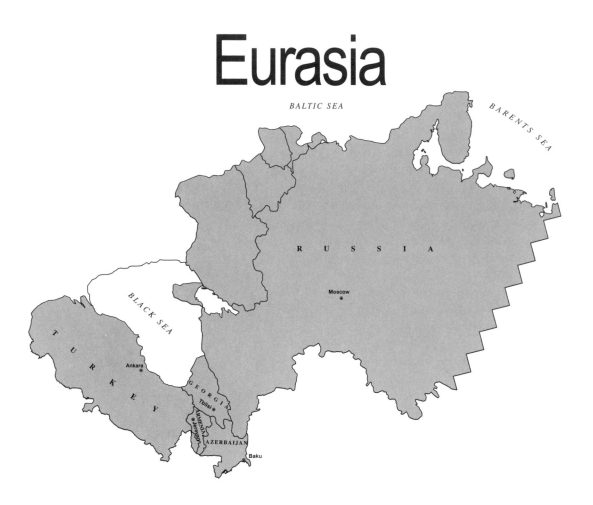

BALTIC SEA

BARENTS SEA

RUSSIA

Moscow

BLACK SEA

TURKEY

Ankara

GEORGIA

Tbilisi

ARMENIA

Yerevan

AZERBAIJAN

Baku

Exhibit 14.20
Business Tips with Greeks

1. Greeks expect foreigners to be courteous, and schedule appointments.
2. Use normal handshake, unless an embrace or kiss on the cheek is offered.
3. Present a business card with Greek wording up, and English on the reverse side.
4. Use titles and surnames, especially with older persons.
5. Be patient for Greeks like to discuss and bargain, as well as to exaggerate somewhat in their story telling.
6. Avoid sensitive subjects that relate to Greek politics and Cyprus.
7. Utilize taverna or coffee houses for business entertaining, or the main meal lunch during a 2 P.M. luncheon; dinner is a lighter meal at 8 or 9 P.M. (If invited to a home for dining, you may be urged to eat more food, and to accept is considered a compliment to the host.)
8. Wear conservative business dress, especially suits for women in subtle colors.
9. Be careful with gestures—though Greeks usually indicate "no" with an upward nod, that is changing with locals who adopt the North American head movements to indicate "yes/no."
10. Be aware that sometimes anger is expressed with a smile, while a puff through the lips may be used to ward off the "evil eye."

Source: G. Nees, *Exploring the Greek Mosaic: A Guide to Intercultural Communication in Greece*. Yarmouth, ME: Intercultural Press, 1996.

Since the Soviet breakup, the countries immediately surrounding the Russian Federation have been in turmoil. Once part of the Czar's empire in the Caucasus, these entities struggle to be nations, like Belarus, Georgia, and the Ukraine, which struggle with a new identity while coping with dictators, internal conflict, and serious economic problems. Besides the Russian Federation, the other key Commonwealth player is ancient Ukraine, populated with Slavic peoples from at least 2000 B.C. Its name means *borderland*, and its beautiful capital is Kiev, the mother city of the old Russian Empire, Slavic Orthodox churches, and Cossacks. This independent neighboring republic encompasses a landmass of 233,100 square miles with some 48 million inhabitants. Native Ukrainians make up 74% of that population, with 21% being ethnic Russians. This split led to a "yellow revolution" in which the Ukrainians voted out strong ex-communists in favor of a reformer president. Though entirely dependent on Russia for oil, gasoline, and natural gas, this new multiparty republic is known as the "bread

Since the Soviet breakup, the countries immediately surrounding the Russian Federation have been in turmoil.

basket" for producing food and supplying iron, coal, and chemical industry equipment. The importance of this republic in the CIS economic alliance is evident not only in the above statistics, but in the fact that it previously manufactured one-fourth of the USSR's agricultural machinery and construction equipment.

Historical Perspectives—Eastern Europe[33]

To understand what is happening in twenty-first-century Russia, one has to comprehend the country's recent history, especially its 1917 revolution. Figes, who did a sweeping cultural survey of Russia for the past three centuries, has raised an astute question: How can this nation, whose elites have consistently looked to foreign countries for their cultural examples, be held together by the unseen threads of native sensibility?[34] Yet, for much of the last century, its totalitarian mind-set and policies dominated political, social, and economic life throughout both Central Europe and Eurasia. When the Union of Soviet Socialist Republics was founded in 1922, Russia, and eventually its East Bloc allies, ensured that all major government and economic decision-making posts were filled by Communist Party members. These enforced its doctrine of centralism, requiring that decisions made at the top not be questioned by the lower echelons. This led to a situation in which a few people at the peak of the pyramid made almost every significant decision, and local initiative was practically nonexistent. The system restricted enterprise and meaningful contact with world market demand and supply. Its state monopoly sought to prevent capitalist countries from influencing the course of economic activities in the whole geographic area, except for what Western science and technologies its spies could steal.[35]

Yet under this repressive regime, the USSR did survive World War II, becoming a superpower and achieving some impressive accomplishments, ranging from education and health care to industrialization and an innovative space. Before its decline, the Soviet Empire had 450 million inhabitants, including some 140 national groups with a mix of European/Asian cultures, and religions ranging from Christians to 50 million Muslims. The USSR's 31 so-called autonomous republics and regions stretched from the Gulf of Finland to the Pacific Ocean. As this great monolith disintegrated, the peoples of Russia and its satellite countries endured disruptions in their lives such as:

- Massive amounts of unpaid work and unemployment.
- Rapid rise in penury and beggary, stress and alcoholism, corruption and crime.
- Deterioration in public services and the economy, especially currency speculation.
- Chaos in political, social, and family life.

The Union of Soviet Socialist Republics was founded in 1922.

■ Initial failure with capitalism, while the "new aristocracy" made up of greedy oligarchs or tycoons mainly prospered.

Since the collapse of the USSR in 1991, the peoples of Central and Eastern Europe have identified increasingly with Western culture and free market enterprises. Their traditional institutions are trying to transform themselves as new entities, missions, and roles are being formulated. There is growing emphasis on protection of freedom, human rights, and the rule of law, as well as on improving the environment and quality of life. Many of today's inhabitants not only are victims of communist cultural conditioning but also suffered the effects from the Cold War between East and West.

The trends, depending on where you are in that area of Europe, are toward reviving the private sector, so that businesspeople cannot only own property, but can also get access to labor, capital, machinery, and raw materials. Increasingly, within their huge, inefficient public sector, governments have undertaken a number of reform experiments, such as:

■ Downsizing bureaucracies to more efficient entities.
■ Modernizing legal systems and procedures, especially regarding private property.
■ Changing legislation to privatize state-owned businesses and to subsidize enterprises that are private or cooperatives.
■ Permitting market forces, instead of the government, to set prices.
■ Creating more flexible and open banking systems that lend money on the basis of fiscal soundness instead of connections.
■ Innovating to attract Western investment, credit, and joint ventures.

Each of these countries is in transition and is experiencing problems institutionalizing reforms. Global managers with vision see new market possibilities in both Central and Eastern Europe, and seek to develop links there with representatives from governments, unions, businesses, churches, environmentalists, and students. Aware of the cultural and intellectual heritage of the region, as well as its potential, they network and encourage entrepreneurs, provide training and services, and promote diversification and outside investment. Trade and education, especially involving the exchange of people, can be a powerful means of facilitating the reform of obsolete systems and practices. The twenty-first century provides a rare chance to work toward peaceful prosperity in this part of Europe for those bold enough to participate in the improvement process.

Many countries in the region are embracing democracy and a market-oriented economy. Realistically in the post-Soviet era, former communists have moved into leadership positions in business and politics, some genuinely accepting the new reforms and practices and

Many countries in the region are embracing democracy.

others fiercely resisting such changes. The challenge for global leaders is to encourage the former, while supporting those noncommunists who seek their country's revival within a larger European partnership.

An early example of such partnership with Russia was Armand Hammer, a physician who became chairman of Occidental Petroleum Corporation in Los Angeles, while developing large-scale economic cooperation between the United States and Marxist countries during the past century. That effort and experience enriched him both personally and financially. Hammer, long deceased, forecast that the culture of free enterprise would take root not only in Russia and its neighboring republics, but also in all of Asia, even the People's Republic of China. Slowly but surely, the old, passive, and submissive mentality of those formerly totalitarian regimes is dying as inhabitants regain their dignity and enthusiasm for freedom and work. Sears refers to this as the passing of the "sleepwalking culture"—dreams/memories persist of Soviet work habits, lacking in real motivation and productivity.[36]

To acculturate the peoples of former communist countries to real democracy and a market economy is a massive reeducation challenge that will take many decades. George Soros, investment broker, has made the case for this. Through his Soros Foundation, this billionaire funds practical projects in this region (and China) initiated by dissenters, journalists, educators, and entrepreneurs. He supports those seeking to bolster battered economies in their transition from socialism to free-enterprise systems. In 1991, for example, at the start of an aborted Soviet coup, his foundation gave photocopiers to then Russian President Boris Yeltsin, so that fliers could be printed to rally Moscow citizens to support the embattled reformers. Since then, this Quantum Fund founder has spent both time and money in development of modern management within Central and Eastern Europe, cultivating entrepreneurial job skills, as well as basic market and consumer literacy. This philanthropist also founded and endowed Central European University, a private graduate school, located in Budapest, Hungary and Warsaw, Poland.[37]

RUSSIA

Russia, bounded by both the Arctic and Pacific Oceans, extends from the European continent into Asia. The country is primarily divided by the Ural Mountains. With a land of some 17 million square miles that spans 11 time zones, it is twice the size of the United States or China. Many countries share borders now with the Russian Federation—Finland, Estonia, Latvia, Belarus, Ukraine to the east; Georgia, Azerbaijan to the south separated by the Caucasus Mountains; and Kazakhstan to the west along with Mongolia and China to the south.

It also maintains sovereignty over the Baltic port city of Kaliningrad, sharing borders with Lithuania, Poland, and the Kuril Islands in the Sea of Okhotsk near Japan.

Apart from oil and natural gas, Russia's enormous natural resources have barely been utilized. Extensive agricultural and manufacturing enterprises add to the potential of this country. One visit to Moscow and St. Petersburg is enough to convince foreigners of the glorious cultural heritage of this people from the days of the Czars. It is evident in the palaces, museums, churches, opera houses, gardens, and many other historic buildings. Besides Moscow, where the seat of government is located in the Kremlin, its other major cities are St. Petersburg, Nizhny Novogorod, Voronezh, Volgograd, Vladivostok, Ekaterinburg, and Saratov. Exhibit 14.21 offers a profile with details and demographics.

EXHIBIT 14.21
PROFILE OF THE RUSSIAN FEDERATION

Area	17,075,200 square miles
Population	143,420,000
Language	Russian
Literacy	99.6%
Life expectancy	67.1 years
GDP per Capita	$10,700
Government	Federation

Cultural Guidelines for Doing Business in Russia and the CIS

Whether the remodeled Russian Federation will be able to modernize further and peacefully meet the immense needs of its varied peoples is an open question. Obviously, this nation and its CIS partners are in the midst of a painful political, social, and economic transition. For centuries the national cultures were autocratic and totalitarian, centered around bureaucratic centralized planning from Moscow. It was a culture with a large underclass of poor peasants led by a wealthy elite (first aristocrats in the monarchy and later Communist Party insiders). The move toward a more open, democratic, free-enterprise society has been slow. Some of the challenges they all face are analyzed in the following sections.

Instability and Transformation

Some immediate problems facing Russia and its Commonwealth partners are as follows:

- Accelerating disintegration of the economy and need for new financial systems and enterprises.
- Deepening crises in food/consumer goods production and distribution, as well as in housing and health services.
- Breakdowns in traditional systems (e.g., legal, banking, business, fuel and transportation) that hinder foreign investment and entrepreneurialism.
- Extensive job dislocation and rising unemployment.
- Political fragmentation and power-seeking by the republics, such as the independence movement in Chechnya.
- Rising crime and political assassinations by a criminal underground *mafia* that extends its power even to émigrés in New York and Los Angeles.
- Development of very powerful "oligarchs" who amassed their wealth by seizure or rigged purchasing of state assets.

But the Russian and CIS transition to a free market system has many positives, such as:

- Incredible human resources of a literate people with a combination of unique traditions and contributions to the arts and sciences, from music and the ballet to space technology and physics.
- Vast natural and material resources, much of which is yet to be developed.
- Sound educational system that provides high-level instruction in mathematics and sciences.
- Codependent economies that foster cooperative alliances, as in a compact signed among five Central Asian republics of Kazakhstan, Kyrgyzstan, Tajikistan, Turkmenistan, and Uzbekistan.
- Growing interest in preserving and protecting the environment and preventing disasters like nuclear accidents.
- Widespread movement toward divesting state industries to private enterprise, and state landholdings to private ownership.
- Majority of the population demonstrating for conservative public decisions made in a democratic way, desiring order and discipline, but not totalitarianism.
- Increasing interest in protecting individual and human rights, while moving in the direction of democratic freedoms and economic pragmatism.
- Resurgence of religion and religious tolerance.
- Expanding entrepreneurialism, even among academics and scientists.

Trade and Business Opportunities

Breaking into the CIS markets, including Russia, takes an enormous amount of perseverance and hard work by foreign firms that have

A sound educational provides high-level instruction in mathematics & sciences.

succeeded by developing long-range strategies. Although the CIS can offer foreign companies and universities much in terms of scientific, technical, and engineering talent, as well as processes, its greatest need from the West and Japan is for capital investment, plus management systems and development.[38]

In the past few years, more than 1300 joint venture agreements have been entered into by Western and Russian companies and institutions. Corporate giants have proven that successful projects can be accomplished within Russia, as Pepsico, Coca-Cola, Dow Chemical, Marriott, McDonald's, and American Express have demonstrated. Most suffered from the Soviet bureaucracy and their regulations but are now achieving superbly. If fledgling democracy and free enterprise are to prosper in the Commonwealth, then business innovators must reach out and take risks for long-term technological and commercial undertakings.

Negotiating Style and Protocol

During the ongoing transition from centralized planning to market economies within the CIS, foreigners can expect much confusion, frustration, and uncertainty. In negotiations, the Russians are noted for patience and stalling, considering compromise a sign of weakness. They expect to "play hardball," continually seeking concessions, and revising "final offers"—the longer the foreigner holds out acceptance, the more attractive the offer. Emotional "walkouts" and dire proclamations are part of their process. So, too, are the use of *blat*, or connections who use influence on your behalf, in exchange for favors, monetary or otherwise. Bribery and corruption are major problems.

There are two stages in business negotiations with the Russians. During the first stage, they try to get as many competitive offers as possible and play one supplier against another, before making a final decision. Nothing may happen for a while after the Western firm has submitted its bid. Then the Russians may notify the firm that it is still interested and resume negotiations. Potential suppliers are expected to provide detailed technical explanations of their products, so that the Russians can evaluate precisely what is being offered. Having collected several competitive offers, the Russians are adept at creating competition among the suppliers. Quotations from competitors are revealed to force bidding suppliers to cut their prices.

The second phase of negotiations begins when the supplier has been chosen. This phase is usually shorter than the first one, but it still takes time to settle all the various points in the final contract. Russian negotiators often negotiate with the weakest competitor first. After concessions are obtained from the weakest, the other companies are notified they also must accept them.

Another maneuver used by Russian negotiators is to first fix the final price the supplier is willing to take for its product. Once this price is

There are two stages in business negotiations with the Russians.

firmly quoted, the Russians may make additional demands for such extra services as free training of technicians or equipment maintenance, which were not originally included in the producer's description and price. Experienced foreign companies make it a standing rule to begin contract talks by discussing the articles of the purchasing agreement before any discussion begins on final price. It should also be made clear at the beginning on which points the supplier is willing to make concessions and on which it is not. The longer an executive postpones talking about demands that are of major importance to his or her company, the more forcefully the Russians may oppose them later.

Each agreement made with the Russians should stand on its own accord. Granting a price discount or making concessions to the Russians to win future business simply does not work. A common Russian tactic is to ask for a bulk price for a product and then to apply the lower price per unit from the bulk price to a smaller lot. It is implied, and sometimes even promised verbally, that more purchases will follow. However, the Russians will honor only written agreements.

It is important to let the Russians know exactly where your firm stands on all issues. The Russians do not respect negotiators who make large concessions because they then believe that initial proposals were inflated or deceptive. The firm should be prepared to stand by its position, and to drop negotiations and cut its losses if necessary. This will impress the Russians far more than slowly acquiescing to their demands. Although the "old" Soviet system may no longer exist, attitudes and cultural perceptions are much more resilient. Russians are very protocol conscious.

However, most of the CIS inhabitants are anxious to find international partners and to learn about Western business practices. No longer having to answer to a centralized government and wanting to move as quickly as possible toward "free enterprise," their business negotiators may be more flexible and accommodating than their Soviet predecessors. Further insights are offered, but for a reality check on the situation in the twenty-first century, consider the observations presented in Exhibits 14.22 and 14.23.

Work Environment

The workweek is generally Monday through Friday, 9 A.M. to 5 P.M. Recently, some banks have begun opening on Saturdays and evenings, Retail stores may be open Monday through Saturdays from 8–9 A.M. to 8–9 P.M.; food stores are also open on Sunday. Although foreigners are expected to show up on time for business appointments, allowance is made to be 15 to 30 minutes late for social events. Your Russian counterpart may be tardy or not show up at all—the previous communist system conditioned people to lateness, not promptness, and endless waiting in lines. Now foreign businesses are training their per-

Exhibit 14.22
The Saga of the Russian Auto Giant

KamAZ, an auto and truck manufacturing giant founded in 1969 at Kama in Central Russia, had developed hundreds of subsidiaries in the Ukraine, Kazakhstan, and Bashkiria. During the "detente" period of the 1970s, it benefited from a multinational consortium of American, West German, French, and Italian firms which provided millions of dollars worth of equipment and 1000 foreign experts. By the 1980s, production of rugged, sophisticated trucks and engines had risen to 250,000 units annually. But with the communist state pocketing the profits, no modernization, and an acute shortage of equipment, the huge enterprise with 170,000 employees and a "company city" of 500,000 began to suffer from deterioration. In 1989, "perestroika" led to more privatization as workers approved leaseholding and empowered management to negotiate for them to take over the state-owned business. Under the innovative leadership of its general manager, Nikolai Beth, a joint stock company was established with shares purchased by its own personnel and 1200 other plans and organizations. In the 1990s, the KamAZ products won prizes at international rallies and competitions, but the worker-owners linked their higher living standards and social protection with growth of production and quality improvement.

Today, their corporate future depends upon penetrating foreign markets with their reliable, heavy-duty trucks, as sales in Saudi Arabia, Senegal, and Egypt prove. For that to happen, KamAZ seeks international partners in trading firms and automotive firms throughout the world. For global managers, this saga of the transformation and requirements of just one Russian business is both symbolic of what is happening throughout the republics within the CIS. There are many similar synergistic opportunities within Central and Eastern Europe for both investment and skill development by businesses from mature market economies.

Source: Excerpt from *Managing Cultural Differences*, 5th ed., pp. 375–376.

sonnel in attitudes of punctuality and prompt customer service. Also allow for delays because of inadequate transportation and distances.

Typically, Russian and CIS officials expect to conduct business with only the highest-ranking executives. On the initial visit, the Western firm's representative is advised to send its top personnel to ensure a favorable first impression (e.g., a regional or East European manager). Final negotiations on larger deals should be handled by a key

EXHIBIT 14.23

RUSSIA: REGENERATION, STAGNATION, OR DECAY?

For more than a decade, Russia has been, more or less, a democracy and a market economy, and on civilized terms with its neighbors. Against the dismal standards of Russian history, that is a big achievement. But so far the fruits have been meager, bringing little comfort to most Russians. All they can see around them is physical, cultural, and moral decay.

The paradox is underpinned by three contradictory trends at work in today's Russia. The first is revival. . . . Freed from totalitarian controls, the energy and brains of millions have brought countless changes for the better. There are plenty of new businesses, and such old ones as have survived are better run than they used to be. There is room for public spiritedness and do-gooders. The crippling fear of the gulag is gradually being eroded by time. And the Russians are beginning to travel, and those who cannot obtain ideas from all over the globe by a mouse-click [on their computer via the Internet]. That has already begun to change their view of the world.

The second trend, though is stagnation. The collapse of communism, it turns out was superficial and partial. Well-connected people and organizations—especially the security services—started clawing back power straight away, and many became rich, as well as powerful. Changes for the better are often stopped in their tracks by greedy bureaucrats, and by the peculiar difficulties and perversities of life in Russia. The state, at all levels, disliked criticism and opposition. Many Russians, for their part, still hanker for the certainties, real or imagined, of the past: tradition, authority, and unity, rather than experiment, competition, and pluralism.

The third trend is accelerating decline. Nobody in Russia's political or economic elite has seriously tried to halt the downward slide that underlay the Soviet Union's defeat in the Cold War. Most of what the Soviet Union built was shoddy to start with, but modern Russia lacks the money and willpower to sustain even that unimpressive standard. . . . Against this depressing background, what chances are there for reforming anything at all? A slew of other big changes are penciled in for the coming years, they include reform of the armed forces (bloated and rickety), banking (good at money laundering), and utilities (mismanaged and corrupt). All are vital. None will be accomplished soon. One reason is sheer complexity of it all. But a more obvious one is lack of political will.

Source: Lucas, E. "A Survey of Russia—Putin's Choice," *The Economist*, July 21, 2001, p. 16.

executive to demonstrate the importance the Western firm is placing on this business. Then the locals may be willing for their chairperson or deputy chairperson to enter the negotiations at some decisive stage.

Business Tips for Russia

The following are some additional cultural clues that may advance synergistic relations:

- *Consumers* are only beginning to get accustomed to higher quality for higher prices. In addition to a plentiful and consistent supply of quality food, they seek modern conveniences and entertainment. Having been subjected to substandard clothing and outdated styles, they hunger for Western adornments that are colorful, stylish, and practical in their climate. However, business dress is conservative (e.g., suit and tie).
- *Business contacts*—Relative to foreign trade, the renamed Russian Market Institute can provide useful data and quotations. Outsiders will have to network and seek direct contacts with new factory owners and entrepreneurs. Emerging there and in the United States are consulting firms/publications to facilitate business in Eastern Europe. The Internet can be a prime source of this information.
- *Currency challenges*—Innovative ways must be developed to convert the volatile ruble and other new monetary units into international hard currency, such as by barter, exchange of services, or third country transfer.
- *Attention to details*—Because of the Soviet cultural conditioning of the past decades, visitors can expect local officials to give much attention to such matters as seating arrangements and invitations; business cards printed in both Cyrillic and one's own language or English; and the caliber of a technical presentation both in writing and orally. Continuity is an important factor, so the visiting team should designate one person as project manager or spokesman in all business dealings.
- *Communication* is facilitated when the foreigner can speak the local language, but many Russians, Ukrainians, and other republic representatives are comfortable speaking English, German, or French. The use of interpreters has both positives (clarifying meaning or building interpersonal relations) and negatives (perceptual slanting by the translator or lack of technical understanding). Orally, Russians may greet foreigners with *gospodin* (Mr.) or *gospozha* (Miss or Mrs.) and ask acquaintances for their *imya* (first name) or *ochestvo* (patronymic). Name listings are similar to those in the West, except for the use of the Russian middle name—a *patronymic* derived from the first name of one's father (e.g., the use of *Ivanovich*, meaning the son of Ivan). Women also add an "a" to their surname, as well as to

Business dress is conservative.

their patronymic middle name (e.g., *Ivanova* for daughter of Ivan). Customarily, the use of the latter, or first name, is indicative of familiarity and friendship.

■ Get to know Russian body language. For example, to the Westerner, the traditional Russian official or executive may appear stiff. Gestures are usually kept to a minimum, and expressions may seem blank and uninterested. Smiles are rare, except between people who are very close. This is the public image Russians seem to convey. In private, they are much more expressive. The modest reserve that they publicly project breaks down under more personal surroundings and socialization.

■ *Time sense* is quite different in Russia, and the locals dislike the quick tempo of Western business or the attitude that time is money. They use the slower tempo to good advantage, especially in negotiations, business, or socializing. The inhabitants quote old Russian proverbs like, "If you travel for a day, take bread for a week," or "Patience and work, and everything will work out." Part of this stoicism and slowness is due to inadequate telecommunications and transportation. Within this colossus of a country, even simple technological advances like fax machines can save much time and facilitate communication, while the computer may expedite matters, if the local has one that functions.

■ *National psyche*—Russians have long suffered from a sense of inferiority (for which they overcompensate); in the days of the aristocracy, the Czar's court turned to things French and German to show how civilized and sophisticated they were. Having been often cut off from outside contacts, the Russians also have manifested xenophobia periodically. Totalitarianism also made many citizens feel like prisoners in their own society. The younger generation is more educated, more open, and more cosmopolitan, as well as more disillusioned and cynical.

Russian leaders are generous hosts with food and beverage.

Russian leaders are generous hosts with food and beverage. Dinners are long and elaborate, and toasts are frequently and generously made to good business relationships and mutual friendships. The visiting foreign businessperson should be prepared to encounter some amiable "imbibing competition" stemming from the Russian prowess for drinking. To better comprehend this complex Slavic people, it helps to read their writers before traveling to Mother Russia.[39]

TURKEY

This bridge between Europe and Asia Minor has Bulgaria on its northeast border; Georgia and Armenia to the west; Iran and Iraq to the southeast; and Syria to the south. Offshore on its southwestern coast is located the large island of Cyprus recently admitted into the EU. Turkey is almost surrounded by water, principally the Black Sea along its northern coast and the Mediterranean Sea on its southern coast.

In its mountainous regions of Anatolia, the highest peak is Mount Ararat, supposedly where Noah's Ark is to be found. Along with alluvial coastal plains, the main rivers are Kizil Irmak, Sakarya, and Seyhan. Typically, the climate is Mediterranean or mild along the coastlines with hot dry summers and warm wet winters, except in the interior plains where the winter can be cold and the summers warm/hot with occasional thunderstorms. Exhibit 14.24 lists other demographics.

EXHIBIT 14.24

PROFILE OF TURKEY

Area	779,452 square miles
Population	70 million
Religions	Muslim, 99%
Languages	Turkish, Kurdish, Arabic, Armenian, Greek
Literacy	86%
Life expectancy	72 years
GDP per Capita	$7,900
Government	Republic

Historical Perspective Overview

Since the dawn of history, the Anatolian Peninsula has been the centerpiece for a series of empires, rebellions, and wars. Because of its strategic location, Byzantium, an independent city-state, was founded here by the Greeks in 600 B.C. Emperor Constantine relocated here to establish in A.D. 320 the Byzantine or Eastern Roman Empire, naming its capital Constantinople. Today that city is called Istanbul. In the modern Republic of Turkey, the magnificent antiquities of Byzantine, Roman, and Turkish cultures can be seen in many ancient ruins and forts, churches and mosques, palaces and museums. Devastating invasions occurred in Constantinople, first the Turks, and in 1204 the Venetian Crusaders, causing its inhabitants who were once 70% Christian to become more than 80% Muslim. Over time, the Turks converted historic churches into mosques, such as Hagia Sophia near the beautiful Blue Mosque.

The Turks, nomadic tribes from Central Asia, adopted Islam as their religion in the tenth century. By 1326, the Ottoman Empire defeated the Romans, and by 1453 it reoccupied Constantinople. Under the reigns of their sultans or caliphs, the Turks extended their empire

The Ottoman Empire defeated the Romans.

westward into Persia and Syria in the Middle East; Algeria, Tunisia, and Egypt in North Africa; as well as into Europe (Balkans, Bulgaria, Greece, Hungary, Romania) and the Crimea. The diminished empire lasted into the twentieth century when Turkey was defeated along with its ally Germany in World War I. The 1918 Armistice led to a brief occupation of Istanbul by France and Britain. After the Turkish War for Independence in 1923, the reformist military leader, Mustafa Kemal Ataturk, founded the Turkish republic as a modern, secular state with Ankara as the capital. This venerated reformist leader introduced the Roman alphabet into the Turkish language, replacing Arabic script. He also changed age-old social and political patterns, especially with regard to dressing in a more contemporary manner (e.g., no fez on men, and discouraging the head scarf on women).

Today, the country's largest cities are Istanbul (9.4 million people), Ankara (3.2 million), and Izmir (2.4 million); smaller urban centers are Adana, Konya, and Bursa. The ancient Mycenaean/Greek/Roman settlement of Ephesus is actually located today within West Turkey. During its 400-year existence, Ephesus became one of the five great cities of the Roman Empire, where the first university and medical school were founded and the Apostles John and Paul preached to early Christians.

In current global geopolitics, as in the past, Turkey occupies a strategic location. This nation controls not only the land bridge from Europe to Asia, but access to the Black Sea where many neighboring countries are dependent on their ports. The way to the Mediterranean is via the Bosporus and Dardanelles, both of which are within Turkish territory. The country is in direct proximity to Russia, Iran, and Iraq. Hence, this is why NATO offered membership to Turkey and why the United States sought military bases on its soil, air space privileges, and use of two ports. When the United States and Britain invaded Iraq in 2003, the Turkish Parliament refused to approve foreign troop deployment. The new and reform-minded prime minister, Tayyip Erdogan, as well as the generals, underestimated the opposition of the deputies, despite offers of billions of dollars in American aid in exchange for such privileges. The Parliament feared going against another Islamic state, as well as their own oppressed minority, the Kurds, who are spread over several countries, including Iraq.

Turkey has opened negotiations for membership in the EU, but despite its geographic importance, the European Commission is concerned about several issues. Objections range from Turkey's past human rights abuses with the Kurds, which make up 20% of its population, and Armenians, as well as its occupation of northern Cyprus in 1974. Within the Union, some have argued that Turkey, a Muslim nation, is not really part of Europe, and if admitted, then Russia might one day become a candidate for membership. Opponents fear that Erdogan, a devout Muslim and conservative democrat, would replace

Turkey has opened negotiations for membership in the EU.

this secular state with one governed by Islamic law. Others counter that neither geography nor religion dictates who may join the EU; it is only necessary that the country subscribe to core values of democracy and freedom. Admitting Eurasian nations is a conundrum for European leaders. The consensus is that within a decade Turkey, already a NATO member, will be welcomed within the EU because of its economic and democratic progress; in addition, it straddles both West and East, with historic landmarks in Europe (on the western side of the Bosporus). To give readers some context and comparisons, Exhibit 14.25 provides an overview of Turkey; neighbors Armenia, Azerbaijan, Cyprus, and Georgia.

EXHIBIT 14.25
PROFILE OF TURKEY, ARMENIA, AZERBAIJAN, CYPRUS, GEORGIA

NATION	ARMENIA	AZERBAIJAN	CYPRUS	GEORGIA
AREA (sq km)	29,800	86,600	9,250	69,700
POPULATION	2,982,904	7,911,974	780,133	4,677,401
CAPITAL	Yerevan	Baku	Nicosia	T'bilisi
RELIGION	Armenian Apostolic, Christian	Muslim, Russian, Orthodox, Armenian Orthodox	Greek Orthodox, Muslim	Orthodox, Christian, Armenian-Gregorian, Muslim
LANGUAGE	Armenian	Azerbaijani, Russian, Armenian	Greek, Turkish, English	Georgian, Russian, Armenian, Azeri
LITERACY	98.6%	98.8%	97.6%	99%
LIFE EXPECTANCY	71.55 years	63.35 years	77.65 years	75.88 years
GDP PER CAPITA	$5,100	$4,600	$21,600	$3,400
GOVERNMENT	Republic	Republic	Republic	Republic

Cultural Insights for Doing Business in Turkey

Turkey is a mixture of modern and medieval, of cosmopolitan and peasant, of secularism and Islamic fundamentalism. Nowhere is this mixture more evident than in beautiful Istanbul, which bridges the tectonic edge between the continents of Europe and Asia on the shimmering Bosporus. Two-thirds of its residents either live in Europe to the west of the seaway or are recent migrants from the traditional countryside. The city reflects the nation's cultural ambivalence and complexity, as rich as the aromas wafting through its spice markets.

Turkey is a mixture of modern and medieval.

Walking on its liveliest street, the contrast is evident in both youthful Turks and villagers; in women's dress, which ranges from form-fitting blouses and midthigh hemlines to *kara carsaf*, the black chadors that fully cover women. There the secular and the sacred are in juxtaposition, as can be seen in skyscrapers teeming with globetrotters who enjoy lively nightlife, while the minarets call the faithful to prayer five times a day. Businesspeople here are often multilingual—besides Turkish and English, German and French are understood. Both business cards and smoking are in abundance. Business entertaining, normally in restaurants, is facilitated by the excellent Turkish cuisine and the national drink of tea (with no milk). Turkish coffee is strong and an after-dinner drink (with or without sugar). Outside of sophisticated cities like Istanbul and Ankara, there is the "other Turkey"—those less cosmopolitan, rural, and less involved in central government. In the eastern region are millions of alienated Kurds who seek independence from the Republic. They are a source of dissension and violence.

Turks also experience a continuing tug of war or power struggle among secularists, militarists, and fundamentalists. In the past 60 years, the nation has been somewhat insulated—it was neutral in World War II, as well as more recently in the Iraq war. However, it responded to UN appeals for troops in the Korean War (1950) and in Afghanistan (2003). As a stable, multiparty democracy, the government generally has been pro-Western in policies. It also seeks to influence the Muslim ex-Soviet republics on its borders, particularly to adopt the Roman alphabet. The Turkish language, part of the Ural-Altaic group, now uses the Latin alphabet in place of the Arabic.

Time Sense and Work Environment

The pace of life is slower in Turkey.

Turks expect foreigners to be on time for appointments, but they themselves may be up to an hour late. The pace of life is slower in Turkey, and promptness is not highly regarded. June, July, and August are holidays for extended vacations. Do not expect to do much business those months, or on the seven Turkish holidays that often begin by noon the day before. Since additional Muslim holidays are computed on the 13-month lunar calendar, be prepared for those special days to fall on different dates each year. *Ramazan* is a Holy Month, observed with fasting from dawn to dusk, so nonbelievers would be considered impolite for eating, drinking, and smoking in a faster's presence; also office hours may be curtailed. During its last three days, a three-day festival occurs called *Sherker Bayram* and banks are closed. The most important secular and religious holiday is *Kurban Bayram*, four days when banks may close and resorts fill up (the feast commemorates the prophet Abraham's offer to sacrifice his son Isaac).

The regular five-day workweek is 9 A.M. to 12 noon; 2 to 5 P.M. Retail stores are open 9 A.M. to 1 P.M., 2:30 to 7 P.M. The fast-growing

Istanbul Stock Exchange functions from 10 A.M. to 12 noon. Although Sunday is the government-mandated day of rest, Friday is the Muslim holy day when business may be conducted.

Work and Social Customs

Business meetings begin with small talk (your journey, lodgings, sports, family and how you like Turkey—be positive, and avoid inquiring about wife or daughters until the local brings it up). Defer to elders since age is highly respected, and the head of the many family-owned businesses may be an elder. Since politeness is also well regarded, be discrete in conversations—avoid openly disagreeing, so the person does not lose face, and discussions about minorities (Armenians, Greeks, or Kurds) and Islamic fundamentalism.

This culture is marked by tenacity, single-mindedness, self-reliance, and constraint among its citizens. Yet, hosts are known for their hospitality with multicourse meals for which they pay, if you are the invited guest.

The country has a growing youth population and market. It is a very male-oriented society; women outside the cities are usually kept in the background or in groups, as strict sexual segregation is maintained. Exhibit 14.26 indicates some of the gender changes underway.

The country has a growing youth population and market.

Economic Prospects

Presently, about 40% of the population is engaged in agricultural work and food processing. Industrial products are now Turkey's chief exports, ranging from textiles to iron, steel and cement. This is also a land of big, family-owned firms—for example, the respected Koc Holding is listed among *Fortune* Magazine's biggest companies outside of America. It is a $10 billion conglomerate with 50,000 employees. Turkey's economy began its turnaround in the 1980s, but its mid-1990's recovery was handicapped in 2001 because of disastrous earthquakes, currency devaluation, and looming debt payments. Yet, the U.S. Department of Commerce listed Turkey as one of the world's 10 biggest emerging markets. Given its size and population, when finally admitted into the European Union this country is likely to be a major player.

CONCLUSIONS

In our opening sections, we have presented both a historical and a contemporary analysis of Europe as it enters the new millennium. The overview includes the ongoing developments within the expanding European Union, both its accomplishments and ambitions.

EXHIBIT 14.26
THE CEO IS A TURKISH WOMAN

Turkish industry is dominated by two vast family businesses, both of which have handed over their top jobs to a new generation of 40-somethings. The Europeanized Koc group passed the reins to Mustafa Koc, the eldest of the chairman's three sons. But in the other Sabanci family business, their heir designate was a niece chosen by an uncle, Sakip Sabanci, before his death. Turks were astonished by the appointment of a woman, Guler Sabanci, to the powerful CEO post in what remains a patriarchal society.

Running a sprawling conglomerate of $12 billion with interests from banking and cars to energy and food is a challenging task. Since age 8, she had been under the care and mentoring of her grandfather who encouraged her in a 27-year business career. Beginning by working in a tire factory, she went on to start her own vineyard "G" and helped found a privately owned Sabanci University, which offers free tuition to 40% of students.

In her executive role, this dynamic middle-aged lady launched many innovative strategies—a joint venture with DuPont to set up a $100 million nylon-yard producer in the port city of Izmit; another alliance with Toyota to export Corollas to the rest of Europe, thereby capturing 6.7% of the local competitive car market; possible acquisition of Telsim, the country's number two mobile phone operator. Ms. Sabanci, described by employees as tough and unpretentious, credits her late uncle for teaching her to be a free thinker, tolerant, honest and fair. Her lifestyle is also unconventional—she lives alone and wears pants, mixes with painters and pop stars and is a reformed smoker. Yet she is a conservative, sharp business woman who takes only carefully calculated risks.

Source: Excerpted from "Face Value—Breaking into a Man's World," *The Economist*, January 29, 2005.

Some key dimensions of European diversity and synergy have been examined, from languages and demographics to immigration and identity. To help global leaders be more effective on this important continent, the chapter then devoted its coverage to cultural and business practices in five separate geographic areas of Europe—the nations and peoples of the west, central, north, south, and east. Profiles were provided for most countries in these locations, while culture-specific information was shared about select countries. This sampling of the continent's complex cultural groupings and national entities may help readers avoid the trap of overgeneralized assumptions about Europeans. If more synergistic relationships are to be developed with their citizens and leaders in industry and commerce, we recommend further data gathering, especially via the Internet. Information collection is the initial step in developing a personal file of business intelligence about countries and cultures in which one wishes to perform well. Whether in Europe or elsewhere, such learning should be continually verified for validity in specific times and places, as well as with different individuals and organizations.

In this opening decade of the twenty-first century, profound economic, social, political, and cultural changes are under way throughout the whole of Europe. Peaceful trade, commerce, and travel there undergird that transformation process. But the European Union is the key mechanism for furthering free enterprise and democracy, as well as the preservation of human rights while respecting diversity among all its inhabitants.

For the next 50 years Europeans are likely to be engaged in struggles to (1) gain continental identity; (2) cope with fertility issues of lower birth rates among the traditional inhabitants and higher ones among the immigrants; (3) control the flow and acculturate these new arrivals from abroad, especially among the Muslim populations; and (4) transform their agricultural and industrial cultures into a continental knowledge culture.

The European Union is the key mechanism for furthering free enterprise and democracy.

MIND AND WORD STRETCHING

1. Why is some understanding of European history so important to comprehending the EU and related continental developments today?
2. What are the implications of changes in the balance of religious adherents within Europe (e.g., Christians, Muslims, and Jews)?
3. How is the development of a single continental market strategy in Europe going to affect the global market?
4. Why are the nations in Northern Europe concerned about the less economically developed countries in Southern Europe?
5. What are some of the specific European countries whose cultures facilitate synergistic relations with neighbors and which ones are seemingly unsynergistic (e.g., more combative, less cooperative)?
6. What impact do geography and climate in various parts of Europe have on a people's culture and economy?

REFERENCES

1. *The Economist*, January 22, 2003, p. 32.
2. "Europe," *Family Reference Atlas of the World*. Washington, DC: National Geographic Society, 2002, pp. 126–141.
3. *Guide to the European Union*. South Burlington, VT: Bloomberg Press/Economist Books, 2004 (www.bloomberg.com/economistbooks); Beech, D. *The Dynamics of European Integration: Why and When EU Institutions Matter*. London: Palgrave Macmillan, 2005.
4. Brunt, F. *San Diego Union-Tribune*, for the New York Times News Service, April 17, 2003, p. A3.
5. "Europe in Transition," *National Geographic*. Map Insert, June 2005; Simons, G. F. *EuroDiversity—A Business Guide to Managing Differences*. Burlington, MA: Elsevier/Butterworth-Heinemann, 2002.
6. Leonard, M. *Why Europe Will Run the 21st Century*. London: Fourth Estate, 2005; Richman, G. "Outgrowing the Union—A Survey of the European Union," *The Economist*, September 25, 2004 (www.economist.com/surveys); Norman, P. *The Accidental Constitution—The Story of the European Convention*. London: Palgrave Macmillan, 2005.
7. Horwirth, J. and Keeler, J. (eds.). *Defending Europe: The EU, NATO, and the Quest for European Autonomy*. London: Palgrave Macmillan, 2005; Carchedi, G. *Another Europe: A Class Analysis of European Economic Integration*. London: Verson, 2001.
8. Bloom, H., Calori, R., and de Woot, P. *EUROManagement*. London: Kogan Page, 1994.
9. Kagan, R. *Of Paradise and Power: America versus Europe in the New World Order*. New York: Knopf, 2003; Storti, C. *Old World/New World-Bridging Cultural Differences: Britain, France, Germany and the U.S.* Boston: Nicholas Brealey/Intercultural Press, 2003; Roger, P. *The American Enemy: The History of French Anti-Americanism*. Chicago: University of Chicago Press, 2005; Chesnoff, R. Z. *The Arrogance of the French—Why They Can't Stand Us and Why the Feeling Is Mutual*. New York: Sentinel Press, 2005; Peddler, S. "The Art of the Impossible—A Survey of France," *The Economist*, October 28th, 2006, 16 pp. insert (www.economist.com/surveys_(http://www.economist.com/surveys)).
10. Brittan, S. "Europe Is Not So Backward After All," *Financial Times*, July 30, 2004.
11. Klausen, J. *The Islamic Challenge: Politics and Religion in Western Europe*. Oxford: Oxford University Press, 2005; Burleigh, M. *Earthly Power—The Clash of Religion and Politics in Europe from the French Revolution to the Great War*. New York: HarperCollins, 2006.
12. Colley, L. *Britons: Forging a Nation, 1707–1837*. London: London School of Economics, 1992; Ferguson, N. *Empire, the Rise and Demise of the British World Order and Its Lessons for Global Power*. New York: Basic Books, 2002; Protherough, R. and Pick, J. *Managing Britannia*. Northumberland, UK: Edgeway Books, Corbridge, 2002.
13. Morrison, T., Conway, W. A., and Douress, J. J. *Dun & Bradstreet Guide to Doing Business Around the World*. Upper Saddle River, NJ: Prentice-

Hall, 1997; Morrison, T., Conway, W. A., and Bordern, G. A. *Kiss, Bow, or Shake Hands—How to Do Business in Sixty Countries*. Holbrook, MA: Adams Media Corporation, 1994; Johnson, M. and Moran, R. T. *Cultural Guide to Doing Business in Europe*. Oxford: Butterworth-Heinemann, 1992.

14. "A Survey of Ireland," *The Economist* (www.economist.com/surveys); Morrison, T., Conway, W., and Douress, J. J. "Ireland," *Dun & Bradstreet Guide to Doing Business Around the World*. Upper Saddle River, NJ: Prentice Hall, 1997, pp. 197–208.

15. Carroll, R. *Cultural Misunderstandings: The French-American Experience*. Chicago: University of Chicago Press, 1987; Asselin, G. and Mastron, R. *Au Contraire! Figuring Out the French*. Yarmouth, ME: Intercultural Press, 2001.

16. D'Iribane, P. *La Logique de l'Honneur*. Paris: Editions de Seuil, 1989.

17. Mesbache, A. "American and French Managers' Self-Perceived Abilities for Effective Functioning in Another Culture: A Comparative Study," unpublished doctoral dissertation. San Diego, CA: United States (Alliant) International University, 1986. Available through University Microfilms International.

18. "A Survey of Germany," *The Economist*, November 19, 1996.

19. "An Uncertain Giant," *The Economist*, December 7, 2002, p. 20.

20. Morrison, Conway, and Douress, J. J. *Dun & Bradstreet Guide to Doing Business Around the World*; Morrison, Conway, and Bordern, *Kiss, Bow, or Shake Hands—How to Do Business in Sixty Countries*; Johnson, M. and Moran, R. T. *Cultural Guide to Doing Business in Europe*. Oxford: Butterworth-Heinemann, 1992.

21. Cottrell, R. "Meet the Neighbours—A Survey of the EU's Eastern Borders," *The Economist*, June 25, 2005 (www.economist.com/surveys); Sears, W. H. and Tamulionyte-Letz. *Succeeding in Business in Central and Eastern Europe—Guide to Culture, Markets, and Practices*. Burlington, MA: Butterworth-Heinemann/Elsevier, 2001.

22. Cagner, E. (ed.). *The Vikings*. Gothenberg, Sweden: Tre Tryckare, Cagner & Co., 1966; Robinowitz, C. J. and Carr, L. W. *Modern Day Vikings—A Practical Guide to Interacting with the Swedes*. Yarmouth, ME: Intercultural Press, 2001.

23. The authors are grateful to Mary Ellen Toffle, MIM, a graduate of the American Graduate School of International Management who originally contributed this section and is presently living in Genoa, Italy.

24. Rocca, F. "The Fading Future of Italy's Youth," *Time Magazine*, April 10, 2006.

25. Diamanti, I. "Chi Siamo," *La Repubblica*, November 29, 2001.

26. Rocca, F. "The Fading Future of Italy's Youth," *Time Magazine*, April 10, 2006.

27. Compagno, G. *Le Guide Xenofobe*. Torino: Edizione Sonda, 2001.

28. Personal interview by Mary Ellen Toffle of Dr. Luigi Giannitrapani, Management Consultant, Genova, Italy, 2003.

29. Gannon, M. *Understanding Global Cultures: Metaphorical Journeys Through 23 Nations*. Thousand Oaks, CA: Sage Publishing, 2001.

30. Compagno, *Le Guide Xenofobe*.

31. Personal interview by Mary Ellen Toffle of Marina Zacco, Managing Director, Associazione Italo-Britannica, 2003.

32. Personal interview by Mary Ellen Toffle of Dr. Annalisa Bardi, Director of Operations and People, Royal and Sun Alliance Insurance Company, 2003.

33. Cottrell, "Meet the Neighbours—A Survey of the EU's Eastern Borders"; Sears, W. H. and Tamulionyte-Letz. *Succeeding in Business in Central and Eastern Europe—Guide to Culture, Markets, and Practices.* Burlington, MA: Butterworth-Heinemann/Elsevier, 2001.

34. Figes, O. *Natasha's Dance: A Cultural History of Russia.* London: Allen Lane/Penguin, 2002; Appelebaum, A. *Gulag: A History.* London: Allen Lane/Penguin, 2003; Kotkin, S. *Armageddon Averted: The Soviet Collapse 1970–2000.* Oxford: Oxford University Press, 2001; McDaniel, T. *The Agony of the Russian Idea.* Princeton, NJ: Princeton University Press, 1997; Aslund, A. *Building Capitalism: The Transformation of the Former Soviet East Bloc.* Cambridge: Cambridge University Press, 2001; Hosking, G. *Russia: People and Empire 1552–1917.* London: HarperCollins, 1997.

35. Holden, N., Cooper, G., and Carr, J. *Dealing with the New Russia—Management Cultures in Collision.* Chichester, UK: John Wiley & Sons, 1998; Granvile, E. and Oppenheimer, P. (eds.). *Russia's Post-Communist Economy.* Oxford: Oxford University Press, 2001.

36. Sears, W. H. and Tamulionyte-Letz. *Succeeding in Business in Central and Eastern Europe.*

37. Soros, G. *Underwriting Democracy.* New York: Free Press, 1991.

38. Holden, Cooper, and Carr. *Dealing with the New Russia.* Granvile and Oppenheimer, *Russia's Post-Communist Economy.*

39. Tolstaya, T. *Pushkin's Children—Writings on Russia and Russians.* New York: Houghton-Mifflin, 2002.

USEFUL INTERNET WEB SITES

www.economist.com/daily/columns/europeview.....www.economist.com/surveys/Britain

15

DOING BUSINESS WITH AFRICANS

North Africa, East Africa, West Central Africa, and Southern Africa

Africa is often called the continent of beginnings. Fossil and bone records there of the earliest humans go back more than 4 million years. Our early upright ancestor, Homo Erectus departed Africa on the long journey that eventually peopled the Earth. It now seems likely that every person today comes from a lineage that goes back to an ancient African. Innumerable cave paintings and petroglyphs, from Sahara to South Africa, provide clues to the beliefs and way of life of these age-old hominids.[1]

LEARNING OBJECTIVES

Our objectives are to appreciate Africa as the cradle of human civilization, not just as a continent of economically developing countries. After a Pan African overview, this chapter will analyze the many political entities of twenty-first-century Africa in terms of its four major regions, North, East, West Central, and Southern Africa. In examining the nations and peoples on this diverse continent, culture specifics will be provided not only to facilitate communications and business with Africans, but also to better understand these remarkable inhabitants, as well as their art, music, and potential.

Continental African Overview

Two hundred million years ago, this landmass split off from the ancient supercontinent of Pangaea. Africa is the cradle of all

Pan Africa

humanity, for we all trace our DNA heritage to this area. Homo sapiens first appeared in Africa some 200,000 years ago, probably in what is today known as Omo Kibish, Ethiopia, where our ancestors' earliest fossils were found. Genetic data indicates that there were two human migrations out of this continent. The first group went no further than what is now Israel, dying out some 90,000 years ago. Descendants of modern humans left Africa some 70,000–50,000 years past. By 50,000 years ago, following a coastal route along southern Asia, they reached what is now Australia; they were a people known today as Aborigines. Some 40,000–30,000 years ago, human inland migration was apparently via Asia and seeded the continent known as Europe. At about the same time, these humans pushed into Central Asia, arriving on the grassy steppes north of the Himalaya. They also traveled through Southeast Asia and China, eventually reaching Japan and Siberia. Genetic clues lead us to believe that humans in northern Asia eventually migrated to the Americas. Between 20,000 and 15,000 years ago when sea levels were low and lands connected Siberia to Alaska, the new arrivals trekked southward down the west coast. The DNA marker M 168 among today's non-Africans proves we all trace our origins to the *mother of the human family*—Africa. Our diverse faces and races come from these first hunter-gatherers.[2]

Africa has largely remained a mystery to the outside world, marked perhaps more by its isolation than by any other feature. This stubborn reality can be traced to the earliest times and is reflected in the hopelessly misrepresented images of ancient cartographers, whose graphic distortions were as errant as the half myths and false science that passed for knowledge about the continent. Ancient civilizations flourished in Africa from Carthage in the north to "empires" in the south.[3] Among these indigenous kingdoms was Great Zimbabwe, which flourished in the eleventh to fifteenth centuries; in the Niger area, the grand states of Yoruba, Ashanti, Hausa prospered, but only Benin survived the longest from the thirteenth to nineteenth centuries. From A.D. 900 onward, the coastal plains contained the Swahili culture and language that dominated from Somalia to Zanzibar, including a mix of local peoples, Arabs, and immigrants. From the sixteenth to nineteenth centuries, the search for riches and a route to India brought European explorers and occupiers, beginning with the Portuguese and extending to the British, French, Belgians, and Germans. Unfortunately, few Europeans appreciated the civilizations and cultures already functioning there, imposing their own ways on the indigenous inhabitants. Although Africans dispersed by natural migration, they were *forcefully* introduced into the Americas, Europe, and the Middle East as a result of the inhumane slave trade.

Africa makes up 20% of this planet's landmass—11,700,000 square miles, lying south of Europe and the Mediterranean Sea, extending a great distance south, bounded on the east by the Red Sea and Indian

We all trace our origins to the mother of the human family—Africa.

Ocean, and on the west by the Atlantic Ocean. Surrounding the continent are 10 island groups: in the northwest, the Madeira, Canary, and Cape Verde Islands; in the west central area, the islands of Book and San Tomé/Principe; in the southeast, the Seychelles, Comoros, Mauritius, Rodgriques, Reunion; and in their midst the largest island of all—Madagascar, just off the Mozambique Channel.

Geographically, this second largest continent is split by the equator, contained between 38 degrees north and south latitudes. Lacking long mountain ranges to wring moisture from passing air masses, Africa has rain patterns that show extreme contrasts. The equatorial rain forest is deluged during two rainy seasons, whereas a single wet season north, south, and east proves quite insufficient. Relief from tropical heat may be obtained in higher altitudes of eastern and southern plateaus, whereas parts of the west coast have currents that transport seawater from cooler regions. For convenient analysis, this huge continent is usually divided into four parts: East, West, North, and Southern Africa. Africa stretches 5000 miles from north to south and 4600 miles from east to west.

Among its dramatic geographic features are the volcanic peaks of Mount Kilimanjaro, in Tanzania, and the East African Rift Valley, which divides the region. Three great rivers, the Niger, Congo, and Zambezi flow through this relatively arid landmass. Beyond its political map, Africa biologically represents 121 distinct areas of communities and plants. Though rich in its diversity of flora and fauna, many African species are threatened by overgrazing, habitat destruction, and extinction, so wildlife preservation in Africa is of global concern.[4] Both large and small mammals are in jeopardy because of the commercial bush-meat trade.

Most of Africa is made up of savanna-high, rolling grassy plains, which, since early times, have been home to the Bantu people as well as the BaMbuti (Pygmies), San (Bushmen), and Nilo-Saharans and Hamito-Semitices (Berbers and Cushgites). Each of these peoples and their tribes have distinctive clothing, music, and art. Two-thirds of the continent's 800 million inhabitants live in the countryside, near coastal regions, lakes, and rivers. Exhibit 15.1 provides an overall profile of Africa in the opening decade of the twenty-first century.

Historical Perspective on Modern Pan Africa

Fifty-three countries share the African continent. National identities are diverse for peoples assembled within borders imposed by departed European imperialists. The outsiders' partitioning of Africa in the past two centuries made little attempt to make national borders coincide with on-site ethnic groups and tribes. Boundaries on this continent are

Fifty-three countries share the African continent.

EXHIBIT 15.1

PAN AFRICAN PROFILE

Population	900 million approximately, 14% of world total; 71% of this population is under age 25.
Urban Growth	Average annual rate of urban growth is 3.5%; Nigeria is the most populous nation with 131 million, and its city of Lagos is the most populous in the whole of Africa at some 16.9 million people.
Life Expectancy	In sub-Saharan Africa, the average is 46 years with infant mortality rate of 102 of 1000 babies born and living until one year old; while in North Africa, it is 67 years with an infant mortality rate of 33 out of 1000 born. Most common cause of deaths throughout the continent is AIDS.
Languages	Over 2000.
Literacy	60% for 16 years or older; most literate is Seychelles with 92%, and least literate is Burkina Faso with 12.8%.
Religions	Muslims = 358 million; Christians = 410 million; remainder animist or indigenous beliefs.
Refugees	15 million, 3.3 million fled their native countries because of violence and conflict; some 12 million are internally displaced.

Source: C. E. Cobb, "Africa in Fact—A Continent's Numbers Tell Its Story," *National Geographic*, September 2005.

being reconfigured as new states emerge. Recently, Eritrea broke away from Ethiopia, and the independent homelands of Swaziland and Lesotho may soon be reabsorbed into South Africa. National names also change rapidly as when Rhodesia became Zimbabwe and Tanganyika became Tanzania.

Africa is home to one-third of the world's sovereign states, but only 19 of them have democratic governments. The World Bank—International Monetary Fund classifies 38 nations worldwide as heavily indebted, poor nations—and 32 of these are on this continent. Most of these countries came into existence in the twentieth century, and currently about half of the governments were formed as the result of coups, principally by the military. The redrawing of colonial boundaries need not mean smaller African states; it could simply mean more rational

Africa is home to one-third of the world's sovereign states.

and viable political communities. The long-term scenario emerging from the crises may be the gradual redrawing of boundaries between Zaire, Rwanda, and Burundi. Unless the Hutu and Tutsi are partitioned into separate countries or federated into a larger, stable, and democratic political community, they are likely to engage in continuous conflict. One scenario calls for the international community to put together a large package of inducements and incentives to persuade Rwanda, Burundi, and Tanzania to create the United States of Central Africa; parts of Zaire could one day seek admission into the new federation. Currently, the Organization of African Unity acts as a coordinating medium for the continental countries, trying to encourage regional cooperation, trading, and political stability. Sovereign states with their bureaucratic controls are the hallmark of mass civilization. But such historical experience was largely absent in sub-Saharan kingdoms before the arrival of European colonialism during the past three centuries. Given this lack of the tradition of strong statehood on the continent, where tribal governance dominated, it is understandable why contemporary Africans struggle with the refinement and administration of government and political institutions.

Although Africans had learned to smelt iron by A.D. 1500, most African missed the industrial stage of development. They were mainly hunter-gatherers, farmers, and herders; only a small minority lived in organized states and urban areas. After a few hundred years of predatory slave-raiding and direct European influence or rule, most Africans only regained their independence and freedom in the past several decades. Thus, a dynamic process is under way throughout Africa to develop modern mass societies with the accompanying political, economic, and technological systems. One needs an *afrocentric* approach to appreciate fully this heritage and experience.[5]

INSIGHTS INTO PAN AFRICA

Africa, a land of great promise and potential, is a continent of immense natural beauty and resources, most of which is still undeveloped. It is a region of contrasts between the primitive and the ultramodern, a place where new industries, technologies, and cities emerge gradually. Yet, in this postcolonial period, it is the misfortune of Africa, which birthed civilization, to remain mired in human suffering and carnage. Although this collective of countries is somewhat disconnected from the world by its unmatched sorrows, its rich mixtures of people have a distinctly African sense of brotherhood and humor.

For global leaders to be effective in their trade and development efforts within Africa, they must be realistic in their analysis of its peoples and possibilities. First, there is great diversity to be found in terms of stages of human and institutional development, manifested in the multitude of tribes, languages, customs, religions, education, and governments. Second, most of the people are generous and traditional, eager to learn, and hardworking. But in the past 40 years, their natural buoyancy and flexibility have been dampened by widespread famine, epidemics, exploitation, and social unrest. The world media often distort our image of Africa by its emphasis on African tragedies—the horror of the mass poverty, the AIDS epidemic, the extensive droughts, the many civil wars, and the millions of refugees. Often overlooked in these reports are the success stories—World Bank and UNESCO projects that work at the local levels, the green revolution that expands agricultural production, the many business enterprises that flourish, the African foreign students who return to apply their Western education, and the shift from failed socialism to democratic and market-oriented policies.

Africa entered this new millennium in a state of intense transition. The changes under way can also be summed up in three words: *tribalism*, *chaos*, and *developing*.

Tribalism

The tribe is the basic sociological unit of Africa that provides one's sense of identity, belonging, and responsibility. When tribal members leave rural areas to go to the city for a job or to study, traditionally their enhanced stature brings with it responsibility for assisting their tribal brothers and sisters at home. Such social pressure on successful Africans may impose a burden to augment income by any means, legal or otherwise. Tribal bonds also lead to intergroup conflict, destruction, and corruption. As the force of tribalism deteriorates in modern, urban environments, Africans search for other substitutes, new institutional loyalties such as membership in a religion, cooperatives, and political parties, often formed along ethnic lines.

For many, tribalism is the bane of independent Africa, with its many tribes and clans involving 2000 language groups—Swahili, Zulu, and Hausa being the most prominent. Leftover from the colonialists are areas where French, English, Portuguese, and a corruption of Dutch are widely spoken. National leaders seek to transform intertribal hostility into collaborative community endeavors. Tribalism is evident in elections when the voting favors the largest tribes, while the winners are only slowly learning that power should be shared with the minority losers. It also is behind failed attempts at ethnic cleansing, authoritarian regimes, and political corruption. The challenge for many Africans is to build upon tribal heritage, while moving beyond narrow tribal loyalties and constraints for the greater common good of the nation and its economic development.

Africa entered this new millennium in a state of intense transition.

Chaos

As Africans seek to move beyond their colonial dependency, while rapidly creating appropriate cultural institutions and opportunities, tumult abounds. The destabilization process is compounded by a combination of factors. Sometimes it is caused by nature, when lack of rain triggers mass famine or monkeys infect entire East African populations through the plague of Acquired Immune Deficiency Syndrome—the AIDS virus that has already killed 18 million on the continent and continues to kill several thousand more each day. Africa is also devastated by many other diseases such as malaria and cholera, often caused by inadequate water systems. In June 2003, a group of African presidents appealed for greater help from the rich G8 nations meeting in Evian, France. Foreign governments have spent billions to fight disease in Africa, mainly through the Global Fund, an organization supporting 150 programs to fight AIDS, tuberculosis, and malaria. But other nations have to match that commitment, which the G8 leaders promised to do. But in some African states, such as in South Africa, the governments have been unable to use the external resources effectively. Other countries on the continent lack a well-organized and functioning health-care system. Many immature political entities do not use donor funds effectively because of a lack of medical personnel and inadequate road and communications infrastructure.

Sometimes the disarray and obstacles to African development come from:

- The rise of extremist Muslim militants and terrorists as in North Africa and Sudan. More recently external terrorists have struck elsewhere, as in Kenya.
- Tribal conflicts in this past decade that escalated into civil wars, as in Rwanda when the Hutu army oversaw the murder of a million Tutsi; in Somalia where tribal warfare led to the collapse of the government and anarchy; and in the Congo where genocide prevailed and 3.5 million died. Distorted ambitions and ideologies of local dictators and guerrillas to crush their opposition in other tribes have led to new tyrannies that occurred recently in Uganda, Nigeria, Liberia, Angola, and elsewhere.
- African infighting and destruction, which are sometimes attributed to religion, as when brown-skinned Muslim Arabs from the north of Somalia raid and destroy dark-skinned Christians in the south of a country with hopeless governance.
- Incompetent strongmen, who take political power through coups or rigged elections and use their positions as head of state to benefit only themselves and their cronies. This lack of authentic leadership has helped undermine national economies and exploitation of the citizenry. Hence, the rule of the "big man" replaces the rule of law,

while the average person suffers. The deterioration of Rhodesia when it became Zimbabwe under its dictator, Robert Mugabe, Zaire when ruled by Mobutu Sese Seko, or Uganda under its despot, Idi Amin, are cases in point.

■ Failure of the current states in terms of borders, governance, and infrastructure. Before the nineteenth century, Africa had been divided into thousands of kingdoms and chiefdoms whose systems of government developed over hundreds of years. For administrative purposes, European colonialists created a few dozen nation states whose borders often divided tribal lands. On all this was grafted European governance models, such as parliamentary democracy, that were alien to Africans, lacking in educated leadership to make it all work. The new regimes proved unstable and dysfunctional, with elected governments giving way to authoritarianism, military takeovers, and assignations. The result undermined the growth of any democratic free-enterprise system, while incumbents became rich and powerful with their private militias and suppressed media, unless they were killed, jailed, or driven into exile.[6]

Often such internal troubles get exacerbated by outside intervention, as when, in past centuries, Europeans imposed their controls on the locals, so that today the influence of European cultures and dependency still may be found in former African colonies of Britain, France, Germany, and Portugal. In the twentieth century, Western powers twice involved Africans in their world wars, as well as in the Cold War between the United States and the former USSR. Or, again, when the United Nations sends relief efforts, but with inadequate peacekeeping troops to such places as the Sudan, Liberia, Rwanda, and Somalia.

The combination of such forces worsens situations because of overpopulation, the need for food because of disruption in farming and fishing, systemic corruption, and widespread unemployment. Mass poverty engenders desperation, which may feed political extremity. All of these factors contribute to the displacement of millions of Africans from their homelands. Many end up as refugees amid poverty on a gigantic scale. One effect of this chaos is the threat it poses to the ecological environment of the continent. Deserts are widening; broad savannas and their communities struggle to survive. Sometimes the confusion is simply *future shock* as tribal cultures and rural peoples try to cope with the demands of an urban, postindustrial way of life. Finally, too many postcolonial nation-states and their political leaders in Africa are failing to liberate, protect, and service their own citizens as well as their country's resources.

But the situation is not all bad: Africans are survivors with remarkable resilience and "make do" capacities. Entrepreneurs abound, humanitarian efforts progress, and some countries are justly and successfully ruled by elected leaders. Peacekeepers and peace enforcers do

Africans are survivors with remarkable resilience and "make do" capacities.

produce some positive results as in Côte d'Ivoire and Congo, and the African Union is training five regional brigades. Outside financial aid from the United Nations, European Union, and other major nations, as well as from nongovernmental organizations (NGOs), are alleviating some of the problems that plague Africa.

Developing

Africa has been classified as the Third World in economic terms—it contributes only 1% of the global economic output. This poor continent often is viewed as a land of tragedy or a land of promise, rich in both natural and human resources still to be developed. The African nations are being crippled by debt to foreign interests. The cause of the current woes goes well into the past with European colonialism and inadequate education of African people. Because of this historical influence, once the majority of Africa gained independence after the 1960s, many of its "leaders" were ill-prepared to lead their countries. They turned toward statism and socialism, favoring state intervention in the economy with bureaucratic controls that stifled initiative, killed incentive, and created chronic, artificial shortages. The situation represents a rejection of the continent's heritage of consensual and participatory democracy, which should embrace *free* markets, trade, and enterprise.[7]

Africa's full potential may be realized in the twenty-second century, if Africans are empowered to build an infrastructure based on their own uniqueness and cultures. Development increases opportunity for people. But to actualize these prospects, Africans will have to learn how to (1) practice synergy among themselves; (2) control their populations; (3) advance their literacy, education, and productivity; (4) build infrastructure, especially roads and transportation; (5) promote conservation and ecotourism; and (6) connect with the information age and its technologies. Consider just one reality to be rectified—less than 10% of the continent's land is formally owned, and only one in ten Africans lives in a house with formal deeds or titles. But Africa's biggest need is for effective, indigenous leadership at all levels of their society. Yet no institution is effectively addressing this need.

There have been promising developments toward progress in Africa, as the next four reports indicate:

■ **Continental Synergy:** In the 1980s, 16 countries joined together to form the Economic Community of West African States, while in the 1990s, 9 more countries launched the Southern African Coordination Conference. In a sense the current African Union (AU) is a case study illustrating in its short history the challenge and the promise of the future since it evolved from prior attempts at unified action. First, there was the Organization of African States founded in 1963, and then later the Organization of African Unity was formed in

1964. Such institutions have been both a disappointment and a modest success—too often their officials have used their positions for demagoguery, posturing, and travel junkets. Yet these unifying efforts, through their economic and technical projects, also have improved the continent's communication and banking systems and the maintenance of interstate peace.[8] The hope is that the renewed African Union, with UN assistance, will become the forum and mechanism for continental recovery and renewal. Today, booming economies in Uganda, Mauritania, Ghana, and Mozambique demonstrate that African countries can thrive, given some measure of peace, stability, and governance. In the year 2000, total foreign investments in Africa were about $6 billion, only 3% of the $235 billion that flowed into Third World economies.

■ *Rebuiling Failed States:* The World Bank lists about 30 "low income countries under stress," while the UK's Department of International Development worries about 46 "fragile states." Many of these today are in Africa, such as Angola, Central African Republic, both Congos, Nigeria, Somalia, Sudan, and Zimbabwe. But some are recovering. After a civil war, Liberia is coming back from misrule, violence, and famine. Its gangsterish president, Charles Taylor, along with other African warlords, are being tried by the International Criminal Court in The Hague, while the Liberian electorate chooses their first female head of state. A large UN peacekeeping force is keeping the nation calm and safe while reconstruction goes forward with external humanitarian aid. Another failed state, Sierra Leone, again with UN help, is holding accountable those war criminals who despoiled it. Ultimately, restoring peace and a measure of prosperity is the responsibility of local citizens.[9]

■ *Private Sector Initiatives:* If foreign aid, debt forgiveness, and trade reform is to help this continent, then a 2005 World Bank Annual, *Doing Business in Africa*, suggests that the private sector must provide leadership. Public sector bureaucracy, ineptness, regulatory obstacles, and red tape contribute to undermining the business climate there. Investors, whether corporate or foundations, realize that if entrepreneurs are to flourish, programs must be undertaken to improve infrastructure, train skilled workers, provide capital support, and curb disease. Yet this report points to 14 sub-Saharan countries where healthy economic growth is under way, because their GNP has increased at least 5% a year since 1990. Botswana and South Africa are at the top when it comes to "best business environment." So a group of multinational companies have formed "Business Action of Africa," to improve business conditions on that continent. In addition, 24 countries outside the region have signed on to a "New Partnership for Africa's Development," aimed at bringing together both the African public and private sectors to improve investment conditions on the continent. Yet, the UN Economic

The private sector must provide leadership.

Commission on Africa calculates that already the foreign direct investment in Africa has on the average a four times better return than in G7 countries and twice as much as in Asia.[10]

■ *African Optimism:* They may not be the richest, but Africans remain the world's staunchest optimists. An annual world survey by Gallup International found that 60% of the African respondents think the present year will be better than the last—twice as much as reported in Europe. Despite 2 million Africans killed by AIDS in 2005, these people are upbeat and hopeful. One reason may be that nine out of ten Africans are religious and know how to transform suffering into recovery.[11]

For foreigners to be more effective in their business and professional relationships with Africans, it is helpful to have some insights into the diverse cultures of this continent. In an earlier chapter we described the Islamic culture, which also dominates North Africa and the Muslim states elsewhere in this area. Within black Africa, there are some common cultural characteristics. The next section will review five dimensions of those African cultures—family, trust/friendship, time, corruption, and respect for elders. This selected analysis may increase awareness and improve interaction not only with Africans, but with the millions of descendants from this heritage who are found throughout North, Central, and South America, as well as in the Caribbean, the United Kingdom, and the Middle East. Be cautious with African generalizations because African cultures are not only diverse, but dynamic, changing to ensure survival as well as to adapt to new times and circumstances.

Be cautious with African generalizations.

Exhibit 15.2 illustrates how quickly the situation can change in Africa, especially when private enterprise is allowed to work.

CULTURAL CHARACTERISTICS OF AFRICANS

Be cautious about cultural generalization. There is no *one culture* on this continent. The northern African states of Mauritania, Morocco, Algeria, Libya, and part of Sudan are closer to the Middle Eastern cultures. Recall that since 300 B.C., the mighty Carthage once prospered and challenged the Roman Empire. Since the first pharaoh united Egypt in 3000 B.C, it has had a distinctive culture from its continental neighbors to the south. Again the ancient kingdom of Ethiopia is also culturally unique, especially among the religions practiced there. The descriptions that follow best apply to sub-Sahara, home of black Africans, like the peoples of Mali, Senegal, Ghana, Congo, Benin, Tanzania, and South Africa. Yet their music and musical instruments

EXHIBIT 15.2

IMPACT OF TELECOMMUNICATIONS IN AFRICA

First radio, then television, and now mobile telephones are trans-forming African communications and business. The wireless age is overcoming the obstacles on this huge continent caused by poor roads, unreliable energy, political instability, and corruption that pre-vented the wiring of landline telephones. The new technologies bypass all this, giving regions and peoples access to phones they never had before. But Africans use this new communication tool for more than mere talking—shepherds in drought-ridden Sahel are using handheld GPS units and cell phones to alert others to good grazing; in Nairobi, customers avoid long lines at their bank by mon-itoring their accounts by text messaging; in Ethiopia, teachers are being trained to use solar-powered satellite radios to receive lessons broadcast to their classes; in South Africa, wives at home use mobile phones to talk in the evening with their husbands who work hun-dreds of miles away; health-care workers use the phones to summon ambulances; fisher women who can't read tell their customers to call their cell numbers to order fish; retailers in the slums can take deliv-ery orders from affluent surbanites. On a continent where some remote villages communicate by beating drums, cell phones are a technological revolution. Cell operators can't put up phone towers fast enough. This phenomenon is causing a sociological and eco-nomic godsend for Africans at large.

Today Africa is the world's fastest growing cell phone market. By 2004, there were 76.8 million mobile subscribers. Others simply buy cell phone time to make each call—buying wireless phone time is like using the grocery list. Used handsets are sold for $50 or less. All this from a people who typically live on $2 or less a day. Domestic cell companies, like MTB and Conteh are not only building telecommu-nications networks, but providing much needed job and national income. International firms, like Vodacom, have 1.1 million sub-scribers in the Congo, adding 1000 new customers daily, and logging 10,000 calls a day. Bicycle-driven and battery chargers are being used in rural areas to provide sufficient electricity to charge the phones. It's all been a boon not only to business throughout Africa, but to families who want to connect with one another.

Source: "Africa—Whatever You Thought, Think Again," *Natural Geographic*, Special Issue, Washington, DC, September 2005; "Cell Phone Frenzy in Africa, World's To-growth Market," *San Diego Union-Tribune*, pp. A1/12.

Mobile telephones are transforming African communications and business.

reflect the diversity of their culture. The African diaspora also brought to the West the popular music that is known today as blues, jazz, R & B, rumba, reggae, and even hip-hop.[12]

Family and Kinship

The basic unit of African society is the family, which includes the nuclear family and the extended family or tribe. In traditional African society, the tribe is the ultimate community. No unit has more importance in society. There may be some loose confederations, but they are temporary and limited in scope. In political terms, the tribe is the equivalent of a nation. It does not have fixed boundaries, but on its sanction rests the law (customary law like the English Common Law). All wars were fought on the tribe's behalf, and the division between "them" and "us" lay in tribal boundaries.

Africans center their communities around villages for food gathering and cultivation. The village elders become judges, mediators, trade masters, and leaders within both religious and tribal life. In some ways, the tribe is more than a nation. In Europe and America, ethical and moral standards are not given by national sanctions but rest on religious and cultural traditions common to the whole continent. But in traditional Africa, except for areas under Islamic control, the family tribe provides the guidelines for accepted behavior. The tribe bears a moral connotation and provides an emotional security. It is also a source of social and moral sanctions as well as political and physical security. The tribe provides its members with rules governing responsibilities, explanations of the responsibilities, and guidelines for organizing the society, and hence, the culture.

The tribe is broken down into different kinship lines. The concept of kinship is important to understanding African societies. It constitutes the primary basis for an individual's rights, duties, rules of residence, marriage, inheritance, and succession. Kinship refers to blood relationships between individuals and is used to describe relationships in both a narrow and a broad sense. Parents and their children are a special kind of kin group. The social significance of kinship covers a wide social field in most African societies. In Western culture, its significance usually does not extend beyond the nuclear family, but in the African culture, it embraces a network of people including those that left the village for urban areas.

The family—father, mother, children—is the ultimate basis of the tribe. But the tribal and family unit organization is being disrupted by changes in the economic organizational structure. The economic organization has tied reward to individual effort and developed road, rail, water, and air communication networks that have increased the range and speed of contact—thereby increasing the rate of intercultural contact and change. The reorganization has also brought tribes together as territorial units, with greater opportunities for migration from one area to another but with a corresponding weakening of family bonds and behavior control.

As this newfound mobility moves more people to the large urban areas, they try to maintain some family ties. This involves a responsibility to support family members still in the villages. It also affects Africans' business relationships with managers from abroad in terms of hiring practices and the need for extra income to support those at home. Earnings from business transactions are often used for this purpose.

Trust and Friendship

Trust and confidence are essential elements needed for successful enterprise in Africa. It is very important to get to know coworkers as individuals before getting down to actual business activities. For Africans, after family, friendship comes next in importance. Often, a friendship continues after specific business activities end. Socializing outside of the office is common. It is under those relaxed conditions that managers talk politics, sports, and sometimes business.

In Africa, interpersonal relationships are based on sincerity. African societies are normally warm and friendly. People generally assume that everyone is a friend until proven otherwise. When Africans smile, it means they like you. When smiles are not seen, it is a clear sign of distrust. Once a person is accepted as a friend, that person is automatically an "adopted" member of the family. A friend can pop into a friend's place anytime. In African societies, formal invitations and appointment making are not common.

One of the most important factors to remember when doing business in Africa is the concept of friendship before business. Normally before a meeting begins, there is general talk about events that have little or nothing to do with the business at hand. This can go on for some time. If the meeting involves people coming together who have never met, but who are trying to strike a deal (an African and a foreigner), the African will try to reach out for friendship first. If on doing so the African receives a cold response, he may become suspicious and lose interest in the deal.

In the traditional village culture, Africans share good fortune and food with other members of the community. This is an example of the wonderful values that modernization may unfortunately change. Society's predators, in the form of rebels and terrorists, greedy politicians, and abusive militias undermine this cultural quality.

Time and Time Consciousness

The way an individual views the concept of time has a major impact on any business relationship. If two businesspeople enter into a situation with complementary goals, abilities, and needs, a successful arrangement can be thwarted if each has different ideas about time. In Africa, time is viewed as flexible, not rigid or segmented. People come first, then time. Anyone in a hurry is viewed with suspicion and distrust. Because trust is very important, individuals who follow inflexible time schedules will have little success. The African wants to sit and talk—to get to know the person before discussing business. Normally, time is not seen as a limited commodity. What cannot be done today can always be accomplished tomorrow. Meetings are not held promptly, and people may arrive several hours late. Often foreigners misinterpret this as laziness, untrustworthiness, lack of seriousness in doing business, or even lack of interest in the venture. However, lateness in meetings should be perceived as part of African life. It is understood among friends that even though everybody agrees to meet at a given time, they will not actually gather until much later.

However, when Africans are dealing with foreigners, they normally try to be on time out of respect for the non-Africans' concept of time. But in the larger cities of Africa, the concept of time is changing. Punctuality is becoming more important. Contact with Western businesspersons has brought an increasing awareness and acceptance of the segmentation of time and its consequent inflexibility. But away from the capital city, time is still viewed in a relaxed and easygoing manner.

Corruption

Corruption in Africa sometimes is related to its poverty and often results from tribal responsibilities that individuals carry with them when leaving the village for a job or schooling in the city. The enhanced stature of city life brings a responsibility of assisting one's tribal family. This obligation often imposes a financial burden on the successful member far in excess of income. The worker is unlikely to resist the pressures of society and is thus forced to augment income, often by means regarded by foreigners as bribery or corruption. However, to the African, it is not. As long as great disparities in income and standards of living continue, the bribe system is likely to continue as it has in many developing economies. In Africa, extra income is swiftly distributed through the extended family system to remote relations living in remote places. The tradition of sharing continues even as individuals move away from their tribal origins.

Corruption may arise because of inadequate compensation for work, causing laborers to seek additional income. Many African state governments have been corrupted by greedy political and military rulers who use public monies and offices to enrich themselves and their families at the expense of citizens and foreign businesspersons. Exhibit 15.3 gives readers some appreciation for the payment of gratuities.

EXHIBIT 15.3
JONES & SMITH FOOD COMPANY

The Jones & Smith Food Company is located in the capital of a large African country. However, they want to expand their headquarters to another state capital. To do this, they need approval from both the federal and the state government. The company sent in a written application a few months ago, but did not get any response.

The manager of the project went several times to the Federal Ministry of Trade and Economic Development but was always told to come back the next day. Mr. Jones became frustrated and mad at the clerks and officials involved. However, in the process of the argument, one of them said, "This is not America. It's Africa. If you want anything done on time, you've got to give a bribe. Kind of like a gratuity tendered before, rather than after, a service is performed."

Mr. Jones, who is not accustomed to such practices, angrily stormed out of the office. In the car, he narrated the incident to the driver who advised him to give the "gratuity" or have the proposal denied.

In an emergency meeting, the company's board of directors decided to offer the gratuity. To the company's surprise, the proposal was approved the next day.

But back in Jones' home culture a board of directors may frown upon such payments, and home country laws may consider such bribes illegal.

Respect for Elders

Age is another important factor to consider in Africa. It is believed that the older one gets, the wiser one becomes—life has seasoned the individual with varied experiences. Hence, in Africa, age is an asset. The older the person, the more respect the person receives within the traditional community, especially from the young. Thus, if a foreigner is considerably younger than the African, the African will have little confidence in the outsider. However, if sincerity, respect, and empathy are shown, the person will receive a positive response. Respect for elders tends to be the key for harmony in African cultures and village life.

Young Africans normally do not oppose the opinion of their elders. They may not agree, but they must respect the opinion. In some cases, especially in rural areas, young people are not expected to offer opinions in meetings. The informal and formal interpersonal relationships in Africa are based on cultural norms of various African societies. As

The older one gets, the wiser one becomes.

EXHIBIT 15.4
BUSINESS TIPS

- Be formal and respectful.
- Be trustworthy—deliver when and what is promised.
- Relax, slow down—Africa is not on the same time schedule as Western cultures.
- Don't be overly sensitive to criticism or advice.
- Don't try too hard to "go African." Remain professional.
- Patience is the key to successful business in Africa.

Africa modernizes—nearly 40 of its cities now have over a million inhabitants—some of the old ways, such as respect and care for seniors, may unfortunately diminish as is happening with other traditional cultures in transition. Exhibit 15.4 offers additional insights for doing business in Africa.

CULTURAL SPECIFICS BY GEOGRAPHIC REGIONS

It is impossible here to cover all the cultural aspects of doing business or humanitarian work in more than 50 African states. Instead, four major geographic areas of Africa will be profiled. In each region, we have selected one country for in-depth analysis for one or more of these reasons: (1) representativeness of a grouping; (2) economic implications for all of Africa; and (3) insights into what is happening in their societies. We will also consider a particular cultural dimension of Africa—business customs, protocols, and prospects.[13]

NORTH AFRICA

Geographically, North Africa contains 11 nations: Algeria, Chad, Egypt, Gambia, Libya, Mali, Mauritania, Morocco, Niger, Senegal, and Tunisia. Nine classify themselves as republics; however, Libya is a Socialist Arab Jamahirya and was once a sphere of Italian influence. Morocco is the only kingdom and is our target culture for analysis. Except for the coastal countries, the area can be characterized as one of high temperatures, vast deserts, Muslim religious practice, and French colonial cultural influence. The economies are developing, centered on textiles, food processing, agriculture, and mining; several are better off for producing or processing crude oil and petroleum.

Northern Africa

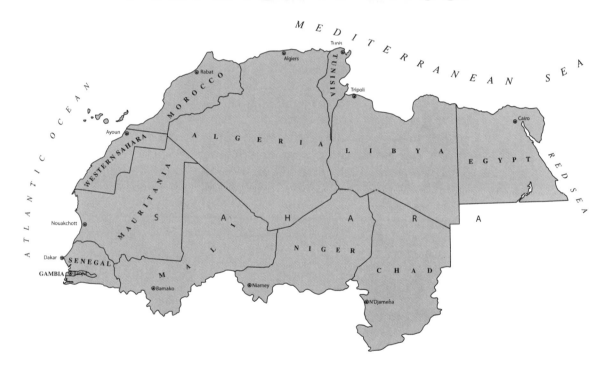

Exhibit 15.5 profiles six nations in the area, chosen for the size of their populations or their gross domestic product.

MOROCCO

Europe and Africa are geographically nearest each other in the narrow Strait of Gibraltar, the strategic passage between the Mediterranean Sea and the Atlantic Ocean. The two continents, once joined are only 22 kilometers apart and converge in the city of Ceuta, Spanish Morocco, often referred to as the gateway to Africa.

Some 50,000 years ago, there is evidence of the Neanderthals in this land, and 10,000 years ago, Stone Age humans dwelt there. From remotest antiquity, a panoply of peoples are represented here: Berbers, Phoenicians, Carthaginians, Romans, Mauretanians, Vandals, Visigoths, Byzantines, Arabs, Portuguese, Spanish, French, Jews, and Hindus. All have found a home in the region of Morocco over many centuries and have left behind vestiges of their rich cultural heritage. For 2500 years, the inhabitants of what is now Spain and Morocco have traded cultures across a narrow channel. After the Carthaginians conquered Iberia, Hannibal brought African elephants over to help in his astonishing assault on Italy. When the Goths declined there, Islam swept across North Africa, leading in A.D. 711 to seven centuries of Moorish domination in Spain. Today, this relatively tolerant multicultural society features Muslim, Christian, Jewish, and Hindu citizens and a semiautonomous government. However, Morocco and Spain are still in dispute over the *Sebta* territory that maintains control over five plazas or North African enclaves, including Ceuta and Melilla.

From this strategic location, one can travel easily to Casablanca, Morocco's largest and most important port city. Perched on Africa's northwest corner, today it is a cosmopolitan center for modern tourism. In 46 B.C. the Roman Empire annexed this region, calling it *Maurentina*. The province was eventually Christianized until the seventh century, when Islam became Morocco's official religion. In 1830, piracy along the coast led to the intervention of France; in 1912, its sultan accepted a French protectorate, which lasted until the country gained its independence in 1956.

Business Tips for Morocco

Moroccan business practices are more Arabic and Mediterranean than typically African. The same business customs, protocols, and etiquette provided in Chapter 11 about Arab culture in the Middle East also apply in this society.

Business conferences are usually held in the office rather than over meals. Breakfast meetings are rare, and lunches are late and long.

Moroccan business practices are more Arabic and Mediterranean than typically African.

Exhibit 15.5
Profiles of Algeria, Libya, Mali, Morocco, Senegal, and Tunisia

NATION	Algeria	Libya	Mali	Morocco	Senegal	Tunisia
AREA (sq km)	2,381,740	1,759,540	1,240,000	446,550	196,190	163,610
POPULATION	32,531,853	5,765,563	12,291,529	32,725,847	11,126,832	10,074,951
CAPITAL	Algiers	Tripoli	Bamako	Rabat	Dakar	Tunis
RELIGION	Sunni Muslim	Sunni Muslim	Muslim, Indigenous, Christian	Muslim, Christian	Muslim, Christian, Indigenous	Muslim, Christian
LANGUAGE	Arabic, French, Berber	Arabic, Italian, English	French, Bambara, numerous African languages	Arabic, Berber, French	French, Wolof, Pulaar, Jola, Mandinka	Arabic, French
LITERACY	70%	82.6%	46.4%	51.7%	40.2%	74.3%
LIFE EXPECTANCY	73 years	76.5 years	48.64 years	70.66 years	58.9 years	74.89 years
GDP PER CAPITA	$7,300	$8,400	$1,000	$4,300	$1,800	$7,600

Appointments should be scheduled, and the foreigner is expected on time, but do not be surprised at delays. Although young local entrepreneurs may speak English because of a Western education, check if you will need an interpreter in Arabic or French. Since there are some nine national holidays, plus four major religious celebrations, it is wise to determine on which days business will be set aside for a local feast or festival; many have dates that change each year because of the lunar calendar. Except for holidays, businesses normally operate Monday through Friday and sometimes Saturday morning. Most will close for lunch from noon until 2 P.M. The currency is the dirham (DH).

Apart from flowing Arab dress, lightweight business attire is favored in this warm climate. Although Moroccan women are beginning to get involved in commerce and professions, foreign females usually have no difficulty here, though a conservative business dress is recommended; a head covering is advised when visiting mosques. Noted for their hospitality, Moroccans often entertain business contacts in their homes.

Finally, remember that the phrase, *in sha'allah*, as in other Arab countries, may mean *yes*, *no*, or *maybe*, depending on the intonation of the speaker. The message is "if God wills or intends it." Other expressions to be heard in communications include: *Bismilah-el-raham er rahim* (in the name of God, clement and merciful); *El-hamdu lilah* (praise to God), an expression of satisfaction; *Allah u akbar* (God is great); and *Allah y jib* (God will provide).

The subtle Arabic language is filled with rhetoric, intricacies, ambivalence, and contradictions in terminology.

EAST AFRICA

This eastern region encompasses a dozen states, just south of Libya and Egypt, and bordering on the Red Sea, Gulf of Aden, and Indian Ocean. The states include Burundi, Central African Republic, Congo, Djibouti, Eritrea, Ethiopia, Kenya, Rwanda, Somalia, Sudan, Tanzania, and Uganda. The area starts in the north with the Sahara Desert of Sudan and ends in the south with the Congo and Tanzania. Except for Eritrea and Somalia, the other 10 countries style themselves as "republics," despite the presence of dictators or military coup commanders. Although Ethiopia was an ancient empire, most East African states were created as national entities by Britain, France, Germany, and Italy during the nineteenth century. Their borders and names have frequently changed as a result of civil wars and other conflicts.

East Africa is a landmass of great natural diversity and beauty, with its deserts and mountains, rivers and lakes, as well as a long, stunning coastline. It has temperatures and precipitation—from 73 to 89°F in the north and from 64 to 69°F in the south. Except for deserts and

East Africa

RED SEA

ERITREA

Asmara ⊛

GULF OF ADEN

⊛ Khartoum

S U D A N

DJIBOUTI
• Djibouti

Addis Ababa ⊛

E T H I O P I A

CENTRAL AFRICAN
REPUBLIC

Bangui ⊛

S
O
M
A
L
I
A

UGANDA
⊛ Kampala

⊛ Mogadishu
Historic capital
No central government since 1991

DEMOCRATIC

REPUBLIC

RWANDA
Kigali ⊛

K E N Y A

⊛ Nairobi

OF THE

BURUNDI
Bujumbura ⊛

CONGO

⊛ Kinshasa

T A N Z A N I A

I
N
D
I
A
N

Dodoma ⊛
Legislative capital

Dar es Salaam
⊛
Administrative capital

O
C
E
A
N

barren lands in five northeastern countries, the predominant land use is grassland, woodland, and forest, with some cropland and wetlands. Agriculture is the primary regional industry, along with mining of copper, gold, fluorite and diamonds. Two manufacturing centers are in Khartoum, Sudan, and Kinshasa, Congo, as well as one processing plant near Lubumbashi, Congo. Resplendent with spectacular landscape, Tanzania with one of the largest populations in the area, boasts the natural wonder of Mount Kilimanjaro.

Some of these countries are landlocked—Central African Republic, Congo, and Democratic Republic of Congo—though the last named does border on Lake Tanganyika. The remainder have coastlines along the Indian Ocean, Gulf of Aden, and the Red Sea. It was from East Africa that humanity spread beyond its origins, conquering five continents in less than 3 million years.

Regional Insights

The nations in East Africa are largely poor countries, but some have substantial, underdeveloped natural and mineral resources; most are dependent on international aid and humanitarian organizations (NGOs); the majority have very poor infrastructure, especially relative to roads and transportation; too many have heads of state who seized power by coup or otherwise with the help of the military and some are dictators, even when there are staged "elections"; their tendency is toward too many political parties for effective governance; many are faced with too many refugees from neighboring countries which require UN assistance; most have differing legal systems and are engaged in disputes with their neighboring states. There is an urgent need for outside forces, such as from the African Union, to disarm gunmen and rebels in the region. Given these drawbacks, one can understand why the region has trouble spots lacking effective governments, such as the following observations will indicate:

■ **Central African Republic** only gained its independence from France in 1960. Since then there has been much misrule and factional fighting between the government and the opposition, leading to a coup in 2003 when General Francois Bozize took over as president. Although the people ratified a constitution in 2004, sociopolitical conditions have not improved very much as regards lawlessness in the countryside. With 4 million recent deaths due to excessive mortality caused by AIDS, there is a desperate need for better health care.

■ **Sudan** was devastated by a 20-year-old civil war between Muslims in the north, where the central government operates, and Christians in the south, where the oil is located. Since 2003, the Arab government has turned a blind eye to the Darfur conflict in the west where a local Arab militia is engaging in monstrous "ethnic cleansing and

Sudan was devastated by a 20-year-old civil war.

genocide" against non-Arab peoples there. Despite both groups being Muslim, these clashes go back to the thirteenth century. Up to 300,000 have died, many from starvation, and 2 million have been displaced from their homeland, with some 200,000 fleeing east to neighboring Chad. Despite condemnation by world governments of the present regime, global politics have prevented the UN from intervening there with a strong force of peacekeepers. The conflict originated over property rights, water shortages, and scarcity of grazing lands—all problems yet to be resolved.

- **Eritrea** is an alluring country with gentle people, whose land is strategically located on one of the world's busiest shipping lanes in the Red Sea. After a 30-year struggle with Ethiopia to gain its independence in 1993, the fledgling nation lost a senseless border war against Ethiopia in 1998, leaving it to face huge unemployment and near famine. Currently, UN peacekeepers protect their border and keep the two parties apart.

- **Rwanda**, after staggering losses from genocide between the Hutu and Tutsi tribes, struggles to adopt a new constitution that ensures more democracy but does not permit either ethnic group to dominate the country. To constrain the Hutu majority population, it attempts to introduce checks and balances in the political system, with measured pluralism permitted by the ruling RPF of Tutsi. About 10,000 Hutu fighters, some of whom took part in the genocide, are now in hiding in eastern Congo. On this pretext in 1994, the Rwandan government invaded that country in pursuit of its rebels.

- **Uganda** is still recovering from the Idi Amin regime that murdered upward of 300,000 people. Because its citizens speak some 50 languages, requiring multiple translations for media and government, innumerable delays are inevitable. Since 1986, Limited General Yoweri Museveni who seized power, has served as "president." He too has threatened to invade the Congo's Kivi Province, but this time in pursuit of Uganda rebels there.

- **Congo** is trying to heal after destructive years of warfare, in which 3.3 million people died after 1998 (Exhibit 15.6). In the Democratic Republic of the Congo, former soldiers face hearings in the International Criminal Court about their past participation in genocide. Having not had an independent election in over 40 years, 25 million registered voters cast a ballot in a December 2005 referendum; over 80% of the people voted to accept a draft constitution to set up new institutions that may lead to a functioning government. Congo is vast (two-thirds the size of Europe) and a former colony of Belgium.

At present, sub-Saharan Africa is also suffering from devastating droughts, plus the largest number of people are afflicted with AIDS in lands devoid of adequate medical assistance. Exhibit 15.7 profiles six key countries with the largest populations in this region. Note the low

EXHIBIT 15.6

CONGO—AFRICA'S WORST WAR

Consider African challenges in terms of one country. As a result of invasions and warfare, the Congo has lost more than 9% of its population since the start of this century. Yet the Democratic Republic of the Congo (DRC) has abundant resources coveted by the rich nations of the world. But this sad story goes back to 1993 when genocide began on its northeast border in small, neighboring Rwanda. There the Hutu-dominated government tried to exterminate the Tutsis, a prosperous minority. The slaughter ended when exiled Tutsis, refugees in Uganda, returned in force to drive the killers into the DRC, while gaining control in Rwanda. Soon six neighboring countries were involved in the cross-border fighting. The senseless game went back and forth, on and on, as marauders from neighboring states and tribes preyed on the poor, especially in the Congo. The latter's economy was disrupted and its infrastructure crumbled. The violence was partially fueled by its greedy neighbors and their warlords seeking the Congo's diamonds, gold, germanium, and other resources.

The United Nations and the European Union decried the situation, especially human rights abuses. The UN Security Council voted in 2003 to send 17,000 French, Belgium, and Canadian peacekeeping troops into the Congo's Ituri's northeastern province—over the previous four years, 60,000 locals in Bunia, its capital, had been murdered, mutilated, or maimed. The African UN secretary general, Kofi Annan, issued a report calling events there a catastrophe for the 4.6 million Ituri inhabitants in the area—600,000 persons had been displaced internally, and half of the health care centers had closed. When neighboring nations withdrew their troops from the Congo, the World Bank and the European Union sent in $2 billion for reconstruction assistance. Projects are underway to renovate the railway from the mineral-rich Katanga to the Benguela port in Angola, which will enable the Congolese to harness their huge, hydroelectric potential. All things are possible if peace can be maintained and the needs of average people met.

In 2006, the Congo is trying to hold its first multiparty election in 40 years. The problem is that 8650 candidates signed up in the capital of Kinshasa to run for the presidency out of a population of 60 million. And the world's largest UN peacekeeping force is still employed there, attempting to ensure a fair election. Finally, the Mbuti Pygmies in the Congo's Ituri forest have managed to survive the civil war and its chaos, but can they cope in a time of peace with a land rush that might overwhelm them?

Source: Partially adapted from "A Report from the Congo" and "Congo's Wars—Peace They Say, But the Killings Go On," *The Economist*, April 15, 2006, p. 48.

Exhibit 15.7
Profiles of Congo, Ethiopia, Kenya, Sudan, Tanzania, and Uganda

NATION	Congo	Ethiopia	Kenya	Sudan	Tanzania	Uganda
AREA (sq km)	2,345,410	1,127,127	582,650	2,505,810	945,087	236,040
POPULATION	60,085,804	73,053,286	33,829,590	40,187,486	36,766,356	27,269,482
CAPITAL	Kinshasa	Addis Ababa	Nairobi	Khartoum	Dar Es Salaam	Kampala (Dodma)
RELIGION	Roman Catholic, Protestant, Kimbanguist, Muslim	Muslim, Ethiopian Orthodox, Animist	Protestant, Roman Catholic, Indigenous, Muslim	Sunni Muslim, Indigenous beliefs, Christian	Christian, Muslim, Indigenous beliefs	Roman Catholic, Protestant, Muslim, Indigenous beliefs
LANGUAGE	French, Lingala, Kingwana, Kikongo, Tshiluba	Amharic, Tigrinya, Oromigna, Guaragigna, Somali, Arabic	English, Kiswahili, numerous indigenous languages	Arabic, Nubian, Ta Bedawie, numerous indigenous languages	Swahili, English, indigenous languages	English, Ganda or Luganda
LITERACY	65.5%	42.7%	85.1%	61.1%	78.2%	69.9%
LIFE EXPECTANCY	51.1 years	48.83 years	47.99 years	58.54 years	45.24 years	51.59 years
GDP PER CAPITA	$800	$800	$1200	$2100	$700	$1700

GDP figures that are indicative of the area's poverty. One country, Kenya, has been chosen for additional cultural analysis.

KENYA

The Republic of Kenya, owing to years of British colonial influence, has East Africa's most modern infrastructure, as well as a large expatriate community because of reasonably priced residential and office accommodations. It is also a popular tourist destination for its national game reserve, safaris, and golf. The coastal beaches, wildlife, and unique scenery are the main attractions, along with access to the magnificent Rift Valley, a site of early human archaeological research. In the global marketplace, Kenya maintains good business and political relations. Representatives from many North American and European countries operate here, using it as a base to access larger markets in both East and Central Africa. The nation's main growth sectors are in agriculture, manufacturing, tourism, and power generation.

Nairobi is not only Kenya's capital, but a huge modern city with a population of 2,818,000. Its largest slum is Kiberia where 800,000 poor but talented citizens live who can "fix anything." This is a primary example of Africa's impoverished rural folk flocking to urban centers to seek a better life. The city may have upwards of 25,000 street children, many of whom lost parents to the AIDS disease. Only 80 miles from the equator and at an elevation of 5500 feet, this site began as a Maasai watering hole and became a camp for workers in 1899 who were building the Mombasa-Uganda Railroad.

Nairobi is also where a new generation of young professionals and businesspeople hope to create the "New Africa."

Nairobi is also where a new generation of young professionals and businesspeople hope to create the "New Africa." In this boisterous metropolis, the middle class is expanding and educated women are pushing ahead. They possess dual personalities, navigating in two languages (African and English) and between two worlds (modern and traditional). Nairobi is also home to the first African woman to win the Nobel Peace Prize, Wangari Maathai, ecologist and activist (Exhibit 15.8).

Despite Kenya's advantages, the crooks with guns and power looking for bribes have contributed to the nation's deterioration and shoddiness. While their corruption flourishes, the roads become potholed and dangerous, the railroad rolling stock has not been upgraded, and the civil servants are for the most part inept, except at wasting aid money or fleecing contractors. Yet the average Kenyan has learned to cope and make do, while hoping for better times. Some spurn death threats, like John Githongo, who as permanent secretary for ethics and governance dared to publicize his investigations on malfeasance by government ministers to the Kenya Anti-Corruption Commission, causing some of

Hard-working, long-suffering African women may lead the resurgence of this continent in the twenty-first century. Already a female has been elected head of state for Liberia, so ravaged by civil war and male power-seekers. In 2004, the Nobel Peace Prize was bestowed on a Kenyan woman for untiring humanitarian efforts on behalf of environmental protection, as well as the prevention of disease, violence, and war. When Wangar Maatha, 64, founder of the Green Belt Movement, received the $1.5 million prize, along with gold medal and diploma, she responded: "Today we are faced with a challenge which calls for a shift in our thinking, so that humanity stops threatening its life support system! We are called to assist the Earth to heal her wounds, and in the process to heal our own, indeed to embrace the whole of creation in all its diversity, beauty, and wonder. This will happen if we see the need to revive our sense of belonging to a larger family of life, with which we have shared our evolution!" Hopefully in Africa, it will be its dynamic women who provide the vision and energy to translate such ideals into positive actions!

Source: Adapted from D. Mellgran, "African Environmentalist Accepts Peace Prize," *San Diego Union*, December 11, 2004.

the misappropriated funds to be recovered. In elections, ordinary Kenyans, with home and school fees to pay, increasingly confront thieving politicans.[14]

Business Tips in Kenya

Kenyan firms are developing expertise in international business, and their buyers expect quality and service. Customary business courtesies are appreciated, including prompt replies for price quotations, orders, and deliveries. Because their markets are price sensitive, ensure that delivery dates are maintained or that buyers are quickly informed of any delays. Also, be prepared to sell here in smaller lots than is customary in the global market.

Their business executives and managers are relatively informal and open, and they do not mind the use of first names. Friendship and trust are highly valued in a productive business relationship. They also maintain a close liaison with local customers, distributors, and representatives.

Basic security precautions are advised, as there is a high crime rate in Nairobi, Mombasa, and Kismu as well as at coastal beach resorts and in some game parks. The border with Somalia has experienced

Basic security precautions are advised.

All of Africa

benefits from the

exceptional

service of

humanitarian

organizations.

violent criminal activity, including kidnappings. Recall the terrorist bombing in 1998 of the American Embassy in Nairobi killing 213 persons, which subsequently caused the embassy to relocate. Also, the Kenyan mail system can be unreliable, and monetary instruments are frequently stolen. If driving, autos travel on the left side of the road; generally, road conditions are poor, especially in the rainy season. Realize that local driving habits are unpredictable and that vehicle maintenance is likely to be inadequate. The use of sealed bottled water is recommended.

All of Africa benefits from the exceptional service of humanitarian organizations; some is UN or government sponsored, and others are under private auspices. Exhibit 15.9 provides some insights into the dedication of such volunteers.

EXHIBIT 15.9[15]
AFRICAN HUMANITARIANS

Not all foreigners in Africa are there to despoil it; for centuries outsiders have also come to help its people and solve its problems, as the next three examples will confirm:

■ The Peace Corps has a 45-year legacy of American service to those in need at home and abroad. One such idealistic representative is Benedict Moran of Scottsdale, Arizona. Each day, 7000 PC volunteers like him work in the developing world to fight hunger and disease, to further basic education, and promote economic security. Motivated by a strong work ethic, these unpaid, optimistic Corps Peace have a commitment to human service, as well as a pragmatic approach in problem solving. After graduation from college, Ben joined and was assigned to a very undeveloped Benin in West Africa. There he worked with local community leaders to bring the benefits of information technology to some 6.6 million people who earn on average less than $2 a day. To assist its largely impoverished and uneducated population, his project in the Peace Corps Partnership program was to improve and upgrade *Radio Rural Locale de Quake,* founded some 10 years ago. That media broadcasting in French and major local languages has a significant impact toward improving health care, girl school enrollment, and use of sustainable agro-forestry techniques. So in his time there, Ben's project sought to replace deteriorating technical equipment in the Quake station, especially computers, music library, information database, and sound quality. Through computer workshops for employees, the Beninese learned new skills, which further empowered them in their business careers.

EXHIBIT 15.9[15]

AFRICAN HUMANITARIANS (CONTINUED)

■ In 1999, Medecins Sans Frontiers (MSF) or Doctors Without Borders was awarded the Nobel Peace Prize for their exceptional, global humanitarian service! Within 72 hours their health-care teams responded to 2005 disasters in Southeast Asia. MSF provided 200 international volunteers and 200 metric tons of aid supplies to assist people in 5 countries who were suffering from tsunami damage. Another of their campaigns is *Access to Essential Medicines*, which offers generic drugs to assist 25,000 patients in 27 countries who are coping with the HIV/AIDS. Many of these recipients are in Africa.

Among its many projects on that continent is one to support the health-care system of Uganda where conflict has raged for 18 years. For example, in the Lira District, MSF runs s 350-bed therapeutic feeding center and program, as well as four clinics and two mobile clinics. In the Gulu District, this nonprofit organization administers a night-shelter for 4000 children in need of a safe place to sleep on the grounds of Lacor Hospital.

■ New York's Fordham University established the Institute of International Humanitarian Affairs in 2001. Its director is an alumnus, Kevin M. Cahill, M.D., who has undertaken medical humanitarian missions for more than 45 years in 60 countries as a member of the MSF. Recently, this "visionary grounded in human realities," wrote a book, *To Bear Witness: A Journey of Healing and Solidarity* (Fordham University Press, 2005). Among Cahill's many true stories, it describes how this physician of Irish heritage treated John Paul II after the 1981 assassination attempt on the Pope's life. Dr. Cahill also pays tribute to his late wife, Kathryn, who often worked with him on his Doctors Without Borders undertakings, saying: "Ours was a marriage made in heaven, and honed to perfection in some of the hell holes on Earth!" These many humanitarian efforts took him to many African countries, such as drought-plagued Somalia, and more recently to serve victims in need after the devastation of U.S. Gulf Coast hurricanes; the earthquake in Kasmir, Pakistan, and India, as well the Iraq war. Here is an excerpt from his new volume: "Those of us privileged to participate in great humanitarian dramas have the opportunity that adversity offers to build a new framework—using and sometimes rediscovering the best of old structures, but realizing that a new spirit and innovative methods are necessary for international discourse in a new millennium."

On the Atlantic side of the African continent, the Gulf of Guinea defines the region. Its coastline has a series of exotic names that reveal something of its history—Grain Coast, Ivory Coast, Gold Coast, and Slave Coast. This is an equatorial area of high precipitation (20 to 40 inches of rain) and high temperatures (75–80°F). It is a landmass primarily of forest, woodlands, and grasslands, plus mixed use, cropland, and wetland. It is an expanse filled with wildlife and fauna—the major crops being bananas, cassava, cattle, citrus fruit, cocoa, coffee, corn, fish, forest products, millet, oil palm fruit, pineapple, rice, rubber, sesame seed, sheep, sorghum, sugarcane, swine, tea, and tobacco. The area is also rich in industry and mining—aluminum, gold, manganese, titanium, diamonds, and petroleum. West Africa is in the midst of an oil boon today, but unfortunately too many corrupt elite benefit instead of improving the lot of the masses. These natural resources are why so many non-Africans have come here and why it is a target of foreign investment.

The region is home to some 14 nations, all of which describe themselves as republics.

The region is home to some 14 nations, all of which describe themselves as republics. However, their rulers range from democratically elected presidents to dictators and military coup masters. The locale extends from Guinea-Bissau in the northwest corner, south of Senegal to another Congo in the southwest that abuts the Democratic Republic of the Congo. Alphabetically, these countries are called: Benin, Burkina Faso, Cameroon, Congo, Côte d'Ivoire, Equatorial Guinea, Gabon, Ghana, Guinea, Guinea-Bissau, Liberia, Nigeria, Sierra Leone, and Togo. The biggest urban center is Lagos, Nigeria, with a population of approximately 10 million. It is not feasible to profile all these countries, so we have selected those with the largest population (Exhibit 15.10). One country in the region, Nigeria, has been chosen for in-depth cultural analysis.

Unfortunately, West Africa is a region of political instability and even civil conflict, often originating from rebel groups in neighboring countries. For example:

- **Côte d'Ivoire**—The central government fights northern rebels, resulting in a violent and wasteful civil war.
- **Liberia**—Warlord President Charles Taylor came to power through a coup and killings but was finally forced into exile with the help of French and American troops; he now faces prosecution in the International Criminal Court. The days of "big man" may be over now that he is the first African head of state to be indicted for *crimes against humanity*. He has been replaced by Africa's first woman elected president who has launched a recovery program.
- **Sierra Leone** is struggling with postwar reconstruction and trying to contain the smuggling of their famous *blood diamonds*.

West Central Africa

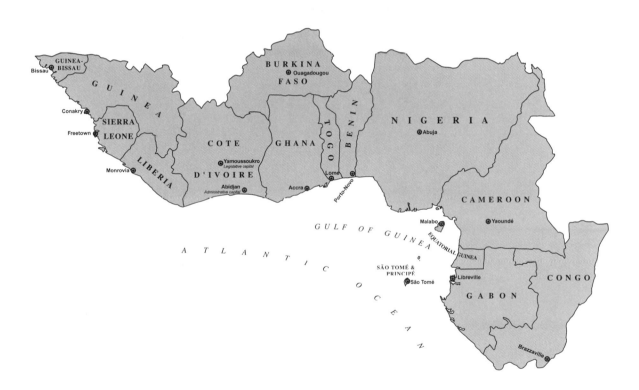

Exhibit 15.10

Profiles of Benin, Burkina Faso, Cameroon, Côte d'Ivoire, Ghana, Guinea, Nigeria

NATION	Benin	Burkina Faso	Cameroon	Côte d'Ivoire	Ghana	Guinea	Nigeria
AREA (sq km)	112,620	274,200	475,440	322,460	239,460	245,857	923,768
POPULATION	7,460,025	13,925,313	16,380,005	17,298,040	21,029,853	9,467,866	128,771,988
CAPITAL	Porto-Novo	Ouagadougou	Yaounde	Yamoussoukro, Abidjan (Admin.)	Accra	Conakry	Abuja
RELIGION	Indigenous beliefs Christian, Muslim	Indigenous beliefs, Muslim, Christian	Indigenous beliefs, Christian, Muslim	Christian, Muslim, Indigenous beliefs	Christian, Muslim, Indigenous beliefs	Muslim, Christian, Indigenous beliefs	Muslim, Christian, Indigenous beliefs
LANGUAGE	French, Fon, Yoruba, Tribal languages	French, native African languages	English, French, 24 major African language groups	French, 60 native dialects (Dioula most widely spoken)	English, African languages	French, various ethnic group languages	English, Hausa, Yoruba, Igbo (Ibo), Fulani
LITERACY	33.6%	26.6%	79%	50.9%	74.8%	35.9%	68%
LIFE EXPECTANCY	52.66 years	48.45 years	50.89 years	48.62 years	58.47 years	49.36 years	46.74 years
GDP PER CAPITA	$1200	$1200	$2000	$1400	$2500	$2200	$1000

■ **Togo**—President General Gnassingbe Eyadema died in February 2005 having shot his way to power. His son took over and the popular election validated his succession in April 2005.

The United Nations is spending over $50 million in the region this year, running camps for refugees and fugitives, numbering more than 200,000. On the positive side, constitutional and multiparty Ghana, Mali, and Senegal stand out as beacons of stability in the area.

NIGERIA

Nigeria's landmass is approximately 356,669 square miles—about twice the size of the state of California. Despite some border disputes with its neighbors over Lake Chad, this West African nation is bounded by Benin, Niger, Chad, and Cameroon, as well as the Atlantic Ocean on its southern edge.

Historical Perspective Overview

The cultural history of this country and its peoples dates back to the seventh century B.C. More advanced cultures have resided in Nigeria since the twelfth century A.D. In 1861, the British seized the principal city of Lagos, supposedly to end the slave trade then flourishing there. The English social, financial, and political cultural impact has been considerable ever since. Even though the locals gained their political independence in 1960, they are still members of the British Commonwealth of Nations, often traveling to the United Kingdom for business, pleasure, or resettlement. English is often the language for business and national affairs, in addition to six different local languages.

Its rapidly growing population of over 130 million is composed of 250 tribal groups of which 65% are the Hausa-Fulani, Ibo, and Yoruba. These also represent three major language groups (Hausa, Zula, and Swahili). There are five main religious influences present: Muslim (50%); Protestant (25%); Roman Catholic (12%); African Christian (11%); and traditional African or indigenous beliefs (10%). (All percentages of the population are approximate.) As with many African countries, foreign missionaries accompanied European colonists in previous centuries. Today Christian churches, schools, hospitals, and social institutions have significant influence on the culture, especially in the south, as do comparable Koranic schooling and enterprises in the north. A quota system guarantees students from the north a share of university places—an undue share, contend the southerners who view their school system as superior.

Its rapidly growing population of over 130 million is composed of 250 tribal groups.

Cultural Guidelines for Doing Business in Nigeria

Nigeria's human resources have great potential, and oil is its main income producer today. The literacy rate has risen to 68% as a result of six years of compulsory education. Over 14 million students are enrolled in elementary (34,240) and secondary (5970) schools and 48 colleges/universities. The Nigerian educational system is based largely on the British system. What was generally described at the opening of this chapter about African culture comes into sharper focus in the context of Nigeria, once considered Africa's most advanced nation.

Social Structure

The family dominates the social structure.

In Nigeria, the family dominates the social structure. Nigerian tradition places emphasis on one's lineage through the male head of the household. In non-Muslim sections, these familial connections form vast networks that serve as a foundation for one's social identity. Marriage is seen as a way of producing more children to contribute to this lineage or network. Sterility is grounds for divorce. Three forms of marriage exist in Nigeria. Among some Christians and non-Muslims, unlimited polygamy is customary. Wives are acquired through the payment of a "bride price" to the bride's parents. Muslim custom differs in that the number of wives is usually limited to four. The Western Christian marriage is relatively uncommon in rural areas, though increasing in the cities.

The stratification of Nigerian society varies with region. In northern Nigeria, rank is more important than it is in the south. In the east, some egalitarian tradition exists, whereas in the west there is a distinct aristocracy.

Groups and Relationships

Among the many tribes, the principal ones are (1) the Hausa, very religious Muslims; (2) the Yoruba, an outgoing, festive people, not secretive about their business activities; and (3) the Ibo, excellent merchants, extremely resourceful, hard working, and conscientious, who understand the value of money.

These important attitudes exist in Nigeria, affecting business relationships:

■ *Old family business tradition.* One does not share information because everyone else is a competitor. (This traditional attitude has often been reinforced by subsequent European influences, as opposed to new American management training which encourages a free flow of information, including the sharing of trade knowledge and more open communications. (Many young Nigerian businesspeople are U.S. trained.)

■ *Muslim attitudes.* Predestination rather than free will; reliance on tradition and precedent; mistrust of innovation; unwillingness to take risks; learning by rote rather than by experiments or problem solving. Some of Nigeria's serious internal strife is not just tribal, but also religious—with Muslims attacking Christians.

Communications

A Westerner in Nigeria should not use words such as *native*, *hut*, *jungle*, *witchcraft*, and *costume*. The connotation behind these expressions tends to be that Africa is still a dark continent. Nigeria, as is true with many other parts of Africa, has made great strides in development and is proud of its advancement. Therefore, it is best to remember that a hut is a home and a costume is really clothing. Nigerians want to be friends with foreign visitors, and they are proud to have them in their homes. They will go to great lengths to be a friend, but they do not want to be patronized.

They do not want to be patronized.

Greetings. Upon meeting a Nigerian business associate, the greeting is Westernized but formal. A simple, "Good morning, Mister Opala, how are you?" is accepted as proper. Asking personal questions about one's family is a common practice. Once you have established some degree of familiarity, you can use a first name if the Nigerian initiates it. Always shake hands when greeting someone. It is extremely rude not to acknowledge a person when entering a room or to fail to shake his or her hand.

Forms of address. Nigerians distinguish the levels of familiarity between one another by their forms of address. Friends will call one another by their first names. Older brothers and sisters are very rarely addressed by their first names. An older brother is addressed as N'da and an older sister as N'se, which means "my senior [brother or sister's name]." This is simply a sign of respect toward seniority and age. The expressions *sir* and *ma'am* are always used when speaking to a businessperson, government official, someone older, or someone in a position of authority.

Social Customs

Nigerians are a proud and self-confident people. Much of this confidence comes from a knowledge that their country is a leader in Africa in many ways. They are extroverted, friendly, and talkative. Nigerians are also known for their hospitality. Strangers are taken in, fed, and lodged for as long as the guest desires. Consequently, it is possible to make many more long-lasting relationships that are less superficial than those in some other cultures.

When a friend, acquaintance, or relative becomes ill, it is customary for that person to receive many, many visitors. Anyone who even remotely knows the sick person will come to visit. It is the Nigerian way of saying, "I want to know for myself how you're feeling."

Gender. As in all of Africa, the role of women in Nigeria is changing with modernization, especially in urban centers. Traditionally, females have always performed the major laboring tasks from farming to road building. Now with increased education and opportunity, they are moving up in commerce and industry, as well as in government and the professions. Perhaps the Nigerian women achieving positions of leadership and influence in the political and economic arena will also set the example for the liberation of women elsewhere on the continent.

Women play a vigorous role in this society, although domestic authority always seems to rest with the husband. There is a network of marketing and trading in commodities that occurs throughout the country. This is the exclusive province of women, who run their own businesses the way they see fit.

Marriage. When two people are considering marriage, a proper procedure must be followed. The first step is for the prospective groom to send an intermediary to the woman's home to present the idea of marriage to her parents. Gifts are sent to the woman, and then the man himself comes to the woman's parents to discuss the marriage. So far, nothing has been said to the woman about the pending marriage. If everything is in order with the prospective bride's family, the woman then goes to live with the man's family to make sure this is where she wants to live. If so, the marriage can occur. The dowry involved in the marriage is not a fixed amount. It is an insurance against maltreatment for the woman. It is not until the wife dies and is buried in her natal land that the dowry is paid to her husband, if she has been treated well.

Currently, intermarriage between tribes is very rare in Nigeria. It is more common for a Nigerian to marry a foreigner than a member of another tribe. There is still a great deal of rivalry between the tribes, and the intent seems to be to try and keep them pure. However, if such an intertribal marriage should occur, oddly enough, the stranger will be treated almost royally by the members of the other tribe. The reason for this is that the nontribe's member is viewed as having made a supreme sacrifice by giving up his or her tribe and their traditions and adopting those of the spouse, as they almost always do in this situation.

Most Nigerian cultures are patriarchal. In some areas, particularly the rural ones, polygamy is still prevalent. However, in urban areas, it is much more common to find one-man, one-woman marriages. Marital age is becoming more of an economic decision. Couples wait until they have an education and can afford a marriage.

Traditions

Nigeria is growing quickly and becoming more modernized and urbanized, but traditions are still very important to the people. Local customs still play a significant role in Nigerian life. One such ritual, though quickly disappearing, is found strictly in the western portion of the country and has to do with tribal marks. When a child reaches the age of two or three years, he or she has the appropriate tribal marks burned into his or her face, very similar to the branding process. These marks reflect tribes or family. When one sees the marks, it is not necessary to ask what the person's last name is or from what tribe he or she comes. It is said that if the child cannot withstand the pain during the ceremony, as there is no anesthesia, he or she is not worthy of that family or tribe. The whole process is very unhygienic and dangerous and seems to be dying out gradually.

Nigeria is a "right-handed" society. As in many cultures, the left hand is considered unclean, as it is the "toilet hand." It is extremely impolite to extend the left hand to others or to eat with it, even if the person is left-handed.

Nigeria is a "right-handed" society.

It is important to reemphasize the matter of age in Nigeria. There is a profound respect for one's elders. Older people are not placed in nursing homes when they become ill. They are taken in by their families, looked after, and revered. The importance of the elderly seems to lie in their capability to pass on family history and tradition.

The custom of eating with one's hands is practiced in Nigeria. If there is a big festival, or even in a private home, where there are foreign visitors not used to this custom, allowances are made and silverware is often provided them. However, an honest effort will be greatly appreciated. A communal bucket is passed around in which everyone washes their hands, prior to the beginning of the meal. Once again, it is important to use only the right hand.

Governmental and Economic Challenges

Despite the long tribal history within this region, the Federal Republic of Nigeria was not established until 1963. The boundaries provided by the British brought together four peoples who have had a continuous rivalry going since then. In 1967, the eastern region seceded to found the Republic of Biafara; the subsequent civil war lasted three years and caused over a million deaths, mainly from starvation. Since its formation, Nigeria has experienced struggles about whether the government should be ruled by civilians or by the military. In 1985, Major General Ibrahim Babangida seized power, and in 1992, when Moshood Abiola, a Yoruba, was elected president, in an election organized by the military, the northern generals annulled the results. Instead, the president was put on trial for treason, and one of the military cabal, General Sani Abacha, became the self-appointed ruler. With his death from a heart attack in 1998, General Abdulsalam Abuubakar was sworn in as Nigeria's tenth head of state, appointed by a provisional Ruling Council of military men.

Nigeria

represents an

enormous

market for

goods and

services.

There is a growing consensus that military rule by soldiers who get rich has had its day—28 years out of the nation's 38 years of independence. Politics has been reduced to matters of stealing, or *chopping*, as it is called here. The reality is that multiparty politics, a product of industrialized societies and often based on social class, has yet to succeed here or in the rest of Africa where loyalties are tribal. Each new general who comes to national power makes noble promises: to break up state monopolies in several industries, to partially privatize big corporations, to introduce competition, and to end the country's crippling domestic fuel shortage. By 2000, a retired general, Olusegun Obasanjo, was serving as president and trying to cope with eight northern states who declared for adoption of *Shariah*, the Islamic legal code. As elsewhere on this continent, there is little trust in their unscrupulous "leaders" whose misrule stirs up ethnic chauvinism, undermining national integration. Finally, in June 2003, elections were held against a backdrop of a failing economy and religious strife.

As Africa's most populous country, Nigeria represents an enormous market for goods and services. Over a hundred companies are doing business there with an investment of some $2 billion, two-thirds of which is in the petroleum industry. Its most important international trading partner is the United States, which imports 40% of its oil production. Expatriates from many countries abounded when Nigeria was awash with oil money, especially in the capital of Lagos. Today, though fewer in number, expatriates remaining are businesspersons, construction engineers, agricultural experts, educators, and technocrats.

Besides petroleum, Nigeria's natural resources are tin, columbite, iron ore, coal, limestone, lead, zinc, natural gas, marble, and fish. Agriculture and foodstuffs are big business, along with major industries in beverages, tobacco, vehicles, chemicals, pharmaceuticals, iron/steel, rubber, printing, building materials, lumber, and footwear. Lewis forecasts that Nigeria, like others of the world's hungriest and most populous markets, has needs, tastes, and requirements that will transform the global economy, including how they work and live.[16]

As a young, struggling democracy, Nigeria has the great challenge of utilizing the country's enormous resources and potential for the benefit of all its inhabitants. If more of the annual national income of almost $10 billion can be diverted into the development of infrastructure, education, and health services, then the new millennium holds promise for this the largest nation in Africa, but with one of its lowest standards of living. A few national problems to be addressed include:

- **Reversing the culture of corruption** so deeply engrained in this society. This pervasiveness ranges from stealing and bribes to scams and swindles, where credit card numbers are subject to theft and fraud. Restoring the nation's financial reputation and retrieving its misdirected income are first steps toward regaining the confidence of international investors who now avoid the country. Tales of massive frauds, drug smuggling, money laundering, and embezzlement make it difficult for Nigerians to obtain visas worldwide. Such reforms must begin at the top levels of government.

■ **Distributing national income** more equitably, so that the fantastically wealthy elite, many of whom stole shamelessly and without punishment from the public treasury, develop some social responsibility toward the poor in their society.

■ **Reforming the public sector,** starting with the electoral, and extending to the criminal justice, law enforcement, and military systems.

Business Tips for Working in Nigeria

Meetings. It will almost always be necessary to deal, in some capacity, with Nigerian government officials. When a meeting is granted, whether with the desired official or someone else, there are important practices to be aware of. First, any significant business transaction is always conducted in person. Any attempt to conduct business either over the telephone or by mail is seen as considering the matter trivial and unimportant. When visiting a colleague's office, tea, coffee, or other refreshments are always available and offered. These refreshments should not be refused, as this may be taken as an offense. Also, refreshments must always be available when the colleague comes to visit the foreign businessperson's office. When commercial visitors are invited to a local colleague's home for dining, if at all possible, the invitation should not be refused.

At state and federal meetings, protocol must be observed. Extreme politeness, respect for authority, and a slower pace are normal. If an authority does not answer your question, it may mean they do not know the answer and do not want to be embarrassed. It is helpful if a foreign businessperson establishes a Nigerian counterpart. One needs expertise in dealing with the Nigerian business community. References should be carefully checked, and choosing someone with influential contacts is important. This local resource will prove invaluable in translating later what was said during a meeting. Even though the official language is English, the Nigerian accent can be difficult to understand. A Nigerian may be insulted when an individual does not comprehend his or her local version of English, often British in origin. It takes a long time to become established in the Nigerian business community, and it is who one knows that will make a difference. Connections are important and should be cultivated. When investing in Nigeria, start at the state government level instead of the federal. Each state operates differently, but all want and need business. Consequently, they are very receptive and can greatly facilitate business formalities.

Negotiations. When conducting negotiations with a Nigerian, the tone of such meetings is generally friendly and respectful. Notice should

Protocol must be observed.

be taken of titles to be sure the appropriate ones are used correctly. Age is highly respected in Nigeria and often associated with wisdom. Therefore, to maximize chances of success, an older person should be sent to meet with prospective businesspersons. Nigerians assume promises will be kept, so be realistic about delivery dates or price specifications. Furthermore, it is not unusual for a Nigerian worker to try to involve his foreign manager or supervisor in politics. It is much better not to participate in these political discussions as sides will undoubtedly be taken and one's role may be compromised. Subsequently, an air of hostility and tension will be apparent.

Decision making. Decision making is based on a centralized system, and delegation of authority is almost nonexistent. Nigerians cling to authority and are dependent on supervision.

A Nigerian manager at a high-level position may feel obligated to find jobs for his or her family and will not hesitate to "pull strings" to employ them. If the Nigerian is very powerful, there is nothing a foreign businessperson can do to stop this practice. This decision-making process based on family responsibilities can be very frustrating to a North American business representative, conditioned to a work environment with a norm of competency and merit selection in advancement and promotions.

Concept of time. In Nigeria this can be summed up as unlimited. Lagos, the center of business, is congested, and traffic jams can hold one up for several hours. Consequently, late appointments are common and usually anticipated, and telephone service is poor and unreliable. Time is, therefore, not of the utmost importance to most Nigerians. As such, punctuality is not prevalent. Although work is important to the Nigerians, so is their leisure. Sports are a favorite way to spend time, including the most popular activities of football, boxing, and horse racing. Hockey, tennis, cricket, polo, golf, rugby, table tennis, and softball are also played.

SOUTHERN AFRICA

The southern tip of the African continent encompasses 11 nations. On the west coast facing the Atlantic Ocean are Angola, Namibia, and South Africa. South Africa is the most modern state bordering on the Indian Ocean and will be the target for our in-depth analysis below. Within that country are the small kingdoms of Lesotho and Swaziland. In the region's interior are Zamia, Malawi, Zimbabwe, and Botswana. On the east coast facing the Indian Ocean, are Mozambique, plus the channel island of Madagascar. In this southern area, the largest population centers are along the northwest and southwest coastlines, as well as in the north.

Southern Africa

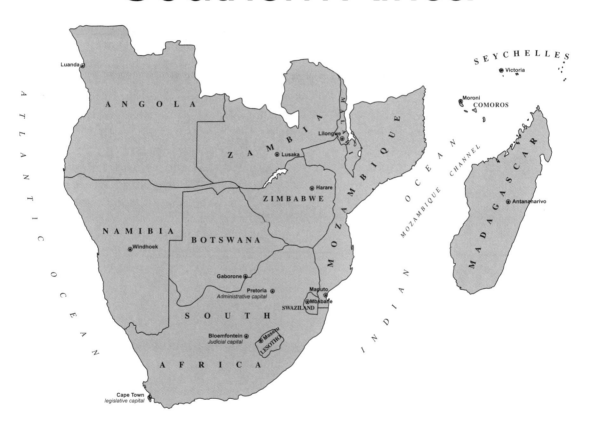

With agriculture and fishing being most prominent, the land use is mixed—some crop growing and ranching, in addition to forest, woodland, and grassland. As elsewhere in Africa, there is an abundance of 18 crops, ranging from fruit to wheat, along with fish, cattle, and sheep. Industry and mining are concentrated in Botswana and South Africa. Mining there is primarily for aluminum, coal, chromite, copper, gold, lithium, mangalese, nickel, platinum, titanium, uranium, and vanadium. Both of the above countries are also engaged in diamond mining, along with Angola. The area's three major manufacturing centers lie within South Africa—Johannesburg, Durban, and Cape Town. Most of the region has heavy precipitation—from 20 to 40 or more inches of rain, except in the southwest coast that usually has less than 10 inches. Temperatures range here from 55 to 78°F, except on the southwest coast where it is 56 to 87°F.

Recall that the area's peace and prosperity has been severely constricted by a 30-year civil war in Angola; a lengthy, costly, but successful struggle to overturn the all-white, Afrikaner apartheid government; and the ongoing civil unrest, killings, land grabs, and economic disasters of President Robert Mugabe's administration in Zimbabwe. An exception to this pattern is Botswana, a small peaceful country of only 1.8 million people, just north of South Africa. It has used its vast diamond wealth wisely to foster education, one of the best on the continent, as well as tourism and friendly business environment. This country is known to be the least corrupt states, but its sparkling image is marred by a high rate of AIDS and its mistreatment of a most vulnerable ethnic group, the Bushmen or San, a hunter-gather or tribal people.

Seven countries are profiled in Exhibit 15.11. With regard to this overview, readers are urged to make comparisons between the states, and seek patterns in the data. For example, contrast population, literacy, and life expectancy with gross domestic income average.

SOUTH AFRICA

There are multiple visions of what South Africa has been and should be. One vision is that it is a land of promise—the most advanced economy on the continent; a country with enormous natural beauty and resources. In the twenty-first century, the African continent needs a strong and prosperous South Africa.[17]

South African society is in the midst of a transformation that could lead to prosperity, if both the white citizen minority who had been in control and the oppressed black majority now ruling, truly shared their nation's sociopolitical institutions and power. By their practice of cultural synergy, both may create a multicultural society of equal oppor-

EXHIBIT 15.11

PROFILES OF ANGOLA, MADAGASCAR, MALAWI, MOZAMBIQUE, SOUTH AFRICA, ZAMBIA, ZIMBABWE

NATION	Angola	Madagascar	Malawi	Mozambique	South Africa	Zambia	Zimbabwe
AREA (sq km)	1,276,700	587,040	118,480	801,590	1,219,912	752,614	390,580
POPULATION	11,190,786	18,040,341	12,158,924	19,506,703	44,344,136	11,261,795	12,746,990
CAPITAL	Luanda	Antananarivo	Lilongwe	Maputo (Leg.)	Pretoria (Admin.), Cape Town	Lusaka	Harare
RELIGION	Indigenous beliefs, Roman Catholic, Protestant	Inidigenous beliefs, Christian, Muslim	Christian, Muslim	Catholic, Zionist Christian, Muslim	Zion Christian, Pentecostal/Charismatic, Catholic, Methodist, Dutch Reformed, Anglican, other Christian, Islam	Christian, Muslim and Hindu, Indigenous beliefs	Syncretic (part Christian, part indigenous beliefs), Christian indigenous beliefs
LANGUAGE	Portuguese, Bantu, other African languages	French, Malagasy	Chichewa, Chinyanja, Chiyao, Chitumbuka, Chisena, Chilomwe, Chitonga	Emakhuwa, Xichangana, Portuguese, Elomwe, Cisena, Echuwabo; other Mozambican languages	IsiZulu, IsiXhosa, Afrikaans, Sepedi, English, Setswana, Sesotho, Xitsonga	English, indigenous languages	English, Shona, Sindebele, tribal dialects
LITERACY	66.8%	68.9%	62.7%	47.8%	86.4%	80.6%	90.7%
LIFE EXPECTANCY	38.43 years	56.95 years	41.43 years	40.32 years	43.27 years	39.7 years	39.13 years
GDP PER CAPITA	$2500	$900	$600	$1300	$11,900	$900	$1900

tunity.[18] One small indicator of progress is the "Buppies," the growing, upwardly mobile, black professionals. In this multiracial democracy, they can even be found at gatherings of "high society," such as the J&B Met Horse Race, an annual sports and fashion extravaganza, formerly the exclusive domain of whites.

Historical Perspective

South Africa has a heritage of pioneering, colonization, wars, and building a modern infrastructure. Thankfully, *apartheid* is gone—a failed policy of separation of white and blacks that was internationally condemned and finally abandoned in the 1990s. Three centuries ago, this land became home to Bushmen and Hottentots, Bantu-speaking black tribes. In the mid-seventeenth century, the European whites arrived; first were the Dutch who built a trading settlement at the Cape of Good Hope. They were joined by Germans and French Huguenot refugees in 1688. Together these colonists would become known as Boers (farmers). The British invaded and captured the Cape in 1806, gaining formal possession of the colony in 1814 as the result of the Napoleonic wars. To avoid English rule, the Boers migrated to the undeveloped interior of the country from 1835 to 1848, defeating the indigenous Zulu and other black tribes in the process. With the discovery of gold and diamonds in that territory, Great Britain annexed parts of that area that led to the Boer War, which they won in 1902. The British then combined their colonies of Cape and Natal with the Boer Republics of Orange Free State and Transvaal, creating in 1910 the Union of South Africa, today called the Republic of South Africa.

Thus, this is a nation of four cultural influences or ethnic groups: the native African majority, the minority populations consisting of the Dutch who were to become known as Boers and *Afrikaners*, along with the British and Asian immigrants, the latter mostly from India and designated later as the *Coloureds*. As British power waned, the Afrikaners increasingly took control of the government after the election of their National Party in 1948. During the 1960s, Afrikaners introduced the oppressive apartheid system separating blacks from whites, creating two unequal communities. Another flawed policy was launched that forced settlement for the majority black African population in separate and supposedly independent homelands (e.g., Lesotho and Swaziland). Since the 1960s, domestic turmoil and violence caused by these inhumane political actions have brought international protests and boycotts, including trade sanctions by the United States and condemnation by the United Nations.

To fight for black human rights, the African National Congress (ANC) was formed in 1955 and eventually coalesced with other black groups' campaigns against the white power government. Finally, the economic and social impact of multinational sanctions led to the resignation in 1989 of the president of the Republic of South Africa (RSA), P. W. Botha. His replacement, F. W. de Klerk, implemented a series of democratic reforms, beginning with the freeing of political prisoners, the desegregating of institutions, and the legal recognition of the ANC as a political party. The outcome was the signing of a peace agreement between the ANC and the ruling elite providing for power sharing, the dismantling of apartheid, and the holding of open elections. In the 1994 election, all RSA citizens voted for the first time, electing ANC leader and former political prisoner, Nelson Mandela, and de Klerk as vice president of a multiethnic government. For their peacekeeping success, both men were awarded the Nobel Peace Prize. Many of the Caucasian settlers left permanently for other countries throughout the world.

Since then a political evolution, not revolution, has been under way. The RSA is a laboratory of social experimentation that has implications for the whole continent. With the ascendancy of the ANC leadership to the national government in 1994, and a new approach to white/black power sharing, the inequitable, segregated, apartheid political and social system is being slowly transformed into a more democratic, multiparty one. Despite an odious and corrosive legacy, here are examples of the change process and progress under way. Suffrage policy was at first limited to whites only, then extended to the *Coloureds*, and now finally includes the blacks, formerly restricted to voting in local "homeland" or township elections. The shift in political parties and power has been from the National Party and Conservative Party to the African National Congress, the Inkatha Freedom Party (Zulu), and the Democratic Party. Overall, the current government is striving to meet educational and training needs for a global economy and a knowledge society.

A political evolution, not revolution, has been under way.

Cultural Guidelines for Business in South Africa

Today there are almost 47 million South Africans, divided equally between males and females who have a life expectancy of only 48 years. This is a relatively young population, about 70% or more are under 50 years of age, with 26% under the age of 10. Approximately 37.2 are black Africans (79.3%); 4.4 million are white (9.3%); 1.2 million are Asian (2.5%); and 4.1 million are colored (8.8%). The Black Africans consist of nine tribal groups—Zulu (the largest), Xhosas, North and South Sothos, Tswanas, Shangaan-Tsongas, Swazis, South Ndebeles, and Vendas. Each has its own special cultural heritage, language, and sense of identity. During the apartheid period, tribal groups had been assigned by the racist government to 10 ethnic "homelands" that were supposed to have self-rule but actually were dependent on the white statecraft; these are being dismantled under the new regime. Although English and Afrikaans (a Dutch derivation) are the official languages, the blacks among the four major tribes speak varying forms of Bantu. The whites have zero population growth but were reserved 85% of the land under the old system. The whites are divided into two groups—the English-speaking descendants of English, Scottish, and Irish settlers and the Afrikaan-speaking offspring of the Dutch, German, and French colonials. The English-speaking *Coloureds* descendants of early white setters, native Hottentots, imported Dutch East Indian slaves and indentured laborers from India (Hindi speakers).

Religion. In terms of religious affiliations, most South Africans are Christians, divided among the Dutch Reformed Church of the Afrikaners and other denominations, including Anglican, Methodist, Presbyterian, and Roman Catholic, as well as African Charismatic, a combination of Christian and traditional African rituals. The Indian community consists of both Hindus and Muslims. There are also a small number of Jews.

Literacy/Education. Compared to most other African nations, the overall literacy rate is high but deceptive. The overall literacy rate is 86.4%, which is among the highest in Africa, but 99% of whites as compared to 50% of blacks are literate. (The other two highest African literacy rates are also in the south—Lesotho, 84.8%, and Zimbabwe, 90.7%; all three countries are former British colonies in which English is widely spoken).

Among the black population, 22.3% have no schooling, 25.4% have some or have completed primary school; 30.4% have some secondary schooling, while only 16.8% have completed their "metrics"; 5.2% has had higher education. Generally, the Indians (41%), the whites (36%), and the coloreds (7%) benefit by passing matric exams and moving on to university or college. Formerly all-white institutions, such as Witwatersrand and Cape Town universities, are still excellent. Historically, black universities have been described as atrocious with serious security problems, so reforms are under way among them. Until recently when Africans replace Afrikaners in the education ministry, only 3.8% of the GDP was devoted to education and 85% of that went to whites; now 20% of the national budget is spent on education regardless of color. Today nearly all the children attend primary school; over 8 million students enrolled in elementary schools, one million plus in secondary, and 282,000 or so in third or higher levels of education. But the quality of that education is questionable. The new education minister claims 30% of the schools are not fit for use, and there is an acute shortage of qualified teachers. The school system is an adaptation of the British educational model but is in transition to integrate more black Africans at all levels. Fifty-eight percent of students matriculating in secondary school do graduate. The apartheid legacy lingers among a lost generation that thought education was right but did not require personal effort and attendance. The situation improves in independent schools, the majority of which charge fees—2000 of them

The overall literacy rate is high.

enroll 4% of the student population. The proportion of blacks in them has risen to 60%, and this system is the best racially integrated. Furthermore, parents are becoming educational entrepreneurs, creating their own avenues of learning opportunities for economic and social mobility. Private business is involved in funding initiatives to improve all types of schooling. Overall, South Africa has one educational advantage; its school systems are flexible and opening to customizing programs to meet national and student needs.

Social Conditions

Consider these cultural insights about contemporary South Africa, especially among the black African majority:

- *Family structure* in the black community has been destabilized by past apartheid policies and its constraints; dislocation caused by job searches contributes to 7 million people living in poverty. In the black extended family, great respect is manifested toward the elderly and obedience to parents is the normal. In contrast, the white community's family is nuclear, close-knit, and privileged, though declining in affluence and influence. The Truth and Reconciliation Commission enabled families from both sides to testify or confess about the brutality of 40 years of apartheid regime, and to try and move on with reconstruction.

- *Emerging middle class* is slowly happening among the black community—up to 40% of the total population. Africans have taken over downtown urban centers, which formerly were only open to them by day. Affirmative action and black empowerment programs have opened up the job market and management positions, but only one black-owned company is a real success—Johnnic Holds, an entertainment, media, and telecommunications group. Today some 70% of the workforce are black Africans, of which 45% are women and 5% disabled. The black share of personal income has climbed and is rising, whereas the white share is declining, falling from 71% (1970) to 50% (2000). With all of the country's problems, including a 25.2% unemployment rate, the trends point toward greater prosperity for black Africans, even with a 0.3% annual growth rate in population.

- *Lifestyle* is better for many black Africans than in the past decade; their society is humming with activity and opportunity amidst poverty. Among the blacks, more vibrancy, naturalness, and brotherhood are evident, but the picture is sometimes marred by inter-tribal conflict and power struggles. Now their government is spending 21% of the national budget on education, which is 5.7% of the GDP. But the rates of crime, violence, and alcohol abuse are up, again partially due to past Afrikaner practices of uprooting people (e.g., putting migrant laborers into hostels, and paying too

Lifestyle is better for many black Africans than in the past decade.

many wages in *papsak* or wine). The dying white-dominated culture kept Africans subordinate, called men *boys*, and undermined their role as protectors, often dumping their wives and children in so-called homelands. Realistically, postapartheid South Africa is experiencing serious threats to family life, which is increasingly breaking down with male violence.

Work environment *is* gradually improving for all employees.

- *Work environment* is gradually improving for all employees. However, in government, the ANC, a former revolutionary party, is still authoritarian and prizes political loyalty over competence. Its officials have not mastered the art of administration and science of management, while being deployed from one job position to another. Their public servants are not open to new ideas outside their own bureaucracy. Their current policies discourage blacks from becoming entrepreneurs, so small and medium enterprises languish. Also there is a severe shortage of native skilled workers, and protectionism is in place to prevent the import of technicians from abroad. This shortage of qualified personnel has led to thousands of job vacancies, especially in the financial and banking sectors. Presently a plan is under way—the Joint Initiative for Priority Skills Acquisition—to develop the needed skill base by recruiting and training more engineers, technicians, and other skilled professionals.

- *Health care and social services* are beginning to deteriorate, though the country has the most organized and functioning health-care system in Africa. The quality of life for average citizens is being severely undermined by the spread of diseases, especially AIDS. The UNAIDS estimates that nearly 4.7 million people are HIV-positive, yet government "leaders" often live in denial. The administration of President Mbeki was absurdly slow in responding to the epidemic of 5.2 million HIV-infected citizens. With 40% so infected, forecasts are that the AIDS deaths will be up to 635,000 by 2010, bringing a vast increase in orphaned children and dysfunctional families. As a result, by the end of this decade, the public health costs are likely to approach 38 billion rand. The health-care and social services systems until recently had no effective plan in place to cope with growing numbers of patients and dying people, no less their youthful offspring who may end up truants, street gang members, and eventually criminals. Within that context, the UN expects South Africa's GDP in 10 years to be lowered by 17%. Except in the gold fields, the nation's workforce is likely to be decimated by this and related diseases, thereby undermining productivity. With about 900 dying daily from this illness, the government is finally waking up to the scourge of AIDS and its implications. A comprehensive regime is under way to combat the pandemic with antiretroviral drugs. But the whole health-care system is inadequate for coping with this plague.

- *Criminal justice* is weak in South Africa. The system suffers from too many criminals who either do not get caught or, when they are arrested, are not likely to be convicted. With the loss of 500 out of 1800 cases prosecuted, half of the 2.2 million crimes reported go unsolved. However, private investment and research into the processing of accused criminals have produced reforms in the justice system and higher conviction rates. The old hatred of police lingers, along with a legacy of firearms. Poorly paid police ranks are riddled by corruption, inadequate equipment, insufficient training, and ineptness. (About a quarter of the police force are functionally illiterate, and large numbers do not even have a driver's license to drive themselves to crime scenes). The cost of crime to business is up approximately to 12 billion rand, while the national police budget is about 16 billion rand. Reforms under way include the appointment of a new national prosecutor, establishment of a new elite investigation force, legislation to mandate minimum sentences, and bail. Poverty and the shantytowns it produced, such as Soweto outside of Johannesburg and Forman Road in Durban, are home to thousands of struggling black Africans and their uneducated and unemployed youth, many of whom turn to criminal activities to survive. In the 1990s there was a crime wave, and Johannesburg became known as the "crime capital of the world." But there has been a remarkable turnaround in that municipality with the formation of Business Against Crime (BAC). It has reduced street crime by 80% after installing 200 surveillance cameras in that city's central business district. Other cities, like Cape Town, have also had success in curbing crime with closed-circuit television monitoring. With a mixture of both private and public sector funding in crime prevention, young professionals have begun to move back into the inner cities, contributing to their renewal. Private security firms have increased and employ some 250,000 people, twice as many as in the regular police force.

Economic and Social Challenges

Economic Development: South Africa still has the strongest and most diversified economy on the African continent. The economy has structurally changed and is more internationally competitive. It is strong not only in minerals and raw materials, but increasingly in high technologies. A strong central bank and legal system, as well as a fair road and transport infrastructure, all contribute to development. Although foreign investments did not grow as anticipated with the lifting of global economic sanctions and diminishing civil protests, the global companies that have come are pleased overall with their experience and are expanding.

The government has succeeded in reducing the national budget, debt, and inflation through disciplined, responsible fiscal and monetary policies. It aims to promote growth, employment, and redistribution. The

South Africa still has the strongest and most diversified economy on the African continent.

Twenty-first-

century

Challenges:

South Africa

produced two of

the greatest

modern African

leaders.

challenge is whether the high standard of living enjoyed by the whites can be shared somewhat by the masses of black citizens, developing in the process a broader middle class. The gross domestic product average is obviously much higher for whites than blacks, but the GDP is growing too slowly overall. With an employment rate between 25 and 35%, 3 million inhabitants are looking for work. Reducing unemployment and job creation, along with new enterprises, are critical for growth within a new multiracial society. In the past, the economy was largely based on varied agriculture, as well as the mining of diamonds and gold, until the manufacturing industries took hold. South Africa has vast natural resources, including chromite, coal, uranium, platinum, natural gas, and fish. Today this diversified economy has a large industrial base—from metal products, chemicals, and foodstuffs to machinery, vehicles, and textiles—all part of a strong exporting program. With a good infrastructure in transportation and communication already in place, as well as an educated population, this nation has great potential for development.

Twenty-first-century Challenges: South Africa produced two of the greatest modern African leaders, namely, Nelson Mandela and Desmond Tutu, both Nobel Peace Prize winners. First African president Mandela and Archbishop Tutu personified the vision of creating a country with a nonracial future. Together they established a Truth and Reconciliation Commission, engaging enlightened leadership like theirs in both the public and private sector. Leadership is South Africa's primary need—leadership that is concerned for the whole citizenry, not just for his or her racial community. That type of leadership would address challenges, promoting:

- **Pluralism and inclusiveness**, which allows for reasonable dissent, compromise, give and take, and protection of human rights.
- **Educational and training improvements** at all levels for the development of a more knowledgeable and competent workforce.
- **Rebuilding strong family life and child care**, especially in those African homes and villages devastated by past-apartheid policies and currently by AIDS.
- **Economic development** without graft and corruption that improves the whole society, especially the black African and colored poor.

Exhibit 15.12 provides an external evaluation of the contemporary scene in this land of great promise.

Business Tips in South Africa

With a continent as vast and diverse as Africa, it is impossible to generalize on the preferred business and trade practices. South African business customs, for example, require some flexibility depending on which ethnic group you are dealing with. The white business protocols

EXHIBIT 15.12
THE NEW SOUTH AFRICA

In the 12 years since the African National Congress triumphantly took power in South Africa's first multiracial democratic elections, the country has plotted its course to relative stability, democracy, and prosperity. It is even beginning to lead the continent in an entirely new way, urging other nations there to emulate its example. Under Nelson Mandela's leadership, the ANC government has campaigned to alleviate poverty and degradation of apartheid victims, without resorting to counterproductive populism. While there have been some improvements, there is growing impatience over the pace of change in South Africa. Mandela's vision of a "rainbow nation" has slowed to a crawl.

Yet, from education to foreign policy to crime-fighting, the inhabitants have found creative solutions to their problems. The government has presided over 87 months of economic growth (currently 5% a year), low budgets deficits, and low inflation. While trying to encourage free enterprise. Buoyant domestic demand has been accompanied by the sort of foreign investment that some thought would never come. But despite a 5% GDP growth, the unemployment rate has risen to 27% of the population. Governance policy has provided more money for social program grants, mainly for child support and pensions to some 10 million people, as well as for public works, mainly to stimulate job creation, consumer demand, and tourism.

Furthermore, there are hopeful experiments to benefit children from squatters camps, such as an extraordinary school called *Sekolo Sa Bonrokgo* in the northern suburbs of Johannesburg. There 25 dedicated teachers inspire black learners to achieve remarkable academic progress. Since the lack of quality education is the single most important thing holding back the country's development, such innovations need to be multiplied.

The continent needs a strong South Africa, one prepared to go beyond traditional agendas and to make a commitment to good governance, humans rights, and democracy as enshrined in the goals of the African Union.

Source: Excerpted and adapted from R. Crokett, "Chasing the Rainbow—A Survey of South Africa." *The Economist*, April 8, 2006, 12 page insert (www.economist.com/surveys).

are comparable to those of Europe and North America, whereas those of Indian heritage may seem more like the commercial environment found in India. However, in what is typically referred to as *Black Africa*, whether in the west, east, or south, the following observations may prove useful. These observations supplement those made earlier in this chapter on "Cultural Characteristics of Africa."

Meetings. Business is normally discussed in an office, bar or, restaurant, but always outside the home. What happens in the home is considered private. When invited to someone's residence for a meal, do not discuss business. When an African is the host of such meetings, he or she will pay for everyone. If a foreigner is the host, he or she should pay. If a foreigner receives an invitation to a *braaivlets* or barbecue, it is an important part of getting to know better business associates without discussing business per se. It is customary for outsiders to bring a token gift, such as beverage or candy.

Communications. Most businesspeople have business cards that are readily exchanged. After some small talk on encountering a foreigner, white South Africans tend to get down to the purpose or agenda for meeting, whereas those of other races may make long inquiries about your health and family before getting down to business.

Attitudes. South Africans generally are low-key in their business discussion, searching for "win–win" opportunities for both parties. They are wary of foreigners who try to take advantage of them, so resist high pressure and cut-throat types, and emotional appeals. Ordinarily in the world of commerce and government, people do not like to be rushed into decisions about some deal. The local merchants of Indian or Chinese heritage are experienced and shrewd traders, and may be more aggressive in their negotiations.

Age commands

respect.

Seniority. As indicated previously, traditional age commands respect. Age and wisdom are seen as identical, and the norms of the elders must be followed to ensure smooth business dealings. Some of this tribal heritage is retained in some business environments.

Gender. As women become better educated and involved in business life, the traditional precedent of male before female is giving way to a more equalitarian approach.

PROSPECTS FOR PAN AFRICAN SYNERGY

In general, Africans are in transition from their traditional cultures based on a rural, agricultural, and tribal way of life. Rapidly, they are moving toward an urban lifestyle that is based on industrial and technological development. For the past 50 years, international business, professional, development, and humanitarian workers have done much to promote greater African prosperity, whether through the United

Nations' agencies, their own governments, multinational corporations, or financial investment. Some foreigners and their governments have also contributed to the exploitation of Africa's enormous resources for their own greedy purposes.

With the onset of this new millennium, there is much discussion of an African Renaissance and rediscovery of its creative past, led by South Africa. If non-Africans wish to participate in that renewal, consider the following arenas to promote:

Effective Leadership—replacement by twenty-first century leaders who are better educated and more competent and honest; more socially responsible; more farsighted and aware of international interdependence. Such new leadership in governance and public service will promote democratic government, being respectful of human and environmental rights. This will require massive cultural changes so that Africans become more goal oriented and less fatalistic. It means the heads of the 53 states must learn to work together synergistically through the African Union.

Environmental Protection/Rural Development—preserving the natural beauty and resources, while stopping further degradation of land and forests. The goal is to manage natural resources for sustainable development and more equitable sharing by the whole population. Less emphasis on urban development and more efforts directed to creating rural opportunity and agricultural production, including providing basic infrastructure for smaller towns and villages (e.g., clean water, electricity, transportation, jobs, education and health services).

Population Control—traditional large families that enlarge tribal power bases have to be regulated, while social security provisions are made for the aged and orphan children. Only then can tough problems related to infant mortality, child abuse, illiteracy, nutrition, and health care be solved in Africa.

Continental Health Crusade—an African Union initiative to control and conquer, with the help of global organizations, the scourges of HIV/AIDS and malaria, to improve water systems and medical treatment, and to provide cheaper drugs. Within Africa, multinational synergistic efforts to defeat the HIV/AIDS epidemic that is devastating Southern Africa, the epicenter of this Pan African tragedy.

Education and Training—promote education and skill development throughout the continent for the technological work environment and the knowledge culture. Such human resource development should include environmental education, civic responsibilities and competencies, intertribal and interracial tolerance, as well as management and administrative skills. The aim would be empowerment of the people, particularly of women and minorities.

If synergy is to occur between the more modern, developed world and Africa, there are lessons to be learned from the observations in Exhibit 15.13.

There is much discussion of an African Renaissance and rediscovery of its creative past.

EXHIBIT 15.13

AFRICA'S POVERTY

Humanitarian assistance should not be confused with economic development assistance. A rampaging disease that respects no international border threatens the survival of Africa. About 70% of AIDS sufferers worldwide are African and fighting the disease has overwhelmed African budgets. At a United Nations Conference on AIDS last June, UN Secretary General, Kofi Annan, called for a global war chest of $7 to $10 billion to battle AIDS. . . .

The state of postcolonial leadership in Africa is not pretty—a hideous assortment of "Swiss bank account" socialists, military vagabonds, quack revolutionaries, and briefcase bandits. Their overriding preoccupation is not to develop their economies but to perpetuate themselves in office, loot the treasury, and brutally suppress all dissent and opposition. . . .

Africa is not poor for lack of resources.

Africa is not poor for lack of resources. Its mineral wealth is immense: hydroelectric power potential; the bulk of the world's diamonds and chromium; substantial deposits of uranium. Gold, cobalt, phosphates, platinum, manganese, copper, and vast bauxite deposits, plus nickel and lead resources. . . . There is also vast oil and natural gas. . . . Yet paradoxically, a continent with such abundance and potential is mired in squalor, misery, deprivation, and chaos.

African leaders prefer to blame the West for Africa's poverty. But in fact, it has little to do with colonial legacies, the slave trade, imperialism, or other external factors. At the 2000 Summit of the Organization of African Unity in Rome, Tongo, Kofi Annan told African leaders they are to blame for most of the continent's problems: "Instead of being exploited for the benefit of the people, Africa's mineral resources have been so mismanaged and plundered that they are now a source of our misery."

The way out of Africa's economic miasma is through investment. . . . Aid to rouge regimes helps nobody. And to trade, a country must first produce the goods required for international commerce. . . . In 1990, only 4 out of 54 African countries were democratic. This number eventually grows to 15. . . . Target aid only to those countries that are democratic. . . . To establish a democratic order, these are most critical: an independent central bank; an independent judiciary; an independent free press and media; an independent electoral commission; a neutral and professional armed or security force; and an efficient civil service.

Source: B. N. Ayittey, "Africa's Poverty." *San Diego Union-Tribune*, INSIGHT, June 16, 2002, pp. G1 & G6.

Africa covers 20% of the world's landmass and has 10% of its people. Yes, it has problems, but nothing that north–south dialogue and collaboration cannot resolve, for Africa is a potentially rich continent. That may explain why the People's Republic of China has stepped up its involvement there. The Chinese are finding not only the resources they require, but business partners in Somalia, Sudan, Zimbabwe, Ethiopia, and Libya. Remember that six centuries ago, Ming Dynasty seafarers reached African shores for trade purposes, and today Chinese vessels ply those same sea lanes to bring back oil, iron ore, and other commodities to satisfy the voracious needs of its huge, expanding economy. Chinese entrepreneurs are pouring billions of dollars into Sino-African cooperative ventures, such as agriculture, anti-AIDS programs, culture, education, infrastructure, and retail projects, as well as investing there in mines, oil production, resort hotels, space satellites, and even military enterprises. Meanwhile the West makes insufficient investments in African human and natural resources, while wondering if the Chinese presence will undermine their own efforts there on behalf of human rights, democracy, peacekeeping, health care, and anticorruption. But Africa should be of global concern for humanity, not just eastern and western nations. Hopefully, the twenty-first century will find Africa moving beyond its colonial past and contemporary problems toward self-sufficiency in a more peaceful environment concerned about protecting the continent's vast natural resources, including its peoples, while at the same time encouraging environmental protection and tourism.[19]

CONCLUSIONS

Africa is the cradle of our civilizations, home to every person in the human family, whether they come to this continent as tourists, professional, humanitarians, or business persons. Accept the diversity among Africans while seeking to understand its inhabitants in an atmosphere of nonjudgmental acceptance.

In this chapter, we examined the vast continent of Africa in terms of its four geographic regions and the multitude of states within it. Profiles of selected countries with the larger populations in each area were presented, along with one in-depth case study of one nation per region. Overall, we also provided general insights into Africa, its current problems and promise, as well as characteristics of its diverse peoples. As a result, global leaders will appreciate the possibilities of Africa's human and natural resources. Synergistic partnerships, such as joint ventures and humanitarian projects, can do much toward contributing to the development of the area and its resources.

When comparing cultures, such as the American and African, and how they affect the business environment, it is necessary to understand that the United States is a low-context culture. It is technologically and futuristically oriented with an emphasis on individual achievement rather than on group participation. In the communication process, a low-context culture places meaning in the exact verbal description of an event. Individuals in such a culture rely on the spoken word. In contrast, Africa's culture is high context. In the communication process, much of the meaning comes not from the words but is internalized in the person. Meaning comes from the environment and is sought in the relationships between the ideas expressed in the communication process. High-context cultures, more so than low-context cultures, tend to be more human oriented and to value the extended family. Perhaps this closing quotation may stimulate readers' thinking about Africa: "No other continent has endured such an unspeakably bizarre combination of foreign thievery and foreign goodwill." (B. Kingsolver, *The Poisonwood Bible*, New York: HarperCollins, 1998).

MIND STRETCHING

Why is it important for all members of the human family, now consisting of 6.5 billion people, to appreciate Africa's past, present, and future potential?

1. How has past European colonialism impacted today's Africans?
2. Where is sub-Saharan Africa, and how does it differ from the rest of the continent?
3. What are the implications that in Africa, 900 million inhabitants live in the countryside, while rapid urbanization is under way?
4. How can those who live outside of Africa contribute to development of its human and natural resources, to combating poverty and disease on this continent, to promoting peace and better governance?

REFERENCES

1. *Family Reference Atlas of the World*. Washington, DC: National Geographic, p. 170.
2. Shreeve, J. "The Greatest Journey Ever Told—The Trail of Our DNA," *National Geographic*, March 2006, pp. 60–73.
3. Oliver, R. *The African Experience—Major Themes in African History from Early Times to the Present*. New York: Icon Editions, 1992; Meredith, M. *The State of Africa: A History of Fifty Years of Independence*. New York: Free Press, 2005.

4. Oldfield, S. (ed.). *The Trade in Wildlife: Regulation for Conservation.* New York: Earthscan, 2003; Peterson, D. *Eating Apes.* Berkeley: University of California Press, 2003.

5. Obradovic, N. (ed.). *The Anchor Book of Modern African Stories,* 2nd ed. New York: Anchor, 2003; Johnson, D. H. *The Root Causes of Sudan's Civil Wars.* Bloomington: University of Indiana Press, 2002; Legum, C. *Africa Since Independence.* Bloomington: Indiana University Press, 1999; Bach, D. *Regionalisation in Africa—Integration and Disintegration.* Bloomington: Indiana University Press, 1999; Pakenham, T. *The Scramble for Africa—The White Man's Conquest of the Dark Continent from 1876–1912.* New York: Avon Books, 1992; Davidson, B. *The Black Man's Burden: Africa and the Curse of the Nation-State.* New York: Times Books, 1992.

6. Recommended readings: "Africa—Whatever You Thought, Think Again," *National Geographic,* Special Issue, Washington, DC, September 2005; Guest, R. "How to Make Africa Smile—A Survey of Sub-Saharan Africa," *The Economist,* January 17, 2004, 16 pp. insert (www.economist.com/surveys).

7. Ayittey, B. N. "INSIGHT; Africa's Poverty," *San Diego Union-Tribune,* June 16, 2002, pp. G1/G6.

8. Davidson, B. *The Search for Africa.* New York: Times Books, 1994.

9. "Rebuilding Failed States—From Chaos, Order," *The Economist,* March 5, 2005, pp. 45–47.

10. "Doing Business in Africa—Different Skills Required," *The Economist,* July 2, 2005, p. 61.

11. "African Optimism—The Hopeful Continent," *The Economist,* January 7, 2006 p. 50.

12. Richmond, Y., Gestrin, P. *Into Africa—Intercultural Insights.* Boston: Nicholas Brealey/Intercultural Press, 1998; Wiredu, K. *Cultural Universals and Particulars: An African Perspective.* Bloomington: Indiana University Press, 1997; Arnoldi, M. J., Geary, G. M., and Hardin, K. L. (eds.). *African Material Culture.* Bloomington: Indiana University Press, 1996.

13. National Trade Data Bank, International Trade Administration, U.S. Department of Commerce, Washington, DC 20230 (Tel: 1/800-USA TRADE #4/5; Web site: www.export.gov—click on "market research" and then "country commercial guide" choosing a particular African state). For hard copy or diskette of any African country guide, call National Technical Information Service (1-800/553-NTIS). There is a country code for information on all nations of Unit 2 and this chapter on Africa (telephone hotline, 1-202/482-1064 or 1860). Major U.S. cities also have local offices of USDC with commercial advisors to provide counseling and resources to businesspersons seeking data or connections abroad in a specific country or area within that target culture. Consult also the local telephone directory under "Government Pages" for the nearest listing of the United States Government Offices, and the Federal Commerce Department. For readers seeking more details about these and other African countries, we recommend an Internet search for specific states in the CIA Fact Book (www.cia.gov/cia/publications/factbook/geos/ct.html).

14. "Kenya—Caught in the Act," *The Economist,* January 28, 2006, pp. 45–46.

15. Paul D. Civerdell Peace Corps Headquarters, 1111 20th St. NW, Washington, DC 20526, USA (www.peacecorps.gov/project#680-120).
   • Doctors Without Borders, 333 Seventh Ave., 2nd Fl., New York, N.Y. 1001, USA (www.doctorswithoutborders.org).
   • "Nota Bene," *Fordham Alumni Magazine*, Fall/Winter 2005/6, Vol. 39:1. (www.fordhamedu/instituteofinternationalhumanitarianaffairs).

16. Lewis, R. D. *The Cultural Imperative-Global Trends in the 21st Century*. Boston: Nicholas Brealey/Intercultural Press, 2003.

17. Sadiman, J. *South Africa's "Black" Market—How to Do Business with Africans*. Boston: Nicholas Brealey/Intercultural Press, 2000, Brown, J. et al. (eds.). *History from South Africa: Alternative Visions and Practices*. Philadelphia: Temple University Press, 1991. The authors acknowledge that the insights for this profile were partially obtained from a "Culturgram for the Republic of South Africa," *Culturgrams*, David M. Kennedy Center for International Studies, Brigham Young University, 280 HRCB, Provo, Utah 84602, USA (Tel: 801/378-6528). For further information about this nation and its culture, contact the Embassy of South Africa (3051 Massachusetts Ave., NW, Washington, DC 20008, USA) and the South African Tourism Board (747 Third Ave., 20th Floor, New York, NY 10017 or 9841 Airport Blvd., Ste. 1524, Los Angeles, CA 90045, USA).

18. Cockett, R. "Chasing the Rainbow—A Survey of South Africa", *The Economist*, April 8, 2006, 12 page insert; Grimond, J. "A Survey of South Africa—Africa's Great Black Hope," *The Economist*, February 24, 2001, 16-page insert. The author acknowledges significant use of these findings in his updating of this South African case study. All such country-specific reports are available from Reprints Department, *The Economist* Newspaper Group, Inc., 111 W. 57th St., 10019, New York, NY 10019, USA (www.economist.com/surveys).

19. "China in Africa—Never two late to Susanble," The Economist, On 28th 2006, pp. 53–54.

OTHER RESOURCES

Besides *Google* search on the Internet for Africa or any country therein, consult www.africaguide.com/; www.joeant.com/DIR/info/get/7375/18588; www.-sul.stanford.edu/depts/ssrg/africa/guide.html.

A very useful learning system is *Africa* produced by Palm World Voices (www.palmworldvoimces.com). This compact packet focuses on African peoples and their business. Each package contains a National Geographic map of African peoples and their music; a booklet with pictures entitled, *Africa the Musical Continent*; a visual DVD and an audio CD on the music of Africa. Inquire about other productions, such as *BabbaMaal: Senegal*.

The National Geographic Society periodically publishes updated maps on Africa (www.nationalgeographic/africa). For example, this map supplement to their magazine in September 2001 was entitled, *Africa Today*, and in September 2005, *Africa the Human Footprint*.

DOING BUSINESS WITH NORTH AMERICANS

The United States and Canada

People may have migrated into North America even before the ice sheets developed more than 20,000 years ago.[1]

LEARNING OBJECTIVES

The purpose of this chapter is to provide an historical overview of Canada and the United States as well as some important cultural similarities and differences.

As the United States is the only remaining "superpower" some perceptions of other nations are suggested. We have provided some "cultural informations on Canada and an overview of Mexico is presented in Chapter 12. These three nations are partners in NAFTA (The North American Free Trade Agreement).

Historical Perspective Overview

The first North American inhabitants of this continent may have migrated thousands of years earlier, possibly from Southern Asia or even Northern Europe. Smithsonian Institution researchers studying other New World human skulls found potential resemblance to archaic Norse populations, as well as the mysterious Ainu aborigines from the Japanese islands. Perhaps these early peoples originated from multiple migrations.[2]

North America

Scholars have found evidence that Phoenician merchants, Viking warriors, Irish monks, and Polynesian seafarers reached the Western Hemisphere centuries before an Italian navigator got the credit for this great feat. Of course, the Eskimos, or Inuit, may have already crossed the Bering Sea and settled in North America long before the Phoenicians, Vikings, Irish, and Polynesians arrived.

Recently, archaeologists from the College of William and Mary uncovered an 11,000-year-old spearhead on Jamestown Island, Virginia. The primitive tool was used by Ice Age inhabitants to hunt mastodon and elk. The English landed in Jamestown much, much later, in 1607.[3]

Although North America geographically includes three nations, Mexico, Canada, and the United States, Chapter 16 covers only those who live north of the Rio Grande River. Although Mexico is geographically and economically part of North America, *culturally* it is aligned with Latin America and South/Central America. (Mexico is covered in Chapter 12 on Latin America.) We begin with a test followed by an overview of the United States and Canada, recognizing that the term *American* can be applied to all the peoples of North, Central, and South America, its popular designation is for citizens of the U.S.A. We begin with queries about the United States and Canada. However, "American" is more often used to refer to those living in the United States.

Although Mexico is geographically and economically part of North America, culturally it is aligned with Latin America and South/Central America.

What Do You Know About Canada?

Question: What is a loonie in Canada?
Answers:
1. An individual who might be viewed as mentally unstable
2. One dollar coin
3. A cell phone
4. Canadian dance move

Question: At a business meal you might notice that Canadians enjoy which of the following condiments with their French fries?
Answers:
1. Ketchup and mustard
2. Gravy or salt with vinegar
3. Hot sauce
4. Mustard only

Question: What are the Mounties?
Answers:
1. Canadian cowboys
2. Men and women who live up in the Canadian mountains
3. Police officers who drive and fly around Canada fighting drugs, gangs, and other problems that face Canada
4. Canadian firefighters

Question: Canada is divided into:
Answers:
1. 10 provinces and 3 territories
2. 10 states and 3 territories
3. 10 states and 3 provinces
4. 10 provinces and 3 states

What Do You Know About the United States?

Question: What do the stars on the U.S. flag represent?
Answers:
1. The fifty colonies
2. The first fifty U.S. presidents
3. The fifty largest U.S. cities
4. The fifty states

Question: Which of the following topics would be good to discuss with a U.S. American that you just met?
Answers:
1. Health concerns
2. Sports
3. Religion
4. Income

Question: Which U.S. city has the largest population?
Answers:
1. Chicago
2. Los Angeles
3. New York
4. Philadelphia

Question: The standard workweek in the United States is how many hours?
Answers:
1. 35 hours
2. 40 hours
3. 45 hours
4. 50 hours

We suggest getting the answers to these simple questions from a Canadian and an American. We also recommend searching the Internet for more information on various Native American or indigenous peoples in both countries as well as minority groups within both countries. In the following material, a much more detailed overview of both countries will be given.

PAN AMERICAN MANAGEMENT PERSPECTIVES

This land body of Canada and the United States that extends almost from the Arctic to Cape Horn was named "America" after the 16th-century Italian explorer and merchant, Amerigo Vespucci. Trade was a dominant force in the discovery and development of these unknown territories between the Atlantic and Pacific Oceans. Although all of today's inhabitants of the Americas have the right to the title "American"—and many think of themselves as such—it was the people in that area of the United States who popularly appropriated the designation.

The Americas—North, Central, and South—have a diversity of cultural heritages, and a synergy of sorts is being forged. It is like a huge laboratory of human relations in which a mixture of cultures from Europe, Africa, and Asia are living side by side. One tends to think of North America as largely "Anglo-Saxons" who speak primarily English. However, Canada is bilingual with French as its second language, while the United States is moving in the bilingual direction with Spanish. The area south of the Rio Grande River is considered Latin America because the language there is mainly of Latin origin. Apart from numerous Indian languages, Spanish is dominant in Mexico, Central and South America, while Portuguese is the primary language of Brazil (with some Italian and Japanese being spoken).

For our purpose, Pan America will designate that landmass of some 15 million square miles from the Arctic Ocean south to the convergence of the Atlantic and Pacific Oceans at Drakes Passage. The Americas comprise approximately 30 *national* cultures, plus Eskimo and Native American cultures.

For global leaders seeking to function effectively in the Pan American market, it is important to understand the geoeconomic and cultural characteristics that will facilitate business and acculturation. To better comprehend the Pan American market, consider these realities.

The Americas— North, Central, and South— have a diversity of cultural heritages.

Economic Development

International agencies and banks generally consider the North American countries to be rich in terms of annual gross domestic product per capita, whereas most of Latin America, from Mexico southward, is thought to comprise developing countries. Despite economic progress in Latin America, a significant percentage of their population is still classified as poor. This helps to explain the economic dependence of the South on the North in the Americas and the flow of illegal immigrants northward in the search of work. It also points up the problems of these nations with the International Monetary Fund and the World Bank relative to difficulties with repayment of loans, rising inflation, and other economic problems. The most significant economic development in the Americas has been the signing of the North American Free Trade Agreement (NAFTA) in 1992, signed by Canada, the United States, and Mexico, to expand trade and financial growth in the three countries.

Human Resources

Canada and the United States have a combined population of approximately 341 million persons, with a natural population increase of less than 1%. Latin America has more than 560 million inhabitants and a rate of increase between 1 and 3%; the most populous countries, at 3% or more, are Mexico, Venezuela, Guatemala, Peru, and Paraguay. Obviously, unless expanding population is brought under control in the South, not only will economic growth there be affected adversely, but continuing social unrest, and political and military turmoil can be expected. There are human assets in Latin America waiting to be capitalized through education and training.

In this hemisphere, the interface between its northern and southern inhabitants is a contrast in opportunities and problems. The opportunities for mutual enrichment are through cultural exchanges, scientific collaboration, educational and economic assistance, and efforts promoting peace between the hemispheres. However, the problems proliferate because issues like these cry out for creative solutions from Pan Americans:

■ Lack of north/south dialogue and synergistic endeavors that benefit the peoples of both continents, such as projects to renew the infrastructures of societies in need, or to provide adequate food and shelter for the poor.
■ Instability in some Latin American countries that suffer from archaic political, justice, and economic systems.
■ Insecurity caused by growing deviant behavior as expressed in antisocial actions such as terrorism and drug trafficking or the expanding struggle between democratic ideals and totalitarian realities.
■ Inability to establish a meaningful north/south dialogue and collaborative exchange in the Americas, instead of exploitation and dependence.

Yet for the most part, Pan America is a free-enterprise system and a market of vast potential. It borders the Pacific Rim on the west and can benefit from the trade shift from the Atlantic to the Pacific.

NORTHERN AMERICA'S INDIGENOUS PEOPLE

Eskimos (Inuits) and Native Americans

From a majority perspective in any society (i.e., as a white, Anglo-Saxon in Canada or the United States), it is difficult to write about indigenous people. However, indigenous people need to be addressed first with respect and in a positive manner and then with openness to the ways we can learn from their culture. History, and how it affected their culture, should also be considered.

Members of the majority and others need to be aware of culturally biased words. *The Color of Words: An Encyclopedic Dictionary of Ethnic Bias in the United States,*[4] explains words and expressions used in the United States today that carry ethnic bias. The words listed illustrate the labeling and classifying of people, these classifications are often for "reasons of manipulation or mischief." There are over one thousand words or phrases listed, and the following are examples of some culturally biased, racist, and inappropriate words.

Coolie, cooly. An unskilled Asian laborer or porter. Dating from the mid-seventeenth century, the term was applied by Europeans in India and China to a native laborer hired at subsistence wages. In California, since the 1860s, Chinese immigrants or sojourners were viewed as a "race of coolies" who threatened white Californian labor.

Coon. A shortened form of *raccoon*. In American English, *coon* is usually dated to 1742. *Coon* has been used derogatorily to refer to a black person, especially a male, since the mid-nineteenth century.

Dink. Derogatory nickname for an Asian or person of Asian descent, but today usually a Vietnamese, as used by American and Australian soldiers during the Vietnam War. (*Note:* "DINK" also describes a social/economic group that has "Dual Income, No Kids.")

In parts of the Americas there are two indigenous peoples caught in a culture gap—the Eskimos (Inuits) and the Native Americans. Both have been harmed and helped by the rapid advancement of "white civilization" into their lives. With the introduction of U.S. and Canadian government health and education programs, their life expectancy and educational levels have risen. But so have their frustration, despair, and social deterioration. Many have succumbed to alcoholism and drug addiction, and the rate of suicide is exceedingly high. Their problems and potentials are similar on or off reservations; whether in the U.S. state of Alaska or the Canadian Northwest Territories; whether above or below the U.S.–Canadian border.

In parts of the Americas there are two indigenous peoples caught in a culture gap.

In April 1999, in an attempt to right past wrongs, Canada divided the Northwest Territory in two and established Nunavut, meaning "our land," giving the Inuit title to 135,000 square miles of their traditional territory. With the creation of Nunavut, the Inuit have won some degree of self-determination. What is remarkable "is that by conventional measures of political influence like the votes they control or the funds they have access to, (the Eskimos) would have been considered almost powerless."[5] However, using traditional Inuit attributes of patience and compromise, they accomplished their goals without long, drawn out court battles or violence.

Weatherford discusses how the misnamed Indians of the Americas transformed the world, stating that the contributions of the Native Americans to our economy and culture have been consistently under-rated, if not ignored.[6] His conclusion is even more telling—the richness of the Indian cultures may be lost due to past wrongs.

The Inuits have given us the snowshoe, toboggan, and kayak, among other things, while Native Americans introduced maize, potatoes, sweet potatoes, and manioc. These crops constitute a large portion of today's staple foods. Cotton was also introduced by Native Americans.[7] The Inuit and Native American have much to teach us about the mind, spirit, and body and about our relationship to the natural world. The Native American philosophy of respect and reverence and cooperation with the earth are finally gaining acceptance in the mainstream.

Tribal or aboriginal peoples everywhere face the same dilemma brought on by accelerating social and technological change. Whether an Inuit in Hudson Bay or a Navajo in northern Arizona, the confrontation with too-rapid cultural change leaves the natives bewildered, confused, and almost overwhelmed. The rate of innovation in traditional societies is slow, while it rises astronomically in modern societies in the midst of transition. The traditional culture is past-oriented, while modern society is future-oriented, interpreting history as progressive movement. Unfortunately, Western ethnocentrism, even among anthropologists, has labeled some of these tribal people as primitive. In fact, these groups are quite developed within their own context and are more in harmony with nature than many people today. They seem to possess a better sense of ecology, energy conservation, food distribution, and overall happiness than many of their so-called civilized counterparts.

In the process of trying to enhance the indigenous peoples of the Americas, one must understand and appreciate the values and assets in such cultures. One is then in a position to create synergy with them relative to their contributions, and both cultures can work together to meet their needs.

The Eskimos (Inuits) and Native North Americans have paid a high price for acculturation. Many of their people suffer mental and physical, as well as economic, handicaps. But with cooperation and col-

Tribal or aboriginal peoples everywhere face the same dilemma brought on by accelerating social and technological change.

laboration by their fellow citizens, these proud and resourceful people can create a new place.

Native Americans

Who is the Native American? Misnamed "Indians" by Christopher Columbus, Native Americans are the indigenous people who were the local inhabitants of the Americas when the Europeans arrived. Ancestors of these Native Americans migrated here from Asia, and possibly Egypt and the Viking homelands. There are obvious cultural differences between the descendants of these aboriginal peoples and modern citizens of North, Central, and South America.

There are approximately 2 million Native Americans in the United States, half of whom live on reservations. The average annual income is below poverty level, and their unemployment rate is the highest in the country.

When America was discovered, there were probably fewer than 1 million Native Americans living in what is now the United States. These peoples were scattered, and their tribal organizations were unrelated. Many early colonists married Native Americans, motivated largely by social and cultural factors. For example, a Native American wife was an asset to a fur trader in teaching him the language and customs of the tribe from which he bought furs. In early New England, however, Native American women had little use in the trading and farming communities, and intermarriage was rare.

The U.S. government, which came into existence with the adoption of the Constitution, began its imperialistic relationship by considering the various tribes as national entities and negotiating with them for land.

There are many fundamental differences between a tribal culture and the dominant culture. The following lists three of these differences:

- In the mainstream culture, time is to be used, saved, and spent. People are paid for their time and generally view time as a continuum that is related to the rising and setting of the sun and to the changes in the seasons.
- In the mainstream culture, decision making is based on authority. Some people have authority to make decisions and others do not. Authority in Native American cultures is more horizontal than vertical because of the necessity of reaching unanimity on a decision before any action will be taken.
- Most Americans live pretty much for the future. We ask our children what they want to be when they grow up. In contrast, Native American children are not asked the same question, because they already "are"—they are children and they do not have to wait "to be."

Native Americans are the indigenous people who were the local inhabitants of the Americas when the Europeans arrived.

Understanding the Native American way of life provides us with a challenge and an opportunity. We can learn to develop skills and to work with them without destroying their dignity, and we can allow them to change at their own pace. An understanding of Native American history, values, and cultural differences can facilitate communication and business with these remarkable people.

Within the continental United States, many Native Americans have passed into the mainstream culture. Today, in many states, gaming and casino operations are managed and owned by Native Americans. For those who still live on government reservations, painful progress is being made to gain greater control over and administration of their own affairs, whether this be in schools and services or within the Federal Bureau of Indian Affairs. With recent financial settlements through the courts over abrogated treaty rights and lost lands, some tribes have established modern corporations to manage their natural resources and to enter into joint ventures with major companies for economic development purposes, even in the field of high technology on the reservations. Native North Americans never had the "white man's" sense of private property. Tribal culture thought in terms of collective responsibility for the preservation of the land and nature's gifts. Today, the ecology and nature movements are catching up to the aboriginal concern for the environment.

More than a half million Canadians are classified as having native ancestry, and three quarters of these people live on reservations. These are grouped by their government in four categories—status (registered formally under the Indian Act); nonstatus Indians who have not registered with the government; Metis (descendants of mixed aborigine and European ancestry); and Inuits (approximately 36,000), a distinct cultural group who generally live north of the tree line and speak primarily their own language (Inuktitut). A 1985 change in Canadian law has caused a dramatic rise in Indian population figures, which includes Indian women who marry Canadians of non-Indian ancestry. Exhibit 16.1, details this historic development.

> We shall learn all the devices the white man has.
> We shall handle his tools for ourselves.
> We shall master his machinery and his inventions, his skills, his medicines, his planning; But we'll retain our beauty AND STILL BE INDIAN.
>
> —A young Indian college student, date unknown

Energy companies, searching for commercial quantities of oil, coal, uranium, and other natural resources, are present on Native American lands. There are apparent differences between the Northern Cheyenne and the oil people who work with them. However, if both groups are respectful and knowledgeable of each other's business motivations,

Tribal culture thought in terms of collective responsibility for the preservation of the land and nature's gifts.

Even equable Canada has its unhappy indigenes: Cree Indians and Inuit fearful of separatism in Quebec; Mohawks farther south in conflict with police over land and smuggling; British Columbia's many tribes which claim, except in a few small areas, they never gave up their rights by treaty and that nearly all of that province's 950,000 square kilometers are rightfully theirs. . . . The "first nations" cannot expect to retrieve title, in the modern sense, to all their land. But they want compensation for it, and recognition of their "aboriginal rights." . . . (I)n remote New Aiyandish, 750 km north of Vancouver, British Columbia's first modern treaty of settlement was concluded. The winners were the Nisga'a, a tribe that has led the fight for aboriginal rights for more than 100 years. . . . Once ratified, the 6000 Nisga'a will collectively own 1992 square kilometers in the Nass River Valley. Along with full power of governance, forest and mineral rights, they will get C$121 m to help build infrastructure in their authorities, and C$190 m grants over the next five years as settlement of their claims. . . . Nisga'as argue they will remain Canadians, with the same rights and subject to the same criminal law as others. They have made other concessions in signing this treaty, including losing their exemption from sales and income tax. . . . Most aboriginal leaders are hailing this treaty as a breakthrough that will speed settlement with 51 Indian groups, covering most of the province. . . . Polls in British Columbia indicate that 90% of the general population favor settling such land claims, for the disputes hinder economic investment and development of the region.[8]

Source: "A New Deal for One First Nation." *The Economist,* August 8, 1998, p. 34.

value systems, and other aspects of their cultures, the possibility of working together for mutual advantage is significantly enhanced. Some energy companies provide education and cross-cultural training for the geologists, landsmen (women), and others who work closely with Native American people in their many phases of intimate contact. These educational seminars involve presentations by Native American leaders, self-assessment exercises, collaborations, team-building exercises, and the distribution of articles and books on the various tribes.

It is impossible to provide here an example of the information presented on all the Native American nations. We have profiled one North American tribe to illustrate the rich background and unique aspects one must consider when contemplating investing in tribal resources, forming joint ventures, and so on. Exhibit 16.2 is a condensed profile on the Northern Cheyenne.[8]

Each Native American culture brings a richness and diversity to the world. An understanding and respect for the differences and similarities can only bring mutual benefit.

EXHIBIT 16.2
HISTORY OF THE NORTHERN CHEYENNE

The name Cheyenne comes from the Sioux word *sahiyela* or *sahyiyena* and means "alien speaker." In their own Cheyenne language, however, the name is *Tsitsistas*.

Originally, the Northern and Southern Cheyenne lived together as one tribe. They were first seen by white men in Minnesota in approximately 1640. In the part of the 17th century, the Cheyenne began migrating to the Western Plains, where they obtained horses and led basically a nomadic life.

The Cheyenne coalesced into two groups; the Northern Cheyenne who lived in Big Horn and Rosebud Counties in Montana and the Southern Cheyenne who lived in the Southern Arpaho in Oklahoma. In the mid-1800s, after several bloody battles with the U.S. Cavalry, the U.S. government ordered the Northern Cheyenne to the reservation of the Southern Cheyenne in Oklahoma. The Northern Cheyenne, longing for their homeland in Montana, left Oklahoma. Eventually, U.S. troops captured the returning Cheyenne and moved them to army barracks at Fort Robinson, while the army petitioned Washington concerning their fate. When Washington decided the Northern Cheyenne should be returned to Oklahoma, about 150 Cheyenne attempted escape and were shot. The remaining Cheyenne were taken to the Tongue River Reservation in Montana that was established for the Northern Cheyenne.

In 1887, Congress passed a law permitting all Native American Indian tribes to divide their land among tribal members. Each member would receive approximately 160 acres. After holding the land for 25 years, the individual could sell the land. Land that was not allocated was owned by the tribe.

The Northern Cheyenne believed that the land that their ancestors had fought and died for should not be divided. Land is mother and is holy. The Indian Bureau informed the Cheyenne that if they divided the land the individuals who owned the land could receive government loans to improve the property. The Cheyenne resisted dividing their land, but in 1926 the tribe gave 1457 members a tract of 160 acres each. The remaining acreage (a little less than half of the reservation) was owned by the tribe. All mineral rights on the

EXHIBIT 16.2

HISTORY OF THE NORTHERN CHEYENNE (CONTINUED)

land belonged to the tribe. After the 25 years passed, there was great pressure on individual Cheyenne to sell their property. Today, less than 2% of the reservation is owned by nontribal individuals, and 70% is owned by the tribe.

Government

The Northern Cheyenne are governed by a tribal council that is headed by a president and elected by the tribal members. There are Indian courts with Indian judges and an Indian police force.

In 1933, the Indian Department became the Bureau of Indian Affairs (BIA). The BIA is the *trustee* of reservation lands. Native American land is *entrusted* to the BIA, which is to ensure that the land is used for the best interest of the Native Americans. Historically, the BIA has not always understood Native Americans or acted wisely on their behalf.

The traditional Northern Cheyenne's view of authority and power was that it was a condition that flowed naturally from one's moral excellence and virtue. Historically, a chief was selected because of his wisdom and honorable actions, and he in turn received the loyalty, respect, and obedience of the tribe.

The People

The Cheyenne's world is a mixture of the American world and the European world. Almost everyone speaks English, although many still converse in the Cheyenne language, and in some schools the Cheyenne language is taught.

The Northern Cheyenne and the Plains tribes are fun loving and enjoy good companionship. They love feasts, happy talk, and story-telling. The efforts of the Northern Cheyenne to preserve their culture are at their height today. Through education, both in the classroom and through the traditions of the tribe, the Cheyenne are attempting to teach and pass on the Cheyenne ways to their children.

Many nontribal organizations, for example, VISTA Volunteers, have offered programs and assistance to the tribe. Many in the tribe, including parents, are concerned that the exposure to nontribal values may create problems or send mixed messages to the young.

The Culture

Historically, the Northern Cheyenne men were hunters who provided for their families and tribe while living on the reservation.

The Bureau of Indian Affairs (BIA). The BIA is the trustee of reservation lands.

EXHIBIT 16.2

HISTORY OF THE NORTHERN CHEYENNE (CONTINUED)

Today, that is a financial impossibility for most, and men and women work on or off the reservation in offices and factories. The Northern Cheyenne, and many other tribes as well, perceive their work in combination with their Native American traditions. Work is to be done so that a harmony exists between one's work and the land, nature, and one's family; a balance. Tardiness on the job is often a problem because of the different perception of time for the Cheyenne. Non-Native Americans view time as a straight line with a past, present, and future, a fast-moving river. Native Americans view time with recurring phases, with one season flowing into the next and one's life leading into another.

In the Native American system, families are extended to include grandparents, aunts, uncles, and cousins, as well as relatives by marriage. In the Northern Cheyenne tribe the word for mother is the same word for aunt, and these aunt-mothers are integral to the child's upbringing.

The naming of a child was an important occasion.

Traditionally, the naming of a child was an important occasion. The first name took place shortly after birth. If it was a male it was named by the father's family, and a female child was named by the mother's. As a child grew older a new name would be given, sometimes describing a brave or important event in his or her life. These new names might be given when the young man or woman entered puberty.

Powwows, a social custom of the past, still are held several times a year. During the summer, a powwow can bring together many different tribes or unite the Southern and Northern Cheyenne and the Sioux. Historically, a powwow was a sacred event, a prayer for protection to the Great Spirit. Also, traditionally, the powwow was a "giveaway," when horses and goods were shared with others in the tribe. Today, the powwows are for feasting and meeting with old friends and for sustaining old traditions.

Another enjoyable old festivity of the Northern Cheyenne was Distribution Day. In the beginning of government annuities, provisions of beef were distributed on the hoof at distribution centers. A bull was released from a chute and the head of each Native American household chased the animal and killed it with a bow and arrow or rifle. Since this was reminiscent of the old buffalo hunting days, the Native Americans enjoyed it immensely. The women would follow and butcher the animal and pack the meat for traveling back to the reservation. At these gatherings there would be singing and dancing and exchange of gossip and news.

PROFILE OF CANADA

Population	33,000,000
Ethnic groups	British Isles origin, 28%; French origin, 23%; other European, 15%; Amerindian, 2%; other, mostly Asian, African, Arab, 6%; mixed background, 26%
Religions	Roman Catholic, 43%; Protestant, 23%; other, 18%
Education	97% literacy rate
Land	9,220,970 sq km
Government	Confederation with parliamentary democracy
Political parties	Bloc Quebecois, Liberal Party, New Democratic Party, Party of Canada, Green Party
Per capita income	$32,800

Cultural Insights

The 19th century was the century of the United States, the 20th century will be the century of Canada.[9]

This prediction was made shortly after Wilfrid Laurier, Canada's first French Canadian prime minister, won the election in 1896. His prediction did not come to pass, but Canada as a country has continued to grow.

Canada is a bilingual and multicultural country, whose more than 30 million people live in ten provinces, three federal territories, the Northwest Territories, and the Yukon.

The identity crisis between its two major cultural heritages—English and French—appears to have subsided. Having lost referenda on separate sovereignty for their province, the hard line French-Canadians have lost much of their power. Earlier attempts at constitutional change in Canada—the Meech Lake and the Charlottetown Constitutional Accords—failed because of the proposed recognition of Quebec as a distinct and different society and culture. There is significant opposition between the federalists and the separatists.

Although Canada was established as a political entity in 1867 through the British North American Act, in 1982 the House of Parliament in the United Kingdom voted to amend it so that the Canadian constitution could be brought home and "patriated." Canada is governed under the Constitution Act.[10]

Throughout Canada, the family is the center of society, and homes are often passed along from one generation to another. Nowhere is this

Canada is a bilingual and multicultural country.

more true than in the central province of Quebec, the heart of French Canada. Canadians tend to be reserved until you get to know them well. The Roman Catholic tradition dominates. The major industries are mining, forestry, hydroelectricity, and agriculture. The country's economic wealth is centered in forests, petroleum, natural gas, and iron ore. Sprawling democratic Canada has one of the world's highest standards of living.

Bilingual (French and English) individuals have an advantage in international commerce. However, English is the dominant language in Canada and the United States. Do people from Canada and the United States speak English the same way with the same accent? *National Geographic* found the following:

- The English spoken in the United States West does not have a uniform regional dialect.
- The U.S. southern accent is strong.
- The U.S. Northeast has many local dialects.
- The dialect of Canadians and Americans, despite frequent contact, are not merging.
- In summary, dialects in Canada and the United States are becoming more pronounced.[11]

Proud of their country, sensitive about their relations with the United States and comparisons to it, fiercely independent while self-deprecating as a people, Canadians resent being lumped together with the other "Americans" below the 49th parallel. Despite that and the U.S. media/ economic dominance, the relations among North Americans are generally good and friendly. The longest unprotected border separates Canada and the United States. These two countries have been friends for over a century. There is tremendous potential for synergy between these neighboring countries, which in many ways are more alike than different.

For those doing business in Canada, it is wise to remember that Canadians are not culturally "just like" their counterparts in the United States. Normally, Canadians are friendly and more reserved than their neighbors to the south. Canadians tend to observe formalities and rules of etiquette that might be overlooked in the United States. Swardon stated it this way:

> Canadians haven't forgotten the social contract of *civility*—there is a collective moral authority in Canada that causes people to act with decorum, whether standing in line or observing a forbidden zone. What is often forgotten in the U.S., is observed here, such as suborning one's own desires for the greater good, respect for authority, and distaste for rugged individualism. Canada's Constitution is based on peace, order, and good government. Good manners are ingrained in the society, and cooperation is preferred to competition.[12]

Canadians are not culturally "just like" their counterparts in the United States.

Canadians everywhere know they can count on the federal government in Ottawa and the Northwest Mounted Police to maintain order. Canadians treat government officials in their 10 provinces with as much gentleness and deference as they do each other. Media commercials downplay both the work ethic and need to overachieve, while emphasizing recreational sports and leisure vacations. Canadian literature also reflects cultural themes of failure, pessimism, and mediocrity. Canadians are all too aware of their southern neighbor and are determined to define themselves differently, but they often lack confidence.

Patriotic, law-abiding, proud of their heritage, Canadians also realize that their nation is vast. With a strong economy and high levels of education and health services, Canadians are confident of their future and welcome foreign business and immigration. Canada is an interesting cultural mosaic. In addition to its main cultural heritage of English and French, there are strong minority ethnic groups of Germans, Scandinavians, Asians, Dutchs, Ukrainians, Poles, and Italians. In 2003, the United Nations ranked Canada second among all nations as having the best "quality of life." Norway was first.

Canada's government operates on the model of the British parliamentary system under a prime minister, the armed forces have been streamlined into a single defense organization, and it does not have a free-market economy, for Canada fears foreign domination of its economy. As a part of the British Commonwealth system, many peoples of those countries, such as India and Pakistan, have relocated to Canada. The latest cultural enhancement to the Canadian west coast is coming from Asia. Apart from Indo-Chinese refugees and Japanese investors, the biggest influx is from Hong Kong residents with Commonwealth passports who are talented and affluent and will invest much in their new country. Exhibit 16.3 shows the diversity among Canadian emigrés.

Canada's government operates on the model of the British parliamentary system.

Tips for Doing Business and Negotiating with Canadians

The following is a profile of a Canadian negotiator based on a framework of variables that can substantially influence negotiations.[13]

There are two dominant cultural groups in Canada. Each of these groups has a "typical" negotiating style. The English Canadian culture is the dominant group in the provinces of Ontario, British Columbia, Alberta, Manitoba, Saskatchewan, Nova Scotia, New Brunswick, Newfoundland, and Prince Edward Island. There is also a strong English Canadian minority in the province of Quebec centered mainly in Montreal. The French Canadian culture is dominant in Quebec where the official language is French. There is a strong French Canadian

EXHIBIT 16.3
PERMANENT RESIDENTS ADMITTED IN 2004

Country	Number	Percentage	Rank
China, Republic of	36, 411	15.44%	1
India	25,569	10.84%	2
Philippines	13,301	5.64%	3
Pakistan	12,796	5.43%	4
United States	7,494	3.18%	5
Iran	6,063	2.57%	6
United Kingdom	6,058	2.57%	7
Romania	5,655	2.40%	8
Korea, Republic of	5,337	2.26%	9
France	5,026	2.13%	10
Total for top 10 countries	123,710	52.46%	
Total for all countries	112,114	47.49%	
TOTAL	235,824	100.00%	

Source: Facts and Figures 2004: Immigration Overview—Permanent and Temporary Residents (www.cic.gc.ca/english/pub/annual-resrport2005/section3.html)

minority in New Brunswick and also in eastern Ontario around the national capital city of Ottawa.

Basic Concept of Negotiation

English and French Canadians tend to confront conflict and focus on points of disagreement as they work through a linear problem-solving process. This process involves identifying the problem or opportunity, the objectives of the negotiation, the alternatives, the decision, and the plan for action. English Canadians tend to focus on abstract or theoretical values and less on the practical facts of key issues that have come out of the negotiation process whereas French Canadians tend to prefer a more instrumental and individualistic approach to negotiating. The goal of French Canadian negotiators is to influence the other party and to focus on relationship building.

Selection of Negotiators

English and French Canadian negotiators are usually chosen for a negotiating team based on their knowledge, expertise, and previous experience concluding successful negotiations. Individual differences such as gender, age, and social class are less important for English than French Canadians. The latter tend to accept greater levels of inequality and ability between different levels of management and are more likely to send no negotiators if the situation precludes their ability to achieve their individual objectives.

Role of Individual Aspirations

Canadian culture encourages individual aspirations and achievement. Most Canadians are expected to represent the objectives of their organizations ahead of their personal objectives. However, the English Canadians may use more cooperative bargaining strategies, while French Canadians may employ more competitive strategies.

Concern with Protocol

English and French Canadians tend to be friendly and informal. English Canadians are less concerned with protocol and usually commence their business with very few preliminaries. French Canadians are more concerned with protocol and ceremony.

Significance of Type of Issue

English Canadians are dedicated to the goal of getting the job done. They seem even less concerned than Americans with building and developing relationships and are both impersonal and task-oriented, as are the French Canadians.

Complexity of Language

English Canadians, like their American neighbors, are generally low-context communicators. The messages sent by the words spoken are the intended messages. French-speaking Canadians are high-context communicators because the spoken word is only one part of the total message.

Nature of Persuasive Argument

Canadians use a rational presentation style with detailed facts and figures organized to support a clearly stated position. A deductive style is favored when parties are expected to be in agreement. This style presents the key recommendations first, followed by the key supporting information. An inductive style is preferred when persuasion is necessary. In this case, supporting information is presented first and then builds toward acceptance of an argument that is presented last.

English Canadians, like their American neighbors, are generally low-context communicators.

English and

French

Canadians tend

to be rigidly

bound by their

schedules and

deadlines.

Value of Time

English and French Canadians tend to be rigidly bound by their schedules and deadlines. Promptness in both beginning and ending meetings is appreciated. If one is made to wait more than five or ten minutes for a scheduled interview, many Canadian businesspeople would assume that a personal slight was intended.

Bases of Trust

Canadian managers believe that trust is an important component in achieving organizational and interorganizational goals. They believe this even when dealing with negotiators from cultures where trust is not a competitive advantage or may even be a competitive liability.

English Canadians tend to trust the information that is being communicated as long as their counterpart uses a cooperative negotiating strategy that emphasizes the free exchange of information. An agreement will result in a contract that can be enforced legally. If, however, English Canadian negotiators perceive that their counterparts are not using a cooperative strategy, then trust is damaged because the counterpart may seem to be more interested in achieving individual outcomes rather than joint outcomes.

French Canadians may tend to distrust information more than English Canadians. French Canadians tend to use more competitive negotiation strategies that place individual objectives ahead of joint outcomes.

THE UNITED STATES OF AMERICA

Profile of the United States

Population	300,000.000
Ethnic groups	White, 81%; Black, 13%; Hispanic, 4%; Asian, 4%; Amerindian and Alaska native, 1%; Hawaiian and other Pacific Islander, 0.5%
Religions	Protestant, 52%; Roman Catholic, 24%; None, 10%; Other, 10%; Jewish, 1%; Mormon, 2%
Education	97% literacy rate
Land	9,158,960 sq km
Government	Federal Republic
Political parties	Democratic Party, Republican Party, Green Party

On September 11, 2001, the United States as a nation and many of its citizens changed. All Americans believe that the events of 9/11 were a serious act of violation of their country.

Now there is a feeling of anxiety among many Americans concerning security. There is some evidence that al Qaeda "sleeper cells" exist in the United States and that their recruitment strategies may have changed from foreign nationals who are in the United States on visas to U.S. citizens.[14] Since 9/11 the United States has also invaded Afghanistan and Iraq, and as a result, the superpower is no longer held in high esteem by many. However, fundamental U.S. values remain unchanged.

The citizens of the United States of America refer to themselves as "Americans," although that term may be claimed by inhabitants of North, South, and Central America. The nation consists of the mainland—the central portion of the North American continent, or 48 states, the state of Alaska in the northwestern tip of the hemisphere; the state of Hawaii, which is located west of the mainland in the Pacific Ocean; and Washington, DC (District of Columbia), the federal capital the United States. Puerto Rico is a self-governing commonwealth, and the U.S. Virgin Islands is a territory. Since the end of World War II, the United States has administered 11 trust territories in the South Pacific, gradually relinquishing control. Between 1975 and 1980, accords were negotiated with the native islanders to establish the commonwealths of the northern Marianas, the Marshall Islands, and the Federated States of Micronesia and the Republic of Palau.

The fourth largest nation in the world, the United States has been referred to as a "melting pot" culture, where people came from many places and melted into the mainstream European cultures of the United States. The "salad bowl" metaphor is perhaps more appropriate and accurate, for it recognizes the contributions of the African, Native, Asian, and Latin cultures, with each culture maintaining its unique cultural markers while striving to work and live in harmony. It is true that it is a land of immigrants—from the time of colonists (English/French/Spanish), plus the African slave and nineteenth-century European influx to the present waves of refugees from Indochina, Cuba, and Haiti. Growing minorities of Hispanics, blacks, and Asians, as well as Native Americans, are rapidly changing the configuration of the population.

Cultural Insight

The United States is a multicultural society. Spanish is emerging as a second language especially in the Southwest, California, Florida, and Puerto Rico. American speech is as varied as the country's geography. French is spoken by many in the state of Louisiana and parts of New England.

An overview of the dominant culture reveals the following.

The United States is a multicultural society.

Goal and Achievement Oriented

Americans think they can accomplish just about anything, given enough time, money, and technology.

Highly Organized and Institutionalistic

Americans prefer a society that is strong institutionally and secure.

Freedom-Loving and Self-Reliant

Americans fought a revolution and subsequent wars to preserve their concept of democracy, so they resent too much control or interference, especially by government or external forces. They believe in the ideal that all persons are created equal, though they sometimes fail to live up to that ideal fully. They strive through law to promote equal opportunity and to confront their own racism or prejudice. Americans also idealize the self-made person who rises from poverty and adversity. Control of one's destiny is popularly expressed as "doing your own thing." Americans think, for the most part, that with determination and initiative, one can achieve whatever he or she sets out to do and can thus fulfill individual human potential.

Work Oriented and Efficient

Americans possess a strong work ethic, although they are learning in the present generation to enjoy leisure time constructively. They are very time conscious and efficient in doing things. They tinker with gadgets and technological systems, always searching for easier, better, more efficient ways of accomplishment.

Friendly and Informal

Americans reject the traditional privileges of royalty and class but do defer to those with affluence and power. Some Americans are impressed by celebrities created by the American mass media. Although informal in greeting and dress, they are a noncontact culture (e.g., they usually avoid embracing in public) and maintain certain physical and psychological distance with others (about two feet).

Competitive and Aggressive

Americans in both play and business generally are oriented to achieve and succeed. This is partially traced to their heritage, having overcome wilderness and hostile elements in their environment.

Values in Transition

Traditional American values of family loyalty, respect, and care of the aged, marriage and the nuclear family, patriotism, material acquisition, forthrightness, and the like are undergoing profound reevaluation.

Generosity

Although Americans emphasize material values, they are a sharing people, as has been demonstrated in the Marshall Plan, foreign aid programs, refugee assistance, and their willingness at home and abroad to espouse a good cause and to help neighbors in need. They tend to be altruistic and, some would say, naive as a people.

Social Institutions

In terms of U.S. social institutions, three are worth noting here. *Education* is viewed as a means of self-development, so participation in the process and within the classroom is encouraged. Education is mandatory until age 16, and 97% finish at least elementary school, so the literacy rate is high. There is a public (largely free of cost) and private school system through the university level; private schools are either independent or affiliated with a religion.

The average *family* is nuclear, consisting of only parents and children; however, the number of single-parent families is increasing. About half of all marriages end in divorce. More than half of American women work outside the home, and women have considerable and improving opportunities for personal and professional growth, guaranteed by law. The society is youth oriented and usually cares for the elderly outside the home, in institutions. It is experimenting with new family arrangements, from unmarried couples living together to group communes.

Politically, the government operates on the Constitution of 1787, which provides a three-branch approach of checks and balances, and the Bill of Rights. Currently, there are increasing problems of disillusionment in political leaders, corruption in public office, and a push toward decentralization or the confederation of states' concept (i.e., emphasis on states' rights and less government regulation over individual lives).

Challenges to the United States

The Americans, too, are in the midst of profound social change, and even an identity crisis. The following factors have contributed to this maturation challenge:

About half of all marriages end in divorce.

- Being the world's sole superpower in a global economy has forced a reassessment of the national self-image. After much success in the two World Wars, Korea and Vietnam proved to be costly and questionable conflicts that the mass media brought into American homes. Support for the war in Iraq is declining in the United States and was never strong abroad. The assassination of the 1960s led to an undermining of the national will, organized public protests, and the need to express national goals. In the 1980s, the American economy was robust, patriotism was high, entrepreneurialism and high-technology ventures flourished, and in the late 1990s the stock market advanced with Internet stocks leading the way. Violence in the streets and in schools continued. Americans were stunned by acts of terrorism on the World Trade Center and at the Federal building in Oklahoma City.
- Latinization of the United States is affecting the character of the country and its communication.
- Social unrest exists, particularly over the increase in violence, racism, and a growing underclass. There is concern about two societies—one colored, one white—that view the American experience quite differently.
- Transition into a postindustrial society is happening first and faster in the United States than in most other countries because of scientific and technological advances. The values and lifestyles created by the industrial stage of development are being reexamined, and new replacements are being sought for more effective coping in cyberculture.

The impact of such contemporary trends depends on where you are in America, for there are considerable regional differences and subcultures. There is an especially big difference between eastern and western lifestyles and attitudes. The eastern United States is thought to be more established, conservative in thinking, overorganized, and deteriorating; the western part of the nation is seen as more casual, innovative, and flexible.

As a result of 9/11, Americans are becoming more isolationist, nationalistic, and provincial in their thinking and actions.

Corporate acquisitions and property purchases by Canadians, Japanese, Europeans, Middle Easterners, and South Africans are considerable, and have even caused some fear and backlash. The influx of refugees and legal and illegal immigrants has strained existing social systems.

Cultural Observations by Other Authors

Anthropologist Margaret Mead proposed that the Americans and British have fundamentally different worldviews. If an American were asked the question "What's your favorite color?" he or she would quickly name a color. If an English person were asked the same question, the

Americans are becoming more isolationist, nationalistic, and provincial in their thinking and actions.

response would most likely be "favorite color of what? a flower? a necktie?" Mead concluded that Americans seek a common denominator.[15]

What is America? Is there a mainstream culture shared by the "average" American? Does the salad bowl theory work in practice? Is the United States a pluralistic society? Is it a multicultural society? What is America?

The following list, taken from Stewart and others, is a summary of what can be called U.S. mainstream cultural assumptions and values.[16] The main categories are the mode of activity, social relationships, motivation, the perception of the world, and the perception of self.

Questions about Activity

1. How do people approach activity?
   concern with "doing," progress, change external environment
   optimistic, striving
2. What is the desirable pace of life?
   fast, busy, driving
3. How important are goals in planning?
   stress means, procedures, techniques
4. What are important goals in life?
   material goals
   comfort and absence of pain
   activity
5. Where does responsibility for decisions lie?
   responsibility lies with each individual
6. At what level do people live?
   operational, goals evaluated in terms of consequence
7. On what basis do people evaluate?
   utility (Does it work?)
8. Who should make decisions?
   the people affected
9. What is the nature of problem solving?
   planning behavior
   anticipates consequences
10. What is the nature of learning?
    learner is active (student-centered learning)

Questions about Social Relations

1. How are roles defined?
   attained
   loosely
   generally
2. How do people relate to others whose status is different?
   stress equality
   minimize differences
   stress informality and spontaneity

3. How are gender roles defined?
   similar, overlapping
   gender equality
   friends of both genders
   less legitimized
4. What are members' rights and duties in a group?
   assume limited liability
   join group to seek own goals
   active members can influence group
5. How do people judge others?
   specific abilities of interests
   task-centered
   fragmentary involvement
6. What is the meaning of friendship?
   social friendship (short commitment, friends shared)
7. What is the nature of social reciprocity?
   real only
   nonbinding (Dutch treat)
   equal (Dutch treat)
8. How do people regard friendly aggression in social interaction?
   acceptable, interesting, fun

Questions about Motivation

1. What is motivating force?
   achievement
2. How is person-to-person competition evaluated?
   as constructive, healthy

Questions about Perception of the World (Worldview)

1. What is the (natural) world like?
   physical
   mechanical
2. How does the world operate?
   in a rational, learnable, controllable manner
   chance and probability
3. What is the nature of man?
   apart from nature or from any hierarchy
   impermanent, not fixed, changeable
4. What are the relationships between man and nature?
   good is unlimited
   man should modify nature for his ends
   good health and material comforts expected and desired
5. What is the nature of truth? goodness?
   tentative (working-type)

relative to circumstances
experience analyzed in separate components and dichotomies

6. How is time defined? Valued?
   future (anticipation)
   precise units
   limited resource
   lineal
7. What is the nature of property?
   private ownership important as extension of self

Questions about Perception of the Self and the Individual

1. In what sort of terms is self defined?
   diffuse, changing terms
   flexible behavior
2. Where does a person's identity seem to be?
   within the self (achievement)
3. Nature of the individual
   separate aspects (intent, thought, action, biographical background)
4. On whom should a person place reliance?
   self
   impersonal organizations
5. What kind of person is valued and respected? What qualities?
   youthful (vigorous)
6. What is the basis of social control?
   persuasion, appeal to the individual
   guilt

Wederspahn suggests, in Exhibit 16.4, where some of these cultural values and assumptions potentially clash with business partners.[17]

EXHIBIT 16.4

CULTURE CONTRAST

Host Country Value	USA Value
Japan: Group orientation	Individualism
Guatemala: Flexible time sense	Punctuality
Saudi Arabia: Relationship focus	Task/goal orientation
Switzerland: Formality	Informality
India: Stratified class structure	Egalitarianism
China: Long-term view	Short-term view
Germany: Structured orderliness	Flexible pragmatism
France: Deductive thinking	Inductive thinking
Sweden: Individual cooperation	Individual competition
Malaysia: Modesty	Self-promotion

In mainstream American society, most people are concerned with "doing." Americans have a preoccupation with time, organization, and the use of resources. In American social relationships everyone is assumed equal, thus removing the need for elaborate forms of social address. Social relationships are characterized by informality, and social reciprocities are much less clearly defined. Mainstream Americans are motivated by achievements and accomplishments. American personal identity and, to a certain extent, one's self-worth are measured by what the individual achieves. The world is material rather than spiritual, and Americans also see themselves as individual and unique.

American culture is in transition.

American culture is in transition, however. Many American families are in crisis, especially in the inner cities. Some also think that the centerpiece of American life, the large middle class, is eroding and under economic threat. Violence is increasing, especially among the young, many of whom lack character education and supervision as parents' attention is directed toward work and earning a living. Under these circumstances, an expanding segment of the population is prone to homelessness, child or spousal abuse, substance abuse, paranoia, crime, hatred, and intolerance. This distressed minority is balanced by a majority of Americans who are relatively affluent and well educated, in contrast to the rest of the world population who are generous in their charity and community service; who are into fitness and wellness regimens; who fight for just causes, such as protecting other species and the environment; who are optimists and futurists. There is growing concern in the United States about the increase in violence and racism. According to Shusta et al., violence motivated by hatred race, religion, ethnicity, or sexual orientation has existed for generations in the United States, as in the rest of the world, and it seems to be increasing.[18]

Subcultures of the United States

By early in the twenty-first century, whites will become a minority in the state of California. In 1900, the state was 90% Caucasian. The number of Hispanics in the workforce will rise from 9% in 1990 to 13.3% in 2010 to 24% in 2050.[19] The emergence of a polyethnic society is evident in Los Angeles where a cacophony of 160 languages is spoken today. California is now home to up to 2.4% illegal immigrants. The transformation of minorities into majorities is also taking place in Texas, Arizona, New York, Nevada, New Jersey, and Maryland. By 2050, half of the U.S. population will likely be nonwhite.[20]

The exceptional uniformity that characterized American society in the post–World War II period has been supplanted by extreme diversity. The most integrated national market in the history of the world is splintering into an array of niches. Immigration, legal and illegal, has eroded the homogeneity of the U.S. population and has multiplied connections between American society and has other societies around the world.[21]

In the United States there are minority cultures of African Americans, Hispanics, Chinese Americans, Japanese Americans, Jews, the physically challenged, and senior citizens, to name but a few. Each of these groups has *aspects* of their lives, priorities, or values that may differ in part from host of mainstream America. To work effectively and develop authentic relationships with any subculture, it is necessary to be aware, accept, appreciate, and respect its uniqueness.

Martin et al. state that labels discursively help define identity and are related to power structures.[22] Most identity labels in the United States are in relation to what is not white.

> It has been argued that this lack of attention to white identity and self-labeling reflects the historical power held by whites in the United States. That is, whites as a privileged group take their identity as the norm or standard by which other groups are measured, and this identity is therefore invisible, even to the extent that many whites do not consciously think about the profound effect being white has on their daily lives.
>
> [W]hite privilege and white standards are so culturally embedded that whiteness has been "naturalized." The racial norm at being white or acknowledging one's whiteness need never be recognized or analyzed by whites because whites generally view themselves as the racial yardstick with which other racial groups are compared.

There are two types of minority groups: those distinguished by the physical—racial groups—and those differentiated by distinct language, religious, cultural or national characteristics. According to Gudykunst and Kim, there are five characteristics of minority group membership:

> First, members of minority groups are treated differently from members of a majority group by members of the majority group. This inequality usually takes the form of segregation, prejudice, and discrimination. Second, members of minority groups have either physical or cultural characteristics that make them stand out from the majority group. Third, because minority groups stand out, membership in them is not voluntary. Fourth, members of a minority group tend to associate with and marry other members of their group. Finally, members of a minority group are aware of their subordinate status, which leads to strong group solidarity.[23]

Often minority groups are not recognized as legitimate and distinct. Instead they are automatically diminished, being judged by their physical appearance rather than with acknowledgment and appreciation of their different culture, language, and ethnic characteristics.

African Americans

The Civil War was fought to presence the union of North and South. Slavery was abolished. However, African Americans are still struggling for civil rights and equal opportunity under the law. A history of infe-

Whiteness has been "naturalized."

rior status is not dissolved easily or simply. Racism has become more subtle within institutions, housing, or educational opportunities. Despite their accomplishments and the growth of the black middle and upper classes, unemployment among black teens and deaths from violence within black communities have also risen. There is much to be done together if all African American citizens are to share in the American dream. Power is not shared; economic access is not equal.

Global events have demonstrated that racism is a significant world problem, as exemplified in the ethnic cleansing in former Yugoslavia and genocide in Rwanda, as well as the "racial profiling" that has become part of world security.

Interestingly, the word *racism* was not listed in Webster's 1939 unabridged dictionary. However, 10 years later, the definition did appear in *Webster's Intercollegiate Dictionary* possibly due to the effects of World War II and the racist philosophy of Nazi Germany.[24] Whether one focuses on individual, institutional, cultural, or symbolic racism, it is a phenomenon that is deeply ingrained throughout many cultures.

Race is an explosive issue in American life today.

According to West, race is an *explosive* issue in American life today.[25] To begin a serious dialogue regarding race, one must establish the terms for racial issues. As long as African Americans are viewed as "them" and the burden falls on blacks to do all the "cultural" and "moral" compromising, healthy race relations will not prevail. We can no longer believe that only certain Americans can define what it means to be American—and the rest must simply "fit in."

Minority groups in many cultures have demonstrated signs of rejecting movements toward assimilation, and some social scientists question whether, in countries like the United States, for example, there was ever as much assimilation as was widely hoped or believed. The number of hate crimes is increasing in many societies. There is a *rage* in many groups that is not being understood or addressed adequately.

This rage is articulated frequently. During the popular Oprah Winfrey television program, on September 15, 1995, Lee Mun Wah, the director of the film *The Color of Fear*, showed excerpts from his film. A white American asked, "Why aren't we just humans? I mean why aren't we just brothers?" An African American responded, "You think—and you think that, 'Hey, it will all be fine when we just treat each other like human beings.' And what that says to me is, 'Don't be yourself. Be like me. Keep me comfortable. Connect when I'm ready to connect. Come out to my place.' . . . You know, I'm not going to trust you until you're as willing to be changed and affected by my experience and transformed by my experience as I am every day by yours."[26]

Much research has been conducted on verbal and nonverbal communication patterns, as well as many other aspects of African American life and culture.[27] It is beyond the scope of this book to write in depth about any culture or the issues faced by people in society. We hope the references cited in this chapter and in the culture specific chapters in Unit 2 will guide readers in their further research.

Hispanic Americans

> Hispanics are moving up in every American business area. Their cultural passion and adaptability with emphasis on family, is ideally suited to both the American and global business scene.[28]

We end this discussion on U.S. subcultures with a brief examination of an emerging majority. Broadly defined, a Latino or Hispanic is an immigrant to the United States, or one whose ancestors came from Spain or Latin America. Most still speak Spanish and reflect the cultural heritage of both Spain and the indigenous peoples of Mexico, Central, and South America. This cultural influence is most evident in California, Florida, Nevada, Arizona, Texas, Puerto Rico, and Guam.

From the viewpoint of creating cultural synergy from cultural differences, the Latino expansion and integration into U.S. culture is not just in the Southwest and Southeast, but also in major urban centers such as Denver, Chicago, and New York, as well as in Miami and Los Angeles, both founded over 200 years ago by Spanish colonists. Many Latinos, whose communities here go back to the sixteenth century, consider themselves "native" Americans. Only 150 years have passed since the United States annexed the Southwest after the Mexican War, and only a century since it occupied Puerto Rico. Today, Latinos represent 11% of the U.S. population, having increased by 60%, and the percentage is projected to further expand by 75% in 2015. Census forecasters expect a Hispanic population in the United States of 96 million by 2050. Spanish-speaking Americans are heterogeneous in terms of skin color and in terms of origin: 65% are from Mexico; 12% Puerto Rico; 12% Central America and other Latin countries; 8% Cuba; and 5% Dominican Republic. They are most diverse in terms of histories, loyalties, and class. Some come from elite and wealthy backgrounds or have ancestors in Mexico, Latin America, or Spain, while many others have come as migrant workers, willing to work hard and long, yet many can find only low-paying and low-status jobs. Once established, they take advantage of American public education and the ability to move ahead economically and socially.

Latin Americans are gaining political power and representation as greater numbers of them vote. Although many are bilingual, they gain a certain cohesiveness through the Spanish language, Roman Catholicism, and family values. They are moving rapidly into middle-class status and home ownership. In most states, the number of Latino-owned businesses has doubled. Since 1990, their buying power has risen 65% and was estimated at $380 billion in 1998, and that is likely to triple by 2010. The Latino consumer market—large and growing—

Latin Americans are gaining political power.

has a reputation for brand loyalty. Consider that by the year 2000 there were 6.9 million Latino schoolchildren, and most of their parents wanted them to be taught in English. Spanish-speaking America is the world's fifth-largest Hispanic nation. Yet, the dialect of choice for millions of young Latinos is *Spanlish*, for they can switch with ease between Spanish and English.[29]

The Hispanic buying power in the United States is estimated to reach $1 trillion by 2010.

Presently, Latinos lack strong leaders. Though well involved in baseball, they are not well represented in mainstream American sports, preferring soccer. As they become more assimilated, Latins are slowly entering the mainstream cultural arts. People of Hispanic background bring a distinct, joyous flavor to the American mainstream. They comprise a varied tapestry reflecting Spanish, Indian, African American, and mulatto heritages.

The Hispanic buying power in the United States is estimated to reach $1 trillion by 2010. This has resulted from a rise in the average Hispanic household income from $14,712 in 1980 to $29,500 in 1996 to over $40,000 in 2003.[30]

Tips for Doing Business and Negotiating with Americans

The following is a profile of an American negotiator, reflecting some of the variables that can occur in business and negotiations.[31]

Basic Concept of Negotiation

American negotiators view conflict and confrontation as an opportunity to exchange viewpoints and as part of the resolution, negotiation, and agreement Americans prefer outlining the issues or problems and processes using a direct approach to reach possible solutions. They are motivated to further the interests of their corporation or government and have a highly competitive nature regarding the outcome or settlement.

Selection of Negotiators

American negotiators are usually chosen for a negotiating team based on their record of success in past negotiations and their knowledge and expertise in the area to be negotiated. Negotiations that are technical in nature require Americans with very specific knowledge and the ability to communicate their expertise. Individual differences, gender, age, and social class are not generally criteria for selection, but individual differences in character (cooperative, authoritarian, trustworthy) can determine whether one is chosen for an American negotiating team.

Role of Individual Aspirations

As a rule, Americans encourage individual aspirations and individual achievements. When representing their corporation or country, Americans temper their individualism and seek to accomplish and/or represent the positions of their company or country.

Concern with Protocol

Generally, Americans are friendly and open. Their etiquette is largely informal, and so is their basic concern for protocol. They are relaxed in their business conduct and do not often adhere to strict or explicit codes of behavior and ceremony.

Americans are friendly and open.

Significance of Type of Issue

The popular American expression "getting the job done" reflects their desire to assess the situation, and get results quickly. In negotiations, Americans may focus on the tangible aspects of the negotiation without spending too much time on the more intangible aspects, such as building relationships during the process.

Complexity of Language

Americans are low-context communicators. The message is primarily in the words spoken and is not overridden by nonverbal communication—the cues of gesture, eye contact, and silence.

Nature of Persuasive Argument

Americans usually attempt a rational presentation with detailed facts and figures accompanied by logical and analytical arguments when persuading one's counterparts.

Value of Time

Every culture has different ways of organizing time and using it. Some cultures are rigidly bound by their schedules and deadlines, while other cultures have a relaxed attitude about detailed plans and schedules. Monochronic time emphasizes schedules, segmentation, and promptness. Polychronic time stresses involvement with people and completion of transactions rather than an adherence to a preset schedule. Americans generally have a monochronic time orientation, and for most Americans "time is money." In negotiations, Americans set schedules and appointments and tend to prioritize events and move through the process "controlling" the time allotted them.

Bases of Trust

In negotiations, Americans generally trust the accuracy of the information being communicated and negotiated, and they assume that the negotiations will have a desirable outcome. If, however, Americans have had a past experience with a counterpart who has not been trustworthy, they will withhold the trust.

Risk-Taking Propensity

Americans are risk takers. In light of their history, their perception of themselves as rugged individualists, and the rewards of capitalism, Americans have embraced risk and are not risk avoidant.

Internal Decision-Making Systems

Decision making is becoming more and more decentralized with authority, within predetermined limits, being given to those with negotiating experience. Most of the final decisions must be cleared with senior executives in the organization.

Form of Satisfactory Agreement

Because their culture is legalistic, Americans prefer and expect detailed contractual agreements to formalize negotiations. A handshake may conclude negotiations, but attorneys are always involved.

CONCLUSIONS

In 1831, a Frenchman, Alexis de Tocqueville, wrote *Democracy in America*. He discovered what he called *habits of the heart*, which form the American character and sustain free institutions—family life, religious convictions, and participation in local politics. Bellah et al. examines individualism and commitment in American life and conclude that rampant individualism within American culture may threaten freedom itself, especially when individual achievement is attained at the expense of the community that provides support, reinforcement, and moral meaning for the individual.[32] Furthermore, within North American society, competition is almost a cultural imperative, but pure selfishness, Bellah argues, does not result in the common good. Yet, he sees new community forces at work within America, such as corporations becoming more personal and participatory, contributing to the renewal of this society and the creation of a new work culture.

In this chapter we have reviewed the diverse cultures of North America—Native Americans, Canadians, and the peoples of the United States. These are complex, and changing populations worthy of careful study by foreign businesspeople, visitors, and students who want to understand Canadians and "Americans."

MIND STRETCHING

Many Americans seem to be anxious about how the world perceives them and are disturbed by what seems to be its declining respect and position in many countries. Some wonder if the end is near for U.S. dominance. The following are some quotations from recently published materials that are worth considering.

- "In Muslim and developing countries the image of America is skewed by north/south, east/west economic inequality, by long-standing, direct grievances over foreign policy."[33]
- "On the surface, President Bush's week-long swing through northeast Asia has been a strong contrast with his recent storming (and, some say, stumbling) excursion with Latin America. And no leader will openly oppose American leadership . . . beneath the polite appearance, however, there is no less a challenge to American leadership in Asia."[34]
- "In developing countries . . . there is much greater awareness now than there used to be of the nature and pervasiveness of imperialism. As a result, in some countries there is mounting reluctance to conform to ideals 'born in the USA.'"[35]
- "One of the trickiest files for the prime minister [of Canada] will be relations with the United States. The two countries are drifting apart."[36]

REFERENCES

1. Gore, R. "The Most Ancient Americans," *National Geographic*, October 1997, pp. 93–97.
2. Murphy, K. "Skeleton Embodies Debate on America's First People," *Los Angeles Times*, August 13, 1997, p. 1/12.
3. Bundle, B. "Spearhead Relic of Last Ice Age," *San Diego Union*. December 14, 1994.
4. Herbst, P. H. *The Color of Words*: *An Encyclopedic Dictionary of Ethnic Bias in the United States*. Yarmouth, ME: Intercultural Press, 1997, pp. 58–59, 69.
5. "Canada's Eskimos Get a Land of Their Own," *The New York Times International*, April 2, 1999.

6. Weatherford, J. *Indian Givers: How the Indians of the Americas Transformed the World*. New York: Crown Publishers, 1988.

7. Tedlock, D. and Tedlock B. (eds.). *Teachings from the American Earth: Indian Religion and Philosophy*. New York: Liveright, 1975.

8. Moran, R. T. and Casey, S. "Profile: The Northern Cheyenne," an unpublished profile, revised 2003.

9. "Holding Its Own," *The Economist*, July 24, 1999, p. 2.

10. Bracken, S. *Canadian Almanac and Directory*. Toronto: Copp Clark Pittman, 1985.

11. "North American Dialects," *National Geographic*, December 2005.

12. Swardon, A. *The Washington Post Weekly*, "It's Nice to be Nice," 1995.

13. The profile of Canadian negotiators was written by Neil R. Abramson, Ph.D., Simon Fraser University, Burnaby, British Columbia, Canada. Excerpted from *Uniting North American Business*. Abbott, J. and Moran R. T. Boston: Butterworth-Heinemann, 2002.

14. Thomas, E. "Al Qaeda in America, the Enemy Within," *Newsweek*, June 23, 2003.

15. Cooke, P. "Coalition of the Differing," *Smithsonian*, June 2003.

16. Stewart, M. *The Age of Interdependence: Economic Policy in a Shrinking World*. Cambridge, MA: MIT Press, 1984.

17. Wederspahn, G. M. *Intercultural Services, A Worldwide Buyer's Guide and Sourcebook*. Houston, TX: Gulf Publishing Co., 2000, pp. 41–42.

18. Shusta, R. M., Levine, D. R., Harris, P. R., and Wong, H. Z. *Multicultural Law Enforcement: Peacekeeping in a Diverse Society*. Englewood, NJ: Prentice-Hall, 1995.

19. dePont, K. *Handling Diversity in the Workplace: Communication Is the Key*. Des Moines, IA: American Media I 1997 (www.census.gov) (U.S. Census Bureau, 2002).

20. Maharidge, D. *The Coming of the White Minority: California's Eruption and the Nation's Future*. New York: Time Books, 1997.

21. Clough, M. "Birth of Nations," *Los Angeles Times*, July 27, 1997, p. M1/6.

22. Martin, J. N., Krizek, R. L., Nakayama, T. K., and Bradford, L. "Exploring Whiteness: A Study of Self Labels for White Americans," *Communication Quarterly*, 44, No. 2 (1996): 125–144.

23. Gudykunst, W. B. and Kim, Y. Y. *Communicating with Strangers: An Approach to Intercultural Communication*, 3d ed. New York: McGraw-Hill, 1994.

24. Katz, P. A. and Taylor, D. A. (eds.). *Eliminating Racism: Profiles in Controversy*. New York: Plenum Press, 1988.

25. West, C. *Race Matters*. New York: Vintage Books, 1993.

26. *The Oprah Winfrey Show*, "The Color of Fear," Burrelle's Information Services, Box 7, Livingston, NJ, 1995.

27. Farley, J. E. *Majority-Minority Relations*, 3d ed. Englewood Cliffs, NJ: Prentice-Hall, 1995; see also Gioseffi, D. *Prejudice: A Global Perspective*. New York: Doubleday, 1993; Henderson, G. *Our Souls to Keep*. Yarmouth, ME: Intercultural Press, 1999.

28. Failde, A. and Doyle, W. *Latino Success: Insights from 100 of America's Most Powerful Business Professionals*. New York: Simon and Schuster, 1996.

29. "A Minority Worth Cultivating," *The Economist*, April 25, 1998, pp. 25–27.
30. Gutierrez, R. "The US Hispanic Market," unpublished paper, 2003.
31. Abbott, J. and Moran, R. T. *Uniting North American Business*. Boston: Butterworth-Heinemann, 2002.
32. Bellah, R. N. et al. *Habits of the Heart: Individualism and Commitment in American Life*. Berkeley: University of California Press, 1985.
33. Gruber, R. "What Europeans Really Think of America," *The New Leader*, August 2002.
34. Sneider, D. "Asia's Polite Reception to Bush Marks Declining US Influence," *Yale Global*, November 2005.
35. Blunt, R. and Mones, M. L. "Exploring the Limits of Western Leadership Theory in East Asia and Africa," *Personnel Review*, 1997.
36. Simpson, J. "Canada's Tests: The World in 2006," *The Economist*, 2006. www.economist/com/surveys/Mexico.

EPILOGUE

We ask our readers to look at a newspaper from anywhere in the world. For the most part, the news is not good with wars, dying, sickness and killing covering many pages.

This book has a simple message. Namely, we must understand our differences, celebrate our diversity, and create partnerships of long-term mutual benefit. Whether at home or abroad, peoples' differences broaden our life experience, be it dress and appearance, foods and festivals, arts and sports, or even commerce and service.

The Genome Sequencing Project now demonstrates that we have common DNA that can be traced to our ancestors who came from Africa some two million years ago. Research now confirms that it was solely geographical constraints that led to the formulation of races.

In the seventh edition of *Managing Cultural Differences*, we have tried to make a case that we all have some responsibility to develop relationships of long-term mutual benefit. We end this book and ask you to consider:

1. *A world of peace*—Instead of warring against nature and each other, the human family needs to develop new skills that will stop violent conflict and its consequences.
2. *A world without poverty*—Many peoples' human needs are not being met. All people have a right to develop their potential within a creative and economically viable environment.

In conclusion, the authors offer for your consideration the counsel of a 13th century sage, Francis of Assisi, who recognized everything and everyone in creation as his sister, brother and friend.

INDEX

ABOUT THE
AUTHORS

Robert T. Moran, Ph.D., is Professor of Global Management, Emeritus at Thunderbird/The American Graduate School of International Management in Glendale, Arizona. As a global consultant, he has worked with some of the world's largest corporations including Aramco, AT&T, Bayer, Boeing, Ericsson, Exxon, Fidelity, General Motors, Intel, Pioneer, Volvo, Singapore Airlines, and many others. A Canadian by birth, Moran's international experiences range from hockey coach in Japan to visiting professor in a French and a Chinese university. A former columnist for the magazine *International Management*, he has edited or authored several books on global management and culture.

Philip R. Harris, Ph.D., a management and space psychologist, is president of Harris International Ltd. in La Jolla, California. A former Fulbright professor to India who has lectured at numerous universities worldwide, he also served as vice-president of St. Francis College in New York, and Copley International Corporation in San Diego. As an international management consultant, Dr. Harris has helped more than 200 clients around the world to better understand and manage the impact of cultural and organizational dynamics. He is the author/editor of some forty books and is on the advisory board of the *European Business Review*.

Sarah V. Moran is currently in a Ph.D. program in Organizational Behavior with an emphasis in Cross Cultural Management at McGill University, Desautels Faculty of Management. She lived 3 years in Taipei, Taiwan, where she worked as the education advisor for the Fulbright Foundation, and also as liaison between the American Institute in Taiwan and the Fulbright office.